INDIA
Art and Culture
1300–1900

INDIA

Art and Culture
1300–1900

Stuart Cary Welch

Prestel

Mapin Publishing Pvt. Ltd.

Sixth Printing

This catalog was published in conjunction with the exhibition *INDIA*! held at The Metropolitan Museum of Art, New York, from September 14, 1985 to January 5, 1986.

The exhibition catalog was made possible, in part, by the Hagop Kevorkian Fund and by the Ford Foundation.

Published by The Metropolitan Museum of Art, New York and Grantha Corporation, 80 Cliffedgeway
Middletown, NJ 07701
in association with
Mapin Publishing Pvt. Ltd.
Chidambaram, Ahmedabad 380 013 India and
Prestel-Verlag
Mandlsraβe 26, D-80802 Munich,
Germany

Published by The Metropolitan Museum of Art, New York
Bradford D. Kelleher, Publisher
John P. O'Neill, Editor in Chief
Emily Walter, Editor, with assistance of Sue Potter
Laura Hawkins, John Holt and Amy Horbar
Gerald Pryor, Designer with assistance of Laurie Jewell
Nan Jernigan, Production
Map drawn by Kathleen Borowik

All Photographs in this volume not otherwise credited in the Photograph Credits on page 478 were specially taken for this publication in India by Sheldan Collins, The Photograph Studio, The Metropolitan Museum of Art.

ISBN: 0-9441-4213-3   (Grantha)
0-1858-2213-1   (Mapin)
3-7913-1253-7   (Prestel)

Typeset in Bembo by U.S. Lithograph Inc., New York.
Printed and bound by Tien Wah Press (Pte.) Ltd., Singapore.

Prestel-Verlag
Mandlstraβe 26, D-80802 Munich
Germany
Tel: (89) 38 17 09 Telefax: (89) 38 17 09 35
and 16 West 22nd Street, New York, NY 10010 USA
Tel: (212) 627 8199 Fax: (212) 627 9866

Prestel books are available worldwide.
Please contact your nearest bookseller or write to either of the above addresses for information concerning your local distributor.

Distributed in India and Nepal by
The Variety Book Depot
A.V.G. Bhawan, M3 Connaught Circus
New Delhi 110 001

Distributed in Asia and The Far East by
Mapin Publishing Pvt. Ltd.
Chidambaram, Ahmedabad 380 013 India
Tel: (079) 755-1833 Fax: (079) 755-0955
email: mapinpub@ad1.vsnl.net.in
web-site: www.mapinpub.com

Cover/Jacket: *Lady Feeding a Bird* (no.196), Deccan, Bijapur, early 17th century, opaque watercolor on paper. Chester Beatty Library, Dublin.

Frontpiece: Pichhavai for a temple or shrine (no.223), Deccan, perhaps Hyderabad, ca. late 18th century, paint on cotton. Museum of Fine Arts, Boston.

CONTENTS

DIRECTOR'S FOREWORD

If it was longing for India that, nearly five centuries ago, led an Italian voyager to discover America for Europe, then surely we in the West have been slow requiters of this historic debt. With our persistent bias toward an axis of world history whose pivotal center swings somewhere between the Atlantic and the Near East, we have for too long disregarded the achievements of early civilization in India because of the mysteries that surround it. Although the Indus Valley, most notably at Mohenjo-Daro, gave birth in the second millennium B.C. to some subtly seductive and finely modeled figures, the culture did not produce masterpieces on the scale of Mesopotamia, Egypt, or Minoan Crete, far less their great monuments. It is only after the Buddha's time that we can speak with any assurance of the history of Indian art. Yet there is the indisputable fact that of the world's five great religions, two were born and nurtured on Indian soil, and one of these, Buddhism, was the first religion to spread beyond the confines of the society in which it originated. An awesome social system, fully evolved by 1000 B.C., to this day regulates the lives of more than 600 million Hindus and even affects, albeit peripherally, the attitudes and assumptions of some Indian Christians and Muslims. Above all, ancient India is with us still, direct and palpable, as is no other early civilization.

An important turning point in prevailing Western attitudes toward Indian art occurred in the early years of this century when the critic Roger Fry, after a brief period of curatorship at the Metropolitan Museum, returned to his native England and reviewed, in an illuminating article, the pioneering studies of Ananda Coomaraswamy and E. B. Havell. Writing in 1910 in *The Quarterly Review*, Fry drew attention to the serious new claims that he believed had to be faced: "We can no longer hide behind the Elgin marbles and refuse to look; we have no longer any system of aesthetics which can rule out, *a priori*, even the most fantastic and unreal artistic forms. They must be judged in themselves and by their own artistic standards."

Today, three-quarters of a century later, the Metropolitan Museum mounts its own particular tribute to India's endlessly rich and varied culture. This impressive artistic heritage, traced from the fourteenth through the nineteenth century, is the subject of the Metropolitan's *INDIA!* exhibition. To date, no other museum in the United States has organized a conceptually comprehensive display of the later art of the Indian subcontinent, bringing together not only masterpieces of its sacred and court traditions but embracing as well its urban, folk, and tribal heritage. The idea for such an exhibition was first proposed in 1980 by Stuart Cary Welch, Special Consultant in Charge of the Department of Islamic Art, and rapidly became the focal point of the nationwide Festival of India, a celebration of India's visual and performing arts to be held in the United States during 1985–86. We are deeply indebted to Mr. Welch, whose pioneering work in the field of painting and the decorative arts has served to prepare the American public for an exhibition of the magnitude and diversity of *INDIA!* and who conceived, shaped, and guided the project to its enormously complex realization. In this latter task, in its every facet, he was aided by Mahrukh Tarapor, Special Assistant to the Director for the *INDIA!* Exhibition, without whose intuitive gift for diplomacy and superb organizational skills it is fair to say the exhibition might never have come to fruition.

In 1981, following discussions with Ted Tanen, American Executive Secretary of the Indo–U.S. Subcommission on Education and Culture, *INDIA!* was brought under the aegis of the Subcommission. Jointly sponsored through the Subcommission by the American and Indian governments, this ambitious project received the unstinting and wholehearted support of friends and colleagues in Indian, European, and American museums.

The government and museums of India have been generous in allowing the Metropolitan to borrow sixty-five paintings and sixty objects from nine private collections, eighteen museums, two churches, and one library. Our negotiations throughout have benefited from the inspired and sympathetic guidance of Pupul Jayakar, Chairman of the Indian Advisory Committee of the Festival of India. Also to be thanked are S. K. Misra, Director General, Festival of India; Niranjan Desai, Minister (Culture), Embassy of India, Washington, D.C.; Vijay Singh, Coordinator of the Festival of India in New Delhi; and senior officials in the Ministry of Education and Culture. Kapila Vatsyayan, Director of the Indira Gandhi National Center for the Arts, provided invaluable guidance in the early stages of the exhibition. We would like particularly to thank the two ambassadors personally concerned with the exhibition: K. Shankar Bajpai, Ambassador of India to the United States, and Harry G. Barnes, Jr., United States Ambassador to India, and their able staffs. Under the able supervision of Laxmi P. Sihare, Director of the National Museum in New Delhi, the loans were secured, collected, and shipped from India, and we recall with pleasure the hospitality extended by him and his colleagues to our curators and professional staff during their frequent visits to India. We would also like to extend our gratitude for the gracious collaboration of Nagaraja Rao, Director-General, Archaeological Survey of India, Government of India. Martand Singh, Secretary, Indian National Trust for Art and Cultural Heritage, long a devoted friend to this exhibition, and to our museum, has made available to us, at all times and on every level, his assistance and expertise. We offer him our sincere and heartfelt thanks.

The Metropolitan Museum is also deeply grateful to a host of other collections, both public and private, throughout Europe and the United States, that together have generously consented to lend to the *INDIA!* exhibition a total of 208 paintings and objects without which the remarkable scope of Mr. Welch's conception could not have been realized.

Under the continuing auspices of the Subcommission, the Metropolitan, along with seven other participating American museums, now looks forward to sending to the National Museum in 1985–86 an exchange exhibition of American painting from the late eighteenth through the twentieth century.

It is a privilege to reaffirm here the magnanimous and enlightened support of the Indian government and the business community in India, without which this exhibition surely would not have materialized. In particular, we express our greatest appreciation to J. R. D. Tata, distinguished Chairman of the house of Tata; to Jamshed Bhabha, Director, Tata Sons Ltd., whose enthusiasm for this project and conviction in its value have been a source of constant encouragement for us; and to the other participating Tata companies, notably Tata Iron and Steel Company, the Taj Group of Hotels, Tata Chemicals Ltd., Tata Tea Ltd., The Tata Oil Mills Company Ltd., Rallis India Ltd., and Excel Industries Ltd. Another good friend in Bombay has been Keshub Mahindra, Chairman of Mahindra & Mahindra Ltd. Additional support from the Indian business community was provided by Brakes India Ltd., DCM Ltd., Gwalior Rayon and Silk Manufacturing Company, Hindustan Aluminium Corporation Ltd., Hindustan Lever Ltd., Lucas Indian Service Ltd., Lucas–TVs Ltd., Sundaran Finance Ltd., Sundaran Industries Ltd., T. V. Sundaran Iyengar & Sons Ltd., United Breweries Ltd., and Wheel India Ltd. Air India has provided assistance toward curatorial travel and is the official carrier for the Indian loans.

Equally vital to the success of this major collaborative enterprise has been the financial support received from friends and contributors in Europe and America. We wish to thank Schlumberger Limited and Mr. and Mrs. Jean Riboud for their early recognition of the exhibition's potential. In the United States, The National Endowment for the Humanities awarded *INDIA!* a major grant. Financial assistance has also been received from the J. M. R. Barker Foundation, New York; George P. Bickford, Cleveland; the Indo–U.S. Subcommission on Education and Culture; and Wendy F. Findlay, New York. A generous gesture on the part of Sheikh Nasser Sabah al-Ahmed al-Sabah and Sheikha Hussa Sabah al-Salem al-Sabah has made it possible for us to include in the exhibition the extraordinary Mughal emerald from the Kuwait National Museum. The exhibition catalogue has been made possible in part by the continuing generosity of The Hagop Kevorkian Fund and by The Ford Foundation.

It is, above all, to the graciousness and cooperation of its lenders that any exhibition owes its being. *INDIA!* is no exception, and we list, with gratitude, the names of fifty-eight institutions and thirty-six private collectors on pages 15–17.

Finally, I acknowledge with pride and pleasure the specialized staff of the Metropolitan Museum, too numerous to name individually, whose combined efforts and expertise have facilitated the mounting of this major show. Some deserve special thanks. Emily Rafferty, Vice President of Development, with Daniel Herrick, Vice President of Finance, assumed the challenging task of insuring the financial viability of the exhibition, both in this country and in India. In addition, Ms. Rafferty, unsparingly and with great good humor, undertook to supervise and coordinate the many complex strands of the Museum's negotiations with India. The editorial staff, under the supervision of John P. O'Neill, assisted Mr. Welch in the planning of the catalogue, and Emily Walter, Associate Editor, organized the diverse aspects of manuscript preparation with patience, tenacity, and skill. John Buchanan, the Museum's Registrar, collaborated with Indian colleagues and handled with customary resourcefulness the innumerable logistical problems that inevitably attend a project of such scale and complexity. Jeffrey L. Daly, Chief Designer, ably assisted by David Harvey, worked closely with Mr. Welch on the exhibition's design and the specific display needs of much of its material. Martha Deese, Administrative Assistant for the *INDIA!* Exhibition, with unflagging energy and exceptional competence kept the exhibition's myriad day-to-day details in exemplary order.

INDIA! is dedicated to the memory of the late Prime Minister Indira Gandhi.

Philippe de Montebello

ACKNOWLEDGMENTS

Six years ago, when Philippe de Montebello, the Director of The Metropolitan Museum of Art, asked me to join the staff of the Museum as Special Consultant in Charge of the Department of Islamic Art, he also asked if I would like to plan a major exhibition. At that moment, with him, *INDIA!* was conceived; and ever since, it has been my preoccupation —and one of his. I am most grateful to him for his constant devotion to one of the most complex exhibitions in the Museum's history.

While our project was forming, a Festival of India for Great Britain was also projected, the inspiration of the late Prime Minister of India, Indira Gandhi—whose interest in the Metropolitan's exhibition was expressed when she announced it at a luncheon in the Museum on July 28, 1982—and of her close friend, Pupul Jayakar, who later became Chairman, India Advisory Committee, Festival of India. During the same summer, the success of the Indian Festival in Great Britain was such that the creative and indomitable Mrs. Jayakar proposed a similar program for the United States. Thus, our exhibition became one of many projects to be carried out with the fullest cooperation and support of the Government of India. The planning of the Festival of India engaged the talented Martand Singh, whose generous spirit, profound knowledge of Indian collections, and quietly effective encouragement have been invaluable. Our exhibition also gained the administrative support of S. K. Misra, Director General, Festival of India; of K. Shankar Bajpai, Ambassador of India to the United States; and of Niranjan Desai, Embassy of India, Washington, D.C.

Although *INDIA!* exhibits hundreds of objects, they are far outnumbered by the people who helped assemble and catalogue them. One of the first to espouse the cause was Ted M. G. Tanen, American Executive Director of the Indo–U.S. Subcommission on Education and Culture, ably and cheerfully assisted by Deputy Director Patrice Fusillo. Their invaluable help at every stage was initiated by their making arrangements in the fall of 1980 for the first of five exploratory visits to India. Accompanied by my ever obliging wife, Edith, I not only visited many museums and private collections but met with Dr. Kapila Vatsyayan, at that time Additional Secretary, Ministry of Culture, Government of India, a vibrantly intelligent lady, art historian, and lithely graceful dancer, who greatly assisted the project during its earlier stages. She apprised me as to which institutions and collectors could be depended upon to lend, and she was encouragingly stimulating with regard to the concept of the exhibition, in which through superb works of art in all mediums we intended to clarify the interrelationships among the artistic traditions of tribes, villages, temples, shrines, and courts.

During the course of the trip, we visited collections and sites in the Deccan in the company of Ziauddin Shakeb and Dr. Annemarie Schimmel, the latter of whom later became Consultant to the Museum's Department of Islamic Art. As diligently generous as she is brilliantly scholarly, Dr. Schimmel's lustrous involvement with *INDIA!* began at that time. Since then, she has contributed essential information to this catalogue, for which she has prepared translations, and—most recently—proven herself not only an eagle-eyed proofreader but also a superb, always smiling, indexer.

In New Delhi, it became evident that *INDIA!* was not only an exciting project but also a way of meeting new friends. Michael Pistor, at that time Counselor for Public Affairs of the American Embassy, New Delhi, provided sound, comradely advice and invaluable help on many levels. He and his wife, Shirley, could not have been kinder or more hospitable; and their efforts on our behalf were paralleled by those of Ted Riccardi, Cultural Affairs Officer, and his wife, Peggy, who were followed in that office by William Thompson.

During the next trip, we met Ambassador and Mrs. Harry G. Barnes, Jr., enthusiasts of India and her culture, without whose continuing and lively concern the progress of our project would have proceeded less mellifluously. Harry and Betsey Barnes reinforced my appreciation of our Foreign Service.

In the meantime, *INDIA!* was being furthered in New York by our departmental staff, and by Wendy F. Findlay, to whom we are most grateful for setting the project in of our project would have proceeded less mellifluously. Harry and Betsey Barnes reinforced my appreciation of our Foreign Service.

In the meantime, *INDIA!* was being furthered in New York by our departmental staff, and by Wendy Findlay, to whom we are most grateful for setting the project in motion. I also wish to thank two friends for their encouragement and participation during the early stages of the exhibition, Alice Heeramaneck and Jacqueline Kennedy Onassis. Mahrukh Tarapor soon joined the exhibition staff as Special Assistant to the Director for the *INDIA!* Exhibition, and it has been she—specialist in Indian art, ambassador plenipotentiary, able translator, a person whose enormous organizational, diplomatic, and personal skills have been essential to the project—who has kept both the exhibition and the catalogue on track, and it is to her that I wish to express my infinite gratitude based on the realization that without her devoted involvement and hard work this exhibition could not have taken place. Marie Lukens Swietochowski, Associate Curator, and Carolyn Kane, Assistant Curator, ably began their researches for the catalogue, the former devoting herself to miniatures and objects of the Sultanate period, the latter to textiles of diverse periods and to compiling the Glossary and the Published section following each entry. Martha Deese, Administrative Assistant for the *INDIA!* Exhibition, soon added her manifold managerial skills to the office, which were later reinforced by Susan Salit, our Administrative Assistant, who in turn was aided by Hilda Feiring. The assistance of George Berard, Principal Departmental Technician, has always been an invaluable help. I am also grateful to Karen Petersen, an enormously helpful volunteer.

On my return, the sheer ambitiousness of our plan dawned on me when I was asked to explain it to the heads of the departments who would assist in carrying it out. Each of them has since earned my ever increasing gratitude for his or her thoughtful, skillful, invariably cheerful professionalism under conditions always strenuous and sometimes worrisome. Compiling their names evokes a multiplicity of happy and engaging anecdotes, the recounting of which, alas, would add to the bulk of an already vast publication: James Pilgrim, Deputy Director; Ashton Hawkins, Vice President, Secretary, and Counsel; Daniel Herrick, Vice President for Finance; Emily Kernan Rafferty, Vice President for Development; Bradford D. Kelleher, Vice President and Publisher; John P. O'Neill, Editor in Chief and General Manager of Publications; Lisa Cook Koch, General Merchandise Manager; John Buchanan, Registrar; Jeffrey L. Daly, Chief Designer; Merribell Parsons, Vice Director for Education; John Ross, Manager, Public Information; James H. Frantz, Conservator in Charge, and Elayne Grossbard, Assistant Conservator, Objects Conservation; Nobuko Kajitani, Conservator, Textile Conservation; Helen K. Otis, Conservator, Paper Conservation; Richard R. Morsches, Vice President for Operations; Linda M. Sylling, Assistant Manager for Operations; Mark D. Cooper, Manager, Photograph Studio; Wen Fong, Special Consultant for Far Eastern Affairs; Barbara Dougherty, Manager, Membership; and Joanne Lyman, Manager, Objects Reproduction and Reproduction Studio.

The register of masterpieces we hoped to borrow was growing in the course of visits to study and photograph collections in Europe, Kuwait, throughout the United States, and particularly in India. A continuing and productive relationship was established with Air India, represented in New York by Pallavi Shah and Nani Mittal, who have never failed to offer invaluable assistance to the project.

Especially auspicious and enjoyable was the first of many encounters with Pupul Jayakar, whose kindness, efficiency, and benevolence toward the exhibition have been unstinting. Without her guidance, this exhibition could not have been. She deserves our additional gratitude for agreeing to lend several of her uniquely marvelous folk bronzes.

The project's roots can be traced to my first trip to the subcontinent in 1957, when in Varanasi I met the now legendary Rai Krishna Dasa, the connoisseurly founder of the Bharat Kala Bhavan, the art museum of Banaras Hindu University, and his son, Rai Anand Krishna. It is satisfying to know that his grandson, Dr. Kalyan Krishna, of Banaras Hindu University, has tendered assistance to the project on many levels. Moreover, thanks to O. P. Tandon, Deputy Director, Bharat Kala Bhavan, Banaras Hindu University, it has been possible to borrow several of the marvelous works of art he collected. *INDIA!* also owes much to early discussions in Bombay with Dr. Pramod Chandra, who most fittingly has prepared an exhibition sister to ours for the National Gallery of Art, Washington, D.C. (*The Sculpture of India, 3000 B.C.–1300 A.D.*).

Other Indian friends, on our various visits to India, have contributed to this project, offering, at all times, warmth, hospitality, information, and enthusiastic support. In addition, many have maintained their invariable record of generosity by lending superb works of art to the exhibition, and we list, with gratitude, their names on page 16.

In particular, we wish to thank Jagdish and Kamla Mittal, whose chowki has been the setting for many exciting hours of aesthetic and art historical stimulation. The inspired creators and donors of the Jagdish and Kamla Mittal Museum of Indian Art, Hyderabad, they and the museum trustees—particularly Naozar Chenoy, Trustee-Secretary —have agreed to lend many marvelous pictures and objects. Jagdish Mittal, moreover, has prepared most informative and insightful entries for this catalogue. Warm memories are aroused by the splendid pictures and objects borrowed from Jaipur, where members of the Jaipur family as well as curators of the Maharaja Sawai Man Singh II Museum in the City Palace have been nobly generous to us over the years. We are particularly grateful to H.H. Colonel Bhawani Singh of Jaipur and to H.H. Gayatri Devi, Rajmata of Jaipur, both of whom have taken deep personal interest in this project. Dr. Asok Kumar Das, Director, Maharaja Sawai Man Singh II Museum, Dr. Chandramani Singh, and Yaduendra Sahai have also provided unfailing and enthusiastic support. We are beholden to H.H. Maharaja Sri Gaj Singhji II of Jodhpur for enabling us to study and borrow a number of objects from both the Mehrangarh Museum Trust and the Umaid Bhawan Museum, and for making our visits to Jodhpur festively enjoyable. We also extend thanks to Naher Singh, Director of the Mehrangarh Museum Trust; to its Manager, Maharaj Prahlad Singh; and to Thakur Raju Singh, Executive Director of the Umaid Bhawan Palace Museum. We are also grateful to Master-craftsman Gokal Ram and his colleagues Chunni Lal, Kishan Lal, and Ghan Shyam, who have carried on the technique of erecting the magnificent tents of Jodhpur.

A great peak of excitement occurred in the Rao Madho Singh Museum Trust at Kotah, when Rajkumar Brijraj Singh showed me the huge, anecdotal painting of his ancestor Maharao Ram Singh II's visit to the Red Fort of Delhi (no. 285), a moment almost exceeded when we learned that we could borrow it. At Kotah, we are most grateful to him, to his family, and to Jaswant Singh. In Mysore, we are indebted to H.H. Prince Sri Srikanta Datta Narasimharaja Wadiyar for helpful accounts of Mysore history and for many courtesies. In Madras, for her infinite helpfulness, we wish to thank Prema Shrinivasan, who greatly contributed to the interest and enjoyment of our visit to South India.

In Bombay, a city of many friends, we are most indebted to Jamshed Bhabha, Director, Tata Sons Ltd., for his continuing and devoted assistance to our project. We are grateful to the Trustees of the Prince of Wales Museum of Western India, particularly to Karl J. Khandalavala, and to its Director, Dr. Sadashiv Gorakshkar, for their help in allowing us access to the museum's collections and for lending several splendid works of art. In Bombay, too, Adi B. K. Dubash very generously made available to us, at many importune moments, his office facilities; Naheed Lalkaka provided friendly administrative assistance; and Ratan Lalkaka helped us secure an important private loan. We also wish to thank Perin and Keki Tarapor, Saryu and Vinod Doshi, Mr. and Mrs. Bal Mundkur, and Ranjan Roy, all of whom, in different ways, have supported and encouraged *INDIA!*

New Delhi, a capital of art as well as of a nation, was searched with pleasure, diligence, and good fortune. Through the good offices of Dr. I. D. Mathur, former Acting Director of the National Museum, we began by viewing the anthropological collections, most helpfully guided by Dr. U. Das. Next, we spent many days seeing textiles and other works of art with Krishna Lal, who was lavishly generous of her time despite other pressures, and to whom we are particularly grateful not only for her kindnesses in Delhi but for her highly informative material for the catalogue. Also in the National Museum, we were shown splendid manuscripts by Dr. Narindar Nath; and Dr. O. P. Sharma, as so often over the years, provided access most generously to a large selection from the thousands of paintings in his care. We are also indebted to Dr. G. N. Pant, whose enthusiasm for Indian arms and armor might be even greater than my own, and who generously guided me through the excellent collection in his charge. At the National Museum, we are also grateful to its recently appointed Director, Dr. Laxmi P. Sihare, whose contributions to this exhibition and to the Festival of India evince his national pride.

In Delhi, too, we are beholden to Dr. Nagaraja Rao, Director-General, Archaeological Survey of India, Government of India, whose previous hospitality and help in Mysore we recollect with great pleasure. Dr. Jyotindra Jain, Senior Director, National Museum of Handicrafts and Handlooms, also has earned our gratitude, as have Prem Jha, Sankho Chaudhuri, Anita Singh of Kapurthala, S. A. Ali, Ebba Koch, Leela Shiveshwarkar, Lalit Sen of Suket, Naveen and Gudu Patnaik, Malvika Singh, Mr. and Mrs. Cyrus Jhabvala —but the list of those who helped in Delhi is too lengthy to compile. However, we would especially like to thank the staff of the Taj Mahal Hotel, New Delhi, for the many services and courtesies, far exceeding their usual responsibilities, that have been extended over the past two years to members of the Metropolitan's curatorial and professional staff.

The most recently founded museum from which we are borrowing is the Dar al-Athar al-Islamiya, Kuwait National Museum, which we visited with immense pleasure shortly after it opened in 1983. We are most grateful to its director, Sheikha Hussa al-Salem al-Sabah, who so informatively guided us through the magnificent al-Sabah Collection, which was formed by her husband, Sheikh Nasser al-Sabah al-Ahmad al-Sabah. We are especially thankful to both of them not only for lending an extraordinary carved emerald (no. 99) but also for making this possible through a generous donation to the Museum.

Many major works of art have been lent by institutions and private collectors in Great Britain and Ireland, all of which are listed on page 16. A long-standing curatorial ambition has been satisfied by the Bodleian Library, and the Bodley's Librarian, J.W. Jolliffe, and Dr. A. D. S. Roberts, Keeper of Eastern Manuscripts, in lending us their painting of a dying Mughal courtier (no. 149b) to be reunited for a few months with the drawing made at the same time of the same unfortunate gentleman (no. 149a). For many major loans from the British Museum, we are especially grateful to its Trustees and its Director, David Wilson, as well as to Dr. J. M. Rogers, Deputy Keeper, Department of Oriental Antiquities, who generously contributed important information for the catalogue entries. We are similarly indebted to the British Library, to its Director and Keeper, Barry Bloomfield, and to Jeremiah P. Losty, Assistant Keeper, Department of Oriental Manuscripts and Printed Books, who also provided vital material for this publication. Particularly warm thanks are also due to the Victoria and Albert Museum, and to its Director, Sir Roy Strong, for lending brilliant material. Robert W. Skelton, Keeper, Indian Department, as always has far exceeded the call of duty in supplying the results of his scholarly researches, for which we continue to be in his debt. For information and encouragement, we are also thankful to numerous friends and several anonymous connoisseurs in London. As in the past, we wish to thank John Robert Alderman, Dr. Mildred Archer, Toby Falk, Sven Gahlin, Michael Goedhuis, Simon Digby, Howard Hodgkin, Lisbet Holmes, Lawrence Impey, Esq., Oliver Impey, David Khalili, Mian Bashir Wali Mohamed, and Dr. Mark Zebrowski.

European museums and collectors have lent outstanding material, and we are happy to acknowledge their graciousness and generosity. With particular pleasure, we express our thanks to Prince Sadruddin Aga Khan, who has lent so generously despite his other commitments to major exhibitions, and to Jean and Krishna Riboud, not only for lending a superb textile (no. 20) but for having been warmly supportive of *INDIA!* at a critical moment in its evolution.

American institutions and collectors have also been outstandingly generous, despite their own plans for celebrating the Festival of India. To them all we express our profound gratitude. In particular, we wish to record our thanks to friends at the Museum of Fine Arts, Boston, and to John Rosenfield, Acting Director of the Fogg Art Museums, Harvard University, for lending so generously at a time of moving and renovation. We are also grateful to Jane

Bowen, Conservators, and to Woodman Taylor, of the Department of Islamic and Later Indian Art, all of whom have devoted much time and effort to *INDIA!*

The globe-trotting phase of exhibition planning was occasionally interrupted by activities within the Museum—meetings with the less nomadic members of the staff devoted to the project. Everyone, from Philippe de Montebello to those concerned with the catalogue, installation design, public relations, and many other departments, was eager for news. Slides of "final" choices were shown (year after year!) until at a dangerously late date the ultimate selection had been made. In the meantime, Emily Walter was appointed editor of the catalogue—a splendid choice. For she is blessed with both firmness and tact, is demonically industrious, and her enthusiasm for the material and for the project could scarcely be exceeded. Her colleagues in this effort include Sue Potter, Laura Hawkins, Joan Holt, Amy Horbar, Nan Jernigan, and the volume's designer, Gerald Pryor.

Although the present publication was initiated as a lavishly illustrated volume, with a short text, the text grew over the years, largely due to the encouragement of the Museum's director and editorial staff, who made every effort to make it visually exciting. We are grateful for their understanding and largess. Sheldan Collins, of the Museum staff, spent a season in India, where he made many excellent transparencies and negatives, assisted by R. K. Saigal, Senior Photographer, Archaeological Survey of India; and on commission, Nicholas Vreeland took many perceptive photographs in this country, for which we are most grateful. Raghubir Singh, the brilliant Indian photographer, accepted our invitation to provide a series of color prints on the theme of India's geography and changing seasons for the introductory section of the exhibition galleries, thereby earning our gratitude.

As already mentioned, Jagdish Mittal wrote thoroughly documented entries on the works of art lent by the Jagdish and Kamla Mittal Museum of Indian Art; and many other distinguished scholars also contributed information to the catalogue. In addition to materials furnished by members of the Department of Islamic Art, we are most grateful for the contributions of Martin Lerner, Curator, Department of Far Eastern Art, and of David Alexander, Research Associate, and Robert Carroll, Armorer, Department of Arms and Armor, at the Metropolitan; Dr. Ali Asani, Department of Near Eastern Languages and Civilizations, Harvard University, Cambridge, Mass.; Milo Cleveland Beach, Assistant Director, Sackler Gallery, Smithsonian Institution, Washington, D.C.; John Correia-Afonso, S.J., Saint Xavier's College, Bombay; Joseph M. Dye, III, Curator of Asiatic Art, Virginia Museum of Fine Arts, Richmond; Daniel J. Ehnbom, former Assistant Professor, McIntire Department of Art, University of Virginia, Richmond; Stephen P. Huyler, New York; Manuel Keene, former Visiting Curator, Dar al-Athar al-Islamiya, Kuwait National Museum; Kalyan Krishna, Banaras Hindu University, Varanasi; Krishna Lal, Curator, Department of Decorative Arts, National Museum, New Delhi; Jeremiah P. Losty, Assistant Keeper, Department of Oriental Manuscripts and Printed Books, British Library, London; Dr. A. S. Melikian-Chirvani, Paris; Veronica Murphy, Indian Department, Victoria and Albert Museum, London; Dr. J. M. Rogers, Deputy Keeper, Department of Oriental Antiquities, British Museum, London; Susan Stronge, Indian Department, Victoria and Albert Museum, London. Woodman Taylor of the Fogg Art Museum not only contributed, with Norbert Peabody, the Chronology to this volume but also supplied useful information for many entries. Norbert Peabody's research on tribal and village India was also invaluable. We are profoundly grateful to Dr. Martin B. Dickson of Princeton University and to Dr. Wheeler Thackston of Harvard University for answering many puzzling questions.

As the catalogue grew, the gallery spaces extended; and each object was imaginatively and in imagination fitted into a series of galleries in the Museum. It has been a pleasure to work with Jeffrey L. Daly and his assistant, David Harvey, who traveled in India to gain an understanding of the relationship between Indian works of art and their settings. Sensitive but discreet, creative as well as practical, they have planned a progression of colors and forms totally in harmony with our projected scheme.

Lengthy as these acknowledgments may seem, it has not been possible to name all the people who have contributed to this exhibition and catalogue. I hope that as they visit the exhibition each one will note his or her influences and be pleased to have helped. For my part, I am most grateful to the many people who have so generously participated in the work.

Stuart Cary Welch
May 30, 1985

LENDERS TO THE EXHIBITION

PRIVATE COLLECTIONS

Prince Sadruddin Aga Khan 116, 151, 161, 294
Michael Archer and Margaret Lecomber 56
Allan Caplan 180
Rainer Daehnhardt 102
Leo S. Figiel 51, 66, 237b
Wendy F. Findlay 258
Sven Gahlin 281b
Jagdish Goenka 225b, 229
Nasli and Alice Heeramaneck 104
Lawrence Impey, Esq. 281c, 281d
J. K. Antiques and Curios Trust 123
Gopi Krishna Kanoria 231, 246, 249, 266, 269
Khalili Collection 215
The Kronos Collections 69b, 164, 225d
Kasturbhai Lalbhai 182, 265, 267
Dr. and Mrs. Aschwin de Lippe 9
Mian Bashir Wali Mohamed 189
Moke Mokotoff 178
Mrs. Krishna Riboud 20
Howard and Jane Ricketts 287, pp. 74–75, 85
Seethadevi Holding 289
H. Peter Stern 260
Colonel R. K. Tandan 256
Paul F. Walter pp. 452, 453, 454
Stuart Cary Welch 225c, 242, 243, 245, 254
Anonymous 2, 18, 22, 30, 32, 33, 34, 35b, 36, 38, 39, 41, 42, 58, 59, 60, 61, 62, 63, 69, 70, 83, 86, 98, 117, 130, 131, 147, 158, 170, 172, 173, 179, 184, 188, 193, 200, 204, 250, 255, 275, 281a, 292, 296

AUSTRIA
Vienna

Kunsthistorisches Museum, Sammlung für Plastik und Kunstgewerbe 77
Österreichisches Museum für angewandte Kunst 112

DENMARK
Copenhagen

The David Collection 186, 187

Bukhara

•Samarkand

U. S. S. R.

Tabriz

Herat

Kabul

CHINA

AFGHANISTAN

KASHMIR

•Srinagar

Jammu

Chamba

Kandahar

Basohli•

Kangra

PAHARI REGION

Lahore•

Guler

HIMALAYAS

Shiraz

PUNJAB

NEPAL

PAKISTAN

Delhi

Indus R.

Bikaner

RAJASTHAN

Fatehpur-
Sikri

NAGALAND

MARWAR

Amber

Agra

Lucknow

Jaipur

Jodhpur•

Banaras

Ganges R.

Kishangarh

Gwalior

MEWAR

Bundi

Jumna R.

Chunar

BANGLADESH

Udaipur•

Kotah

BIHAR

Dacca

•Raghugarh

BENGAL

MALWA

INDIA

Calcutta.

•Burhanpur

GUJARAT

GULF
OF
CAMBAY

Ahmadnagar

ARABIAN

Bombay•

DECCAN

ORISSA

BAY

Godavari R.

SEA

Golconda

OF

Kistna R.

Bijapur

•Hyderabad

BENGAL

GOA

ANDHRA

•Vijayanagar

KARNATAKA

Mi. 0   100   200   300

Km. 0 100   300

200

Madras

MALABAR COAST

Ootacamund

Calicut

TAMIL
NADU

KERALA

SRI
LANKA

INDIAN

OCEAN

I.   THE GREAT TRADITION

II.   TRIBE AND VILLAGE

III.   THE MUSLIM COURTS

IV.   THE RAJPUT WORLD

V.   THE BRITISH PERIOD

Dimensions: Height precedes width precedes depth.

Catalogue entries for works lent by the Jagdish and Kamla
Mittal Museum of Indian Art, Hyderabad, were written by
Jagdish Mittal.

For full citations of the references that follow each entry,
see Bibliography.

THE GREAT TRADITION

TRIBE AND VILLAGE

India: Art and Culture 1300–1900 documents six critical centuries of artistic synthesis, change, and survival. The exhibition opens with two South Indian bronzes that exemplify the endurance and vitality of the all-encompassing Great Tradition: stirring images of the Hindu god Shiva and his consort Parvati, sculpted by anonymous craftsmen who used age-old techniques and prescribed canons of iconography and proportion to give shape to a sacred inner vision. It closes with two photographs that epitomize adaptability in the face of profound disruption: an enigmatic portrait of a sensitive young prince and a brooding study of swagged Victorian curtains leading only to a forbiddingly blank wall. Both photographs were taken in about 1890 by Lala Din Dayal, virtuoso of a new-fledged Western technique. Bracketed by these extremes of the traditional and the nontraditional are hundreds of pictures and objects, each of which, from a miniature commissioned by an emperor to a wood carving created by a village artisan, is a work to be judged in its own right. Spanning all parts of the subcontinent, the exhibition demonstrates not only the many paths artistic creativity has taken in India but the fundamental familiality of Indian art and the profound spirituality that is its essence. If a drably colored folk bronze surprises with its soaring spirit, some shimmeringly rich ornament might prove equally, or even more, transcendental.

The dominant characteristic of traditional Indian art and culture is its spirituality. From birth to death, life is keyed to shrine, temple, or mosque, enriched by prayer, chanting, and spiritual exercises, and enlivened by rites of passage and religious festivals. Artists and craftsmen reared in a spiritual milieu instill their work with its essences, and many patrons in India, regardless of their specific religion, encouraged this tendency. Most of the works of art brought

together here either portray gods and goddesses, were used as aids to meditation or worship, or were intended to remind beholders of their sacred obligations. Even portraiture emerged from depictions of donors on shrines. Though the religious connection is not immediately apparent, even ragamala (garland of melody) series of miniature paintings represent a synesthetic merging of poetry, music, and painting that developed from Hindu temple practice, in which architecture, painting, sculpture, and literature, as well as music, dance, and costume, were combined to honor the deities. Spirituality is not always associated with formal religion: one often senses it in objects as outwardly worldly as Mughal jade carvings or as mundane as quilts and water vessels.

These objects offer more than aesthetic delight, and they are more than reflections of a remarkable cultural ethos. Rather, they are highly charged sources of spiritual energy and potent, almost animate ambassadors from a land that can be envisioned as a noble mountain inhabited by a hierarchical but interdependent and infinitely varied society, a cultural, linguistic, and ethnic blend that began at least as long ago as three and a half millennia, when Aryan tribes from Central Asia invaded India and found what we now know was an already highly developed civilization.

At the airy summit of the mountain, peopled by the worldly (and at times the otherworldly), the pace is swift and dangerous, fraught with temptation and prone to violence. Alive, radiant as a peacock's tail, rich with gold and emeralds, the pinnacle is alluring and curiously welcoming, but it is no place for permanent shelter. Nearer the less brilliantly hued base, the mountain gains in solidity and earthiness. Life moves more slowly, with less stimulating variation, but the footholds are more secure and companionship is plentiful. This exhibition offers works of art from all levels of the mountain, from the villages and remote tribal areas that form its solid base to the courts and palaces perched more precariously near the top.

The bounty of the Indian subcontinent, a triangular peninsula 2,000 miles long suspended beneath the vast Central Asian land mass, has since ancient times attracted horde after horde of immigrants and ambitious seekers of empire. The Bay of Bengal forms India's eastern border; the Arabian Sea lies to the west, the Indian Ocean to the south. Across the top of the wedge-shaped peninsula, 1,600 miles of mountain ranges—the Hindu Kush, Karakoram, and Himalaya—barricade India from the rest of Asia. Migrants from Turkistan and the Central Asian steppes began to scramble through the Khyber and Bolan passes in India's northwest corner during the second millennium B.C. and continued to pour in until as late as the seventeenth century.

After struggling through the hazardous mountain passes, each family, tribe, or army usually faced another epic test in "the cockpit of India," the narrow corridor between the Indus and Ganges river basins: angry settlers determined to protect the lands they had in turn wrested from earlier arrivals. But in India the bitter and the sweet often blossom from a single stem. Within the seductive walled paradise, as hard to leave as it is to enter, a culture of cultures was nurtured, ever gaining in intensity and savor over the centuries as wave upon wave of ethnically and linguistically varied people eventually laid down their arms, settled, and were assimilated.

Geography and climate contribute to the form and substance of culture and art. In the north of the Indian subcontinent rise the world's highest peaks, and below them stretch some of the most luxuriant valleys and arid deserts, flattest plains and densest jungles. The monsoon winds contribute to the pattern of extremes, scorching the land for part of the year, then from June to October bringing essential, cooling rains up from the south that wash the mountainsides, crumbling the rich loam the holy Ganges River carries to one of the world's lushest plains. But the monsoon is capricious, sometimes bringing floods with an excess of bounty, sometimes withholding its liquid blessing for so long that parts of the fertile paradise become hells of drought and famine. It is not surprising that in the ancient religions of India such erratic behavior was attributed to deities who personified the forces and spirits of nature. When the gods smiled, the monsoon was good; if their wrath was not appeased, it brought floods or drought.

In the face of such extremes, it is also not surprising that the flavors of Indian art are so pronounced—even her classicism is excessive in its restraint—or that Indians developed the metaphysical concepts of maya and karma. Hindus see the physical world as a form of maya, or illusion, from which man's greatest hope is to escape and to become one with the Supreme Soul, the only true reality, beyond which nothing exists. Only through liberation from the continuous cycle of creation and destruction can man transcend karma, the inevitable consequences of his every action, either in this life or in the ones that follow.

The ancient Aryans were probably the last of the invaders and immigrants of the early period whose ways were not gradually absorbed, or Indianized, entirely beyond recognition. The Vedas (literally, knowledge), the four sacred books of the Aryans, written in Sanskrit, are fundamental to Indian thought and are still revered by Hindus. The earliest of the Vedas, the *Rig Veda*, which was probably compiled sometime between 1500 and 1000 B.C., contains the oldest hymns in the world, songs of praise to Indra, Lord of the Heavens, and to other Aryan gods. The Vedas are also a rich source of historical information, if one allows for their bias.

The Vedic texts describe the Aryans' attacks on the fortified towns of dark-skinned, "broad-nosed, and bull-lipped" barbarians, hostile cattle breeders who were terrified by the unfamiliar horse-drawn chariots of the militant and efficiently organized conquerors. In the nineteenth century, however, archeologists uncovered evidence at the pre-Aryan sites of Mohenjo-Daro and Harappa in the Indus Valley that presents quite a different view, implying that in fact the Aryans were the barbarians and their victims were peaceful, prosperous people who lived in highly organized communities with wide streets and advanced drainage systems and were in contact with nations in western and Central Asia. Among the many objects excavated at Mohenjo-Daro are a dancing girl or goddess cast in bronze and a steatite bust of a bearded man, which could be a royal portrait, that date to the late third or early second millennium B.C. They rank among the masterpieces of Indian art.

Scholars speculate that the "original Indians" encountered by the first raiders were Australoids, akin to the people of Australia, New Guinea, and parts of the East Indies. Following the Aryan invasions, these people were either killed, enslaved, blended into the community by intermarriage, or driven off, usually to less luxuriant regions. Descendants of the so-called Dravidians can be found in remote tracts of the subcontinent among India's tribal people, whose traditional lore often refers to their times of greatness and whose lively and timeless arts are represented here in the section called Tribe and Village. Of similar lineage are the Dravidians of South India, whose lives were not interrupted by invasions. Examples of their cultural heritage are included in the Great Tradition section.

Although some elements of the caste system may have existed before they came, the Aryans are usually credited with this specifically Indian concept, which has become less influential in modern times. By about 900 to 600 B.C., when the three later Vedas were compiled, Aryan society was led by priests whose complex rituals had become accepted as indispensable to tribal prosperity. Aryan priests divided humankind into four still familiar major social classes, each further subdivided into many castes and subcastes. The scholars and priests who devised and perpetuated the system constituted the highest class, the Brahmins. Warriors and rulers made up the second, the Kshatriyas. The third class, the Vaishyas, was composed of farmers and merchants, and the laborers and serfs who worked the land were the fourth class, the Shudras. The English word caste comes from casta, Portuguese for lineage. The Aryans used the Sanskrit word varna, which means color. The darker, "uncivilized" aboriginals whom the fair-skinned Aryans had defeated were relegated to a fifth group, the Panchama, outside the caste system.

Despite its diversity, Indian culture is composed of interlocking cells. In India each separate part of the whole, each element of life, each idea or thing, is relegated to its own niche, either in the phenomenal world or in the realm of soul and mind. However rigid the order might seem, much of its strength lies in its flexibility. Within the caste system, for instance, new categories have evolved for those who do not fit into earlier schemes: outlaws, foreigners, practitioners of new occupations, even transvestites. Furthermore, each segment of the community is linked to and often depends on the others, and the hierarchy is in constant flux, varying not only in time but in space and in the mind. Many tribal people, heedless of the caste system, see themselves as the mighty rulers of their domains. And however deep India's divisions along religious lines, Muslim prime ministers were often employed at Hindu courts, and Hindu officials at Muslim courts. Hindu painters worked for Muslim patrons, and Muslim artists painted Hindu subjects for Hindu employers.

India's many religions—Hinduism, Jainism, Islam, Christianity, Zoroastrianism—reflect her racial, linguistic, and cultural variety. Hinduism and Islam, the major religions, are divided into many sects and branches, whose teachings over the centuries have blended with the timeless beliefs, often ecstatic and magical, of animists who worship the spirits of trees, rivers, animals, or ancestors. In all likelihood many of the highly evolved rituals, sacrifices, and spiritual disciplines, such as yoga, pranayama (breath control), mantras (words of power), and trance, were adapted from the practices of animists. India's exploration of spiritual techniques—meditation, yantras and mandalas (psychocosmograms, or sacred diagrams of the cosmos), ecstatic dance, numerology, the use of mind-expanding herbs and mushrooms—has been sustained and profound. All that is "good" and all that is "bad" and every shade between— from focusing on points of light to firewalking and antinomian coprophagy, to over- and underindulgence in almost everything from foods and liquids to the senses of sight, sound, smell, and touch—has been analyzed, codified, and tested.

After the fourteenth century, as Hindu literature and religious texts were increasingly written in or translated into the vernacular dialects, Hinduism underwent a revival. Bhakti, or devotional, cults grew in popularity and achieved respectability under the influence of such mystics as Chaitanya (1485–1534) and Kabir (1440–1518), who sought to abolish caste and taught that the way to salvation was through bhakti-marga, the road of fervent devotion to God, rather than through knowledge or asceticism. Chaitanya, a poet who was born a Brahmin in Bengal, revered Krishna and his divine consort Radha. Kabir, who was born a Muslim, allowed his followers a choice of worshiping the Hindu gods or Allah. At his death, according to legend, Kabir's Hindu followers were determined to cremate his body; the Muslims insisted upon burial. But when they drew back the sheet that covered the corpse they found it had turned to flowers. Half the blossoms were burned, the rest were buried.

Most Indians are Hindus, followers of a religion as hard to define as the shape and texture of sunlight. Penetrating every chink, its brilliance dazzles but also casts deep shadows. In keeping with India's diversity, Hinduism adjusts to time, place, and personality. Like the land it is all-welcoming and all-transforming. Even Christians and Muslims have been touched by its influences. An evolved and evolving faith, without set creeds, dogmas, or prac-

tices, with no church, no standardized worship, no single prophet or holy book, Hinduism could be described as a nonreligion that has absorbed every stage of Indian cultural and doctrinal belief, from animism to Brahminism, to the sectarianism of the Shaivites and Vaishnavites, on through reformed Hinduism and the more recent phase, which amalgamates metaphysics with patriotism. It could be argued that every Hindu creation is imbued with devotional spirit. Many Hindus follow a guru, and they tend to be guided by what they regard as their moral duty, or dharma, determined by their caste and stage of life: student, the time of celibacy and learning; householder, the years of marriage, parenthood, and worldly responsibility; hermit or ascetic, the phase of gradual withdrawal to the forest for meditation; or pilgrim, the stage of renunciation, when one breaks all ties with the world and prepares one's soul for dissolution into the universal spirit.

Inasmuch as life is but illusion to Hindus, neither worldly phenomena, including works of art, nor the hours or weeks required to make them, matter as much as in the West. Infinite amounts of time and skill are often expended on ephemera, especially when they are related to religion. In Bengal, for instance, extraordinary marriage pavilions of jute—as intricate as they are impermanent—are prepared for brides and grooms. Painstakingly detailed images of the goddess Kali are modeled in clay, polychromed, adorned with finery, and then, after a brief puja (worship), borne in procession to the riverbank and immersed. Holy earth reverts to mud. Perhaps because damaged images lose potency, damaged objects are not highly regarded. A Westerner or a Japanese might repair a fine but broken teacup; an Indian, reared in a tropical climate where deterioration is swift and immaculate cleanliness essential, would throw it away. Similarly, patinations on bronzes that would delight Western or Far Eastern connoisseurs are often cleaned in India. Indians are also less apt to venerate "old-fashioned" designs; a prince's inherited jewels are as likely as a villager's silver ornaments to be sent to the jeweler for redoing in celebration of tomorrow's wedding.

The extended family is the nest of Indian culture, a legacy from pre-Aryan times. Family members share a residence, whether a hut or a palace complex, eat food from the same kitchen, hold property in common, and join together in worship. Within the family, which usually includes several generations as well as those adopted into it, seniority is strictly observed, and everyone, from the male elder in charge to the most junior of wives, carries out his or her assigned tasks. If privacy is rare, the family provides security and companionship in high degree. Villages, where most families live, are the modules of existence. Village life is regulated by nature, by the sun and moon, by the cycle of seasons, by birth and death, and by human needs. Houses, usually built of mud and thatch, conform to the land and are scaled to people and domestic animals. Walls are soft-edged and curved as human arms, legs, or bellies. In such congenial settings, villagers gather by lamplight for storytelling and dramatic performances of ancient myths and legends.

The values of village India extended up to all levels of society, affecting even Rajput princes and Mughal emperors. Examples abound of the influence of villages on art. The rustic thatched roof was translated into stone at Akbar's imperial City of Victory, Fatehpur-Sikri, and Indian princes often ate and drank from dishes and cups composed of leaves—though their leaves were carved from jade. The feathers, shells, yak hair, beetle-wing cases, and other natural materials used to adorn palaces and their occupants were all originally rural improvisations. The physical dimensions of art also reveal the impact of the villages, where every household maintains a small shrine, and size bears little relationship to importance. Just as the tiny tulsi plant symbolic of the goddess Lakshmi, consort of Vishnu, is more revered than the mighty banyan tree, so a small bronze image might be more monumental than one of towering proportions.

Indeed, it would be difficult to exaggerate the impact on art of villagers, who in effect filter out its impurities, frequently breathing new life into sophisticated but tired themes from the courts or cities. This process is in evidence even today. Recently we took a motor trip from Chandigarh to the Punjab Hills. Near the metropolis the road signs cautioning "Sound Horn" were decorated with naturalistically curvaceous horns, admirable examples of fine academic dullness. As we progressed into the hinterlands, the horns on the signs, now the work of village painters, gradually changed, becoming more and more simplified until in remote areas they seemed humanized, battered and bent by use, with delightful, emphatic little squiggles—the toots— emerging from them.

The works in this exhibition date from 1300 to 1900, a period when India's invariable openness and vulnerability, and her genius for absorbing and transforming people and ideas, were again demonstrated as she faced yet two more waves of foreigners, the Muslims and the Europeans.

Muslims first came to India in 712, less than a hundred years after the death of the Prophet, when Arab traders reached Sind in what is now Pakistan. Over the next three centuries, the teachings of Muhammad spread throughout Central Asia, and the armies of Islam gathered strength. In the eleventh and twelfth centuries, far greater forces led by rugged Turks and Afghans raided India through the northwestern mountain passes, destroying as they pushed eastward and southward magnificent medieval Brahminical and Buddhist temples and monuments, erasing forever part of the legacy of India's Great Tradition. The Muslim invasions dealt the final blow to Buddhist culture in North India, and at the outset of the fourteenth century, as now, most Indians were Hindus, Muslims, or animists whose tribal and folk traditions, always fundamental to Indian culture, flowed on almost impervious to distracting change. As the conquerors adjusted to their new surroundings, Islam's cultural heritage enriched and blended with India's, and by 1300 truly Indo-Muslim idioms were emerging in the art and architecture of the sultanates of North India and the Deccan.

Another, far more vigorous Muslim invasion began in 1525, when Babur, from the kingdom of Fergana in Russian Turkistan, marched his army into northern India and occupied the Punjab. A year later, Babur defeated the last sultan of the weakened Lodi dynasty at Panipat and founded the Mughal empire. Babur was not only a mighty prince, descended from Timur (Tamerlane) and Chinghiz Khan, he was also a scholar and a poet, and we know from his autobiography that he considered life in his newly acquired territories inferior in many ways to the cultivated society he had left behind. Babur died in 1530, but his four-year reign initiated one of the most creative periods in India's cultural history, during which indigenous and foreign ideas intertwined in fresh patterns of great beauty and profundity.

Meanwhile a subtler invasion had already started in the south. Vasco da Gama's visit to India in 1498 seemed a minor event at the time, but when he landed at Calicut, on the Malabar Coast some three hundred miles north of India's southern tip, he opened the country to direct European trade. Portuguese, Dutch, French, British, and other European merchants all vied for the India trade, and in the wake of the trading vessels came armies and navies. As had so often been the case, India's many kingdoms failed to unite against the new influx of foreigners, who established seaports and trading centers and gradually moved inland. During the second half of the eighteenth century, ish not only overcame most of their European competitors but took over the by then splintering domains of the Mughals. By the mid-nineteenth century they dominated all of India, and after the failed Mutiny of 1857 they tightened their control. In 1877 Queen Victoria proclaimed herself empress of India, and by the turn of the century India was the resplendent —and lucrative—mainstay of the British empire.

Although for six hundred years the accumulated incursions of Muslims and Europeans rocked the traditional social and cultural mountain, and many of those at the summit were cut from their roots, those nearer the bottom survived the quake. And because most of India's artists and craftsmen come from the base of the mountain, they adjusted to each change in patronage and carried on with their habitual tenacity and ingenuity. Viewing the works of art brought together here evokes the men and women for whom they were created: priests and saints in temples and hermitages, tribal chiefs in jungle dwellings, sultans and maharajas in opulent city palaces. And one can envision the creators: weavers working to the accompaniment of gently clicking shuttles, artists seated cross-legged before drawing boards, enamelers pigmenting gold vessels in the glow of hot kilns, jade carvers working bow drills with their feet, jewelers cutting and polishing emeralds, armorers hammering and shaping elegant watered steel blades.

The energy and inventiveness of India's traditions, whether animist, Hindu, or Muslim, are the greatness of her art. The Great Tradition and the tribal-village continuum are at once a huge storehouse, a vast repository of ancient motifs, techniques, and ideas, and a mighty dynamo providing immense power. Strong in the way tides and the sun are strong, this natural resource is so pervasive as to have remained in effect invisible, and its most potent element—the people who created it—have often been taken for granted. From their ranks many of India's master artists and craftsmen have moved to the cities, shrines, and palaces to do their illustrious work, sometimes for generations, before quietly returning to the countryside in an ebb and flow over the centuries. The importance of the family and the caste system and the value placed on spiritual mysteries and hermetic knowledge have encouraged generation after generation of artists and craftsmen in family and guild workshops to invent, refine, preserve, and improve upon arcane skills and techniques. The virtuosity of these masters astonishes, and their creations often verge on the miraculous.

1

THIS IMAGE OF Shiva and a Parvati, also from Vijayanagar (no. 2), brilliantly represent South Indian bronze casting. Although their stylistic precursors, the renowned bronze sculptures created under the Chola kings who ruled in South India from about the ninth to the thirteenth century, are often considered to exemplify the peak moment of such art, one could argue that post-Chola sculptures such as these also mark peaks. With the passage of time, the prescribed canons of proportion for images became more complex, with ever more exacting stipulations not only for trunk, limbs, and neck but for facial features as well, and the human (or divine) form tended to be interpreted more stiffly, with increased formality.

It is appropriate that our first example of the art of Vijayanagar is an image of potentially destructive Shiva, who descended from the Aryan storm god Rudra (the Roarer). Shiva is shown here in his calmer aspect as the auspicious one, bearer of happiness, but he is also the creator-destroyer, responsible for ending each age, or yuga, once it has run its cycle (the current age is kali-yuga, a black period that began in 3102 B.C.). The history of Vijayanagar is itself a demonstration of cyclical change, of the way in which the mighty tumble, giving way to more vigorous stock. Vijayanagar was founded in 1336 by two brothers, Harihara and Bukka, feudatories of the Hoysala kings of the Deccan, who in turn had succeeded the reputedly invincible Cholas. The empire flourished, and the capital city, on the banks of the Tungabhadra River on the site of the modern town of Hampi in Andhra Pradesh, became a luxurious metropolis, a center of Hindu art and culture. In about 1520, the Portuguese traveler Domingo Paes visited Vijayanagar and reported that the city was as large as Rome, with markets overflowing with jewels, textiles, spices, horses, and other riches, most of them brought by Portuguese traders from places as distant as Lisbon, Peking, Alexandria, Pegu, and Ormuz.

In 1565 the great Vijayanagar empire, the last Hindu bulwark against the encroaching armies of Islam, was finally overtaken after two centuries of resistance. At the terrible Battle of Talikota, an alliance of sultans from the Deccani kingdoms of Ahmadnagar, Bijapur, and Golconda at last wrested the remainder of the Deccani plateau from Hindu political control. The melee lasted only four hours. The king was captured and decapitated, and his head was flaunted on a spear before his demoralized forces. Only two years later, an Italian traveler named Caesaro Federico wrote that the city was "not altogether destroyed, yet the houses stand still and empty, and there is dwelling in them nothing, as is reported, but tygres and other wild beasts."[1]

1. Sewell, *A Forgotten Empire*, p. 208.

Published: *Rarities of the Asian Art Museum*, p. 22, fig. 17.

1.
SHIVA
Vijayanagar, 14th–15th century
Bronze, height 35¾ in. (90.8 cm.)
Asian Art Museum of San Francisco,
The Avery Brundage Collection (B69.S14)

NO ONE COULD deny the immense artistic and human appeal of this masterfully cast, crisply modeled and chased sculpture, with its sweetly compelling expression, superbly lissome yet ample figure, luxuriantly sinuous jewelry and coiffure, and costume vibrant with form-hugging folds. Late as it may be within South India's tradition of bronze casting, this is a powerful and movingly feminine envisionment of Shiva's consort Parvati, who represents generic woman—shakti, the tangible and noblest form of cosmic divine power—and is the benign aspect of Kali. Although as a tool for meditation (dhyana) the goddess could have been represented in other worshipful forms, she is embodied here as a stunning figurative image, a pratima. A devotee who is sufficiently pure in heart and able to take power from within can through the image's suprasensual beauty achieve the goal of worship: samadhi, or the merging of the perceiver with the perceived. At a yet higher spiritual level, this union of the divided divine can be affected without the image, by envisioning it in the mind's (or soul's) eye.

According to Tantric philosophy (as more widely practiced in the north

2.
PARVATI
Vijayanagar, ca. 1450
Bronze, height 33¼ in. (84.5 cm.)
Private collection

2, front

2, back

in medieval and post-medieval India), it is also possible to attain such release through worshiping a living woman, a human image: "On a Friday [the worshiper] is to invite and summon a beautiful maiden pleasing to his eye, in the bloom of youth, of great charm bedecked with all the auspicious symbols . . . and past puberty. He is to cleanse her body with bathing and ointments and place her upon the ceremonial seat. He is to adorn her according to the instructions, with perfumes, flowers, garments, and ornaments, and following this, adorn himself as well with ointments, flowers, and so forth. He is to install the deity into the maiden and offer her sacrifices through the ritual of touching. Once he has worshiped her in the proper ritual sequence, and sacrificed incense and candles to her . . . in his belief that she is the deity, he is to delight her, in his loving devotion, with things to eat, each of which possesses one of the six types of flavors, with meat and other foods and sweetmeats. When he sees her delight at its peak, he is to utter the Goddess' sacred formula, himself filled with the joy of youthful vigor, and his thoughts totally immersed in the ritual image of the deity. Once he has with unwavering attention offered up to her the spoken formula, among other things, one thousand and eight times, let him pass the night with her. Whoever worships in this way for three, five, seven, or nine Fridays receives benefits beyond measure deriving from his piety."[1]

1. *Kularnava Tantra* X.39–45. See: Zimmer, *Artistic Form and Yoga*, pp. 211–12.

IN INDIAN ART, as in life, things are not always what they seem. This emaciated crone baring her fangs is in fact a representation of the sixth-century poetess Karaikkalammaiyar, the earliest of sixty-three Shaivite saints who lived between the sixth and ninth centuries and composed devotional hymns in the Tamil language for use in temple rituals. Their fervent outpourings of

3.
KARAIKKALAMMAIYAR
South India, ca. 14th century
Bronze, height 16⅜ in. (41.5 cm.)
The Nelson-Atkins Museum of Art, Kansas City, Missouri, Nelson Fund (33.533)

3

devout love contributed to the growth of the bhakti (devotional) cults, which espouse an ecstatic mode of Hindu worship, that began early in the Christian era and continue to this day.[1]

Karaikkalammaiyar's original name was Punitavati, and she was the daughter of the chief of Karikal, a village on the southeastern coast of India near the city of Nagapattinam. Devoted even as a child to Shiva, after her marriage to a rich merchant named Paramatattan she continued her devotions to the god. One day, when Paramatattan received two mangoes as gifts from a customer, Punitavati gave one of them to a Shaivite ascetic. When her husband asked for the mango, she prayed to Shiva, and a deliciously ripe fruit appeared in her hand. Paramatattan, alarmed, became so fearful of his wife's divine powers that he abandoned her. Punitavati asked Shiva to replace her now useless beauty with the misshapen form of a demon. At once her flesh melted away and she became a skeleton. Flowers showered from the sky, thunder resounded, and the ascetics and troops of Shiva danced with joy around her. Her parents offered their homage, and she was then left alone to begin a new life as a religious mendicant.

Punitavati began to compose poems in praise of her divine master Shiva, and soon she set forth on a pilgrimage to his abode atop Mount Kailash in the Himalayas. To avoid defiling the sacred mountain with her footsteps she climbed the steep slopes on her hands. Shiva sighted her and was amazed. Beckoning to her, he called, "Come, Mother!" And henceforth Punitavati was known as Karaikkalammaiyar (the mother of Karikal). As a boon she asked only that she might always stay close by Shiva's feet as he danced. Shiva assented and instructed her to go back to South India, to Tiruvalangadu, the site of his sublime victory in a dance contest with the goddess Kali. There the saint dwells to this day, and sculpted reliefs often show her emaciated figure seated beneath the upraised legs of Shiva Nataraja (Lord of the Dance), playing her cymbals and singing with joy.

1. Fickle, "Karaikkalammaiyar, Saint and Poetess," from which much of the information in this entry has been taken.

Published: Kramrisch, *The Art of India*, p. 212, pl. 150; *Art of the Orient*, p. 140; Rowland, "Indian Art," p. 974.

4.
A PAIR OF DVARAPALAS
Kerala, probably 16th century
Bronze, height 44½ in. (113 cm.)
State Museum, Trichur

AMIABLY FORCEFUL, THESE bronze guardian figures from Dravidian India, where many regional styles evolved, exemplify the vigorous school of Kerala. Combining folkloristic power with opulence and stark simplicity with dense elaboration, they should be envisioned in their original setting, at the doorway of a temple or shrine that was probably built of wood and round in ground plan. They once provided coruscating accents to backgrounds so unadorned and subtly proportioned as to remind one of Zen gardens or Cycladic marbles.

The doors (dvaras) of temples, palaces, or homes were believed to be unlucky unless they were decorated with auspicious symbols. According to the *Rig Veda* (X.110.5), gods enter the temple enclosure "like morning light passing through the portals of the western sky." The lower segments of doors were considered particularly vulnerable and hence required doorkeepers, or dvarapalas, which in the south were placed outside the main temple unit. Dvarapalas usually bear the insignia of the gods whose sanctuary they protect; these two figures have the third eye of Shiva on their foreheads.

Of all the bronzes known from Kerala, the Trichur dvarapalas, with their demonic energy, wrestler's agility, and flamboyant ornaments, are the most impressive. Their bold earrings sprout lions and elephants, both symbolic of unknowable power in the iconography of Kerala. The inverted arches of their exuberant belts, from which draperies and jeweled tassels flare with cosmic force, are held together by lionlike "faces of glory," the kirttimukhas that are a potent symbol of Shiva. Their armbands are shaped like makaras, crocodilian monsters of the primeval waters, from whose gaping mouths pour forth frothing strings of pearls and festoons.

Local authorities say that these dvarapalas originally belonged to the Thekkadeth temple of Shiva, which was destroyed along with many others

4

4

4, detail

during Tipu Sultan's devastating march through the territory of Cochin (now part of the state of Kerala) in 1789 (see no. 188). They were discovered during the cleaning of a well, where they may have been placed for safety, and were brought to the Trichur Museum in 1916.

RELIGIOUS REVERENCE AND human warmth join in this honey smooth image. The sculptor dared to approach the divine with startling intimacy, breaking through the usual barriers that separate men and gods. Following nature more than traditional canons, he envisioned Krishna and his foster mother Yashoda as a familiar infant and wetnurse, not as idealized sacred images. Their flesh is palpable; their expressions are truer to life than to the realm of the gods. The artist's zest for the subject is clear not only in the lively figures but in the sensuous undulation of hair and the swoop of Yashoda's hemline.

The treatment is appropriate. Lord Krishna, whose name means dark, is the most accessible of the Hindu deities, a god of youth who gradually emerged from ancient sacred mystery and legend. It is believed that in pre-Aryan times Krishna was adored by a tribe that deified cows. In the Vedic literature of ancient India, he appears as a worshiper of cattle. In the *Mahabharata* (The Book of Wars; see no. 21), he is referred to as a lowly cowherd, one of whose wives is an untouchable. In the *Harivamsa* (The

5.
YASHODA AND KRISHNA
Karnataka, 14th century or later
Copper, height 13⅛ in. (33.3 cm.)
The Metropolitan Museum of Art, New York,
Purchase, Lita Annenberg Hazen Charitable
Trust Gift, in honor of Cynthia Hazen and
Leon Bernard Polsky (1982.220.8)

5

Genealogy of Hari) and the *Bhagavad Gita* (The Song of the Lord), Krishna is the eighth avatar of Vishnu, who took his form to slay the tyrant Kamsa.

When a sage warned Kamsa, the tyrannical ruler of Mathura, that he would be slain by one of the sons of Devaki, he ordered that Devaki's first six offspring be murdered at birth. But when Balarama, the seventh son of Devaki and Vasudeva, was conceived, Vishnu arranged a miracle and the fetus was transferred to the womb of Rohini, Vasudeva's second wife. When Devaki's eighth son, Krishna, was born, Devaki and Vasudeva were imprisoned. Vishnu again interceded. Their chains broke and clattered to the floor, the guards fell asleep, and Vasudeva spirited the babe to safety across the Jamuna River, whose waters obligingly parted for him. Krishna was delivered for safekeeping and nursing to Yashoda, wife of the cowherd Nanda, who protected him from Kamsa's order to slaughter all infants. Krishna grew up in the sacred groves of Vrindavan (the herd forest), in the world of the gopis and gopalas (herdswomen and herdsmen), where he developed his talents as the Divine Lover. Krishna's initial miracle was the destruction of the demoness Putana. Unaware when she offered him her breast to suckle that her milk was poison, he indulged his healthy thirst, draining Putana to the last drop—and reducing her to a desiccated heap of skin, hair, gristle, and bones.

Published: Pal, *The Sensuous Immortals*, pp. 128–29, no. 74; *Notable Acquisitions 1982–1983*, cover and pp. 80–81.

An entire exhibition could be held of Indian oil lamps, so remarkable are their variety and quality, and the lamps of Kerala are among the most appealing and imaginative. There are lamps for prayer and for offerings, lamps in the form of the goddess of wealth for shrine entrances, lamps to illuminate the inner sanctuary, peacock lamps, swan lamps, tower-shaped lamps, and the brass lamps, their handsome, simple shapes perfected over the centuries, that throw light, at just the right level, on the actors' faces at kathakali performances.

This bronze lamp in the form of a two-story wooden temple, raised from the wick and oil container by two pairs of horses and hanging from chains of continuous links cast in a single mold, once glowed in the central shrine of a temple. With its lion masks, curling finials, roof tiles, and crowd of worshipers, the lamp transports one to Kerala, where such scenes are part of life. The squat, spirited figures and folkish energy are typical of Kerala bronze sculpture, as is the dark, rugged patination, suggestive of black earth.

6.
LAMP IN THE FORM OF A TEMPLE
Kerala, 15th century
Bronze, height without chain 28 in. (71.7 cm.), diameter 16½ in. (41.9 cm.)
State Museum, Trichur

6

7

7.
CHARAKKU
Kerala, probably 17th–19th century
Bell metal, height 16½ in. (41.9 cm.),
diameter 52 in. (132.1 cm.)
State Museum, Trichur

KERALA BRONZES RANGE from flamboyantly rich, darkly patinated figures (such as the dvarapalas, no. 4) to austere, often nobly spare utilitarian objects like this charakku, one of a pair. Charakkus are used for cooking and serving feasts at religious festivals and at marriages. Temples and families often specially commissioned charakkus for such occasions. This majestic vessel, whose stark planes and rhythmic spatial nuances call to mind the wooden architecture of Kerala, stands out not only for its size and architectonic perfection but for its excellent craftsmanship and superbly modeled detail. The functionally sturdy but animatedly scrolling handles and the reliefs beneath them, which seem to be birds' heads reminiscent of "animal-style" art of the Migration period, are as unusual in form and shape as in artistic quality. The salamander and the solar and lunar symbols cast in relief on the sides may be maker's marks. Such objects are very hard to date, for their designs have changed little over the centuries; this bell metal charakku might have been made as early as the seventeenth century or as late as the nineteenth. Although the demand for them has lessened, craftsmen in Kerala still make handsome charakkus by the traditional cire perdue technique (see no. 51).

8.
KINDI
Kerala, ca. 18th century
Bell metal, height 8¼ in. (21.1 cm.)
Jagdish and Kamla Mittal Museum of Indian
Art, Hyderabad (83.2)

THIS EWERLIKE VESSEL for holding and pouring water represents one of the most elegant of several types of metalware objects that have been made for centuries in Kerala. Kindis are still made in sizes varying from three to twelve inches high. They are used for both domestic purposes and rituals and are a common sight in homes and temples all over Kerala and the neighboring districts.

The artisans traditionally engaged in bell metal casting, for which Kerala is well known, are the Moosaris, one of the occupational communities of the Kammala caste, whose name means maker of an article pleasing to the eye. Their achievements in alloying metals and in shaping, casting, and finishing objects, large and small, are unrivaled in India.

The belly of this kindi is a compressed globular shape, its gently grooved neck is high and shapely, and the upturned pouring spout attached to the belly is long and tapering, like a tender shoot. A channeled rim around the neck ornaments the vessel, and a flaring foot ring acts as a base, completing its classically elegant profile. It is difficult to assign precise dates to kindis because the same shapes and alloys have been used for hundreds of years.

J.M.

8

HOODED COBRAS WITH intertwining tails dance in attendance around this wooden mask of Kali (the Black One), the goddess who is the terrible aspect of Parvati, wife of Shiva (see no. 2). Wood, which was plentiful in Kerala, was used more often than stone or bronze for both building and image making. Indeed, the chunky opulence of Kerala bronze figures often stems in part from prototypes in wood, which could be carved and modeled with ease. But the tropical climate, insects, and political upheavals have dealt harshly with objects made of wood, and very few have survived. In the absence of comparable material it is difficult to date this lintel with precision. Although Kali's enormous earrings are embellished with lion and elephant motifs similar to those on the dvarapalas (no. 4), it seems likely that this piece, once polychromed, is earlier. Its rhythms are even bolder, its forms broader. All bulbous eyes, upturned fangs, and snakes, it must have been awesome in its original position above a temple door, where soft light from below would have increased its daunting magnificence.

9.
KALI WITH COBRAS
Kerala, probably 14th century
Wood, traces of polychrome, 21⅝ × 56⅝ in.
(55 × 144 cm.)
Collection Dr. and Mrs. Aschwin de Lippe,
Paris

9

10.
IVORY THRONE LEG
Orissa, 13th century
Height 14½ in. (36.8 cm.)
Philadelphia Museum of Art, Gift of
Mrs. John B. Stetson, Jr. (60–96–1)

IVORY CARVING IS an ancient craft in India, and rarely was the art raised to the heights it reached in medieval Orissa, where this throne leg was carved on royal commission. Although lions and elephants, with their natural majesty and symbolic consequence, frequently inspired Indian painters and sculptors to peaks of accomplishment, few outshine this carving, an extraordinary composition in which fleeting royal worldliness perfectly coalesces with cosmic, eternal truth.

The gaja-simha, the war elephant of kings and the king of beasts himself, lends his power to the ruler's throne by triumphing over the enemy, a wild man decked out in plumes and necklaces. In India's mythological jungle one frequently meets compound beasts such as this gaja-simha, in which the wisdom and might of the elephant are joined with the supreme solar energy of the lion, whose mane flares like sunlight and whose claws seem invincible. Gaining strength, like Hercules, from contact with the rugged earth below, the divine zoomorph supports the enthroned king not only physically but morally by defeating the terrible demon, the rakshasa.

The sculptor took advantage of the massive tusk's natural bend not only to increase the leg's strength as a support but to emphasize the ele-

10, front

10, side

phant's head and trunk and the generous belly of the writhing demon. Observed realities—muscles, flashing eyes, fleshy amplitude; the feel of skin, fur, and hide; rhythmically repeated beads; waves of hair, folds of cloth, foliage, and crags—are in harmonious balance with the sculptor's inner vision of sinuous plastic power.

Orissa, where this sculpture was made, has often been the setting of conflict between aboriginals and waves of newcomers eager to push them ever farther into remote districts. Narasimha I, who ruled Orissa from 1238 to 1264 and probably commissioned the magnificent Temple of the Sun at Konarak, not only controlled the tribal people but fought off the Muslims of Bengal. On the basis of its stylistic affinities to other Konarak sculptures, the Philadelphia throne leg has been ascribed to Narasimha's reign.[1]

1. For related sculptures from Konarak, see: Zimmer, *The Art of Indian Asia*, pl. 365. For a later, more elaborately detailed but less sculpturally powerful throne leg, now in the Freer Gallery of Art, Washington, D.C., see: Lippe, *The Freer Indian Sculptures*, pp. 41–46, figs. 41–47.

Published: Kramrisch, "Early Indian Ivory Carving," pp. 55–66; Van Lohuizen-De Leeuw, "Indian Ivories," pp. 195–216; Kramrisch, *Indian Sculpture*, p. 83, no. 39, pl. 58.

11, front   11, back

VOLUPTUOUS IN SHAPE and feel, this ivory comb must have prepared many a lover for rendezvous as countless as their fragrantly oiled hairs. Few materials are as sensuous as ivory, and none so improves through devoted handling. In this instance, the intrinsic seductiveness of the material is reinforced by the scenes carved in relief on both sides of the comb, which can be attributed to a spirited ivory carver working in the delightfully forceful style of Orissa, where the Great Tradition survived into the nineteenth century.

The carving on one side illustrates the story of Krishna as Vastraharana (Thief of Clothes), an especially popular incident in the adventures of Krishna as a boy growing up among the cowherds of Vrindavan, tales in which the Dark God takes on qualities sometimes associated with the Greek god Apollo. One day at dawn the gopis went to the Jamuna River, where each of them prayed to Devi to grant her fondest wish, to have Krishna as her husband. They then doffed their clothing and jumped playfully into the river, unaware that their beloved Krishna had followed them and was enjoying the scene from high in a nearby kadamba tree. Krishna descended stealth-

11.
IVORY COMB
Orissa, 17th century
3¼ × 3 in. (8.3 × 7.6 cm.)
National Museum, New Delhi (74.96)

ily from his hiding place, gathered up their clothes, and climbed back into the branches, which he decorated with his brightly colored spoils. Seeing their skirts and scarves flapping like banners in the tree, the girls were appalled, and fascinated. Love and embarrassment were in the balance when the playful god made matters worse by offering to return the clothes if the gopis would come to him. The bashful young ladies refused, pleading that they were cold and that the joke had gone too far. But the smiling, bantering god was adamant, and one by one, covering their nakedness as best they could, the gopis inched toward the tree. Clever Krishna then accused them of offending the river spirit with their nudity, promising he would be appeased if they raised their arms worshipfully above their heads. Mortified, the girls reached awkwardly for the sky, but with one arm only, struggling to retain a degree of modesty with the other. But again Krishna was dissatisfied, and in the end the shy, well-brought-up young girls of Vrindavan complied with Krishna's wishes, for which they received the promise of his divine love. The other face of the comb is carved with three figures amorously entangled in a pavilion, their scarves waving in the breeze like the gopis' clothing.

Published: Banerjee, *The Life of Krishna*, p. 99.

12.
PANEL OF A COSMETICS BOX
Tamil Nadu, probably Madurai,
probably late 17th century
Ivory, 6 × 12⅜ in. (15.2 × 31.4 cm.)
Virginia Museum of Fine Arts, Richmond,
The Glasgow Fund (80.171)

AFTER THE FALL of the Vijayanagar empire in 1565 (see no. 1), many of the Hindu governors of its two hundred or so southern provinces formed separate kingdoms. Even before the Battle of Talikota, the Nayaks (literally, governors), some of whom were members of the Vijayanagar royal house, had exerted considerable independence. Now they became all-powerful. Most of the Nayaks continued their lavish patronage of music, dance, literature, and art; some built major architectural complexes. At Madurai, under Tirumala Nayak (r. 1623–59), a cultural flowering that extended to all the arts produced a great double temple dedicated to Shiva and his consort Minakshi, as well as many ivories.

This carved panel from a cosmetics box (probably the front, as it is fitted with a keyhole) is believed to be from Madurai. The pairs and trios of figures, long limbed, slightly bulbous and steatopygic, stooping, and cramped by the archways in which they stand, are the stylistic descendants of stone sculptures commissioned by Tirumala Nayak. In the small museum recently opened

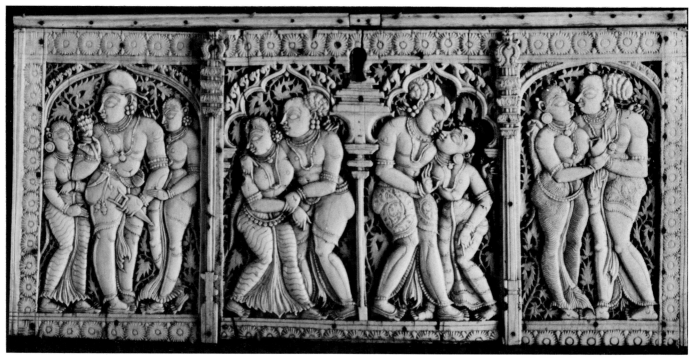

12

at the temple at Madurai are several excellent ivories from a small coffer of the Nayak period that are similar in style to the Virginia panel,[1] and in the temple museum at Srirangam is an ivory carving, also in a style much like this, that has been identified as a depiction of Tirumala Nayak with his queen.[2]

1. The coffer was found recently at Bath; other sections from it are in a London collection and in the Museum of Fine Arts, Boston.
2. For the Srirangam carving, see: Sivaramamurti, *The Art of India*, pl. 58. For paintings in a similar style, see: Sivaramamurti, *South Indian Paintings*, figs. 78, 79.

Published: "Art of Asia Acquired," p. 97, fig. 47.

13, detail

SOUTH INDIAN TEMPLE complexes are bustling centers not only of worship but of the arts, music, dance, and virtually all of life. Often vast in size, with large courtyards and a tank for purifying baths, they provide areas for meditation, contemplation, study, conversation, and rest, as well as for rituals. If temples are active from day to day, with continuous rites lasting into the night, they are even busier at festival times, when crowds of pilgrims gather from far and wide for services and feasting. Each temple has a large staff of priests who carry out both religious and administrative duties, and there are many attendants (some of whom look after the temple elephants stabled within the compound). Masons, sculptors, bronze casters, painters, and other artists and craftsmen—all on the staff—devote their lives to maintaining the temple's sculptures, wall paintings, and ritual implements, and they add to its artistic wealth whenever a donor offers to endow a new palanquin or jeweled gold crown for an image, or whenever the trustees and priests express the need for an additional shrine, carving, or picture.

13.
TEMPLE HANGING WITH EPISODES FROM THE *RAMAYANA* (THE STORY OF RAMA)
Probably Tamil Nadu, 18th century
Cotton, embroidered and appliquéd,
6 ft. 7 in. × 33 ft. 2 in. (2.07 × 11.09 m.)
National Museum, New Delhi (62.538)

This magnificent textile hanging was probably commissioned by an important temple complex, if not made in its own workshop, sometime in the eighteenth century. An oblong of well-woven cotton more than thirty feet long and six feet high, it is a masterpiece of skillful appliqué work and embroidery in a wide range of stitches. Mythological scenes patterned on contemporaneous mural paintings fill the large central panel (illustrated here) and the three smaller ones flanking it on each side, as well as the borders running across the top and bottom edges. The scenes appear to depict episodes from the *Ramayana* (The Story of Rama), one of the greatest Hindu epics. The hanging was probably made to embellish a decorative arch or a hall or cloister in a temple during a Vaishnavite festival. Its exact provenance is not known, but it is reported to have come from a site on the border between Tamil Nadu and Andhra Pradesh. The style of the figures, lively despite their usually frontal poses, and of the geometric ornament arranged in tiers recalls the Nayak wall paintings in the seventeenth-century Kapardisvara temple at Tiruvalanjuli, near Tanjore in Tamil Nadu.[1]

The adventures of Rama, the legendary hero of the *Ramayana*, have been illustrated countless times in many mediums in Indian art (see, for example, nos. 24, 58, 232, 268, 272, 277). Rama, the eldest son of Dasaratha, king of Kosala, spent his childhood in the capital city of Ayodhya, preparing to inherit his father's throne. But when the guileful Kaikeyi (one of Dasaratha's four wives) had her own son Bharata declared heir apparent, Rama, his wife Sita, and his half brother Lakshmana were exiled to the Dandaka Forest. There they lived in idyllic peace until Sita was carried off by Ravana, the demonic monarch of Lanka (Sri Lanka). Rama and Lakshmana sought the aid of Sugriva the monkey king, and with Hanuman (Sugriva's counselor) and a host of monkey troops they stormed the fort at Lanka, killed the king, and rescued Sita. After years in exile, the three returned to Ayodhya, where Rama regained his kingdom.

13, detail

13, detail ▷

The *Ramayana* is generally believed to have been part of the indigenous oral tradition, to have first been given literary form, in Prakrit, by Buddhists, and then to have been reworked and translated into Sanskrit in the first or second century. The Sanskrit epic, a poem of 48,000 lines arranged in seven books, was long considered the work of a single author, Valmiki (who is said to have been a robber, probably of non-Aryan origin, before his poetic talent was recognized by a sage), but most scholars now agree that it must have undergone many stages of development. In later versions, under Brahmin influence, Rama, originally a human hero, "the jewel of the Solar kings," was deified as an incarnation of Vishnu; his rival, King Ravana, became a demon; and Rama's rescue of Sita was reinterpreted as an Aryan triumph over the barbarians. Regional variations also exist. Whoever designed this temple hanging probably drew both from the text ascribed to Valmiki and from local South Indian versions.

At the top left corner of the hanging, the story opens with Rama's first meeting with the monkey god Hanuman, after Sita has been abducted. The rest of the upper border seems to be an account of Rama's and Lakshmana's stay at Kishkindhya, home of Sugriva, the monkey king, where they help Sugriva defeat his tyrannical half brother Bali, see him installed as king, and finally persuade him to aid in the search for Sita. In the scenes embroidered on the left side of the bottom border, Sugriva dispatches monkeys to look for Sita, and Rama gives his ring to Hanuman. When the monkeys learn where Sita is concealed, Hanuman leaves for Lanka, where he finds Sita in an ashoka grove. Hanuman gives her Rama's ring, she entrusts her jewel to him, and, after destroying the grove, he allows himself to be captured. The last scene on the right side of the border shows an astonished Hanuman beholding Ravana, the ten-headed demon. For the largest, most elaborate illustration (the center panel shown here), the designers seem to have chosen the climactic episode of the *Ramayana*: the coronation of Rama after the exiled hero's glorious return to Ayodhya.

1. For the wall paintings at Tiruvalanjuli, see: Sivaramamurti, *South Indian Paintings*, figs. 84–86.

Published: "Decorative Arts," pp. 13–14, 16–20.

I am grateful to Jagdish Mittal for having brought this important textile to my attention, and to Krishna Lal, whose account of the hanging I have followed, for her perceptive and enthusiastic comments.

14.
LINGAYAT PENDANT IN THE
FORM OF NANDI
Northwestern Karnataka, probably
Hubli-Dharwar, early 17th century
Silver, cast, chased, and engraved,
height 4⅛ in. (10.4 cm.)
Jagdish and Kamla Mittal Museum of Indian
Art, Hyderabad (76.1456)

THIS IMAGE OF the bull Nandi is not a sculpture for worship but a pendant worn by a Lingayat guru (spiritual teacher) or jangama (itinerant priest). The Lingayat (lingam wearer) religion started also as a sociocultural movement in the twelfth century at Kalyani, the capital of the western Chalukya kings. Basavanna, the Chalukya officer who founded the revolutionary Shaivite faith, revived an old form of lingam worship, and he is believed to have introduced the practice of wearing the lingam (a stylized phallic symbol of Shiva). With a brave band of four saint reformers, Basavanna soon found a large following in the region that is now Karnataka state, and today there are also many Lingayats in Andhra Pradesh and Tamil Nadu. Lingayats elevate their clergy to a special position: a jangama is regarded as a form of Shiva, "a moving temple."[1]

The lingam is worn around the neck in a silver box, usually a chauka, which is a peculiar shape with two pointed projections and two ornamental knobs at the top, or a gundgurdgi, which is egg-shaped. Lingayat clergy don large pendants, laity smaller ones, the size varying according to the wearer's means. Our pendant is the only known example that is shaped like a recumbent bull instead of a chauka or a gundgurdgi. Its significance lies not only in its rarity but, even more, in the exquisite execution and sensitive rendering of the Nandi as an image rather than a mere ornament. It was evidently made, possibly as a gift, for some very important clergyman,

14

more than likely at Hubli-Dharwar in northwestern Karnataka, a region still well known for its silversmiths.

The Nandi fulfills its function as Shiva's vahana (vehicle) in more than one way. In its theophany as Nandin, it is the Happy One in the presence of Shiva. Some consider that the bull was the theriomorphic form of Shiva, which later became his vehicle, some that it represents the fertility aspect of Shiva. According to others, the Nandi is an embodiment of dharma (moral law); as Stella Kramrisch interprets it, "Nandin/Dharma corresponds to the twofold meaning of the linga, its sexual power transmuted into intellectual command."[2] For Lingayats the bull has added meaning, for they believe Basavanna to be an incarnation of Nandi.

In this pendant, the elaborately bejeweled Nandi is seated upon a rectangular pedestal enriched with four ornamental knobs, two on each end, and two rows of foliate motif incised on the sides. The pendant opens at the base, and the detachable underside is richly ornamented: within a narrow border, a central floral medallion is flanked by rampant lions, and between their heads a double-headed mythical bird, the ganda-bherunda, is surmounted by two scalloped arches with floral ornament on the spandrels. From constant use Nandi's mouth and legs are worn, and two detachable knobs are missing, one from each side.

J.M.

1. Ishwaran, *Religion and Society*, p. 62.
2. Kramrisch, *Manifestations of Shiva*, p. 29, no. 26.

SHORT, STURDY ELEPHANT goads, or ankuses, terminating in daggerlike blades and massive hooks are the traditional implements employed by mahouts (elephant drivers) to steer, prod, or poke their mounts. These two examples, made by the same workshop if not by the same sculptor-craftsman, go far beyond the basic form of such objects. Their royal splendor suits them to great occasions such as Dasara, the festival celebrating the war between good and evil which at Mysore is marked by a grand, brilliantly colorful parade of caparisoned elephants bearing the maharaja and other dignitaries.

Chiseled, carved, engraved, pulled, twisted, hammered, inlaid with gold or silver, alive with deities and "faces of glory," the kirttimukhas symboliz-

15.
TWO ELEPHANT GOADS
Tanjore or Mysore, probably 17th century

a. Cut steel, length 25 in. (63.5 cm.)
   Government Museum, Madras

b. Forged and cut steel, inlaid with silver and gold, length 27 in. (68.5 cm.)
   Musée Guimet, Paris (p. 426)

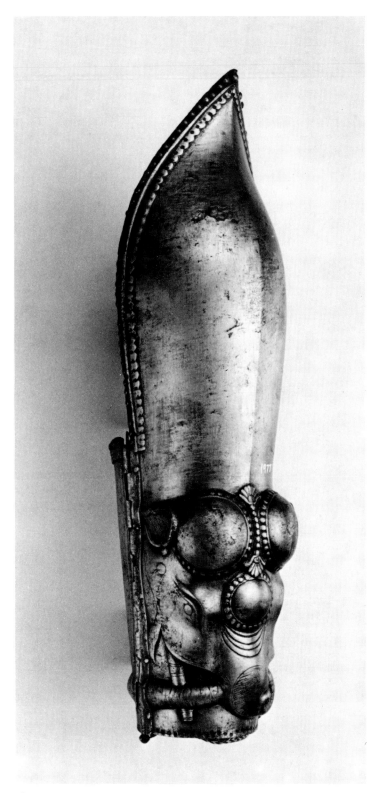

15b

15a   16

ing the destructive aspect of Shiva, as well as lions, tigers, and vegetal ornament, these two goads, along with four or five others of the same facture, represent Indian steelwork at its most intricate. Although they have long been admired by specialists, their specific provenance is not known. A few of the other examples came from the armory of the Nayaks of Tanjore, and some of them are associated with the Wodeyar dynasty of Mysore. The workmanship here is similar to that on some South Indian katars that have been dated to the seventeenth century.[1]

1. For other goads of this sort, as well as a vambrace and katars in related styles, see: Watt, *Indian Art*, pp. 461–62, pls. 4, 67.

Published:
b. Auboyer and Goepper, *The Oriental World*, pp. 70–71, no. 50.

A SEVENTEENTH-CENTURY Indian battle was an assemblage of the creations of armorers, chariot makers, weavers, artists, and many other craftsmen who worked for years to prepare the weapons and banners and hundreds of other objects sacrificed to the fray. A master armorer shaped this thick steel armguard with the potent mask of a heaving, crushing war elephant. The vambrace is believed to have been part of the armory at Tanjore, where the Nayak dynasty assumed power after the fall of Vijayanagar in 1565.

16.
VAMBRACE
Probably Tanjore, late 17th century
Steel, length 15¾ in. (40 cm.)
Government Museum, Madras (1977)

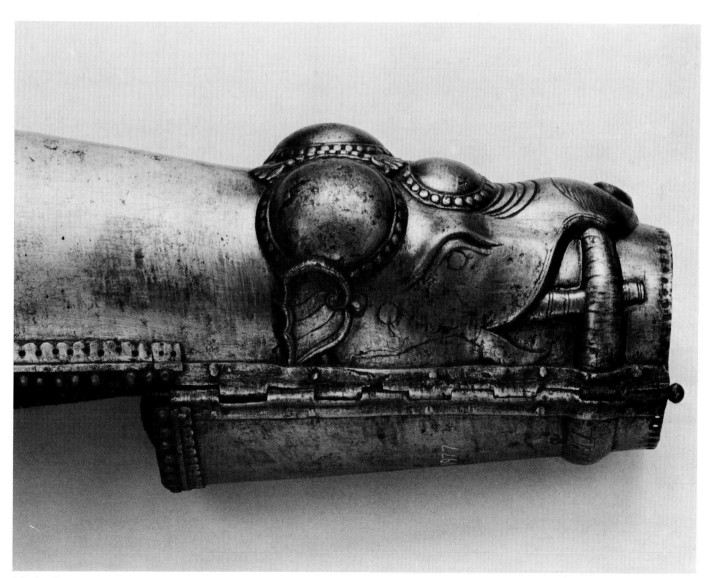

16, detail

17.
SWORD WITH ZOOMORPHIC HILT
Inscribed: "Adoni"
Vijayanagar, mid-16th century
Steel, hilt of gilded bronze, length 33 in.
(83.8 cm.)
Government Museum, Bikaner (B.M.650)

ON THE BASIS of the inscription, it seems reasonable to assume that this splendid sword was captured with other swords and daggers in 1689 at the siege of the Bijapur fort of Adoni by a Rajput who served with Aurangzeb's armies in the Deccan. The sword was surely at Adoni prior to 1568, when Sultan ʿAli ʿAdil-Shah I of Bijapur (r. 1558–80) captured the fort from the rajas of Bijanagur, then a lingering outpost of the Vijayanagar empire.

The hilt brings to mind the bronzes and architecture of Vijayanagar, which are rooted in the earlier manner of the Cholas. Unlike the richly jeweled later hilts seen here (nos. 127, 130, 133), which are rarely adorned with more than one animal, this one of gilded bronze teems with life. Its mélange of animals recalls the symplegma of beasts in "animal-style" art, which was probably brought to India in ancient times by the Scythians and in this instance preserved in the south. Entangled in the design are a snake, a peacock, and a lion carrying a small elephant in its paw.

Published: Goetz, *The Art and Architecture*, fig. 63.

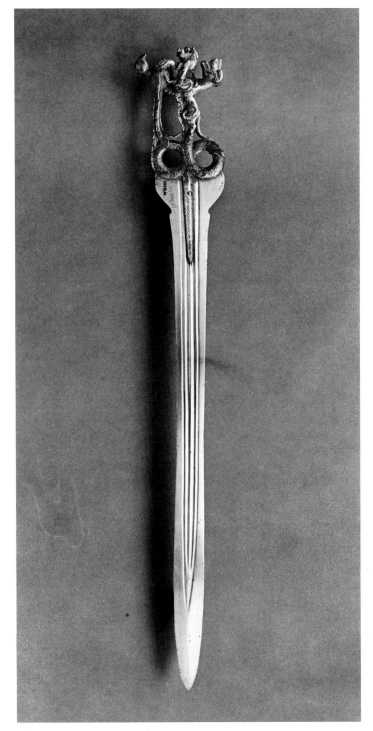

17, detail

17

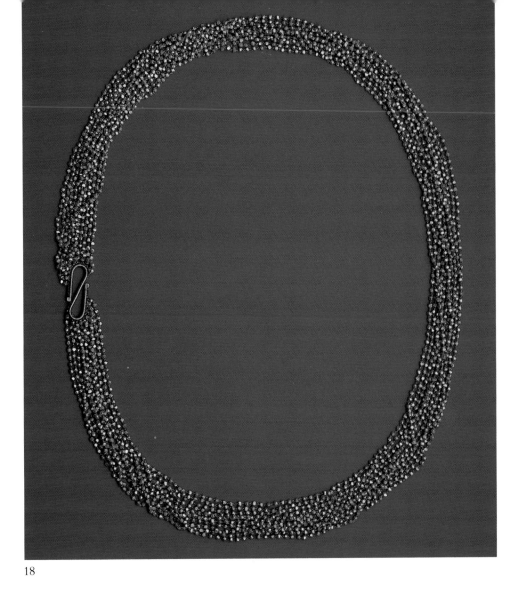

18

GOLD JEWELRY HAS been enjoyed and treasured in India since ancient times. Not surprisingly, considering the retentiveness of the Indian tradition, a number of gold objects from Harappa in the Indus Valley, which could date to as early as 2300 B.C., are identical to modern versions from village India. For more than four thousand years, Indian artisans have shaped and soldered gold into glittering, eye-catching forms that take full advantage of the material. Pieces from the first century B.C. reveal astounding technical and artistic brilliance, equaling the most remarkable specimens of the same period from other parts of the ancient world.[1]

Of South Indian provenance, this necklace probably dates to the seventeenth century. Stylistic affinities with theatrical jewelry seen in kathakali performances suggest Kerala as a possible point of origin. Very little gold jewelry from this period is available for inspection, and our knowledge of it depends largely on representations in sculptures and paintings. At up-to-date Indian courts, "old-fashioned" jewelry was often melted down and reshaped, and most of the dazzling pieces, often cast, chiseled, and chased, sometimes inset with jewels and enamel, that have been preserved in private collections and in the great temple treasuries are inaccessible.

Like most Indian gold jewelry, this necklace should be seen in use, with its rhythmic tumble of sparkling accents and flowing chains conforming to and enhancing the wearer's anatomy. Superb in overall design and craftsmanship, it can be assigned to a workshop that specialized in working with gold wire. The S-shaped clasp, deftly wrapped with gold strands, is so subtly magnificent that it may have been placed against the chest rather than behind the neck.

1. For a pair of gold ear ornaments, see: Lerner, *The Flame and the Lotus*, pp. 20–21, no. 2.

18.
GOLD NECKLACE
South India, probably 17th century
Length 43¾ in. (111.1 cm.)
Private collection

Overleaf, 19, detail ▷

A FAMILY OF MINSTRELS of the Kunepullalu caste once owned this splendid painted scroll made from fine handwoven cotton. Moving from village to village in the Telangana region of northwestern Andhra Pradesh, in the heart of the Deccan, the storytellers earned their living staging performances for members of the Padmasali community. Each evening for a week the Padmasalis, who are a subcaste of the Salis, a caste of weavers, would gather to watch and listen as the performers recounted, in prose, verse, and song, episodes from the life of the rishi (sage) Bhavana, their legendary progenitor.

When the sage Markandeya, so the story goes, wanted to provide the gods with clothing he performed a ritual. From the flames of the sacrificial fire Bhavana issued forth, holding a ball of thread he had manufactured from the fibers of the lotus (padma) that sprang from Vishnu's navel, and with this thread Bhavana wove celestial garments for the devas. Bhavana married Bhadravati, daughter of the Sun, and she bore him one hundred and one sons. One son was the first of the Pattusalis; one hundred sons were the forefathers of the Padmasalis.

Performances by the storytellers always opened with prayers to Ganesha, the elephant-headed Hindu deity who is invoked before any undertaking. Ganesha's large image appears on the first panel of the scroll. Speaking in the vernacular Telegu, the narrator then began to tell the story. Three or four other members of the family played instruments or occasionally joined in the singing. As the drama unfolded, the scroll, suspended from poles or affixed to a wall, was slowly unrolled, event by event.

An inscription on the bottom of the scroll reveals that it changed hands on November 13, 1644, in the Mahbubnagar district of Telangana. The original inscription, which would perhaps have given the date the painting was finished and the name of the artist, has been erased. In recent years, several

19.
THE MARKANDEYA AND BHAVANA
RISHI LEGEND SCROLL
Andhra Pradesh, probably Mahbubnagar
district, ca. 1625
Paint on cloth, 27 ft. 8 in.× 36¼ in.
(8.45 m. × 92 cm.)
Jagdish and Kamla Mittal Museum of Indian
Art, Hyderabad (76.469)

19, detail

legend scrolls have been discovered in the region; seven others, painted from about 1775 to 1900, are in the Mittal Museum.[1] Until about fifty years ago, several painter families lived in the villages and temple towns of Telangana. Now only one family paints scrolls. A scroll was completed as recently as early 1985.

Painted scrolls have been used in India to provide religious and ethical education, as well as entertainment, since ancient times. Buddhist, Brahminical, and Jain texts dating to centuries before the birth of Christ all contain abundant references to painted scrolls, or pata-chitras, and in classical Sanskrit literature one finds descriptions of yama-patas, scrolls that narrate the journey to heaven and the punishments in hell. Indian artists in several parts of the country still paint scrolls illustrating local versions of tales from Hindu and Jain mythology, but these from Andhra Pradesh are the only scroll paintings we know of that depict the legends and heroic exploits of the ancestors of particular castes.

The paintings on all of the Telangana scrolls are in a fairly sophisticated style that can hardly be termed "folk." It is evident that they were painted by the same artists commissioned by the Hindu aristocracy, the powerful landlords who fostered Hindu art and culture in the villages of the region. None of the scrolls show any sign of the painters' having been influenced by the work done at the courts of the Muslims who ruled the predominantly Hindu population of this area for more than four hundred years, from 1518 to 1948. Both the overall effect and many details of the illustrations on this scroll reflect the artists' debt to paintings produced for the Hindu rulers of Vijayanagar in the fifteenth and sixteenth centuries. The later scrolls owe much to the styles evolved in South India under the Nayaks from the late sixteenth to the eighteenth century.

Agile, powerfully limbed heroes and heavenly beings adorned with towering crowns and lavish jewelry people these scenes, and the sweep and swing of their striped garments and fluttering girdles create the illusion of movement. No attempt has been made to model either figures or accessories, but they are so well drawn one can almost feel their rounded forms. A firm, vigorous outline encloses areas of bright, flat color set against a dominant cinnabar red ground, but the line is never allowed to disturb the rich two-dimensional texture of the painted surface. The scroll's twenty-two panels are further enhanced by a pervasive rhythmic unity.

J.M.

1. For other scrolls with the same theme as this one, see: Talwar and Krishna, *Indian Pigment Painting*, pp. 119–20, pls. 133a, 133b, colorplate XII.

19, detail

20

THE BRILLIANT DRAWING in this delightful fragment of a kalamkari (literally, worked with a pen) appears to have flowed from the artist in effortless strokes. The dashing, spontaneous brushwork can be ascribed to the energy and expertise acquired over centuries in South Indian textile workshops, where unselfconscious craftsmen devoted lifetimes to composing lively, crowded scenes like this procession passing a palatial façade. At the bottom of this section from a hanging that was as large as a bedspread, a princely figure stands beneath his royal umbrella holding an elephant goad. Behind him is an attendant bearing a chauri (yak-tail fly whisk). Both were probably mounted on an elephant, for in front of them is a canopy, along with a flying bird and part of a billowing cloth standard. Beyond a painted screen eight swaggering, bright-eyed soldiers (and part of another) march dizzily along, waving their typically South Indian straight-bladed swords, threatening flights of insects with their fly whisks, and gesticulating with broad good humor.

From ancient times, textiles have been one of India's thriving industries. If international trade in fabrics developed under the Phoenicians or even earlier, India's history as a producer of textiles is surely yet more ancient, as is apparent from the apparel represented in Indus Valley works of art, some of which imply block printing. Today many villagers wear cottons decorated with patterns passed down for generations.

Arab, Persian, Indonesian, and Chinese dealers braved India's coasts and rivers, eager to acquire Indian textiles and pepper in exchange for East African ivory and gold, South Arabian coffee, Bahrain pearls, Chinese porcelains and silks, Ceylonese cinnamon, Indonesian nutmeg, mace, and cloves, Persian silk, wine, and rosewater, or Arab horses. Although the many varieties of South Indian and Gujarati silks were greatly admired, cotton fabrics

20.
FRAGMENT OF A KALAMKARI
South India, ca. 1660
Cotton, resist dyed, 20⅛ × 18⅞ in.
(51 × 48 cm.)
Collection Mrs. Krishna Riboud, Paris

were also in demand and were widely made. Indian expertise in preparing fibers to absorb dyes through mordants (a trade secret), as well as the appealing inventiveness of Indian designers, painters, and block printers and their eagerness to accommodate special needs, brought Indian cottons well-deserved international markets. Block printing was the specialty at Gujarat on the west coast; centers on the east coast concentrated on painted cottons.

The artisans of the Riboud kalamkari fragment worked in a milieu somewhere between the robust workshops that supplied villagers and those that catered to sophisticated court ateliers. The dashingly brushed, densely packed figurative composition, although it was influenced by the rapidly changing painting styles at Nayak palaces and major temples, suggests that these painters were master craftsmen in the urban bazaar. They may on occasion have supplied goods for the courts and priests, but we can assume that more often they sold their work to well-to-do local clients and perhaps to wholesalers, probably including foreigners.

Published: Varadarajan, "Figurative Kalamkari," pp. 67–70, fig. 161; Gittinger, *Master Dyers*, pp. 121–27, figs. 113, 116.

21.
TWO FOLIOS FROM A MANUSCRIPT OF THE *MAHABHARATA* (THE BOOK OF WARS)

Karnataka, probably Seringapatam, dated 1670
Jagdish and Kamla Mittal Museum of
Indian Art, Hyderabad (76.528, 529)

a. FOREST LANDSCAPE WITH RIVER
   From the *Aranyaka Parva* (?)
   Opaque watercolor on paper
   Folio: 7½ × 18⅛ in. (19.2 × 45.9 cm.)
   Miniature: 4½ × 6¼ in. (11.3 × 15.8 cm.)

b. BATTLE SCENE
   From the *Drona Parva* (folio 280)
   Opaque watercolor on paper
   Folio: 7½ × 16 in. (19 × 40.6 cm.)
   Miniature: 4⅛ × 6⅛ in. (10.4 × 15.5 cm.)

THESE TWO ILLUSTRATIONS and the other folios to survive from the same *Mahabharata* manuscript, all painted in a mature, highly sensitive and individual style, provide a basis and direction for the study of South Indian miniature painting.[1] The manuscript's colophon page not only bears the name of the scribe—Govind Sharma, son of Ratnaker, resident of the village of Chalitgram—but also provides a firm date: Samvat 1592, which corresponds to 1670. Although lavish and extensive paintings still exist on temple and palace walls in South India, illustrated manuscripts, either palm leaf or paper, dating to before the end of the eighteenth century are extremely rare.

The manuscript was written and illustrated in Mysore (now the state of Karnataka), probably at Seringapatam, which became the capital of the Wodeyar dynasty in about 1610 and continued to flourish as a center of art and culture under Devaraja Wodeyar, who ruled the kingdom from 1659 to 1673. The Brahmin for whom the manuscript was produced, one Timmaji Pandit (perhaps an important priest or official of the Wodeyars), is depicted —by a different artist from the one who illustrated the text—on the chapter colophon pages along with a saintly figure identified as Vyasa, the sage who is traditionally credited with compiling the *Mahabharata*.

The vast collection of myths and legends that make up the *Mahabharata* was probably compiled between 200 B.C. and A.D. 200, although opinions vary as to its date and author. The great classical Sanskrit epic contains many plots and subplots, but the main theme concerns the struggle between two families, the Kauravas and the Pandavas, for control of upper India, called Bharata in the poem (whose title translates literally as the Great Bharata but which is generally known as The Book of Wars). On the orpiment yellow ground of the pages from this *Mahabharata* manuscript, the Sanskrit text is written in black Devanagari script around the illustrations, and the principal characters' names are given above them.

The first of these two illustrations could be from the *Aranyaka Parva* (Forest Chapter), which narrates the life of the Pandavas during their exile. The grove of flowering trees beside a river alive with fish and a crocodile could be one of the three forests the Pandavas stayed in: Kamyaka, Dwaitvana, or Naimisa. Pure landscapes like this are rare in Indian art, where nearly every painting has a figural subject. In the battle scene from the *Drona Parva* (a chapter named after one of the Kaurava war leaders), Ashvatthama, a Kaurava, furiously charges two of the Pandava brothers, Bhima and Arjuna. The rivals fight with bows and arrows from elaborate gold chariots. Ashvatthama's flying banner bears the symbolic face of a lion; Arjuna's is decorated with the striding figure of green-bodied Hanuman, the monkey god.

The stark profiles, beaklike noses, and large oval eyes of these figures, as well as their partially frontal poses, betray the painter's debt to the

21a

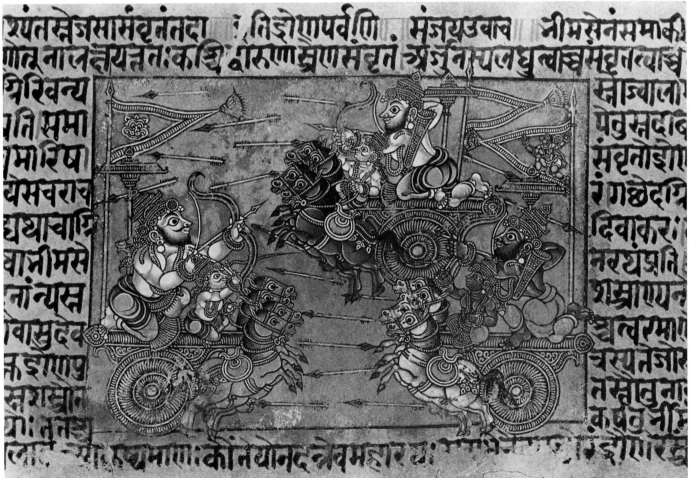

21b

Vijayanagar tradition, but otherwise the *Mahabharata* illustrations show little affinity with Vijayanagar painting. Though both figures and objects are highly stylized, they are charged with great freedom of movement. Emphatic arcs define the contours of the solid, short figures, and the unusual modeling and rounded drawing infuses them with superhuman strength and vigor. Though the figures are small, even finger- and toenails have been meticulously rendered, and the costumes are particularly naturalistic, carefully drawn with full understanding of their folds.

The painter used only a few intense yet mellow colors, usually against a salmon background. Modeling is done in shades darker than the ground colors, and highlights are suggested with white or a lighter color. Figures are elaborately jeweled and crowned, and there is a profusion of gilding. Instead of applying the gold leaf directly to the painted surface, the artist applied it first to thin paper, which he then cut into the desired shapes and pasted onto the picture, a technique found only in Karnataka paintings.

J.M.

1. The folios are dispersed in museums and private collections; for those that are published, see: Mittal, *Andhra Paintings*, fig. 5; Rawson, *Indian Art*, p. 104; Karanth, *Karnataka Paintings*, pls. 30, 31; Sharma, *Indian Miniature Painting*, no. 24, pl. 24; Czuma, *Indian Art*, no. 124.

22

22.
A MAN LISTENING TO A VINA PLAYER
Andhra Pradesh or Tanjore, late 18th century
Opaque watercolor on cloth, 11¾ × 16½ in.
(30 × 42 cm.)
Private collection

THIS BUXOM YOUNG musician and her admirer could be stone temple sculptures flattened into pictorial form. In South India the Great Tradition survived far longer, and with greater purity, than was the case at Mughal and Rajput courts of northern India, where the traditional mode was submerged, or at least cosmetically covered. The picture rings with visual excitement. Curving lines, bold stripes, and glowing color convey the forceful rhythms, tones, and mood of the music. For Indian viewers, the painting evokes a cluster of poetic similes: "eyes like pipal leaves," "breasts full as baskets of rice," "bowstrings buzzing like bees."

Published: Khandalavala and Chandra, *Miniatures and Sculptures*, p. 24, no. 70.

THE DASAVATARA SERIES these two pictures belong to, a sequence of about fifteen cotton panels painted on both sides, was originally joined together like an accordion. In addition to the ten avatars of Vishnu, the series depicts other forms of Vishnu and Krishna, the minor gods Hanuman and Garuda (Vishnu's half-human, half-avian vehicle), fashionably dressed bhaktas (devotees), and naked saints.[1] The series, which comes from Karnataka and was probably painted at Seringapatam in the early eighteenth century, is of such high quality that it must have been executed for a Mysore ruler or high official. The patron may have been one of the prosperous Maratha chiefs who settled in Mysore after Bijapur conquered part of the kingdom in the 1640s and Shivaji became governor of the region.

At the left, the infant Krishna sucks his toe as he floats on a banyan leaf in the cosmic ocean. The theme of this graceful picture is found in the *Markandeya Purana*, in the myth of the sage Markandeya who sees the Creator as a small child resting on the branch of a banyan tree in the vastness of the primeval sea. On the reverse (not shown here), a bhakta, perhaps Markandeya, adores the image of the god Venkatesvara. In the background, a sahastradal-kamal (thousand-petaled lotus), a large hamsa (the sacred goose that is Brahma's vehicle), and a serpent symbolize the story of the creation according to Vaishnavite mythology: as Vishnu lies asleep on the coils of Ananta, the cosmic serpent, floating effortlessly in the primeval waters, from his navel sprouts a wonderful lotus of a thousand petals in which the Creator, Brahma, is seated.

The scene depicted in the painting at the right is Krishna's slight of Indra, king of the gods and lord of the clouds, whose worship Krishna has persuaded the cowherds to abandon in favor of the spirit of Mount Govardhan. Incensed, Indra retaliated by sending down torrents of rain. Whereupon Krishna, knowing the deluge to be the work of Indra, uprooted the mountain and held it effortlessly aloft on the tip of his little finger to shelter the earth below. The foreground and the rocks on either side of Krishna are filled with animals — cows, deer, peacocks, a bear, a leopard, a serpent, and an elephant—and the mountaintop holds a sadhu (a Hindu ascetic), a tiger, and a hare. In the picture on the reverse (not illustrated), a bearded bhakta or mahanta (priest) wearing a red jama, his hands folded in adoration, stands beneath an arch decked with flowers.

The style of the *Dasavatara* paintings carries on the distinctive tradition seen first and at its best in *Vishnu Rescuing the King of the Elephants*, a large painting on cloth (now in the State Museum at Hyderabad and as yet unpublished) that has been dated to between 1625 and 1650, and in the 1670 *Mahabharata* manuscript (no. 21). The style continues in some twenty-five paintings executed in about 1800,[2] and the last phase is represented in a manuscript on paper of the tenth chapter of the *Bhagavata Purana* (Legend of the Lord), with seventeen illustrations, that dates to about 1825.[3] The last two groups, however, have lost the flamboyance and mood of religious absorption found in the earlier paintings. They have become instead mere icons, almost incapable of inspiring reverence.

In the half century that separates the *Mahabharata* manuscript from these paintings, the style changed very little. The figures are no longer stunted, and they are larger in scale, but these are portraits of deities, not illustrations of a narrative. In most of the *Dasavatara* paintings, a single figure stands under an arch decorated with floral garlands, as if in a shrine, filling almost the entire picture space. Some of the gods face front with a hypnotic stare; others are shown in stark profile, with their feet twisted sideways, one slightly forward, and their bodies in the combined front and side view that harks back to late Vijayanagar style. Whereas the figures' bodies are modeled strictly according to the formula adopted by the *Mahabharata* artist, the heavy modeling on the costumes has been completely discarded, and folds of fabric are rendered with a series of lines that suggest the contours of the body beneath. The only other change is in the palette. A wider range of colors has been used in the *Dasavatara* series, and they are more vivid than the somber shades of the *Mahabharata* pages. Lapis lazuli rather than indigo covers large areas in some of the pictures, an unusual feature not seen in other medieval South

23.
TWO FOLIOS FROM A *DASAVATARA* SERIES
Karnataka, probably Seringapatam, early 18th century
Paint on cotton, 10⅛ × 6⅝ in. (25.7 × 16.8 cm.)
Jagdish and Kamla Mittal Museum of Indian Art, Hyderabad (76.535, 537)

a. THE INFANT KRISHNA FLOATING ON THE COSMIC OCEAN

b. KRISHNA LIFTS MOUNT GOVARDHAN

23a

58

23b

Indian miniatures or wall paintings, and rare even in paintings done at the neighboring Muslim courts of the Deccan.

The artist has fully achieved his purpose, for these paintings, with their power-inflated figures and vigorous designs, not only provide aesthetic pleasure but evoke spiritual visions of the deities they portray. The sensuous celestial forms, drawn according to the South Indian iconographic canons popular since the Vijayanagar period, remind one of Karnataka sculpture. Some of the figures are based on the stone images in the Venkatesvara temple at Tirupati, in Andhra Pradesh. The god at Tirupati was greatly revered by the Vijayanagar and Mysore rulers, as well as by the people of Karnataka.

J.M.

1. Seven other paintings from the group are in the Mittal Museum in Hyderabad, one is in the collection of Naozar Chenoy of Hyderabad, and another is in the Cleveland Museum of Art. The whereabouts of the others is unknown. All the pictures have flyleaves with Sanskrit verses written in black Devanagari script.
2. The paintings are dispersed in several collections. See: Kramrisch, *Unknown India*, no. 119; Spink, *Krishnamandala*, fig. 21; *Indian Painting*, no. 89.
3. See: Doshi, "Illustrated Manuscripts," figs. 2a–d. The manuscript is now in the Karnataka Historical Research Society, Hubli-Dharwar.

24.
RAVANA AIMS AN ARROW AT RAMA
Folio from a *Ramayana* manuscript
Southern Andhra Pradesh, ca. 1725
Watercolor on paper, backed with cloth
Folio: 8⅛ × 5⅝ in. (20.8 × 14.2 cm.)
Miniature: 7⅜ × 5⅜ in. (18.7 × 13.8 cm.)
Jagdish and Kamla Mittal Museum of Indian Art, Hyderabad (76.540)

WALL PAINTING WAS the favorite means of pictorial expression in South India. Although painted miniatures from the area are rare, the best examples compare favorably with works produced anywhere else in India. This painting, executed in southern Andhra Pradesh in the early eighteenth century, may once have been part of an incomplete *Ramayana* manuscript that is now in the State Museum, Hyderabad.[1] All of the *Ramayana* illustrations, which have text written above them in small captions in Telegu script, are done on handmade European paper backed with cotton cloth. The paintings clearly demonstrate that a sophisticated school of Hindu miniature painting existed in Andhra Pradesh.

Although until shortly before these paintings were made most of the state had been under the Qutb-Shahi rulers of Golconda and was at the time controlled by the nawabs of Carnatic, who were also Muslims, the literature, music, and art of the Hindus of Andhra Pradesh reflected their staunch adherence to the traditions of the Vijayanagar kings.

Figures, costumes, and ornaments in the miniatures from the *Ramayana* manuscript all follow conventions that the local painters adopted from the post-Vijayanagar traditions evolved in the seventeenth century under the Nayak rulers of South India. The style is a highly sophisticated one, related in some ways to a series of paintings done at Madras for Niccolao Manucci between 1701 and 1706,[2] and close as well to the wall paintings dating to about 1625–50 that were discovered recently at Chengam in Tamil Nadu.[3] Most of the *Ramayana* paintings are executed in watercolor rather than gouache, and the backgrounds are unpainted. The color scheme is somber, and gold and silver are altogether absent. The compositions bespeak the artist's unique sense of design.

Like other war scenes from the manuscript, this dramatic depiction of multiheaded, multiarmed Ravana, the demon king of Lanka, is imbued with tremendous force and energy. Ravana, mounted on a horse-drawn chariot, aims an arrow at Rama, who was probably shown on the facing page. Rama's arrows fly through the air, wreaking havoc in Ravana's camp. Action and mood have been conveyed not so much by facial expression as by posture and gesture. The winging arrows and the corpses and severed heads that lie scattered in the foreground and draped over the chariot intensify the drama. Using but a few colors, relying almost entirely on the power and expressiveness of line, this highly imaginative painter has succeeded in re-creating the tension and ferocity of battle. (See also no. 13.)

J.M.

1. See: Mittal, *Andhra Paintings*; and Welch, *Indian Drawings*, no. 3, which may also belong to the manuscript.
2. Archer, "Company Painting."
3. Nagaswamy, "Tamil Paintings," p. 117, figs. 11a, 11b.

24

25

25.
PLANE IN THE SHAPE OF A MAKARA
Andhra Pradesh, ca. 18th century
Bronze, length 12⅝ in. (32.1 cm.)
Jagdish and Kamla Mittal Museum of Indian
Art, Hyderabad (83.1)

THIS REMARKABLE OBJECT, actually a metal plane in the shape of a crouching makara (a crocodilian sea monster), is unique. Most planes are made of wood (though they may sometimes have a metal plate on the smooth sole), and metal planes were rarely used in India by either carpenters or metalsmiths. Perhaps our plane was made by a metal caster as a gift for a fellow craftsman. The shape is whimsical, but the wide-open mouth, flat sides, and two loops on top also make it very functional. Watching thin shavings emerge from the makara's mouth as the tool was used to smooth wood or metal must have been exciting, especially for the artisan's young sons who were later to learn his craft.

The makara is a symbol of happiness and an auspicious sign, for it is the vehicle of several Hindu deities. It takes precedence over all other water animals as a motif in Indian art, particularly sculpture, and figures prominently on panels, torans, medallions, gargoyles, throne backs, and jewelry. As in later sculptures, the depiction here is highly conceptual. The makara is shown with scanty details, yet there are beaded ornaments on the neck and about the hindquarters, and all the parts of the body, the legs in particular, have been imaginatively sculpted to achieve the illusion of movement. The iron blade and the wooden wedge that held it in place are missing.

J.M.

26.
MANUSCRIPT: *GITA GOVINDA* (THE SONG OF THE COWHERD) OF JAYADEVA, WITH THE COMMENTARY OF NARAYANADASA (81 folios)
By Dhananjaya
Orissa, ca. 1690
Opaque watercolor on palm leaf, covers of wood inlaid with ivory, 1½ × 11⅝ in. (3.8 × 29.5 cm.)
Orissa State Museum, Bhubaneshwar

PROBABLY THE EARLIEST dated Orissan manuscript, and one of the few surviving examples to be signed, this copy of the *Gita Govinda* (The Song of the Cowherd) was written and illustrated by an artist named Dhananjaya in about 1690. Like other early books from South India, the manuscript has folios made from palm leaves. The leaves were dried, boiled, redried, then flattened and burnished with agate or polished shell, and the stack of finished pages, trimmed to uniform size and protected between wooden covers, was pierced with holes so that the long, narrow book could be bound with cord.

In the Orissan style, both script and illustrations were cut into the smoothed surfaces of the leaves with the pointed end of an iron stylus (the knife on the opposite end was used for trimming pages). The artist or scribe held the implement stationary with his right hand and moved the leaf beneath it with his left, doubling his control and allowing him to achieve the graceful roundness that characterizes Orissan writing and drawing. On many manuscripts, the last step was to blacken the incised lines by rubbing soot, ground charcoal, or burned cowdung into the grooves; on others, the artist added a few accents of yellow, green, or white with a brush. This manuscript, enriched with an unusually lavish palette that includes shades of blue and red as well as yellow and green, is especially sumptuous. Most of the eighty-one folios have incised drawings on both sides, in addition to one or two lines of text in Oriya script with commentary above and below, and in some cases not only costumes and figures but entire backgrounds have been enlivened with color.

Dhananjaya may have been influenced by Rajput or Mughal pictures, for by the late 1600s the Mughal empire was firmly established even in Orissa. The *Gita Govinda*, a lyric love poem composed in the late twelfth century by Jayadeva, a court poet at Bengal, is set in the idyllic groves of Vrindavan and describes the love of Krishna and Radha. Radha languishes when Krishna flirts with the other herdswomen, but in the end she and the Blue God (whom Dhananjaya has sometimes painted green, sometimes yellow) are reconciled. Though Dhananjaya worked within a tradition of set formulas for figures, trees, animals, and even entire compositions, he managed to infuse his often monumental designs with imagination, vitality, and humor.

Published: Losty, *The Art of the Book*, p. 137, no. 114; Sharma and Vatsyayan, *Krishna* (manuscripts), no. 20.

26

26, detail

27a

27.
FOLIO FROM AN ARTIST'S
SKETCHBOOK
Orissa, 1st quarter of 18th century
Paint on cotton, 5 × 6¼ in. (12.7 × 15.8 cm.)
Jagdish and Kamla Mittal Museum of Indian
Art, Hyderabad (77.1)

a. DURGA SLAYING MAHISA, THE BUFFALO
   DEMON (recto)

b. LOVERS (verso)

EVEN THE INCORPORATION of Orissa into the Mughal empire in 1592 did little
to affect the staunch Hindu orthodoxy and conservatism of the population.
Like its architects, musicians, poets, and sculptors, the painters of this remote region of eastern India evolved their own styles and techniques. Tradition bound, rigidly adhering to age-old conventions for depicting figures
and ornament, the work of Orissan artists is difficult to date. Based on the
color scheme, certain details of costume and jewelry, and the overall vitality
of the two paintings on this cloth page from an artist's sketchbook, we have
attributed it to the first quarter of the eighteenth century.

The painters who lived in villages outside the Orissan seacoast town of
Puri catered to the demands of both the court and the masses. The same
artists who were hired by wealthy patrons to create technically sophisticated
illustrations for palm-leaf or paper manuscripts and fine murals for the walls
of shrines or palaces also produced brilliantly colored, quickly worked cloth
paintings called patas to sell in the bazaar. Large numbers of patas depicting
either Hindu deities or the great shrine of Jagannath (Lord of the Worlds, a
form of Krishna) at Puri were sold as mementos to the pilgrims who flocked
to the city. In sketchbooks much like the one this page must have come

27b

from, the painters kept iconographic drawings of the important Hindu gods in their various forms as well as sketches for both wall paintings and patas. The sketchbooks were used not only as aides-mémoire but for training apprentice artists, and they were also shown to clients, who could leaf through the drawings to select themes and images.

On the front of this page an eight-armed image of the Great Goddess Durga, elegant but powerful, her ponderous yet shapely limbs emanating strength, slays Mahisa, the buffalo demon. Durga Mahisasuramardini (She Who Crushes Mahisa; see also no. 65) was, and is still, a favorite subject of sculptors and painters in Bengal and Orissa. This artist's rhythmic drawing, well composed, sparingly colored, rendered with the assured, angular lines that are a hallmark of Orissan painting, is among the most convincing portrayals of the goddess as envisioned by the people of eastern India. In the picture on the reverse, a man and a woman make love. The coy, contemplative girl who sits at the right could be a servant or may be the same woman before the arrival of her lover. The gently flowing lines give the drawing a lyrical quality, and a few symbolic, suggestive colors enhance the romantic mood.

J.M.

28.
A PROCESSION OF HOLY MEN
Orissa, perhaps Buguda district,
probably 18th century
Tinted drawing on paper, 7¾ × 11½ in.
(19.7 × 29.2 cm.)
Asutosh Museum of Indian Art,
University of Calcutta

TOUCHED WITH THE elegant grotesqueness and sinuous curvilinearism that characterize Orissan art, this drawing, like the wall paintings depicting episodes from the *Ramayana* in the Viranchi-Narayana temple at Buguda, is done in a style that is close to the traditional painting of South India.[1] Working with a brush on paper, which allowed him far greater freedom than stylus on palm leaf, the chitrakara (a member of the painter caste) who sketched this delightful procession of Indian ascetics or holy men, called sadhus, has noted every detail of toilette, gesture, and personality, from the dour concentration of the leader thumping his tambourine to the militancy, inspired fervor, or sweet devotion of the others. Marching to the rhythm of drum and handbells, the sadhus file past, wearing little more than ornaments, tilakas (caste marks), and licks of ash, their remarkable lengths of hair braided, curled, pomaded with ash or ghee, or shaped into Shaivite protrusions.

There were sadhus in India even in pre-Aryan times. Today most of these antinomian nomads are devotees of popular Hindu beliefs, albeit in their more extreme forms, and, like the rest of Indian society, they have absorbed elements from other cultures and religions. Most shun material possessions: a sadhu is likely to carry only a shroud, a danda (staff), an achal (a short crutch used to support the chin while one meditates), prayer beads, a fan to ward off evil spirits, a water pot, a drinking vessel (sometimes a human skull), and a begging bowl.

1. For the wall paintings at Buguda, see: Fischer, Mahapatra, and Pathy, *Orissa Kunst*, pls. 459, 460, 567–73; Das, *Puri Paintings*, pl. 4.

29a

29b

RARELY HAS THE sacred eroticism of Jayadeva's *Gita Govinda* (The Song of the Cowherd) been more ecstatically illustrated than in these four unfinished pictures, painted on both sides of a pair of folios from an artist's sketchbook. The enchanted, willowy herdswomen of Vrindavan, high-stepping deer, melodiously chirping birds, buzzing dragonflies, peacocks symbolic of Lord Krishna, and, in the final composition, the passionate Blue God himself celebrate divine love in flowery bowers by the banks of the Jamuna. The lissome, graceful gopis, their long hair in braids, amble, sit, or stand, with their oddly reticent backward lean, and chat in a world of expectant reverie made all the more mysterious because the artist never dotted in the pupils of their eyes. The artist's handling of the brush suggests that he may have been a painter of murals. He began gently, his brush touching the sized and burnished paper with the agility of an alighting bird, leaving faint, deft strokes of tan and orange-brown. Gradually, as his inner visualization clarified and the pictures emerged, he added greens, reds, and blues to the palette, which

29.
TWO FOLIOS FROM AN ARTIST'S SKETCHBOOK
Orissa, perhaps 18th or 19th century
Opaque watercolor on paper, 7⅜ × 11¾ in.
(18.7 × 29.9 cm.)
Asutosh Museum of Indian Art,
University of Calcutta (T.284)

a. FIVE GOPIS IN AN ARBOR (recto)

b. SEVEN GOPIS SEATED BY THE RIVERBANK (verso)

c. SIX MAIDENS BY THE FULL MOON (recto)

d. THE LOVE OF KRISHNA (verso)

Overleaf, 29d ▷

29c

he then highlighted in lively white. In flickering, painterly strokes that resemble densely intertwining, curling tendrils, he built up tremulous, animated banks or clusters of forms. Flowering vines so profuse they seem to burst forth from the page echo the ecstasy of Krishna and Radha. The fervent mood of bhakti, all-consuming devotion, permeates these sketches; every living thing seems to move as though aware of Krishna's immanence.

Published:
a. *The Art of India and Pakistan*, pp. 101–2, 182, no. 865, pl. 80; Barrett and Gray, *Painting of India*, pp. 73–75; Das, *Puri Paintings*, pp. 169–70, pl. 27.
c. Ghosh, "Orissan Paintings," p. 197, pl. xiv facing p. 114; Barrett and Gray, *Painting of India*, pp. 73–75; Chaitanya, *A History of Indian Painting*, p. 23, pl. 18; Banerjee, *The Life of Krishna*, fig. 130.

30.
LOTA
Probably Uttar Pradesh, 17th century or earlier
Tinned bronze, diameter 6¾ in. (17 cm.)
Private collection

THE SECTIONS OF this lota, as wide as it is tall and resembling a ridged fruit, relate to one another like the beats of an Indian drum. The shapes of lotas have changed hardly at all since the first millennium; this one, a particularly excellent example, was probably made in the seventeenth century. The vessel fits the hand, and even when wet it is not slippery. Over the years, used daily for pouring drinking water, for baths, and for ritual ablutions, it has softened to the touch.

30

31a, detail

JAINISM HAS ITS roots in concepts developed in India some three millennia ago. Jains share with Hindus and Buddhists a view of life as a unity, a continuum of generation and regeneration in which the most minute creature is capable of evolution; their devotion to ahimsa (nonviolence) is perhaps the ultimate expression of that belief. So as not to harm even air-borne microorganisms with the force of their breath, Jain monks and nuns cover their faces with gauze. Jain means descendant of jinas (conquerors), the epithet given to the twenty-four great Jain teachers, or tirthankaras, who conquered all passions and attained liberation, or nirvana. Vardhamana, known as Mahavira (Great Hero), the twenty-fourth tirthankara, was a contemporary of the Buddha in the sixth century B.C. When he was thirty, Mahavira renounced his wealth and took up the life of an itinerant monk. After thirteen years of asceticism and sacrifice, he became a jina, and for the next thirty years he traveled the Gangetic kingdoms teaching the doctrines of the twenty-three saints who had preceded him. Mahavira is believed to have died from self-starvation at Pava, near Rajgir in northeastern India.

The lives of the tirthankaras and the legends that surround them are recounted in the *Kalpasutra*, the Book of Ritual of the Shvetambaras (White-robed Ones), the Jain sect that was once separate from the more austere Digambaras (Sky-clad Ones), who eschewed even clothing. Traditionally ascribed to the sage Bhadrabahu and compiled in about 300 B.C., the *Kalpasutra* also gives rules for monks and records the succession lists of the Jain pontiffs.

These three folios belong to a *Kalpasutra* manuscript so close in style to one written and illustrated at Mandu, in Central India, in 1439 that there is little doubt it was produced there as well, at about the same time.[1] The manuscript's seventy-four paper folios have text on both sides, written in gold Nagari script on a colored ground and arranged in double columns. Twenty-eight of the pages have an illustration on one side; one page, the last, obviously a replacement, has miniatures on both sides in a style associated with early nineteenth-century Jodhpur painting.

The painting on folio 28, the first of those shown here, depicts the lustration of the infant Mahavira. On the night the tirthankara was born, Indra, lord of the heavens, called Shakra (the Potent One), lulled Mahavira's mother into a deep slumber with a charm and took the child from her, placing a substitute by her side. Indra multiplied himself fivefold, and the five gods carried the baby to Mount Meru, where they anointed him with marvelous unctions. Here one Indra, flanked by two others bearing pitchers, holds Mahavira on his lap. The peaks of Mount Meru, the mythical abode of the gods, rise at the bottom of the picture, and at the top are two bulls, apparently two of the four crystal bulls Shakra created to stand at the four

31.
THREE FOLIOS FROM A *KALPASUTRA*
(THE BOOK OF RITUAL) MANUSCRIPT
Madhya Pradesh, Mandu, ca. 1440
Opaque watercolor on paper, 4 × 9⅞ in.
(10.2 × 25 cm.)
Jagdish and Kamla Mittal Museum of Indian Art, Hyderabad (76.816)

a. MAHAVIRA ON MOUNT MERU (folio 28v)

b. MAHAVIRA CARRIED ON A PALANQUIN (folio 33r)

c. MARUDEVI, ON AN ELEPHANT, ON HER WAY TO MEET RISHABHA (folio 52v)

31a

points of the compass. The episode illustrated on folio 33 marks the start of Mahavira's years as an ascetic. When Mahavira perceived that the time for his renunciation had come, he distributed his possessions. Seeing his preparations, the gods descended to his home, where Shakra created a divine throne and placed Mahavira upon it. He bathed Mahavira with pure water and precious oils, robed him in the lightest of figured muslins, and adorned him with garlands of pearls and gems. After fasting for three days, Mahavira took his seat in a splendid palanquin called chandraprabha (moon radiance), another of Shakra's magical creations. The illustration shows Mahavira being carried swiftly to the park where he will obtain diksha, or be initiated. Gods bear the front of the palanquin, men the back, and Shakra stands behind Mahavira waving a fly whisk.

Other *Kalpasutra* manuscripts depict Shakra as a four-armed god, not the very human king he has become here, and that the artist has included the scene showing Marudevi mounted on an elephant (folio 52) is equally unusual. These are only two of the iconographic peculiarities this manuscript has in common with the 1439 *Kalpasutra*, which Jeremiah Losty concludes was illustrated by an artist who "was obviously not a Jaina, nor did he have access to a standard illustrated version of the text."[2]

Filled with grief at the thought of her son Rishabha's suffering as an ascetic, Marudevi wept herself blind. When Rishabha attained enlightenment, he sent his son Bharata to bring Marudevi to him, and in the painting on folio 52 she rides to meet the tirthankara, an offering in each hand. Bharata, holding a chhattar (umbrella), sits behind her. In the presence of Rishabha, Marudevi's blindness vanished, washed away by tears of joy. She immediately died and achieved salvation, for her spiritual blindness had vanished as well.

Most Jain manuscripts were produced in western India, chiefly in Gujarat, where prosperous Jain merchants and shipbuilders filled whole libraries with copies of the sacred texts. But this *Kalpasutra* and the few other fifteenth-century manuscripts to survive from centers outside western India were also clearly executed by first-rate calligraphers and artists hired by wealthy patrons.[3] For several decades after paper and blue pigment were imported to India from Iran in about the mid-1300s, artists in western India, no longer hampered by the difficulties of working on a palm-leaf surface or limited to the leaves' thin horizontal format, made steady improvements in design, draftsmanship, and painting techniques. As demand grew, however, and paper manuscripts were produced in greater numbers, the work became stereotyped,

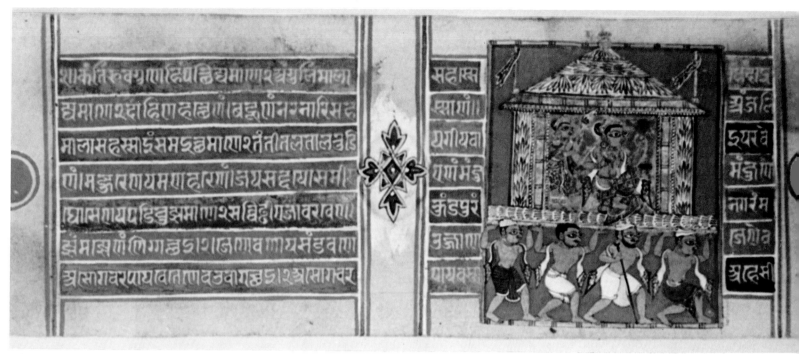

31b

the execution rougher. These illustrations, with their vitality, wider range of colors, and beautifully rendered contemporary textiles and furniture—all very different from what was being done in Gujarat at the time—prove that it was creative painters at places like Mandu who kept the best strains of Western Indian painting alive.

J.M.

1. See: Chandra, "Notes"; Khandalavala and Chandra, "A Consideration"; Khandalavala and Chandra, "New Documents of Indian Painting," pp. 17–22, figs. 9–19.
2. Losty, *The Art of the Book*, p. 60.
3. In addition to the 1439 Mandu *Kalpasutra* (see notes 1 and 2), this rare group of manuscripts includes a *Kalakacharyakatha* from Mandu; folios (now in the Los Angeles County Museum) from a *Kalpasutra* also produced at Mandu; and a *Kalpasutra* from Jaunpur dating to 1465. See: Chandra, "A Unique Kalakacharyakatha Ms."; Chandra and Ehnbom, *The Cleveland Tuti-nama*, nos. 6–8; Khandalavala and Chandra, "An Illustrated Kalpsutra."

31c, detail

Overleaf, Members of the Naga tribe. Unidentified photographer, 1860s. Albumen print, 8½ × 10½ in. (20.6 × 26.7 cm.). Collection Howard and Jane Ricketts, London

THE NAGAS (see photograph, pages 75–76), noted for their fierce independence, their courage as warriors, their talent as dancers and musicians, and their artistry, lived until quite recently as slash-and-burn (swidden) agriculturists in the jungle-covered hills of northeastern India between Assam and Burma. Together with other Indian aboriginals, they have had a reputation for being wild and unapproachable, a reputation strengthened by their "eccentric" dress and their headhunting practices. In Mughal paintings such people are depicted as ferocious hunters dressed in leaves, "bogeymen" with whom to frighten ill-behaved children.

Intended to be worn by a Naga warrior in a heroic dance, this splendid headgear should be seen in stately but turbulent motion, with feathers spinning, brass disk flashing, and black hair flying in the breeze. Traditionally, hornbill feathers could be worn only by warriors who had taken a human head, an act deemed essential in the life of a young male Naga (in recent times monkey heads have been substituted).

Prior to British and Indian government influence, the wearing of hornbill feathers was the prerogative of warriors, who were permitted one feather for each head taken—up to five, after which feathers could be added for each corpse touched in war. Other sumptuary laws concerning dress and ornament were related to the practice of headhunting. Only warriors who had taken heads were allowed to wear certain types of shawls or to bear distinctive tattoos, and only they could wear brass or wooden trophy masks (see nos. 33, 34).

THE MOST STRIKING adornments of Naga warriors are miniature trophy masks symbolic of their prowess as headhunters—worn singly or in groups of two or more, mounted as pendants on necklaces. According to Naga belief, the human soul is divided into two parts, known in the Wanchu dialect as yaha (the animated aspect) and mio (the spiritual aspect). When a Naga dies, the yaha travels to the land of the dead while the mio remains in the village. Abundant mio is considered beneficial to the prosperity and fertility of the Nagas and their crops, and Nagas zealously preserve the supply of mio in their village. When someone dies incantations are recited lest the mio wander off into the forest, and throughout the year ritual hospitality is lavished upon ancestors to insure that their spiritual force remains contentedly at home. In the past, because Nagas believed that mio resided in the head, the spirit reservoir of the village was augmented by the taking of heads. When a head was brought into a Naga village, the spirit of the slain victim was ritually told that although his relatives no longer cared for him, he should feel welcome among his new friends. In the same vein, during headhunting forays Naga warriors would cut off and carry away heads of dead comrades lest they fall into rival hands and thus increase the mio of an enemy village.

Inasmuch as trophy heads represented the village's wealth, they were displayed with pride. Skulls were (and still are) stacked like books on a shelf in the village morungs (longhouses where young boys lived), and it was not uncommon for a morung to have 150 skulls. Because the Naga morungs were made of wood, bamboo, and thatch, fires often destroyed these all-powerful inventories, and the Nagas would lovingly carve substitutes (see no. 34) that were deemed as spiritually efficacious as the originals. Miniature replicas of heads, such as the one illustrated here, were similarly imbued with mio, assuring the wearer of health, fertility, prosperity, and success in hunting.

Poignantly expressive as a Käthe Kollwitz self-portrait, the present example is by far the earliest and most moving Naga brass trophy mask we have seen. Unlike later trophy masks, it is a wholly convincing portrait, the reduced simulacrum of a real face, modeled in wax and cast by the cire perdue method (see no. 51). It is possible with one's fingers and thumbs to experience the modeling of the wax, to feel as the sculptor did the contours of bony struc-

32.
FEATHERED HEADDRESS
Nagaland, perhaps Angami tribe, 19th century
Hornbill feathers, brass, human and goat hair, Job's tears, unidentified red seeds, wood, basketwork, cotton thread, and copper wire, with recent Naga repairs in pink thread, 54¾ × 25⅝ in. (139.1 × 65.1 cm.)
Private collection

33.
BRASS TROPHY MASK
Nagaland or Tirap district of Arunachal Pradesh, Wanchu Naga tribe, perhaps 17th century
Cast and chased brass, repaired with plates of brass, fibers, and wire; suspended on a necklace of tubular orange glass beads, height 2⅞ in. (7.3 cm.); necklace, length 23¾ in. (60.2 cm.)
Private collection

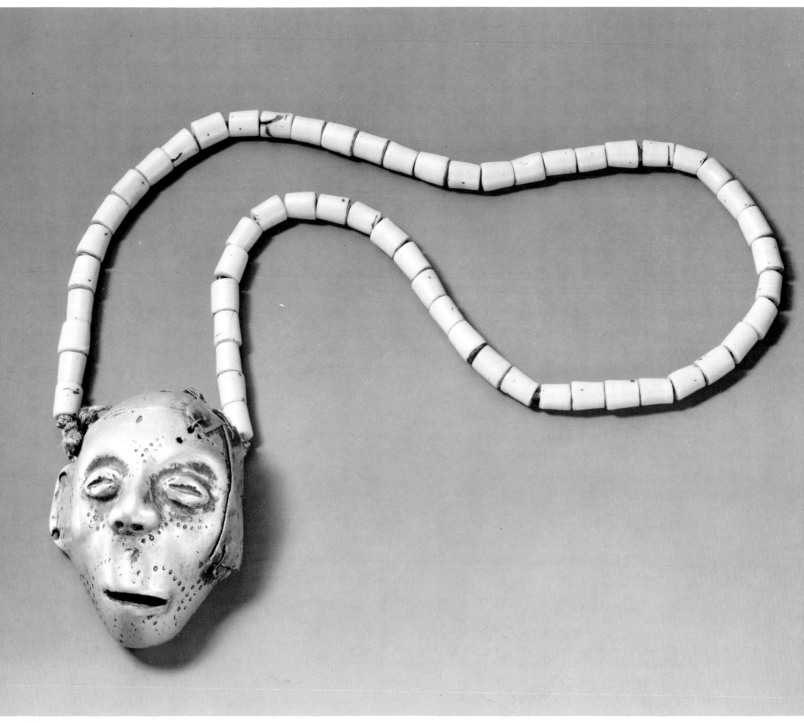

33

ture, nose, and mouth, and to trace his skillful incision of the tattoos. With sensitivity and conviction, the village artist conveys violence and transcendence simultaneously, achieving a work of art that can be compared, in its universality, with another reflection on man's mortality, the portrait of the dying Mughal courtier ʿInayat Khan (no. 149).

Trophy masks were handed down from one generation to another; here the metal has been worn through by frequent use. Much revered, the mask was ingeniously and carefully repaired with small, irregularly shaped plates of brass attached by village-made copper and steel wire and by sinewy bamboo(?) fibers.

UNLIKE THE BRASS mask (no. 33), which probably was commissioned by a Naga from a Nagaized but non-Naga village brassworker, these wooden masks were carved by Nagas, perhaps by the warriors who had taken the heads they represent. From these pendants much can be learned about the ethnic background of the Nagas, an Indo-Mongoloid group that, it is believed, incorporates elements of the Mongoloids, the proto-Australoids, and the Negritos. Because the Nagas are a preliterate people whose history has been largely ignored by archaeologists, the question of how these groups came together remains unanswered. Origin myths are contradictory. Some Nagas claim to have come from the south by way of the Bay of Bengal; others say they arrived from Burma, to the east; and still others argue a northern origin. Perhaps there are elements of truth in all these myths, and the Nagas as we know them arrived from various places. It is also possible that they are descended from the stock that spawned another isolated highland headhunting society of Southeast Asia—the Ifugao of the Philippines. So similar are some of their customs and beliefs, their appearances, and their extremely chaste art styles—quite unlike the ornate idioms of neighboring peoples—that one senses a common heritage.

The sculptors of these trophy masks captured not only the physical appearance of their fallen foes, but—like Indian portrait painters—their spirits as well. One characterization is clownishly rambunctious, another dourly warlike, and the Janus-like pair seem gentle and serene. To increase spiritual power, the sculptors inserted strands of human hair into these masks, converting them into anthropomorphic reliquaries.

34.
THREE WOODEN TROPHY MASKS
Nagaland or Tirap district of Arunachal Pradesh, Wanchu and Konyak Naga tribes, 19th century
Average height 2⅞ in. (7.3 cm.)
Private collection

34

35a

35b

35.
TWO PAIRS OF BRACELETS AND BANGLES

a. **PAIR OF MASSIVE IVORY BRACELETS FOR THE UPPER ARM**
Nagaland, Naga tribe, 18th–19th century
Height 5⅞ in. (14.9 cm.), diameter 4½ in. (11.4 cm.)
The Knellington Collection, Courtesy Harvard University Art Museums, Cambridge, Massachusetts

b. **PAIR OF CAST AND ENGRAVED BRASS BANGLES**
Nagaland, Naga tribe, early 19th century
Height 2½ in. (6.4 cm.)
Private collection

TRIBAL BRASS OR ivory bangles are often more impressive, and more beautiful, than court jewels, however many rubies, emeralds, or diamonds the latter might contain. A pair of Naga bracelets for the upper arm exemplifies potent elegance to a degree not seen in Mughal or Rajput equivalents. Sawed from the wide end of a tusk, then shaped and stained to bring out the superb grain of the ivory and rubbed for lifetimes against the wearers' skins until the inner edges took on a jewellike transparency, they endowed their warrior owners with regal authority.

Also Naga are a pair of bracelets of very heavy cast and engraved brass, lined inside with lac, presumably to buffer the skin. Their Noguchi-like masses are as impressive sculpturally as they must have been serviceable in a brawl.

YOUNG NAGAS OF both sexes enjoyed colorful ornaments, which were traditionally worn with appealing flourish. They adapted unpromising foreign objects to their own use with admirable inventiveness and taste. Broken tumblers of thick glass were ground down into ear ornaments; and necklaces such as these, of colorful glass trade beads, were strung on cords of local fibers fastened by British Indian coins. Swathed in several twisted strands of these indigo, orange, and purplish beads, which blend harmoniously with traditional ornaments, a Naga village belle brings to mind the magnificent women of ancient Indian sculpture, who wore comparably simple, powerfully massed forms.

36.
GLASS BEAD NECKLACES
Nagaland, late 19th century
Average length of strand 22¼ in. (56.5 cm.)
Private collection

36

37

37.
EAR ORNAMENTS
Manipur, Koboi Naga tribe, ca. 1900
Feathers, bark, wool, and hemp fiber,
diameter 4½ in. (11.5 cm.)
National Museum, New Delhi (64.1541)

38.
EAR ORNAMENT
Nagaland, Phom or Chang Naga tribe,
late 19th century
Shell, bamboo, string, and glass(?) bead,
2⅞ × 2¼ in. (7.2 × 5.8 cm.)
Private collection

39.
**WOODEN HAIR ORNAMENT WITH
TROPHY MASKS**
Nagaland, Konyak Naga tribe, 19th century
Length 13½ in. (34.4 cm.)
Private collection

TRADITIONAL INDIANS, TRIBAL or otherwise, often go to nature for their raw materials. Feathers—ephemera radiant as jewels—delighted the Nagas as much as they did maharajas (see no. 184), and one can scarcely imagine more eye-catching ornaments than these. To preserve their jungle freshness, a special wooden box, almost as pleasing as the ear ornaments, was made for them.

SHELLS FROM THE sea have always been valued by the Nagas, perhaps in remembrance of a distant past lived by the Bay of Bengal. Nagas have used them to make ornaments, occasionally commissioning brassworkers to cast their forms in metal. This ear ornament, one of a pair, was shaped from the center of a shell, smoothed, and then incised with a human figure, probably representing a defeated enemy. As with so many Naga objects, its exquisite proportions, line, and surface have gained soft lustrousness from handling. The ghostly but lively stick figure also appears as a motif in cowrie shell sewn on black cloth and as a tattoo on the chests of warriors.

THE RAMAYANA (see no. 13) DESCRIBES an almost mythical non-Aryan people —perhaps the ancestors of the present-day Nagas—who inhabited the hilly jungle tracts of northeastern India as terrible tiger-men, with hair done up in pointed topknots. The description brings to mind the wooden hair ornament shown here. Smoked black and much rubbed by use, it was skewered through a warrior's topknot. Trophy heads at each end, to which feathers were once attached, reminded onlookers of the wearer's brave deeds. The carved faces

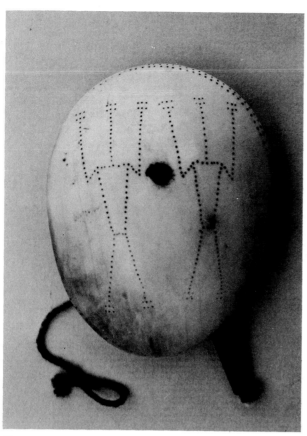

38

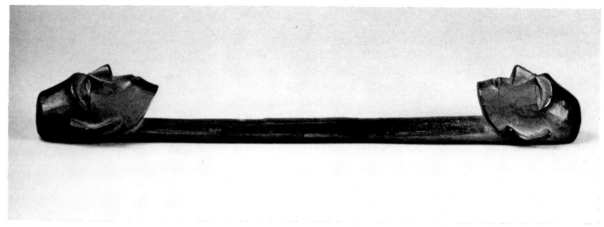

39

with their sharp-edged, harmoniously abstract forms are markedly Oceanian in style. They appear to be calling out—or, perhaps, ecstatically releasing mîo to their new friends (see no. 33).

THIS BOLDLY SIMPLIFIED representation of a warrior wears on his chest two trophy masks and at his waist a belt, on the back of which are attached seven skulls on a belt plate. His hair ornament is of the same basic shape as no. 39. Apparently a commemorative portrait of a village hero, the sculpture probably stood in a boys' morung, where it was protected from the elements. Originally, the figure carried a dao in the right hand, which is carved to grasp it. Like the small trophy masks of wood (no. 34), it is a truthful likeness with individualized features, carved by a Naga who may have known the admired personage he portrayed. The warrior's gaze is intense and arresting, and one seems to hear his call.

Published: Barbier, *Art of Nagaland*, pp. 82–83, nos. 50, 51.

40.
WARRIOR
Nagaland or Tirap district of Arunachal
Pradesh, Wanchu or Konyak Naga tribe,
date unknown
Carved wood inlaid with shell and bone, human
or goat hair, feathers, and black pigment,
height 25⅝ in. (65 cm.)
Musée Barbier-Müller, Geneva (2503–28)

40, front

40, back

Members of the Toda tribe. Photograph by Samuel Bourne,
1860s. Albumen print, 9¼ × 11¼ in. (23.4 × 28.7 cm.). Collection
Howard and Jane Ricketts, London

IT HAS BEEN said that tribal Todas—who are thought to be of Aryan descent
—live and dream cattle. Their principal form of wealth has been their buffalo
herds, and their religion centers on cattle and dairies; dairymen serve as the
priests, and most rituals are associated with their animals. The Toda diet is
lactovegetarian, and although cattle are sacrificed on the occasion of family
deaths and rites of passage, as well as at frequent festivals, the corpses of the
animals are given over to members of the neighboring Kota tribe, who
either feast upon them or sell the meat at the nearby hill station, Ootacamund, or "Ooty" (Udagamandalam).

In return for the buffalo meat, Kota tribesmen traditionally provided
services to the Todas, with whom in many ways they lived symbiotically.
Without Kota musicians, Toda celebrations would have been silent affairs;
and without Kota metalworkers, the Todas would have had to purchase
many tools from more distant markets. Kota jewelers also made the brass,
silver, and gold ornaments worn by Todas of both sexes.

This caparison for a sacrificial buffalo is of Kota manufacture, given
perhaps in exchange for a Toda buffalo, or—considering its weight and
workmanship—several buffaloes. It is composed of three massive flowers
of cowrie shells sewn onto roundels of black cotton cloth fitted over an
armature of wickerwork, weighty polygonal silver and gold beads strung
on ropelike cotton, and silver pendants suspended on silver chains from the
cowrie-shell disks. A large silver and gilded silver pendant hangs from the
smaller flower, the only one of the three with cowries on both sides. No
photographs showing such trappings in use have been found, perhaps because
of the sanctity of the occasions on which they were used. It is believed,
however, that the necklacelike rope, with its silver and gold beads, silver
pendant, and smaller cowrie-shell disk hung in the form of a triangle—said
to symbolize the Mother Goddess Thekkis—between the sacrificial animal's
forelegs, and that the larger disks were attached to its horns.

41.
TRAPPINGS FOR A SACRIFICIAL
BUFFALO
Tamil Nadu, Nilgiri Hills, Toda, made by
Kota tribe, ca.1875
Silver, gold, cowrie shells, black cotton thread,
and cloth; larger disks, diameter 16½ in.
(42 cm.); smaller disk, diameter 10½ in.
(26.7 cm.); length of necklace 8 ft. 6 in.
(2.59 m.); weight 30 lbs.
Private collection

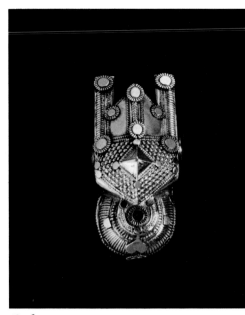

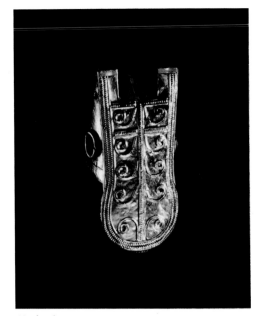

42, front   42, back

COMPOSED OF THIN sheets of gold and a tube of silver, through which it was suspended, this appealingly geometric object is designed in the form of a stylized buffalo mask. The back is decorated with a repoussé tree of life motif based either on the sacred tudr or kias tree or on kakar grass, worshiped by the Todas. According to Rivers, whose anthropological study of the Toda tribe published in 1906 remains definitive, kakar promoted speedy delivery at childbirth, and was used by young girls to sweep the threshold of the sacred dairy at the time of the migration ceremony.[1]

Ornaments were used by the Todas at the most important occasions and rites of passage. After a dairyman had held office for eighteen years, his long celibacy was ended in a special ceremony. It was essential that the young woman who participated in the ceremony be finely clothed and adorned with ornaments before the rite could be celebrated.[2]

Ornaments were also brought out when a Toda was close to death, at which time he was dressed in all the household jewelry. If he recovered, he was entitled to sport the family ornaments for the rest of his life (or, one suspects, until he tired of wearing them).[3] And before they were burned, corpses were similarly adorned. (The jewels were removed a moment before the pyre was ignited.)

When Rivers visited the Todas at the turn of the century he observed, "Formerly, gold ornaments seem to have been commonly worn, and so far as one can judge from older accounts and illustrations, it seems that Toda jewellery has greatly degenerated."[4] From the inventiveness and sensitivity of design, we ascribe this pendant to the late nineteenth century. Like the trappings for a sacrificial buffalo (no. 41), this object is in harmony with the stately arched houses of the dignified Todas (see photograph, page 85).

1. Rivers, *The Todas*, p. 435.
2. Ibid., p. 103.
3. Ibid., pp. 341–42.
4. Ibid., p. 579.

THE KONDS ARE a Dravidian people, originally from the coast of eastern India, forced by the Aryan invaders into the wild and remote upper hill tracts of the Eastern Ghats, where the rivers were unnavigable and had a tendency to flood as high as twenty feet, often without warning. The climate, too, was brutal, with temperatures ranging from over 100 degrees Fahrenheit in the shade to below freezing. Even today, this area has few roads and most of it can be traveled only by footpaths.

42.
GOLD PENDANT IN THE FORM OF A
BUFFALO MASK
Tamil Nadu, Nilgiri Hills, Kota tribe,
late 19th century
1⅞ × ⅞ in. (4.7 × 2.2 cm.)
Private collection

43.
GROUP OF BRONZE FIGURES, BIRDS,
AND ANIMALS
Orissa, Kutiya Kond tribe, ca. 1900
Maximum height 12 in. (30.5 cm.),
minimum height 1⅝ in. (4 cm.)
Victoria and Albert Museum, London

The Hill Konds, or Maliah Konds, preserved their ancient culture —including their language, Kui, which is related grammatically to Telegu, Tamil, and Kanarese—through the centuries. Although their inaccessible land protected them from acculturation, it brought other hazards. Wild boars ravaged root crops; jackals, hyenas, and leopards threatened their goats and cattle; and bears occasionally attacked villagers, ripping their scalps, gouging their eyes, and inflicting wounds that too often festered into blood poisoning. Elephants, tigers, and cobras and kraits were also dangerous, but worst of all were the malarial mosquitoes. It is no wonder that the Aryans left these lands to them; nor is it surprising that the Konds gained a reputation for independence to the point of intractability.

In the mid-nineteenth century, the British were astonished to learn that the Konds practiced human sacrifice on a massive scale, presumably to propitiate the gods and invoke their blessings. With considerable difficulty, a few dedicated civil servants, backed up by soldiery, persuaded the tribal people to substitute animals for human beings.

The fancifully engaging bronzes shown here fall into two groups: those representing peacocks, which are believed to have been used in connection with the sacrificial rites, and those which are totemic in nature. Kept on altars inside family houses, they were important items for dowries. As was usually the case in tribal India, bronze casting and other metalwork was not done by the tribal people themselves but was commissioned from neighboring villagers, who served in this capacity from generation to generation.

Published: Kramrisch, *Unknown India*, p. 60.

44.
MASK
Rajasthan, Bhil tribe, ca. 1800
Polychromed wood inlaid with mirror
fragments, 8¾ × 8¾ in. (22.3 × 22.3 cm.)
Maharaja Sawai Man Singh II Museum, Jaipur
(M.470/78)

ACCORDING TO LEGEND, the god Mahadeva was reclining in the forest one day when a beautiful damsel appeared, the very sight of whom eased his pain. Many children were born to the couple, and one of them was exceptionally ugly and disagreeable. He killed Mahadeva's favorite bull and was exiled to the mountains. His descendants are the Bhils, once known as "the thieves of Mahadeva."

44

Today the Bhils are thought to be descended from the Dravidian race, driven from their lands by the Aryan Rajputs. Although many Bhils now live in towns and cities and have taken on urban life styles, traditional members of the community still celebrate their dramatic festivals and worship Mataji and Devi under the guidance of their priests. It is still essential that the Bhils, as the former lords of the land, give the ceremonial tika, a mark of blessing on the forehead, to certain Rajput princes.

This mask was worn by a Bhil at a traditional festival, where it might have portrayed the warrior saint Gugaji; the Bhils, however, are widespread in Rajasthan, and their deities probably differ from one branch of the tribe to the next.

CREATED TO SATISFY the curiosity of foreigners and their eternal itch for souvenirs, this artfully sculptured slice of life transports us to Bengal to explore a timeless Indian scene. Most of India is rural; and most Indians, including those of tribal background, live in villages, work the soil, or tend herds. Wherever they live, whatever their religion, caste or subcaste (if indeed they are within the caste system at all), and social or economic lot, their lives are influenced profoundly by the seasons. A Bengali glancing at this photographically accurate village market could tell from the fruits and vegetables the season or even the week represented.

Not usually accepted as "art," such objects are known to have been made as early as 1821, when James B. Briggs began to collect the five life-sized examples "copied from nature by a distinguished native artist of Calcutta" that he gave to the East India Marine Society (later the Peabody Museum of Salem).[1] Like the paintings made for William Fraser (see nos. 49, 50), they prefigure photography, and their creation can be ascribed to the desire for "scientific" visual documentation that contributed to the invention of the camera.

Highly naturalistic sculptures of this sort were made at Krishnaghur, a village near Calcutta, as well as at Hatwa, Datan (near Saran), Muzaffar-

45.
A VILLAGE MARKET
Bengal, Calcutta area, Krishnaghur, ca. 1875
Polychromed pottery, wood, thatch, and cloth,
13 × 32 × 32 in. (33 × 81.3 × 81.3 cm.)
Peabody Museum of Salem (E7676)

pur, Dacca, Burdwan, and, later, Lucknow and Poona. They resemble eighteenth- and nineteenth-century crèche figures made in Naples, which are similarly detailed and dressed in cloth garments. Perhaps an Englishman familiar with the Neapolitan examples—standard memorabilia from the Grand Tour—and aware of both the very skillful Bengali makers of polychromed clay images and the naturalistic Mughal tradition inspired this art form.

1. Archives, Peabody Museum of Salem.

I would like to thank Susan Bean for providing much of the information used in this entry.

46.
MORTUARY PAT: A LADY FROM MIDNAPUR
West Bengal, Midnapur, mid-19th century
Opaque watercolor on paper, 15¾ × 30¾ in. (40 × 78.1 cm.)
Asutosh Museum of Indian Art,
University of Calcutta (T.2573)

IN WEST BENGAL, a humble caste of roving Jadupatuas, or painter-storytellers, painted scrolls showing legendary or topical events to illustrate their dramatic recitations for village audiences. To earn extra money, these enterprising entertainers, on learning of a death in a tribal village, would scurry to the house of the deceased and offer the family a pat, or memorial portrait, the fee determined by a rapid evaluation of the family's bullocks, ornaments, and cooking pots. Once the portrait had been produced, it was apparent that the eyes lacked pupils, and the wily artist would explain that the late lamented was fated to be a blind wanderer in the other world, a problem that he could correct—for an additional sum—by painting in the eyes. Usually, such pictures were powerful silhouettes, true to type but not actual likenesses, showing one or two figures—if tragedy had struck twice—set against the bare and very cheap paper. This example is altogether exceptional in showing a lady who must have been of considerable importance within her Midnapur community, attended by servants or family members, in a house rich with European style oil lamps and other signs of wealth.

46

47

EMBROIDERED QUILTS CALLED kanthas were once made by country women—of all castes and classes, both Hindus and Muslims—in all parts of Bengal, usually for their own domestic use or as special gifts. Large kanthas served as bedspreads or as wraps to be worn, smaller ones as cradle cloths or covers for books or mirrors. The women of the Tanti (weaver) and Dhobi (washerman) castes were especially adept at embroidering them; the best come from East Bengal (Bangladesh), where the Kayastha women, from the homes of middle-class clerks and scribes, produced the most ornate of the known examples. No kantha made before the nineteenth century survives, and by the early decades of the twentieth century kantha making was discontinued.

Kanthas were made from carefully selected old and discarded white cotton dhotis. The cloth from women's saris was never used, but colored threads meticulously drawn out from the borders of old saris were used for the embroidery. To achieve the required thickness, several layers of white cloth of uniform fabric and texture were laid evenly on a mat, patched if necessary, and stitched together around the edges with white thread. The surface was compartmented, and geometric, floral, or figural designs were drawn in with thin lines of charcoal. The actual embroidery was started at the center, usually with a traditional medallion, and the work proceeded outward.

All the patterns and figures on a kantha are imbued with symbolic meaning. The form and placing of the motifs and the combination of colors and stitches were dictated by the imagination of the embroiderer and thus reflect her personality. The ingeniously employed stitches not only reinforce the white cloth but give the kantha an overall liveliness and a distinctive character. The patterns were filled in with running stitches in colored thread and then defined by back stitching. In the intervening spaces on the white field, closely parallel running stitches in white thread were made to follow the outlines of the figures and motifs, producing the effect of modeling and

47.
KANTHA WITH DESIGN OF BIRDS AND ANIMALS
Bengal, late 19th century
White cotton, quilted and embroidered with colors, 15¾ × 25⅝ in. (40 × 65 cm.)
Jagdish and Kamla Mittal Museum of Indian Art, Hyderabad (76.1514)

giving the textured surface of each kantha a tonality all its own. In the early nineteenth century, the designs were embroidered mainly in madder-dyed red and indigo blue thread; in the latter half of the century, yellows and greens were added.

Designed by the women themselves, kanthas are infused with the vitality and spontaneity of the folk art for which Bengal is so famous. No two kanthas are alike, but because repertoires of designs, colors, and stitches were often handed down from one generation of women to the next, kanthas from the same village or district have features in common. Some are embroidered only with ancient Hindu symbols and with objects popular in Bengal, some illustrate Hindu myth and ritual, and some show scenes of contemporary everyday life. Our kantha belongs to a fourth group, in which stylized plants and symbols surround archaic figures, sometimes, as here, just animals and birds, sometimes human beings as well.

This coverlet is a masterpiece among small kanthas. Birds, animals (a cow, a fish, a butterfly, and other creatures), and floral motifs are embroidered in red, yellow, green, and black on the white field, which is enclosed by a border of two broad bands, one purplish brown, the other green, both edged in yellow. Closely spaced running stitches in white thread, cleverly made to run along the contours of all the figures, enliven the design. The woman who designed this small coverlet and executed it with her needle created much more than a traditional kantha. Her flight of fancy is like folk painting at its best.

J.M.

48

48.
SIX BATTLING WARRIORS
Rajasthan, late 19th century
Watercolor on paper, 4¼ × 10 in.
(10.8 × 25.4 cm.)
Jagdish and Kamla Mittal Museum of Indian Art, Hyderabad (76.209)

THE STYLE OF this picture, done in watercolor on an unpainted ground, fits no known Indian folk idiom, nor are there any of the clues—subject, palette, details of costume and ornament—that usually link folk paintings to a particular region or village. Unsophisticated, naïve, innocent as a child's painting, this is obviously not the work of a professional. Yet in spite of his lack of training and limited knowledge of technique, the village artist managed to infuse his six dynamic warriors, fiercely battling with their fists and what could be either maces or swords, with unusual vitality and directness.

J.M.

AUTHENTIC AS DUST in sunlight, this group portrait of villagers brings with it a notable snippet of history. On a quiet evening in 1835, Sir Thomas Theophilus Metcalf, a typical English squire transplanted to Delhi—where he served as British resident at the Mughal court—was enjoying his collection of Napoleonic memorabilia when servants interrupted. William Fraser, for whom this picture was painted, his friend and a fellow agent of the governor-general, had been shot dead. Fraser, who was born in Scotland in 1784 and arrived in India in 1799, was known as an erratic, often wayward, gregarious fellow, admired by his many prestigious English and Indian friends but

49.
TAX COLLECTORS AND VILLAGE ELDERS
From the Fraser Album
Probably by Ghulam ʿAli Khan
Delhi or Haryana, early 19th century
Opaque watercolor on paper
Folio: 20¾ × 15¼ in. (52.7 × 38.7 cm.)
Miniature: 10½ × 15¼ in. (26.7 × 38.7 cm.)
The Knellington Collection, Courtesy
Harvard University Art Museums,
Cambridge, Massachusetts

49, detail

reputed to be a ruthless and tightfisted manager of his own extensive estates in Haryana. Whole villages, it was claimed, packed up and moved to avoid his merciless tax collectors.

Fraser's murder was ascribed not to outraged villagers but to assassins in the hire of a young nobleman, Shams ad-Din, nawab of Firozpur, who believed Fraser had blocked his inheritance of title and fortune. A remarkably colorful career during a most vital period of British India had ended at its zenith.

William Fraser is important as the patron of superb gouaches that sweep one back to northwestern India of the 1810s to 1830s. William shared the artistic sensibility of his brother James Baillie Fraser, whose appealing romantic landscape prints still enliven bedroom walls of Rajput palaces and old-fashioned Indian hotels. He hired at least two artists trained in the Mughal imperial ateliers, the brilliant Ghulam ʿAli Khan and an unidentified lesser hand. Accompanying Fraser on his missions to the Punjab and the Himalayas, they were kept very busy recording the activities of Indian people in a series of more than one hundred accurately rendered studies. Leafing through Fraser's nostalgic album, one meets the inhabitants of the world he encountered: musicians, soldiers, yogis, Sufis, merchants, murderers, dancing girls, princes, courtesans, and—above all—villagers, sketched on the move, in characteristic settings and costumes. The earliest of these album pictures, on English paper, were painted in purely Mughal opaque watercolor technique, but soon the artists adjusted to Fraser's taste for transparent washes.

In this group portrait Jat and Rajput elders, probably headmen from Fraser's own villages, suffer the attentions of his agents, a clerkish scribe and a sleek Muslim. Except for the Muslim's outmoded costume, everything here can be seen today in the villages of Haryana. As was customary, the patron numbered each portrait and diligently penciled the subjects' names on the attached protective page. Despite the business at hand, the characterizations represent Fraser's sympathetically warmhearted mood, communicated to his artist and well served by the latter's remarkable ability to reach the sitters' inner spirits.

Published: Sotheby's, London, July 7, 1980, lot 4.

For an account of William Fraser and his circle, see: Spear, *The Twilight of the Mughals.*

MORE CONVINCING AND informative than any photograph, this picture represents one of two village complexes rendered to William Fraser's meticulous specifications (see no. 49). The artist was trained in the Mughal tradition, which ordinarily eschewed genre subjects (but see nos. 140, 159, 160), and one assumes that he was shown English or European townscapes on which to base perspective and composition. Painting from life, in English watercolor technique but with a miniaturist's attention to minute detail, the artist noted distinctive vignettes that to this day fascinate travelers in rural India: a peacock strutting on a skewed and weathered thatched roof; an old lady pounding meal to make chapatis; huge sculptural earthenware grain-storage jars; meandering bullocks, cows, and camels; and mud walls looking as though they had grown in place. Most appealing of all, of course, is the multitude of villagers going about their chores in a camouflage of sweat and dust.

Published: Sotheby's, London, July 7, 1980, lot 22.

50.
RAUNEAH, A VILLAGE IN THE PUNJAB
From the Fraser Album
Probably by Ghulam ʿAli Khan
Punjab, early 19th century
Opaque watercolor on paper, 12⅜ × 16½ in.
(31.5 × 42 cm.)
The British Library, India Office Library and Records, London

50

51.
DEMON
South India, perhaps 17th century
Brass, height 13½ in. (34.3 cm.)
Collection Leo S. Figiel, Atlantis, Florida

THIS FOLK IMAGE expresses the awesome, even terrifying potency of a primeval village demon. His help might have been sought to cure malaria or smallpox, to promote fertility, to appease—or torment—a threatening money lender, or to hasten a delayed monsoon. When worshiped, the image was probably housed in the chamber of a small shrine, lighted by flickering clay oil lamps, partly shined by the touches of devotees, and partly hidden beneath accumulated dust, and offerings of ghee, vermilion powder, and flower petals.

Most Indian bronzes are made by the cire perdue, or lost wax, process, which usually entails modeling the core of the object, somewhat smaller than the proposed metal one, in medium rough clay mixed with dung. The core is then covered with a skin of fine clay, after which the clay model is covered with a layer of wax (beeswax and dammar resin from the sal tree), sometimes enriched by rolled wax pellets or wirelike elements, and worked in detail with bamboo and tamarind wood tools. The mold is then built up with a coating of soft clay (three parts clay to one part powdered pottery, ground together), into which metal strips or nails are inserted, reaching into the wax image. An opening is made in the base of the image and mold, and after the whole has dried, the wax is melted out. The mold is then heated and inverted. Molten metal is poured in, in a steady stream, so that it reaches every area once filled with wax. Heavier images are made by modeling in solid wax, without a core. Once the object has been cooled by sprinkling it with water, the craftsman carefully chisels away the clay crust, or mold, and cuts away the metal strips or nails. Cleaning, chasing, and polishing follow.

Published: Kramrisch, *Unknown India*, p. 91, no. 89, pl. XXII; Christie's, New York, December 1, 1982, lot 164.

Kerala is a land of dance. Best known for kathakali, its evolved dance-drama, it is also noted for many folk traditions. At festival times, like flowers suddenly in bloom, villagers dressed in magnificent masked headdresses such as this one performed ancient religious dances. Relying on designs passed down for generations among families of craftsmen and dancers, villagers fashioned the headdresses from available materials—plantain leaves, cotton cloth, wood, fibers, and indigenous dyes and pigments.

Many of these folk traditions, such as the Mudiyettu, a stylized dance-drama devoted to the Puranic story of Darika-Vadha, in which the goddess Kali slays the demon Darika, are still performed at certain temples. Less formal and less complex traditions retain elements of spontaneous trance, exorcism, and release. This headdress, which brings to mind the art of New Guinea and New Ireland, seems to belong to an early, vital stage in the evolution of dance.

An exciting discovery of some 150 life-sized wooden sculptures of divinities, attendants, and animals was made not long ago at Basrur, a village by the sea surrounded by forest. The sculptures belonged to a shrine named Mekkekattu, where local fishermen and their families worshiped.[1] One of the livelier figures is this ample chauri bearer, holding up her yak-tail whisk to honor one of the deities. Her simplified, extravagant form recalls the

52.
HEADDRESS AND MASK FOR A DANCE
Kerala, ca. 1900
Painted wood, cloth, peacock feathers, glass beads, shells, paper, silver foil, cord, and cane fiber, height with feathers 66½ in. (168.9 cm.)
State Museum, Trichur

53.
CHAURI BEARER
Karnataka, 18th century
Wood, originally polychromed, height 5 ft. 3 in. (1.6 m.)
Folklore Museum, Mysore

53

sculpture of the Baga tribe of Africa, and her ruggedly geometric features bring to mind the expressive profiles of early Rajput paintings, such as are shown in the large battle scene from Uttar Pradesh (no. 225), a stylistic affinity spanning considerable time and distance.

1. Other sculptures from Mekkekattu are in the Folklore Museum, Mysore, and in the Crafts Museum, New Delhi. See: Kramrisch, *Unknown India*, nos. 113–16.

54, three-quarters   54, front

54.
GRAVE EFFIGY: FIGURE OF A WOMAN
Nicobar Islands, 19th century
Wood and red ochre, height 44⅞ in. (114 cm.)
National Museum, New Delhi (80.579)

THIS NOBLY IMPRESSIVE statue of a woman was collected by Sankho Chaudhuri, who has told us that it was found under a tree on the island of Katchall. On Katchall, it is the duty of young men to install in front of the family alpanan (house on stilts) wood carvings that depict their fathers, so that families virtually live with their dead parents. As spirit members of the household, these images are given propitiatory offerings of food and drink every day; and sometimes, according to Chaudhuri, little bottles containing alcohol are suspended from their outstretched arms. When a new effigy is installed, earlier images are removed. Statues of women, such as this one, are extremely rare.

55.
SORCERY FIGURE
Malabar Coast, Mappilla, 19th century
Wood, height 60 in. (152.4 cm.)
Government Museum, Madras (605)

SPECTRAL IN ITS silent, geometric power and lean harmony of proportion, this piece so struck the museum world of India in the days when objects of this sort were usually denigrated as ethnographic curiosities that it was collected for a great museum. Edgar Thurston, then superintendent of the Madras Government Museum, which acquired it, discussed and illustrated it in his monumental anthropological study, attributing it to the Mappillas, or

56

Mohplas, who are described as "the hybrid Mahomedan race of the western coast. . . . The Mappilla jins and shaitans correspond to the Hindu demons, and are propitiated in much the same way. One of their methods of witch-craft is to make a wooden figure to represent the enemy, drive nails into all the vital parts, and throw it into the sea." Of this work in particular he goes on to say: "In 1903, a life-size nude female figure, with feet everted and turned backwards, carved out of the wood of *Alstonia scholaris*, was washed ashore at Calicut. Long nails had been driven in all over the head, body, and limbs, and a large square hole cut out above the navel. Inscriptions in Arabic characters were scrawled over it."[1]

1. Thurston, *Tribes and Castes*, vol. 4, p. 489.

Published: Thurston, *Tribes and Castes*, vol. 4, p. 489; Mookerjee, *Indian Primitive Art*, p. 68, pl. XXXVIII.

THIS TOMB COVER was being used as a canopy over a stall when Mr. and Mrs. William G. Archer came upon it at a village fair in the vicinity of Bahraich in the early 1930s. Timeless as it may be artistically—the cheerfully ani-mated design recalls Alexander Calder's *Circus*, Matisse's cutouts, and Greek geometric painted pottery—one can be specific about its purpose and histori-cal background. According to legend, Salar Mas'ud, a nephew of Mahmud of Ghazni, was slain in battle in 1033 or 1034. By 1325, a cult had evolved

56.
KANDURI
Uttar Pradesh, Bahraich, ca. 1900
Cotton, embroidered and appliquéd, 15 ft.
3 in. × 6 ft. 1 in. (4.65 × 1.85 m.)
Collection Michael Archer and Margaret
Lecomber, London

around his tomb. Despite the august recognition of Muhammad Tughluq and Firoz Shah in the late fourteenth century, the cult tended to be regarded very critically by orthodox Muslims.

It is said that the tomb is located on the site of an old temple to Surya, the sun god, and that the saint was slain on the night of his marriage to Zahra Bibi of Rudauli, whose tomb is nearby. In his name, spears were taken out and paraded, and it is claimed that he converted the Mewatis near Delhi, who continue to honor his memory with their spear ceremonies. When the saint's anniversary is celebrated, offerings of flags are made in honor of his flagstaff, one of the shrine's relics. During the celebration, the flag is also known as a kanduri, or tablecloth, because of the offerings of food and incense made to it. After the initial offering has been ceremonially buried, the rest is distributed on the new cloths brought by the devotees. People suffering from leg trouble make pilgrimages to Salar Mas'ud, and when they are healed they make little horses of wheat flour boiled in syrup called khule ghore (frisky horses)—like those embroidered here—which are blessed with the Fatiha and then distributed.

Ordinarily, kanduris are deeply stained by food and singed by incense. The Archer piece is a particularly large, splendid, and well-preserved example.

Published: Wheeler and Jayakar, *Textiles and Ornaments of India*, p. 28; Kramrisch, *Unknown India*, pp. 74, 100, no. 195, pl. xl.

57.
CARVED DOOR

Madhya Pradesh, Gondwana, Bastar area, perhaps Gond tribe, early 20th century
Wood, 40⅛ × 24¼ in. (102 × 61.5 cm.)
Zonal Anthropological Museum, Jagdalpur
(1163)

ALTHOUGH EACH TRIBAL group in India lives according to a slightly different pattern, most of them possess a communal house where the young people gather. At once an entertainment center, community hall, and music room, its door and walls are usually adorned with appropriate motifs, which today are likely to include airplanes, bicycles, and buses. Examples such as this one, suggestive of a premechanistic age, offer timeless animals, a plow, wheels, a comb, and a hunter aiming his rifle at a buck. In their vital simplicity, these configurations recall punch-marked coins of the Mauryan period (320–183 B.C.).

Unusually large and complex in its casting, this vibrantly expressive bronze describes the fourteen-year exile in the Dandakaranya Forest of Rama, the central figure of the *Ramayana*, the ancient epic known to every Hindu villager, for whom it is a perennial source of entertainment and moral instruction (see no. 13). Although he is the legitimate heir to the throne of Ayodhya in northern India, Rama is banished through the unscrupulous machinations of his stepmother and condemned to exile and futile wandering. Rama cheerfully accepts his fate, and the privations to which he and the heroine Sita are subjected are alleviated by his loyal brother Lakshmana and by the monkey god Hanuman—all of whom are shown here in the wilds, represented by trees and a tiger. One is reminded by the seemingly masked personages —mustachioed Rama and Lakshmana, gentle Sita, and submissive Hanuman —of folk dance-dramas still current in India.

58.
RAMA, SITA, LAKSHMANA, AND HANUMAN IN THE DANDAKARANYA FOREST
West Bengal, Purulia District, 17th century
Bronze, 4¾ × 9⅞ × 3⅛ in. (12 × 25 × 8 cm.)
Private collection

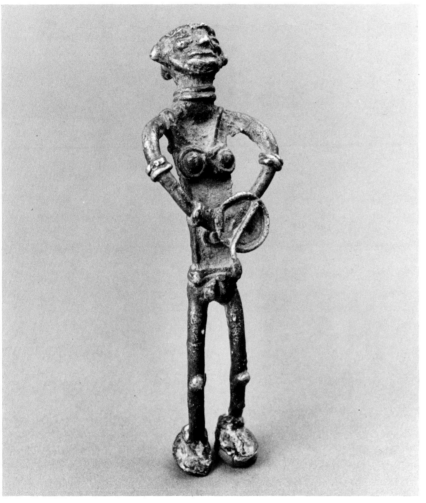

59

Although court art, with its swift changes of fashion, can be dated almost to the year, works of art by sculptors closer to nature and to the soil defy the art historian's desire for chronological exactitude, demonstrating the continuity in spirit and form through the centuries.

Singing or chanting as she holds a bowl and stick, this thin-limbed, loose-jointed bronze representation of a village goddess, her breasts reduced to pellets, her torso to a thin strip of metal, radiates an enigmatic, earthy power. In her lean vitality, she recalls the beguiling naked maiden from Mohenjo-Daro, of the late third or early second millennium B.C. This goddess also defies spatial boundaries, for despite its smallness, it is spiritually one of the most monumental figures here.

Published: Jayakar, *The Earthen Drum*, pp. 266–67, fig. 279.

59.
THE VIRGIN GRAMA DEVATA
Maharashtra, date unknown
Bronze, height 2¾ in. (7 cm.)
Private collection

60

60.
HORSE
Provenance and date unknown
Bronze, height 3 in. (7.5 cm.)
Private collection

61.
BOAR
Provenance and date unknown
Bronze, height 4⅜ in. (11 cm.)
Private collection

62.
KHANDOBA (KHANDE RAO)
Maharashtra, Jejuri, 17th century
Bronze, height 4½ in. (11.5 cm.)
Private collection

PROUD AS A king of beasts, this stocky, lively horse was modeled with firm persuasiveness from a chunky fistful of wax. In the process, the animal's chest and back took on, in reverse, the organic hollow of the sculptor's cupped palm, which also smoothed and rounded the forms with its melting warmth. His large noble head held high, eyes confronting us with a touch of disdain, he seems about to neigh disapproval of our attempt to assign a provenance. When a sculpture is so reduced to essentials, it is especially hard to place; and if the Indian origin of this one were not secure, one might find a look of China in the treatment of the eye and muzzle, or a touch of Egypt in the swelling girth.

BRONZE ANIMALS ON wheels (missing in this example) have been excavated from Bronze Age sites in India. As with so many Indian artifacts, the lines are blurred between the secular and the religious. Was this uncharacteristically amiable boar, with its well-rubbed mask and spine, a plaything for some fortunate child; was it an offering for a shrine; or does it represent the manifestation, or avatar, of the god Vishnu as Varaha, the boar, in whose form he slew the demon Hiranyaksha? One suspects that it served in all three capacities, for this imposing object was made to last. After its current phase as an objet d'art, nourishing to aesthetes, it may one day return to one or all of its traditional roles—if, indeed, it does not find a new one.[1]

1. For objects from the Daimabad hoard, datable to about 1000 B.C., see: Allchin and Allchin, *The Rise of Civilization in India*, figs. 10.14a–c, 10.15. In nineteenth-century miniature paintings depicting Shri Nathji of Nathadwara, one often sees bronze "toys" as offerings.

SO RUGGEDLY SHAPED in wax as to resemble candle drippings, this slowly advancing warhorse with its two stern and weighty riders brings to mind encounters in rural India with sturdy village headmen riding similarly robust horses on their daily rounds of the fields. The sculptor must have thought of such impressive local potentates when he modeled this image of Khandoba, or Khande Rao (the Maratha name for the god Shiva), holding a trident and drum in his right hand and accompanied by his consort, Parvati, with an

61▷

62

63

attendant and a hound. The platform bears a Shiva lingam as well as symbols of the sun and the moon.

Inasmuch as the Marathas are known for their military prowess (even today they are well represented in the Indian army), it is natural that their favorite deity—to whom a cluster of temples at Jejuri, near Poona, are dedicated—should be Lord Shiva, god of creation and destruction, seen as a well-armed, hard-riding cavalryman (see also no. 204).

63.
GODDESS OFFERING FOOD
Orissa, 16th century
Bronze, height 4⅜ in. (11.3 cm.)
Private collection

SOME FOLK BRONZES startle; others awe, or disturb, or excite fear. This image of a mother goddess, symbolic of divine feminine energy and fecundity, offers food with sweet generosity. The mood is reinforced by the softly lustrous patination—the result of fond, gentle worship over many generations. Her devotees probably belonged to a single family, whose shrine she occupied. Her ropelike ornaments are similar to those still in use by aboriginal tribes.

The relationship of this piece from Orissa to small pottery sculptures from Bengal, not far away, reveals the close connection between the modeling of clay and the modeling of wax for bronze casting by the cire perdue process. In each case the material is malleable, easy to roll between the palms of the hands and form into a conical base, such as the one seen here, or to shape into flattened pellets to be attached as cheeks or eyes, or as beads of a necklace.

This HEAD OF a village deity, whose identity is not known, was produced in eastern Madhya Pradesh, where the forested region is chiefly inhabited by the Gond tribes. Several places in Madhya Pradesh have a long and distinguished tradition of making bronze images; in the Bastar region, cire perdue metal casting is still a living art form. For centuries the Gonds have been buying ritual objects and images of their deities made by the local hereditary community of metal artisans.

Neither naturalistic nor abstract, this admirable head sculpted in the round is at once one of the most delightful and most powerful examples of metal folk art from Bastar. The bearded face, with its mysterious smile, seems to change its expression in different lighting conditions and at different hours of the day. The prominent oval eyes, encased in a grooved band on the upper eyelid and double wire on the lower, impart a hypnotizing stare to the face, while the discreet beaded ornament on the nose, eyebrows, earlobes, and neck, and the circular rings on the forehead add to the overall effect. All these and other details combine to enhance both the sculptural quality and the distinct godly identity of the image.

J.M.

64.
HEAD OF A VILLAGE GOD
Bastar, 18th century
Brass, height 5¼ in. (13.2 cm.)
Jagdish and Kamla Mittal Museum of Indian Art, Hyderabad (76.979)

64

65

65.
THE BUFFALO DEMON MAHISA
Rajasthan, 16th century
Bronze, height 6⅞ in. (17.5 cm.)
Jagdish and Kamla Mittal Museum of Indian
Art, Hyderabad (76.899)

ALTHOUGH THE IDENTITY of this unusual animal figure baffles us at first glance, we are convinced that it is from a Mahisasuramardini composition, in which the Great Goddess Durga, accompanied by her vehicle the lion, is depicted killing the buffalo demon Mahisa. (The companion figure of the lion, cast separately, is also in the Mittal Museum, but the whereabouts of the main figure, Durga, are not known.) The legend is narrated in the *Markandeya Purana*:

> After Mahisa, Lord of Demons, defeated all the gods, angered energy arose from their bodies like a burning mountain. It filled heaven and earth and, gathering its blaze into one, it became a woman, the Great Goddess Durga. Each of the gods presented her with his weapons, and with all of their arms, as if in merest play, she fought the army of Mahisa, the invincible —and covetous —demon, who had taken the shape of a buffalo (mahisa). When Mahisa attacked the lion —the vehicle of Durga —she flung her noose over him. He abandoned his buffalo shape and suddenly became a lion, then a man; but she slew him in every form he took. He resumed his buffalo shape; she leaped on him and, kicked by her foot, he issued forth from his own mouth. The goddess struck off his head.[1]

This monumental figure of the demon has been conceived with a touch of fantasy. The agitated energy of the awesome Mahisa pervades the abstract, compact, almost rocklike form of the buffalo, which extends its left front foot and turns its head backward as Mahisa, his hair pulled up, dramatically issues forth from his own mouth to face the onslaught of the goddess and fight his last battle for survival.

J.M.

1. Kramrisch, *Manifestations of Shiva*, p. 96.

As BEFITS HER position as Mahadevi, the Great Goddess trots along with utter assurance. Alternatively mild—as Uma (Light), Gauri (the Yellow or Brilliant), Parvati (Shiva's consort on Mount Kailash), or Haimavati (the Mother of the World)—she is shown here in her destructive aspect, as Durga, a beautiful yellow woman mounted on a tiger, perhaps on her way to destroy the terrible demon Mahisa (see no. 65). This vital little image, which exemplifies Indian rural art, is, in effect, a portable, always available "dry-cell battery" of religious and artistic power.

THE PUNJAB HILL states are well known for their paintings. The region also had a great bronze tradition, both classical and folk, and Kulu, Chamba, and Kangra were particularly active centers for metal casting. This tall slim girl, who wears little jewelry, originally held a chhattar (umbrella) behind a deity, though which one we do not know. When in actual use in a temple, the figure would have been clothed, but the garments could not have affected her erect, animated stance or disturbed the expression on her face, which is full of humility as she gazes downward with a gentle smile. The unique conception of the shaping and positioning of the arms, legs, and torso gives this sculpture a special abstract quality and strength. The girl's tubular, exaggeratedly elongated limbs and her serene, sharp-featured head are rare in a Pahari bronze. Her face is in fact reminiscent of the bashfully graceful charm and liveliness of the female figures in early Pahari paintings.

J.M.

66.
DURGA RIDING HER LION
Himachal Pradesh, perhaps Chamba,
16th–18th century
Brass, height 4 in. (10.2 cm.)
Collection Leo S. Figiel, Atlantis, Florida

67.
STANDING FEMALE CHHATTAR
BEARER
Punjab Hills, 16th century
Bronze, height 9⅝ in. (24.5 cm.)
Jagdish and Kamla Mittal Museum of Indian
Art, Hyderabad (76.1048)

66

67

68

THE ELEPHANT-HEADED Ganesha, lord (isha) of hosts (ganas), is venerated chiefly by Hindus, but Buddhists also worship him. No other deity has been so often portrayed in Indian sculpture and painting in such a variety of forms. The legends about Ganesha's origins are numerous: according to one tradition, he was born of Shiva and his consort Parvati; another says he was fashioned by Parvati herself. Ganesha, also called Vighneshvara, lord who creates and removes obstacles, is worshiped in innumerable ways. On auspicious occasions all worship must begin with invocation of Ganesha, and his idols are worshiped with great pomp on the fourth lunar day of the month of Bhadrapad (August–September). Large images in stone and metal are enshrined in temples; smaller ones, mostly in metal, are used in household shrines or carried on travels. In the houses of the well-to-do, Ganesha is carved in wood on doorjambs, and in many places likenesses of him are painted above entryways. At weddings in Gujarat, he is embroidered on panels hung on the wall and worshiped by the bride and groom.

A wealth of creative imagery is used to depict Ganesha in the small folk bronzes made for worship in homes or village shrines. Representations are often humorous, but, like this one, they can also be aesthetically moving. Our image was used in the Panchayatana Puja, a Hindu ritual wherein Ganesha is worshiped either alone or in the company of Vishnu, Shiva, Aditya, and Shakti. The style of this remarkably fine example from eastern India is distinctive and unusual. Panchayatana images, most of them small, are commonly made in Maharashtra, or sometimes in Karnataka or Central India, but they rarely come from Bihar, where this bronze was made.

In some Panchayatana images, Ganesha is given a higher place in the hierarchy of the gods, as he is here. Ganesha sits on his vehicle, the rat, atop a high, footed pedestal. He has two arms, and his tubular trunk is coiled in a frontal position. At his right is a trident; at his left are a peacock (the vehicle of his brother, Karttikeya) and Parvati, seated with her hands folded in salutation. In the center, a naga shelters a lingam, symbol of Shiva, and in the foreground stand a lion (Parvati's vehicle) and a bull (Nandi; see no. 14). Ganesha's prominent crown, a trefoil composed of spiraling wire, and the rhizomelike shaping of all the elements of the composition are typical of the bronzes made at Tatijharia for the villagers of southern Bihar.[1] The bronze has acquired a blackish patina from being kept continuously in a small shrine filled with smoke.

J.M.

1. Only a few examples of Tatijharia bronzes are known. For two others, see: Reeves, *Cire Perdue Casting*, p. 63, pl. 36; Getty, *Ganesa*, pl. 13b.

BANGLES AND ANKLE bracelets alone could make a representative exhibition of Indian art, for these infinitely varied, often remarkably sculptural works can be found everywhere in India and in all sectors of the population. Many materials could be represented: twisted cotton or other fiber, bone and ivory, brass and bronze, silver and gold, enamel and jewels. Some are massive and astonishingly heavy. But wearing them on wrists, upper arms, or ankles is not enervating but empowering; and dancing with several pounds of metal just above one's thudding feet fuses soul to soil, a source of exalting energy.

Designed to fit against the inner surface of the wrist, the finials pressing against the outside of the forearm, is a pair of brassy bronze bangles (a) perhaps from Madhya Pradesh. They were modeled in wax, stamped with designs reminiscent of those on Mauryan punch-marked coins, and cast by the cire perdue process. The shapes are suggestively ambiguous: are they snakes, or grain, or tuberous roots? Whatever they represent, the village sculptors who devised this wondrous design over the centuries gave tangible expression to the rhythms of growth and life.

Two monumental ivory bangles (b) from southern Rajasthan or Gujarat, not a true pair, would once have formed part of the dowries of well-to-do

68.
TWO-ARMED SEATED GANESHA
Bihar, Tatijharia, early 19th century
Brass, height 5⅝ in. (14.3 cm.)
Jagdish and Kamla Mittal Museum of Indian Art, Hyderabad (76.1082)

69.
GROUP OF BRACELETS AND BANGLES

a. PAIR OF BRONZE BANGLES
Perhaps Madhya Pradesh, 19th century
Height 2¾ in. (7 cm.)
Private collection

b. IVORY BANGLES
Southern Rajasthan or Gujarat, 19th century
Height 4½ in. (11.4 cm.), diameter 3⅝ in. (9.2 cm.)
Private collection
The Kronos Collections, New York

c. PAIR OF BRASS CHAIN-LINK
ANKLE BRACELETS
Rajasthan, 18th–19th century
Diameter 5½ in. (14 cm.)
Private collection

d. PAIR OF ELEPHANT(?) BONE BANGLES
WITH SHELL AND GLASS BEADS
Nagaland, Naga tribe, early 19th century
Height 2 in. (5.1 cm.)
Private collection

e. BRONZE BANGLE OR WRIST GUARD
Nagaland, Naga tribe, probably 17th century
Height 4⅛ in. (10.5 cm.)
Private collection

69 a–e

village girls. Splendidly ample, they suggest two great egg cups that might have been commissioned from Brancusi. From Rajasthan comes a pair of heavy chain-link ankle bracelets (c). Sturdy as anchor chain, but tighter and more complex in construction, they follow the contour of any ankle; and when worn, another quality emerges: their sound, which brings invigorating rhythmic bell clanks to the ancient choreographed ritual of the harvest when swaying, singing village women, balancing the grain on their heads in sheaves, parade in single file from the fields at dusk.

The much worn, naturally polished bangles, perhaps made of elephant bone (d), fastened around the wrists with fiber cord strung with tubular shell and blue glass beads, have taken on the appetizing hue of milk chocolate. The Art Deco shape brings to mind a three-fingered clenched fist. A Naga bangle (e), finely cast of silvery bronze and probably dating to the seventeenth century or earlier, is lightweight and thin, but threatening. The wrist-guard form, ornamented with meandering spirals, sprouts a series of belligerent "mushrooms," harmless to brush against but damaging in combat.

ONE OF THE pleasures of visiting rural India is to observe the changing designs of costumes, textile patterns, and ornaments as one moves from region to region. Still seen occasionally in Tamil Nadu are traditional ear ornaments of the sort shown here, objects of startlingly cubistic design made by village silversmiths according to traditional patterns slightly adjusted over the centuries. This pair made from brazed sheets of silver seem to represent birds, perhaps peacocks savoring worms, now so stylized as to be barely discernible. The craftsmanship is as remarkable as the design.

70.
EAR ORNAMENTS
Tamil Nadu, 19th century
Silver, height 1⅝ in. (4.1 cm.)
Private collection

70

Overleaf, 110, detail ▷

THE MUSLIM COURTS

THE SULTANATE PERIOD: 1192–1526

Islam reached the Indian subcontinent in several successive waves. In the eighth century Arab armies, representing the new militant faith, invaded Sind. They remained there and gradually settled to live in relative harmony with the Indian peoples. Early in the eleventh century, the repeated onslaughts of Mahmud of Ghazni considerably reduced the power of the Rajput chiefs, themselves descended from other Central Asian tribes, whose separate clans ruled small kingdoms in northwestern India. But this hardly modified the pattern of Indian culture. India's religious life remained relatively unaffected for another two centuries, except for the continuing decline of Buddhism and the rise of the popular Tantric cult, named after its scriptures the Tantras, which centered on incantations and magico-religious rites and rituals as a means to salvation.

It was only at the end of the twelfth century, after the invading armies of the Ghaznevid ruler Shihab ad-Din Ghori defeated the Rajput forces of Pritvi Raj at the Battle of Tarain in 1192, that Muslim rule was firmly established in India, eventually extending over the major part of the subcontinent for the next 500 years.

Delhi became the seat of power of the Turkish sultans, no doubt because of its strategic position allowing access both to the Ganges Valley and to Central and western India. Within a decade Banaras was sacked, the great fortress of Gwalior captured, and Bihar annexed, with a massacre of monks that virtually ended Buddhism in India. Early in the next century, Bengal was added to the Turkish empire. Under Sultan Iltutmish (r. 1211–36), the great Sultanate of Delhi became the largest and most powerful dominion in India. Hindu kingdoms—Gujarat, Malwa, Mewar, Jaunpur, and Gaur, for example—survived within it on a tributary basis.

The Delhi sultans dreamed of establishing an empire that would embrace all of India, but, under constant threat of Mongol invasion in the north and northwest, they were never able to extend farther south than the tableland of the Deccan. A new dynasty of Turks, the Khaljis, came to power in 1290, and the reign of ʿAlaʾ ad-Din Khalji (1296–1316) marks the height of the Sultanate's political power, both territorially and in terms of the sultan's absolute sovereignty, which was subject only to the tenets of the Shariʿa, the Holy Laws of Islam. One of ʿAlaʾ ad-Din's ablest commanders, Malik Kafur, a Hindu convert from Gujarat, organized numerous expeditions to South India from 1302 to 1311, even attacking the city of Madurai, the seat of the Pandyas. But disturbances in the northern Rajput kingdoms once again weakened the Sultanate's hold, and the campaign was ultimately unsuccessful. The Tughluq dynasty (1325–98) replaced the Khaljis and continued the efforts to annex the whole of the southern peninsula, but with the establishment of the Hindu kingdom of Vijayanagar in 1336—the dominant power in the South for the next two centuries—the Sultanate dream of empire came to an end.

The sultans earned India's gratitude by staving off the Mongol scourge, which would have been far grimmer than Timur's horrific sack of Delhi in 1398. Although in 1241 the Mongols raided and destroyed Lahore, establishing an encampment just beyond her borders that was an omnipresent threat for half a century, paradoxically they stimulated a major cultural flowering. Iltutmish and his successors welcomed the scholars, poets, architects, and master craftsmen who had fled Mongol persecution in Khurasan, Iran, ʿIraq, and Afghanistan. Many of the new arrivals were not Turks but Tajiks, Persian-speaking intellectuals whose talents as administrators as well as litterateurs were put to use. But these urban sophisticates were not always welcomed by the soldierly and spirited Turks, and conflicts led to bloody feuds.

From the works of chroniclers and historians attached to the cosmopolitan court at Delhi, we know that political institutions and practices under the Sultanate, though modeled after other regional monarchies ruled by Turks and Afghans, evolved in response to Indian conditions. Hindu rulers, if they paid fealty to the sultans, were welcome at such festive royal activities as hunts, polo games, parades, and animal combats, which in many instances derived from Rajput customs. Eventually, many Hindus spoke Persian and cultivated the graceful manners of Iranian culture. Lesser nobles continued to enjoy local power under Muslim suzerainty, and many Hindus found posts in the administrative system.

Conversion to Islam sometimes came about by intermarriage, but far more subtly persuasive was the implication that acceptance of Islam led to success at court and in the marketplace. The pre-Islamic tradition in India of gurus (religious teachers) and sannyasis (ascetics) prepared the way for the acceptance of Muslim pirs and shaikhs. The Sufis, Muslim mystics who advocated ascetic practices and intense love of God, and whose delight in poetry and music created a highly emotional approach to religion, attracted many Hindus. Sufi doctrines of union with God through loving devotion seem to have influenced the growth of the already existing Hindu cult of bhakti, with its emphasis on love as the basis of the relationship with God, and bhakti in turn lent imagery to Indian Sufi poetry. Indeed, if the two religions ever achieved spiritual synthesis, it was through such figures as the mystic poet Kabir (1440–1518), according to legend a Hindu by birth but a Muslim by upbringing, who preached a religion of loving devotion that transcended all creedal differences.

The most powerful unifying force in Islamic life and art has always been the Muslim faith itself. Muslims are a people of the book, and Islam demands a commitment to the revealed message of the Qurʾan, the book of God and the conveyor of both spiritual and social law. The Qurʾan, with the Hadith, the Sayings of the Prophet, forms the basis of the Holy Law which regulates all aspects of the life of every Muslim. Qurʾanic law also prescribes an image of the cosmos, a total order made up of all the planes of human and material existence, within which the arts too are integrated. Contrary to popular belief, the Qurʾan makes no specific pronouncements on the prohibition of representational art in Islam, but a few passages indicate that the Prophet Muhammad associated statues with pagan idols, and that God alone is the true mussawwir (creator) of life in all its forms.

Within Islam are two main divisions, the Sunni orthodoxy, based primarily in areas not influenced by Iran, and the Shiʿa, the party of ʿAli, cousin and son-in-law of the Prophet. The two divisions developed gradually on divergent lines although both adhere to the Qurʾan and rely upon the Sunna, the way or example of the Prophet as reported in the Hadith. The Shiʿites believe that the rights of ʿAli to the succession were unlawfully contravened by Abu Bakr and Umar, two in-laws of Muhammad, when they named themselves his two first successors, or caliphs. The Shiʿites developed the concept of the infallible imam, the leader of the community from among ʿAli's descendants, sent by God to guide the faithful. According to mainstream Shiʿite philosophy, the twelfth imam disappeared mysteriously in 873. Other Shiʿite groups, such as the Ismailis, believe in the presence of a living imam in our time.

Twelver Shiʿa was made the official state religion in Iran in 1501, under the Safavids, but already it had reached the Deccan. Although most of the Turkish and Afghan sultans and the Mughal emperors of India were Sunni, a new influx of Shiʿite nobles occurred in the sixteenth and seventeenth centuries, and Hyderabad and Lucknow became strongholds of Shiʿite doctrine.

With their religion, the Muslim sultans also brought to India the arts of calligraphy and manuscript illumination that already by 1200 had reached impressive heights in Egypt and Iran. Although not much has survived from the first two centuries of Muslim rule, perhaps because of the destruction of Delhi by Timur in the late fourteenth century, it is likely that the early sultans replaced the indigenous Hindu and Jain tradition of painting on palm leaf with painting on paper imported from Iran. Under the Tughluqs and later under the Lodi dynasty (1451–1526), ateliers and workshops were set up at the imperial courts; Persian and Arabic texts were copied and illustrated in Iranian styles, although Indian characteristics became increasingly evident. In one of the loveliest of all Sultanate manuscripts, the sixteenth-century *Chandayana* of Mulla Daʾud (see no. 80), Iranian and Indian elements reflect a balanced synthesis.

The Turko-Afghans brought with them, in addition to the art of the book, new architectural ideas that were to transform the Indian landscape. The dome, the arch, and the minaret were hitherto unknown forms to Hindu builders, long accustomed to working in the indigenous trabeate mode, in which space is spanned by means of beams laid horizontally. But the early Muslim settlers introduced the principle of the radiating arch, thus initiating a cooperation of indigenous and alien forms that was to evolve into one of the outstanding creative achievements of the Indo-Muslim period. Eventually, Sultanate experimentation gave way to a dynamic synthesis under the Mughal emperors. Perhaps more than in any other art form, the fusion of architectural forms and motifs inspired by the Delhi Sultanate symbolizes the nature of the pluralistic world inhabited by Hindus and Muslims under the sultans, especially during the fourteenth and fifteenth centuries.

THE MUGHALS: 1526–1857

India on the eve of the Mughal invasion was a country of uneasy political balance. The Lodi Afghans, under Sikandar Lodi (r. 1489–1517) and Ibrahim Lodi (r. 1517–26), held together a large but restive empire that extended from the banks of the Indus River across the northern plains to the borders of Bengal and whose southern boundary was marked by the Chambal River. Hindu states through much of the North had lost sovereignty. Only the Rajput kingdoms of Rajasthan remained independent, but even here clan divisions and territorial and dynastic disputes weakened any effective opposition to the Afghan power in Delhi. In the Deccan, the Bahmanid Muslim kingdom, itself a successor state to the Delhi Sultanate but long debilitated by factional politics, was replaced in the early sixteenth century by the smaller independent states of Berar, Bidar, Ahmadnagar, Bijapur, and Golconda. Farther south, embracing what today are the states of Karnataka, Tamil Nadu, and Kerala, was the Hindu empire of Vijayanagar. The City of Victory, whose kings built massive multipillared temple complexes to their patron deity, Shiva, enjoyed its period of greatest prosperity during the reign of Krishnadeva Raya (1509–30), but after this it was continually alert to the threat of attack from an alliance of the five sultanates of the Deccan. It finally collapsed in 1565. Meanwhile, Portuguese traders, coming to India by sea in the late fifteenth century, settled in Travancore and Calicut in the south and by 1510 had established themselves at Goa, halfway up the west coast, so beginning a long struggle for control of the maritime trade of India.

In 1526, Babur, a Muslim prince from Fergana, now in Russian Turkistan, and descendant of the two great Central Asian conquerors, Timur and Chinghiz Khan, defeated Sultan Ibrahim Lodi at the Battle of Panipat, about fifty miles from Delhi, and declared himself ruler of India. Although his army was small, his men were able warriors. Skilled in the use of firearms and matchlocks, still a novelty in Indian warfare, they easily put to rout the Lodi sultan's mighty army of more than 100,000 men. The following year, Babur took on the more formidable confederation of Rajput chiefs, briefly united under Rana Sanga of Mewar, and defeated them at the momentous Battle of Kanhua, which ended the last hopes of the Rajputs to restore Hindu supremacy in northern India and established the Mughal dynasty on the throne of Delhi. By the time of Babur's death in 1530, he ruled an empire extending eastward from Badakhshan and Kabul through the Punjab to the borders of Bengal.

Babur's grandson, Akbar, the third and greatest of the Mughal emperors, ascended the throne in 1556, at the age of fourteen. Much of Babur's domain had by this time been lost by his son Humayun (r. 1530–56) to the Afghan rebel Sher Shah Sur. Humayun's reign was interrupted by a brief period of exile in 1544 at the Safavid court of Shah Tahmasp in Tabriz. This fact was to prove of immense significance to the history of Mughal painting in India, for when Humayun was able to regain his dominions in 1554, he brought with him two painters from the Iranian court, Mir Sayyid 'Ali and 'Abd as-Samad. Thus were introduced into India the latest developments in the Iranian book tradition: high standards of calligraphy and illumination, draftsmanship of extreme refinement, the use of colored or gold-sprinkled paper, exquisitely illuminated and illustrated margins, and decorated lacquer bindings. The large painting on cloth *Princes of the House of Timur* (no. 84) is the earliest known work by these Safavid artists for Humayun, and its style is wholly Iranian.

The achievement of consolidating an empire that extended over half of India and of shaping the distinctive cultural traditions that have influenced her ever since belonged to Akbar (r. 1556–1605). By initiating a remarkable series of Rajput alliances, culminating in his own marriage to a Jaipur princess, he pressed the Rajput chiefs into the service of the empire and by 1576 was master of all of Rajasthan, with the exception of Mewar. Gujarat was secured in 1573 and Bengal was attacked the following year, so that by the age of thirty-four Akbar ruled the whole of northern India from the Indus to the mouth of the Ganges and from the Himalayas to the Vindhya mountains on the edge of the Deccan plateau.

The Mughal empire, as it continued to be ruled by his successors and as its power and grandeur became legendary in contemporary Europe, was the creation of Akbar. Unlike the Delhi sultans, whose kingdoms, however vast, were essentially held together by military might, Akbar established a central bureaucratic administrative system, controlled by himself. Its principal officers, the mansabdars (holders of command), ruled the twelve provinces into which the empire was then divided. This official aristocracy represented the imperial will and spread across the empire, like its impressive network of waterways and highways, to work the administrative machine. The provinces divided and subdivided into sarkars (districts) and parganas (subdistricts), and the division of authority penetrated the many levels of bureaucracy, with responsibilities assigned to both Hindus and Muslims.

There is perhaps no surer documentation of the history of Mughal rule, its dramas and vicissitudes, and of the colorful personalities of its talented sovereigns than the art they commissioned, much of which is seen in the following pages. The century and a quarter between Babur's invasion of India in 1526 and the death of his grandson Shah Jahan in 1666 saw the publication of two monumental autobiographies, the Turki *Babur-nama* (History of Babur) and the Persian *Tuzuk-i Jahangiri* (Memoirs of Jahangir), as well as two biographies, the *A'in-i Akbari* (Statutes of Akbar) by Abu'l-Fazl, court historian of Akbar, and the *Padshah-nama* (History of the Emperor), an official account of the reign of Shah Jahan by a pupil of Abu'l-Fazl's, 'Abd al-Hamid Lahori. The *Babur-nama*, recording in detail the events of Babur's life, was translated into Persian and lavishly illustrated by court artists during Akbar's reign. Akbar's own biography, popularly known as the *Akbar-nama*, was illustrated in imperial albums commissioned by the emperor himself. These documented his heroic campaigns and reflected the interest in various religious faiths and cultures, including Hinduism, Zoroastrianism, Christianity, and Judaism, that prevailed in the enlightened and cosmopolitan atmosphere of Akbar's court. The *Memoirs of Jahangir*, at once intimate, spontaneous, and connoisseurly, reveal that emperor's insatiable and somewhat eccentric interest in things, events, and people. The imperial copy of the *Padshah-nama* is the last of the great Mughal illustrated histories. Its text and paintings are almost exclusively limited to the great occasions of state—darbars, processions, and military campaigns—that reaffirmed the imperial status, and they reflect the refined but coldly formal taste of Shah Jahan himself.

The great achievement of the Mughal period, the individual accomplishments of its legendary rulers notwithstanding, was the dynamic and dramatic synthesis it effected between indigenous and Islamic forms. While it would be unrealistic to expect a cultural fusion of the ideologies of Hinduism and Islam, we have already seen that bhakti and Sufi thought and practice influenced each other. In the new mystical system he founded, the Din-i Ilahi, Akbar went even further by making a deliberate effort to integrate facets of both faiths. Persian, the language of the Delhi Sultanate, became far more widely used because of the vast Mughal administrative network. Replacing Sanskrit as the official language, it came to be used by Hindu rulers and the Hindu ministerial class. But here too there was coalescence, represented by the emergence of a new language, Urdu, literally the camp-language. It was a combination of Hindi grammar with Persian and Arabic vocabulary and dated back to the late thirteenth century, when it became the lingua franca of the Delhi Sultanate. In the course of time, Urdu became a court language, and even today in India it is considered the language of poets. In the arts, the early domination and eventual assimilation of Iranian forms can be traced in miniature painting of the sixteenth and seventeenth centuries. In early Mughal architecture, likewise, Iranian components are at once discernible.

In 1658, Shah Jahan was deposed by his third son, Aurangzeb (r. 1658–1707), whose numerous military campaigns in the Deccan depleted the empire's resources. Puritanical and orthodox by nature, he offered little support to the court arts, and by the end of the seventeenth century many painters sought patrons at provincial centers in the Punjab Hills, Rajasthan, Oudh, and Bengal. The reign of the pleasure-loving and ineffectual Muhammad Shah (r. 1719–48) witnessed the collapse of central authority, the sack of Delhi in 1739 by the Iranians under Nadir Shah, and the emergence of Maratha power in the south. From 1748 to 1762, northern India was repeatedly invaded by the Afghans, while the Marathas, making a bid for the control of Delhi, devastated central and northern India. The west, meanwhile, was rocked by Rajput rebellions. But even as Mughal power continued its rapid decline, ending only with the deposition and exile of its last emperor, Bahadur Shah II, in 1857, no indigenous power emerged that was capable of restoring its administrative authority. A vacuum was thus created, into which a wholly new power was to step. British dominion, slowly on the increase since the mid-eighteenth century, evolved into the virtual assumption of full authority throughout India by 1820 and culminated in the rule of empire that was to open India irrevocably to the impact of the West.

THE SULTANS OF THE DECCAN: ca. 1500–1686

The emergence in the fourteenth century of independent kingdoms in the Deccan and in South India (notably Vijayanagar) was directly related to the failure of the Delhi Sultanate to control the southern regions. In 1347, a Turkish governor of the Deccan revolted and founded the independent Bahmanid dynasty, which was to rule the northern Deccan for two centuries, with its capital first at Gulbarga (1347–1422) and later at Bidar (1422–1512). Imposing architectural remains at both sites attest to the wealth and culture of the Bahmanid sultans, though no manuscripts, miniatures, or metalwork are known from their courts. The gradual decline of the Bahmanid kingdom and the rise to power of Vijayanagar under Krishnadeva Raya were parallel developments. Undermined since the late fifteenth century by the repeated thrusts, province by province, of Vijayanagar's armies, the Bahmanid kingdom eventually splintered into five separate sultanates. First to break off was Berar, under a Hindu convert named Fathullah ʿImad-Shah, who declared his independence in 1484. The ʿImad-Shahis were absorbed by the sultanate of Ahmadnagar in 1574. Ahmadnagar itself was founded by Malik Ahmad, the son of a Hindu slave converted to Islam and the governor of Junnar under the Bahmanids until he declared his independence in 1490. Yusuf ʿAdil-Shah, Bahmanid governor of Bijapur, followed his example in the same year.

According to the historian Ferishta, who wrote the definitive *History of Muhammadan Power in India* while serving at the court of Ibrahim ʿAdil-Shah II in the late sixteenth century, the founder of the ʿAdil-Shahi dynasty of Bijapur was the younger son of the Ottoman Sultan Murad II, who fled Turkey at the time of the accession of his brother, Sultan Muhammad II. Golconda developed in the ruins of the Hindu kingdom of Warangal, which had been defeated by the Bahmanids in 1424. It was founded by Quli Qutb-Shah, who was descended from the Turkman rulers of Tabriz and was governor of Telangana under the Bahmanids. He set up his own state in 1512. The three major sultanates —Ahmadnagar, Bijapur, and Golconda—belonged to the Shiʿa sect of Islam and maintained close political and cultural relations with the Safavid dynasty of Iran (1501–1722) against the Sunni Mughal empire of northern India. Part of Ahmadnagar fell to Akbar in 1600, and Bijapur and Golconda were captured by Aurangzeb in 1686–87.

Except for a period of about four decades (1687–1724) following its conquest by the Mughals under Aurangzeb, the Deccan remained politically independent of northern India until the twentieth century. As a result it evolved, within an Islamic context, its own distinctive cultural milieu and artistic styles. Its population was a mixture of Indian Muslims and Hindus, and Turks, Persians, Arabs, and Africans. The Arab link, notably absent in northern India, had been forged through centuries of trade across the Arabian Sea with Egypt, Yemen, and ʿIraq, making the Deccan, until the Mughal conquest of 1687, one of the great centers of Arabic learning outside the Middle East.

There was, in addition, the proximity of the Hindu South. The Deccani sultanates, constantly engaged in petty squabbles against each other, combined efforts only once in their regrettably short-lived history when, in 1565, they disposed of the kingdom of Vijayanagar. Following its fall, it is likely that many Hindu painters and craftsmen from that wondrous city were recruited to the capitals of the Deccani sultans, taking with them traditions that derived from the early pre-Muslim styles of classical India. This new influx may have been something in the nature of a catalyst, for after this date a great flowering of miniature painting occurred at Ahmadnagar, Bijapur, and Golconda, the earlier Iranian styles giving way to superb masterpieces reflecting the new, typically Deccani conventions of line and gorgeous color.

While the Nizam-Shahi sultans of Ahmadnagar are accepted as the earliest and most original of the Deccani patrons, the ʿAdil-Shahis of Bijapur and the Qutb-Shahis of Golconda also commissioned important works. The most outstanding single patron was Ibrahim ʿAdil-Shah II of Bijapur (r. 1580–1626), who maintained a court rich in its patronage of music, literature, and the arts where Iranian and Mughal artists were welcomed. Lush landscapes, both subtle and splendid, and sumptuous colors touched with gold to catch the light give Bijapuri painting its mysteriously lyrical and introspective character. After 1636, when Bijapur came under Mughal control, the mature style of Mughal portraiture increasingly influenced contemporary work at Bijapur and Golconda. Appropriate to the lavish style favored in life by this intensely creative and romantic ruler is the vast complex of his tomb and the adjoining mosque, known as the Ibrahim Rauza (see fig. 6, page 453).

Architecturally, the Ibrahim Rauza is an example of the new forms initiated by the Bijapur sultans, combining tomb, mosque, and a cistern for ablutions all situated together on a plinth. The tomb structure itself reflects another Bijapuri innovation, the surrounding of the square monument of the tomb by a pillared arcade.

At Golconda, where the reign of Sultan Muhammad-Quli Qutb-Shah (1580–1612) ushered in a period of great luxury and splendor, painting continued in a mixture of Safavid, Turkish, and Mughal styles, always retaining echoes of the Turkman origins of this dynasty. Better known, perhaps, than the miniatures that scholars only recently have begun to assign specifically to Golconda are its paintings on cotton for use as curtains, wall hangings, and floor spreads. Created for export in the seventeenth and eighteenth centuries, these were covered with landscape and figural designs drawn not only from Indian and Iranian but from Chinese and European decorative conventions. Like Bijapur, Golconda evolved an independent architectural style, most in evidence today in the city of Hyderabad.

After the Mughals conquered the Deccan in 1686–87, the artistic traditions of Bijapur and Golconda, already on the wane from the 1650s, were finally disrupted. Hyderabad, emerging as an independent kingdom in 1724, became a new center of artistic patronage, its paintings combining the flamboyant flavor of the former Golconda school with the increasing rigidity of the provincial Mughal style. Following the collapse of centralized Mughal authority in the eighteenth century, other independent states were established in the Deccan, Bengal, and Oudh, ruled by powerful nobles who patronized art forms that increasingly were a blend of late Mughal and European elements. In this last phase of the great Mughal empire, its provincial courts paid only nominal allegiance to Delhi, a poignant throwback to the Delhi Sultanate on the eve of Babur's historic invasion. India's new masters, carrying her into the modern age, were the British. Unlike the Muslim rulers, they did not stay. But their impact was to be as profound as that of any of their predecessors.

THE DELHI SULTANATE

THE MUNIFICENT MUSLIM sultans who ruled the Deccan in the Middle Ages prided themselves on attracting the best available literary and artistic talent to their courts, and they also kept in close touch with cultural developments in the central Islamic lands. Among the scholars, poets, and artists they welcomed each year from Iran, Turkey, and Arabia were calligraphers who worked alongside local scribes and artisans to create both architectural inscriptions and illuminated manuscripts for the royal libraries. Some of the finest inscriptions that have survived at Bidar, which served as the capital of the Bahmanid dynasty from 1424 until its demise in 1538, were composed in Arabic by a Persian calligrapher in the 1430s and executed in stone by craftsmen who spoke only the vernacular Telegu. The inscriptions are in Thuluth, one of several styles of cursive Arabic script that were developed in Baghdad between the tenth and the thirteenth century and became known as classical. Calligraphers aspiring to master the classical method of writing Arabic were taught to practice the circles, arcs, and measuring dots that governed the shape of each letter of the alphabet before attempting to write whole words. In a text written in classical Thuluth, Naskhi, Nastaʿliq, Muhaqqaq, or Rihani script, each word is an artistic, harmonious construction of perfectly formed individual characters.

This Qurʾan, illuminated with a breadth and magnificence that suggests it was copied for a patron of high rank at one of the princely courts, is apparently the only manuscript to survive from the Bahmanid period, which began about 1350. Although it was written in the late fifteenth century, long past the peak of Bahmanid power, the manuscript, with its stately opening page, seems as sturdy as the great fort at Daulatabad. Sustained by the force of the holy verses themselves, the dynamic script seems imbued with conviction. The style is Bihari, which has been used by calligraphers in India since the early Middle Ages. On the opposite fringes of the world of Islam, in North Africa and Spain, scribes also wrote Arabic texts in a style of their own, called Maghribi. In Bihari, the characters are wedge-shaped, more angular than the classical rounded forms, and writers of both Bihari and Maghribi script depart from the rules by treating each word not as a carefully constructed sum of its letters but as an entity in itself. What could be seen as a lack of classical perfection and harmony in Bihari and Maghribi texts is often more than offset by the vigor of the writing and the sometimes daring use of colorful decoration.

The writing style may be particularly Indian, but the design of these pages, a forceful arrangement of two lines of large script alternating with

71.
QURʾAN
Sultanate, Deccan, dated A.H. 888 (1483)
Opaque watercolor and gold on paper,
18¾ × 12¼ in. (47.6 × 31.1 cm.)
Archaeological Museum, Bijapur (912)

Overleaf, 71 ▷

امرأتى عاقرا و قد بلغت من الكبر
عتيا قال كذلك قال ربك
هو على هين و قد خلقتك من قبل
و لم تك شيا قال رب اجعل لى
آية قال آيتك الا تكلم الناس
ثلث ليال سويا فخرج على قومه
من المحراب فاوحى اليهم ان سبحوا
بكرة و عشيا يا يحيى خذ الكتاب
بقوة و آتيناه الحكم صبيا و حنانا
من لدنا و زكوة و كان تقيا
و برا بوالديه و لم يكن جبارا
عصيا و سلام عليه يوم ولد
و يوم يموت و يوم يبعث حيا

بِسْمِ اللَّهِ الرَّحْمَٰنِ الرَّحِيمِ

كهيعص ۝ ذِكْرُ رَحْمَةِ رَبِّكَ
عَبْدَهُ زَكَرِيَّا ۝ إِذْ نَادَىٰ رَبَّهُ نِدَاءً
خَفِيًّا ۝ قَالَ رَبِّ إِنِّي وَهَنَ
الْعَظْمُ مِنِّي وَاشْتَعَلَ الرَّأْسُ
شَيْبًا وَلَمْ أَكُنْ بِدُعَائِكَ رَبِّ
شَقِيًّا ۝ وَإِنِّي خِفْتُ الْمَوَالِيَ مِنْ وَرَائِي
وَكَانَتِ امْرَأَتِي عَاقِرًا فَهَبْ لِي
مِنْ لَدُنْكَ وَلِيًّا ۝ يَرِثُنِي وَيَرِثُ مِنْ
آلِ يَعْقُوبَ وَاجْعَلْهُ رَبِّ رَضِيًّا ۝
يَا زَكَرِيَّا إِنَّا نُبَشِّرُكَ بِغُلَامٍ اسْمُهُ
يَحْيَىٰ لَمْ نَجْعَل لَّهُ مِن قَبْلُ سَمِيًّا ۝
قَالَ رَبِّ أَنَّىٰ يَكُونُ لِي غُلَامٌ وَكَانَتِ

three of small, has been borrowed from classical texts. Muslim scribes took great pride in writing the Qurʾan as artfully as possible and in inventing eye-catching calligraphic designs for copies of the sacred book. This design, which became very popular in Ottoman Turkey for single pages of religious poetry or the Prophetic Traditions (Hadith), seems to have originated in the early fifteenth century. The idea may have come from medieval Arab poets, who often inserted their own verses between the lines of classical, preferably religious, poems, the so-called takhmis. Two lines of original poetry written in large script would be followed by three lines of secondary poetry, in smaller script, enlarging on the classical text. The traditional designers used two distinct styles of script, always in the same combinations: the large script was usually Thuluth, the small Naskhi, but on rare occasions two lines in large Muhaqqaq preceded three in small Rihani. The Deccani artist who transcribed this Qurʾan has applied the same technique, which he no doubt learned from a Persian or Turkish colleague, but he has written both the large and small script in his accustomed Bihari style.

72.
CHESSMAN
Inscribed, on the bottom: "from the work of Yusuf al-Bahlili"
Sultanate, northwestern India, late 11th or early 12th century
Ivory, height 6⅛ in. (15.5 cm.)
Bibliothèque Nationale, Paris, Cabinet des Médailles (Chab. 3271)

WITH A FIERCE battle raging about him, a proud, mustachioed nobleman, perhaps a king, sits with remarkable poise on the howdah of his war elephant. The angry-eyed beast, a great battle tank, lumbers into the melee, flanked by four horsemen, ensnaring an enemy rider in its crushing trunk, while the mahout, gymnastically pitched forward from his seat atop the elephant, attacks from above, tugging at the rider's hand even as he holds on for dear life. Nothing could better represent the mighty grandeur of the Indian sultans than this forceful chess piece carved from a cross section of a great elephant tusk. The carving is packed with detail: one of the horses, for instance, his head bowing animatedly, is crested with a superbly simplified bird, and battle-axes, swords, jewels, costumes, and horse and elephant caparisons are all precisely noted. The relief around the outer edge of the howdah, a repeat pattern of foot soldiers brandishing swords and shields, bespeaks the caliber of the stout but muscular occupant, whose triumph over the enemy is implied by the twisted limbs crushed beneath the elephant's hind legs. Warmly patinated over the centuries, the noble ivory has also suffered the buffets of time. The front part of the base has split off, as have the legs of the endangered horseman's steed, and fragments of an arm and a leg on the top of the elephant's head suggest there was once a second mahout.

Although this chessman, either the king or a rook of what must have been a staggering set, has long been recognized as a masterpiece of great artistic and historical importance, its provenance has never been definitely established, and it has been assigned dates ranging from the eighth century to the fifteenth. Few would now make the claim, but Souren Melikian-Chirvani reminds us that in the nineteenth century the piece was widely believed to have been part of a set presented as a gift to Emperor Charlemagne by the fifth Abbasid caliph, Harun ar-Rashid, who ruled from Baghdad between 786 and 809. That it was listed in the 1505 inventory of the treasury of the royal abbey at Saint-Denis, France, where it had been preserved, immediately after a now lost ivory chess game that was recorded as having belonged to Charlemagne probably accounts for the confusion.

Melikian-Chirvani points out that the piece itself contains several clues which may provide at least a tentative solution to the complex puzzle of where and when it was made, though he is careful to reserve final judgment until a more exhaustive study has been done. The signature in Arabic on the carving's underside, for example, which reads, "from the work of Yusuf al-Bahlili," indicates that the date cannot be later than the end of the eleventh or the beginning of the twelfth century: neither the style of the plain Kufic lettering nor the signing formula "from the work of" was in general use by the twelfth century. Although aesthetically this object has nothing to do with Iranian art as we know it, several details provide links to the eastern Iranian world. The armed footmen encircling the howdah wear boots of an early eastern Iranian type, and their stylized marching position—one leg

72

straight, the other bent at a right angle—also closely follows an Iranian convention. Even more telling are the standard Iranian horse trappings: the stirrups, the disks hanging from the straps, and the rectangular saddle cloths, which occur on representations of horses on Sassanid silverware and on vessels associated with pre-Islamic Central Asia and eastern Khorasan. Based on this and other evidence he has gathered so far, Melikian-Chirvani concludes that it is reasonable to suggest that the chessman was made in the late eleventh or early twelfth century at a center in northwestern India where Iranian military equipment was used, probably in some dependency of the Ghaznevid sultanate. After the conquests of Mahmud of Ghazni, who reigned from 998 to 1030, the Ghaznevid sultans, from their capital at Ghazni in what is today Afghanistan, ruled a kingdom stretching from the Tigris to the Ganges that endured until 1173, when it was overrun by Muhammad of Ghor.

Published: Barrett, "A Group of Medieval Ivories," no. 42, pl. XVII; *Arts de l'Islam*, p. 187, no. 267; Kühnel, *Die islamischen Elfenbeinskulpturen*, pp. 30–31, no. 17, pl. VI (showing the base), pl. VII; *L'Islam dans les collections nationales*, pp. 174, 176, no. 377; Tardy, *Les Ivoires*, p. 153, no. 5; M. Pal, *Crafts*, no. 42, pl. XVII.

73.
RUSTAM THROWN INTO THE SEA BY
THE DEMON AKVAN
From the Schulz *Shah-nama* (Book of Kings)
Sultanate, Delhi or Malwa, first half of
14th century
Opaque watercolor on paper
Folio: 8 × 5⅜ in. (20.3 × 13.7 cm.)
Miniature: 1⅞ × 4¼ in. (4.8 × 10.8 cm.)
The Metropolitan Museum of Art, New York,
Bequest of Monroe C. Gutman (1974.290.17)

CHEERED ON BY a squawking duck, Rustam—the principal champion of
Firdausi's great eleventh-century Iranian epic the *Shah-nama* (Book of Kings)
—fights for his life. In this episode Rustam, exhausted by his strenuous
search for the terrible div Akvan, lies down for a nap. As Rustam sleeps, the
div comes upon him, and with devilish care cuts out the turf around him
and lifts him, ground and all, into the air. With gentlemanly consideration,
Akvan then asks Rustam whether he would prefer to be flung to his death
onto the mountaintops or drowned in the deep sea. Knowing that whichever
he chooses, the demon will do the opposite, Rustam requests the former,
whereupon Akvan tosses him into the sea. After battling with crocodiles,
Rustam swims to freedom.

The artist portrays the scene with the utmost humor and economy.
Akvan's arms have barely released his victim, yet his optimistic face is already
shadowed by a hint of dismay. The jumble of waves calms obediently where
Rustam swims, and although the weeds just beyond the nasty, lionesque
water creature stab aggressively at the hero, the blossoms near him peep out
in tender encouragement.

All the known miniatures from the manuscript to which this painting
belongs, called the Schulz *Shah-nama* after the distinguished German scholar

73

who once owned it, are in The Metropolitan Museum of Art. They are the best drawn, among the most vigorous, and probably the earliest of surviving pictures from the Sultanate period. The date of the miniatures can be hazarded on the basis of related early fourteenth-century material usually associated with Iran, a group that includes two now dispersed copies of the *Shah-nama* in a similar small format and illustrated in an equally lively but more fastidious style, with less stocky figures.[1]

Inasmuch as paintings of the early Sultanate period in India are extremely rare, one can do no more than speculate on the provenance of the Schulz *Shah-nama*. The bright, flat colors, with large areas of vermilion, look ahead to seventeenth-century pictures from Malwa, in Central India, which was annexed by ʿAlaʾ ad-Din Khalji (r. 1296–1316) in 1305 and continued to be governed from Muslim Delhi until it became independent in 1401, three years after Timur's sack of Delhi. In all likelihood these small pictures belong either to the Khalji tradition or to that of the Tughluqs who succeeded them in 1320. They were probably painted either in Delhi or at Malwa, where the style spawned many stylistic descendants. The artist is likely to have been trained in Iran and to have undergone an emboldening change of style after he came to India. Already strongly Indian are the ruggedly patterned vermilion sky, the large flowers reminiscent of Western Indian painting, the well-observed elephants (which are unknown in Iranian painting), and the exhilarating overall gusto.

1. For the two small *Shah-nama* manuscripts, see: Simpson, *The Illustrations of an Epic*; Robinson, "A Survey of Persian Painting," p. 21; Robinson, "Areas of Controversy." For another group of *Shah-nama* illustrations (Staatsbibliothek Preussischer Kulturbesitz, Berlin), which stands midway between the Schulz *Shah-nama* and the other two small manuscripts, see: Ipsiroglu, *Saray-Alben*, pl. 1, figs. 1, 2; pl. 2, figs. 3–5; pl. 3, fig. 6.

Published: Schulz, *Die persisch-islamische Miniaturmalerei*, vol. 1, p. 14, vol. 2, pl. 14; Pope, *A Survey of Persian Art*, vol. 3, p. 1834, vol. 5, pt. 2, pl. 832E; Dimand, "An Exhibition," p. 85; Grube, *Muslim Miniature Painting*, p. 29, no. 20.

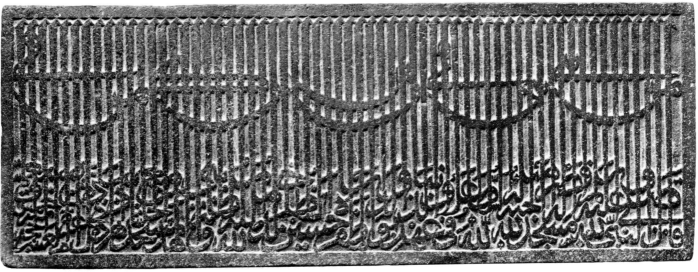

74

THE INDIAN GENIUS for working in stone, so renowned under Hindu and Buddhist patronage, was applied in very different ways under the Muslim rulers, as is apparent in this dedicatory slab from a mosque in Bengal. The inscription, worked with chisels, files, and abrasives, begins with words taken from the Hadith, or Prophetic Traditions: "The Prophet, the blessing of God and peace be upon him, said, 'Whosoever builds a mosque for God, God will build for him a palace the like of it in Paradise.' In the reign of Sultan ʿAlaʾ ad-Dunya waʾd-Din Abuʾl-Muzaffar Husain Shah al-Sultan, may

74.
DEDICATORY INSCRIPTION FROM A MOSQUE
Sultanate, Bengal, Gaur, dated A.H. 905 (1500)
Schist, 16⅛ × 45⅜ in. (41 × 115.3 cm.)
The Metropolitan Museum of Art, New York, Purchase, Gift of Mrs. Nelson Doubleday and Bequest of Charles R. Gerth, by exchange (1981.320)

God perpetuate his rule and sovereignty, Prince Daniyal, may his honor endure, built this congregational mosque on the tenth of Dhu'l-Hijja of A.H. 905 [July 7, 1500]."

Composed in Arabic and written in a special Bengali variant of the Tughra script known as "bow and arrow," the inscription is still as legible as it is visually arousing. Designed within a long rectangle by a master calligrapher whose sensitivity to rhythm and proportion recalls a painting by Uccello, Mondrian, or Gris, it brings to mind an army of the faithful on the march, their standards raised high over a bustling throng of horsemen and elephants.

According to Annemarie Schimmel, the slab illustrates a particularly successful example of the "rhythmic parallelism" cited by Richard Ettinghausen and Irma L. Fraad as characteristic of Indian calligraphy: "Vertical hastae [have been] elaborated into a regular pattern that is then interrupted and shaped regularly by the long backward strokes of the letter *ya* and superimposed *kaf*, a feature also found in predominantly Indian manuscripts. A bowlike design is achieved by placing the round letter *nun* in the upper register. Regularity is rarely, if ever, achieved; at best, five hastae are grouped into one unit. Our stone has exactly sixty verticals of equal length, through which five 'bows' are set, each comprising twelve hastae with two very minor variants. The central 'bow' consists of two superimposed, slightly rounded wide letters; each of the other four 'bows' has a straight horizontal letter, forming a kind of bowstring. The pattern thus assumes a perfect harmony, and can be considered the finest of all published inscriptions from Bengal."[1]

With the weakening of the sultanate of Delhi, the provincial governors became independent, not only politically but culturally. In Bengal various dynasties replaced the Delhi governorships between 1340 and 1526, when the first Mughal emperor, Babur, entered the Indian scene. Particularly admired among the Bengali kings was ʿAlaʾ ad-Din Husain Shah (r. 1493–1518), a Sayyid of Arab descent. Husain Shah was made king after the tyrannical Shams ad-Din Muzaffar Shah, a former slave from Abyssinia under whom Husain had served as vizier, was deposed and slain. During his long rule, Bengal prospered. At the capital, Gaur, and in other parts of Bengal, he and his family built splendid mosques, tombs, and palaces, some of which have survived. Simon Digby, who first translated the inscription, has identified Prince Daniyal, who built the mosque for which this piece was the dedicatory inscription, as one of Husain Shah's eighteen sons. The tomb of Shah Nafa at Monghyr, dated 1497, also bears the prince's name. During the nineteenth century, Gaur became a quarry for contractors from Calcutta, and it was probably then that this stone was carried off and in due course sent to England.

1. Schimmel, in *Notable Acquisitions 1981–1982*, pp. 13–14.

Published: Digby, "The Fate of Daniyal," pl. I; *Notable Acquisitions 1981–1982*, pp. 13–14; Skelton and Francis, *Arts of Bengal*, pp. 30–31, no. 33.

75.
BAZUR THE TURANIAN WIZARD
From a manuscript of the *Shah-nama*
(Book of Kings) of Firdausi
Sultanate, ca. 1430–35
Opaque watercolor on paper, 7¾ × 8⅛ in.
(19.7 × 20.6 cm.)
The Metropolitan Museum of Art, New York,
Bequest of William Milne Grinnell (20.120.246)

THE LONG STRUGGLE between the Turanians and the Iranians is a continuing theme through much of the *Shah-nama*. Numerous armies of countless paladins stain endless fields with their blood. At times, supernatural techniques heighten the encounters. Here, the warlock Bazur, at the order of the Turanian commander in chief, Piran, ascends a mountain and casts spells to engulf the Iranians in darkness, cold, and dense snow. The devastating weather issues in vigorous noxious squiggles from the yogilike shaman's bottle, producing ornamental blobs of snow that have already begun to disturb the intrepid Iranian cavalry and make some of the hidden grotesques in the craggy mountains shiver.

The dispersed manuscript from which this miniature comes has been recognized since the 1950s as being from one of the sultanates. Well before 1430, painting from what might be described as the Turkish-Iranian tradition was being carried out in many fresh sultanate idioms at centers in Kashmir, the Punjab, Delhi, Bengal, Malwa, Gujarat, and the Deccan. These workshops were often staffed not only by Indians but by artists trained in Iran at Shiraz,

75

Tabriz, Herat, or even beyond, who adjusted their styles to the more intense Indian cultural clime. Neither this manuscript nor a related *Shah-nama*, of about 1450, also dispersed, can be assigned a precise provenance.[1]

1. For the related *Shah-nama* of ca. 1450, see: Fraad and Ettinghausen, "Sultanate Painting," fig. 152.

FEW OBJECTS BETTER reveal the synthesis between imported Islamic forms and shapes indigenous to India. A typical zoomorphic incense burner of the sort made by the Seljuk Turks has undergone an Indian metamorphosis:[1] the erstwhile highly stylized lion mask has taken on the pop-eyed and horned aspect of the apotropaic kirttimukha, the "face of glory" associated with Lord Shiva, and the lion's salutatory right paw and the tonguelike folds on his neck, pierced beneath the edges to allow smoke to escape, are also Indian adaptations. Rows of similarly saluting leonine beasts add their august pres-

76.
INCENSE BURNER IN THE FORM
OF A LION
Sultanate, Deccan, 15th century
Bronze, height 6⅞ in. (17.5 cm.)
Fogg Art Museum, Harvard University,
Cambridge, Massachusetts, Purchase, Friends
of the Fogg Art Museum (1964.44)

ences to *The Throne of Prosperity*, folio 191 of the *Nujum al-ʿUlum* (Stars of Science), a manuscript dated 1570–71 that was in the royal library of Bijapur, where it was probably written and illustrated.[2] Like the incense burner, many of the *Nujum al-ʿUlum* miniatures fuse Muslim and Hindu motifs.

The lion's tongue, wobbling on a pivot, is a humorous Indian touch, reminiscent of the tongues on a pair of large stone waterspouts in the form of grotesque water monsters that are now in the Archaeological Museum of Bijapur. The incense burner's lid, which was attached to the animal's tail, is now missing, and the left rear leg is a wooden substitute.

1. For a Seljuk prototype, see: Pope, *A Survey of Persian Art*, vol. 6, pl. 1304.
2. For the *Nujum al-ʿUlum*, see: Arnold, *The Library of A. Chester Beatty*, vol. 2, pl. 4.

77.
ROCK-CRYSTAL ELEPHANT
Sultanate, Deccan, late 15th–16th century
Rock crystal, with 16th-century European mounts in gold and enamel, height 2⅞ in. (7.3 cm.)
Kunsthistorisches Museum, Sammlung für Plastik und Kunstgewerbe, Vienna (2320)

THIS RECUMBENT ROCK-CRYSTAL elephant is the first of the objects and pictures here to have reached the West. Because it is unique and because rock crystal takes on no signs of age, it is also one of the hardest to place in time. The object is clearly Indian in style and workmanship. The carving could only have been done by a lapidary aware of the way Indian elephants look and move: after studying the animal's exceptional—and very obliging—pose, he abstracted it, echoing the pleasing roundness of head and trunk in the almost circular space between trunk and chest. Inasmuch as there are no signs of Mughal naturalism, which would have lent individuality, suggestions of texture, and greater accuracy of proportion, the piece is almost certainly of Sultanate manufacture. The gold and enamel mounts were added in Europe during the sixteenth century, when the elephant was fashioned into a saltcellar.

The elephant once belonged to the younger brother of Hapsburg Emperor Maximilian II, Archduke Ferdinand of Tirol (1520–1595), who was a notable collector in the days of the *Wunderkammer* and *Kunstkammer* (cabinets of curiosities and arts), the forerunners of modern museums. The archduke began acquiring systematically while serving as regent at Prague. At Ambras, his castle near Innsbruck, he arranged and installed his remarkable discoveries, which included many objects from Asia gathered through his family's diplomatic and commercial contacts. His favorite objects were kept on the shelves of eighteen very large cabinets, one of which contained rock-crystal elephants, horn goblets, coconuts, muscat nuts, and bezoar stone amulets and cups, most of which were set in European mountings.

Archduke Ferdinand's Indian material probably came through Goa, which enjoyed close relations with the Deccani sultans. This plump, benevolent

pachyderm bears stylistic affinities to later Deccani depictions of elephants, such as that of Atash Khan, painted for Sultan Ibrahim ʿAdil-Shah II of Bijapur (no. 194), and we are strongly inclined to assign it to one of the sultanates of the Deccan, perhaps to the Bahmanid dynasty that ruled from 1345 until the first quarter of the sixteenth century. It is very likely that many objects made for the pre-Mughal sultans have been incorrectly assigned to Muslim centers outside India.

Published: Born, "Some Eastern Objects from the Hapsburg Collections," p. 275, pl. IID; Lach, *A Century of Wonder*, p. 27, pl. 9.

IN INDIA, WORLDLY pleasures were often explored as diligently as otherworldly pursuits. We have a hedonistic father and son to thank for the renowned *Niʿmat-nama* (Book of Delicacies) to which this miniature belongs. The *Niʿmat-nama*, one of the few such books on gastronomy and related matters to survive, was commissioned by Ghiyath ad-Din Khalji of Malwa (r. 1469–1500) and expanded for his son Nasir ad-Din Khalji (r. 1500–1511). The manuscript contains fifty miniatures relating to cookery and the preparation of aphrodisiacs, drinks, and perfumes.[1] No men are to be seen in the pictures other than the sultan, who surrounded himself with women who attended to his every need. He is reputed to have kept in his harem some fifteen hundred women, whom he educated not only in singing and dancing but also in such matters as finance and the military arts.

78.
THE SULTAN'S LADIES FLAVORING WATER
From a manuscript of the *Niʿmat-nama* (Book of Delicacies) of Nasir ad-Din Shah
Sultanate, Malwa, ca. 1495–1505
Opaque watercolor on paper
Folio: 10⅞ × 7½ in. (27.5 × 19 cm.)
Miniature: 8⅛ × 5½ in. (20.5 × 14 cm.)
The British Library, India Office Library and Records, London (Persian ms. no. 149)

The *Ni'mat-nama* manuscript was copied in a bold Indian variety of Naskhi script and illustrated in a local variant of a well-known Iranian idiom described by B. W. Robinson as the "Turkman style," which seems to have been centered at Shiraz but was widely disseminated.[2] Merchants sold manuscripts illustrated in this manner far and wide, and considerable numbers of painters trained to practice it found employment at courts as distant as Turkey and India. In this picture the dragonish clouds, formulaic flowers, tidily brushed outlines, and bright, clear colors, as well as the scale of the figures and their relationship to the landscape, owe much to the Turkman mode. But the ornamentally patterned leaves on the tree and the ground are as Indian as the cooking pots, bringing to mind not only Indian textile patterns but also the enticing and alluring compositions Indian sellers of pan still devise for their displays of the lustrous and delicate leaves in which betel nut and supari are wrapped. The large-eyed ladies silhouetted in Malwa costume, one of them waving a large Indian fan, reveal the influence of the indigenous style that is also apparent in *Bilhana Makes Love with Champavati* (no. 227), painted some fifty years later.

1. For a discussion of the *Ni'mat-nama* and other published illustrations from it, see: Skelton, "The Ni'mat nama"; Barrett and Gray, *Painting of India*, pp. 60–61; Khandalavala and Chandra, *New Documents of Indian Painting*, pp. 58–64, pls. 11, 12, figs. 131–39; Losty, *The Art of the Book*, p. 67, no. 41.
2. Robinson, "Origin and Date."

Published: Skelton, "The Ni'mat nama," no. 4.

79.
MANUSCRIPT: *BUSTAN* (THE ORCHARD) OF SA'DI (229 folios, 43 miniatures)
Scribe: Shahsuvar al-Katib
Sultanate, Mandu, ca. 1500–1503
National Museum, New Delhi (48.6/4)

THE PATRIARCH ABRAHAM PLAYS HOST TO A FIRE WORSHIPER
Opaque watercolor on paper
Folio: 13⅝ × 9⅝ in. (34.6 × 24.5 cm.)
Miniature: 7⅝ × 6⅜ in. (19.4 × 16.2 cm.)

THE MORALISTIC TALES of Sa'di of Shiraz (ca. 1200–1290) amused and enlightened readers throughout Islam, and several illustrated manuscripts of his *Gulistan* (The Rose Garden) and *Bustan* (The Orchard) were brilliantly illustrated in India (see also no. 139). This illustration describes the humiliation of Abraham, a proudly hospitable old gentleman so keen to entertain a guest that when he sighted a frail, white-haired vagabond crossing the desert he invited him to dine. While grace was being said, Abraham noted his guest's silence, and he soon realized that the old fellow was a despised Zoroastrian. Outraged that his purity should be defiled by his eating with such a being, he forced the hungry old man back into the desert, whereupon an angel appeared and admonished him: "For a century God has provided this fire worshiper's daily bread, and now you presume to withhold the hand of bounty?"

This copy of the *Bustan* was written in unusually bold but graceful Nasta'liq script by Shahsuvar al-Katib (Shahsuvar the Scribe) for Nasir ad-Din Khalji of Malwa (r. 1500–1511), the second patron of the *Ni'mat-nama*. Nasir ad-Din's name and honorifics are given within a shamsa on folio 1r. Inasmuch as the colophon page contains an inspection date of A.H. 908 (1502–3), the manuscript must have been completed early in the sultan's reign. Inscriptions on folios 1 and 190r give the name of the painter and illuminator as the same Haji Mahmud, working at Mandu, who illustrated the *Ni'mat-nama*. The other forty-one pictures appear to be by the same workshop if not by the same hand.

The stumpy trees on the horizon in some of the miniatures, the essentially logical handling of space and architecture, and the ornament and figural types reveal a faint but recognizable awareness of the work of Bihzad, the late Timurid master of Herat. As it is most unlikely that the Mandu patrons and artists had actually seen Bihzad's paintings, echoes of the great artist's style would have to have been transmitted at second or third hand. It is a tribute both to the power of Bihzad and to the level of artistic appreciation at Mandu that his invention reached so far.[1]

1. For a miniature of the sort that might have been the source of Bihzadian influences at Mandu, see: Sakisian, *La Miniature persane*, fig. 109. Marie Lukens Swietochowski has suggested that the artist of the *Bustan* was in this manuscript modifying examples of a now lost early phase of Bukhara painting.

Published: Ettinghausen, "The Bustan Manuscript," pp. 40–43; *Manuscripts from Indian Collections*, pp. 94–95; Losty, *The Art of the Book*, pp. 67–68, no. 42.

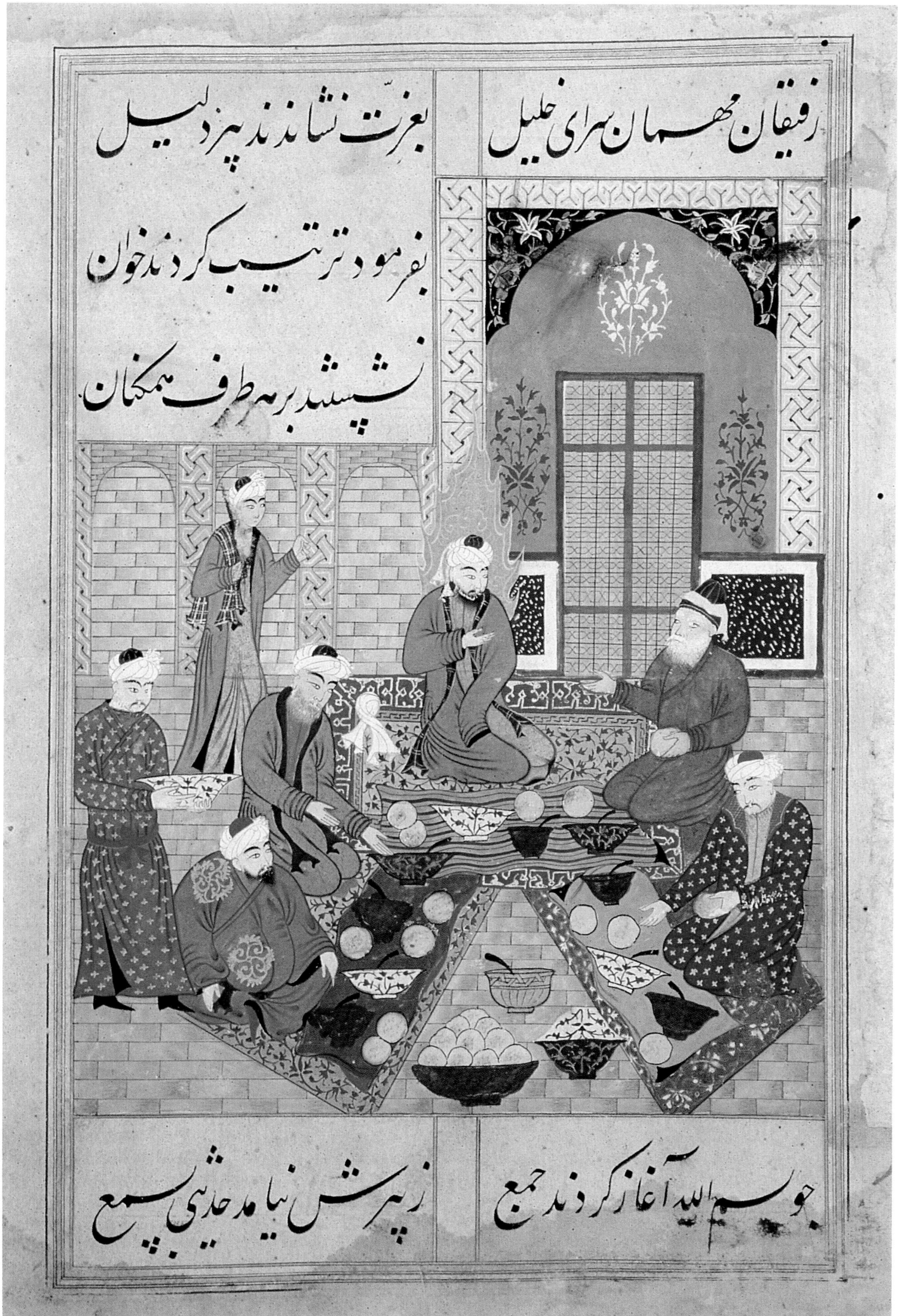

رفیقان مهمان سرای خلیل

بعزّت نشاندند پرد دیل

بفرمود ترتیب کردند خوان

نشستند برمه طرف بمکان

چو بسم الله آغاز کردند جمع

زپرسش نیامد حدیثی بسمع

80

WHILE JOURNEYING THROUGH a forest, the hero Laur and his beloved Chanda rest beneath a tree, from whose branches Laur has suspended his buckler, when a gang of soldiers suddenly attacks them. Violence has rarely been painted more lyrically. The action unfolds beneath a sky of arabesques and a tree flowering with songbirds. Despite the impending slash of Laur's scimitar, his victim reclines with terpsichorean grace, either honored to be slain by so perfect a hero or unable to adjust his mood to life's reality. Like the fallen soldier, the artist seems to have been oblivious to the mundane—even more so than were the Iranian artists from whose style his took flight. The illustrations to this well-known manuscript of the *Laur Chanda* soar farther beyond the daily world than is usual even in Iranian art. The tree in this miniature brings to mind a lollipop craning to become a great rising full moon, the sky could be the work of a skilled embroiderer, and the flowers are scattered rhythmically as drumbeats. For the delectation of a passionately aesthetic patron, a happy, engaging view has vanquished everything inartistic or even slightly unpleasant.

The *Laur Chanda*, or *Chandayana* (The Story of Chanda), was composed in the Avadhi dialect of Hindi in 1377–78 by Mulla Daʾud, who dedicated the story to Jahan Shah, vizier of Sultan Firoz Shah Tughluq of Delhi. Its popularity is attested to by the fact that in a field noted for a paucity of material, parts of at least five illustrated pre-Mughal copies of the romance have survived. Sixty-eight miniatures from this copy were acquired from Bhopal by the Prince of Wales Museum in 1957.[1] Although opinions vary as to when they were painted, the date cannot be far from 1535 to 1540. The

Iranian elements (such as the tree trunk here, which looks back to comparably curved Turkman precursors) are no more than vestigial, and the female figures are painted in a style related to that of the *Chaurapanchasika* series, which has been dated to the mid-sixteenth century. Mandu, Malwa, Delhi, and Jaunpur have all been proposed as possible places of origin. Wherever they were painted, the pictures imply a patron who was not only interested in illustrated books but also devoted to other artistic pleasures. (See also no. 224.)

1. See: Khandalavala and Chandra, *New Documents*, figs. 165–70, 172–75, pl. 24; Khandalavala and Chandra, "A Ms. of the Laur Chanda."

Published: Losty, *The Art of the Book*, p. 69, no. 45.

ONE OF INDIA's contributions to the world is the fable book, the most renowned of which is the classic *Kalila wa Dimna*, named after the two jackals whose exploits it recounts. *The Leopard's Court* depicts a climactic moment in Dimna's career. Having ingratiated himself with the lion-king, Dimna introduces him to an ox. But when the two become boon companions, the Iago of jackals seethes with jealousy, and with lies he so arouses the king against the ox that he kills him. On discovering his friend's innocence, the

81.
TWO MINIATURES FROM A
MANUSCRIPT OF THE
KALILA WA DIMNA OF BIDPAI
Sultanate, Gujarat, mid-16th century
Opaque watercolor on paper, 12 × 8⅞ in.
(30.5 × 22.5 cm.)
The Metropolitan Museum of Art, New York,
The Nasli Heeramaneck Collection, Gift of
Alice Heeramaneck (1981.373)

a. THE LEOPARD'S COURT (folio 51r)

b. BURZUYA'S INDIAN MISSION (folio 5v, 6r)

81a

81b

sad lion-king orders Dimna to stand trial for causing the lamented ox's death. Dimna is found guilty and sentenced to death by starvation. Here, within a zestful arabesquescape of flowers, fruit, and cypress trees, a resolute leopard sits in judgment on the devious jackal, from whom an outraged hare turns away in disgust.

According to legend the tales of Karataka and Damanaka, as the jackals were originally called, were written by Vidyapati (Bidpai), a Brahmin sage who figures in the stories, which are in fact largely based on the even older fables of the Sanskrit *Panchatantra* (Five Books), in which human vices and foibles are instructively revealed through the personalities and activities of birds and beasts. In the sixth century, according to the *Shah-nama*, the sage Burzuya, at the order of the Sassanid ruler Nushirvan, located a copy of Bidpai's book in India and brought it back to Iran, where it was translated into Pahlavi. Ironically, the extant Sanskrit versions are translations from the Pahlavi text, which was also the basis for an eighth-century Arabic translation by ʿAbd Allah ibn al-Muqaffaʿ, whose version spread Bidpai's tales to Turkey, Egypt, and other parts of the Islamic world. Nushirvan's copy of the *Kalila wa Dimna* would have contained marvelous pictures, which probably established the compositions for later illustrations. With each later version, however, the original designs changed, even when artists tried to be accurate by using tracings.

Most of the seventy-eight painted folios in the manuscript these two miniatures come from, which was painted in western India in the mid-sixteenth century, were derived from designs traceable to Egypt, to Mamluk prototypes that may in turn have been based on long-lost Indian originals.[1] But the Heeramaneck manuscript contains many delightful, sometimes comical, innovations. Of particular interest is the strong Ottoman flavor, especially apparent here in the windblown tulips in *Burzuya's Indian Mission*, a double-page miniature in which the artist has caught the sage at a particularly puzzled moment in the course of his search for Bidpai's book. Other miniatures include characteristically Ottoman textile patterns and architectural elements, sometimes in conjunction with figures wearing unmistakably Safavid turbans. Dominating this stylistic melting pot, however, is an overwhelmingly Indian spirit. The smoldering palette is rich in burnt orange and colors otherwise known to us only in paintings from Sirohi, in the southwestern corner of the present-day state of Rajasthan, not far from the Gujarat border.[2]

The Heeramaneck *Kalila wa Dimna*, combining vitality, cosmopolitan style, courtly refinement, and popular élan, is as informative and historically significant as it is appealing. Masterful pictures like *The Leopard's Court*, as rhythmically ornamental as embroidery, provide evidence of a major Gujarati stylistic synthesis. *Burzuya's Indian Mission* not only represents a fusion of Ottoman and indigenous styles but its potent juxtapositions of ornament, horses, and figures look ahead to the elements Gujarati artists brought to Akbar's imperial ateliers at Fatehpur-Sikri following the Mughal annexation of Gujarat in 1572.

1. For characteristic Mamluk sources, see: Atil, *Kalila wa Dimna*.
2. For a characteristic Sirohi picture, see: Lee, *Rajput Painting*, no. 53. A mid-seventeenth century miniature from a *Bhagavata Purana* series reveals many traces of the Gujarati elements apparent in the Heeramaneck manuscript. See: Welch and Beach, *Gods, Thrones, and Peacocks*, no. 15.

Published: *Notable Acquisitions 1981–1982*, pp. 15–16; "Art of Asia Acquired," p. 105, fig. 43.

ARCHITECTONIC AS A building, this sumptuously restrained box was made to house the tools of the calligrapher's trade: reed pens, fine knives and a small block of hardwood for pointing and trimming them, and, perhaps, inks. Like other qalamdans made for discerning and affluent penmen, this one is inscribed with its maker's name and the date of its execution as well as a virtual anthology of appropriate Arabic and Persian verses. The inscriptions, written in Nasta'liq script, are executed in ivory and mother-of-pearl inlay that is as fine as illuminated calligraphy.

The quatrain at the top of the front panel, which is only partly legible, opens with the poet's admonition to himself not to bring out his tongue (that is, not to speak) lest he divulge the taste of the beloved's sweet lip, and continues with verses implying that the waist of the beloved is so slender as to seem invisible, although it is improper even to mention so tender a secret. The name Humayun appears in the third line, and this poetical conceit may have been composed by the second Mughal emperor, Humayun. The lines below the quatrain announce, "The deviser of this . . . pen case is Shaikh Muhammad Munshi Ghaznavi / On the date of Sha'ban of the year 995 [July 1587] it found completed form."[1]

In the corners to the right and left of the central inscription, the couplets read, "When I try the ink / I draw night over the face of day," and "When I tried the ink / I remembered your black tresses." The images are traditional: the calligrapher's ink-black script as it fills the white page is like night falling over day, and like the black curls hiding the beloved's pale complexion.

The inscription in the lower cartouche, placed obliquely to catch the eye, begins with the formula "God is too lofty and high for whatever they describe," and goes on to quote the opening lines of the Sufi mystic Jalal

82.
QALAMDAN
Sultanate tradition, Gujarat,
dated A.H. 995 (1587)
Wood, inlaid with mother of pearl,
14⅛ × 25⅝ in. (36 × 65 cm.)
Benaki Museum, Athens (10181)

ad-Din Rumi's *Mathnavi-yi ma'navi* (The Spiritual Couplets): "Listen to the lamentation of the reed / How it tells of the ache of separation." Rumi was referring to the Sufi's reed flute; here his words also evoke the sound of the scribe's reed pen as it moves across the paper.

Verses fill the cartouches in the upper border, although parts of them are now illegible. The inscription at the upper right on the front of the box alludes both to a Prophetic Tradition, "Man is between two of God's fingers," and to the pen, with which God writes whatever He wills: ". . . had made its place between His two fingers." In the verse in the next cartouche either the poet or the hollow reed of a pen or flute could be speaking: "You see, there is nothing in me of my own essence / He is in me, breath of my breath." And the metaphors continue with the boast of the pen: "I make the camphor-white page black as musk. . . . I trace limpid water ornamental as the wild rose. . . . Sometimes I interpret the state of longing [and] track scars on the soul."

The artisans of Gujarat, where this pen box was made, were well known for their beautiful mother-of-pearl inlays, and inlaid tables, chests, and other objects made in the region were sold by merchants to clients all over India and beyond. The earliest known examples of Gujarati inlaying are two superb shields of the early sixteenth century, one now in the Bargello Museum, Florence, the other in the Topkapi Sarayi Museum, Istanbul, which also has in its collection a tabouret topped with an inlaid Indian game board and floral designs similar to those on this qalamdan.[2] Gujarati inlaid work was much admired by the Mughals, who brought specialized craftsmen to Fatehpur-Sikri, Agra, and Delhi to carry out major commissions. Shaikh Salim Chishti's tomb at Fatehpur-Sikri contains a magnificent inlaid wooden cenotaph by Gujarati artisans.[3]

1. Annemarie Schimmel has translated the inscriptions and made invaluable suggestions as to their interpretation.
2. Ettinghausen, *Treasures of Turkey*, p. 235.
3. For other examples, a pen box and a chest from the seventeenth century, see: *The Indian Heritage*, p. 162, nos. 549, 550.

THE MUGHALS

ZAHIR AD-DIN MUHAMMAD BABUR (1483–1530)—the first Mughal emperor —was born with conquest in his veins. Descended from both Timur (Tamberlane) and Chinghiz Khan, he inherited the minor throne of Fergana (now in Soviet Turkistan) in 1494, when he was twelve. Already restive and ambitious, Babur (the Tiger) soon led his small army against Samarkand in an attempt to recover the capital of Timur from the Uzbeks, an attempt that was ultimately unsuccessful. His first major triumph was the capture of Kabul and Ghazni in 1504, valuable base camps for further military forays. In 1519, prompted by India's richness and vulnerability and by his ancestor Timur's exploits in India, he led his small, eager army on an unsuccessful campaign via the time-honored route, the mountain passes of the northwestern frontier. A second attempt, in 1525, led to his great achievement, the founding of the Mughal empire.

In 1526, at Panipat, near Delhi, Babur's cavalry and artillery overwhelmed the combined forces of the Muslim sultan of Delhi and the Hindu raja of Gwalior; and a year later, at Kanhua, his hold over Hindustan was consolidated by his defeat of an alliance of Rajput princes. Although he died only a few years later, in 1530, Babur had established what was to become the largest, most powerful, and longest lasting Muslim kingdom in Indian history.

In the absence of any works of art commissioned by him, Babur's greatest memorial, more permanent than his empire, is his autobiography, the *Waqi'at-i Baburi*, written in Chaghatai Turkish and later translated into Persian as the *Babur-nama* (The History of Babur) by order of his grandson, Emperor Akbar, for whom it was illustrated by court painters. Although Babur also wrote and loved poetry, his sparkling, precisely observed and astonishingly candid prose is more compelling. The descriptions of people, flora and fauna, and events in his memoirs are written in sensitively naturalistic, reportorial style—the mode of expression that set the pattern for Mughal art and literature down through the years.

A determined huntsman as well as warrior and author, Babur recorded the hunt depicted in the present miniature, which was painted by one of Akbar's most inventive artists, perhaps Miskin, for the earliest known copy of the translation prepared for Akbar in 1589, probably the earliest of Mughal historical manuscripts. We quote Babur's own description of the incident, which reveals how forcibly, sensitively, and credibly Mughal painters carried out the commissions of their exacting patrons: "A hunting-circle was formed on the plain of Kattawaz where deer (*kiyik*) and wild-ass are always

83.
BABUR SLAYS A WILD ASS
From a manuscript of the *Babur-nama*
(The History of Babur)
Mughal, ca. 1590
Opaque watercolor on paper
Folio: 13⅝ × 9 in. (34.5 × 23 cm.)
Miniature: 9⅝ × 5⅝ in. (24.6 × 14.4 cm.)
Private collection

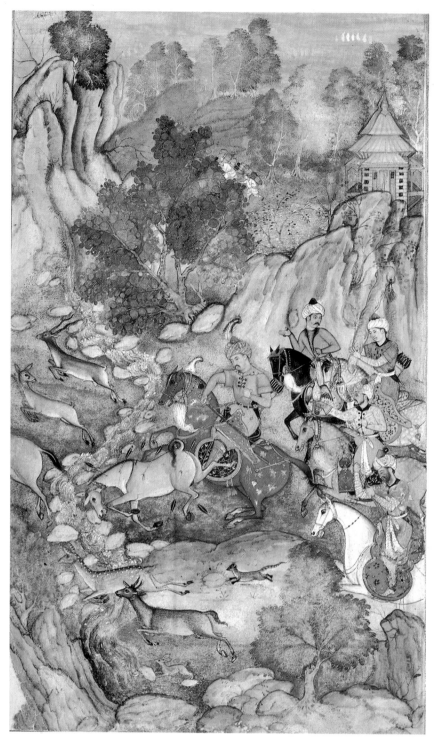

83

plentiful and always fat. Masses went into the ring; masses were killed. During the hunt I galloped after a wild-ass, on getting near shot one arrow, shot another, but did not bring it down, it only running more slowly for the two wounds. Spurring forwards and getting into position quite close to it, I chopped at the nape of its neck behind the ears, and cut through the windpipe; it stopped, turned over and died. My sword cut well! The wild-ass was surprisingly fat. Its rib may have been a little under one yard in length."[1]

1. Babur, *The Babur-nama*, vol. 1, p. 325.

Published: Smart, "Six Folios," pp. 120–21, no. 95.

THE SECOND MUGHAL emperor, Nasir ad-Din Muhammad Humayun (1508–1556), was left an empire scarcely worthy of the term; and he was hardly the man to strengthen it. Temperamentally an inheritor rather than a founder, Humayun delighted in art, literature, good company, and royal ways. In character he reminds us of his great-grandson, the quintessential aristocrat, Shah Jahan. He commissioned a tent complex within which his court could be arranged not only by rank but also according to astrological sign. Although the court astrologers prophetically drew up a highly favorable chart for his first son, Prince Akbar, Humayun himself was not born under winning stars. His brothers Hindal and Mirza Kamran coveted his position, as did an aspiring Afghan nobleman, Sher Khan, once in the service of Babur, who seized Bengal, assumed the title Sher Shah, and led his army against the Mughals. In 1537, he forced Humayun back to the Mughal capital of Agra, and later drove him toward the Punjab. Dependably troublesome, brother Mirza Kamran then sealed off the Punjab and the road to Kabul, forcing Humayun into the deserts of Sind.

In Sind, Humayun's prospects were bleak. Accompanied by his pregnant wife, a few attendants, and an ever diminishing army, he improvised. In 1542, under these inauspicious circumstances, Prince Akbar was born. Perhaps the prince's good fortune was infectious. Life improved. Shah Tahmasp, the mighty Safavid ruler of Iran, offered refuge. This was an event of art-historical as well as political consequence, for the artistically discerning Mughal emperor went to the shah's court at just the time when Tahmasp's once intense and highly creative interest in painting was lagging. Humayun was thrilled by the brilliance of the shah's artists' work; and the painters responded to his connoisseurship. Although Mughal prospects were slim, several of the greatest Safavid artists tentatively accepted Humayun's invitation to join his entourage.

84.
PRINCES OF THE HOUSE OF TIMUR
Probably by 'Abd as-Samad
Mughal, ca. 1545–50
Opaque watercolor on cotton, 42¾ × 42½ in.
(108.5 × 108 cm.)
Trustees of the British Museum, London,
Presented by the National Art Collections Fund
with a contribution by W. Graham Robertson,
Esq. (1913.2-8.1)

84

84, detail

Shah Tahmasp's generous treatment of Humayun was motivated at least in part by political expediency. Threatened by the Ottoman Turks on his western border and the Uzbeks to the east, he was eager to be on good terms with the ruler of Hindustan. In 1545, Shah Tahmasp helped Humayun capture Kandahar, the strategic fortress guarding the gateway to India, which Humayun had agreed to turn over to the Safavids. But Humayun disappointed the shah. He kept the fort and marched upon Kabul, which he took from his nettlesome brother Mirza Kamran.

In 1546, Emperor Humayun sent for the Safavid artists whom he had met at the shah's court. They set off in 1548 from Tabriz for Kandahar, where they lingered until calm had been restored at Kabul. There they joined Humayun in 1549, and in 1554 they accompanied him on his successful return to Hindustan.

The *Princes of the House of Timur* dates from the earliest known phase of Mughal painting, soon after Emperor Humayun's formerly Safavid artists had reached the imperial court. Its size, innovative conception of portraiture, and close observation of incidental figures—the cooks, waiters, and minor courtiers—reveal Humayun's effectiveness as a Mughal patron reared in the tradition of Babur's all-seeing pattern. No purely Safavid miniature would have recorded the precise gestures and expressions of menials, or shown this festive scene so believably arranged.

Although the *Princes of the House of Timur* has been somewhat cut down and repainted, it can be assigned to one of Humayun's émigré Safavid artists, ʿAbd as-Samad, working under the influence of his colleague Mir Sayyid ʿAli. Typical of ʿAbd as-Samad are the bold arm gestures of the figures, the flight of birds at the top of the picture, the treatment of trees and vegetation, and, above all, the convincing arrangement of forms in space.

Revered as an artistic and historical document, this picture may have been painted, as has been suggested by Michael Rogers, at Kabul, prior to Humayun's return to India.[1] Although the central figure has usually been identified as Humayun, Rogers intriguingly suggests that it may be a portrait of Babur, characteristically shown in one of his garden palaces. Facing him, within the pavilion, are Emperor Akbar, his son Emperor Jahangir, and grandson Prince Khurram, who later reigned as Shah Jahan. These later portraits are imperial work of the Jahangir period, and can be dated to about 1607, when Khurram, who is not fully grown, was fifteen years old, and his father, who must have commissioned them, was thirty-eight. Many other faces were retouched or overpainted at the same time. Rogers has pointed out that the foreground, now missing, would have shown musicians and entertainers, and would have added another twenty to twenty-five centimeters to the height of the picture.

1. Letter, December 20, 1984.

Published: Binyon, *A Persian Painting of the 16th Century: Paintings from the Muslim Courts of India*, pp. 22–23, no. 1; Rogers, *Islamic Art*, pp. 71–72, no. 60.

85.
HUMAYUN AND HIS BROTHERS IN A LANDSCAPE
From the Berlin Album (folio 15r)
Attributed to Dust-Muhammad
Mughal, ca. 1550
Opaque watercolor on paper
Folio: 16⅛ × 10 in. (41 × 25.5 cm.)
Miniature: 15¾ × 8⅝ in. (40 × 22 cm.)
Staatsbibliothek Preussischer Kulturbesitz, West Berlin

IN THE FOREGROUND of a craggy, somewhat ominous landscape, Emperor Humayun sits on a rustic stone throne, receiving his brothers. The ladies of the household entertain one another in a picturesquely rustic zenana, or harem; musicians perform; and attendants await orders. Three small boys, one of whom must be Prince Akbar, romp beneath trees, near a life-sized elephant concealed in the rocky setting, prophetic of Indian days ahead.

Such hidden grotesques were admired by Shah Tahmasp, the former patron of the painter of this miniature, who can be identified as Dust-Muhammad. A distinguished master artist, calligrapher, and man-of-letters, Dust-Muhammad had studied at Herat with the great Timurid painter Bihzad before moving to Tabriz, the Safavid capital. A further adventure in his picaresque career brought him to the court of Humayun, for whom he painted this and other pictures, attributed to him on the basis of earlier, inscribed works.

This splendid, somewhat spooky picture is one of Master Dust-Muhammad's liveliest and best. Prior to being mounted in Emperor Jahangir's album, it probably was housed at Agra, where Humayun's palace included a three-building complex known as the Khana-i tilism, or Magic House.[1] One of the buildings, intended for merriment, comfort, and pleasure, contained a special room on the uppermost level in which Humayun kept books, gilded pen cases, portfolios, albums with pictures (muraqqaha latif ma'i taswirha), and beautiful specimens of calligraphy.

A nomad by temperament, Dust-Muhammad was fated not to remain long at the Mughal court, which was at Kabul when this picture was painted in about 1550. A decade or so later, at the age of seventy, he apparently returned to Iran, where he spent his remaining years piously copying out Qur'ans at Qazvin.[2]

1. For Humayun's Magic House, see: Ansari, "Palaces and Gardens of the Mughals."
2. For further information about this artist, see: Dickson and Welch, *The Houghton Shahnameh*, vol. 1, pp. 118–28.

Published: Kühnel and Goetz, *Indian Book Painting*, p. 5, pls. 4 (det.), 32.

86.
LOVING MUSICIANS
Mughal, ca. 1550
Opaque watercolor on paper, 7⅝ × 4⅝ in.
(19.5 × 11.8 cm.)
Private collection

WERE IT NOT for the characteristic turban unique to Emperor Humayun and his court, this miniature might be ascribed to the Uzbek tradition, centered at Bukhara. Instead, the pleasingly moon-faced musicians, with their deftly drawn bird-beak noses, fingers suitably shaped like plectra, and gracefully arcing brows, must be assigned to the little-known early phase of Mughal art. One senses non-Uzbek verve in the lyrically dancing trees keeping time with the music, in the zestful interaction of the lovers, and in the spritely duet of tambourine and lute.

A copy of Jami's *Yusuf and Zulaikha* (New York Public Library), inscribed with the name of Mirza Kamran, brother of Emperor Humayun, contains illustrations in the same style, perhaps by the same hand, though lacking Mughal turbans. Considering the origins of Emperor Babur, it is likely that his artists worked in a slightly earlier variant of this style. Another closely related picture, also with Bukhara turbans, is in the collection of the Museum of Fine Arts, Boston.[1]

1. For the Boston miniature, see: Coomaraswamy, *Catalogue of the Indian Collections: VI*, pl. 24, no. 15.29.

I am grateful to Michael D. Willis for calling my attention to Mirza Kamran's copy of Jami's *Yusuf and Zulaikha*.

87.
AKBAR HUNTING TIGERS NEAR NARWAR
From a manuscript of the *Akbar-nama* (The History of Akbar) of Abu'l-Fazl
Designed and partly painted by Basawan; colored by Tara Kalam
Mughal, ca. 1590
Opaque watercolor on paper
Folio: 14¾ × 10 in. (37.6 × 25.3 cm.)
Miniature: 12⅜ × 7½ in. (31.6 × 19 cm.)
Victoria and Albert Museum, London
(I.S. 2–1896 17/117)

ABU'L-FATH JALAL AD-DIN MUHAMMAD AKBAR (1542–1605), known as Akbar the Great, inherited the Mughal throne from his father Humayun in 1556, at the age of fourteen. At the time, his empire was less consequential than either his lineage or his personality, and had he not been able to greatly expand his territories and establish an effective government, Mughal India would be known only to specialists. Akbar, however, was in every way remarkable. He was at once supremely practical and a visionary, a conqueror and a patron. In temperament, he was more of a founder than an inheritor; indeed, he can be said to have refounded the Mughal empire. Before his twentieth year he had pushed his borders far into Central India, and he was to continue an aggressively expansionist policy until he died, at the age of sixty-three, in 1605. Had he lived to the age of one hundred fifty, as his astrologers predicted, India's map, and perhaps that of the rest of the world, would have been even more extensively redrawn. By the time of his death, perhaps by poisoning, the Mughals controlled all of northern India and vast territories to the west, in what are now Pakistan, Afghanistan, Iran, and parts of the Soviet Union.

Possessed of the force of nature, Akbar was a man of total conviction and self-confidence. The territories he conquered were effectively joined to the empire by the wisdom and power of his statesmanship. Despite differ-

86

87

ences of language and custom, the people of Akbar's realm were brought together by his policy of unification, one of his continuing preoccupations, which he furthered in every conceivable way. By marrying into the ruling families of captured territories, he linked himself to Kshatriya dynasties, thus availing himself not only of wives but of brothers-in-law, many of whom became officers in his ever growing, always busy armies. The policy of marrying Hindu wives not only joined the Mughal house to important indigenous ones but also hastened the Indianization of his initially foreign dynasty and culture.

Akbar in his youth far preferred outdoor activities to bookish education. Riding, hunting, swordsmanship, shooting matchlocks, dancing, playing drums, and listening to music—all were preferred to what was usually considered "educational." Fortunately, his regent, Bairam Khan, was helpful, sympathetic, and extremely capable; and young Akbar was able to satisfy his phenomenal curiosity about all aspects of the world in suitably imperial style. There was no need to learn to read: books on any subject he desired were read aloud to him by specialists, poetry was recited, and fantastic tales were spun for his pleasure. However great his physical energy may have been, his mind was in scale with it.

Akbar's broad interests included the arts, which he encouraged with the same degree of intelligence and energy expended on his state. Like a magnet he drew to his court architects, craftsmen, and artists from most of India and beyond. Basawan, who designed and partly painted this brilliant reconstruction of one of Akbar's youthful exploits in the hunting field, was probably the most gifted of the imperial workshop's hundreds of artists.

Abu'l-Fazl, who was so close a friend to Akbar that his biography, the *Akbar-nama* (The History of Akbar), is the equivalent of an autobiography,

87, detail

describes the notable events of Akbar's life in the grandiloquent style of the time. Illustrated by the imperial artists, Akbar's own copy was the most immediate and impressive volume in a magnificent series of historical manuscripts. We quote Abu'l-Fazl on the subject of the tiger hunt shown here, one of its vital pictures:

"When [Akbar's] crescent standards cast their rays on the territory appertaining to the fort of Narwar, a tiger such as might terrify the leopard of heaven came out of the forest with five cubs and onto the track by which the cavalcade was proceeding. His Majesty, the Shahinshah who had the strength of the lion of God in his arms and the coat of mail of the Divine protection on his breast, went alone out without hesitation in front of that lion-clawed, fiery-natured wild animal. When the spectators beheld this the hair on their bodies stood erect and sweat distilled from their pores. His Majesty with swift foot and alert arm attacked the brute and killed it by one stroke of his sword.

"The wild beast so great and terrible, fell bleeding to the dust before the strength of his arm and the might of his courage, and a shout arose on all sides. This was the first beast of prey which His Majesty personally attacked. Its cubs were killed by the swords and arms of a number of brave men who were in attendance on the sublime stirrup."[1]

1. Abu'l-Fazl, *Akbarnama*, vol. 2, pp. 222–23. For an account of Akbar, see: Schimmel and Welch, *Anvari's Divan*. Basawan is discussed in Welch, "The Paintings of Basawan."

Published: Welch, "The Paintings of Basawan," figs. 11, 13, 14 (dets.); Welch, *The Art of Mughal India*, pp. 28, 163, no. 11A; *Paintings from the Muslim Courts*, p. 39, no. 35; *In the Image of Man*, p. 153, no. 204.

AKBAR'S VITALITY AND charisma reach out to us through time and space, whether transmitted by his extraordinary architecture, as at his wondrous City of Victory, Fatehpur-Sikri; through the hero-worshiping Abu'l-Fazl's florid but impressive prose; or by means of the many works of art that have survived from his prodigious reign. Akbar commissioned manuscripts, miniatures, and objets d'art just as he fought battles—unhesitatingly and with total clarity of command. A supreme patron, he in effect entered the minds and souls of great artists, through whom he painted pictures precisely as he liked them.

The emperor's fearlessness and electric energy are splendidly conveyed in Basawan's double-page composition showing a horrendous episode: Sighting an enraged elephant which had run amok and was about to cross a bridge of boats, Akbar leaped onto its back and gained control. The artist and his excellent assistant express the splash, the bobbing and hurtling, even the frenzied noise in one of the most vigorous of all Mughal compositions. Akbar's muscular strain gains emphasis by his proximity to the prominent figure of the boatman struggling with a pole to avoid capsizing.

Basawan often returned to paintings he had outlined or designed, and enjoyed coloring parts that especially appealed to him, such as the dashingly brushed wood piling lashed with ropes in the left foreground near the distraught spectators. Like his imperial mentor, Basawan created as naturally as the wind blows.

Published: Brown, *Indian Painting*, pl. XXXIX; Welch, "The Paintings of Basawan," fig. 9; *Paintings from the Muslim Courts*, pp. 39, 42–43, no. 39; Welch, *Imperial Mughal Painting*, pp. 62–65, pls. 12, 13.

88.
AKBAR'S ADVENTURES ON HIS ELEPHANT HAWA'I
Double-page miniature from a manuscript of the *Akbar-nama* (The History of Akbar) of Abu'l-Fazl
Designed and partly painted by Basawan; colored by Chatar Muni
Mughal, ca. 1590
Opaque watercolor on paper
Folio: 14¾ × 9½ in. (37.5 × 24 cm.)
Miniature: 13⅝ × 8½ in. (34.5 × 21.5 cm.)
Victoria and Albert Museum, London (I.S. 2–1896 21/117, 22/117)

88, left

88, right

89

90

89.
AKBAR ORDERING THE SLAUGHTER
TO CEASE
From a manuscript of the *Akbar-nama*
(The History of Akbar) of Abu'l-Fazl
Attributed to Miskin
Mughal, ca. 1590
Opaque watercolor on paper
Folio: 16⅜ × 11⅜ in. (41.5 × 29 cm.)
Miniature: 12⅜ × 7½ in. (31.5 × 19 cm.)
The British Library, India Office Library and
Records, London (Johnson Album 8, no. 4)

NOT IN EXHIBITION

AKBAR OFTEN BROKE with the conventional patterns of his time. In a world of ardent hunters who protected the villagers from tigers while delighting in the sport, he was daringly expert. But one day near Bhera, in 1578, when Akbar was thirty-six, a great qamargah had been arranged, a traditional Mongol hunt prepared by an army of beaters who drove all sorts of game from miles around into an enclosure. Aided by huntsmen and trained cheetahs, the swiftest of animals, Akbar stormed through the enclosure, firing arrows and swinging his sword at deer, nilgai, and other captive animals. Violence triggered revulsion. In disgust, Akbar stopped the hunt. As Abu'l-Fazl described it, "A sublime joy took possession of his bodily frame. The attraction of cognition of God cast its ray." Afterward, heeding the emperor's wishes, "Active men made every endeavor that no one should touch the feather of a finch and that they should allow all the animals to depart according to their habits."[1]

Following Akbar's visionary experience, which took place at the time in life when others have been blessed with comparable revelations, he gave much gold to the holy men and poor of Bhera; and on returning to Fatehpur-Sikri, he filled a large tank in the palace with coins for charity.

Miskin, to whom this picture can be attributed on the basis of style, was Akbar's most understanding animal painter. The dead or dying buck confronting Akbar could hardly be a more tragic object for contemplation. Although representations of the pensively Buddha-like emperor—lent a vibrant aura by the wave-edged red coverlet on which he sits—and the concerned train of huntsmen winding from the distance are sensitively dramatic, Miskin's animals are painted with closer observation and deeper sympathy. One senses that on this occasion he shared the emperor's view; his animals happily enjoying their freedom constitute a deeply felt painted sermon.[2]

1. Abu'l-Fazl, *Akbarnama*, vol. 3, pp. 346–47.
2. Another miniature designed and mostly painted by Miskin, from the *Akbar-nama* series in the Victoria and Albert Museum, London, shows Akbar slaying animals in the enclosure; reproduced in Welch, *Imperial Mughal Painting*, pl. 14.

Published: *The Art of India and Pakistan*, p. 151, no. 672, pl. 130; *Paintings from the Muslim Courts*, p. 52, no. 48; Falk and Archer, *Indian Miniatures*, p. 47, no. 3, pl. 1.

No OTHER MUGHAL battle scene so compellingly expresses the tumultuous energy and terrible chaos of armies and elephants clashing against one another. As members of Akbar's staff, the artists would have accompanied him on campaigns and sketched the horrors and exultations. Abu'l-Fazl, the emperor's boon companion, also served stints as reporter in the field and was expert in military matters. In the *Akbar-nama*, he describes the episode shown here, a culminating event in the rebellion of two Afghan brothers, 'Ali-Quli Khan and Bahadur Khan, whose behavior so offended the emperor that he led his army in person from Agra to Jaunpur to punish them. When the rebels "saw the majesty of the army and the onset of the elephants they understood that it was the sublime cortege of the Shahinshah, and that His Majesty in person had set the foot of victory in the stirrup of conquest. 'Ali-Quli Khan and Bahadur Khan set their hearts on death and stood in the plain of rebellion."[1]

Bahadur Shah's horse was struck by an arrow. It reared up, flinging the rebel leader to the ground, where he was surrounded and captured. "'Ali-Quli Khan . . . in the pride of his disloyalty was inquiring after . . . Bahadur Khan, [when] a mast elephant [one in the rutting season] called Citranand, which was one of the royal elephants, rushed against the elephant Gaj Bhanwar . . . [which] fled, followed by Citranand. Gaj Bhanwar's driver drove his elephant among the ranks of the rebels, [who] opposed to Citranand the elephant Udiya. Citranand left Gaj Bhanwar and ran at Udiya and with one mountain-breaking blow stretched him on the dust of destruction. A great discomfiture ensued among the rebels, and many of their leaders became the harvest of the sword."[2]

1. Abu'l-Fazl, *Akbarnama*, vol. 2, p. 431.
2. Ibid., p. 432.

AKBAR DELIGHTED IN fancifully imaginative tales. According to the *Akbar-nama*, in 1564 he relaxed after an elephant hunt at Narwar by listening to the *Dastan-i Amir Hamza*, or *Hamza-nama* (The Story of Hamza), a Persian epic that relates the exploits of Hamza, an uncle of the Prophet Muhammad, conflated with those of an adventurous namesake from Sistan. Although it is difficult to ascertain exactly when Akbar's grand series of illustrations on cloth to the *Hamza-nama* was begun and completed, its twelve volumes containing 1,400 illustrations were his most majestic and inspired project in the field of painting. Although less than ten percent of the original number has survived, and many of those have been damaged, repainted, or both, their surging vitality, dramatic impact, and detailed handling underscore Akbar's preeminence as a patron. Like his empire, they represent a new synthesis of elements from far and wide. Akbar's painting ateliers were directed by two of his father Humayun's Safavid artists, Mir Sayyid 'Ali and 'Abd as-Samad, who trained and supervised painters of talent recruited from within the land and from abroad. Whenever Akbar's forces added a city or province to the empire, its most gifted artisans were brought to court, where they participated in the ongoing creation of the Mughal cultural synthesis under the magnetically compelling influence of the emperor himself.

Although the *Hamza* pictures were invariably designed and sketched by

90.
THE MAST ELEPHANT CITRANAND
From a manuscript of the *Akbar-nama* (The History of Akbar) of Abu'l-Fazl
Designed by Kesu Kalan; colored by Chatar Muni; with special touches by Kesu Kalan
Mughal, ca. 1590
Opaque watercolor on paper
Folio: 14¾ × 9⅝ in. (37.6 × 24.4 cm.)
Miniature: 12½ × 7½ in. (31.8 × 18.9 cm.)
Victoria and Albert Museum, London
(I.S. 2–1896 115/117)

91.
THE PROPHET ELIAS RESCUING NUR AD-DAHR FROM THE SEA
From a manuscript of the *Dastan-i Amir Hamza*, or *Hamza-nama* (The Story of Hamza)
Composition attributed to Mir Sayyid 'Ali
Mughal, ca. 1570
Opaque watercolor on cotton gauze
Folio: 29 × 22¾ in. (73.6 × 57.9 cm.)
Miniature: 26⅝ × 20½ in. (67.6 × 52 cm.)
Trustees of the British Museum, London, Presented by the Reverend Straton Campbell
(1925.5–29.01)

master artists and finished with the help of others in the royal workshop, it is sometimes possible to recognize the hands of specific masters. In this hauntingly poetic yet turbulent portrayal of the Prophet Elias saving a prince from the sea, into which he had been hurled by a demon, the prophet's proportions, gestures, and such details as his hands and the stumpy trees on the shore bring to mind the work of Mir Sayyid ʿAli, who must have laid out the composition and painted parts of it. More agitated sections of the miniature—the leaping fish, swirling water, and twisting tree trunks—bring to mind the work of Akbar's Indian masters, such as Miskin, who may have painted them and the splendid birds and animals. Partially hidden in the animatedly ornamental, tapestrylike jungle, they recall a series of marvelous panels carved in red sandstone in the so-called Turkish sultana's pavilion at Fatehpur-Sikri, which can be assigned to the same designer or designers, working at approximately the same time. Like this miniature—one of the half-dozen or so most compelling of the series—they perfectly balance Safavid nuance with indigenous flights of vision.[1]

1. For the panels at Fatehpur-Sikri, see: Smith, *The Moghul Architecture of Fathpur-Sikri.*

Published: Arnold, *Painting in Islam*, frontispiece; Stchoukine, *La Peinture indienne,* pl. VI; *Paintings from the Muslim Courts*, p. 28, no. 11; Losty, *The Art of the Book*, pp. 85–86, no. 54, ill. p. 76.

THE EXPANSIVE STYLE of Akbar's *Hamza-nama* series is also seen in these two miniatures from a manuscript of *Duval Rani Khizr Khan*, by the sultanate poet Amir Khusrau Dihlavi. The hero of the verse is depicted in Mughal setting, everyone but the angels dressed as though at Akbar's court. As in the *Hamza-nama*, characterizations are portraitlike and often verge on caricature. The potbellies, sneers, giggles, and raised eyebrows must have entertained the fortunate owners of this remarkable manuscript.

According to seals in the book, it was in the library of two emperors, Shah Jahan and Aurangzeb. Earlier, it belonged to a prestigious lady of the imperial family, Salima Sultana Begum, a granddaughter of Emperor Babur and wife of Emperor Akbar.

Amir Khusrau Dihlavi, perhaps India's most renowned Muslim poet,

92.
MANUSCRIPT: *DUVAL RANI KHIZR KHAN* OF AMIR KHUSRAU DIHLAVI
(157 folios, 2 miniatures)
Scribe: Sultan Bayazid ibn Nizam
Mughal, dated A.H. 976 (1568)
National Museum, New Delhi
(L53.217)

KHIZR KHAN AND DEVALDI ENTHRONED, HONORED BY ANGELIC VISITORS
Opaque watercolor on paper
Folio: 12⅜ × 8¼ in. (32.2 × 21 cm.)
Miniature: 12¼ × 7⅝ in. (31 × 19.3 cm.)

92, detail

was the son of a Turkish officer and an Indian mother. He was born in Patiala in 1253, and he became court poet to virtually all the sultans of Delhi who reigned between 1270 and 1325. A disciple of Nizam ad-Din Auliya, who called him "God's Turk," he was praised for the sweetness of his language as Tuti-yi Hind, (India's Parrot). Prolific and experimental, he wrote a great number of lyrics, an imitation of Nizami's *Khamsa* (Quintet), a treatise on correspondence, and numerous historical works. He was the first to compose mathnavis not only on traditional themes but also on contemporary events.

His third mathnavi of this sort was the love poem, or ʿashiqa, *Duval Rani Khizr Khan*, finished in 1314. It recounts the tragic romance of Khizr Khan, a son of Sultan ʿAla ad-Din Khalji and Devaldi, a Hindu princess. The poem is admired for its intense, tender romanticism and for its praise of things Indian.

The miniature depicts the enthroned lovers honored by angelic visitors. Presumably, it was painted for Emperor Akbar. He later presented the volume to Salima Sultana, who must have enjoyed it with her friends and attendants in the harem. The picture invites speculation about Mughal women as patrons. Was Akbar's poetically minded wife also a keen devotee of painting, and might not she have been directly involved in the illustration of this superb manuscript, the only one in a style markedly similar to the *Hamza-nama* to have survived?

Published: *Manuscripts from Indian Collections*, pp. 96–97; Chandra, *The Tuti-nama*, p. 72, pl. 36; Losty, *The Art of the Book*, pp. 86–87, no. 56; Nath and Khandalavala, "Illustrated Islamic Manuscripts," pp. 38–39.

93.
MANUSCRIPT: *ANVAR-I SUHAILI* (THE LIGHTS OF CANOPUS) OF HUSAIN WAʿIZ-I KASHIFI
(349 folios, 27 miniatures)
No scribe's name given
Mughal, dated A.H. 978 (1570–71)
Manuscript: 14 × 9 in. (35.6 × 22.9 cm.)
School of Oriental and African Studies, University of London (Ms. 10102)

a. THE THIEF, THE DEMON, AND THE DEVOTEE (folio 174)
   Attributed to Basawan
   Opaque watercolor on paper

b. MAIMUN, THE PATRIOTIC MONKEY, LURES THE BEARS TO THEIR FATE (folio 182)
   Opaque watercolor on paper

AKBAR'S EXTENSIVE, CONSTANTLY growing library included many categories of literature and learning: biography, theology, comparative religion, science, mathematics, history, astrology, medicine, zoology, and anthropology. Many of the volumes were illustrated. And if certain projects required no more than matter-of-fact illustrations, others so excited the emperor that he encouraged his artists to ever new heights. The *Hamza-nama* challenged the painters to release all their inventive powers; and the *Akbar-nama*, with its miraculously detailed descriptions of Akbar's reign, populated by a myriad of portraits, opened their eyes wide to life's fascinating hurly-burly.

Active as a storm while engaged on military campaigns or attending to matters of state, Akbar in his hours of relaxation was also creatively busy. He is said to have needed very little sleep, and during restful moments he enjoyed commissioning and looking over volumes of literary classics, books of poetry, and of fables and other diverting tales. Intended for sustained and close scrutiny, they were of a size to hold rather than to view from a bookstand, and their miniatures differed from those for the larger scaled projects in being true "masterpieces," the work of a single master artist instead of a joint effort designed or outlined by a master and then colored by one or more assistants.

Akbar's *Anvar-i Suhaili* (The Lights of Canopus) of 1570–71 is the earliest dated example of this sort, carried out when Humayun's formerly Safavid artists were strongly influential in the royal library. In every respect, it represents a major effort to produce for Akbar an Indian manuscript of a subject of Indian origin equal to Shah Tahmasp's elegant volumes of Iranian poetry, to which Mir Sayyid ʿAli and ʿAbd as-Samad had contributed during their years at the Safavid court. Paper, illuminations, pigments, and compositions, which often break into the margins—all are in keeping with Safavid practice. Although a few of the miniatures are by an artist trained at Bukhara who had not adjusted his style to the Akbari synthesis, the others are by artists of the most progressive wing of the royal workshop, closely directed by Mir Sayyid ʿAli and possibly by ʿAbd as-Samad.

This rustic scene from the manuscript can be assigned to one of Akbar's recruited artists, almost certainly Basawan, trying most assiduously to follow the strict directions of Mir Sayyid ʿAli. It illustrates the story of a thief and a demon whose paths cross when each is bent upon swindling a devotee, the first by stealing his fat young she-buffalo, the second with fiendish temptations. The pair rejoice over their apparent partnership in crime but soon bicker, arousing their victim as well as his neighbors, who forces them to flee. Down to the last brushstroke, the Hindu painter strives for Safavid exquisiteness. Pigments of purity and brightness unusual for the Mughal workshops at this date are applied with enameled hardness, and the architecture is a virtual translation of Indian fences and thatched huts into the Safavid idiom.

Nevertheless, Basawan's artistic personality shines through—his roundedly powerful intertwining trees, adapted from Mir Sayyid ʿAli's; his animals brimming with individual character; and his animated portraits—all familiar from the *Hamza-nama*. Notwithstanding the strictures of his mentors, Basawan's dashingly liberated brushwork is also apparent. But he was struggling; and we suspect that Akbar sympathized with his plight. For the radically innovative patron's aesthetic is clear not only from his commissions but, indirectly, from his thoughts on literature, as quoted by Abu'l-Fazl: "Most old authors who string out their words . . . and display a worn-out embroidery, give all their attention to the ornamentation of words, and regard matter as subservient to them, and so exert themselves in a reverse direction. They consider cadence and decorative style as the constituents of eloquence, and think that prose should be tricked out like the works of poets."[1] Clearly, Akbar's preference for the unadorned coincided more closely with Basawan's aesthetic than with Mir Sayyid ʿAli's elegant interpretation of the world in arabesque. Although one is grateful for the Iranizing fineness of this miniature and many others in the manuscript, and although Basawan must have learned a great deal from painting it, one is relieved—with Akbar and Basawan, we suspect—that the lessons in Safavid discipline soon ended (see also nos. 87, 88, 108, 110).

Indian artists and sculptors invariably excelled in characterizing animals, as is apparent in the spritely *Maimun, the Patriotic Monkey, Lures the Bears to Their Fate*, one of the illustrations to a complex and enlightening fable in which monkeys avenge the slaughter of their companions by bears, who are enticed into a desert to expire in the heat. Although Mir Sayyid ʿAli—who must have directed the painting bear by bear—was himself an exceptional animalier, most of the brushwork is probably by Miskin, an Indian-born "student." Like Basawan, he was one of Akbar's leading artists, who here adapted to Safavid ways. But beneath the fine, smoothly textured brushwork, almost Tabriz-style rocks, and strongly Safavid treatment of space, the churning water, overall burst of energy, and markedly Indian bears proclaim Mughal origin (see also nos. 89, 103, 109).

1. Abu'l-Fazl, *Akbarnama*, vol. 2, p. 553.

Published: *The Art of India and Pakistan*, p. 142, no. 636, pl. F; Wilkinson, *Mughal Painting*, pl. 3; Losty, *The Art of the Book*, p. 87, no. 57.

Overleaf, 93a,b ▷

دیو نیز فریاد کرده که اینجا در دست مینخواهد که کار و ترا برود زاید از عربۀ ایشان بیدار شد و خروشیدن در گرفت همسایکان در آمدند و ایشان هر دو بکر تخیستند و نفس و مال از این سبب اختلاف

دشمنان سالم و محفوظ مانذ نظم چو در لشکر دشمن افتد خلاف چرا تیغ باید کشید از غلاف چون و زیر بپیم این سخن پاک رسانید

وكسم تَوبِرصواب آنست كه كمر ملازمت بربندیم وبقیهٔ العمر درخدمت
ملازمان ملک کذرانیم و درسایهٔ دولت اوازتنکبات زمان آسوده بکوبه شه

وتوشه بسازیم بنظم در بناه دولت صاحبدلان ماه جو بدم که هست از عاقلان

کرتو درکلشن درآیی کل بری پسوی بستان کذری سنبل بری ملک از

94.
TAMARUSA AND SHAPUR AT THE
ISLAND OF NIGAR
From a manuscript of the *Darab-nama*
(The History of Darab) of Abu Tahir
(folio 34r)
By Basawan
Opaque watercolor on paper
Folio: 14⅛ × 9 in. (36 × 23 cm.)
Miniature: 9⅞ × 7½ in. (25 × 19 cm.)
The British Library, London (OR.4615)

OF ALL AKBAR'S manuscripts, the *Darab-nama* (The History of Darab) may be the most personal to him. In contrast to the sumptuous *Anvar-i Suhaili* (no. 93), with its minutely finished pictures painted under the rigid control of Akbar's Safavid émigrés, the *Darab-nama* is ruggedly experimental and unselfconscious, less formally "imperial," and more expressive of Akbar's wishes. While turning its pages, one senses his mood during the later years at Fatehpur-Sikri and soon after his move to Lahore in 1585. Although the manuscript bears no dates, it was probably initiated in the later 1570s, when the emperor was in his late thirties. Still youthfully dynamic and experimental, he was eager for new adventures, and—following his vision of 1578 (see no. 89)—brimming over with conviction. Life was at its fullest for Akbar and for the empire, which continued to expand. The government was running smoothly, and Akbar had entered the active quarter of life associated in India with the "householder."

Akbar was amplified, not changed, by his vision. More appreciative than ever of otherworldly delights, he could now more effectively relate them to day-to-day life. Fantastic tales entertained him as before, and those illustrated in the *Darab-nama* indicate his increased ability, through his artists, to make the unbelievable credible. If the *Hamza-nama* series represents Akbar's mood prior to his vision, and the 1570–71 *Anvar-i Suhaili* exemplifies the same mood under the very calming direction of Mir Sayyid 'Ali and 'Abd as-Samad, the *Darab-nama* reflects the newly integrated, virtually reborn, galvanic Akbar. The whirlwind style of the *Hamza-nama* has given way to more restrained rhythms and subtler colors, and characterizations have gained in depth and nuance. Dragons incredibly—if delightfully—outrageous in the *Hamza-nama* are believably menacing in the

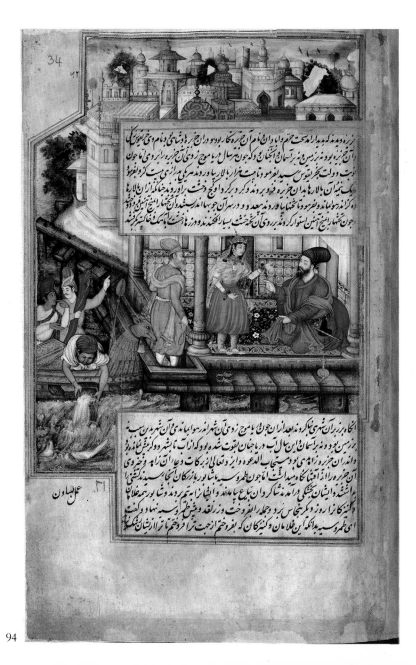

94

Darab-nama; and nude figures, rare subjects in Mughal art, are rawly, embarrassingly naked.

Preeminent artists contributed to the *Darab-nama*: Basawan, Nanha, and Miskin. Basawan's persuasiveness as a dramatist, analyst of personality, and storyteller are always balanced by serious concern for pure painting. In *Tamarusa and Shapur at the Island of Nigar*, he has perfectly harmonized the fantasy of the island, its crystalline city built on pilings, with the fetching heroine, the voluminous and portentous Shapur gracefully entwined by a brushed gold shawl, and the innovatively foreshortened boy. Basawan instilled everything with life; the rooftops sprout, and the prow smiles responsively.

Published:
a. *Paintings from the Muslim Courts*, p. 29, no. 17; Welch, *Imperial Mughal Painting*, pp. 50–51, pl. 6; Losty, *The Art of the Book*, p. 88, no. 59.

95

AKBAR SURROUNDED HIMSELF with magnificent works of art, great and small. A superb dagger or a carved sandstone panel for a pavilion was as artistically significant to him as a painting. To outfit all his forts and palaces and satisfy his aesthetic cravings, Akbar staffed his workshops with artist-craftsmen from all of Mughal India and beyond. The *A'in-i Akbari* (Statutes of Akbar), the last section of Abu'l-Fazl's *Akbar-nama*, describes several of the workshops, including the farrashkana, which was responsible for the manufacture and maintenance of tents and carpets, many of which were artistically extraordinary. Akbar did not confine men of talent within narrow specialties; artists, illuminators, and calligraphers provided motifs to stonecutters and weavers.

Tangible evidence can be seen in the thirteen or so surviving fragments of a carpet (or pair of carpets) composed in a vast, surging arabesque as dynamic as the *Hamza-nama*—a phantasmagorical zoo of birds, serpents, oxen, elephants, rabbits, and other creatures, relieved by flowers and vases.[1] Full of life, the motif of six bird heads flowering from the mouth of an animal can be interpreted on many levels. Most of the beasts are apparently disgorging or consuming one another as actively as its patron was swallowing up much of India. If it were music, one would hear martial drumming, the clash of cymbals, and trumpet salvos. The drawing of birds, beasts, and flowers projected from many angles, and the grandeur of the overall

95.
FRAGMENT OF AN ANIMAL CARPET
Mughal, ca. 1585–90
Cotton warp and weft, wool pile, 31½ in. × 10 ft. 1 in. (80 cm. × 3.02 m.)
The Fine Arts Museums of San Francisco, Gift of Arthur Sachs (1952.35)

arabesque—a Safavid design gone wild—can be traced to Mir Sayyid ʿAli, whose Tabriz miniatures reveal so many of its elements.

It has been suggested that the fragmented animal carpet might have been made at Lahore, during the reign of Emperor Jahangir.[2] Although the fragments are technically and coloristically similar to later imperial Lahore carpets, their unleashed energy and lively fantasy far surpass the later ones, which seem calmer and almost mechanically refined in comparison. Very likely, these fragments, marred by the technical flaws of a new workshop, represent the farrashkana of Lahore soon after Akbar's move from Fatehpur-Sikri in 1585. The demonic mask invites comparison to the masks in the border of the famous, slightly later pictorial carpet in the collection of the Museum of Fine Arts, Boston, showing figures, architecture, and fantastic animals.[3]

1. Further fragments are in the Museum of Fine Arts, Boston; Textile Museum, Washington, D.C.; Burrell Collection, Glasgow; Detroit Institute of Arts; The Metropolitan Museum of Art, New York; The Hermitage, Leningrad; Musée du Louvre, Paris; Collection C. L. David, Copenhagen; City Art Museum, Saint Louis; private collection, Cambridge, Mass.; and other private collections. See: *The Indian Heritage*, p. 74, no. 191.
2. Walker, "Classical Indian Rugs," p. 255.
3. For the Boston carpet, see: Welch, *The Art of Mughal India*, pp. 31, 165, pl. 22.

96.
BRONZE LION
Mughal, ca. 1575
Height 18¾ in. (47.6 cm.)
The Knellington Collection, Courtesy
Harvard University Art Museums,
Cambridge, Massachusetts

THIS SPIRITED, SLEEK, somewhat threatening bronze lion may have guarded Akbar's throne, or looked down imposingly from a column upon his assembled courtiers. For the image on the Mughal imperial standard, as recorded by a British visitor in the early seventeenth century, bears a close resemblance in pose and character to the present bold animal. In style, it combines

96

naturalistically observed musculature, proportions, and ribs with passages of extreme abstraction. The lion's ears, shredded by triumphant encounters in the jungle, have been metamorphosed into pleasingly Muslim rosettes; the proud chest is shaped as a curving ridge; and dangerously bladelike underedges add force to the lion's forearms. As in other Mughal works of this period, there are traces of European influence, both in the overall concept and in the pose, which recalls lions rampant of heraldry.[1]

A sinuously agitated mane brings to mind the formulas for water seen in the giant illustrations to the *Hamza-nama* (see no. 91). One is reminded, too, of far earlier Indian prototypes—the stately and powerful Mauryan lion and bull capitals associated with another philosopher-king, Ashoka. Inasmuch as Akbar visited places where Mauryan pillars stood, it seems likely that he admired the sculptures and realized the applicability of Mauryan state symbolism to his own empire.

A pair of gilded bronze lion masks, certainly from the same workshop as this lion, is in the collection of the Museum für Östasiatische Kunst, Cologne. Presumably, they once adorned the tops of columns at Agra or Fatehpur-Sikri.[2]

1. A pair of possibly related South German bronze lions cast from models by Hubert Gerhardt stand in front of the entrance to the Residenz of the former electors of Bavaria in Munich. A similar pair attributed to Hans Krumper was sold at Sotheby's; see: *Art at Auction: The Year at Sotheby's & Parke-Bernet, 1970–71*, pp. 288–89.
2. For the Cologne masks, see: Bernheimer, *Romanische Tierplastik*, pp. 126–27; Welch, "A Lion-King's Lion," forthcoming; Lowry and Brand, *Akbar's India: Art from the Mughal City of Victory,* forthcoming.

THIS MASSIVE, HEAVY object could crack an enemy's helmet, unhorse him at a single blow, or dent an elephant. With such possibilities in mind, the armorer cast its handsomely architectonic form in one piece and adorned the classic arabesque flanges with suggestions of elephant heads in profile. Brobdingnagian warriors wield maces of corresponding heft in several of the miniatures from the *Hamza-nama*, swinging them in fierce struggles against demons, giants, and polycephalous dragons. Others are illustrated in the *Darab-nama*.

Comparably giantesque weapons, once wielded by stout Turkish champions, are exhibited as part of the Ottoman armory in the Topkapi Sarayi Museum in Istanbul.

97.
MACE
Mughal, ca. 1575
Cast iron, length 21¼ in. (54 cm.),
diameter at top 5⅛ in. (13 cm.)
The Knellington Collection, Courtesy
Harvard University Art Museums,
Cambridge, Massachusetts

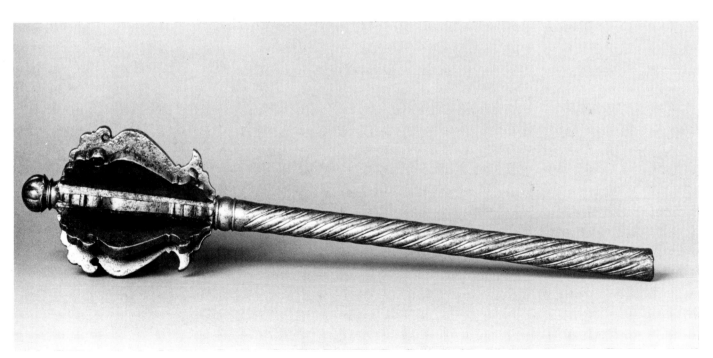

97

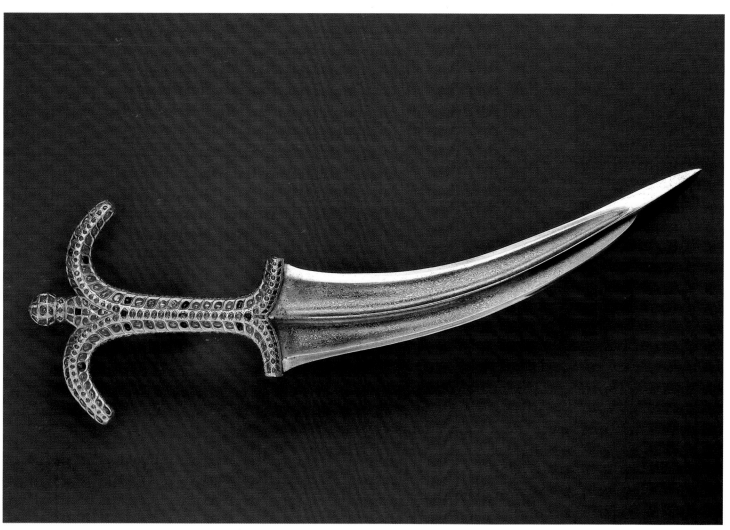

98

98.
DAGGER
Mughal, ca. 1585
Watered steel, gold, emeralds, and rubies,
length 13½ in. (34.3 cm.)
Private collection

SPLENDID WEAPONS WERE appreciated by the Mughals for both utility and beauty. During the early Akbar period, swords and daggers were intended primarily as tools, secondarily to delight the eye. Along with robes of honor, jewels, and villages, they were frequent royal gifts. In the *Hamza-nama* miniatures and other early paintings, one often sees daggers of exactly this form, lethally springy, with hilts ending in finials that snugly fit the hand. As with this one, their blades and hilts were forged for greater strength from single pieces of steel.

Most early Mughal blades—as well as helmets, shields, and even scissors—were made by watering steel, a technique that was believed to strengthen them and to produce sharper edges and points, and which enhanced them with attractive ripple patterns. Two methods were used. In the first, pieces of hard and soft iron were combined by welding, folding them, and sometimes cutting the results into bars at rhythmic intervals. In the second, various types of iron (even meteoric ore) were combined in an ingot that was slowly heated and then hammered out to the shape desired. The heavy, curved blade of the present example was thickened near the point to pierce armor and chain mail.

After the blade and hilt had been formed on an anvil, they were fitted into a stone slab indented to their shape, and held fast with gum, to be refined by grinding with abrasives and files. The hilt was then covered with gold and set with precious stones. By about 1600, this form of hilt sprouted a knuckle guard (see no. 127). Even peaceful Tansen, Akbar's greatest musician, faced life securely with a dagger like this one—perhaps an imperial gift—tucked into his belt (see no. 106).

THE EMPERORS, SULTANS, and rajas of India vied with one another to possess beautiful and important gems, which were set into thrones and weapons; valued as compactly portable state and personal wealth; given and received as the ultimate presents; and—as the final accents of royal splendor — worn. This jewel is not only intrinsically beautiful; artistry has made it into a deeply moving object, a brilliant garden or oasis—surely magical — for majestic contemplation. Emeralds were particularly admired by Muslims. In Sufism, an emerald mountain stands for the final level of spiritual aspiration, when man has passed through the blackness of annihilation and emerged in paradise, at last able to view the world as through the eye of God. More practically, according to popular belief, emeralds can blind snakes and dragons.

This emerald is assuredly the most extraordinary gem of its kind in the world. Color and quality are unparalleled; and according to the noted gemologist Manuel Keene, there is no likelihood that an emerald of this size and quality will again be mined. The hexagonal form "is not purely the choice of the designer, but rather comes naturally from the fact that [it] is a sawn cross section from an emerald crystal, the crystallographic habit of which is to take the form of a hexagonal prism."[1]

This gloriously dark green gem was formed and found in Colombia, where Spaniards first obtained emeralds in 1514 and began mining them about forty years later. Presumably, it was carried by merchants to India during the second half of the sixteenth century. And soon after its arrival there, the extraordinary relief of tall, windswept palm trees was carried out by a masterful lapidary through drilling, rotary grinding, and the use of polishing points and wheels.

The artist-craftsman elevated this emerald from the world of gems to the world of art, transforming it into an emblematic fusion of the organic and the crystalline, of the kinetic and the static. Asymmetric trees, growing ever upward and outward, suggest the transitory but vital force of life in contrast to the eternal but inactive hardness of the stone into which they are cut and in which the artist has made them immortal while he has at the same time imprisoned them. This huge emerald, in short, is a microcosmic allegory, something for princes to ponder, and from which to learn that without living light, not even a great jewel is radiant.

99.
EMERALD WITH DESIGN OF
SPREADING TREES
Probably Mughal, ca. 1585
233.45 carats, 2¼ × 2 in. (5.7 × 5 cm.)
The al-Sabah Collection, Dar al-Athar al-Islamiya, Kuwait National Museum
(LNS.28.Hs)

99

Where was it cut, and when? In the absence of historical evidence and related material, one can only suggest, on grounds of style, that it is either Mughal or Deccani—probably the former—and that the movement of the trees and suggestions of landscape conform to what we know of Akbar's taste during his most vital period, about 1585. It was for him, we believe, that the inspired lapidary, perhaps in consultation with a court painter, infused this monumental stone with its joyous, talismanic power.

1. Letter, January 1985.

Published: *Islamic Art in the Kuwait National Museum*, p. 124.

100.
MADONNA AND CHILD
Mughal, ca. 1580
Opaque watercolor on paper
Folio: 14¾ × 8¾ in. (37.5 × 22.2 cm.)
Miniature: 7¼ × 4¼ in. (18.4 × 10.8 cm.)
The Knellington Collection, Courtesy
Harvard University Art Museums,
Cambridge, Massachusetts

AT FATEHPUR-SIKRI, from 1575 through 1582, Akbar brought together representatives from every sect of Islam and from Hinduism, Buddhism, Zoroastrianism, and Christianity for all-night religious debates in a special hall, the 'Ibadat Khana (House of Worship). He first met with Portuguese Christians in 1572 in Cambay. The following year he negotiated peace with Father Antonio Cabral at Surat, an encounter so promising that the Portuguese viceroy soon dispatched the priest to Fatehpur-Sikri for further talks in the hope of converting Akbar, and through him all of Hindustan.

The Portuguese Jesuits were pleased when Akbar celebrated the Feast of the Assumption by setting up a picture of the Virgin given to him by Father Rudolf Aquaviva—whose mission was at court from 1580 to 1583—and ordering his relations and courtiers to kiss it. On March 3, 1580, Father Rudolf gave Akbar a copy of Plantin's *Royal Polyglot Bible*, printed in the sixteenth century for Philip II of Spain, from which he subsequently directed his artists to copy pictures of Christ and of the Virgin Mary. A letter recorded at Goa in 1580 from Father Francis Henriques to Father Lawrence Peres says that on entering the church, Akbar was "surprised and astonished and made a deep obeisance to the picture of Our Lady that was there . . . as well as to another beautifully executed representation of Our Lady brought by Father Martin de Silva from Rome, which pleased him no end. . . . He was so taken up that he came in again with a few intimates and his chief painter and other painters, of which he has many excellent ones, and they were all thunderstruck and said that there could be no better painting nor better artists than those who had painted the said pictures."[1] The second picture is believed to have been a copy of the Byzantine Virgin said to be in the Borghese chapel of the basilica of Santa Maria Maggiore in Rome. It was made by order of Francis Borgia with the permission of Pope Pius V, and was sent to Goa in 1578.

This *Madonna and Child*, with its markedly Byzantine character, is likely to have been painted immediately following the incident described in Father Henriques's letter. Stylistically, it can be dated to about 1580; it is the earliest Christian subject we have seen that can be assigned to a Mughal artist. The artist, probably a Vaishnavite Hindu, was so enthralled by the Christ Child that he interpreted him as a beguiling infant Krishna, merely substituting white skin for blue.

Two further missions from Goa followed, a brief one in 1591, and another, led by Father Jerome Xavier, which arrived in 1595 and stayed until 1614, by which time Muslim orthodoxy had taken such a hold at the imperial court that conversion was unlikely. Nevertheless, Jesuits remained at the Mughal court until 1803.

1. Correia-Afonso, *Letters from the Mughal Court*, p. 31.

Published: Welch, *Room for Wonder*, pp. 18–19, fig. 1.

101.
CORPUS OF CHRIST
Probably Indian, Goa, 16th century
Polychromed wood, height 38½ in. (97.8 cm.)
Museum of the Basilica Bom Jesus, Goa

ALTHOUGH ONE MIGHT suppose that Christianity was foreign to India, in fact it is of greater antiquity there than in any place other than Palestine. It is sometimes believed that Christ himself assigned the teaching of the Gospels in India to the Apostle Thomas. According to tradition, Thomas reached India in 52 A.D., eventually settling in Malabar, where he had many con-

100

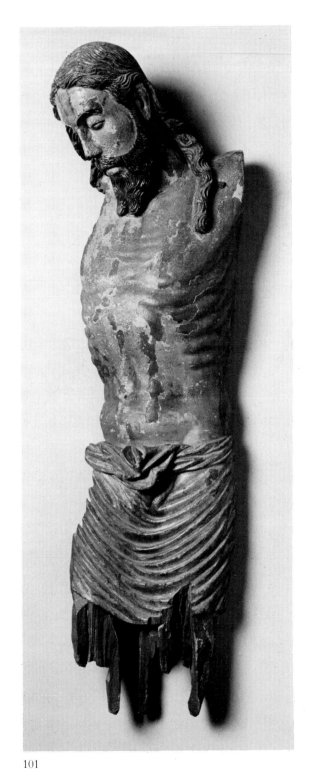

101

verts and founded churches before expanding his missionary activities as far as China. He is thought to have been martyred by Brahmins at Mylapore, near Madras, when he returned to India in 72 A.D.

Strongly reminiscent of European Gothic sculpture, this *Corpus of Christ* was probably carved and polychromed at Goa by Indian craftsmen working under Catholic patronage, who infused it with their innate spirituality. Craftsmen of Goa specialized in wood carving to supply a clientele eager for sculptures and reliefs of the Virgin Mary, the Christ Child, the Crucifixion, the pantheon of saints, and many other subjects suited to altars and shrines for ecclesiastical as well as domestic use. Greatly varied in size and shape, their styles reflect those then evolving in Europe.

102

102.
CABASSET
Goa, ca. 1560
Gilded copper, 7⅞ × 11¾ in. (20 × 30 cm.)
Collection Rainer Daehnhardt, Belas, Portugal

BECAUSE SPICES—particularly pepper—were so essential in Europe to preserve meat after it had been soaked in brine, venturesome Portuguese traders, who knew of Indian spices because of their contacts with the Arabs, worked their way to India. In 1486, Bartholomew Diaz rounded the Cape of Good Hope; and Vasco da Gama, seeking among the Syrian Christians of Travancore allies against the Arabs, reached Calicut in 1498.

The resentment of European competition by Arab traders who had long prospered in their monopoly of the spice trade forced the Portuguese to send warships and establish fortified ports. The Portuguese in 1510 seized Goa, the principal station in a network that eventually included Malacca in the East Indies, Ormuz on the Persian Gulf, and outposts in East Africa on Socotra off the Red Sea, Diu in Gujarat, and Colombo in Ceylon. All this was masterminded by Affonso d'Albuquerque, who also wisely promoted close relations with local people. In India, Portuguese sailors, soldiers, and merchants were encouraged to intermarry, and Goa developed into a strongly Indianized Catholic community, which, as we have seen, was eager to proselytize, especially at seats of great power, such as the Mughal court.

This gilded copper cabasset, alive with ornamental animals and scenery, is typically Portuguese in shape, though the repoussé decoration bears the stamp of its Goanese origin. A hero's chariot harks back to village bullock carts, and the flowers, trees, and beasts, and a huntsman aiming his matchlock at a flying bird all glow with Indian character. This is believed to be the sole surviving example of five such "golden helmets" made in the viceregal armory of Goa for the Portuguese viceroys of India between about 1550 and 1580. It was probably commissioned in about 1560 for Don Diogo De Menezes, who later led the Portuguese armies during the reign of King Antony. Following the capture of the fortress of Cascais in 1580, Don Diogo was beheaded by the duke of Alba. The helmet is thought to have been taken by King Antony to the Azores, where it remained until recently. A similar helmet, presumably captured by the Dutch, was owned by Rembrandt, who painted it in his *Man Wearing a Golden Helmet* (Staatliche Museen, West Berlin).

Published: *Os Descobrimentos portugueses e a Europa do Renascimento*, p. 81, no. 80.

I am grateful to Rainer Daehnhardt for providing information for this entry.

THESE SNORTING, STAMPING buffaloes—two varieties of the same species—were drawn and tinted by Miskin, Akbar's best animal painter, in recollection of an actual combat staged for the entertainment of the emperor and members of his immediate circle. Animal combats, whether between elephants, buffaloes, tigers, or smaller beasts, were frequent events at court, viewed by the emperor and his guests from a terrace or rampart. Sketching from life, the artist must have sat near the noble onlookers, who took bets on the outcome—as did the animals' grooms—and encouraged their favorites with ardent loyalty.

Miskin's draftsmanly style is unmistakable, and his gift for conveying both the inner spirit and outer form of animals probably inspired Akbar to summon him for the present assignment. Not even the great Basawan, represented here by his stunning elephant chase (no. 88), surpassed Miskin in capturing such dramatic details as the buffaloes' expressions of victorious exultation and gored despair. The loser in such a combat might be turned into a mashk—a leather waterbag, such as the one shown here being used to keep down the dust.

By delicate modulations of tone, achieved with invisibly small brushstrokes, Miskin modeled the animals' masks and bodies into tautly rounded forms reminiscent of Achaemenid animal reliefs, curvaceously ornamental yet starkly powerful. But unlike the Achaemenids, the Mughal stopped action at the most telling instant, and achieved a degree of empathy that enables us to hear the animals' bellowing.

Published: Sotheby's, London, November 24, 1952, lot 107; Parke-Bernet, New York, December 15, 1962, lot 285; Sotheby's, London, June 20, 1983, lot 143; "Recent Sales," p. 308, no. 29; *Notable Acquisitions 1983–1984*, pp. 6–7; Heeramaneck, *Masterpieces of Indian Painting*, p. 158, pl. 167.

103.
BUFFALOES IN COMBAT
Attributed to Miskin
Mughal, late 16th century
Brush and ink with color on paper,
6⅞ × 9½ in. (17.5 × 24.1 cm.)
The Metropolitan Museum of Art, New York,
Harris Brisbane Dick Fund (1983.258)

103

COMFORTABLY AT EASE, reclining in a bamboo grove, a sleekly groomed and well-fed lion awaits his next adventure—be it another meal or an amorous lioness. Like the birds, bamboo, and grass, he has been interpreted midway between the naturalistic and the ornamental modes: his alert eye, wrinkled cheeks, fur, and decorously crossed paws are sharply observed; but the stylized animal design (janvar-sazi) of Iranian tradition is apparent in the elegant twist of spine and calligraphic sinuosity of tail and lips.

Attributing this beguiling beast—far too docile to terrorize a village—is difficult; but Iranian graces in conjunction with acute study from life bring to mind early work by Mansur, the Mughal natural history painter usually associated with the reign of Emperor Jahangir (see nos. 141–45).

Published: Heeramaneck, *Masterpieces of Indian Painting*, p. 161, pl. 195.

THE MUGHAL EMPERORS assembled albums as well as manuscripts. These varied in size and character, but most of them combined calligraphy, miniatures —some of which had been removed from manuscripts—drawings, prints, and at times European watercolors. Most of the miniatures were Mughal, with occasional Iranian ones to add variety. The Mughal material ranged in subject from portraiture to studies of flora and fauna to picturesque fancies.

Special book craftsmen were responsible for composing, trimming, and gluing the bits and pieces, which had been selected for inclusion by the emperors themselves; and illuminators—some of whom also painted miniatures—were responsible for the borders, surrounds, and other ornamental passages. Completed folios were brought to the emperor for his approval, and he frequently took reed pen in hand to note identifications or add personal comments. Although the album from which this folio comes is known both as the Berlin Album, due to its location, and as the Jahangir Album, it contains many pre-Jahangiri Mughal pictures, and it was probably initiated for Akbar toward the end of the sixteenth century. The borders, mostly commissioned by Jahangir, are marvelously varied, often combining arabesque ornament with landscape, figures, animals, or—as here—twittering birds.

The majority of the portraits in Mughal royal albums are formal depictions of the emperor and his circle (comparable to those we keep in family photograph albums), of rival dignitaries, or of notable calligraphers, artists, musicians, poets, and craftsmen. The present folio includes two portraits of elderly courtiers, a pleasing band of landscape, perhaps snipped from a miniature, and the earliest portraits known to us of Mughal artists at work —all assembled in a nearly convincing ensemble, with trees and flowering plants improvised here and there to cover the joins.

One of the painters wears spectacles while drawing a Madonna and Child, and we assume that magnifying glasses were also used. Both artists sit typically cross-legged, surrounded by the tools of their trade, with the work in progress fastened to a comfortably propped-up drawing board. Pigments, composed of finely ground minerals, gold, silver, earths, and certain organic substances (crushed insects, animal urine, and so forth), were kept for ready access in clamshells, in close proximity to a cup of water and a jar of the glue employed as binding medium. Brushes were made by the artists themselves from squirrel or kitten hairs, carefully graded and fastened into bird quills.

Moderately complex miniatures required a month to complete. After burnishing the paper with a smooth rounded stone against a large rectangular one of comparable texture, the artist made an underdrawing in faint gray or brownish red brushstrokes. Often, he worked from earlier sketches made from life; but occasionally he employed charbas, or tracings on gazelle skin, which were pricked along the outlines so that black pigment could be pushed through to transfer the design. Occasionally, too, Indian painters worked directly from life.

Errors were easily corrected by covering them over with opaque white

104.
A LION AT REST
Mughal, ca. 1585
Opaque watercolor on paper
Folio: 15 × 10¼ in. (38.1 × 26 cm.)
Miniature: 8 × 6 in. (20.3 × 15.2 cm.)
Collection Nasli and Alice Heeramaneck, New Haven

105.
ARTISTS AT WORK
From the Berlin Album (folio 21r)
Mughal, ca. 1585
Opaque watercolor on paper
Folio: 23⅝ × 16½ in. (60 × 42 cm.)
Miniature: 16⅛ × 10 in. (41 × 25.5 cm.)
Staatsbibliothek Preussischer Kulturbesitz, West Berlin

pigment and redrawing—a practice that lent spontaneity to the finished work. Once the underdrawing had been laid in, the paper was given a thin wash of opaque white. This was set by burnishing, a process done to maintain a smooth finish and to bind one layer of color to the next. The depth of color so enjoyable in Indian miniatures was achieved by building up enamellike intensity with repeated layers of pigment.

Gold and silver pigments were made by pounding bits of the metal between sheets of parchment into thin leaves; these were ground with salt into fine powder with a mortar and pestle. The salt was then washed out and the resultant pigment mixed with glue in aqueous solution. Gold was often used in two or more tones, a lighter tone made by adding silver, and a richer, yellower one by adding copper. To avoid the tarnishing of silver pigment, artists of the eighteenth century and later sometimes substituted zinc for silver.

Metallic pigments usually were applied late in the development of a miniature. When brushed on in solution, gold and silver seem dull; but once lightly rubbed by the smooth agate or crystal burnisher, they take on magical brilliance. A steel needle with a rounded point was used to make striations in the metal or to create glittering points of light. Pearls and other raised passages were made by brushing on small globs of thick white pigment. Occasionally, actual jewels—rubies, emeralds, diamonds— or jewellike beetle-wing cases were attached to miniatures for special opulence (see no. 265).

Published: Kühnel and Goetz, *Indian Book Painting*, pp. 9, 12, pl. 39 (dets.).

DURING THE SEVENTH year of Akbar's reign, a notable event at court was the arrival of Tansen, the illustrious musician and leading exponent of the dhrupad style associated with Gwalior. Abu'l-Fazl described the circumstances as follows: "Inasmuch as the holy personality of His Majesty the Shahinshah is a congeries of degrees, spiritual and temporal, and a collection of divine and terrestrial excellences so that when matters are discussed the master of each science imagines that the holy personality has devoted his whole attention to his particular subject, and that all his intellect has been expended on it, the knowledge which His Majesty has of the niceties of music, as of other sciences, whether of the melodies of Persia, or the various songs of India, both as regards theory and execution, is unique for all time. As the fame of Tansen, who was the foremost of the age among the kalawants [noble musicians] of Gwaliar came to the royal hearing, and it was reported that he meditated going into retirement and that he was spending his days in attendance on Ram Cand the Rajah of Pannah, His Majesty ordered that he should be enrolled among the court musicians. Jalal Khan Qurci, who was a favourite servant, was sent with a gracious order to the Rajah for the purpose of bringing Tansen. The Rajah received the royal message and recognized the sending of the envoy as an honour, and sent back with him suitable presents of elephants of fame and valuable jewels, and he also gave Tansen suitable instruments and made him the cheek mole of his gifts.

"Tansen [later] did homage and received exaltation. His Majesty the Shahinshah was pleased and poured gifts of money into the lap of his hopes. His cap of honour was exalted above all others. As he had an upright nature and an acceptable disposition he was cherished by long service and association with His Majesty, and great developments were made by him in music and in composition."[1]

Tansen died on April 26, 1589, and "by His Majesty's orders, all the musicians and singers accompanied his body to the grave, making melodies as at a marriage. The Joy of the Age was overcast, and His Majesty said that his death was the annihilation of melody. It seems that in a thousand years, few have equalled him in sweetness and art."[2]

A Mughal living legend, Tansen was also greatly revered by Akbar's son, Jahangir, who described in his *Memoirs* a remarkable episode. Shaikh Salim Chishti, the saint who was considered by Akbar to have made possible the birth of the prince by interceding with God, once requested that

106.
TANSEN OF GWALIOR
Mughal, ca. 1585–90
Opaque watercolor on paper
Folio: 6⅞ × 4⅜ in. (17.5 × 11.1 cm.)
Miniature: 4⅝ × 2⅝ in. (11.8 × 6.7 cm.)
National Museum, New Delhi
(50.14/28)

106

Tansen come to sing for him. He also invited Akbar to attend; and when both had arrived, the shaikh said, "'The promised time of union has come, and I must leave you. We have made Sultan Salim [the prince] our successor, and have made him over to God, the protector and preserver.' Gradually, his weakness increased, and the signs of passing away became more evident, till he attained union with the 'True Beloved.'"[3]

In keeping with Akbar's desire for truthful, penetrating likenesses—as compared to the Iranian tradition, which tended to idealize—this characteristic early Mughal portrait vividly conveys the great musician's appearance, gestures, and spirit. According to Abu'l-Fazl, "[Akbar] himself sat for his likeness, and also ordered to have the likenesses taken of all the grandees of the realm. An immense album was thus formed: those that have passed away have received a new life, and those who are still alive have immortality promised them."[4] Like Tansen's portrait, probably once contained in the album, the figures are isolated against simple green grounds, to be studied like butterflies mounted in rows on pins.

1. Abu'l-Fazl, *Akbarnama*, vol. 2, pp. 279–80.
2. Ibid., vol. 3, p. 816.
3. Jahangir, *The Tuzuk*, vol. 2, p. 71.
4. Abu'l-Fazl, *A'in-i Akbari*, pp. 108–9.

Published: Delhi Museum of Archaeology, *Loan Exhibition*, pp. 120–21, no. C.502, pl. LII(f); Brijbhushan, *The World of Indian Miniatures*, pl. 45.

AKBAR'S PORTRAIT ARTISTS were instructed to record their sitters' innermost natures, a task they sometimes carried out with embarrassing scrupulousness. Inasmuch as Raja Man Singh was one of Akbar's Nauratan, or Nine Jewels, his boon companions, one would not expect Akbar's artists to treat him less than admiringly, even though he and the emperor occasionally differed in opinion. He joined Akbar's court in 1562, when Akbar married the eldest daughter of Raja Bihar Mal of Amber, who had adopted Man Singh. Raja Man Singh received command of seven thousand horse, a very prestigious rank in the imperial hierarchy. Nevertheless, the senior Rajput nobleman, Rana Pratap Singh of Mewar, refused to eat with him—or even to receive him—on the grounds that he was a turncoat to the Rajput cause, in league with the despised Mughals.

Akbar ordered Man Singh to lead a Mughal army against the unyielding Rana Pratap; and at the Battle of Haldigat, twenty-two thousand Mewar warriors were slain. The rana escaped—much to the dismay of Akbar, who believed that Man Singh's loyalties to the Rajput cause interfered with duty. Raja Man Singh also distressed the emperor by refusing to join the Divine Faith, a religion devised by Akbar to strengthen the empire by unifying Muslims, Hindus, and other religious groups. Although a slight coolness developed between Akbar and Raja Man Singh, he was appointed governor of Bengal, a major post he held during the rest of the reign. Under Emperor Jahangir, he served in the Deccan, where he died during the ninth regnal year. Sixty wives mounted his funeral pyre in rites of sati.

This small portrait was part of an album prepared for Prince Khurram (later Shah Jahan), and it contained a number of calligraphies written in the prince's own hand, some of them dated 1611–12. Presumably, most of its miniatures, a few of which are as early as about 1575, were gifts from his grandfather, Akbar, who knew of the young prince and Man Singh's friendship.[1] The other side of the folio contains verses probably copied by the prince himself in characteristically Mughal Nasta'liq script tending toward Shikasta. Before Akbar's death, Man Singh tried to persuade him to appoint Prince Khurram his successor, bypassing the young man's father, Prince Salim, who inherited the throne as Emperor Jahangir. A final link between the old raja and Prince Khurram was forged after Khurram had come to the throne. On the death of his favorite wife, Mumtaz-Mahal, land that had belonged to Raja Man Singh was acquired as the site for her tomb—the Taj Mahal.

1. For Prince Khurram's album, see: Welch, *Indian Drawings*, pp. 34–35, no. 7; Beach, *The Grand Mogul*, p. 74.

Published: *Notable Acquisitions 1982–1983*, pp. 10–11.

MUGHAL ART IS FAMED for its animal studies, the earliest of which, exemplified by this ram, are datable to the reign of Akbar. Babur's memoirs, with their observant descriptions of flora and fauna, suggest that Babur would have commissioned such pictures; and one knows from the memoirs of Humayun's servant Jauhar that once, when a bird had been caught, "[Humayun] took a pair of scissors and cut some feathers off the animal; . . . [he] sent for a painter, and had a picture taken of the bird, and afterwards had it released."[1]

107.
RAJA MAN SINGH OF AMBER
Mughal, ca. 1590
Opaque watercolor on paper
Folio: 9¼ × 5⅝ in. (23.5 × 14.3 cm.)
Miniature: 4⅞ × 3⅛ in. (12.5 × 7.8 cm.)
The Metropolitan Museum of Art, New York, Purchase, Gift of Jacques L. Galef and Bequest of Charles R. Gerth, by exchange (1982.174)

108.
AN IMPERIAL RAM
Attributed to Basawan
Mughal, Agra, ca. 1585
Opaque watercolor on paper
Folio: 8⅛ × 10⅜ in. (20.6 × 26.4 cm.)
Miniature: 5⅛ × 7¼ in. (13 × 18.4 cm.)
Maharaja Sawai Man Singh II Museum, Jaipur (AG.1413)

شبیہ راجہ مانکلہ

108

This tethered ram, perhaps a champion admired for its strength in combat, can be attributed to Akbar's most gifted painter, Basawan, whose ability to paint rounded, believably tactile forms and to instill life into his subjects is nowhere more apparent than here. A later, fragmentary variant of this picture is in the collection of the Museum of Fine Arts, Boston.[2]

1. Jauhar, *The Tezkereh*, p. 43.
2. For the Boston *Ram*, see: Coomaraswamy, *Catalogue of the Indian Collections: VI*, p. 51, no. 17.3104, pl. XLII.

Published: Das, *Treasures of Indian Painting*, ser. 4, pl. II.

AKBAR'S APPRECIATION OF all the world's wonders, as well as his desire to promote unifying understanding between Muslims and Hindus, led him to commission illustrated translations of Hindu epics, such as the *Ramayana* and the *Mahabharata*, which fired the imaginations of his artists as much as had the fantastic tales from the *Hamza-nama*. The many illustrations to these thrilling manuscripts dating from the late 1580s, now in the Maharaja Sawai Man Singh II Museum of Jaipur, and to the slightly later, now dispersed, *Harivamsa*, an appendix to the *Mahabharata*, radiate religious intensity.

Krishna Lifts Mount Govardhan is one of the illustrations to the *Harivamsa* (The Genealogy of Hari). According to legend, the young god Krishna asserted his power over the god Indra by convincing the gopis (herdswomen) near Mount Govardhan to worship the spirit of the mountain in his place, after which Krishna transformed himself into the Mountain Spirit—and took delight in their offerings. Enraged by the upstart god, Indra scoffed at him before the gopis and raised up a terrible storm, threatening the land and people. The gopis and their families pleaded for Krishna's help, which he gave unstintingly. As though it were a large umbrella, he lifted Mount

109.
KRISHNA LIFTS MOUNT GOVARDHAN
From a manuscript of the *Harivamsa*
(The Genealogy of Hari)
Probably by Miskin
Mughal, ca. 1590
Opaque watercolor on paper, 11⅜ × 7⅞ in.
(28.9 × 20 cm.)
The Metropolitan Museum of Art, New York,
Purchase, Edward C. Moore, Jr. Gift
(28.63.1)

Govardhan and, balancing it on his little finger, protected them from the storm.

This painting is probably by Miskin, who gave to it its miraculous credibility by couching it in characteristically Mughal everyday terms. The villagers, animals, and trees might all be encountered while wandering in rural India today.

Published: Breck, "An Early Mughal Painting," pp. 133–34; *The Art of India and Pakistan*, p. 151, no. 673; Metropolitan Museum of Art, *Art Treasures*, p. 240, no. 208, pl. 208; Welch, *The Art of Mughal India*, pp. 28, 164, no. 13, pl. 13; Welch, *Imperial Mughal Painting*, p. 60, pl. 10; "Islamic Painting," p. 39; Schimmel and Welch, *Anvari's Divan*, pp. 27–28, fig. 2; Chaitanya, *A History of Indian Painting*, pl. v.

A MORE ACCURATE view of Mughal court life could not be found than this dramatically stirring scene, in which an argumentative man stands in the gaping jaws of a black arabesque carpet. In it every figure attests to the brilliant artist Basawan's perceptive eye for humanity. The expressions of the musicians are archetypal, and the animated studies of courtly gestures could illustrate a book on Indian body language. Down to the last wine cup, moreover, it is an unrivaled source of information on the paraphernalia of Akbar's court.

By the last decade of the sixteenth century imperial artists, illuminators, binders, and other craftsmen had achieved unprecedented degrees of refinement. Although manuscripts of jewellike elegance are known from Iran as early as the Timurid period, only now did Akbar's studios have full access to the finest of pigments, papers, and other materials required to produce volumes of comparable splendor.

Such perfectionism can be traced to 1588, when a superb little manuscript of Anvari's *Divan* was produced in the ateliers of Lahore. Although the manuscript was illustrated by Akbar's most admired artists, the subtleties of its miniatures imply the guidance of another patron, doubtless the discerning Prince Salim, who was nineteen years old at the time and still on close terms with his father, with whom relations deteriorated after 1591, when Akbar accused Salim of trying to poison him. In the 1580s and 1590s, Salim would have been welcome in the royal ateliers, where he surely discussed art at great length with such revered masters as Miskin and Basawan, and with his contemporary, Basawan's son Manohar, who became one of his ablest artists.

When Akbar's magnificent *Anvar-i Suhaili* was illustrated in 1596–97, Prince Salim was in better odor with his father, largely due to the yet more upsetting behavior of his younger brothers, Murad and Daniyal. His influence in the painting studios therefore remained strong, and even revered Basawan, the painter of *A Crisis at Court*, must have gained from his discerning encouragement.

The fullest account of Basawan was written by Abu'l-Fazl in the *A'in-i Akbari*: "In designing and portrait painting and coulouring and painting illusionistically and other aspects of this art [Basawan] became unrivalled in the world and many connoisseurs prefer him to Daswanth." Inasmuch as Daswanth was considered by the same critic to have "surpassed all painters and become the first master of the age," this was high praise.[1]

Basawan's career sheds light on the role of the artist in Akbar's India. According to Pramod Chandra, his name links him to the Ahir caste of Uttar Pradesh, whose members are noted as herdsmen and agriculturists.[2] His artistic talent earned him recognition, and he was recruited for the imperial Mughal ateliers as early as 1565 to 1570, when he worked on the *Tutinama* (Tales of a Parrot), now in the Cleveland Museum of Art. Although there are traces of his pre-Mughal style in his miniatures for the Cleveland manuscript, he had already formed a strongly individualized idiom fully in keeping with the Mughal synthesis, to which he had contributed important elements. His psychologically acute—even Rembrandtesque—characterizations, painterliness, three-dimensional treatment of space, and swelling roundness of form are all apparent in *A Crisis at Court*, which exemplifies

110.
A CRISIS AT COURT
From a manuscript of the *Anvar-i Suhaili*
(The Lights of Canopus)
By Basawan
Mughal, Lahore, dated A.H. 1005 or 1006
(1596–97)
Opaque watercolor on paper, 9⅞ × 5⅝ in.
(25 × 14.2 cm.)
Bharat Kala Bhavan, Banaras Hindu University, Varanasi (9069/3)

the peak of his career. Basawan continued to develop artistically into the early seventeenth century, when he either retired from painting or died at approximately the age of seventy.[3]

1. Abu'l-Fazl, A'in-i Akbari, p. 114. Translation by Robert Skelton.
2. Personal communication.
3. For a study of this artist, see: Welch, "The Paintings of Basawan."

Published: Welch, "The Paintings of Basawan," p. 11, pl. A.

As AKBAR AGED, his taste became increasingly refined. In his more worldly and military younger days, lacquer bindings such as this one, with its shiny, densely adorned surfaces, might have caught his fancy momentarily, but he would hardly have urged his craftsmen to create them, any more than he would have urged his painters to work in the evolved and subtle manner of the twenty-one miniatures it contains. By the end of the century, however, when he approached sixty, his tastes had changed, and, influenced by his son Salim, he enjoyed seeing and handling highly refined works of art.

Miniature-like, this binding presents two worlds. One face shows a prince interrupting a successful hunt to visit a holy man; the other describes aerial and aquatic struggles between divs and angels in a paradisiacal landscape. Both are by a court painter who had turned his hand to the lacquerer's art, working in gold and colors over a deep red ground. He followed Safavid prototypes in creating this miniaturistic binding, which is one of the finest and best preserved to have survived from Akbar's court.[1]

During the late sixteenth century, there was a vogue at the imperial court for pictorial ornament, as can be seen in this binding and in carpet design (see no. 112). Lacquer painting had been used for bindings and playing cards by Safavid artists, who brought the technique to India.

1. For the finest Safavid lacquer prototype, see: Pope, A Survey of Persian Art, vol. 5, pl. 972.

Published: The History of Bookbinding 525–1950 A.D., p. 40, no. 94, pl. XXII; Ettinghausen, "Near Eastern Book Covers," p. 126, pl. 12; Welch, The Art of Mughal India, pp. 26, 163, no. 7.

111.
BINDING FOR A *KHAMSA* (QUINTET) OF AMIR KHUSRAU DIHLAVI
Scribe: Muhammad Husain
Mughal, dated A.H. 1006 (1597–98)
Lacquer over pasteboard, 11¼ × 7¾ in. (28.6 × 19.7 cm.)
The Walters Art Gallery, Baltimore (W.624)

111, front

111, back

PRINCE SALIM'S INFLUENCE as a young man on his father's workshops must have spread beyond the painters' ateliers, even though his first love was painting. His influence would also have extended to the armorers, jade workers, and carpet weavers, and the designers who provided them with motifs.

Although both Akbar and Salim, as well as their artists, would have been well versed in the technical problems inherent in each discipline, they were also daringly innovative. The patron—and we sense Prince Salim's aesthetic acumen here—and artist responsible for this magnificent carpet approached the difficult challenge of combining traditional arabesques and pictorialism with admirable sensitivity and discrimination. Excitedly aware, certainly, of European tapestries, they avoided the pitfall of creating a woven miniature rather than a suitably two-dimensional carpet design. And they achieved a movingly lyrical work of art.

The composition and the drawing of birds, trees, and arabesques all point to a late sixteenth-century date, as does the thoughtful originality of conception, which far transcends later, primarily ornamental, pictorial carpets, in which excellence of craftsmanship replaces divine spark.[1]

1. For a discussion of Safavid artists as carpet designers, see: Welch, "Two Shahs, Some Miniatures, and the Boston Carpet."

Published: Riegl, *Oriental Carpets*, no. 1, pl. 1; Sarre and Trenkwald, *Old Oriental Carpets*, vol. 1, pls. 35, 36; *The Arts of Islam*, p. 116, no. 98; Gans-Ruedin, *Indian Carpets*, pp. 76–77.

112.
LANDSCAPE CARPET
Mughal, late 16th century
Cotton warp and weft, wool pile, 7 ft. 8½ in. × 61½ in. (2.35 m. × 156.2 cm.)
Österreichisches Museum für angewandte Kunst, Vienna (Or. 292)

MOST PORTRAYALS OF Akbar show him actively doing things—hunting, leading armies, directing building programs, or receiving distinguished guests. Here, in his early sixties, gray and worn, he leans against a bolster within a red sandstone throne-pavilion. He receives a dignified and serious gentleman identifiable as ʿAli of Gilan, his doctor, who probably came to discuss the stomach condition from which Akbar died in 1605. In the foreground, a sleek hunting dog turns away from an attendant bearing a matchlock, aware that it is not the time for an outing. Behind stand two fond grandsons,

113.
AKBAR IN OLD AGE
Inscribed: "the work of Manohar Das"
Mughal, ca. 1605
Opaque watercolor on paper
Folio: 9⅝ × 5⅞ in. (24.5 × 14.8 cm.)
Miniature: 7¼ × 4¾ in. (18.4 × 12.1 cm.)
Cincinnati Art Museum, Gift of John J. Emery (1950.289a)

113

Prince Khusrau, age eighteen, waving a chauri (yak-tail fly whisk)—an object both practical and symbolically regal—and thirteen-year-old Prince Khurram. The former, after rebelling against his father, died young from drink, the family weakness; the latter, who is known to have been particularly close to his grandfather, eventually reigned as Shah Jahan, and can be seen further on in imperial grandeur occupying his Peacock Throne, an elaboration, characteristically extravagant, of Akbar's austere platform (see no. 154). Both young men look gravely concerned about their grandfather's health, and one wonders if they were aware of the dread rumor at court that to hasten his own path to the throne their father, Prince Salim, was poisoning the emperor.

Manohar's pensively affectionate characterization of Akbar, under whose patronage he had grown up, may be the very one that established the model for posthumous portraits. Endowed with much of his father Basawan's psychological understanding, he recorded Akbar's pained but mannerly resolve and malaise, and the doctor's concerned humility. Khusrau's already puffy face is shadowed by underlying impatience and hostility; Khurram, even then bejeweled, appears conscientious, aristocratic, every inch a sovereign.

Published: Beach, *The Grand Mogul*, pp. 132–33, fig. 11; Welch, *Imperial Mughal Painting*, p. 69, pl. 15.

114.
THE BIRTH OF JAHANGIR
From a manuscript of the *Tuzuk-i Jahangiri*
(The Memoirs of Jahangir)
Attributed to Bishndas
Mughal, ca. 1615–20
Opaque watercolor on paper, 9⅞ × 6⅞ in.
(25 × 17.6 cm.)
Museum of Fine Arts, Boston, Francis Bartlett
Donation of 1912 and Picture Fund (14.657)

WHEN PRINCE SALIM inherited the throne as Emperor Jahangir (World Seizer), like his father he commissioned an illustrated account of the events of his reign, a manuscript known to us only from a dozen or so miniatures, many of them damaged. Consciously connoisseurly in his enthusiasm for the arts and a passionate collector, Jahangir swiftly adjusted the imperial workshops, releasing many artists whose work did not meet his standards, and welcoming "old masters" such as Manohar, whose careers he had encouraged and influenced when he had access to his father's ateliers at Lahore and Agra. Large numbers of proficient painters trained in the imperial studios found work elsewhere, some in the bazaars of Agra or at Rajput courts in Rajasthan, others in Central India or the Punjab, thus disseminating the Mughal style far and wide.

Jahangir's approach to life and art differed greatly from Akbar's. While Akbar had inherited a small, virtually unestablished realm at fourteen, Jahangir was thirty-six when his father left him a vast, superbly organized, smoothly functioning, and rich dominion that required little more than supervision. Its problems were barely discernible signs of institutional aging and of built-in factors such as the recurrent struggles for power within the imperial household. The scramble for the throne by Emperor Humayun's brothers and their factions was repeated through the generations, forcing successive emperors to cruel decisions. Rivals were blinded, murdered, or imprisoned in Gwalior Fort, where oblivion and eventual death followed daily doses of poust—an opium concoction enjoyed by Akbar and Jahangir in smaller quantities. Conceivably, these skeletons in the Mughal closets encouraged the hyperaestheticism that made uncertain, perhaps brief, imperial lives as blissful as possible. But they may also have sparked spiritual concerns, the other side of cruelty. Jahangir's candid, erratic, often painfully realistic, and at times self-deluding memoirs, the *Tuzuk-i Jahangiri*, describe his reverence for holy men, whom he often visited, as well as terrible episodes, as when he ordered rebellious Prince Khusrau's followers to be impaled, and forced the prince to watch their agonies.

The trivia recorded in Jahangir's memoirs and paintings surprise and delight: a combat between a spider and a snake encountered on the roadside; his beloved wife Nur-Jahan's Annie Oakley-like marksmanship; the sending of his portrait to the rival sultan of Bijapur "so that [he might] see me spiritually"; a jeweled rose; a boy raised from the dead by a holy man; a corpse that would not rot; and a yogi who copulated with a tiger—all are described in lively detail. Although Jahangir was not catalyzed by challenges

114

equal to those his father faced, he may have been as intelligent, and assuredly he was at least as curious about the world.

The *Birth of Jahangir* is one of the fullest revelations of harem life, piling vignettes of wifely and motherly behavior atop anecdotal observations on astrologers, maidservants, and infantdom. Where else can one find a gold crib set with precious stones, or see exactly how neem leaves were mounted over gateways to celebrate a birth? When Bishndas recorded all this, and far more, for the official illustrated history of the reign, one can be sure that he did so with Jahangir often at his side. Of all the documentary-minded emperors, in a dynasty that kept as many records as the Romans, Jahangir was the most insistent upon lively accuracy and completeness.

Published: Coomaraswamy, *Catalogue of the Indian Collections: VI*, p. 17, no. 14.657, pl. III; Welch, *The Art of Mughal India*, pp. 71, 166, no. 26; Beach, *The Grand Mogul*, p. 63, no. 15; Welch, *Imperial Mughal Painting*, pp. 70–71, pl. 16.

115.
EMPEROR JAHANGIR IN DARBAR
From a manuscript of the *Tuzuk-i Jahangiri* (The Memoirs of Jahangir)
Attributed to Manohar
Inscribed: "done by the most humble of the house-born"
Mughal, ca. 1620
Opaque watercolor on paper, 13¾ × 7¾ in. (34.8 × 19.8 cm.)
Museum of Fine Arts, Boston, Francis Bartlett Donation of 1912 and Picture Fund (14.654)

AKBAR'S COURT AT Fatehpur-Sikri must have seemed informal or even casual; but as the empire matured, it became harder for visitors to approach the emperor. By 1620, no stranger could bypass the system of guards and attendants who screened would-be guests. Ordinarily, the emperor could be viewed daily from a distance when he appeared briefly at the jharoka window of the ramparts and gazed down to assure the multitudes of his continuing presence and good health. Closer inspection of the emperor was possible at formal audiences, or darbars, as shown here—under strictly controlled conditions. Family members and close attendants stood nearest to the royal presence; distinguished foreign visitors and courtiers were arranged on a

115

lower level, according to rank and prestige; and less important visitors were placed yet farther away, beyond a railing.

William Finch, who visited India between 1608 and 1611, described his experience as a visitor: "[After passing through a third gate] you enter into a spacious court with atescannas round about, like shops or open stalls, wherein [Jahangir's] captaines according to their degrees keep their seventh day chokees [watch]. A little further you enter within a rayle into a more inward court, within which none but the Kings addees and men of sort are admitted, under paine of swacking by the porters cudgells, which lay on load without respect of persons. Being entred, you approach the Kings derbar or seat, before which is also a small court inclosed with railes, covered over head with rich semianes to keep away the sunne; where aloft in a gallery the King sits in his chaire of state, accompanied with his children and Chiefe Vizier (who goeth up by a short ladder forth of the court), no other without calling daring to goe up to him, save onely two punkaws to gather wind; and right before him on a scaffold is a third, who with a horse taile [in fact, yak tail] makes havocke of the poore flies. On the right hand of the King, on the wall behind him, is the picture of our Saviour; on the left of the Virgin. Within these railes none under the degree of foure hundred horse are permitted to enter."[1]

Jahangir urged his artists to paint him realistically, as is apparent in this mirror-accurate portrait, with its pouched eyes, incipient jowels, benevolent majesty—and grandfatherliness. For he gazes thoughtfully upon four-year-old Shah Shuja‛, who had narrowly escaped serious injury when he fell from a fort window but was spared by landing on a carpet spreader and his carpet, an episode described in the doting grandparent's memoirs.

1. Finch, in Foster, *Early Travels in India*, p. 184.

Published: Welch, *The Art of Mughal India*, p. 167, no. 30; Beach, *The Grand Mogul*, pp. 61–63, no. 14; Welch, *Imperial Mughal Painting*, pp. 72–73, pl. 17.

ONE WINTER, ON seeing an elephant shivering during its bath, Emperor Jahangir ordered that henceforth the water be warmed; and in comparably benevolent mood, realizing his inaccessibility to people in need, he ordered golden bells to be made, with a golden "Chain of Justice" reaching down to a spot near the Jamuna River, so that petitioners could attract his attention.

As portrayed by Jahangir's favorite artist, Abu'l-Hasan, one of "the house-born" whose precocious talent had been nurtured since childhood by Emperor Jahangir, the effect of this nobly intentioned plan was not wholly successful. The elephant seems to laugh as crowds of courtiers, tidily arranged by seniority, gather for a morning view of the emperor at his jharoka (window of appearances), while a servant armed with a stick drives away the bell-ringing rabble.

The left-handed Abu'l-Hasan, along with Mansur and Farrukh Beg, was one of the emperor's most admired artists. Jahangir wrote of him in the *Tuzuk*: "On this day Abu-l-Hasan, the painter, who has been honoured with the title *Nadiru-z-Zaman*, drew the picture of my accession as the frontispiece of the *Jahangir-nama*, and brought it to me. As it was worthy of all praise, he received endless favours. His work was perfect, and his picture is one of the *chefs-d'oeuvres* of the age. At the present time he has no rival or equal.... His father, Aqa Riza'i of Herat, at the time when I was a prince, joined my service. There is, however, no comparison between his work and that of his father.... My connection was based on my having reared him, till his art arrived at this rank.... Truly he has become *Nadiru-z-zaman* ('the wonder of the age')."[1]

Abu'l-Hasan's pictures run the gamut of Mughal subjects. Here, we see his astonishing mastery of a densely packed, humorously anecdotal historical view; but he was also a subtly objective analyst of people, as is apparent from his portrait studies; and his natural history pictures match those of the more specialized Mansur. No other artist tells us as much about Jahangir's palaces, textiles, and weapons and other objects. The view of Agra Fort, for

116.
EMPEROR JAHANGIR AT THE JHAROKA WINDOW
From a manuscript of the *Tuzuk-i Jahangiri*
(The Memoirs of Jahangir)
Inscribed: "Nadir az-Zaman"
(Wonder of the Time)
Mughal, ca. 1620
Opaque watercolor on paper
Folio: 21⅞ × 13¾ in. (55.5 × 35 cm.)
Miniature: 12¼ × 7⅞ in. (31.2 × 20 cm.)
Collection Prince Sadruddin Aga Khan, Geneva

116, detail

116

instance, is fascinatingly accurate. From it one knows, for example, that the Khas Mahal pavilion was based upon a canopied prototype, and that the essential form of the Samman Burj, from which the emperor looks down, existed during Jahangir's reign.

1. Jahangir, *The Tuzuk*, vol. 2, p. 20.

Published: Delhi Museum of Archaeology, *Loan Exhibition*, p. 92, no. C.508, pl. XXXVIII(a); Martin, *The Miniature Painting*, vol. 2, pl. 216 left; Beach, *The Grand Mogul*, pp. 64, 91; Welch and Welch, *Arts of the Islamic Book*, pp. 212–15, no. 70.

117.
ANUP RAI SAVES THE LIFE OF EMPEROR JAHANGIR DURING A LION HUNT
Attributed to Abu'l-Hasan
Mughal, ca. 1610
Brush and ink with color on paper, 7 × 7¼ in.
(17.9 × 18.5 cm.)
Private collection

ABU'L-HASAN, SON OF a well-known Iranian artist in Jahangir's service, Aqa-Riza Jahangiri, grew up under the emperor's artistic guidance. Precocious, he drew and painted masterfully by the age of thirteen; and along with the imperial flora and fauna specialist, Mansur, who was given the title Nadir al-'Asr (Wonder of the Age), he was in the forefront of Jahangir's artists. Abu'l-Hasan often accompanied his patron, whether on visits to Kashmir or shorter expeditions to the hunting field. During Jahangir's fifth regnal year, the artist might have gone with his patron and Prince Khurram on a late afternoon hunt, which provided the incident depicted here and is described in the *Tuzuk*: "Anup Ray . . . one of my close attendants was heading the men who were with him in the hunt . . . when . . . he saw a half-eaten bullock.

Near it a huge, powerful lion [sher] got up out of a clump . . . and went off. [Knowing of] my liking for lion-hunting, he and some of those who were with him surrounded the lion and sent someone . . . to give me the news . . . . I rode there at once in a state of excitement and at full speed, and Baba Khurram [Prince Khurram] . . . and one or two others went with me. On arriving I saw the lion standing in the shade of a tree, and wished to fire at him from horseback but found that my horse was unsteady, and dismounted and aimed and fired my gun. As I was standing on a height and the lion below, I did not know whether it had struck him or not. In a moment of excitement I fired the gun again, and I think that this time I hit him. The lion rose and charged, and wounded the chief huntsman, who had a falcon on his wrist and happened to be in front of him, sat down again in his own place. In this state of affairs, placing another gun on a tripod, I took aim. Anup Ray stood holding the [gun]rest, and had a sword in his belt and a baton in his hand. Baba Khurram was a short distance off to my left, and Ram Das and other servants behind him. . . . When I was about to fire, the lion came roaring towards us and charged. I immediately fired. The ball passed through the lion's mouth and teeth. The noise of the gun made him very savage, and the servants . . . fell over one another, so that I, through their pushing and shock, was moved a couple of paces from my place and fell down. In fact, I am sure that two or three of them placed their feet on my chest and passed over me. I'timad Ray and the huntsman Kamal assisting me, I stood up. At this moment, the lion made for those who were on the left hand side. Anup

117

Ray let the [gun]rest slip out of his hand and turned towards the lion. The lion, with the same activity with which he had charged, turned on him, and he manfully faced him, and struck him twice with both hands on the head with the stick he had in his hand. The lion, opening his mouth, seized both of Anup Ray's arms with it, and bit them so that his teeth passed through both, but the stick and the bracelets on his arms were helpful, and did not allow his arms to be destroyed. From the attack and pushing of the lion Anup Ray fell down between the lion's fore-feet, so that his head and face were opposite the lion's chest. At this moment, Baba Khurram and Ram Das came up to the assistance of Anup Ray. The prince struck the lion on the loins with his sword, and Ram Das also struck him twice with his sword. . . . On the whole, it was very warm work. . . . Anup Ray with force dragged his arms out of the lion's mouth and struck him two or three times on the cheek with his fist, and rolling over on his side stood up by the force of his knees. . . . When he stood up, the lion also stood up and wounded him on the chest with his claws, so that these wounds troubled him for some days."

But the lion was far from dead. When a lampman, on his evening rounds, chanced upon the scene, the lion knocked him down. And, according to the *Tuzuk*, "to fall and give up this life were the same thing. [But] other people came in and finished the lion's business. As Anup Ray had done this service to me and I had witnessed the way in which he offered his life, after he had recovered from the pain of his wounds and had the honour of waiting on me, I bestowed on him the title of Aniraʾi Singh-dalan. Aniraʾi they call in the Hindi language the leader of an army, and the meaning of Singh-dalan is a lion-slayer."[1]

Abuʾl-Hasan's interpretation of the episode transforms it into a guardedly naturalistic ballet, choreographed to the imperial taste. Jahangir trots bravely onto the scene, matchlock in hand; Prince Khurram single-handedly slashes the lion; Anup Rai with utmost composure retains his dignity before the imperial gaze and beneath the crushing weight of the terrifying animal. The artist's quick eye for gesture, his lilting but accurate brushed line, the logical spatial composition, and the solid grounding of figures who firmly grip sword and matchlock support the attribution to Abuʾl-Hasan.

1. Jahangir, *The Tuzuk*, vol. 1, pp. 185–88, where the word "sher" is incorrectly translated as "tiger."

Published: Hofer, "A Collector," p. 35, fig. 15.

118.
EMPEROR JAHANGIR WEIGHS PRINCE KHURRAM
From a manuscript of the *Tuzuk-i Jahangiri* (The Memoirs of Jahangir)
Attributed to Manohar
Mughal, ca. 1610–15
Opaque watercolor on paper
Folio: 17⅜ × 11⅝ in.(44.2 × 29.7 cm.)
Miniature: 11⅛ × 5 in. (28.4 × 12.8 cm.)
The Trustees of the British Museum, Bequest of P. C. Manuk Esq. and Miss G. M. Coles, through the National Art Collections Fund (1948.10–9069)

EMPEROR JAHANGIR DESCRIBED this episode, which took place in 1607, in the *Tuzuk*: "On Friday . . . I came to the quarters of Khurram [later, Shah Jahan], which had been made in the Urta Garden. In truth, the building is a delightful and well-proportioned one. Whereas it was the rule of my father to have himself weighed twice every year, [once] according to the solar and [once according to the] lunar year, and to have the princes weighed according to the solar year, and moreover in this year, which was the commencement of my son Khurram's sixteenth lunar year, the astrologers and astronomers represented that a most important epoch according to his horoscope would occur, as the prince's health had not been good, I gave an order that they should weigh him according to the prescribed rule, against gold, silver, and other metals, which should be divided among faqirs [Muslim holy men] and the needy. The whole of the day was passed in enjoyment and pleasure in the house of Baba Khurram, and many of his presents were approved."[1]

Jahangir's artists vied with one another to please their demanding but appreciative patron, whose eye searched out such details as the portrayal of the blanc de chine figurines in the niches, or the array of presents offered to him by the prince. He would also have scrutinized, and admired, the remarkable golden scales, the portraits, and the ethereal patch of garden.

We attribute this informative and touching miniature to Manohar, the son of Basawan, who had become one of Jahangir's finest portrait painters. Although his work is found in most of Jahangir's albums and manuscripts, he was not singled out for mention in the memoirs. It seems likely that he

not only responded, as here, to the challenge of Abuʾl-Hasan's extraordinary historical scenes but sensed that no other artist could equal that "Wonder of the Age" in their patron's esteem.[2] (For other work by Manohar, see nos. 113, 115; for Abuʾl-Hasan, see nos. 116, 117.)

1. Jahangir, *The Tuzuk*, vol. 1, p. 115.
2. For Manohar, see: Beach, *The Grand Mogul*, pp. 130–37.

Published: Barrett and Gray, *Painting of India*, pp. 103–4; *Paintings from the Muslim Courts*, pp. 68–69, no. 112; Welch, *Imperial Mughal Painting*, pp. 74–75, pl. 18; *The Indian Heritage*, p. 37, no. 40, pl. 2.

119.
WINE BOWL (JAM)
Mughal, probably 1st quarter of 17th century
Copper, height 6½ in. (16.5 cm.), diameter
13⅜ in. (34.6 cm.)
Trustees of the Prince of Wales Museum of
Western India, Bombay (56.61)

119

AMPLY PROPORTIONED, SEDUCTIVELY curved, and balancing on an elegantly small foot, this bowl is unsurpassed in quality by other early Mughal copperwork. Its hunting frieze of horsemen and attendants pursuing deer and of an elephant carrying a caged lion in a craggy landscape is vividly executed; and both the arabesques and Nastaʿliq calligraphy are superb—fit for royal use.

Easy to enjoy as a work of art, the bowl has challenged those determined to date and place it with precision. Recently, however, A. S. Melikian-Chirvani has studied the piece and arrived at convincing conclusions. He points out that both the shape and the engraving are strongly Western Iranian in style. Indeed, were it not for the characteristically Mughal hunting scene it would be assigned to a Safavid workshop. He believes the hunt to be in honor of a Safavid prince, and suggests that the bowl may have been commissioned as a gift to a member of the Safavid royal family.

The inscriptions, echoing the engraved scenes, support his theory. Although most of the Mughals belonged to the Sunni sect as opposed to the Shiʿite, a Shiʿite prayer alternates with Shiʿite invocations in the upper register of calligraphy and other inscribed lines are from a *Saqi-nama* (Invocation of the Cupbearer), a mystical poem in praise of wine. Four of the twelve distichs are by Hafiz (d. 1389), Iran's most famous lyrical poet.

Inasmuch as Melikian-Chirvani argues that several of the other verses are from the *Tazkira-yi Meykhana* (and appear in precisely the same order),

119, detail

an anthology composed by the Persian poet Molla Fakhr az-Zaman-i Qazvini in Patna in 1618–19, he finds it difficult to assign an earlier date to the bowl —despite the rather crudely incised inscription added after its completion, saying that it had been donated to the shrine of Ba ʿAbdullah Husain by one Safiya Begum "in the year 991" (1583). On the basis of style and costume, the earlier date is clearly unreliable, and Melikian-Chirvani suspects that the clumsy engraver may have intended it to read as 1101 (1689).

In principle, we fully agree with him, while adding that the engraved animals, figures, and landscape are somewhat archaic in style, and were it not for the inscriptions and costumes—incontrovertible evidence—we should be content with a date closer to 1600. The bowl's strongly Iranian flavor is fully consistent with Jahangir's court, where a powerful Iranian faction associated with the emperor's favorite wife, Nur-Jahan, belonged to the Shiʿite sect.

Published: Chandra, "Two Early Mughal Metal Cups," pp. 57–60; M. Chandra, *Indian Art*, pl. LXVIII; *The Indian Heritage*, p. 144, no. 488; Mittal, "Indo-Islamic Metal and Glassware," p. 71, no. 23.

PIERCED STONE SCREENS were useful and appealing Indian architectural elements long before the Mughal period. They cast mysterious, ever changing patterns of light and shade as the sun moved by day or lantern bearers passed by night. Practical, too, jalis allowed gentle breezes to flow, cooling in the summer and warming in the cold season; and they gave a degree of privacy. At court, where intrigue and flirtatiousness flourished, their peepholes catalyzed guards, servants, the amorously bold, and the coy.

Architects and stonecutters, with ingenuity and skill, created jalis in a great variety of shapes, sizes, and patterns, which can be dated decade by decade. Those made for Akbar at Fatehpur-Sikri, for instance, are ruggedly geometric, masterly cut but powerfully simple; while Jahangir's gained in refinement, delicacy, and precision, at the same time retaining Akbari might. Shah Jahan preferred floral and arabesque motifs, virtuosic and graceful (see no. 164).

Zigzagging diagonals in the present example set up a powerful waving rhythm that sets spinning the interlocking rosettes and crosses. Like all excellent jalis, this one encourages the eye and mind to roam, and to discover the idiosyncratic, inner repertoire of forms. It was cut from a large slab of makrana marble quarried near Jaipur, and it can be dated on the basis of identically patterned red sandstone windows in Akbar's tomb at Sikandra. That splendid complex was commissioned by Jahangir and visited by him during the third regnal year. Considering the ambiguity of feeling between the father and son, it is particularly interesting to read the latter's comments in the *Tuzuk*: "I went on foot [probably from Agra, a distance of five miles] on my pilgrimage to the enlightened mausoleum of the late King. If it had been possible, I would have traversed this road with my eyelashes and head. My revered father, on account of my birth, had gone on foot on a pilgrimage to the shrine of Khwaja Muʿin ud-Din Sanjari Chishti, from Fathpur to Ajmir, a distance of 120 kos [about 200 miles]: if I should traverse this road with my head and eyes, what should I have done? When I was dignified with the good fortune of making this pilgrimage, I saw the building that had been erected in the cemetery. It did not come up to my idea of what it ought to be, for that would be approved which the wayfarers of the world should point to as one the like of which was not in the inhabited world. Inasmuch as at the time of erecting the aforesaid building the affair of the ill-starred Khusrau took place, I started for Lahore, and the architects had built it after a design of their own. At last . . . a large sum was expended, and work went on for three or four years. I ordered that experienced architects should again lay the foundations . . . on a settled plan. By degrees, a lofty building was erected, and a very bright garden was arranged round the building of the shrine, and a large and lofty gateway with minarets of white stone was built. On the whole they told me the cost of this lofty edifice was 1,500,000 rupees."[1]

120.
JALI
Mughal, probably Agra, ca. 1610
Marble, 48⅜ × 26½ in. (123 × 67.4 cm.)
The Metropolitan Museum of Art, New York,
Rogers Fund (1984.193)

120

It is likely that the Metropolitan Museum jali was made for Jahangir's private apartments in Agra Fort, a section of the palace replaced by order of Shah Jahan. Architectural elements of this quality, satisfying in themselves as sculpture, suggest the character and quality of Mughal buildings. Presumably, this jali was stored in Agra Fort until, after Mughal power had weakened during the second half of the eighteenth century, it was carried away by looters.

1. Jahangir, *The Tuzuk*, vol. 1, pp. 151–52.

LIFE-SIZED AND MADE from a single great lump of jade, this powerfully carved sculpture stands apart from most other Mughal hardstone objects, which were made for use. It is tempting to suppose that it was commissioned to enhance the water channels of a princely garden. The sculptor observed a living terrapin with typical Mughal intensity, and conveyed its unhurried spirit and movements down to the slight but characteristic turn of the head and the gait of its webbed, flipperlike feet.

Uninscribed and unique, the terrapin is difficult to date and place. According to records in the British Museum for June 12, 1830, it was "brought from India by Lieutenant Gen. Kyd, found in a tank and brought to him while working on fortifications of Allahabad." Clearly Mughal in style, it was probably made at Allahabad, built by Akbar's order and long a provincial Mughal center crowned by a fortress overlooking the confluence of the Ganges and Jamuna rivers. In the early seventeenth century, Allahabad was Prince Salim's capital when he rebelled against his father; and in 1622, his eldest son Khusrau died there, perhaps a victim of Shah Jahan's ambition. Inasmuch as the terrapin is a noble object and would have suited his taste, it is likely to have enlivened Prince Salim's gardens there. The compact massing of simplified, naturalistic forms and the expansive energy invite comparison to the bronze lion (no. 96), which argues for an early date.

Published: "Exhibition of Islamic Jades," pp. 202–3.

I am indebted to Michael Rogers for supplying crucial information for this entry; Rogers independently assigned an early date to this frequently neglected object.

121.
JADE TERRAPIN
Mughal, early 17th century
7⅞ × 19⅛ × 12⅝ in
(20 × 48.5 × 32 cm.)
Trustees of the British Museum, London
(1830.6–1.6)

121, side

121, front

122

122.
INKPOT OF EMPEROR JAHANGIR
Inscribed, in cartouches around the body: "for
King Jahangir [son of] King Akbar in the
fourteenth year of Jahangir's reign correspond-
ing with the year 1028 of the Flight the form
[of the inkpot] attained completion"; under the
foot: "the work of Mu'min in the service of
Jahangir"
Mughal, dated A.H. 1028 (1618–19)
Dark green nephrite, mounted in gold, height
2½ in. (6.4 cm.), diameter 3¼ in. (8.3 cm.)
The Metropolitan Museum of Art, New York,
The Sylmaris Collection, Gift of George Coe
Graves (29.145.2)

FOR YEARS ON end, Jahangir never handled a knife, cup, or buckle, never
wore a turban, shoe, or robe that would not now grace an art museum. This
compact, powerfully rounded jade inkpot, just the right size and weight for
ink, and to dip reed pens into without tipping it over, may have been used
by the emperor when writing his *Tuzuk* or signing imperial decrees. Although
Jahangir is better known as a lover of painting, he was an equally discerning
admirer of useful but superb objects.

In the *Tuzuk*, objets de vertu are mentioned as frequently as pictures or
architecture; and inspecting those made or collected for him was part of his
daily round. India's genius for sculpture was expressed during the Mughal
period in objects of this sort, which are imbued with the same serious grasp
of form and understanding of nature admired in the arts of other periods in
less deceptively "ornamental" or even "frivolous" guise.

A very hard stone, difficult and slow to work, nephrite was imported
from Khotan and from the K'un-lun Mountains on the southern border of
Sinkiang, where it was found in river beds into which it had tumbled due to
erosion. It is still worked by craftsmen in Agra and Varanasi (Banaras). They
sit on the ground, first cutting the material into convenient form with a bow
saw fitted with two metal strings and an abrasive of sand moistened with
water. Shaping and ornamenting is then accomplished with a bow lathe powered by one hand pulling back and forth on the bow while the other holds
the object against the cutting wheel. Hollowing out an object such as the
inkpot was accomplished with drill-like implements, similarly powered. (For
a comparable bow being used by a turner, see no. 280b.)

Published: Upton, "A Gift of Jade," p. 22; Skelton, "The Relations Between the
Chinese and Indian Jade Carving Traditions," p. 104, pl. 27A; "Islamic Jade," p. 48;
A. Welch, *Calligraphy in the Arts*, pp. 184–85, no. 79; *The Indian Heritage*, p. 117, no.
352.

Although tobacco was brought to the Deccan by the Portuguese in the sixteenth century, it did not reach the Mughal court until 1604, upon which Akbar's physicians told him that it was bad for his health. Nevertheless, smoking became a favored pastime; Indian smokers particularly enjoyed aromatic tobaccos in which spices, perfumes, and crude molasses syrup were blended. Conceivably, the cool-smoking water pipe developed from the ancient Indian smoking technique in which the substance to be smoked was burned in a small clay vessel planted into the earth or snow and the smoke was drawn through a small tunnel dug into the soil by means of a tube or straw extension. Tobacco could also be inhaled through a hand-held chillum, made of clay or bronze, which was fitted into the opening on top of the base (see no. 270).

The use of the huqqa was described in 1616 by Reverend Edward Terry, chaplain to Sir Thomas Roe, who was ambassador from King James I to the court of Jahangir: "They have little Earthen Pots [with] a narrow neck and an open round top, out of the belly of which comes a small spout, to the lower part of which they fill the Pot with water; then putting their *Tobacco* loose in the top, and a burning coal upon it, they having first fastned a very small strait hollow Cane or Reed . . . within that spout . . . the Pot standing on the ground, draw that smoak into their mouths, which first falls upon the Superficies of the water, and much discolours it. And this way of making their *Tobacco*, they believe makes it more cool and wholsom."[1]

In 1811 another European traveler, Solvyns, wrote: "Cette manière de fumer est extrêmement commune . . . on la nomme Hubble de Bubble."[2] Whatever the name, whether the onomatopoeic hubble-bubble or the more correct, originally Persian, huqqa, this paraphernalia led to the production of many works of art, none more splendid than this one.

Shaped like the most perfect melon ever grown—we very nearly inhale its perfume—this dark green jade huqqa base was carved with walls thin as eggshell. Its expanding shape gives the semblance of growth, and one might suppose that the snakelike tube that once joined it to the mouthpiece was the stem by which it was nourished. Perfection of form invites speculation that it was made for Emperor Jahangir.

1. Yule and Burnell, *Hobson-Jobson*, p. 428.
2. Ibid.

123

To Jahangir, drinking cups were favorite possessions, imperial attributes; and new ones frequently were commissioned or received as gifts. In the *Tuzuk*, he wrote of a crystal cup acquired for him by a roaming agent in ʿIraq. When Shah ʿAbbas I saw it, he told the Mughal ambassador that if "his brother [Jahangir] would drink wine out of it and send it to him, it would be a great mark of affection."[1] The cup was sent, after being fitted with a special lid and saucer. If the drinking of intoxicants was forbidden to most orthodox Muslims, many royal personages believed that upon touching their lips they became water—and they were quaffed accordingly.

The dark, very heavy, and massively solid Bharat Kala Bhavan cup was apparently designed to withstand the hazards of being dropped by a trembling hand. Jahangir was appealingly candid about his weaknesses. In the *Tuzuk* he wrote: "I had not drunk [wine] till I was fifteen [in fact, eighteen], except when in the time of my infancy two or three times my mother and wet-nurses gave it by way of infantile remedy . . . mixed with water and rose-water to take away a cough. . . . [Years later] when I had moved about a good deal and the signs of weariness had set in, a gunner . . . said to me that if I would take a cup of wine it would drive away the feeling of being tired and heavy. It was in the time of my youth, and as I felt disposed towards it ordered . . . an intoxicating draught . . . the amount of one and a half cups of yellow wine of sweet taste in a little bottle. I drank it and found its quality agreeable. After that I took to drinking wine, and increased it from day to day until wine made from grapes ceased to intoxicate me, and I took to drinking arrack [potent spirits distilled from palm sap or rice] and by degrees my potions rose to twenty cups of doubly distilled spirits, fourteen during the daytime and the remainder at night. . . . In that state of matters no one had the power to forbid me, and . . . in that crapulous state from the excessive trembling of my hand I could not drink from my own cup, but others had to give it to me to drink, until I sent for Hakim [Dr.] Humam . . . and informed him of my state. 'Lord of the world' [he said] 'by the way in which you drink spirits, God forbid it, but in six months matters will come to such a pass that there will be no remedy for it.' As his words were said out of pure good-will, and sweet life was dear to me . . . from that day I began to lessen my allowance and set myself to take filuniya. In proportion as I diminished my liquor, I increased the amount of filuniya."

But what is filuniya? Apparently, the word was synonymous with opium, of which, once he had reached the age of forty-six, he ate "eight surkhs [a red berry used as a weight] . . . when five gharis of the day have passed, and six surkhs after one watch of night."[2] Even if Jahangir's account of his wine and opium habits was written at a time of remorse, he must have been considerably addicted. And he was fully aware of the dangers of opium, as is apparent from such passages in the *Tuzuk* as the description of ʿInayat Khan's death (see no. 149) and remarks on Jalal ad-Din Masʿud, who died in 1608: "He was an opium-eater, and used to eat opium after breaking it in pieces, like cheese, and it is notorious that he frequently ate opium from the hand of his own mother."[3] A contemporary painting of Jahangir shows him, supported by girls in the harem, staggering about in cheerful obliviousness.[4]

Although inscribed at Mandu, the Bharat Kala Bhavan cup was not necessarily made there, even though its color, powerful rhythms, and simplified lotus form perfectly suit the mood of that great complex of fortified sultanate palaces.

1. Jahangir, *The Tuzuk*, vol. 1, p. 374.
2. Ibid., pp. 308–10.
3. Ibid., pp. 141–42.
4. The painting is in the Chester Beatty Library, Dublin. See: Arnold, *The Library of A. Chester Beatty*, vol. 2, pl. 56.

Published: Morley, "On Applied Arts of India in Bharat Kala Bhavan," p. 114, pl. 10; Nigam, "The Mughal Jades of India," p. 81, fig. 15.

I am extremely grateful to Robert Skelton for his precise description of the shape and material of this cup, as well as for his reading of the inscription.

124

125   126

EMPEROR JAHANGIR'S CONNOISSEURSHIP extended to calligraphy, the most admired of all arts in the Islamic world, although his own unmistakable handwriting was more imperial than masterful (see no. 140 for a specimen). The sides of this superb small cup are inscribed with verses in Tughra script. They have been translated by Robert Skelton: "By command of His Majesty, the Great Khaqan, Lord of the Kings of the World, Manifestor of Divine Favors in the Offices of Caliphate and Kingdom, the Sun in the Firmament of World Sovereignty, the Moon in the Sky of Justice and Felicity, Abu'l-Muzaffar, son of King Akbar, Nur ad-Din Muhammad Jahangir the Emperor, Warrior of the Faith, the form of the cup attained completion [in the] year 1016."[1] The Persian quatrains are in four cartouches alternating with quatrefoils, which contain the inscription "The wine cup/of the Emperor/of the age/second [regnal] year." The upper quatrain reads: "See, this cup's body imbued with spirit—a jasmine leaf suffused with [purple of] the Judas tree. No, no, I err! Through extreme fineness the cup is watery [i.e., as limpid as water], pregnant with flowing fire [wine]." The lower quatrain reads: "Through wine, the tulip grows on thy face. It is like a rose petal: dew grows on it. If the hand which took the cup from thine should become dust, a cup will grow from it."

The earliest dated wine cup among those that belonged to Jahangir, it is also the most restrained in spirit, representative of Jahangir's responsibly imperial self.

1. *The Indian Heritage*, p. 117, no. 350.

Published: Sotheby's, London, December 16, 1971, lot 70; Skelton, "The Relations Between the Chinese and Indian Jade Carving Traditions," pp. 103–4, pl. 26d; *The Indian Heritage*, p. 117, no. 350; Metropolitan Museum of Art, *The Guennol Collection*, vol. 2, pp. 62–67.

NEVER AT A loss as to what to do, Emperor Jahangir one day shot a nilgai that contained two unborn fawns, he summoned the royal cooks to prepare a du-piyaza (meat cooked with onions), and later commented, "[It] certainly was not without flavour."[1] His interest in novelty was well known; and regularly as the tides, curiosities were brought to his attention. According to the *Tuzuk*, "Masih uz-Zaman produced before me a cat, and represented that it was a hermaphrodite, and that in his house it had young ones, and when it had connection with another cat, young were born to the latter."[2]

125.
WINE CUP OF EMPEROR JAHANGIR
Inscribed with verses, the titles of Jahangir, and the date
Mughal, dated A.H. 1016 (1607–8)
Mottled gray-green nephrite, height 2⅛ in. (5.5 cm.), diameter 3 in. (7.5 cm.)
The Brooklyn Museum, New York, Anonymous loan (L78.22)

126.
WINE CUP OF EMPEROR JAHANGIR
Mughal, dated A.H. 1021 (1612–13)
Green hardstone, height 2⅞ in. (7.3 cm.), diameter 4¾ in. (12.2 cm.)
Museum of Art, Rhode Island School of Design, Providence, Helen M. Danforth Fund (84.163)

Unusual materials were also brought—and often imaginatively transformed. Jahangir's opium cup (no. 124) probably came to him as a lump of pleasing stone, and in all likelihood the Rhode Island cup—shaped from a jadelike material supposed until recently to be rock crystal dyed green by some secret Indian technique—arrived the same way. Consultations with lapidaries followed, to plan the curve and thickness of the walls, the ornamentation, and the inscription, which may have been composed by the emperor himself.

The shape is consistent with Jahangir's penchant for dignified, massive forms—a taste also evident in his buildings and throne platforms. Over it is engraved a delicate skin of ornament and calligraphy: eight arabesquelike flowering plants framed within graceful but forceful surrounds and six couplets inscribed in Nastaʿliq script. A lotus flower is engraved under the foot. The verses have been translated by Robert Skelton.[3]

On the upper band, beneath the rim:

> This is the cup of water [of life], nourisher of the soul,
> Of King Jahangir, [son] of King Akbar,
> Who can see from its shadow the dome of heaven.
> [It is] the world-displaying cup [i.e., Jamshid's cup]
> [Showing the events] on the face of the Earth.
> Having poured the cup of his munificence over the world,
> He has caused the fountain of the spirit to flow.
> Since this cup was completed at his command,
> May it be full of the Water of Life for ever.

On the lower band, above the foot:

> May the seven climes be according to his desire.
> May his cup be passed around eternally.

Its Hijra year is obtained from the numerical value of the words of the imprint, "The seventh year of the king's reign."

1. Jahangir, *The Tuzuk*, vol. 2, p. 275.
2. Ibid., vol. 1, p. 374.
3. *The Indian Heritage*, p. 122, no. 372.

Published: *The Indian Heritage*, p. 122, no. 372.

127.
JEWELED DAGGER AND SHEATH
Perhaps by Puran and Kalyan
Mughal, ca. 1619
Watered steel blade, hatched and overlaid with koftgari work; hilt of gold; scabbard of wood overlaid with gold (back worked in repoussé); hilt and scabbard engraved and set with ivory, agate, diamonds, rubies, emeralds, glass, and enamel, length 14 in. (35.5 cm.)
The al-Sabah Collection, Dar al-Athar al-Islamiya, Kuwait National Museum (LNS.25.J)

A STUNNING MASTERPIECE of jewelrylike weapon making, this dagger must have been commissioned by Emperor Jahangir, perhaps in 1619. A microcosm for the belt, it is so inventively and intricately designed as to require hours of study to discover all its hidden trees, animals, birds, insects, flowers, and arabesques. The baluster-shaped hilt and pommel form a tree of life, burgeoning with birds and flowers, while the knuckle bow emerging from the finial of the quillon—a stylized elephant mask—is in the shape of a graceful horse's neck and head, barely touching the end of the pommel above. On the other side of the quillon a stylized tiger mask growls, its teeth of ivory and its tongue carved from one ruby, the inside of its throat and mouth set with three more.

In the *Tuzuk*, Jahangir devotes many passages to daggers, which he presented to members of his family and to courtiers and also received as gifts. He mentions the skilled craftsmen who made them with the same high regard accorded his favorite artists, as indicated in a passage written in the fourteenth regnal year (1619): "I ordered the Ustads [masters] Puran and Kalyan, who had no rivals in the art of engraving, to make dagger-hilts of a shape that was approved at this time, and has become known as the Jahangiri fashion [probably the shape of the present hilt]. At the same time the blade and the sheath and fastening were given to skilful men, each of whom was unique in his age in his art. Truly, it was all carried out according to my wish. One hilt came out coloured in such a way as to create astonishment. It turned out of all the seven colours, and some of the flowers looked as if a

127 ▷

skilful painter had depicted them in black lines round it with a wonder-working pencil. In short, it was so delicate that I never wish it to be apart from me for a moment. Of all the gems of great price that are in the treasury I consider it the most precious. On Thursday I girded it auspiciously and with joy round my waist, and the masters who in their completion had exercised great skill and taken great pains were rewarded, Ustad Puran with the gift of an elephant, a dress of honour, and a golden bracelet for the wrist, which the people of India call *Kara*, and Kalyan with the title of ʿAja ʾib-dast [Wondrous Hand], and increased *mansab* [rank], a dress of honour, and a jewelled bracelet, and in the same way every one according to his circumstances and skill received favours."[1]

The quality of this magnificent dagger suggests that it may indeed have been made by these two great masters. The basic design, with its remarkable knuckle bow, is an intensely aesthetic development from the opulent but workmanly earlier form, shown in a portrait of Akbar's musician Tansen (no. 106) and exemplified by no. 98. The more refined shape no longer fits the hand as snugly, nor does the dagger seem so lethal; but Jahangir was less likely than his father to put a blade to the test.

1. Jahangir, *The Tuzuk*, vol. 2, pp. 98–99.

Published: *Islamic Art in the Kuwait National Museum*, p. 126.

128.
CEREMONIAL SPOON
Mughal, early 17th century
Gold, engraved and set with rubies, emeralds, and diamonds, length 7¼ in. (18.4 cm.)
Victoria and Albert Museum, London
(I.M.173–1910)

SIMILAR TO THE al-Sabah dagger (no. 127) in workmanship and material, and probably from the same workshop, this spoon—except for the inside of the bowl—is adorned with an all-over skin of jeweled arabesques, without, however, the bird or animal forms. Annemarie Schimmel has suggested that it might have been used to distribute sweets over which the Fatiha had been recited, and which therefore conveyed blessings, either in the name of the Prophet or of a saint. Less intricate than the dagger, it is likely to be earlier.[1]

1. Personal communication, 1984.

Published: Welch, *The Art of Mughal India*, pp. 31, 165, no. 20, pl. 20; Gascoigne, *The Great Moghuls*, p. 226; *The Indian Heritage*, p. 112, no. 322, pl. 12a.

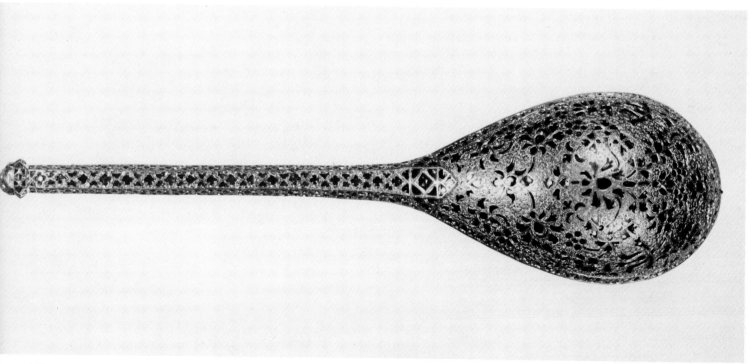

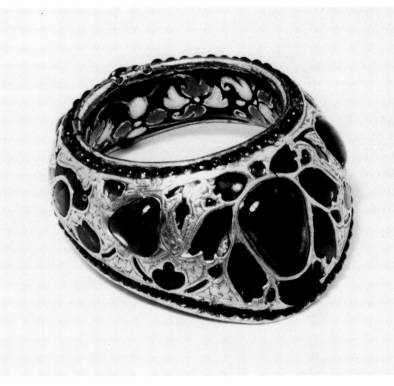

129

THUMB RINGS WERE used in archery to release the arrow with precision; but they were also admired for their artistry, and presented as tokens of appreciation by the emperors. One sees them not only in use (see no. 205) but also dangling ornamentally from a sash or patka (see no. 105), perhaps signaling the wearer's rank, or at least his closeness to the throne.

This one is especially rich, the goldsmithing and jewel setting recalling those of Jahangir's daggers (nos. 127, 130, 133) and of the ceremonial spoon (no. 128). The inner surface is enameled with a design of acanthus leaves derived from Italian Renaissance ornament, as seen, for example, in the engraved acanthus rinceaux of Enea Vico, probably struck in Rome in about 1540.[1] Designs of this sort were frequently employed by Mughal designers and craftsmen, who must have had access to European pattern books.

1. For possible sources of the Renaissance pattern, see: Byrne, *Renaissance Ornament Prints and Drawings*. The Windsor Castle *Padshah-nama* of ʿAbd al-Hamid Lahori (fols. 146v, 193v, and 216v) includes scenes of Jahangir and Shah Jahan giving audience near marble railings carved in relief with similar designs. All are by the artist Murad, whose name is inscribed on fol. 193v as the pupil of Nadir az-Zaman (Abuʾl-Hasan) and whose ornamental and architectural passages are so knowingly accomplished as to suggest that he was also employed as architectural designer.

Published: Hambly, *Cities of Mughal India*, pp. 130–31, pl. 109; *The Indian Heritage*, p. 109, no. 303.

LARGE IN SIZE, sturdy in construction, and inlaid with elegant but tautly designed arabesques, this dagger more effectively balances the ornamental and the utilitarian than the al-Sabah artistic tour de force (no. 127). After the late sixteenth century, hilts and blades of Mughal daggers were no longer made from a single piece of watered steel. Hilts took on additional importance and splendor; and daggers, as is awesomely apparent from no. 127, had become collaborative efforts of armorers, jade workers, and jewelers. In Mughal and Rajput silahkanas (armories), blades were matched to hilts and were easily interchanged, their tangs held in place with resin. In a seventeenth-century miniature of a bazaar (Collection Howard Hodgkin), a shopkeeper offers a tidy row of dagger hilts ready for fitting to suitable blades.[1] Accumulations of dark grease on hilts suggest that daggers were covered with rust-preventing pomade for storage.

129.
THUMB RING
Mughal, ca. 1625
Gold, chased and engraved and set with rubies and emeralds, the inside enameled in opaque white, blue, pale green, and black, height 1½ in. (3.7 cm.), diameter 1⅛ in. (3 cm.)
Victoria and Albert Museum, London
(I.M.207–1920)

130.
JADE-HILTED DAGGER
Mughal, ca. 1625
Watered steel blade, hilt of light green nephrite inlaid with gold and jewels, length 16⅝ in. (42.2 cm.)
Private collection

130

131

To adorn jade hilts, gold inlays, either shaped or as wire, were fitted into prepared grooves that were beveled to lock in the precious metal. Jewels were set into gold, held fast by similar beveling or crimped in by hammering of the soft metal. Gold was inlaid in steel by damascening, a technique also known as koftgari, by which a thin sheet of gold is applied by being delicately hammered into a surface prepared by filed hatchings.

1. For the miniature, see: *The Indian Heritage*, p. 64, no. 160, pl. 4.

Published: Hendley, *Ulwar and Its Art Treasures*, pl. XXXVII.

ALTHOUGH MUGHAL AND Persian portraits often show knives of this shape —along with more menacing daggers—at the belts of princes, human-headed finials were exceedingly rare. This one is so very similar to the kard worn by Prince Salim in a posthumous portrait painted for Shah Jahan by Bichitr (Victoria and Albert Museum, London) that one wonders if the artist did not employ it as the model, presumably at the suggestion of his patron, who would have inherited it.[1] The knife is fitted deeply into its richly decorated sheath, with only the superbly carved head, its hair arranged in snaillike ringlets, peeping out. The ferrule is inlaid in gold with a band of floral scrolls, chamfers with two fish. The finely watered blade is inlaid with the imperial parasol, which is often found in combination with imperial inscriptions and may indicate imperial ownership.

The inscription on the blade tells us that the kard belonged to Shah Jahan. Born under most auspicious astrological circumstances—the conjunction of the two felicities, Jupiter and Venus—he was known through his life as second Lord of the [Auspicious] Conjunction, the first having been his ancestor Timur. On the basis of style, it seems likely that this noble knife was commissioned by Jahangir for his heir—prior to February 22, 1621, when the emperor's increasing ill-will toward his son, encouraged by his all-powerful wife Nur-Jahan, came to a head. In a moment of drunkenness, Jahangir had turned over to him his younger brother and potential rival Sultan Khusrau, who died, probably of colic, while in his charge. Thereafter, Shah Jahan was known to his father as Bi-Daulat—the Wretch.

1. For the portrait of Prince Salim, see: Hambly, *Cities of Mughal India*, p. 72, fig. 47.

Published: *The Indian Heritage*, p. 128, no. 406.

DAZZLING FROM AFAR, jewels can only be appreciated by intimate study. This teardrop-shaped Colombian emerald, of remarkable transparency and purity, was carved with a flower of trembling sensitivity, its petals and leaves as limpid as the material they adorn. Perhaps made as a pendant to a necklace, it might equally have been intended, as Manuel Keene has suggested, as a finial.[1] A miniature by Balchand in the Windsor *Padshah-nama*, of Jahangir receiving Shah Jahan prior to his campaign against Mewar, shows a eunuch behind the emperor holding up a rod terminating in a jeweled bird (folio 43v).[2]

1. Letter, January 1984.
2. The miniature is unpublished.

MUGHAL HISTORY OCCASIONALLY chills the blood, telling us that however ravishingly artistic we find their talwars, katars, khanjars, and kards, the edges were kept serviceably sharp. When and where they were worn and how employed were symptomatic of the state of the Mughal ethos. During the early Akbar period, weapons were sported by the emperor and his circle, and usually peaceful men of letters or the arts carried arms—and for good reason. Abu'l-Fazl the biographer, who also served as a general, was ambushed and hacked to death at the order of Prince Salim. Even Akbar occasionally drew his sword in hot blood, an act unimaginable by Emperor Jahangir, whose violent moods were given expression by accomplished specialists

131.
KARD
Inscribed: "sahibqiran-i thani"
Mughal, ca. 1620–30
Watered steel blade inlaid with gold, jade hilt, length 11½ in. (29.2 cm.)
Private collection

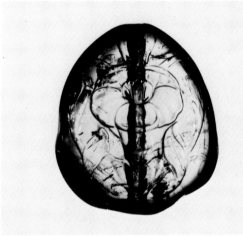

132

132.
EMERALD WITH DESIGN OF A FLOWER
Mughal, 2nd quarter of 17th century
109.7 carats, 1⅜ × 1¼ in. (3.6 × 3.2 cm.)
The al-Sabah Collection, Dar al-Athar al-Islamiya, Kuwait National Museum
(LNS.35.Hs)

133.
DAGGER
Mughal, ca. 1620
Watered steel blade; gold hilt, locket, and chape, inlaid with emeralds, rubies, spinels(?), and glass, length 14 in. (35.6 cm.)
The Metropolitan Museum of Art, New York, Purchase, Harris Brisbane Dick Fund and The Vincent Astor Foundation Gift (1984.332)

133, detail

133

who knew how to stab or slash—and circumspectly carried out their missions beyond the imperial eye.

Gradually, an etiquette of weaponry evolved, and circumstances determined whether or not the emperor or courtier wore a dagger or knife, or carried a sword. In formal portraits of the Jahangir and Shah Jahan periods, both daggers and knives and often swords are worn as standard accouterments; even very young princes toy with weapons scaled to size. And at family gatherings, such as at the weighing of Prince Khurram (no. 118), the prince and his father have kards at their belts, but no daggers. Their prestigious courtiers, however, are fully equipped to protect the imperial family. On friendly formal occasions, the emperor wore a knife but not a dagger, and often a nearby attendant carried his sword, concealed in a sumptuous cloth bag like the one borne for Jahangir by ʿInayat Khan (no. 148). It was considered inappropriate for the emperor or prince, while visiting or receiving individual holy men, but when Shah Jahan honored his religious orthodoxy, he wore a dagger, and his sons and courtiers were fully armed. Mullas and holy men ordinarily did not bear arms.

At a glance, one can read a dagger's significance. This splendid straight-bladed dagger is clearly from the imperial workshop, presumably commissioned by Jahangir for his own use. Less fantastic than the al-Sabah dagger (no. 127), with its birds, beasts, insects, and flowers, it nevertheless can be assigned, along with the ceremonial spoon (no. 128), to the same circle of craftsmen. In miniatures, both Jahangir and Shah Jahan often wear daggers of this type (see nos. 115, 117), which, with its bifurcated pommel, brings to mind Turkish yataghans as well as European examples.

JAHANGIR TOOK DELIGHT in unusual materials, which he eagerly collected and sometimes had made into useful objects, such as one dagger hilt sculpted from meteorite and another—the gift of Shah ʿAbbas I—created from a piebald "fish's tooth" (tortoiseshell?). He was thrilled to receive a "coloured tooth of great beauty [which] a stupid stranger bought in the open bazaar . . . for a trifle."[1] Mottled, crystallike narwhal ivory, from the sea unicorn of the arctic Cetacea, must have intrigued the emperor, and it is not surprising therefore that an archer's thumb ring made from it is in the Jaipur armory. Adorned with angels bearing offerings at either side and a Michelangelesque face of Christ as Pantocrator at the front, it is perceptively and very finely carved in the style of the early part of Jahangir's reign. A typical Mughal repeat pattern of trefoils surrounds the upper edge.

1. Jahangir, *The Tuzuk*, vol. 2, p. 96.

I would like to thank Asok Kumar Das for having called my attention to this piece, which he was the first to identify.

134.
THUMB RING
Mughal, ca. 1615
Narwhal ivory, height ¾ in. (2 cm.), diameter 1¾ in. (4.5 cm.)
Maharaja Sawai Man Singh II Museum, Jaipur (S.1950)

134, front

134, back

135

135.
CANDLESTICK
Mughal, ca. 1625
Bronze, height 4¾ in. (12 cm.), diameter 5 in.
(12.7 cm.)
The Knellington Collection, Courtesy
Harvard University Art Museums,
Cambridge, Massachusetts

136.
CARPET
Mughal, ca. 1620
Silk velvet on satin weave foundation, surfaced
with metallic thread in twill, 15 ft. 3½ in. × 8 ft. 6 in.
(4.66 × 2.59 m.)
The Metropolitan Museum of Art, New York,
Purchase, Joseph Pulitzer Bequest (27.115)

MUGHAL ART IS best seen under the lighting conditions originally intended. This bronze candlestick—apparently the only such piece to have survived from Mughal times—should be seen at night, with its candle lit. Only then is the decoration on its sloping drum—a low relief of lively alternating poppy and iris plants framed by arches of graceful lance-shaped leaves—flickeringly at its best. Basing the form upon classical Muslim prototypes, the designer and bronze caster softened and rounded the usually straight-edged profile, adding notes of sensuousness and intimacy.

In Mughal pictures, one sees candlesticks arranged in rows; and it seems likely that the present example was one of a set.

JAHANGIR, ON A New Year's day, visited his brother-in-law Asaf Khan, who had covered the road between his house and the palace with gold brocade and velvet. This delicately sumptuous floor spread introduces us to an extraordinary tale of success at the Mughal court—and to the Iranian taste of Asaf Khan's sister, Nur-Jahan, the favorite wife of Emperor Jahangir, whose influence on Mughal art was almost as great as it was on the emperor.

Born with the name Mehr un-Nisa, she was the daughter of Ghiyath Beg, an aspiring but untried Iranian nobleman, who brought her to Mughal India with the rest of his family. She became the young bride of Sher Afkan, whose accidental death in 1607 led to her moving from Bengal to the Mughal court as lady-in-waiting to one of Akbar's widows. There, in 1611, at a fancy bazaar at which the ladies coyly played at being shopkeepers, selling trinkets to the emperor and his family and to the nobles of the court, she met Jahangir, a mutually soul-stirring encounter. One of the great royal marriages of world history soon followed; and Mehr un-Nisa received the title Nur-Mahal (Light of the Palace), which was soon increased in refulgence to Nur-Jahan (Light of the World). Magnetic, witty, a crack shot with a

136

matchlock, artistically discriminating, hardly selfless but socially responsible (she established institutions for orphaned girls), she was above all subtle. And she enchanted her imperial husband, at whose side she was always present. When he, a Muslim ruler, struck coins bearing his own effigy holding a wine cup, it was considered extreme; but it was far more irregular when coins were minted in her name.

The Metropolitan Museum carpet, with its scintillating eight-lobed medallions and floral rosettes, is one of a set of three (with those in the Museum of Decorative Art, Copenhagen, and the Musée du Louvre, Paris) that bring to mind the artistic character of one of the finest Mughal buildings, the tomb commissioned and closely supervised between 1622 and 1624 by Nur-Jahan for her mother and her father, I'timad ad-Daula (Pillar of

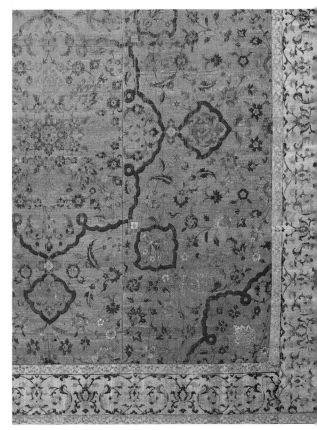

136, detail

Government), one of Jahangir's most powerful nobles. Known for its *pietra dura* inlays in muted, often mottled buff, black, gray, and brown stone, it is preferred by many connoisseurs to the better-known Taj Mahal, the tomb of his granddaughter. Especially marvelous is the upper chamber, containing the cenotaphs of the late chief minister and his wife. The walls are huge, richly geometric jalis, and the floor a stunningly bold, vital, but stately arabesque in stone inlay for which the building is especially admired. The mind and eye that conceived this magnificent room—in which constant changes of light, by day and night, scatter rays through the screens, lending unearthly voices to the fugal pattern of the arabesques—would also have enjoyed the Metropolitan's superb carpet, with its once shimmering silver and gold threads playing against red velvet.

Published: Dimand, "A Persian Velvet Carpet," pp. 247–51, no. 10; Gans-Ruedin, *Indian Carpets*, pp. 142–43.

I am grateful to Edmund de Unger, who on seeing this carpet several years ago suggested its Indian rather than Iranian origin.

137.
COURT COAT
Mughal or Deccani, ca. 1630–60
White satin, embroidered with colored silks in fine chain stitch, length 38⅛ in. (97 cm.)
Victoria and Albert Museum, London
(I.S.18–1947)

MIRACULOUSLY, IT HAS survived. This resplendent coat is the only one of imperial quality that has come down to us from the age of Shah Jahan, at whose court magnificence was commonplace. The form of the coat, we have learned from Veronica Murphy, whose expertise is followed here, is that of a kurdi, of which there is a clear description in Jean-Baptiste Chardin's *Travels in Persia*, dating from the 1660s: "They put over the Robe a short, or close-bodied coat, and without sleeves, which they call Courdy.... These close-bodied coats are wide at Bottom, and narrow at Top, like Bells; they are made of cloth, or Gold Brocade, or a thick Sattin, and they daub them all over with Gold or Silver Lace, or Galloons, or they embroider them."[1]

The chain-stitch embroidery, repeated with slight but enlivening

137

208

variations, is in markedly Safavid style, reminding us of the close relationship between the Mughal court and Iran. Also significant is the Iranian background of Nur-Jahan and her niece Mumtaz-Mahal, which fostered the Mughal vogue for Iranian designs. But other Iranians also held high positions in Mughal India, including Mirza Rustam, a relative of the Safavid royal family, whose daughter married Shah Jahan's son, Prince Shah Shujaᶜ. Moreover, embassies came and went from Iran, invariably bearing and receiving gifts; and it must not be forgotten that the sultans of the Deccan —especially those of Golconda (see nos. 209–16)—maintained close contact with the Safavids, and were clothed in styles that brought together Iranian, Mughal, and local characteristics.[2]

1. Chardin, *Travels in Persia*, pp. 212–16.
2. For a related Golconda coat, with a fur collar such as this one might once have had, see: Raghaven, *Srngaramanjarai of Saint Akbar Shah*, pl. c.

Published: *The Art of India and Pakistan*, p. 214, no. 1017, pl. 66; Irwin, *Indian Embroidery*, no. 1, fig. 1, pl. I; Welch, *The Art of Mughal India*, pp. 75, 169, no. 41; Victoria and Albert Museum, *Indian Art*, pl. 58; *The Indian Heritage*, pp. 94–95, no. 252.

MUGHAL CULTURE IS too often interpreted as primarily mundane, emphasizing power, elegance, and aestheticism; for intense religiosity—an anodyne to worldliness—is a frequent undercurrent, as in this prayer rug. Gloriously sumptuous, fit for imperial knees, it is far more than an appurtenance of a princely mosque. Vibrant blossoms, stalks, and leaves and visionary colors surely stimulated spiritual feelings both in the worshipers who used it and in

138.
PRAYER RUG WITH FLOWERING PLANT
Mughal, ca. 1625
Silk warp and weft, wool pile, 49 × 35⅝ in.
(124.5 × 90 cm.)
Thyssen-Bornemisza Collection, Lugano

138

those who designed and knotted it. Although it has been suggested that Mughal art and architecture are monuments to the oppressive control by a few over many, it could be argued that those who created Mughal works of art, such as this rug, gained almost as much from the experience as the patrons. Without their elation, this sublime carpet could not have been made.

May Beattie has suggested that this carpet, once known as the Aynard prayer rug, was part of a saf, or prayer rug with multiple niches.[1] Daniel Walker has proposed that it represents the imperial level of Lahore work.[2]

1. Beattie, *The Thyssen-Bornemisza Collection*, pp. 69–72.
2. Walker, "Classical Indian Rugs," pp. 256–57.

Published: Migeon, *Exposition des arts musulmans*, pl. 83; Beattie, *The Thyssen-Bornemisza Collection*, pp. 69–72, pl. IX; *The Arts of Islam*, pp. 62, 118, no. 100; Gans-Ruedin, *Indian Carpets*, pp. 114–15; *The Indian Heritage*, p. 76, no. 199.

139.
MANUSCRIPT: *BUSTAN* (THE ORCHARD) OF SAʿDI
(132 folios, 3 miniatures)
Scribe: Mir-ʿAli al-Husaini, copied for
Sultan ʿAbd al-ʿAziz
Mughal, Bukhara, 1540–50
Fogg Art Museum, Harvard University,
Cambridge, Massachusetts, Gift of Philip Hofer
in honor of Stuart Cary Welch (1979.20)

SAʿDI'S VISIT TO AN INDIAN TEMPLE
Attributed to Bishndas, working over an
earlier painting by Shaikh-Zada
Opaque watercolor on paper
Folio: 11¾ × 7¼ in. (29.9 × 18.4 cm.)
Miniature: 11¼ × 6⅞ in. (28.6 × 17.5 cm.)

JAHANGIR, THE "WORLD SEIZER," was in fact more interested in acquiring works of art than additional territories. The most aesthetically discriminating member of a dynasty of great patrons, he was also the outstanding collector, and his agents searched widely in his behalf, with the thoroughness of latter-day art dealers. This copy of Saʿdi's *Bustan* (The Orchard) was one of his cherished possessions, inscribed in his own hand with the statement that he received the manuscript in 1605. An inscription under the shamsa of Akbar on the lower part of the page also indicates that the manuscript came to him after the death of his brother Prince Murad and that it was "most of the time in my presence and is constantly being read, and the eye enjoys the beauty of its incomparably beautiful calligraphy." The manuscript was later admired by other emperors, including Shah Jahan.

Notable for its three superb miniatures and its illuminations, magnificent calligraphy, and marvelously varied borders, the manuscript was commissioned for Sultan ʿAbd al-ʿAziz of Bukhara, who could be considered the Jahangir of the Uzbek dynasty. It was illustrated by Shaikh-Zada, a major Iranian artist who began his career at Herat working with the great Bihzad and later moved to Safavid Tabriz, where he contributed to several of Shah Tahmasp's greatest manuscripts and trained several important Safavid masters. In about 1530 he moved to Bukhara, the Uzbek capital, probably at the invitation of Sultan ʿAbd al-ʿAziz, where he was instrumental in bringing about a new artistic synthesis.

Although Jahangir greatly admired this *Bustan*, its miniatures did not entirely satisfy his taste for psychological depth. In two of them, *Dara and the Herdsman* and *Garden Scene*, signed by Shaikh-Zada, several faces were discreetly repainted in the current Mughal mode, probably by Bishndas.[1]

The third miniature is the only work of art known to us that has been *improved* by extensive repainting, a demonstration of Jahangir's and his artist Bishndas's daring conviction and inventiveness. *Saʿdi's Visit to an Indian Temple* illustrates Saʿdi's witty morality tale in which unprincipled priests are revealed to have rigged a lucrative "miracle": an image whose arm could be raised—by secretly pulling a cord. All of this was set forth by Shaikh-Zada in a splendid "temple," an orientalist fantasy of arabesques, pillars, and tiles. These met with imperial enthusiasm, but the figures did not, and they were almost entirely translated into Mughal idiom by Jahangir's admirable portrait painter Bishndas, who created an affecting assemblage of sensitively portrayed priests, devotees, and casual visitors. Shaikh-Zada's figures are now buried without a trace beneath those of Bishndas, who discreetly retouched surrounding areas to assimilate them into the setting. Although this brilliant picture is unsigned, our attribution of the repainting is supported by comparison with *Shaikh Phul in His Hermitage* (no. 140). The *Birth of Jahangir* (no. 114) can also be ascribed to him.

1. For *Dara and the Herdsman*, see: Martin, *The Miniature Painting*, vol. 1, fig. 28; for the *Garden Scene*, see: Grube, *The Classical Style*, pp. 39, 204, pl. 97.2.

Published: Welch, *The Art of Mughal India*, pp. 70–71, 165–66, no. 23; Grube, *The Classical Style*, pp. 39, 204, no. 97; Das, "Bishndas," pp. 184–85, fig. 356.

139

پیش دل مخزو بس که در اکبر منی

140

MUCH OF THE appeal of Mughal paintings stems from their all-encompassing view of India and its people, as observed through acute eyes and perceived by minds at once curious, objective, and poetic. Jahangir, who directed this miniature much as Satyajit Ray directed the film *Pather Panchali*, brought to bear the same intelligence that sparkles in his *Tuzuk*. Pertinent "inconsequentials" engaged the emperor's, his artist's, and now our attention: the crumbling brick wall beyond the inspired devotee; its mysterious door, leading nowhere; the beautifully wrinkled, baffling bits of cloth laid by the shaikh at the edge of his platform; the seated figure (the devotee's devotee?) to the right of the house-shrine; the trio of shy but enthralled ladies in the distance at the left.

Jahangir was fully aware of his artists' potentials, and of their weaknesses. He admired Bishndas for his portraiture, and for his ability to catch dusty colors and winding village spaces. From 1613 until 1620, Bishndas, who was a nephew of the artist Nanha, served as artist with Jahangir's embassy to the court of Shah ʿAbbas I, where he painted and drew the most penetrating portraits ever made of a Safavid ruler.[1]

1. For Bishndas, see: Beach, *The Grand Mogul*, pp. 107–11.

Published: Mehta, *Studies in Indian Painting*, pl. 37; Das, "Bishndas," pp. 186–88, pl. 18; Das, *Mughal Painting*, pl. 62; Skelton, "Shaykh Phul," pp. 123–29.

140.
SHAIKH PHUL IN HIS HERMITAGE
By Bishndas
Inscribed by Jahangir: "a painting of the majdhub [attracted by God] Shaikh Phul, who lives at present in the city of Agra, by Bishndas"
Mughal, ca. 1610
Opaque watercolor on paper, 14⅜ × 10⅜ in. (36.5 × 26.5 cm.)
Bharat Kala Bhavan, Banaras Hindu University, Varanasi (5410)

141, detail

JUSTIFIABLY, THIS MINIATURE and Mansur's *Peafowl* (no. 144) are the most renowned of Jahangir's natural history pictures, brought together here for the first time since the eighteenth century or earlier. Both reflect the emperor's delight in animals and birds, and the effectiveness of his encouragement of the two artists he most admired. According to the emperor, Mansur was "unique" in the art of "drawing," a word he chose carefully, for Mansur's pictures are draftsmanly rather than painterly. Unlike Abu'l-Hasan, who could paint anything, Mansur was highly specialized, the equivalent in the arts of a Thoreau or a Fabre, happiest and most at ease with the world of nature. Although he occasionally depicted people, especially as a young man during the reign of Akbar, he saw them through eyes attuned to the animal and vegetable kingdom rather than to mankind, landscape, or abstract form. His most exhilarating pictures—meditations brushed onto paper—grew from direct responses to animals, birds, and flowers. By analyzing the pictures, one can follow their development from the first faint brushstrokes suggesting gesture and proportion to firmer, darker ones defining form and texture. When his bird or animal moved, Mansur countered by whiting over his first lines and redrawing, an enlivening procedure that increases the effect of motion.

Mansur stalked birds and animals in the field, where he and his subjects were more comfortable and behaved more naturally than in Jahangir's zoological gardens; and it was there that he accomplished much of his work, adding the finishing touches—resplendent passages of gold or lapis lazuli, and landscape backgrounds—in his studio. Whereas Basawan or Abu'l-Hasan studied the psychological interplay between people, Mansur analyzed and recorded the gestures and expressions of the animal world—the looks of squirrels when one has a nut and the other covets it, or a peahen's sudden hungry rush when her mate has caught a luscious little snake.

Mansur's early works, datable to about 1585–90 (see no. 104), offer another significant clue to his artistic personality: his gracefully calligraphic brushwork, verging in its rhythms on arabesques. Perhaps because arabesques are distilled from natural forms and movement, Mansur found them congenial; and when he sketched flora and fauna, he often infused them with the reciprocal twists and turns familiar from this appealing mode. It is very marked in the springing tails of the squirrels, the essential actors in this picture who lend it universal appeal.

The inscription on the back, "The work of Nadir al-ʿAsr [Wonder of the Age], Nadir az-Zaman [Wonder of the Time]," which gives the titles bestowed by Jahangir upon both Mansur and Abu'l-Hasan, has caused much academic ink to flow on the question of the attribution of the picture. Although the inscription probably dates from the eighteenth century, it conforms to

141.
SQUIRRELS IN A PLANE TREE
By Abu'l-Hasan and Mansur
Inscribed: "the work of Nadir al-ʿAsr [Wonder of the Age], Nadir az-Zaman [Wonder of the Time]"
Mughal, ca. 1610
Opaque watercolor on paper
Folio: 18½ × 12⅝ in. (47 × 32.2 cm.)
Miniature: 14¼ × 8⅞ in. (36.2 × 22.5 cm.)
The British Library, India Office Library and Records, London (Johnson Album 1, no. 30)

the visual evidence. Painterly Abu'l-Hasan seems to have worked jointly on the picture with his more draftsmanlike and animal-minded older colleague. Passages such as the mysterious figure climbing the tree (an artist gathering squirrel hairs with which to make brushes?), as well as the tree itself, would seem to be his, while the squirrels must be assigned to Mansur. (For Abu'l-Hasan, see nos. 116, 117; for Mansur, nos. 142–46.)

Published: Brown, *Indian Painting*, pl. xv; Wilkinson, *Mughal Painting*, pl. 9; Welch, *The Art of Mughal India*, pl. 25; *Paintings from the Muslim Courts*, p. 65, no. 100; Welch, *Imperial Mughal Painting*, pp. 74, 168, no. 35; Chaitanya, *A History of Indian Painting*, p. 66, fig. 54; Falk and Archer, *Indian Miniatures*, pp. 59–60, 369, no. 34, pl. 4.

142.
A NILGAI
By Mansur
From the Kevorkian Album
Inscribed, upper left: "Jahangir Shahi"; lower left: "the work of the servant of the court, Mansur, the Wonder of the Age"
Mughal, ca. 1615
Opaque watercolor on paper
Folio: 10 × 15¼ in. (25.4 × 38.7 cm.)
Miniature: 7¼ × 9½ in. (18.4 × 24.1 cm.)
The Metropolitan Museum of Art, New York, Purchase, Rogers Fund and The Kevorkian Foundation Gift (55.121.10.13)

MANSUR'S INTENSE GAZE, a scientist's and poet's combined with a painter's, concentrated on this magnificent animal, probably within the confines of Jahangir's deer park. In his fervent interest in animals and birds, the artist isolated the nilgai, hinting of the field in which he stands only with a few clumps of weed near and far. The palette is seductive: modulated blue-grays and whites against a thin pale pink ground, now streaked with khaki (an Indian word meaning "dusty") in pigment darkened by time. Mansur's crystal-clear image of the calmly appealing animal emerges from an infinitude of fine brushstrokes, rarely covering the paper underneath and never failing to define bony structure, musculature, or textures. Flexibility of ears, wrinkled at the base; luster of eye; hardness of horn and skull, felt through the short hairs covering the bridge of the nose; brushlike bristles of mane; and softness of tail—all are faithfully and knowingly conveyed.

When Mansur's *Nilgai* was incorporated into its royal album, a superb border was prepared. Harmoniously blending arabesques and classical motifs as interpreted in Renaissance Europe, its red, violet, white, and blue flowers show off the painting to spectacular effect. It is difficult to assign a precise date to the border, which is likely to have been commissioned not by Jahangir but by Shah Jahan, who particularly admired floral arabesques of this sort, which are known from other borders and from textiles and marble carvings.

143

MANSUR'S AFFINITY FOR nature extended to creatures as small as the butterfly threateningly ogled by this chameleon. The picture's plot is evident, and characteristically unsentimental. Like most Indians, Mansur understood and accepted nature's cruel moments as well as its wisdom and humor. *A Chameleon* exemplifies Mansur's exquisite handling of both pigment and line. The spritely lizard's skin is exactingly, tactilely dotted all over with shaded green spots, and his spine is saw-toothed from neck to tail with perfect points of color. How firmly the chameleon grasps his branch! Surely, Mansur knew no rival —not even Abu'l-Hasan—as a painter of wildlife.

Published: *The Art of India and Pakistan*, p. 160, no. 724, pl. 135; Welch, *Indian Drawings*, frontispiece, p. 46, no. 15.

EYED BY HIS hen, the cock lunges down the page, a delicious tidbit wriggling in his beak. Beautiful as they may be, neither bird is temperamentally alluring. With terrible sharp beaks and scrawny but powerful "drumsticks," both are hungry and unfriendly. The hen's ballerina graces are marred by her scratchy claws and a gimlet gaze that would strike terror into a snake.

Few artists have depicted motion as well as quick-eyed Mansur, whose peafowl are a study in kinetics as well as avifauna. The peacock's forward rush and the peahen's split-second turn are recorded with lightning speed. The unnervingly palpable bone, muscle, and sinew of their legs are accelerated by smoky grays scumbled over Mansur's corrected underdrawing.

After sketching directly from life and dashing in suggestions of landscape, with rocks and trees angled to enhance yet balance the dynamic forms of the birds, the artist took this half-finished work into the studio. With continuing delight, he completed the patterns and textures of feathers, and lavished gold and lapis lazuli on the peacock's tail and full-throated neck—one of the bluest of blues, made iridescent by highlights of vermilion.

Mansur's flowers in the foreground should be compared to the *Western Asiatic Tulip* (no. 145) and to his floral borders for the self-portrait by Farrukh Beg (no. 147), upon which the later floral borders here, for an album of Shah Jahan, were based.

Published: Brown, *Indian Painting*, pl. XXIII; *Persian and Mughal Art*, p. 184, no. 99; Beach, *The Grand Mogul*, pp. 140–41, no. 47; Welch, *Imperial Mughal Painting*, pp. 90–91, pl. 26.

143.
A CHAMELEON
Inscribed: "Ustad [Master] Mansur"
Mughal, ca. 1610–15
Brush and ink with color on paper, 4⅜ × 5⅜ in. (11 × 13.7 cm.)
Her Majesty Queen Elizabeth II, Royal Library, Windsor Castle (RL.12081)

144.
PEAFOWL
Attributed to Mansur
Mughal, ca. 1610; border ca. 1645
Opaque watercolor on paper
Folio: 14⅜ × 9⅞ in. (36.5 × 25 cm.)
Miniature: 7½ × 4¼ in. (19.1 × 10.8 cm.)
The Knellington Collection, Courtesy Harvard University Art Museums, Cambridge, Massachusetts

144

144, detail ▷

145.
WESTERN ASIATIC TULIP (TULIPA
MONTANA)
Inscribed by Mansur
Mughal, ca. 1620
Opaque watercolor on paper
Miniature: 10¼ × 6¼ in. (26 × 15.9 cm.)
Maulana Azad Library,
Aligarh Muslim University

AFTER DESCRIBING THE flowers of Kashmir, a province he especially enjoyed visiting, Jahangir wrote in his memoirs that "those that Nadiru-l-ᶜasri Ustad Mansur has painted are more than one hundred."[1] Unless the emperor included flowers in borders, only three have come to light, studies of an iris and of a narcissus in the Imperial Library, Gulistan Palace, Tehran, and the present painting.[2] As in the animal and bird studies, Mansur here beamed all his perceptive powers toward botanical and entomological life, probing their secret wonders in a manner both scientifically faultless and imaginatively entrancing. Against a late afternoon lemon sky, a scavenging dragonfly cuts the air while, near enough to touch, a frail butterfly, majestic as a galleon with all sails set, hovers over the festive tulip. Beneath insects and blossoms, an aspiring bud aims skyward, resembling a helium balloon tugging at its cord. Flowers and bud, empowered by their sinuously reaching leaves, become an emblematic silhouette. Mansur's study has overshot—so magnified and lofty that it carries us above the earth.

However closely we look, the prospect delights. Each fragile petal, ithyphallic stamen, cleanly arcing stalk, and agitated green leaf has been passionately studied and defined. As in his treatment of the peacock's tail (no. 144), with its flashing jewels of gold and lapis lazuli, the tulip contains passages of gemlike brilliance.

1. Jahangir, *The Tuzuk*, vol. 2, p. 145.
2. For the *Iris*, see: Goddard, "Un Album de portraits des princes timurides," pp. 273–74, fig. 113; the *Narcissus* is unpublished.

Published: Mehta, *Studies in Indian Painting*, pl. 31; Das, *Mughal Painting*, p. 199, pl. 66.

145

145, detail

146

WHILE THE HUNTSMAN futilely shakes his talwar, a lion takes pleasure in his meal, just as a family cat might toy with a mouse. Nanha conveys empathy as effectively as Basawan, sending a shudder through us in his vision of the prey turning the tables on the hunter. Although Nanha magnifies the graceful lion and shows the man as a squirming, terrified creature, the drama is nightmarishly convincing. We even accept the small, seemingly scurrying bush in front of the man, and the ghoulish hidden profiles on the horizon.

Nanha convinces us of his distortions by tweaking our sympathies and drawing attention to small, undeniable realities: the pathetic little fist clutching a useless scabbard, the lion's cruel fangs and claws, and the ravaged pleading of the hunter's expression. Although Nanha painted for Akbar, Jahangir, and probably Shah Jahan, he always adjusted his style to the prevailing mode without weakening his artistic individuality. One of his earliest pictures, from the *Divan* of Anvari (Fogg Art Museum, Harvard University, Cambridge, Mass.), contains a cook—with arms as exaggeratedly large as this lion—robustly stirring a caldron.[1] Even as early as about 1588, Nanha could move us by artful distortions, inciting appetite rather than wincing.

1. For Nanha's cookery scene, see: Schimmel and Welch, *Anvari's Divan*, p. 105, pl. 9, p. 107 (det.).

Published: Coomaraswamy, "Notes on Mughal Painting: 2," p. 212, fig. 20; Beach, *The Grand Mogul*, pp. 148–49, no. 50.

ARTISTS' LIVES ARE often stranger and more intriguing than those of kings, and Farrukh Beg's, as understood from a few documents and a handful of paintings, was one of the most varied and puzzling. This recently discovered picture is inscribed as his work at the age of seventy in 1615. Allowing for the adjustment of Hijra dates to our own system, he must have been born in 1545, presumably in Iran; and one knows from Abu'l-Fazl's words in

146.
PERILS OF THE HUNT
Signed by Nanha
Mughal, ca. 1615
Opaque watercolor on silk
Folio: 9⅝ × 14⅝ in. (24.5 × 37.2 cm.)
Miniature: 7⅜ × 11½ in. (18.7 × 29.2 cm.)
The Free Library of Philadelphia, Rare Book Department (M.36)

147.
FOLIO FROM AN IMPERIAL ALBUM
Mughal, dated A.H. 1024 (1615)
Opaque watercolor on paper
Folio: 15 × 10⅛ in. (38.2 × 25.6 cm.)
Miniature: 7⅝ × 5½ in. (19.4 × 14.1 cm.)
Private collection

a. AN OLD SUFI (recto)
Inscribed, top right: "the work of the Wonder of the Age [Nadir al-ʿAsr] Farrukh Beg in his seventieth year inscribed after the opening . . . in battle in the tenth regnal year Hijra 1024 [1615]"; inscribed, lower inner border, in the hand of Shah Jahan: "Farrukh Beg," with seal of Nadaram Pandit

b. CALLIGRAPHY IN NASTAʿLIQ (verso)
Signed by ʿAli; with floral borders, perhaps by Mansur; with the seal of Jahangir

147b

Farrukh Beg. *Sufis in a Landscape*, ca. 1601–4.
Opaque watercolor on paper. Saltykov-Shtshedrine
Public Library, Leningrad

the *Akbar-nama* that he arrived at Akbar's court in 1585, probably after a career that had led from Shiraz to Khorasan. For Akbar he contributed two paintings to the *Akbar-nama* and others to several exceptionally fine literary manuscripts. Nevertheless, this Iranian master's style may not have greatly appealed to the emperor, who would have urged him to observe the real world more closely, and to record it with fewer Iranian flourishes. For this reason, as Robert Skelton suggested in 1957, Farrukh Beg gladly accepted an invitation to move to the Deccan in the early 1600s to work for Sultan Ibrahim ꜥAdil Shah II of Bijapur, who admired many styles of painting, including those with Safavid flavor. For Ibrahim, it seems, he painted the astonishing *Sufis in a Landscape* (left), which was influenced by and contributed to the extraordinary Bijapuri style. He remained at Bijapur, if Skelton is correct, until 1608 or 1609, well after Akbar's death, when he returned to the Mughal court, now a great artistic center where he could expect enthusiastic patronage from Jahangir. At last, according to the inscription mentioned above, he was granted the recognition he believed he deserved. In company with Abu'l-Hasan and Mansur—and a favorite imperial elephant—he became one of Emperor Jahangir's "Wonders."

Farrukh Beg's artistic style is the most quirkily personal in Mughal art. His characteristic figures are shaikhs (spiritual guides), not their youthful counterparts, shahids (beloveds), whom he also painted. Middle-aged or older, they are angular and attenuated, leaning precariously forward on slippered feet, with inwardly searching faces, unfocusing eyes, aquiline noses, and long, artfully coiffured white beards. Their hands are those of an artist: sensitive, capable, and unexpectedly strong. Although these mystics are silently cocooned in their auras, the world about them is noisily vital. Steep cliffs rumble upward like clenched hands from the murk, with knuckles and joints arranged to cast dramatic, occasionally comical, silhouettes. They hark back to Dust-Muhammad's rocks (see no. 85), which also emanated from the great Safavid Sufi painter Sultan-Muhammad—except that Farrukh Beg's rise from dreams, not nightmares.

One of the most introspective and profound Mughal miniatures, this psychic self-portrait by Farrukh Beg was painted at the Mughal court under very strong Bijapuri influence. This is especially apparent in the lyrically otherworldly character of the miniature and in the *changeant* off-black stones, which take on a purplish glow like that of Sultan Ibrahim ꜥAdil Shah's tomb in a warm, late afternoon light. The subject is a gray-bearded Sufi of approximately the artist's age, careworn and pensive, slumped in a chair under a fantastic tree. Its leaves grow in unlikely red, green, and yellow cabbage shapes, so clustered as to seem an infinity of forests—the illumined thoughts of a mystic floating heavenward. Behind the old gentleman, a book and two pairs of spectacles hint at his eye-straining occupation, while his hennaed dog and cat doze contentedly nearby. In the left foreground, suckling sheep and goats poignantly refer to a more active stage of life. On his desk, a corpulent and aging cat—an ambulatory supply of hairs for paint brushes —stalks a puddle of spilled milk, a metaphor perhaps for Farrukh Beg's soon to be spilled life.

This dramatically inventive, darkly glowing miniature, the only picture by Farrukh Beg based on European sources, is in effect an homage to Albrecht Dürer, partly as reinterpreted by Marten de Vos (1532–1603) in his *Dolor* (Hollstein 209; facing page) and engraved by Raphael Sadeler I (1560–ca. 1630).[1] In all likelihood, Farrukh Beg was familiar not only with the Sadeler but also with the Dürer engravings that had inspired de Vos: *Saint Jerome in His Study* (Bartsch 60), *Melencolia I* (Bartsch 74), and *Erasmus of Rotterdam* (Bartsch 107).[2] Although Akbar's and Jahangir's artists frequently copied or borrowed elements from the emperor's collections of European engravings, Farrukh Beg, like Sadeler and de Vos, has here made the sources his own, using them according to his needs as though he were quoting passages from his own tradition. The Sufi-like head, the flames of hair, the cap, and the hands are based on the *Erasmus*; the sleeves, cuffs, and swelling folds of his robe are adapted from *Melencolia I*. The angle of the head and the sloping shoulders evolve from the *Saint Jerome*, whom Farrukh Beg converted from Christian saintliness to Muslim Sufihood and whose slippers he borrowed, taking them from their shelf in the engraving and putting them on the feet of their transformed owner. With further artistic sleight of hand,

Farrukh Beg lent additional sweetness to Sadeler's and de Vos's hound—based on Dürer's sleeping terrier. The chair, boxes, book, walking stick, basket, cup, and bottles he also adapted from Sadeler and de Vos, who had in turn reshaped most of them from the *Saint Jerome*. Perspective lines traveled along the same route, from Dürer to de Vos to Sadeler to Farrukh Beg. But as the picture progressed, he increased its spatial ambiguity and wondrousness by burying many of the lines under his infinitely expanding tree, converting the saint's sunlit study into an arboretum of the soul.

Farrukh Beg was always a masterful technician, and in old age there was no diminishing of artistic control, as is evident in the lovingly minute brushwork of the gilded wicker chair, in the graining of the wooden panels of desk and cabinet, and above all in the hypnotically subtle mottled painterliness—representing months of meditative industry—of the stones, tree, and foliage. These, too, were influenced by Dürer, whose work with the burin, forming an all-encompassing, unifying pellicle of minute strokes, was reinterpreted in color. Close inspection reveals that the goat was painted over a highly burnished gold ground, and each hair of the dog was highlighted in an almost invisible golden stroke, a further recollection of Dürer's minute handling.

Farrukh Beg belongs in the company of the world's mystical artists: Sultan-Muhammad, Altdorfer, and Hercules Segers. As with them, subject matter—the portrait, landscape, or story—provided solid ground from which to leap into space. Devotedly, he poured all his creative strength into this plangent, melancholically personal picture, perhaps sensing it to be his final major production. It is his purest achievement, a summary and culmination of his artistic and spiritual growth. Iranian graces, Mughal observation, Dürer's minute handling, and Bijapuri coloring and fantasy combine harmoniously in this most visionary of Mughal paintings.

The lengthy inscription, presumably in the artist's hand, not only tells us that Farrukh Beg was seventy years old in 1615 but also refers to a battle, the name of which is illegible. Since the only major clash of arms during Jahangir's tenth regnal year was at Roshangarh, near Khirki (where the imperial forces roundly defeated a Deccani alliance that included Farrukh Beg's former employer, Sultan Ibrahim ʿAdil-Shah), the artist's words must have increased Jahangir's enjoyment of the miniature, reminding him not only of a victory but that he had hired away an enemy's most renowned artist.

This folio from one of Emperor Jahangir's albums is surrounded by borders as exceptional as the miniature. It is surrounded by flowers drawn in gold on an indigo ground and is further enriched by lines of verse and by floral arabesques. On the verso, superb lines of Nastaʿliq calligraphy, signed by ʿAli, are set within a field scattered with colorful flowers outlined in gold. Unlike most such Mughal borders, which are more ornamental than naturalistic, this one contains closely observed flowers—none of which is repeated—growing believably and organically, with palpable stems, leaves, and blossoms. They snap with freshness, gesticulate, dance, reach for the sun, and exchange views on botanical life. Evidently a very early—perhaps the first—instance of this kind of border, it forcibly brings to mind flowers painted by Jahangir's great natural history specialist, Mansur, the Wonder of the Age, to whom we also assign the border around the miniature, a tribute from one "Wonder" to another.[3]

Marten de Vos (1532–1603). Dolor (Hollstein 209). Engraving. The Metropolitan Museum of Art, New York, Department of Prints and Photographs, Harris Brisbane Dick Fund (44.62.6)

1. *Hollstein's Dutch and Flemish Etchings, Engravings and Woodcuts*. Comp. Dieuwke de Hoop Schieffer. Amsterdam, 1980, vol. 21. I am grateful to Margaret Erskine for calling to my attention Marianne Kuffner's identification of the Sadeler engraving as the source on which the miniature is based.
2. Bartsch, Adam Ritter von. *The Illustrated Bartsch*. Ed. Walter L. Strauss. New York, 1980, vol. 10 (formerly vol. 7, part 1).
3. The flowers in the borders may be compared to Mansur's *Western Asiatic Tulip* (no. 145) and to strikingly similar flowers in the foreground of his *Peafowl* (no. 144).

Published: Sotheby's, London, October 15, 1984, lot 36.

For the pioneering monograph on this fascinating artist, containing bold speculations, many of which have proved to be correct, see: Skelton, "The Mughal Artist Farrokh Beg"; the Sufi element so essential to the appreciation of Farrukh Beg's pictures is discussed in depth in Schimmel, *Mystical Dimensions of Islam*.

148

148.
FOUR PORTRAITS OF COURTIERS
From the Kevorkian Album
Inscribed, upper left: "Raj Singh, by Balchand";
upper right: "'Inayat Khan, by Daulat"; lower
left: "'Abd al-Khaliq, by R . . . D . . . M . . . ";
lower right: "Jamal Khan Qarabul, by
M . . . ra . . ." (probably Murad)
Mughal, ca. 1615
Opaque watercolor on paper
Folio: 15¼ × 10⅜ in. (38.7 × 26.4 cm.)
Miniature: 9⅞ × 5⅛ in. (25.1 × 13 cm.)
The Metropolitan Museum of Art, New York,
Purchase, Rogers Fund and The Kevorkian
Foundation Gift (55.121.10.29)

JAHANGIR CONTINUED HIS father's portrait albums, encouraging his artists to
explore psychology ever further, and to note quirks of appearance and costume
with fuller detail. The almost invariable isolating green grounds behind early
Akbari figures slowly gave way to suggestions of landscape and to variations of color. As before, the subjects' names were noted, often in Jahangir's
own hand.

These small, informative characterizations, usually of courtiers standing
at attention as though before the emperor, often indicate the sitters' stations
and activities as well as their temperaments. Jamal Khan Qarabul (lower
right), for example, not only bears a hunter's name but carries the tool of his
trade, a matchlock. 'Abd al-Khaliq (lower left) looks comfortably, plumply
reverential, while Raj Singh's (upper left) dignity is touched with pride.
Holding the emperor's sword in a richly figured bag is 'Inayat Khan (upper
right), whose features suggest those of an obliging aristocratic rabbit, a
glimmer of the psychic weakness that brought tragic days ahead (see facing
page for portraits of this courtier shortly before he died).

149a

149b

149.
TWO PORTRAITS OF ʿINAYAT KHAN

a. ʿINAYAT KHAN DYING
Probably by Govardhan
Mughal, 1618
Brush and ink with color on paper, 3¾ ×
5¼ in. (9.5 × 13.3 cm.)
Museum of Fine Arts, Boston, Francis Bartlett
Donation of 1912 and Picture Fund (14.679)

b. ʿINAYAT KHAN DYING
Probably by Govardhan
Mughal, 1618
Opaque watercolor on paper
Folio: 14½ × 14 in. (36.8 × 35.6 cm.)
Miniature: 5 × 6¼ in. (12.7 × 15.9 cm.)
Curators of the Bodleian Library, Oxford
(Ms. Ouseley 171b, 4v)

JAHANGIR, IN HIS *Tuzuk*, describes the scene shown in this drawing and painting: "On this day news came of the death of ʿInayat K[han]. He was one of my intimate attendants. As he was addicted to opium, and when he had the chance, to drinking as well, by degrees he became maddened with wine. As he was weakly built, he took more than he could digest, and was attacked by the disease of diarrhoea and in this weak state he two or three times fainted. By my order Hakim Rukna applied remedies, but whatever methods were resorted to gave no profit. At the same time a strange hunger came over him, and although the doctor exerted himself in order that he should not eat more than once in twenty-four hours, he could not restrain himself. He also would throw himself like a madman on water and fire until he fell into a bad state of body. At last, he became dropsical, and exceedingly low and weak. Some days before this, he had petitioned that he might go to Agra. I ordered him to come into my presence and obtain leave. They put him into a palanquin and brought him. He appeared so low and weak that I was astonished. 'He was skin drawn over bones' [verse] or rather his bones, too, had dissolved. Though painters have striven much in drawing an emaciated face, yet I have never seen anything like this, or even approaching to it. Good God, can a son of man come to such a shape and fashion?

"As it was a very extraordinary case, I directed painters to take this portrait."[1]

Although Jahangir implied that more than one painter took the dying man's portrait, both the sketched and painted versions here appear to be by the same hand. The drawing, made directly from what remained of life, to serve as a guide for the finished painting, was probably not intended for presentation to the emperor, whose royal albums contain unfinished paintings but virtually no drawings. It is more dramatic and immediate, revealing ʿInayat Khan's pained lassitude, his jaw and mouth sagging, his eyes glazed. In the painting, with the artist's connivance, he makes a last effort at courtliness. He sits upright, hair tidied, eyes straight ahead, still obedient to Jahangir's command. Even the bolsters and pillows are at attention.

Not for a moment has the artist's intense interest in his subject diminished in the painted work, in which coloristic beauty, a marvelous arabesque carpet, and glass bottles in niches are effective foils to the pitiable theme. The muted palette of whites, off-whites, and dusty tans enriched by bold accents of richer colors brings to mind the work of Govardhan, who is noted for his profound portraits of ascetics and holy men. Many of them share ʿInayat Khan's emaciation—reached along another road.

Other earmarks of Govardhan's manner are also apparent here: his liking for boldly scaled arabesques, the precise flow of his wrinkled textiles, and his tendency to draw unnaturally thin fingers.

The drawing and the painting are exhibited together here for the first time.

1. Jahangir, *The Tuzuk*, vol. 2, pp. 43–44.

Published:
a. Coomaraswamy, *Catalogue of the Indian Collections: VI*, p. 42, no. 14.679, pl. XXXII; Welch, *The Art of Mughal India*, errata, p. 72, no. 28; Welch, *Indian Drawings*, p. 47, no. 16; Beach, *The Grand Mogul*, pp. 162–63, no. 60; Welch, *Imperial Mughal Painting*, p. 27.

b. Martin, *The Miniature Painting*, vol. 2, pl. 200; Binyon and Arnold, *Court Painters of the Grand Moguls*, pl. XXIV; Brown, *Indian Painting*, pl. L; *The Art of India and Pakistan*, p. 162, no. 733; *Paintings from the Muslim Courts*, p. 72, no. 125; Welch, *Imperial Mughal Painting*, pp. 84–85, pl. 23; Chaitanya, *A History of Indian Painting*, p. 60, fig. 38; *In the Image of Man*, p. 148, no. 191.

150.
A SCRIBE
Attributed to Bichitr
Mughal, ca. 1625
Opaque watercolor on paper
Folio: 12½ × 9⅛ in. (31.9 × 23.1 cm.)
Miniature: 4⅛ × 2¾ in. (10.5 × 7 cm.)
The Knellington Collection, Courtesy
Harvard University Art Museums,
Cambridge, Massachusetts

SMALL MUGHAL PICTURES are sometimes memorably forceful. The intense characterization of this very old man carries across a room and makes it a fit neighbor to the haunting studies of ʿInayat Khan (no. 149). Respect, not pity or sadness, inspired the portrait of this old calligrapher, probably one long associated with the imperial library.

We seem to hear the scratch of the reed pen on paper as the wiry figure intently copies from one folio to another. He hunches forward, shoulders

150

and elbows sharpened by age, knotted into a pose held daily for most of a long life. His lean face is foreshortened, a challenging but dramatically effective angle seldom represented in Mughal painting. The artist confronted it brilliantly, noting the furrowed brow, wrinkled cheeks, and piercing pupils, lustrously black as the scribe's ink.

Bichitr is not ordinarily known for intimately moving portraits, but rather for impressively formal ones. Here, removed from the court, underlying compositional geometry and adept handling of textures—as in the stiff silk coat with deeply ingrained wrinkles that record the gentle old man's arduous work—demonstrate the artist's warmth of feeling toward the sitter. Although it is usually unwise to base attributions on lesser details, Bichitr can be recognized from his unique way of depicting hands, as here, with an inordinately large and flat flap of skin between thumb and forefinger.

Published: Brown, *Indian Painting*, pl. XLVIII; Saksena, *History of Shahjahan of Dihli*, p. 267; *Persian and Mughal Art*, pp. 194, 213, no. 118; Beach, *The Grand Mogul*, pp. 168–69, no. 66; Welch, *Imperial Mughal Painting*, pp. 96–97, pl. 29; Das, "Calligraphers and Painters," p. 97, fig. 287; *The Indian Heritage*, pp. 44–45, no. 65.

SMILINGLY CONTENT WITH life, a sumptuously accoutered princely young man sets off at a prance for a day of hawking. A cypress tree arcs gracefully, blossoms sparkle: nature heralds his adventures in the field. Muhammad ʿAli carries us to a world completely different from those of suffering ʿInayat Khan (no. 149) and the industrious scribe (no. 150), both of which portraits are affectingly individualistic. In comparison, the prince is a prettified type rather than a particular man. Nevertheless, the picture is superb, ecstatic with ara-

151.
A PRINCE HAWKING
Attributed to Muhammad ʿAli
Mughal, ca. 1625; border ca. 1640
Opaque watercolor on paper
Folio: 14⅜ × 10¼ in. (36.6 × 26 cm.)
Miniature: 7½ × 6⅜ in. (19.2 × 16.3 cm.)
Collection Prince Sadruddin Aga Khan, Geneva

besques, massed foliage, burgeoning flowers, sparkling metalwork, and a most ornamental huntsman astride a Nijinsky of a horse.

Muhammad ʿAli the painter remains a mysterious figure, known only from a few pictures, one of which—a tinted drawing of a young girl in the Binney collection—is signed "work of Muhammad ʿAli Jahangir Shahi."[1] It confirms that the painter was in Jahangir's employ, even though the style of the painting would seem—like that of this miniature—to be more to the taste of Shah Jahan. In any event, both these pictures, *A Thoughtful Man* (no. 152) and the *Reading Youth with Fâlcon* (Freer Gallery of Art, Washington, D.C.), exude the heady bouquet of the Deccan, where Prince Khurram (later Shah Jahan) served.[2] Perhaps, in a bountiful moment, he recruited the artist as a human offering to placate his distressed father.

1. Binney, *Indian Miniature Painting*, no. 123.
2. For *Reading Youth with Falcon*, see: Ettinghausen, *Paintings of the Sultans*, pl. 9.

Published: Stchoukine, "Portraits mughols," pp. 202–3, pl. 69, fig. 6, no. XI; Skelton, "The Mughal Artist Farrokh Beg," p. 400, fig. 9; *Persian and Mughal Art*, pp. 178–79, no. 92; Welch and Welch, *Arts of the Islamic Book*, pp. 198–200, no. 65.

MUHAMMAD ʿALI'S MOST memorable picture depicts the spiritually enlightened old man. He is surrounded by a superb still life—water bottles, pen box, water jar, and book—and backed by ecstatically flowering bushes, his ascending thoughts transformed. Like the court coat (no. 137), this profound and compact picture could as well be assigned to the Deccan as to the Mughal court. Inasmuch as an attached remnant of floral border indicates that it belonged to the Mughal emperor, we place it here rather than among the Deccani pictures (nos. 193–95, 197). But the palette of golden buff, pale

152.
A THOUGHTFUL MAN
Inscribed: "the work of Muhammad ʿAli"
Mughal, ca. 1610–15
Opaque watercolor on paper
Folio: 6⅛ × 5⅞ in. (15.5 × 15 cm.)
Miniature: 4½ × 3⅞ in. (11.4 × 10 cm.)
Museum of Fine Arts, Boston, Francis Bartlett
Donation of 1912 and Picture Fund (14.663)

152

blue, and purplish blue-gray is as Bijapuri in style as the sensitive flare of the pensive graybeard's scarf. Evidence of this Deccani connection is supported by the very strong influence on Muhammad ʿAli of Farrukh Beg, who painted for Sultan Ibrahim ʿAdil-Shah II of Bijapur as well as for Akbar and Jahangir and many of whose pictures also reveal affinities with both traditions (see no. 147). Inasmuch as Farrukh Beg specialized in portraying wise old gentlemen and because the clump of flowers in the lower right corner of this picture is painted precisely in his manner, it seems possible not only that the felicitous younger painter worked at Bijapur with the older artist but that he accompanied him when he returned from the Deccan to Jahangir's court.

Published: Coomaraswamy, *Catalogue of the Indian Collections: VI*, p. 35, no. 14.663, pl. xxv; Skelton, "The Mughal Artist Farrokh Beg," p. 339, pl. 8, fig. 17; Barrett and Gray, *Painting of India*, p. 125; Beach, *The Grand Mogul*, pp. 144–45, no. 48; Welch, *Imperial Mughal Painting*, pp. 96–97, pl. 20.

153.
FRAGMENT OF AN ARABESQUE
CARPET
Mughal, ca. 1625
Silk warp and weft, wool pile,
18 ft. 9½ in. × 49¼ in.
(5.73 m. × 125.1 cm.)
Calouste Gulbenkian Museum, Lisbon (T.72)

ARABESQUE CARPETS SUCH as this one offer a little-explored garden paradise of floral scrolls, trellises, palmettes, and cloudbands, to mention but a few of its dazzling elements. This large, extremely well-preserved section of a carpet should be imagined in a Mughal palace over a white marble floor, where it would have been laid out only for certain occasions, perhaps special feasts or celebrations. Like European rulers of the early seventeenth century, the Mughals did not eat in places specifically intended for dining. Rather, food was brought to favorite spots, selected according to mood, time of day, moon and stars.

Precise dating of Mughal pictures and objects on stylistic grounds is often difficult, and this carpet could as well be from the reign of Shah Jahan as from that of his father. But on the basis of its vitally resonant design and color with strong Iranian flavor, we associate it with the court of Jahangir and Nur-Jahan rather than with the more formal period of Shah Jahan. Whoever the patron, it is magnificent, with the impassioned, almost distracting chromaticism that separates it totally from Iranian classicism.

Published: Perdigão, *Calouste Gulbenkian Collectionneur*, pl. facing p. 152.

154.
SHAH JAHAN ON THE
PEACOCK THRONE
Attributed to Govardhan; border attributed to
the Master of the Borders
Mughal, ca. 1635; border ca. 1645
Opaque watercolor on paper
Folio: 14¾ × 10 in. (37.5 × 25.4 cm.)
Miniature: 6½ × 4⅞ in. (16.5 × 12.4 cm.)
The Knellington Collection, Courtesy
Harvard University Art Museums,
Cambridge, Massachusetts

SHIHAB AD-DIN MUHAMMAD SHAH JAHAN (r. 1628–58), the quintessence of the "Great Mogul," reigns to this day in the public mind as the embodiment of royal grace, grandeur, and power. Two of his creations are as renowned as he: the superb white marble tomb known as the Taj Mahal, built for his deeply beloved wife, Mumtaz-Mahal (Chosen One of the Palace); and the Peacock Throne, which he occupies in this miniature. During his thirty-year reign the empire achieved its peak of glory. These were the years of the Pax Mogulica, when the government was just but firm and life was secure. Shah Jahan's court poets, artists, and sculptors devised emblems for this golden age: scales of justice and a mighty lion so disciplined that he relaxes peacefully near an appetizing goat.

The ultimate aristocrat in his tastes, appearance, and way of life, Shah Jahan (Ruler of the World) was sufficiently practical to be coldly ruthless when circumstances demanded. As Prince Khurram, he—in typical Mughal fashion—plotted ways to power; and just as Jahangir's relationship with his father Akbar had turned bitter, so did Khurram's with Jahangir, whose antagonism toward him was encouraged by Nur-Jahan. At his father's death, Prince Khurram's followers, led by Asaf Khan, eased him to the throne. Once he occupied it, orders were issued to do away with potential rivals, a brother, two nephews, and two cousins.

Hardy, alert, and practical, Shah Jahan also fancied the good life, within limits. Although his father died of heart trouble at the age of fifty-eight, after years of overenthusiastic indulgence, Shah Jahan reached seventy-four,

153, detail ▷

a considerable age in those days, and one that supports belief in his temperateness, despite gossip at the time of his death that it was brought on by a surfeit of aphrodisiacs. He lived in an age of moderation, when the Mughal ethos continued the move toward orthodoxy in every area—from social conduct to religion to art, a trend initiated during the later years of Akbar's rule. These changes can be traced in stone by following the development of palaces from Akbar's buoyantly powerful, organically arranged red sandstone buildings at Fatehpur-Sikri to Shah Jahan's crystalline halls of white marble at Agra or Delhi (Shahjahanabad).

Painting and social deportment exemplify the same pattern, as can be seen by comparing *Shah Jahan on the Peacock Throne* with *Akbar in Old Age* (no. 113). While the grandfather, whom he greatly admired, seems relaxed even in ill health, Shah Jahan exudes decorum. Arranged in pure profile, he is pleasantly austere—isolated in his wealth and glory. According to a reliable eighteenth-century Mughal biography of Bebadal Khan Saidai Gilani, a poet who also served as the darogha, or superintendent, of the goldsmiths' office in the royal establishment, "the jewelled throne—known by name as the Peacock Throne—was finished by him in the course of seven years at the cost of a kror of rupees, or 333,000 tumans of Persia, or four krores of the khani coinage of Transoxiana . . . so valuable and adorned a throne was never seen in any other age."[1]

The Peacock Throne (Takht-i ta'us) was commissioned shortly after the jewel-loving Shah Jahan's accession and first used on March 12, 1635, at the celebration of the New Year, when it was set in a pavilion along the southern wall of the lower court at Agra. By the end of March in 1648, when Shah Jahan moved his court to Delhi, the throne was installed in the diwan-i khas (hall of private audience) of the Red Fort. One of the major symbols of Mughal wealth, might, and artistry, it was occupied by Aurangzeb, Shah Jahan's most effective and at times ruthless son and successor, as well as by later emperors. When it was carried off to Iran in 1739 by Nadir Shah, the Mughal empire lost far more than a superb treasure of jewels and gold. It was replaced by a sad pastiche replica worthy of the operatic stage—a poignant reminder of vanished power, sat upon by a puppet king. In Iran, it became a convenient mine for diamonds, rubies, emeralds, and gold, some of which were incorporated into the thrones of Fath 'Ali Shah of the Qajar dynasty and of his successors. By now, only the legend remains.

Shah Jahan on the Peacock Throne must have been painted soon after the completion of the throne. It not only depicts the king in all his glory, and his new creation, but it also contains studies of the once hoarded gems that were set into the gold masterpiece to impress and delight spectators. Govardhan, to whom the picture can be attributed by comparison with signed works, set actual precious stones and pearls into Shah Jahan's rings, necklace, and earring to make the portrait all the more lavish. The border, a schematized garden planted with flowers and aflutter with pleasing birds, can be attributed to the Master of the Borders, a mysterious painter and designer whose career seems to have begun in the Deccan (see nos. 151, 161).[2]

Although several late copies of the picture have survived, this is the original.[3]

1. Shah Nawaz Khan, *The Maathir-ul-umara*, vol. 1, pp. 396–97.
2. For further work by the Master of the Borders, see: Welch and Welch, *Arts of the Islamic Book*, nos. 56, 57, 62, 65, 72, 73.
3. For early nineteenth-century copies of this painting in the Victoria and Albert Museum, London, and in The Metropolitan Museum of Art, New York, see: Clarke, *Indian Drawings*, pl. 10; Hambly, *Cities of Mughal India*, pl. 48. Both are finely worked but the figure drawing is soft and boneless. The painting *Timur Hands His Imperial Crown to Babur*, from the Minto Album (Victoria and Albert Museum, London), attributed to Govardhan in Shah Jahan's own hand, is especially valuable in making the attribution. See: Welch, *Indian Drawings*, p. 48.

Published: Brown, *Indian Painting*, p. 90, pl. xxv; *Persian and Mughal Art*, pp. 181, 208, no. 95; *The Indian Heritage*, p. 43, no. 57.

155.
ROSETTE (SHAMSA) BEARING THE NAME AND TITLES OF EMPEROR SHAH JAHAN

Opening page from the Kevorkian Album
Inscribed: "His Majesty, Shihab ad-Din
Muhammad Shah Jahan, the King, Warrior of
the Faith, may God perpetuate his kingdom
and sovereignty!"
Mughal, ca. 1645
Opaque watercolor on paper, 15⅜ × 10½ in.
(39.1 × 26.7 cm.)
The Metropolitan Museum of Art, New York,
Purchase, Rogers Fund and The Kevorkian
Foundation Gift (55.121.10.39)

As PATRON, SHAH JAHAN is best known for his great buildings, especially the Taj Mahal and the mosques and palace and fort complexes of Agra, Lahore, and Delhi. But he was also a highly discerning patron of jewelers, jade craftsmen, metalworkers, and textile makers, as well as of painters and calligraphers. Too often, paintings made under his guidance are dated to his father's reign; and he is insufficiently credited with innovative marvels such as the present shamsa (little sun) from one of his albums. The illuminator, whose name is unknown, lavished many months of devotion on it, losing himself in a myriad of rosettes, garlands, and swooping birds, which should be viewed from several angles to appreciate the varied work of the gold. It is a superb painting, to be ranked with the finest Mughal figural miniatures, and to be compared with other masterpieces of arabesque design, such as the floor spread (no. 136) and the carpet (no. 153).

Although many Iranian prototypes for this rosette could be cited, they differ strikingly in spirit. Shah Jahan's illuminator envisioned the sunburst not flat, as in Iranian prototypes, but with characteristically Mughal three-dimensionality; and his coloring is tropically warm as opposed to the cool blues and golds of the Iranian mode, which seem in comparison classically restrained. Shah Jahan's shamsa is romantic, even passionate, radiating sunlight and expressive of the emotional undercurrents at his court and in his temperament.

The Kevorkian Album contains a second, very similar rosette, bearing the titles of Emperor Aurangzeb. Two other rosettes, uninscribed but apparently by the same patient, highly disciplined but visionary artist, are in the Windsor Castle *Padshah-nama*, and a third was formerly in the Rothschild collection.[1]

1. The second Kevorkian example will be reproduced in the full study of the Kevorkian Album now in preparation. The shamsas in the Windsor Castle *Padshah-nama* have not been published. For the Rothschild shamsa, see: Beach, *The Grand Mogul*, cover.

Published: Welch, *Imperial Mughal Painting*, pp. 98–99, pl. 30; *The Indian Heritage*, p. 44, no. 66.

156.
SILK HANGING

Mughal, perhaps Gujarat, ca. 1625-30
Silk, 6 ft. 11 in. × 38¼ in. (2.12 m. × 97 cm.)
Staatliche Museen Preussischer Kulturbesitz,
Museum für Indische Kunst, West Berlin
(MIK.I.364)

IF SHAH JAHAN crossed the time barrier and revisited his palaces, he would probably deplore them as starkly barren shells. The proportions and details of carving would please him, but he would be shocked by the condition of many *pietra dura* inlays—picked out by generations of looters and tourists—and by the absence of dazzling gold and silver adornments. He would also miss the stunningly colorful textiles, virtual flower gardens once stretched on the floors, hung in doorways and windows, and worn by throngs of courtiers and attendants—more than an intimation of which is provided here by a miraculously preserved imperial tent (no. 165). Designers devised ever richer and more inventive variations usually on botanical themes, and weavers on imperial looms were constantly busy. Agents as a matter of course acquired the finest work, usually on commission, from textile centers all over India and beyond; and visiting dignitaries brought bolts of superb cloth along with peerless elephants and horses, splendid objects, and other royal gifts, which were punctiliously inspected, admired—and, often as not, recycled in the rounds of imperial benevolence.

Shah Jahan's miniatures in the Windsor Castle *Padshah-nama*, the official illustrated history of his reign (see no. 162), offer vivid glimpses of the splendors of court life as it was lived, replete with exquisitely detailed renderings of all the vanished glories. From the miniatures, it is apparent that silk hangings such as this one hung in doorways or windows to provide shade or privacy. Even now, in the forts of Agra and Delhi, one sees small hooks and stone fastenings for setting the acres of festive hangings that made Shah Jahan's white palaces resemble paradisiacal vessels in full sail.

Often, as here, designers "improved" nature, borrowing leaves and blossoms from flowers of the mind rather than the garden. Carolyn Kane has pointed out that the central hybrid might be based upon the tobacco plant, introduced to India during the late Akbar period, but that the spandrels

155

are filled with three distinct varieties of leaves and buds.[1] Very similar textiles are in the Calico Museum, Ahmedabad; the Government Museum, Karachi; and private collections.

1. Personal communication, November 1984.

Published: *Katalog 1971: Ausgestellte Werke*, no. 150, pl. 25; *The Arts of Islam*, no. 93.

157

THIS GATHERING, shown in a cool, fragrant garden as dusk approaches, perfectly exemplifies the civilized pleasures of princely Mughal life. The royal
host, perhaps a reminiscence of Jahangir as Prince Salim, enjoys a mushaira,
or poetry reading, enhanced by music and good things to eat and drink.
Bichitr, the Mughal Van Dyke, who portrayed every eminent personage
during the reigns of Jahangir and Shah Jahan, has itemized each paintable
delight: the wise and witty company; their elegantly decorous attendants; a
superb dhurrie, beneath yet more marvelous carpets with arabesque designs,
one of them entirely in whites; a black pedestal table, apparently of Mughal
workmanship; gold, jade, and glass utensils; and—in the event that all this
begins to pall—an invitingly placed charpoi (cot) beneath a canopy at
the end of the garden.

Bichitr's brilliance of technique is apparent everywhere, especially in
the trompe l'oeil handling of still life, a European approach to painting usually avoided by other Mughal artists. The guard dressed in white, left
foreground, wears a quilted collar far wider than those worn prior to the
reign of Shah Jahan. The drawing of his hand, with sinuous, tapering fingers,
is one of many convenient earmarks of Bichitr's artistic personality. More
fundamental, however, is the geometric substructure of his compositions, as
here and in the unusually intimate depiction of an old scribe (no. 150).

Published: Arnold, *The Library of A. Chester Beatty*, vol. 1, p. 29, vol. 3, no. 7, pl. 58;
Welch, *Imperial Mughal Painting*, pp. 110–11, pl. 36; James, *Islamic Masterpieces of the
Chester Beatty Library*, p. 41, no. 51c; *The Indian Heritage*, pp. 40–41, no. 49.

157.
A YOUNG PRINCE WITH SAGES IN A
GARDEN
From the Minto Album
Inscribed: "the work of Bichitr"
Mughal, ca. 1630
Opaque watercolor on paper
Folio: 15 × 10⅝ in. (38 × 27 cm.)
Miniature: 11 × 8 in. (28 × 20.2 cm.)
Chester Beatty Library, Dublin (Ms. 7, no. 7)

158c

158d

158e

158f

158.
MANUSCRIPT: *GULISTAN*
(THE ROSE GARDEN) OF SAʿDI
(114 folios, 6 miniatures)
Scribe: Sultan ʿAli ibn Muhammad al-Mashhadi
Herat, dated A.H. 873 (1468)
Private collection

a. SAʿDI MEETS A FRIEND IN A GARDEN
By Govardhan; signed in lower margin[1]
Opaque watercolor on paper, 5⅛ × 2⅝ in.
(12.9 × 6.7 cm.)

b. A PROPHET TEACHES SEVEN DISCIPLES
Attributed to ʿAbid[2]
Opaque watercolor on paper, 4⅜ × 3½ in.
(11.2 × 9 cm.)

c. AN ARGUMENT COMES TO BLOWS
By Payag; signed on coat of older man[3]
Opaque watercolor on paper, 3⅞ × 2⅝ in.
(9.8 × 6.6 cm.)

d. A PRINCE WHILE RIDING COMES UPON A
MAN RESTING UNDER A TREE
By Balchand; signed beneath the horse[4]
Opaque watercolor on paper, 4⅛ × 2¾ in.
(10.5 × 6.7 cm.)

e. A REVERED OLD MAN IS DISCOVERED
IN A DRUNKEN STATE
By Lalchand; signed in lower left corner
Opaque watercolor on paper, 3⅝ × 2⅝ in.
(9.3 × 6.6 cm.)

f. A WARRIOR FRIGHTENED BY TRIBESMEN
By Murad; signed in lower left corner
Opaque watercolor on paper, 3¾ × 2⅝ in.
(9.5 × 6.6 cm.)

ACCORDING TO INSCRIPTIONS, this manuscript was given by Emperor Akbar to one Muʾmin Khan. It also bears the name of Jahangir, presumably as owner, from whom it would have passed to Shah Jahan. Shah Jahan's eighth regnal year (1636) is noted, as are the names of Prince Dara-Shikoh and Princess Jahanara.

Like his predecessors, Shah Jahan enjoyed reading especially rich, pocket-sized copies of literary classics. This superb fifteenth-century manuscript, copied by an illustrious scribe in 1468, contains six small miniatures that are painted over damaged Timurid pictures, discernible from the backs of the folios.

In all likelihood, the repainting followed a terrible episode in the palace at Agra in the summer of 1644: Legend has it that one evening the manuscript was being read by Princess Jahanara, who had served as first lady at Shah Jahan's court since 1631, the year that her mother, Mumtaz-Mahal, died while bearing her fourteenth child. The princess's dress brushed against a candle flame and ignited. Attendants scurried to help, and two ladies-in-waiting threw themselves onto the blaze, saving their mistress's life but dying from their burns. For four months the princess lay on the verge of death, during which time Shah Jahan spent hours each day attending her and praying for her recovery. In late November her return to health was celebrated at court, with honors and exchanges of gifts.

On this occasion, presumably, the manuscript became sopped with water, and its borders and miniatures were disturbingly stained. In the aftermath of the dousing, Shah Jahan commissioned his artists to treat the manuscript with as much care as his physicians had treated the princess. Stylistically, the pictures by his court artists, most of whom also contributed to the Windsor Castle *Padshah-nama*, can be dated to the mid-1640s, just the time of the fire in the harem. Each represents its painter at his most intimate and his best, moved to outdo himself at a time of imperial tragedy.

1. The style and handling are wholly characteristic of this master; see also nos. 149, 154, 159, 160.
2. The smoothly rounded, inwardly smiling, parchment-hued faces in this miniature are unmistakably those of ʿAbid. A scarcely legible inscription, however, gives the name Aqa-Riza Jahangiri, perhaps as master of ʿAbid. This miniature has suffered more than the others, and appears to have been retouched after 1645.
3. For this romantically inclined painter, see: Welch, *A Flower from Every Meadow*, pp. 110–12, no. 66; Beach, *The Grand Mogul*, pp. 151–54.
4. For this artist, see: Welch, *A Flower from Every Meadow*, pp. 108–9, no. 65; Beach, *The Grand Mogul*, pp. 95–100.

Published: *Paintings from the Muslim Courts*, p. 82, no. 148.

I would like to thank Robert Skelton, with whom I examined this manuscript many years ago, at which time I observed that the miniatures were painted over Timurid pictures. I am also grateful to B. W. Robinson, whose identifications of the subjects of the miniatures I have followed.

159.
A RUSTIC CONCERT
Inscribed: "the work of Govardhan"
Mughal, ca. 1630
Opaque watercolor on paper
Folio: 15 × 10⅝ in. (38 × 27 cm.)
Miniature: 9 × 6⅝ in. (23 × 16.7 cm.)
Chester Beatty Library, Dublin (Ms. 7, no. 11)

MUCH OF THE appeal of Mughal painting stems from its sympathetic and accurate documentation of Indian life. Govardhan, whose artistic career spanned three reigns, from Akbar's well into Shah Jahan's, recorded rural and ascetic genre with a degree of curiosity and sympathy unequaled until the early nineteenth century, when William Fraser's artists explored similar marvels (see nos. 49, 50).

With his favorite palette of whites and dusty grays, Govardhan celebrated some of the pleasures of the road, perhaps in the course of a royal cavalcade to Kashmir. In the foreground, observed by the artist as though he sat with his patron on a platform in an improvised garden enclosed by a rustic fence, a Gorakhpanthi yogi and an attendant (the royal valet?) with a pet bird listen to a singer accompanied by a rababi. Beyond, servants set up the royal tents, one of which is red, signifying the presence of a Mughal prince; and on the horizon elephants are tended following the day's march.

This nostalgic miniature presumably was painted for Shah Jahan's

159

eldest son, Crown Prince Dara-Shikoh, who shared his great-grandfather Akbar's ambition to bring together Muslim and Hindu religious tenets, especially on the mystical level. Although Prince Dara-Shikoh's religious tolerance was increasingly at odds with Mughal orthodoxy—and ultimately provided compelling arguments for his execution—he spent many years exchanging ideas with Hindu as well as Muslim devotees. Several of Govardhan's more profound portrait groups record members of his religious circle, who often gathered in his beloved Kashmir. It is not farfetched to assume that Prince Dara-Shikoh also commissioned them. Govardhan must have been available to him through the generosity of his admiring father, who encouraged in him characteristics he had admired in his beloved grandfather, Akbar. (See also nos. 149, 154, 158, 160.)

Published: Arnold, *The Library of A. Chester Beatty*, vol. 1, p. 30, no. 11, frontispiece to vol. 3; Welch, *Imperial Mughal Painting*, pp. 94–95, pl. 28; James, *Islamic Masterpieces of the Chester Beatty Library*, p. 39, fig. 51b; *The Indian Heritage*, p. 39, no. 47.

GOVARDHAN HAS ASSEMBLED four distinct human types. The gray-bearded astrologer, astrolabe in hand, who sits quietly in his hermitage, represents the intellectual. He is attended by three reverential followers: the loyal assistant, happy to serve, who slowly turns the crisp pages of a manuscript; the dedicated man of nature, scantily dressed, close to the sun and the earth; and the spiritual ecstatic, his face wrinkled with fervor. The painting is characteristic of Govardhan, and seems to have been painted for Prince Dara-Shikoh in Kashmir, probably in one of the shaded groves along watercourses near Dal Lake in Srinagar.

Spurred on by Prince Dara-Shikoh, Govardhan in his later series of pictures of ascetics furthered Mughal psychological portraiture in the steps of Basawan and Daulat, whose work he seems to have studied. Although he also painted imperial grandeur (see no. 154), and his gaunt sitters were not all saints (see no. 149), his studies of Hindu and Muslim holy men are among

160

244

the highest achievements of Indian painting. In these spiritual evocations, he eschewed rich gold, lapis lazuli, and malachite, limiting his palette to varying tones of smoke, seeming to load his brushes from the ashes that were the sole raiment of many Hindu devotees. He also avoided sensuous glitter and luster, applying the pigments to produce more of a matte surface than in his imperial subjects, and scarcely touching them with the needle or burnishing stone.

Govardhan's work is best recognized from its spirit, but certain habits of mind and hand also provide useful clues to his artistic personality. In addition to his preference for a subdued palette of dust colors and gold and his predilection for unusually lean fingers, his treatment of the nude human form is innovative in Mughal painting. Most of all, we esteem his painterliness, especially in the layered network of whites and off-whites boldly brushed on in thin washes and in lyrically sinuous runs, often in the wrinkles and folds of clothing. Related to them is a recurring organic pattern fundamental to his overall compositions but also found in textiles and other ornamental passages, in foliage, and in clouds. Its liquid forms resemble marbleizing and bring to mind the cosmically charged motifs of wind, water, and vegetable life known from Gujarati stone reliefs.

Published: Hôtel Drouot, Paris, November 23, 1960, lot 63; *Arts de l'Islam*, p. 227, no. 357; *L'Islam dans les collections nationales*, pp. 288–90, no. 693.

THIS DIALOGUE BETWEEN a fragile, ladylike iris and a loomingly regal tulip, attended by an embarrassed little *tulipa montana*, far transcends botany. The artist has so elevated and humanized these flowers that we approach them as we should Shah Jahan himself, his very distinguished lady friend, and an estimable servant, who averts his glance and seems not to know quite what to do with his foliage. The poetic and amusing encounter is set out of doors against a golden sky—in fact the bare paper—with a scrub of trees stretching across a far horizon.

We attribute this miniature to an anonymous artist dubbed the Master of the Borders because all of the other works assignable to him are borders for calligraphies or for miniatures, such as the one surrounding *Shah Jahan on the Peacock Throne* (no. 154). Like this bewitching convocation of three flowers, the borders were painted in a highly personal idiom, usually suggesting more than meets the eye. The border framing Shah Jahan on his throne implies a formal garden through which he, or the viewer, might stroll to inspect its flowers and birds, all painted in potent colors—note the strange acid greens and reds startlingly juxtaposed with orange—that sing out in higher tones than those of other Mughal artists.

Whatever his name or history, this cheerful painter is easily distinguished through his delicate but notable grace notes in Shah Jahan's albums and from designs supplied to decorate the walls of palace apartments. He stands out as a lyrical poet among masters of prose.

His career seems to have begun in the Deccan, where his talents were recognized by Akbar's—and later Jahangir's—enlightened courtier, the statesman-soldier-poet-patron 'Abd ar-Rahim, the Khankhanan (Lord of Lords; 1556–1627), for whom he created many fantastically inventive borders. (For a portrait of the Khankhanan, see no. 118, where he is shown standing directly in back of Prince Khurram.) These borders, which can be dated to about 1615–20, and even more extraordinary ones for the Khankhanan's now dispersed manuscript of Jami's *Subhat al-Abrar* (The Rosary of the Righteous), are the most imaginatively poetic works by this peculiarly gifted artist, whose ornamental fantasies would appeal to Japanese taste.[1]

Further light on the career of the Master of the Borders is shed by a series of smaller, simpler borders for a dispersed copy of the *Fawaʾid-i Qutb-Shahi* (The Benefits of Qutb-Shah), copied for Sultan 'Abdullah Qutb-Shah of Golconda in 1629–30.[2] Revealing slight traces of Mughal naturalism in their bird painting, they can be assigned to him and to his workshop before he joined the staff of Shah Jahan, who as prince spent many years in the

161.
TULIPS AND AN IRIS
Attributed to the Master of the Borders
Mughal, mid-17th century
Opaque watercolor on paper
Folio: 12⅝ × 8 in. (32 × 20.2 cm.)
Miniature: 10⅜ × 6⅜ in. (26.4 × 16.1 cm.)
Collection Prince Sadruddin Aga Khan, Geneva

161

Deccan, where he probably met the Master of the Borders through the connoisseurly courtier.[3]

1. See Arnold and Grohmann, *The Islamic Book*, pls. 84–87. For the *Subhat al-Abrar*, some pages of which contain small studies of birds and animals, see: Hassan, *Moslem Art*, vol. 1, pls. 16, 17. Other folios are in the collections of Mr. and Mrs. Ralph Benkaim and The Metropolitan Museum of Art.
2. Seven folios of the *Fawaʾid-i Qutb-Shahi* are in the collection of Edwin Binney, 3rd. See: Binney, *Indian Miniature Painting*, p. 149, no. 125. For the manuscript, see: Bukhari, "An Unpublished Illuminated Manuscript," pp. 8–11.
3. Other borders by this artist are illustrated in Welch and Welch, *Arts of the Islamic Book*, pp. 198–200, no. 65, pp. 220–23, no. 73.

Published: Welch and Welch, *Arts of the Islamic Book*, pp. 217–20, no. 72.

LIKE AKBAR AND JAHANGIR, Shah Jahan commissioned a great illustrated manuscript documenting the history of his life and reign; and like those made for his progenitors, his has come down to us less than intact. The largest portion, containing forty-four pictures, was bound and cased at Lucknow in the late eighteenth century, and has been in the Royal Library at Windsor Castle for over a century. Before it was bound, several miniatures went astray, among them the two here, which were adorned with Lucknow borders. Both illustrate episodes late in the reign.

Shah Jahan's notion of subjects appropriate to an official history differed from his father's. Jahangir's appreciation of the quirky and trivial led him to commission pictures of, for example, interviews with holy men and his discovery of a confrontation between a snake and a spider, whereas his more formal son concentrated on state occasions, battles, and family celebrations, which his artists painted with almost compulsive, hence delightfully informative, attention to detail.

Sprawling, rich, and managed by an increasingly complex officialdom, the Mughal empire now moved at the stately pace of an aged tortoise. Whereas Akbar took off at a moment's notice at the head of a vigorous army, Shah Jahan's military establishment required months to get under way; and all too often, the results were less than triumphant. The motivation had changed, too. Akbar's active expansionism had been replaced by quiescence, occasionally interrupted by massive attacks upon places such as Kandahar, in Afghanistan, the possession of which had long been contested with Iran; by the pursuit of traitors to the empire; or by rodomontade campaigns against the rival sultans of the Deccan, whose lands had been coveted by the Mughals since the sixteenth century.

Shah Jahan also felt romantic territorial longings for Samarkand, capital of his ancestor Timur. They were sparked to life by outbreaks in Transoxiana, which justified a series of campaigns led by a succession of princes. The first to go was Murad Bakhsh, who at twenty-two led fifty thousand men into Badakhshan. But the climate was disagreeable and the going arduous. The prince begged permission to return to India without reaching Samarkand. Shah Jahan ordered him to persevere. Murad rebelled, and returned alone to Lahore—for which he received a stern paternal reprimand, was denied access to the court, and was replaced by his energetic brother, Aurangzeb.

For the *Padshah-nama*, however, a rosier episode was chosen, the triumph of Qulij Khan Turani, the devoted follower of the emperor, whose army boasted an elite corps of one thousand Uzbeks, all wearing heron plumes. Noted for piety and fasting, they were equally renowned for gambling and whoring. In the miniature, Qulij Khan accepts the keys of a conquered city, probably Bust, which was captured in the eleventh year of the reign from Mihrab Khan, one of the Iranian shah's abler generals. In the foreground, the Mughal general accepts his enemy's submission, while the background itemizes incidents of the siege: mines exploding the fort's outer walls, and the breach of the inner ones; Mughal forces invading the city; and the capture of Mihrab Khan, who had sought refuge in the citadel. All of this is set forth with verve and sunlit clarity by Murad, who inscribed another of his pictures for the project (*Jahangir Receiving Shah Jahan*, Windsor *Padshah-nama*,

162.
TWO FOLIOS FROM A MANUSCRIPT OF THE *PADSHAH-NAMA* (HISTORY OF THE EMPEROR) OF ʿABD AL-HAMID LAHORI

a. QULIJ KHAN ACCEPTS THE KEYS TO A CITY IN BADAKHSHAN
Attributed to Murad
Mughal, ca. 1646
Opaque watercolor on paper
Folio: 18⅞ × 12⅜ in. (48 × 31.5 cm.)
Miniature: 13⅜ × 9½ in. (34 × 24.2 cm.)
Musée Guimet, Paris

b. THE SIEGE OF KANDAHAR
Attributed to Payag
Mughal, mid-17th century
Opaque watercolor on paper
Miniature: 13½ × 9⅜ in. (34.3 × 23.9 cm.)
The Knellington Collection, Courtesy Harvard University Art Museums, Cambridge, Massachusetts

162a

folio 193v) as by "Nadir az-Zaman's pupil, Murad." The Guimet miniature is easily attributed by comparison with his signed *Siege of Daulatabad*, folio 143r of the Windsor manuscript.

If Murad's siege raised the spirits of his imperial patron, Payag's view of an episode in 1649, during the unsuccessful attempts to recapture strategic Kandahar must have lowered them. Although Murad was noted for his cheerful portrayals of grand events at court—and, we suspect, as a designer of architectural ornament, which he painted so inventively—Payag is admired for portraits of holy men and ravaged old soldiers, and for views of war in all its horror.

Bleached skeletons, unsettling relics from a previous Mughal misadventure, occupy the center of this battle scene, set in a visionary, Altdorfer-like landscape of Badakhshan. Payag offers other mettlesome vignettes: a toothy drummer pounding the kettledrum with sticks; bright-eyed elephants proud in their war paint; and rank upon rank of portraitlike foot soldiers, ever diminishing as they clamber up the hill through puffs of smoke toward glory, or death.

Published:
a. Blochet, *Collection Jean Pozzi*, p. 34, no. 21, pl. XXXIX; Soustiel, Paris, 1970, sale cat., *Catalogue de la collection Jean Pozzi: miniatures indiennes et orientales*, lot 76; *Arts de l'Islam*, p. 226, no. 358; *Rarities of the Musée Guimet*, no. 69; *L'Islam dans les collections nationales*, p. 196, no. 435.

b. Blochet, *Collection Jean Pozzi*, pl. XXXV; Welch, *A Flower from Every Meadow*, pp. 110–12, no. 66; Beach, *The Grand Mogul*, pp. 81–84, no. 25; Welch, *Imperial Mughal Painting*, p. 105, pl. 33.

162b

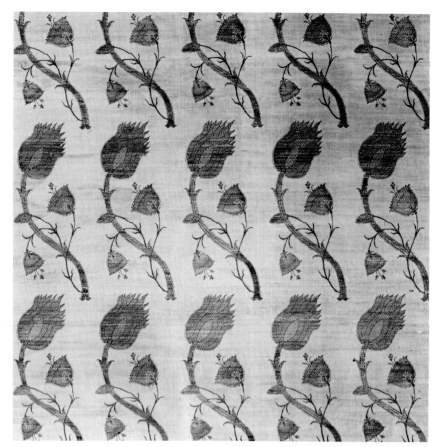

163, detail

163.
LENGTH OF FLOWERED SILK
Mughal, mid-17th century
Silk and metal-wrapped yarns, 27¼ × 29½ in.
(69.2 × 74.9 cm.)
The Metropolitan Museum of Art, New York,
The Nasli Heeramaneck Collection, Gift of
Alice Heeramaneck (1982.477)

A THOUGHTFULLY PHILOSOPHICAL designer devised this symbolic pattern of boldly masculine curving stems enlaced by gracefully ladylike smaller flowers and culminating in blossoms with flamelike petals. Whether it was intended to cover a puffy bolster, a prestigious courtier, or the emperor himself, this length of fabric increased the artistic glory of court life. Its forcefulness was perhaps influenced by Ottoman textiles, reminding us that the Mughal imperial style not only equaled or surpassed other royal modes but was part of a widespread international artistic complex that included the Ottomans, the Safavids, and the Deccani sultanates.[1]

1. For a related textile, shown in a miniature, appropriately covering a bolster for royal lovers on a terrace, see: Welch, *Imperial Mughal Painting*, pl. 35.

164.
JALI
Mughal, Agra, ca. 1630–35
Marble with hardstone inlay, 57 × 43⅝ in.
(144.8 × 110.8 cm.)
The Kronos Collections, New York

THIS SUPERB MARBLE jali, with hardstone inlays in its borders, probably once enriched the mood of Shah Jahan's private apartments in Agra Fort. It may have preceded, or even inspired, the almost identical twenty-four panels forming a screen around the cenotaphs in the famed Taj Mahal tomb complex. Mumtaz-Mahal's death in 1631 at Burhanpur in the Deccan while bearing her fourteenth child brought terrible sadness to Shah Jahan, who returned to Agra in June 1632 and at once initiated the project of her great tomb, which was also to be his own. Although the emperor spent approximately half of his thirty-year reign away from his capitals, he was in Agra from June 1632 until January 1634, and much of his time must there have been spent planning the tomb in detail. Conceivably, the Kronos jali was made at that time, as a promising substitute for the jeweled gold railing originally intended to surround Mumtaz-Mahal's cenotaph. Curiously, by 1648, the year of the tomb's completion, Shah Jahan had decided to move his capital from Agra to Delhi, a decision believed by some to mark the beginning of imperial decline.

Shah Jahan's serious illness in 1657 led to rumors of his imminent death, which precipitated the wars of succession, one of the more agonizing episodes in Mughal history. On his sickbed, Shah Jahan appointed Prince Dara-

Shikoh his heir, and this was followed by a scramble for power on the part of his four sons. Aurangzeb proved to be the hardiest—and most ruthless—and he defeated the others in a series of pitched battles, intrigues, and killings. In June 1658 he besieged Agra Fort, where his father, who had now recovered his health, was protecting the imperial treasure. By blocking access to the water of the Jamuna River, Aurangzeb forced him to capitulate. Imprisoned thereafter by Prince Aurangzeb, Shah Jahan was to spend the last years of his life (from June 1658 until February 1666) within Agra Fort, where this screen imparted both beauty and sad associations.

Jalis were characteristically Indian architectural elements, ornamental as well as useful, enheartening designers and stonecutters to conjure up ever fresh ideas, guided by imperial aesthetes. The boldly geometric jali (no. 120) marks Jahangir's taste in about 1610. Now we hurtle forward, omitting several stages of the development, to the 1630s, when vegetal forms once treated with classical strictness break out in almost rococo florescence. Flowers and leaves twist, turn, and undulate in a virtuosic stone lace of writhing intensity, a tree of life become orchidaceous.

Denaturalized flowers, stems, buds, and leaves are arranged in repeated arabesques, conveying essences of growth and calling to mind earthier cousins—the folkloristic bangles that combine vegetal and serpent forms in a romp of fertility (no. 69). But the decorative vitality of the imperial screen brings to mind other, very disparate traditions: the swagging vegetation of Gandharan and Mauryan art, Caesar Augustus's Ara Pacis, and Enea Vico's engravings of acanthus ornament (published in Rome about 1590)—all of which contributed to the Mughal artistic synthesis.

Published: Lerner, *The Flame and the Lotus*, pp. 156–57, no. 60.

165.
A ROYAL TENT
Mughal, mid-17th century
Silk velvet, embroidered, with metal-wrapped yarns and cotton, 12 ft. 8 in. × 24 ft. 9 in. × 24 ft. 6 in. (3 m. 80 cm. × 7 m. 42.5 cm. × 7 m. 35 cm.)
Mehrangarh Museum Trust, Fort, Jodhpur, on loan from Maharaja Sri Gaj Singhji II of Jodhpur (L21/1981)

THIS PORTABLE CLOTH palace, among the grandest monuments of the Shah Jahan period, is one of the very few imperial tents to have survived. Its miraculous preservation can be ascribed to centuries of protection in the noble fort at Jodhpur, where it and several others have been maintained since they were taken from the Mughals in the seventeenth century. But before recounting the drama of their coming to Jodhpur, we must recall that Shah Jahan took pleasure in hunting, campaigning, and traveling to distant parts of the empire, and that, like his ancestors, he lived for several months of each year in the airy coolness of tents. They were designed and constructed in the farrashkana, a special branch of the imperial workshops to which, it appears, architects, textile designers, and even artists—all under the supervision of the emperor himself—contributed ideas.

Red tents such as this one were the prerogative of imperial princes. The form and magnificence of this tent suggest that it provided the artistic—indeed, theatrical—climax to a vast encampment through which visitors would have been led along increasingly splendid pathways as they approached the temporary imperial quarters. Together forming the diwan-i ʿam (hall of public audience) of the complex, within which an imperial prince or the emperor himself transacted affairs of state and received visitors, the tent's sides are festive with seven gracefully lobed archways. Entering the tent from bright sunlight or nocturnal darkness must have been awesome. Even after hundreds of years of mellowing, the inner walls still dazzle us. Their overall pattern of sensitively observed yet ornamental golden yellow flowers, embroidered in gold over a yellow silk core, is artfully designed. Narrow borders of similarly embroidered light blue silk relieve the intense red and yellows. Tassels, brilliantly twisted and sewn, fringe the lower edge of the ceiling where it meets the walls.

165, detail

Amid the splendor of the interior walls is the colonnaded inner chamber, where the emperor or prince—the jewel within the setting—sat upon the richly covered bolsters composing the gaddi, or throne, and greeted honored visitors.

The exterior walls and sloping roof of the tent were originally covered with red and yellow striped masharu (cotton and silk fabric). The flat top of the roof is a square of red velvet, identical in its dimensions to the inner chamber beneath. Despite its age, the tent is in excellent condition except for the striped masharu, which has been replaced. To lend enlivening authenticity, seventeenth-century window and door hangings, made of bamboo splints to form floral patterns, have been added at the suggestion of H. H. Gaj Singhji, who not only discovered this tent and several others in Jodhpur Fort but has also taken personal interest in its restoration and mounting.

Seen in the light of Rajput history, as recounted by James Tod in his *Annals*, the tent evokes the heroic and dramatic times when Maharaja Jaswant Singh of Marwar (1638–1678), all of his sons, and many other noble Rajputs lost their lives during the Mughal wars of succession and in their aftermath.

How did this magnificent tent reach Jodhpur, and when? Fortunately, the design and artistry combine with historical evidence to provide the answers. Maharaja Jaswant Singh, who acquired it, was the senior prince of the House of Rathor and ruler of Marwar, the capital of which was the mighty fort at Jodhpur. Although a great Rajput nobleman, and of course a staunch Hindu, he conformed to the frequent Rajput practice of serving the Mughals. His career began under Shah Jahan, whom he first served in the Peshawar war.

In 1657 Shah Jahan fell seriously ill, and his sons and their ambitious followers initiated struggles for the throne. Prince Dara-Shikoh, senior son

165, detail

and heir apparent, became regent. A serious student of religion, keen to reconcile the differences between Hindus and Muslims, he was admired by Rajputs, whose company he enjoyed and whose support he sought against his rival brothers. He appointed Maharaja Jaswant to the viceroyalty of Malwa; and when Dara-Shikoh's ambitious, soldierly, but religiously intolerant younger brother, Prince Aurangzeb, threatened, Dara-Shikoh appointed Jaswant commander of the imperial armies.

But fate intervened at the Battle of Dharmat, when the raja's vast army, composed mostly of Rajputs, was vanquished by the smaller force of Prince Aurangzeb, a surprising outcome that altered the course of Indian history. According to legend, when Maharaja Jaswant returned to Jodhpur as a fugitive —although he retained his shield and his honor—his proud wife was so dismayed by the defeat that she barred the gates of the fort.

Aurangzeb soon captured Malwa. At the Battle of Jajau he again defeated the imperial armies; afterward, he drove off Prince Dara-Shikoh, who was eventually captured and slain. Next, he deposed Shah Jahan and imprisoned him in Agra Fort, where he died in 1666.

After usurping the throne, Aurangzeb pardoned Maharaja Jaswant and asked his help in the campaign against yet another brother, Shah Shuja͑. Jaswant, remaining secretly loyal to Prince Dara-Shikoh, warned Shah Shuja͑ of the plot. At the outset of the Battle of Khajwa, thirty miles north of Allahabad, Jaswant launched a surprise attack upon the rear flank of Aurangzeb's army, led by Prince Mu͑azzam. After hacking his way through Aurangzeb's army, Jaswant dashed ahead to the splendid and unprotected imperial camp and plundered it. A considerable part of the loot was the present tent, which was packed with the others onto camels and carried off to Jodhpur Fort.

Maharaja Jaswant's struggles against Emperor Aurangzeb had not ended. Within a few years, according to Colonel Tod, Jaswant Singh's son and heir, Prithi Singh, was summoned to the imperial court, where he was presented by the seemingly benevolent emperor with a khil͑at (robe of honor). Soon after donning it, Prithi Singh expired in great pain, envenomed through his pores. Not long thereafter, Jaswant Singh's only remaining son succumbed to the harsh climate of Afghanistan, where he had been sent with his father by Aurangzeb to quash a rebellion. In 1678 the brokenhearted Jaswant Singh died at Kabul. Aurangzeb's revenge was complete. But in Jodhpur Fort the tents remain, mutely dramatic memorials of Rathor resistance to the Mughals.

A note on the tent's later history: Maharaja Abhey Singh, son of Maharaja Ajit and grandson of Maharaja Jaswant Singh, is recorded as having used this tent in 1734 at the village of Horda near Ajmer for a meeting of the princes of Jaipur, Kotah, Bikaner, and Kishangarh. When Emperor Muhammad Shah (see no. 182) learned that the red Mughal tent had been the site of the signing of a Rajput treaty promising mutual assistance in times of war, he indicated his displeasure—until he was assured by the diplomatic maharaja that the tent had served to unite the princes under the imperial insignia against a common enemy, the Marathas. This so pleased the emperor that he issued a proclamation bestowing a khil͑at upon him.[1]

1. Ren, *History of Marwar*, part 1, pp. 347–48; reference generously supplied by Maharaj Prahlad Singh, Director, Mehrangarh Museum Trust, Jodhpur.

166.
ROCK-CRYSTAL BOWL
Mughal, mid-17th century
Height 3¼ in. (8.3 cm.), diameter 5⅞ in. (14.9 cm.)
Victoria and Albert Museum, London
(I.S. 986–1875)

DURING THE REIGN of Shah Jahan, floramania ran riot. Artist-craftsmen specializing in hardstone abraded and cut jade and rock-crystal reliefs of poppies, tulips, irises, and lilies into a treasure of splendid vessels. When Shah Jahan was in residence at Agra, Delhi, or Lahore, he regularly met with the daroghas in charge of the studios and with their craftsmen to inspect the fruits of their labors, only a very small sampling of which has survived. Each piece was unique, its compositional nuances the result of soulful dedication. After approval by the emperor, these objects reappeared in the hands of sensitively attuned servants when the mood was suitably convivial or introspective and when the lighting emphasized an object's color and design.

The vertical lobes of this rock-crystal bowl are embellished with rhyth-

166

mically aligned lilies, and the base whirls with acanthus leaves that call for sunlight. Especially brilliant when filled with red or even white wine, it was designed to be drunk from or eaten from in changing light. Regrettably, such pieces are now so revered that only a few specialists touch them, while wearing white gloves.

Published: *The Art of India and Pakistan*, p. 232, no. 1218, pl. 75; Hambly, *Cities of Mughal India*, p. 106, pl. 75; Zebrowski, "Decorative Arts of the Mughal Period," p. 187, fig. 210; *The Indian Heritage*, p. 122, no. 373.

THIS WHITE NEPHRITE wine cup probably was made in connection with the "Glorious Darbar" marking the end of the first epoch of Shah Jahan's reign. The event was celebrated at Delhi in late April 1657, the date inscribed on the cup. It is probably the most moving and artistically elevating of all Mughal jades, an object of unabashed splendor, voluptuous elegance, and tenderness. In it, the vegetal world metamorphoses into the animal, a sleight of hand and mind accomplished so slitheringly that transitions from gourd to goat are subtler than dusk.

Highly stylized and unmistakably Mughal, it is also articulately naturalistic. The goat bleats plaintively, appreciative of Shah Jahan's sadnesses earlier in life, and lamenting painful times to come.

Published: Welch, *The Art of Mughal India*, pp. 103, 176, fig. 5; Skelton, "The Shah Jahan Jade Cup," pp. 109–10, fig. 8; Skelton, *Shah Jahan's Jade Cup*; Zebrowski, "Decorative Arts of the Mughal Period," pp. 186–87, fig. 209; *The Indian Heritage*, pp. 118, 151, no. 356, pl. 12b.

167.
WINE CUP OF EMPEROR SHAH JAHAN
Inscribed with the monogram of Shah Jahan:
"Second Lord of the [auspicious] Conjunction"
Mughal, dated A.H. 1067 (1657)
White nephrite, height 2½ in. (6.4 cm.), width 5½ in. (14 cm.)
Victoria and Albert Museum, London
(I.S. 12–1962)

LIVELY ANIMAL SCULPTURE has been a staple of Indian art, not least under the Mughals, who loved, respected, and understood animals, often in the paradoxical way of hunters. Inasmuch as their religious tradition did not encourage large-scale figurative sculpture, their sculptural objects took on special importance. If small it must be, let it be wondrously small! was the credo of connoisseurs who usually conceived things either as big or little, not in between —vast forts and palaces, little pictures, and objects preciously small as jewels.

Those made to be carried brought particular pleasure. A fine dagger at the belt, accessible to eye and hand, was aesthetically satisfying as well as necessary. Like jewels, daggers indicated a Mughal's position at court. Although very fine weapons were available in the bazaars, the best ones

168.
DAGGER WITH JADE HILT IN THE FORM OF A NILGAI
Mughal, mid-17th century
Length 15 in. (38.1 cm.)
The Metropolitan Museum of Art, New York,
Gift of Alice Heeramaneck in memory of
Nasli Heeramaneck (1985.58a)

167

came from the imperial workshops, and wearing one signaled imperial approval. Thus, a courtier knew another's standing at a glance. A nobleman close to the emperor might have worn a jewel-sized portrait of Shah Jahan, while a member of Dara-Shikoh's faction proclaimed his loyalty with that prince's likeness on his turban.

A close look at the many hundreds of elegant personages thronging the miniatures of the *Padshah-nama* reveals that by far the most common form of dagger worn was the katar (no. 178), with the curved khanjar (no. 98) next in popularity, followed by the straight-bladed kard (no. 131). Only a small number of hilts with animal finials are known, and these include examples with a horse or nilgai, worn by Dara-Shikoh and Shah Shuja[c].[1] Although animal-hilted daggers—ordinarily with horses—proliferated during the seventeenth and eighteenth centuries, they were exceedingly rare during the reign of Shah Jahan. A superbly sculptured hilt such as this one portraying a nilgai, or blue bull, with its acutely sensitive observation of the animal and its marvelous craftsmanship, could only have been made in the imperial ateliers.[2]

1. In the Windsor Castle *Padshah-nama*, both Dara-Shikoh and Shah Shuja[c] wear daggers with nilgai hilts in a miniature that shows Shah Jahan receiving an embassy of Europeans (folio 115v); and in a darbar scene by Balchand, Dara-Shikoh is portrayed wearing a horse-hilted dagger (folio 72v). Few other animal hilts can be found in the manuscript, which is our most reliable source of information.
2. Another nilgai hilt, carved in lighter, blue-green jade, is in the collection of Bharat Kala Bhavan, Varanasi. See: Morley, "On Applied Arts of India in Bharat Kala Bhavan," p. 117, pl. 12.

169.
SILVER FLASK FOR ANTIMONY
Mughal, Agra or Delhi, mid-17th century
Height 3½ in. (8.9 cm.)
The Knellington Collection, Courtesy
Harvard University Art Museums,
Cambridge, Massachusetts

JAHANGIR'S AND SHAH JAHAN'S palaces contained silver furniture, ornaments, and vessels. Whatever survived into the eighteenth century caught the eyes of looters, who tossed virtually all of it into melting pots. This small screw-topped bottle somehow survived. It was made to contain antimony, a solution of kohl applied cosmetically by women and on the eyes of infants to protect them from the sun. It was cast in five parts: the stopper, which was designed so that its lobes are perfectly aligned with the acanthus leaves below; the body of the piece, melon shaped, with a stylized acanthus leaf design, cast in two parts almost invisibly fused across the middle; a disklike filler between the body and the base; and the base itself, an openwork acanthus design, riveted to the body. It was finished with a chisel file and graving tools.

Despite its small size, the flask is architectural in conception. The upwardly swelling form recalls Mughal domes and the stately, almost baroque columns of the Sawan Pavilion in the Red Fort of Delhi. Sturdily constructed and weighty, it shows signs of long use, especially near the neck, where it was repeatedly and firmly knocked against the edge of another receptacle, creating a network of royal—and humanizing—dents.[1]

1. Related to this object is part of the silver finial of a courtier's stick (Collection the Marquess of Tavistock and the Trustees of Bedford Estates) inscribed, "Carolus Rex AD 1632, Dieu et Mon Droit; Carolus Rex; Natuis Nov. 1600." The stick, however, appears to have been assembled from various places over several centuries. See: *The Indian Heritage*, p. 162, no. 552. Another notable piece of Mughal silver is the covered beaker in the Victoria and Albert Museum, London. See: Welch, *The Art of Mughal India*, pl. 61; *The Indian Heritage*, p. 112, no. 323, p. 155, pl. 14c.

169

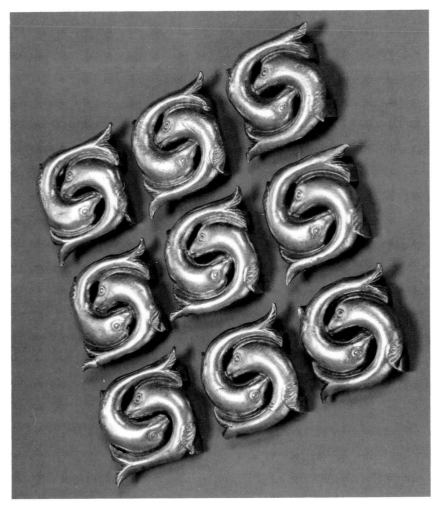

170

Paintings indicate that Mughal horses and elephants were as richly caparisoned as the princes who rode them. Bridles were often brightened with
rows of ornaments such as these, forming a rhythmic repeated pattern that
is both eye-catching and meaningful. Very similarly arranged fish, the zodia-
cal configuration of Pisces, are found on a talismanic bowl of the Jahangir
period.[1] The fish is also seen as a standard in Muslim India (see no. 219); and
during the eighteenth and nineteenth centuries, it was the heraldic symbol
of the Muslim rulers of Lucknow. One wonders if these excitingly designed
earlier examples, which bring to mind the ancient "animal style," might not
have been associated with their owner's astrological sign.

1. For the talismanic bowl, see A. Welch, *Calligraphy in the Arts*, pp. 186–87.

170.
SYMPLEGMA OF FISH: ORNAMENTS
FOR A BRIDLE
Mughal, mid-17th century
Silver with mercury gilding, diameter 1 in.
(2.5 cm.)
Private collection

Village women are frequently seen carrying huge earthen or brass vessels
of well water on their heads, a graceful balancing act—and feat of strength
—achieved with the help of a doughnut-shaped ring, or ondoni, made of
wood padded with cloth. When the huqqa, or hubble-bubble, was invented,
it was only natural that forms derived from these round waterpots and ondonis
became part of the smoking apparatus.

Against medical opinion, tobacco became greatly popular during the
seventeenth century, and princely households vied with one another in the
splendor of their smoking equipment. The simple earthenware of mouthpieces
and waterpots was transformed into jewel-encrusted jade or other precious
substances, the snakelike tube extending from pot to mouthpiece was often
adorned with jewels or pearls, and ondonis were equally opulent. The present example is the noblest we have seen, made of massive gold enriched
with marvelously enameled poppies against a white ground.

171.
RING FOR A HUQQA BOWL
Mughal, mid-17th century
Gold with vitreous enamel, height 1⅛ in.
(3 cm.), diameter 5¾ in. (14.5 cm.)
The al-Sabah Collection, Dar al-Athar
al-Islamiya, Kuwait National Museum
(LNS.2.J)

171

Although enameling was not unknown to the Mughals, and the hilt of Jahangir's dagger (no. 127) contains accents of enamel in several colors, imperial jewelers usually employed thinly sliced rubies, emeralds, and other jewels, or jewellike bits of colored glass.

Published: *Islamic Art in the Kuwait National Museum*, p. 127.

172.
OPIUM CUP IN THE FORM OF A POPPY
Mughal, mid-17th century
Jade with rubies and emeralds set in gold,
height ¾ in. (1.8 cm.), diameter 2½ in.
(6.4 cm.)
Private collection

THIS COMPACTLY POWERFUL little cup, shaped appropriately like an opium poppy, sparkled and shimmered when used to serve kawa, a potent blend of wine, spices, and opium. The handle, in the shape of a serrated poppy leaf, is inlaid with thinly sliced emeralds set in gold. It grows from the sensitively carved stem on the bottom of the cup, from which also emerge the fragile petals forming the bowl. Within, rubies and emeralds set in gold over reflective gold foil repeat the poppy motif. A central emerald, of brilliant color and purity and shaped like a mushroom, is brightened by light reflected from the surrounding white jade. The jewels, including a row of slightly rounded rubies just below the inner rim, are set with gold wire, skillfully hammered flat at the surface and often finely engraved.

This brilliant bauble, made in the imperial ateliers for the use of the emperor or someone within his immediate circle, raises the topic of opium. In small quantities, it encouraged the dreamy indolence associated with Mughal palace life; in somewhat larger doses, it eased pain; but for those considered threatening to the throne, enforced daily quaffs brought oblivion and death.

173.
GUNPOWDER FLASK
Mughal, mid-17th century
Gray-green jade, diameter 4⅜ in. (11.1 cm.)
Private collection

BY THE MID-SEVENTEENTH century, Mughal objects tended to be more splendid than practical, as is demonstrated by this powder flask in the shape of a turtle, which would have cracked if knocked too vigorously against the matchlock it served to load. Artistically moving and technically extraordinary, it was made from a large chunk of gray-green jade, appealingly enriched with mottled streaks dark as rainclouds.

172, inside

172, outside

After envisioning his design, the maker roughed in the basic shape, allowing for the floral ornament, neck, and pair of fittings shaped like lotus buds on the flat underside through which straps could be inserted. He then drilled and abraded a round opening less than an inch in diameter through which he hollowed out the inside, leaving only the very thin outer walls. After making a plug to fill in the hole and refining the reliefs of flowers, including a stylized lotus on the rounded back, he completed the flask with a final polishing. The stopper, now lost, was probably made of gold.

The flask is based on Far Eastern prototypes, exemplified by polychromed wooden Korean examples that are more explicitly formed, with heads, feet, and tails. Both probably derive from a Chinese prototype.[1]

1. Shah 'Abbas of Iran wears a similar flask at his belt in a portrait by Bishndas. See: Goddard, "Un Album de portraits des princes timurides," pp. 194–95, fig. 68. A later seventeenth-century powder flask of this shape, in white jade inlaid with jewels and enamel, is in the Victoria and Albert Museum, London. See: *Joyaux et saris de l'Inde*, p. 33, no. 4. For a Korean powder flask in the shape of a turtle, see: Moes, *Auspicious Spirits*, no. 114.

173, top

173, bottom

174

174.
FRAGMENT OF A SHAWL BORDER
Mughal, Kashmir, ca. 1640–50
Pashmina, 7¼ × 28⅜ in. (18.5 × 72 cm.)
Jagdish and Kamla Mittal Museum of Indian
Art, Hyderabad (81.2)

VERY FEW OF the brilliantly designed shawls made in Kashmir for the Mughal court have survived from the seventeenth century, and this fragment from a shawl's end border (pallav) may be the earliest known example. The masterful workmanship on loom, so appropriate for the sensitive, beautifully drawn flowering plants, gives some indication of the virtuosity and versatility of the Kashmiri shawl weavers. We can now see only in the mind's eye the many other elegant shawls these masters must have created, but we can imagine that the technique may even have excelled this exquisite work, and that each of the designs was different, for the Mughals admired not only perfection but exclusiveness.

The white ground, now turned cream, is worked in twill tapestry weave. Narrow bands filled with undulating stems bearing leaves and small, three-petaled flowers act as a surround, and the field is patterned with an evenly spaced row of delicate, naturalistic plants whose stems bend slightly under the weight of clusters of blossoms. (The borders on a complete shawl dating to the late seventeenth century that is now in the Museum of Fine Arts, Boston, each have eleven plants;[1] this border may have had the same number.) The crimson outlines on the clustered pink petals and the sprouting buds could almost be brushstrokes, and the stems and curling, scalloped leaves, in a light blue-green edged in deeper green, have been woven with the same mature skill and confidence.

The fabric is so deceptively soft, at first glance one thinks it is silk. Pashmina fabric, the fine woolen cloth used especially for Kashmiri shawls, has for centuries been prized for its lightness, warmth, and softness, and the Kashmiris have long specialized in weaving it, but the shawls made from it during the Mughal period were exceptional. Both the colored pattern and the white ground of this border are woven of shah tus (goat's fleece for a king), the rare and astonishingly fine wool collected in the Himalayas from thorn bushes on which mountain goats have scratched their beards, leaving small quantities behind. Although shawls made from less costly grades of pashmina cloth were richly embroidered, shah tus was considered so beautiful in itself and its natural colors, ranging from whites to golden tans to darker

hues, were so admired that floral patterns, like this one, were added only at the ends.

The shawl in Boston and the few other seventeenth-century shawls that survive all have the shallow borders that appear to have been the fashion until the end of the eighteenth century.[2] The borders seem to have become broader with each decade. In 1668, F. Bernier reported that Kashmiri shawls were "ornamented at both ends with a sort of embroidery, made in the loom, about a foot in width."[3] This border measures just over seven inches.

When exhibited at the Victoria and Albert Museum in London in 1982, this fragment and a group of shawls shown with it were attributed to the late seventeenth or early eighteenth century.[4] We would date the other shawls in the group from 1675 to 1700, but we believe this piece was produced earlier. The detailed, realistic execution of the flowering plants, by a weaver who seems to have faithfully followed the design he was given, perhaps by a Mughal artist, is more characteristic of Mughal decorative arts from about 1625 to 1650. By the last two decades of the seventeenth century the designs on shawls, like those on the known examples of brocades and velvets from the period, had already become stiffer, more standardized, and the outlines more angular. In overall quality and refinement, this extraordinary fragment matches the Shah Jahani carpets and velvets.[5] The superb weaving of the design and ground, in the most luxurious of materials, assures us that it was made for an enlightened patron, perhaps even Shah Jahan himself.

J.M.

1. Irwin, *The Kashmir Shawls*, pls. 5, 6.
2. Ibid., pls. 1–4, 7. For other early examples, see: Murphy, "A Note on Some Recently Discovered Tipu Shawl Fragments," pp. 161–69.
3. Bernier, *Travels in the Mogul Empire*, p. 403.
4. *The Indian Heritage*, pp. 100–101, no. 282.
5. Ibid., nos. 195, 199, 203, 219, 220.

Published: *The Indian Heritage*, pp. 100–101, no. 282, ill. p. 79.

175

175.
MIRROR
Mughal, mid-17th century
Dark green jade with gold trellis pattern inset with white jade and rubies; mirror of rock crystal, 5⅛ × 4⅜ in. (13.1 × 11.2 cm.)
Victoria and Albert Museum, London
(I.S.02587)

MUGHAL TASTE OCCASIONALLY oscillated between austerity and almost vulgar sumptuousness. Here, opulence is overshadowed by perfection of proportion and craftsmanship—and by the look of crisp, smooth, touchable coolness.

Silvered mirrors were first brought to India from the West during the Akbar period. Their success as presents and trade items was at first considerable; but too many were imported, and their novelty had so worn off by the 1620s that they were barely acceptable at court as gifts. Nevertheless, every palace worthy of the term had a shish mahal (chamber of mirrors) in which small pieces of mirror were set into the walls in arabesque patterns —magically effective by candlelight. Accounts of European travelers tell us that Shah Jahan's palace at Agra also contained many large decorative mirrors.

Published: Grube, *The World of Islam*, pp. 160, 170, no. 105.

176.
EMPEROR AURANGZEB SHOOTING NILGAI
Attributed to Hashim
Mughal, ca. 1660
Opaque watercolor on paper
Folio: 15 × 20⅛ in. (38 × 51 cm.)
Miniature: 11 × 15⅛ in. (28 × 38.5 cm.)
Chester Beatty Library, Dublin
(Ms. 11, no. 27)

MUHYI AD-DIN MUHAMMAD AURANGZEB (r. 1658–1707), who ascended the imperial throne as 'Alamgir I, was the sixth child and second son of Shah Jahan and Mumtaz-Mahal. Born in the course of an imperial progress from Gujarat to Agra in 1618, he soon experienced the realities of Mughal court life. When he was four, his father's embittered relationship with Emperor Jahangir led to open rebellion, and disrupted what might have been a joyous imperial childhood. In 1626, he and his elder brother, Crown Prince Dara-Shikoh, were demanded by Emperor Jahangir as hostages, and they remained at the imperial court, watched over by Nur-Jahan, until after Jahangir's death.

Highly intelligent, Aurangzeb (Jewel in the Throne) learned Arabic, Persian, Chaghatai Turkish, and Hindi; his calligraphy—in Naskhi, Nasta'liq, and Shikasta script—was excellent. At an early age, he mastered the Qur'an and the Prophetic Traditions (Hadith). But he was not a withdrawn intellectual. At fourteen, while attending an elephant combat at Agra with his father and brothers, he ventured too close to the hulking beasts, one of whom, Sudhakar, charged him. Aurangzeb held steady, controlling his terrified horse, and hurled a spear at the advancing brute. With a sweep of his tusks, the elephant knocked down the prince's horse. Aurangzeb got to his feet, drew his sword, and confronted his outraged and colossal attacker. Astounded observers soon came to his rescue. Prince Shuja' cantered over and thrust a spear into the elephant's trunk, for which brave act he was tossed to the ground; Raja Jai Singh of Amber joined the fray—as did a throng of imperial guards armed with spears and poles topped with spinning fireworks, a standard device for controlling elephants. The episode ended when Suratsundar, the maddened elephant's opponent, renewed his attack and drove Sudhakar from the field. Aurangzeb's bravery was established.

Other qualities contributed even more to his success. Unlike his older brother Dara-Shikoh's spiritual proclivities which followed the pattern of religious toleration set by Akbar, Aurangzeb's rigorous Muslim orthodoxy conformed precisely to the spirit of his time. All through life, he copied out Qur'ans, which he presented to holy shrines at Mecca and Medina and in India. Once, during a pitched battle, he astounded the enemy by calmly getting down from his mount, spreading his mat, and praying. History has shown that Aurangzeb could also be ruthlessly practical, and at times brilliantly devious.

In the perspective of time, Aurangzeb emerges as a complex and fascinating man, and a highly controversial one. Was he a marble-hearted, power-mad bigot? Or a highly intelligent, troubled figure struggling to conform to an elevated, fiercely puritanical code, even more demanding of himself than of others? During his reign, the Mughal empire reached its peak in size and wealth. At last, the rival sultanates of the Deccan were defeated and joined to the empire. But Mughal power was in decline. Aurangzeb spent most of his years struggling to control sprawling, often rebellious provinces; and as he lay dying, at the age of ninety, he wrote troubled letters confessing that his grand schemes had failed.

Aurangzeb was forty when he seized power from his ailing father and carried out his cruelly effective plots against his brothers. A fabulous empire was his, with all its magnificent treasures, superb cities, forts, and palaces, and vast human resources. At first, apparently, he found pleasure in his new grandeur. He mounted the Peacock Throne, wore the imperial jewels, viewed the treasures of the library, inscribing his name in many of its great manuscripts, listened to the court musicians, and carried on the traditions of artistic patronage. His enthronement as Emperor 'Alamgir (Seizer of the Universe), the culmination of two months of festivities, was held at Delhi on June 5, 1658, a day declared astrologically auspicious. The ceremony was notable for its splendor, outdoing all previous imperial Mughal celebrations. The richest jewels and objects of art were assembled from the royal treasuries, jeweled gold globes and magnificent textiles were suspended from the ceilings and arches, musicians and dancers performed, and fireworks turned the skies over the Jamuna River into a fiery paradise.

In 1659, Aurangzeb commissioned a small but superb mosque in the Red Fort at Delhi, a building that took five years to complete and represents the emperor's usually unexpressed—and too seldom recognized —taste for the arts. The mosque's intimate scale and white marble reliefs, with succulent still-life carvings of fruits and almost rococo ornament, sheds appealing light on the usually austere, self-denying emperor.

Aurangzeb was also a perceptive and enthusiastic patron of painting—at the outset of his reign. *Emperor Aurangzeb Shooting Nilgai* completely belies its patron's reputed lack of interest in the arts. The landscape, probably in the southern Deccan, stretches out past a perspective view of imperial elephants, a town, and a fort, all painted in copious and accurate detail. The young ruler has just fired the bullet, striking his quarry through the heart. Ahead of him the tame nilgai, which had lured his fellow creature to the kill, seems startled, and cognizant of his role in the plot.

This great picture can be ascribed to Hashim, a remarkable artist who also painted a famous portrait of Aurangzeb receiving his son, Muhammad A'zam, with an assemblage of courtiers.[1] Just as Govardhan, who specialized in ethereal portrayals of holy men, can be associated with Prince Dara-Shikoh, so can Hashim, known for his keenly observed depictions of courtly magnificence, be linked to Aurangzeb, for whom he painted these two ex-

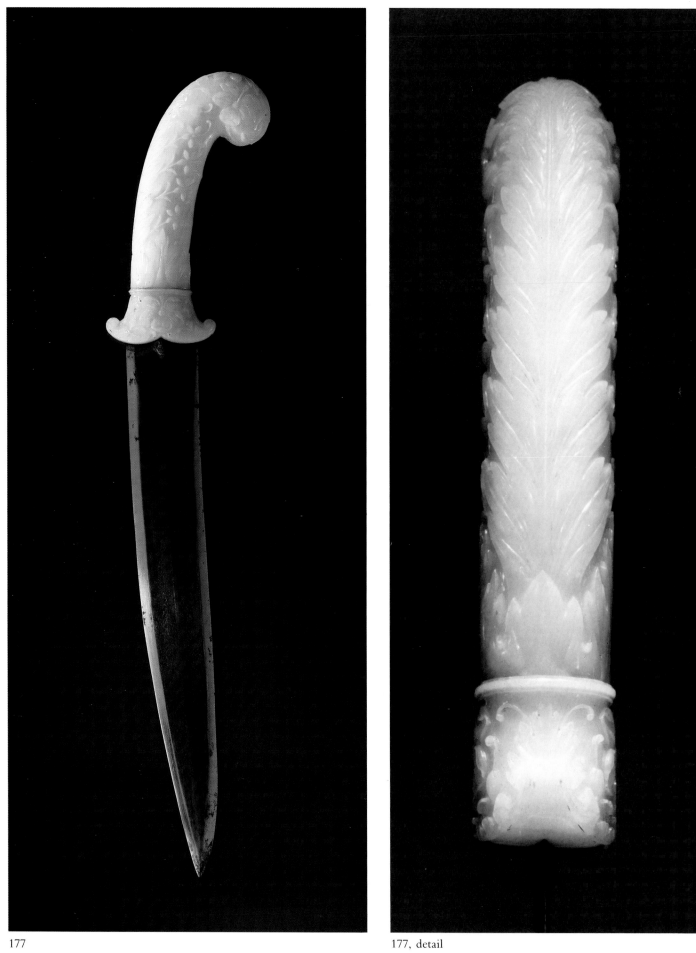

177

177, detail

traordinary miniatures before the emperor's enthusiasm for painting was smothered by puritanical orthodoxy.

1. For Hashim's portrait of Aurangzeb and his son, see: Welch, *Imperial Mughal Painting*, pl. 37 (there attributed to Bichitr).

Published: Arnold, *The Library of A. Chester Beatty*, vol. 1, p. 48, no. XXVII, vol. 3, pl. 90; Welch, *The Art of Mughal India*, pp. 122, 176, fig. 6; Welch, *Imperial Mughal Painting*, pp. 114–15, pl. 38; *In the Image of Man*, p. 155, no. 212.

IF WEAPONS CAN be lyrical, this one is. Organic as a seashell, with its row of gently swaying flowers along the grip, acanthus leaves, and unexcelled craftsmanship, this dagger is the finest of the pistol-grip type. It can be assigned to an imperial artist-craftsman, perhaps to the genius who made Shah Jahan's gourd-into-goat wine cup (no. 167). Presumably, it was carved for Aurangzeb, who is shown wearing a very similar weapon in the portrait of him hunting nilgai (no. 176). A thorough search through the miniatures of the Windsor *Padshah-nama*, the best source for weaponry at Shah Jahan's court, reveals no examples of this form of hilt, which first appears in portraits of Aurangzeb. The origin of the form can be traced to the Deccan, where it must have been admired by Aurangzeb and adapted for his use during his years there as viceroy. In early stages of their evolution, which probably began in the southern Deccan, pistol grips terminated not in the familiar rounded abstract shape but in parrot heads, complete with beaks and eyes. Deccani examples of the seventeenth century (such as no. 202) already incorporate this change. After Aurangzeb had established a vogue for them, pistol-grip hilts became common at the Mughal court during the late seventeenth and the eighteenth century; some of them archaistically repeat the original parrot design.

Published: *Notable Acquisitions 1982–1983*, pp. 12–13.

177.
KHANJAR
Mughal, ca. 1640
Watered steel and white nephrite,
length 14⅜ in. (36.5 cm.)
The Metropolitan Museum of Art, New York,
Purchase, Mr. and Mrs. Nathaniel Spear, Jr.
Gift (1982.321)

THIS RICHLY JEWELED katar, with its attractive white enameling and jewels set in gold, is of a sort especially favored by Shah Jahan. Lighter in weight and with a less thick blade than most katars, it was designed to be impressive at court, not, like workaday examples, to stab. Its basic form is unique to India, and it is represented frequently in the *Hamza-nama*, as well as in other early Mughal manuscripts. The type, with its peculiar triangular blade and hilt composed of two straight uprights, to protect the hand and wrist, with crossbars between, probably originated in southern India. Many examples, with richly ornamented steel hilts, are known from Tanjore. We have not found them in paintings from pre-Mughal Rajput, Sultanate, or western Indian sources. They seem to have been common, however, in the Deccan and at Rajput courts of the Mughal period.

178.
KATAR
Mughal, mid-17th century
Steel blade, gold and enamel hilt with rubies,
emeralds, and diamonds, length 15¾ in.
(40 cm.)
Collection Moke Mokotoff, New York

179.
FLOOR SPREAD
Probably Burhanpur, late 17th or
early 18th century
Cotton, resist dyed, 9 ft. 10¼ in. × 12 ft. 8 in.
(3 × 3.86 m.)
Private collection

179

To SIT AND EAT upon at courts of the Mughal period, printed and painted cotton dastarkanas, or floor spreads, sometimes referred to as "summer carpets," were stretched out, held down at the edges by ornamental weights, or mir-e farsh (lords of the carpet). During the luxurious late seventeenth century, scores of artistically marvelous textiles, representing months or even years of work by skilled craftsmen, were used once or twice, and discarded as too worn for princely use. Those in charge of the palace stores, however, laid up stocks of floor spreads, dress lengths, velvets, and other yardage in untold numbers and looked after them so well that a few—like this one—survived pristinely in godowns to this day.

With its central pattern of naturalistically drawn block-printed poppies silhouetted against a white field, and its sensuously scrolling blossoms, vines, and leaves against the muted earth green of the border, the design of this floor spread is bold enough to stun at a distance and fine enough to enjoy close at hand. The flowers, with their carefully modeled petals, spirited leaves, and vestigial roots, bring to mind the painted poppy from the Rajput court of Kishangarh (no. 248). That the painted poppy is presumably by an artist who had migrated from Burhanpur, the major Mughal center in the Deccan, further supports the supposition that this dastarkana is from the same city, which was noted for its printed and drawn cottons in Mughal style.[1]

1. Sections of very similar floor spreads are in the National Museum of India, New Delhi; Calico Museum of Textiles, Ahmedabad (see: Irwin and Hall, *Historic Textiles of India*, pp. 33–34, nos. 23, 24, pl. 9); Victoria and Albert Museum, London; The Metropolitan Museum of Art, New York; and private collections.

179, detail

180, front

180, back

EMERORS, SULTANS, AND their courtiers were passionate collectors and connoisseurs of precious stones, which they bought, wore, gave and received as gifts, and ordered carved in pleasing patterns. This remarkably large, splendidly carved emerald, of excellent color and quality, is adorned on one side with conventionalized flowers in Mughal style and on the other with a Shiʿite inscription with blessings for the twelve imams.

At the top appears "The Merciful One, The Compassionate One"; beneath:

> O God
> God bless Muhammad and ʿAli
> and Fatima and al-Husain
> and al-Hasan and ʿAli
> and Muhammad and Jaʿfar
> and Musa
> 1107 [1695]
> and ʿAli and Muhammad
> and ʿAli
> and al-Husaini and the steadfast Mahdi.

A Colombian emerald, it might have reached India as part of the stock of an international gem dealer, such as Jean-Baptiste Tavernier, whose six voyages to India between 1641 and 1667 enabled him to write *Travels in India*, a fascinating firsthand account of the country and its people. In 1665, before leaving India, he was summoned by the emperor, who was eager that he be shown the imperial jewels. Tavernier was conducted into a small apartment, where the emperor was seated on his throne. "I found in this apartment ʿAkil Khan, chief of the jewel treasury, who, when he saw us, commanded four of the imperial eunuchs to bring the jewels, which were carried in two large wooden trays lacquered with gold leaf, and covered with small cloths made especially for the purpose—one of red and the other of green brocaded velvet. After these trays were uncovered, and all the pieces had been

180.
INSCRIBED EMERALD
Mughal, dated A.H. 1107 (1695–96)
217.8 carats, 2 × 1½ in. (5.1 × 3.8 cm.)
Collection Allan Caplan, New York

counted three times over, a list was prepared by three scribes who were present. For the Indians do everything with great circumspection and patience, and when they see any one who acts with precipitation, or becomes angry, they gaze at him without saying anything, and smile as if he were a madman.

"The first piece which ʿAkil Khan placed in my hands was the great diamond [apparently the famed Koh-i Nur, a large part of which is now set in the British crown], which is a round rose, very high at one side. At the basal margin it has a small notch and flaw inside. Its water is beautiful, and it weighs 319½ ratis, which are equal to 280 of our carats. . . . When Mir Jumla, who betrayed the King of Golconda, his master, presented this stone to Shah Jahan . . . it was then in the rough, and weighed . . . 787½ carats; and it had several flaws."

Tavernier continued his account of his viewing of the Mughal jewels with a description of the cutting of the "great diamond" by one Sieur Hortensio Borgio, who "spoilt the stone, which ought to have retained a greater weight; and instead of paying him for his work, the Emperor fined him 10,000 rupees, and would have taken more if he had possessed it . . . he was not a very accomplished diamond cutter." He was then shown a pear-shaped diamond, "of good form and fine water," other fine diamonds, several jewels composed of diamonds, and some splendid pearls, one of which "of a lively white . . . is the only jewel which Aurangzeb . . . has himself purchased on account of its beauty, for the rest either came to him from Dara-Shikoh, his eldest brother, he having appropriated them after he had caused his head to be cut off, or they were presents made to him after he ascended the throne. I have elsewhere remarked that the Emperor has no great regard for jewels, priding himself only on being a great zealot of the law of Muhammad."[1]

Because the present emerald is inscribed with Shiʿite formulas, more appropriate at courts of the Deccan, such as Golconda, it might have been carved for a Deccani prince.

1. Tavernier, *Travels in India*, vol. 1, pp. 314–19.

Published: Caplan, "An Important Carved Emerald," pp. 1336–37; Bancroft, "Great Gems and Crystal Mines," p. 165; Sinkankas, *Emerald and Other Beryls*, p. 113; *Sweat of the Sun,* pl. 5; Bari and Poirot, *Larousse*, pp. 132–33.

181.
JAR AND COVER
Mughal, ca. 1700
Cloisonné enamel on gold, height 5⅝ in. (14.3 cm.)
The Cleveland Museum of Art, Purchase from the J. H. Wade Fund (62.206)

THIS SMALL JAR belies its size and the elegance of its decoration by sitting assertively. The crisply articulate enameling—in white, green, translucent yellow, and pink—reminds us of both Mughal carpet designs and manuscript illumination. Although the technique was employed at the Mughal court at least as early as the Jahangir period (see nos. 127, 129), few early examples have survived, both because of the imperial preference for jewels and because of its fragility, for enamel cracks and splinters as easily as glass.

The technique is complex, and in India is practiced by family workshops whose secrets have been passed on from one generation to the next. After the object to be enameled has been made by a metalsmith, preferably of gold, with its wall-like enclosures to contain the enamel, the surface is prepared by the master craftsman. He engraves designs and neatly scars the surface with striations to hold fast the enamels, which are made of finely ground colored glass or minerals. While a small tubular charcoal-burning oven, open at the front, heats up to the required temperature, the enameler selects his glassy materials from the small flasks in which they are stored and mixes them with water on a palettelike receptacle. With a fine spatula, he then fills the enclosure walls with the slightly gritty substances, which must be applied and fired one by one in prescribed order, lest the progressive applications of heat damage the less hardy ones. Gripping the object with tongs, he then places it in the oven, allowing it to heat just long enough to vitrify into a desirably smooth surface. He inspects the work frequently, and progresses from one color to the next until the work is done.

Published: Welch, *The Art of Mughal India*, pp. 123, 172, no. 62; *The Indian Heritage*, p. 112, no. 324.

182

THE MUGHAL EMPIRE, after the death of Aurangzeb in 1707, could be likened to a magnificent flower slowly wilting and occasionally dropping a petal, its brilliance fading, its stalk bending ever lower. The grand legend persisted. The empire was still admired for its civilization; it remained awesomely rich and was even feared for its lingering might; but the nine emperors who ruled between 1707 and the exile of the last Mughal ruler in 1858 lacked stature. The infinite vision of Babur and Akbar had narrowed; Jahangir's imperial curiosity, Shah Jahan's refined sense of governmental responsibility, and Aurangzeb's ambition, piety, and sadness—all were replaced at best by specimens of poignant weakness, royal foolery, admirable stoicism, and tragicomic reveling.

Raushan Akhtar Muhammad Shah (r. 1719–48), known as Rangila (the Pleasure Loving), perfectly exemplifies a wilting imperial blossom, especially in this twilight image. One sympathizes both with the ladies assigned to carry their bulky, rather adenoidal king and with Muhammad Shah, whose lot was less easy than this picture suggests. At the age of eighteen, he had been placed on the Mughal throne by two unscrupulous and ambitious governors, the Sayyid brothers, who saw him as a docile puppet. They were mistaken. Assisted by Nizam al-Mulk of Hyderabad, the kingmakers were disposed of by assassination and poison. For this service, the nizam was appointed vizier; but in 1722 he withdrew to Hyderabad to strengthen his own now virtually independent kingdom. Sadly for the empire, and for Muhammad Shah, other rich provinces of the empire, Oudh and Bengal, also became in effect separate domains. Moreover, the Marathas spread their power far and wide; Agra was captured by the Jats; the Rohilla Afghans founded Rohilkhand; and in the Punjab, the Sikhs usurped the central power. Without these territories Muhammad Shah's empire had reverted to a size not much larger than that inherited by Akbar.

182.
EMPEROR MUHAMMAD SHAH
CARRIED IN A PALANQUIN BY LADIES
Mughal, ca. 1735
Opaque watercolor on paper
Folio: 16 × 20 in. (40.6 × 50.8 cm.)
Miniature: 10⅜ × 14 in. (26.4 × 35.6 cm.)
Collection Kasturbhai Lalbhai, Ahmedabad

Although weakened, Muhammad Shah persevered. But he realized that his and the empire's great days were over, and he decided to make the best of it. Blessed with a talent for pleasure, Muhammad Shah yielded to most temptations, some of which were respectable, or even admirable. He supervised the creation and re-creation of beautiful gardens; and he delighted in the conventional triad of joys: the wine was excellent, as were the women, and for him song was especially rewarding. He was a gifted musician and poet. If Mughal power was failing disastrously, Mughal culture was not.

Acceptance became Muhammad Shah's policy. As his political strength waned, he found ever greater diversion in gardens, poetry readings, recitals, gastronomy, painting, and lovemaking. With such consolations and the advice of holy men, Muhammad Shah stood fast—until the combination of imperial wealth and weakness sparked trouble. Nadir Shah of Iran, a greedy Turkman soldier of fortune, led an army into India in 1739. The imperial forces gave way, and the piratical Iranian marched into Delhi, where Muhammad Shah played the roles of host and victim. Despite efforts to suppress violence, a scuffle led to wholesale slaughter. When Nadir Shah and his armies finally left, they carted off enough treasure to enrich dozens of great libraries and art museums. Muhammad Shah especially regretted the loss of a favorite series of pictures, Akbar's *Dastan-i Amir Hamza* (see no. 91). A small parade of exceptionally strong camels labored under the dead weight of another major imperial possession, now dismantled—that splendid symbol of Mughal supremacy, the Peacock Throne (see no. 154).

Although historians dwell on Muhammad Shah's political and military failures, art connoisseurs judge him less severely. For Rangila's artists served him well, blending moods with the expertise of a skilled perfumer. In this riverside view at dusk, nostalgia, dissolution, and poignant luxury are concocted by a gifted painter from marvelous women, superb ornament, and the wistful, not quite obese emperor.[1]

1. For other pictures of Muhammad Shah, see: Welch, *The Art of Mughal India*, nos. 77, 78; Welch, *Imperial Mughal Painting*, pl. 39; Falk and Archer, *Indian Miniatures*, no. 160.

183.
TURBAN JEWELS: JIGHA AND SARPATI
Mughal, Bengal, Murshidabad, ca. 1757
Gold and silver set with diamonds, emeralds, rubies, sapphire, and pearl; champlevé enamel on reverse, height 8⅛ in. (20.6 cm.)
Victoria and Albert Museum, London
(I.S.3–1982)

"A ROSE AND plume composed of diamonds, rubies, sapphires, and emeralds, which though not of great value made a pompous appearance"—such was the contemporary description by Edward Ives of this turban ornament, a bauble vibrant with history. The provinces of Mughal India were being dismembered bit by bit, and the ornament was a reward from an elderly Mughal nobleman, Mir Ja'far 'Ali Khan, to Admiral Charles Watson, who with Robert Clive had set him up as nawab of Bengal following the Battle of Plassey in 1757. The appointment of this amenable gentleman to replace the defeated nawab Siraj ad-Daula, the last Mughal governor of Bengal to stand up against the British, marked the transition from Bengal as a state allied to the British to one sponsored by them and wholly under their control. Henceforth, the British were committed to ruling not only Bengal but in due course all of India.

Jewels waxed in size, if not in quality, as Mughal power waned, and their designs decreased in inventiveness and authority. Nevertheless, these feather and flower ornaments, enlivened with pendant emerald and baroque pearl, are both impressive and engagingly playful. The plumelike jigha was intended for the upper front part of the turban; the sarpati, designed as three flowerlike elements, each with a large central stone surrounded by petals set with diamonds, was held beneath it by ropes of pearls swagged around the turban. However "pompous" the jewels might have seemed to some eighteenth-century British eyes, Admiral Watson, once home, included them in a family portrait.

Published: Stronge, "Mughal Jewellery," pp. 2–6; Sotheby's, London, April 22, 1983, lot 274, with illustration showing a portrait of Admiral Watson wearing Indian dress, including these jewels.

I am indebted to Susan Stronge for her generosity in making available to me the results of her extensive and original research.

ARTFULLY SNIPPED FROM the wing covert of a male Impeyan pheasant[1]—a bird found in the Himalayas at eight to ten thousand feet in Afghanistan, Tibet, and Bhutan—the electrifyingly vivid metallic greens and copper red of this sarpech blaze in sunlight, outdazzling comparable turban ornaments made from precious stones set in gold. In paintings, rajas in the hunting field wear feathered turban ornaments, perhaps in the hope that such natural adornments will not alarm the lions or tigers. Frequently, in pictures, Lord Krishna, splendid as a peacock, is crested with feathers; and it is conceivable that this sarpech was intended for a devotee dancing the role of the god during a festival or rite.

1. Named after Mary, Lady Impey; see no. 281.

184.
FEATHER SARPECH
Mughal or Rajput, Rajasthan, 18th century
Height 5 in. (12.7 cm.)
Private collection

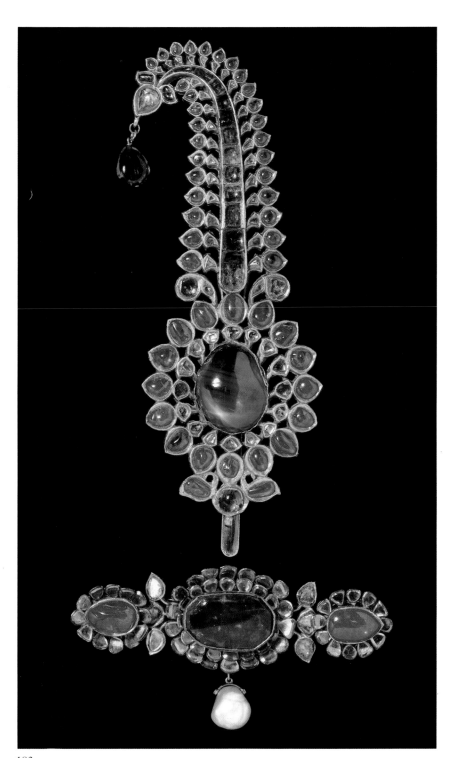

183

184

185

185.
HUQQA BOWL
Mughal, 18th century
Painted glass, height 8 in. (20.3 cm.), diameter
6¾ in. (17.2 cm.)
Los Angeles County Museum of Art, from
the Nasli and Alice Heeramaneck Collection,
Museum Associates Purchase (M.76.2.12)

THE GLASS BLOWER of this piece made a rewardingly perfect shape; and the enamel painter decorated it with rhythmically lively lotus flowers harmoniously matched to the rounded bowl. Not intended for the isolation of a museum vitrine, the bowl once added a small accent to an ambience crowded with exciting objects: a striped or flowered floor spread, trays of sweetmeats, wine bottles and cups, an incense burner, lamps, and, most ornamental of all, the prince and his courtiers and attendants.

Glassmaking in India can be traced back to Chalcolithic times. Glass bangles have been found in southern Baluchistan, and vitreous material was unearthed at Harappa. During the Akbar period, European glass was brought to the Mughal court in the form of spectacles, drinking glasses, and mirrors. Seventeenth- and eighteenth-century Mughal and Rajput pictures show glass flasks and cups of many varieties, most of which appear to be of Indian manufacture.

Published: Welch, *The Art of Mughal India*, p. 174, pl. 81; *The Arts of India and Nepal*, no. 234; Dikshit, *History of Indian Glass*, p. xib; *The Indian Heritage*, pp. 124–25, no. 386.

186.
IN A HAREM GARDEN
Attributed to Faiz Allah
Mughal, Faizabad, ca. 1765
Opaque watercolor on paper, 17¾ × 12⅝ in.
(45 × 32 cm.)
The David Collection, Copenhagen (46/1980)

WHILE THE MUGHAL empire weakened at the center, major provincial capitals flourished at Faizabad and Lucknow in Oudh, Murshidabad in Bengal, and Hyderabad in the Deccan. Poets, dancers, musicians, and artists, lured by generous patronage, moved from Delhi to these new centers of culture and power, where nostalgia for home often added to the temper of their work.

The pattern of events in Oudh was characteristic. Emperor Muhammad Shah appointed Saʿadat Khan Burhan al-Mulk to the governorship in 1724. Three years later, he had become its autonomous ruler, while retaining the title of governor, and established a dynasty that survived until the British exiled Wajid ʿAli Shah to Calcutta a year before the Sepoy Rebellion of 1857.

Although Saʿadat Khan is not known as a patron, his successors made their marks on the arts. Safdar Jang (r. 1739–54) is noted for his fine tomb and garden in Delhi. Under his son, Jalal ad-Din Haidar Shujaʿ ad-Daula (r. 1754–75), and grandson, Asaf ad-Daula (r. 1775–97), Lucknow and Faizabad developed from provincial Mughal centers into courts notable for their particularly perfumed "nawabi" extremes. During the late eighteenth century, following the Battle of Baksar in 1764, the British presence was felt; and by 1775, the culture of Oudh was becoming markedly cosmopolitan, exotic, and eccentric.

In a Harem Garden so swarms with late Mughal pleasantries it fairly bursts its borders. Begums of every degree of seniority and their myriad attendants inhabit a multilevel suite of idealized palaces surrounded by formal gardens and set within a landscape that stretches across the world. The ladies loll, smoke huqqas, perform and listen to music, draw, fly kites, play with yo-yos, and long for their beloveds, who are probably among the lively hunters barely visible beyond the bridge. They are delicately reminded of love's pangs by the peacock on the roof, who turns masterfully to his hen. Wherever we look this pictorial aviary, containing as many cranes and ducks as women, hints of the birds' freedom—in contrast to the ladies' imprisonment in their Indian rococo cage, as is evident from its adamantine walls and even more adamantine amazons who bracket the foreground.

Faiz Allah, to whom this wedding cake of a picture can be attributed, created here a wonderland of perspective. Colonnades, watercourses, verdant allées, and many-storied pavilions dance to the rhythm of his vanishing points, sprinkled like confetti and charging the already festive atmosphere. Another European technique—the diminution of forms in space—is also applied here, in the elfin junior wives at play on looming pavilion terraces.[1]

1. For a signed painting by Faiz Allah, see: Welch, *Room for Wonder*, no. 33.

A HAPPY AND ornamental young couple long for one another with well-bred discretion in an idyllic setting rustling with flowers in the breeze and suggestively amorous animals. With beguiling coyness, the lovers sit under a decorative tree joyously stocked with songbirds while listening to a not distractingly beautiful musician. In creating this eighteenth-century Lucknow "Valentine," Mir Kalan flirts daringly with romantic tenderness that edges on sentimentality and archness, a considerable achievement—and one characteristic of the late Mughal culture of Oudh. To do so, he plucked ideas and motifs from many sources. The mood is akin to that of Lucknow gazals, sweetly spiced love lyrics, while the couple was translated from Riza ʿAbbasi's languorously cloying seventeenth-century Safavid counterparts. With additional touches of eighteenth-century French boudoirie, Mir Kalan produced a thoroughly delightful fantasy. Pleasure-bent as the picture might seem, it also can be interpreted mystically: the couple loving one another in their garden become souls loving God in paradise.

Iranian elements frequently contributed to the zest of Lucknow art, which often reflected the frivolity of the later Safavid court. This link to Iran, which was shared with Hyderabad, gained strength from the fact that the nawabs of Lucknow, like the Safavid shahs, were Shiʿite rather than Sunni Muslims. On the other hand, one might ascribe the fundamental seriousness of most imperial Mughal art to the dynasty's firm Sunni affiliations, and to their rivalry with the Safavids.

THIS SPLENDIDLY CAST pair of bronze cannon unites European, presumably French, rococo elegance with imaginative Indian splendor. Cast for Tipu Sultan, who was known as "the Tiger," their muzzles, trunions, and cascabels and even the dolphins on the barrels end in tigers' heads. One barrel is marked with the sword of ʿAli, the other with a dagger within a field of tiger stripes. More to the Mughal taste, the muzzle astragals are in the form

187.
LOVERS IN A LANDSCAPE
By Mir Kalan Khan
Mughal, Lucknow, ca. 1775
Opaque watercolor on paper, 8¾ × 6 in.
(22.2 × 15.2 cm.)
The David Collection, Copenhagen (50/1981)

188.
A PAIR OF CANNON
Mysore, Seringapatam, late 18th century
Bronze, with brass bearing, length 46 in.
(116.8 cm.), diameter 18 in. (45.7 cm.)
Private collection

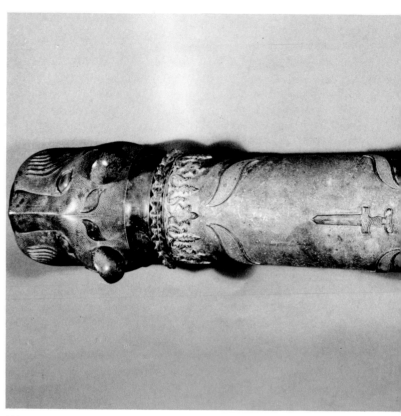

188

of chains, edged with a pattern of flowers and leaves. Like the turban ornament from Bengal (no. 183), the cannon, which were probably made in Tipu's own foundries at Seringapatam, bring to notice an important chapter of history.

Muslim power was not limited to northern India. During the mid-eighteenth century, in the peaceful and prosperous Hindu state of Mysore, Haidar ʿAli, an illiterate but canny Muslim soldier of fortune, entered the service of Nanraj, the prime minister. Courageous, obliging, and burningly ambitious, Haidar took over the powers of Nanraj and, expanding his territories by the sword, subjugated many adjoining principalities. A suddenly militant and Muslim Mysore alarmed the Marathas, the nizam of Hyderabad, and the British, who saw it as a threat to Madras. In 1765 the Marathas invaded Mysore, forcing Haidar to forfeit lands and pay a generous indemnification. A year later, the British joined with the nizam and repeated the plot; and soon, a triple alliance further menaced the Muslim upstart, who countered by buying off the Marathas. But partners changed as at a cotillion: when the British and the nizam's armies invaded Mysore in 1767, the nizam turned coat, siding with Haidar. The British triumphed, and they now allied with Haidar, promising to come to his aid if another power attacked.

When the Marathas assailed Haidar in 1771, however, the British did nothing. Haidar's mounting displeasure broke forth in 1779, when he joined the Marathas and the nizam in a grand confederacy against them. In July 1780, Haidar, at the head of 80,000 men and 100 guns, attacked the British in the Carnatic. He seized Arcot, so alarming the British that Warren Hastings dispatched an army under Sir Eyre Coote, commander-in-chief in India. Haidar was defeated at Porto Novo in 1781.

Haidar's day was ending. Within two years he succumbed to cancer. But the wars continued. Haidar was succeeded by his son Tipu Sultan (1749–1799), who was equally brave and warlike and who became a legend of cruelty in England, where his polychromed wooden tiger, devouring an Englishman who screeches at the turn of a crank, is a popular exhibit in the Victoria and Albert Museum. For the time being, however, the British favored peace. In 1784 they signed the Treaty of Mangalore with Tipu, to the

displeasure of Lord Cornwallis, governor-general of India, who differed with this policy. Fearing the alliance between Tipu and the French, and believing an attack was imminent, he sought alignment with the nizam, so offending Tipu that in 1789 he invaded Travancore, a state under British protection. Cornwallis, the nizam, and the Marathas now conspired against Tipu in a campaign that lasted two years.

The alliance was potent and relentless. Bangalore, Tipu's metropolis, was captured in March 1791, and by May 13 Lord Cornwallis's armies neared his capital, Seringapatam. But Tipu's abilities as strategist and diplomat held them at bay; and although forced to surrender half his dominions to the alliance in 1792, he remained alive and independent.

Ever resourceful, Tipu rebuilt his fortifications and armies. He also revived his alliance with the French, thereby outraging yet another Englishman, Lord Wellesley, who had succeeded Lord Cornwallis. Wellesley joined with the Marathas and attacked. Tipu lost two battles before withdrawing to Seringapatam, where against discouraging odds he fought bravely to the death.

Admired in India as a pioneer anticolonialist, Tipu Sultan in the West has evoked responses mixed as those to hot chillies—mouth-puckering but strangely appealing. In his day, he caught the public fancy; and his renown has been kept alive by the many works of art associated with his life and death. Scores of English engravings, lithographs, drawings, and paintings document his wickedness while depicting his slayers' glory. His polychromed wooden tiger still roars while its prone Englishman howls, his tent and other souvenirs are prized by the descendants of Lord Clive, and at Seringapatam, visitors stroll fascinated through his palaces, gardens, and mosque. His pair of cannon, perhaps dating to the time of his alliance with the French, evokes Tipu's elegance, and recall his quixotic stand against incomparably greater forces.[1]

1. An almost identical pair, found in the fort at Seringapatam along with 371 other "brass guns" and a large number of other weapons, is illustrated in Porter, *The Storming of Seringapatam*, p. 139.

Published: *The Indian Heritage*, p. 140, no. 467.

THE SULTANS
OF THE DECCAN

189.
RAHL
Deccan, probably Ahmadnagar,
ca. 1588–89
Bronze, inset with turquoise,
height 18½ in. (47 cm.)
Collection Mian Bashir Wali Mohamed, London

IT IS APPROPRIATE that the rahl to support the holy book of a religion from the stark desert lands of Arabia should be a simple stand of crossed boards, a sensible furnishing designed to hold a Qurʾan open to a chosen folio in a mosque, in a madrasa, or at home. Rahls were initially made of wood, perhaps by makers of camel saddles. Although the fundamental structure remained as sparely practical as the saddle which may have inspired it, in time Qurʾan stands were enriched with carved arabesques and made from materials that were scarcely austere. Some Indian rahls, honoring the book's sanctity while proclaiming the owner's or donor's piety and wealth, were made of precious metals or jade, occasionally inlaid with gems.

This rahl, of cast and chased bronze inlaid with turquoise, is embellished with pierced arabesques and calligraphic inscriptions in Naskhi script. Although most of the inscriptions are invocations to God and praises of Shiʿite imams, one of them reads, "During the time of the sultan of the time, Shah Sultan Husain Dinparvar [Protector of the Faith]." It seems likely that this object was commissioned by Sultan Husain II, who reigned at Ahmadnagar for only one year, in 1588–89. The working of the calligraphy and the style and material of the stand relate to metalwork from the Deccan.

Ahmadnagar was one of the five Deccani sultanates that broke off from the Bahmanid kingdom during the late fifteenth and early sixteenth centuries. In 1490, Malik Ahmad routed the Bahmanid army and established himself, with the title of Ahmad Nizam-Shah, as an independent ruler at Junnar, north of Poona. He later moved the Nizam-Shahi capital eastward to his new city of Ahmadnagar. In 1499, Ahmad strengthened his dominions by capturing the great fortress of Daulatabad. Although the Nizam-Shahi dynasty ruled until 1636, when its territories were finally annexed by Shah Jahan, decline had set in by the late sixteenth century. Following a brief but debauched reign, Husain Shah II, who was married to the sister of Sultan Ibrahim ʿAdil-Shah II of Bijapur, was imprisoned, blinded, and put to death (see also nos. 193–95).

190

190.
THE SULTAN OF AHMADNAGAR,
PROBABLY BURHAN AL-MULK II
Inscribed, on the back: "Burhan Nizam al-
Mulk . . . the earliest work of the Deccan"
Deccan, Ahmadnagar, late 16th century
Opaque watercolor on paper
Miniature: 9¼ × 8⅛ in. (23.5 × 20.5 cm.)
Bibliothèque Nationale, Paris, Cabinet des
Manuscrits, Section Orientale.
(Supp. Persan. 1572)

ROUNDER THAN THE bolster behind him, this Ahmadnagar prince, probably
Burhan al-Mulk II (r. 1591–95), exemplifies good living and conveys an air
of authority that extended at least as far as his kitchens. Pictorially, his
massiveness seems weightless; and compared to contemporary figure paintings from the Mughal court, it lacks muscle. Although the picture delights
the eye, its qualities lack the vital surge of Akbar's art. However rotund the
forms, they are scarcely palpable; and against the golden ground, Burhan's
throne hovers in limbo, suggesting uneasily that if its occupant became flesh,
bone, and blood, the thin gold legs would bend and snap.

Burhan al-Mulk II, whose name is inscribed on the back of this portrait, was the brother of Murtaza Nizam-Shah I of Ahmadnagar, who was more admirable for his patronage of the arts than for his statesmanship. The chronicles of Murtaza's reign wobble from rhapsodies on his judiciousness, wisdom, and generosity to poets and musicians to lurid accounts of episodes worthy of the Grand Guignol. The year 1588 brought horrific melodrama. Ill and deserted by his followers, Murtaza was locked in a hammam (bath) by his son, Prince Miran Husain, who ordered a fire built in the chamber below. The sultan was smoked to death—after which he was buried with full pomp. Prince Husain came to the throne at sixteen, and soon gained the reputation of an Elagabalus, achieving new heights of excess and dissoluteness. As a demonstration of loyalty the young sultan's vizier, Mirza Khan, put to death fifteen potential rivals before imprisoning the debauched youth in one of his own palaces—a prelude to his blinding and decapitation.

Sultan Husain was replaced in 1589 by a twelve-year-old cousin, Burhan al-Mulk's son, Ismaʿil Nizam-Shah. Following further gory episodes, a new kingmaker, Kamal Khan, had taken charge; and Mirza Khan was paraded through the streets on assback before being cut into sections, which were mounted for public edification on Ahmadnagar's public buildings.

In the meantime, Burhan al-Mulk waited in the wings, keen for power. In 1585, Burhan accepted an invitation to visit the Mughal court at Lahore, but aware of the Mughal emperor's scheme to use him as an imperial puppet in the Deccan, he turned down the offer of an army with which to seize Ahmadnagar. In 1591, at the Battle of Rohankhed, Burhan and his allies defeated the army of Jamal Khan. Burhan's son, the sultan, escaped from the field with the help of a court eunuch, who then left him stranded in a village. He was captured, brought to Burhan, given a paternal kiss on the forehead, forgiven—and packed off to prison in the fort of Bhakar.

Finally, at the age of thirty-five, Burhan succeeded his own son. As sultan he reneged on his promises to Akbar, waged war against Bijapur, which had supported his rise to the throne, and exhausted himself in constant rounds of dissipation. In 1595, bedridden with dysentery, he chose another son, Ibrahim, as successor, a decision so repugnant to his son Ismaʿil's faction that they gathered an army and attacked. Burhan rose to the occasion, leading his army against the rebels and roundly defeating them. But the effort was exhausting. Burhan al-Mulk II died on April 18, 1595.

One of the very few surviving miniatures of the Ahmadnagar school, the Paris portrait bears traces of Mughal influence, in recollection of Burhan's visit to Lahore. The roseate palette, the soaring flyflapper held by the attendant, the massive gold belts, and the rippling skirt edges are the work of a master.[1]

1. For a portrait of Burhan al-Mulk at the Mughal court in 1585, see: Schimmel and Welch, *Anvari's Divan*, p. 49. This miniature shows a younger Burhan (center, facing ʿAbkarhud), already stocky, accompanied by his entourage. It is folio 74a in the *Darab-nama*.

Published: Blochet, *Les Enluminures*, pp. 153–54, pl. cix; Goetz, *Geschichte der indischen Miniaturmalerei*, pl. 3; Barrett, *Painting of the Deccan*, pp. 14–15, pl. 5; Chaitanya, *A History of Indian Painting*, p. 86, fig. 4; Zebrowski, *Deccani Painting*, pp. 19–23, figs. 4, 6–9, pl. II.

FEW INDIAN MINIATURES so pulsate with the energy of spring. Birds, lovers, and insects vibrate almost musically in this renowned painting, once part of a Ragamala (Garland of Melody) series. Indian music is improvised, according to prescribed rules, on classical musical modes, or ragas, each of which evokes a mood, or "colors" the mind with a certain emotion, and is meant to be performed during a particular season at a particular time of day. Poets gave verbal imagery to the melodies (see no. 211), and artists in turn interpreted them pictorially, improvising on predetermined compositions much as musicians created variations on the basic melodic themes. Ragamala paintings usually came in sets of thirty-six, representing the human situations associated with the thirty-six fundamental ragas and raginis ("wives of ragas," or subordinate modes).

The styles and traditions for both musical improvisation and ragamala

191.
HINDOLA RAGINI
From a Ragamala (Garland of Melody) series
Deccan, Ahmadnagar, ca. 1590
Opaque watercolor on paper
Folio: 10⅜ × 7⅞ in. (26.4 × 20 cm.)
Miniature: 9⅝ × 7⅜ in. (24.5 × 18.7 cm.)
National Museum, New Delhi
(BKN–2066)

painting differed from region to region (see also no. 228). This illustration of Hindola Ragini, invariably depicted as a woman seated on a swing with her lover, was painted at Ahmadnagar in about 1590. Muslim rule in the Deccan was by then centuries old, but this remarkable composition, still close to pre-Muslim Deccani art, shows few traces of "foreign" idiom. Though it seems likely that this set of ragamala paintings was commissioned by an important Hindu family, the court at Ahmadnagar was so appreciative of indigenous traditions that the series could also have been painted for a royal patron. Chronicles of Ahmadnagar refer to marriages between Hindus and Muslims, as well as to the prominence of Hindus at court.

The still life of spray guns at the lower right of the picture refers to Holi, the festival celebrating spring and fertility. To this day, the Holi saturnalia marking the end of winter is a time when distinctions of class and caste are tossed aside and everyone—from prince to shopkeeper to cowherd—joins in the festivities, gleefully spraying each other with red coloring (once made from tessu blossoms).

Published: *The Art of India and Pakistan*, p. 173, no. 804, pl. 142; Barrett, *Painting of the Deccan*, pp. 12–13, pl. 4; Barrett and Gray, *Painting of India*, pp. 118, 121; Ebeling, *Ragamala Painting*, p. 156, no. 9/6; Dahmen-Dallapiccola, *Ragamala-Miniaturen*, p. 264, no. 21.6; Chaitanya, *A History of Indian Painting*, p. 86, pl. VIII (here called Vasanta Raga); Zebrowski, *Deccani Painting*, p. 40, fig. 26, pl. V.

191

192

EXCAVATED NEAR THE Chini Mahal, in Bijapur, where quantities of broken Iranian and Chinese shards were found, this powerfully ornamental jali, with its sturdy arch and spiraling vines, infuses imported arabesques with an indigenous Indian intensity. Although no other Bijapuri iron jalis are known to have survived, its silhouette conforms to the vigorously inventive Bijapuri arabesques which adorn most of the city's superb monuments. Apparently, it was made by pouring melted iron into a mold of stone or sand, after which it was refined with files and abrasives.

This jali has served for many years as a screen in All Saints Church, Bijapur, where it is mounted in a heavy wooden frame.

Published: Cousens, *Bijapur*, p. 66, fig. 15.

192.
JALI
Deccan, Bijapur, late 16th or early 17th century
Iron, 55 × 34 in. (139.7 × 86.4 cm.)
All Saints Church, Bijapur

193

ROUND-FACED, BEAK-NOSED, not yet fully bearded, and exuding good will and confidence, Ibrahim ʿAdil-Shah II (r. 1580–1626) is seen at the age of seventeen or eighteen, when he was beginning to assert his statesmanly independence. Following the sordid murder of his uncle, Sultan ʿAli ʿAdil-Shah I of Bijapur, he suddenly came to the throne at the age of nine. Although the issueless Sultan ʿAli had groomed him as heir, his early years as sultan were dominated by firm and ambitious regents who probably encouraged his penchant for the arts in order to keep him from meddling in affairs of state. He was admired and protected by the late sultan's widow, Chand Bibi, a lady of great charismatic power who was revered by the people of Bijapur for her heroic stand against the Mughals. Although she returned permanently to her native Ahmadnagar when Ibrahim's sister married Prince Husain of Ahmadnagar in 1584, she had served Ibrahim devotedly and well during his vulnerable years.

Few rulers possessed Sultan Ibrahim's engaging charm, which one senses through adolescent plumpness from his bright eyes and direct gaze, and from his betel-stained, smiling lips. A merry monarch, he glows with optimism, a justifiable mood. For Sultan Ibrahim inherited the throne of Bijapur at an auspicious time, prior to the Mughal campaigns later in the century. He and Malik Ambar of Ahmadnagar together were sufficiently powerful and diplomatically astute to protect the Deccan. Moreover, Sultan

193.
SULTAN IBRAHIM ʿADIL-SHAH II OF BIJAPUR
Deccan, Bijapur, ca. 1585–90
Opaque watercolor on paper,
10⅜ × 6½ in. (26.5 × 16.5 cm.)
Private collection

194

Ibrahim's tolerant religious policies enabled him to maintain good relations with his predominantly Hindu subjects, who admiringly dubbed him Jagat Guru (Spiritual Leader of the World).

Sultan Ibrahim was passionately devoted to the arts, especially music, and his aesthetic accomplishments rank with those of Akbar and Jahangir. His tomb and the adjoining mosque, the Ibrahim Rauza, are among India's greatest buildings, and we know of no unexceptional picture painted for him. In this portrait, each eyelash and jewel and twist of arabesque enhances the characterization. One senses Ibrahim's musicianship in the lyrical runs of flowering vines on his typically Bijapuri turban and in the matching pattern of his collar. Note, too, the trippingly paced calligraphy, in white, a truly melodic passage of Nasta'liq.

Published: Gray, "Deccani Paintings," p. 75, pl. B; M. Chandra, "Portraits of Ibrahim Adil Shah," pl. I; Soustiel and David, *Miniatures orientales*, pp. 30–31, no. 25; *Paintings from the Muslim Courts*, p. 91, no. 176; Zebrowski, "Transformations," p. 171, fig. 412; Zebrowski, *Deccani Painting*, p. 73, fig. 49, pl. VI.

194.
SULTAN IBRAHIM 'ADIL-SHAH II RIDING ATASH KHAN
Deccan, Bijapur, early 17th century
Opaque watercolor on paper
Folio: 6¾ × 5⅜ in. (17.2 × 13.7 cm.)
Miniature: 5½ × 3¾ in. (14 × 9.5 cm.)
The Knellington Collection, Courtesy Harvard University Art Museums, Cambridge, Massachusetts

SULTAN IBRAHIM REVELED equally in indoor and outdoor activities. Here, he rides his enormous elephant, Atash Khan, upon whom he so doted that he wrote verses about him in his book of songs, the *Kitab-i Nauras* (Book of Nine Sentiments). With legs resembling helium balloons, strawberry-pink mask and trunk festooned with jangling gold chains and bells, and wearing a rich blanket adorned with Ottoman tiger stripes, Atash Khan is no ordinary beast. Ibrahim's artist scanned the heights of fantasy and experimented with scale: blossoms are as big as human heads, deer are as large as men. Atash Khan looms like some great hill in a magician's landscape, dwarfing the sultan, his simian mahout, and the minuscule attendants. Beside him even his mate, Chanchal—who sadly was given under duress to Akbar in 1604—seems runtish. But a few feet away, we come upon the trunk of a chanar tree which if painted in full would reach far beyond the picture and reduce the royal animal to midgetdom.

Published: Zebrowski, "Transformations," p. 173, fig. 415; Zebrowski, *Deccani Painting*, p. 96, figs. 71, 72 (det.).

195.
SULTAN IBRAHIM 'ADIL-SHAH II IN A FANTASTIC LANDSCAPE
Deccan, Bijapur, ca. 1610–15
Opaque watercolor on paper, 6¾ × 4 in. (17 × 10.2 cm.)
Trustees of the British Museum, London (1937.4–10.02)

WHEREVER SULTAN IBRAHIM stepped, flowers and leaves preened to the rhythms of his kartal (clapper)—or so it would appear from this superb portrait, in which, without appearing to be a clotheshorse or a fop, he stuns us with his magnificent gold shawl, pink britches cut in Portuguese style, and transparent robe edged with embroidered arabesques. To Ibrahim, whose music, pictures, mosques, palaces, and tomb proclaim the perfection of his eye, even the designing and manufacture of a shoe was an event. Glimpsing his sultanly feet through the veil of his jama compares to viewing a mountainscape through windswept mist, or a waterfall through snow.

Published: Gray, "Portraits from Bijapur," p. 184, pl. LIIIA; Gray, "Deccani Paintings," p. 77, pl. B; *The Art of India and Pakistan*, pp. 137, 139, fig. 149; Skelton, "Documents," pp. 117–18, fig. 5; Barrett and Gray, *Painting of India*, pp. 127–28; *Paintings from the Muslim Courts*, p. 91, no. 176; Zebrowski, *Deccani Painting*, p. 81, fig. 59, pl. VIII.

196.
LADY FEEDING A BIRD
Deccan, Bijapur, early 17th century
Opaque watercolor on paper
Folio: 17⅜ × 12⅝ in. (44 × 32 cm.)
Miniature: 12⅝ × 8⅞ in. (32 × 22.5 cm.)
Chester Beatty Library, Dublin (MS. 11A, no. 31)

FRESH AND ORIGINAL as it might seem, the artistic synthesis of Bijapur drew from many traditions: from Iran and Turkey; from other courts of Hindu and Muslim India, north and south; from Europe via the Portuguese and via the Mughals, through whom it also received elements from Tibet, Nepal, and Central Asia. China, too, is represented in Bijapur's amalgamation of styles, as is strongly apparent here. Far Eastern motifs arrived by various routes. The sensuously sprawling peonies with their liplike leaves and ornamentally broken spikes of foliage may have reached the Deccan directly, on imported textiles, ceramics, or gilded bronze vessels; or they may derive from Iranian variants on Chinese motifs, which were admired particularly at

195

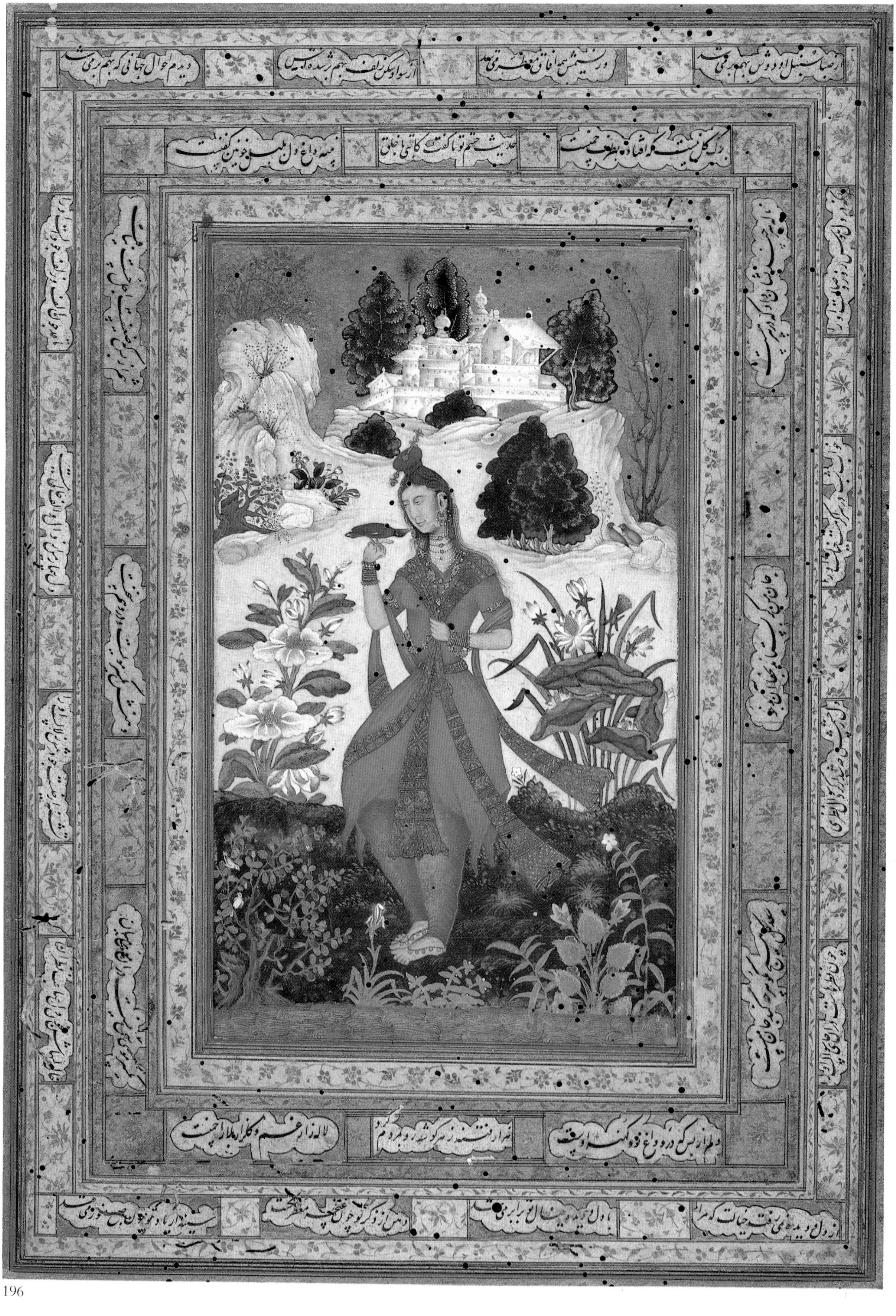

Tabriz in the fifteenth century and then transmitted from the Turkman court throughout the Islamic world.

Like Ibrahim 'Adil-Shah II (see nos. 193–95), the lady of this picture incorporates many moods. Her ash-hued skin and her topknot designate that she is a yogini, or female Hindu ascetic, a devotee frequently associated with the renunciation of all that is mundane. And yet, like many ascetics, she suffers worldliness. Her golden dopatta arcs gracefully in the breeze, the points of her chakdar jama (four-pointed skirt) reach out flirtatiously, and she is weighted down with gold necklaces, anklets, earrings, and bangles. Only the bird on her hand, which pecks at her mouth, amorous as a royal lover, can fathom the mystery of her smile. Who will accompany her to the otherworldly white palace in the hills?

The verses around the painting were chosen with care and typify the amorous conceits of Muslim courts from Turkey through India from the fifteenth century onward. One of these ghazals coos that the beloved's curly black hair, disheveled by the morning breeze, is like hyacinths that perfume the air while, because tangled, it lends confusion. The dreamy vision of the beloved is ever in the lover's eye and heart; from continually reciting the beloved's name, his mouth is fragrant as a rosebud; and remembering her, his heart is radiant as the morning. The second four couplets further elaborate the image: those with spiritual insight dream of drinking from the fountain of the beloved's lips; and the ailing heart of the lover is never without the letters alif and dal, because the beloved's stature is straight as the former, her tresses curved as the latter.

Published: Arnold, *The Library of A. Chester Beatty*, vol. 1, pp. 49–50, vol. 3, pl. 93, no. XXXI; Skelton, "The Mughal Artist Farrokh Beg," p. 399, pl. 8, fig. 16; Barrett, *Painting of the Deccan*, pp. 18–19, pl. 7; Chaitanya, *A History of Indian Painting*, fig. 65; Zebrowski, *Deccani Painting*, p. 103, fig. 82, pl. XII.

197.
A NOBLEMAN OF BIJAPUR
Deccan, Bijapur, ca. 1615
Opaque watercolor on paper, 6¾ × 4 in.
(17.1 × 10.1 cm.)
Trustees of the British Museum, London
(1937.4–10.03)

THE RASAS (FLAVORS) of Bijapuri art range widely. This austerely aristocratic, sternly noble courtier, eagle-nosed and calm, stands firm as a mountain beneath a pair of gracefully hovering yellow and white birds. All is quiet. A graceful shawl flows soft as a waterfall from his shoulders, and the merest ripple enlivens the end of an understatedly sumptuous sash. But beneath the powerfully simple wrapping of his turban, behind his eye—Egyptian as Ikhnaton's—we sense expectation. Something is about to crack the silence; and the courtier's strong hands, as used to the sword as to the wine cup, will seek action.

Published: Gray, "Deccani Paintings," p. 76, pl. A; Barrett and Gray, *Painting of India*, pp. 126, 128; *Paintings from the Muslim Courts*, p. 91, no. 174; Zebrowski, *Deccani Painting*, p. 81, figs. 55, 56.

198.
A FAT BEGUM
Inscribed: "Hur Khanum Mughalani"
(The Mughal Lady Hur)
Deccan, Bijapur, ca. 1625
Marbling, with touches of gold, silver, and opaque watercolor on paper, 9⅛ × 5⅜ in.
(23.2 × 13.5 cm.)
Jagdish and Kamla Mittal Museum of Indian Art, Hyderabad (76.408)

ALTHOUGH THE PORTRAYAL is essentially a caricature, we can almost feel the dignified presence of this obese begum, a lady of high rank of some royal house, perhaps the royal harem of Bijapur. Her massive, rocklike body dominates the picture space, and her sharp, scanning eyes belie her plump, motherly visage. Resplendent with necklaces, a nose ring, tassels, prayer beads, scarves, and a plumed Chaghatai headdress, she sits holding a sprig of flowers delicately between thumb and forefinger. But it is the marbling on her clothing, the flowers, and the foreground that makes this miniature worthy of further study. Complete paintings produced by this highly complex process are very rare.

Marbled paper was often used in India, Turkey, and Iran for book bindings and for decorating the borders of album pages. Its hypnotic effect was also used imaginatively in India as a background for elegant calligraphy on manuscript pages (see no. 214). Interest in the ancient art of marbling has been revived in recent years in Japan, Turkey, Pakistan, India, and the United States.

The first recorded use of marbling in the Deccan is in the *Kulliyat*

(Collected Works; Salar Jung Museum, Hyderabad), a book of poetry by Muhammad-Quli Qutb-Shah, the sultan of Golconda (r. 1580–1612), that was compiled sometime between 1590 and 1600. On one of the eight illustrations in Bukhara style that enrich the manuscript, the iridescent wings on some of the birds are actually pieces of marbled paper pasted onto the surface.[1] Deccani artists seemed to have had a particular interest in creating entire paintings with marbling. At one time it was thought that the idea was imported to the Deccan from Turkey, but recent research has shown that marbled paper was then used in Turkey only for colorful book bindings and borders.

Marbled paintings were a Bijapuri specialty. All of the known examples —no more than twenty-four including this one—were produced between about 1625 and 1650.[2] There must have been at least one artist or patron at Bijapur who was fascinated by the complicated process. Even some of the other paintings done at Bijapur during this twenty-five-year period have clouds painted with swirling patterns and colors that imitate marbling. One of the marbled paintings, *Rustam Lassoing Wild Horses* (National Museum, New Delhi), bears the name of the artist Shafiᶜ.[3]

To create a painting as impressive as this portrait of a begum, the artist first chose an absorbent paper, which he treated with a mordant to insure better adhesion of the colors. He covered the areas to be left unadorned, in this case the unpainted background and the begum's hand, her head and throat, and all but part of her headdress, with a resistant gum. Using brushes or droppers, he then floated pigments mixed with ox gall on the surface of a vat of water mixed with size, a pasty substance that served to slow down the movement of the pigment, and swirled the colors with a stylus or comb to create his design. When he had the pattern he wanted, he placed his specially prepared sheet of paper directly in contact with the floating colors for a short time, then lifted it off and rinsed away any excess size. Finally, after the marbling had dried, the artist drew in the outlines, painted the solid areas of color and the shading on the face and hand, and heightened other details necessary for clarity with gold and a few deft strokes of color.

J.M.

1. For the manuscript, see: Zebrowski, *Deccani Painting*, p. 165, figs. 126–28.
2. For other examples, see: Zebrowski, *Deccani Painting*, pp.135–38, figs. 102–6; Welch, *Indian Drawings*, p. 74, no. 34; Binney, *Indian Miniature Painting*, p. 153, no. 128, pp. 155–56, no. 129.
3. Zebrowski, *Deccani Painting*, p. 138, no. 14.

Published: Welch, *Indian Drawings*, p. 75, no. 35.

ALTHOUGH NONE OF the jeweled gold objects admired in Bijapuri paintings have been found, several bronze and copper vessels are known. Most are inscribed with Qurᵓanic verses in Naskhi script of such striking boldness and monumentality they resemble the stone-cut inscriptions on Bijapuri architecture. Forceful yet ornamental, with their repeated curves and uprights, they bring to mind Ottoman calligraphy and suggest that Turkish scribes were employed by the ᶜAdil-Shahis. Although the inscriptions on the tomb and mosque of Sultan Ibrahim ᶜAdil-Shah II are the high water mark of the art at Bijapur, excellent work was done until the ᶜAdil-Shahi dynasty fell in 1686.

Fanning out from a characteristically Bijapuri stylized flower, eight human-headed fish lend uniqueness to this dish, which can be dated to about 1600, during the reign of Sultan Ibrahim. It was probably intended to serve offerings of food or flowers in the shrine of a Bijapuri saint. Related to it iconographically is a pair of large stone waterspouts in the Government Museum of Bijapur. Also human-headed, these gigantic fish—whose tongues, drilled and mounted on rods, undulated when water coursed through their mouths—once graced a building. The inscription, which for compositional reasons omits the last sentence of the famed Throne Verse (Sura 2:255), reads as follows:

199.
DISH WITH CALLIGRAPHIC INSCRIPTION AND A WHORL OF FISH
Deccan, Bijapur, ca. 1600
Tinned copper, diameter 10¾ in. (27.3 cm.)
Fogg Art Museum, Harvard University, Cambridge, Massachusetts, Purchase, Philip Hofer Fund for Islamic and Indian Art, the Fund for the Acquisition of Islamic Art, and the Discretionary Fund of the Islamic Department (1983.27)

199

Allah! There is no God save Him, the Living, the Self-subsistent. Neither slumber overtakes Him nor sleep. Unto Him belongs what is in the heavens and what is on earth. Who is it that intercedes with Him except with His permission? He knows what is before them and that which is behind them, and they do not encompass anything of His knowledge save what He will. His throne encompasses the heavens and the earth, and He wearies not of preserving them. [He is the Exalted, the Mighty.][1]

1. The Qur'anic verses were identified and translated by Annemarie Schimmel.

200.
SULTAN MUHAMMAD 'ADIL-SHAH
AND IKHLAS KHAN RIDE
AN ELEPHANT
Signed: "Haidar Ali, Ibrahim Khan, Bijapur"
Deccan, Bijapur, ca. 1645
Opaque watercolor on paper, 11 × 12¼ in.
(28 × 31 cm.)
Private collection

As HE LAY dying, Ibrahim 'Adil-Shah II named his fifteen-year-old second son to succeed him as Sultan Muhammad 'Adil-Shah (r. 1627–56). Sultan Muhammad inherited a state troubled by factions from within and by the threat of Mughal attack from without. Psychologically not unlike his chief persecutor, Shah Jahan, Muhammad retained his dignity and composure against terrible odds. In 1636, he was forced by the Mughal ambassador to enter a degrading alliance with the imperial power, a diplomatic defeat balanced by his successes in the South, where he won fealty and tribute from the rajas of the Carnatic kingdoms.

Like Shah Jahan, Muhammad 'Adil-Shah was an inspired patron, particularly of painting and architecture. His tomb, the vast Gol Gumbaz (Round Dome), the largest domed structure in India, begun shortly after his accession, was not completed when he died thirty years later. The dramatic mihrab in Bijapur's Jami' Masjid (Great Mosque), also built during his reign, is adorned with calligraphies in gold and with trompe-l'oeil niches showing books, vases of flowers, and censers and chains.

Portraits of Sultan Muhammad reflect his taste for a sumptuous yet hard-edged style richly embellished with gold and notable for its stately curves.

Surviving examples combine great splendor with formality, qualities achieved by both his artists and Shah Jahan's portraitists. In this picture, he and his vizier, Ikhlas Khan, are shown riding a noble, splendidly caparisoned elephant that steps forward with firm and stately tread, propelled by undulating, swaying rhythms; the haloed sultan, ankus in hand, mans the animal with dignified authority. In their costumes, sparkling with tooled and burnished silver and gold, the two men continue the sartorial tradition notable in the portraits of Sultan Ibrahim ʿAdil-Shah II. Typical of Bijapuri painting are the rich deep reds and blues employed to suggest shadows within the creases of gold brocades.

Sultan Muhammad became seriously ill in 1646; and until his death ten years later, he was barely able to rule. The begum Bari Sahiba, his senior wife, headed the regency in his stead. But it was during these years that the Maratha leader Shivaji gained strength; a major chapter of Indian history might have been altered had not the Bijapur sultan been incapacitated.

Published: *Paintings from the Muslim Courts*, p. 92, no. 179; Zebrowski, "Transformations," p. 177, fig. 429; Zebrowski, *Deccani Painting*, pp. 131–32, fig. 100; Topsfield, *An Introduction to Indian Court Painting*, pp. 25–26, pl. 17.

201.
BRONZE LAMP
Deccan, Bijapur, Gol Gumbaz, probably
early 17th century
Height without chain, 24⅞ in. (63.2 cm.)
Archaeological Museum, Bijapur

OIL LAMPS BY the thousands once brought soft, flickering light and lively shadows to nocturnal Bijapur. Made from hammered and cut sheets of metal, this lamp, from the Gol Gumbaz, is so architectonic in design that it brings to mind seventeenth-century Bijapuri buildings. Polygonal panels with arabesque and geometric ornament are divided by narrow flanges decorated in silhouette with particularly appealing animal heads, characteristic of Bijapuri inventiveness and wit. Light in weight, it would have swung from the chain on which it was suspended, scattering beams of light.

201

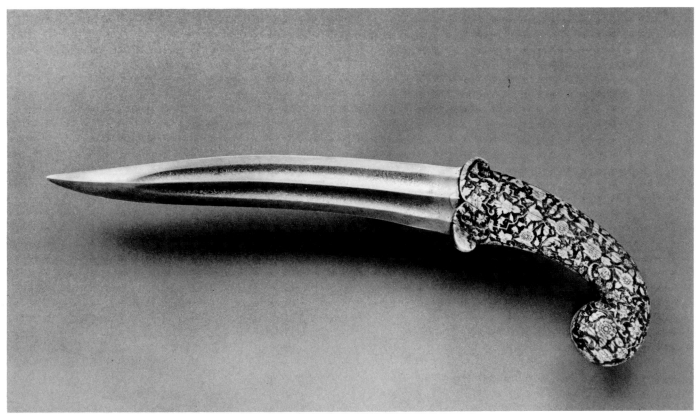

202

"KHANJAR" IS AN Arabic word used in the Islamic countries for different weapons. In Persia and India the name is applied to a dagger with a double-edged, slightly recurved blade and, usually, a pistol-grip hilt made from metal, ivory, or jade or some other hardstone. Jade hilts may be plain, carved, or set with jewels; fewer khanjars were made with ivory hilts, and they generally have a simple shape. Khanjars were commonly used in India from about 1600. Daggers with hilts of gold, silver, jade, or ivory were worn at court or in ceremonies, not carried on the battlefield. The hilt of this khanjar is so well rubbed that it must have been used often, perhaps by an official attending the court.

This dagger is a unique example of an ivory-hilted khanjar. The finely wrought watered steel blade is ribbed and has a slight double curve. The hilt is embellished with an exquisite allover arabesque pattern of minutely drawn flowers and foliage carved in low relief against a dark brown stained ground. The same floral ornament, derived from the standard Persian type, was used for both Mughal patrons and the contemporary Deccani sultans, but the feeling and general appearance differed. Our piece seems to be Deccani, more than likely from Bijapur.

J.M.

Published: *The Indian Heritage*, pp. 130–31, no. 419.

202.
KHANJAR
Deccan, probably Bijapur, early 17th century
Steel with ivory hilt, length 14⅝ in. (37 cm.)
Jagdish and Kamla Mittal Museum of Indian
Art, Hyderabad (76.1527)

IT IS A paradox that things endowed with the power to hurt or kill are often exceedingly beautiful. Daggers, knives, swords, maces, arrows, and other weapons seen here, for example, are elegantly shaped and lavishly adorned either by their makers or according to the fancy of rich, opulence-loving patrons. Most such arms were meant to be used as weapons; others, like this elephant goad, were made for ceremonial use, or to herald their owners' power. It is therefore baffling to learn that this ankus was made not for a monarch but for a Sufi saint.

The ankus is remarkably crafted and well proportioned: the octagonal

203.
ANKUS
Inscribed with Qur'anic verses and the name
of Shah Amin ad-Din A'la
Deccan, Bijapur, ca. 1625–40
Steel, length 33⅛ in. (84 cm.)
Jagdish and Kamla Mittal Museum of Indian
Art, Hyderabad (76.1530)

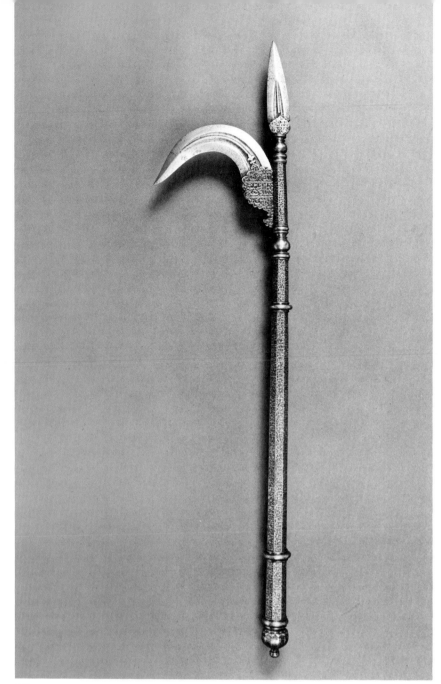

203.

shaft tapers from a domical, faceted knob at one end to the two pointed blades, or hooks, at the other. In the compartments created by the ring moldings along the shaft's length, a series of Qur'anic verses in Thuluth script is chiseled in low relief. In the lobed cartouches on both sides of the ornamental plate that reinforces the curved blade, the inscription reads: "Allah, Muhammad, 'Ali, Shah Amin ad-Din A'la."

Shah Amin ad-Din A'la (1597–1675) was a prominent descendant of the Chishti Sufi family who had their hospice on Shahpur Hillock at Bijapur. Several works in the Dakhni language have been attributed to him, but little is known of his activities during the first half of the seventeenth century, when this ankus was made. Some of Amin ad-Din's teachings, such as his protest against the idea that the mosque was the exclusive house of God, were merely unconventional. Others were more extreme. Amin ad-Din A'la claimed to have achieved union with God, and both manuscript and epigraphic sources suggest that his followers believed in the lofty spiritual status of their pir (teacher of the Sufi way). Accommodating toward Muslims and non-Muslims alike, the cult that coalesced around his figure consisted of at least a dozen khalifas (disciples who may induct others into the order) and numerous murids (pupils). There seem to have been especially close ties between Shahpur Hillock and the Kannada-speaking Hindu Lingayat population of the region; one of Amin ad-Din's foremost khalifas was a man named Qadir Linga, who had been a cavalryman in the Bijapur service. Even today, both Muslims and Hindus assemble in large numbers at Shah Amin ad-Din A'la's shrine on the anniversary of his death to commemorate his 'urs (marriage) with God. The ceremony is one of the major events in Bijapur.[1]

The question of who commissioned this ankus and had it regally inscribed with the saint's name is problematic. Shah Amin ad-Din A'la had no contact with the courts of Ibrahim 'Adil-Shah II and his son Muhammad 'Adil-Shah at Bijapur. But in spite of Amin ad-Din's detached attitude to the court, one of them could have offered him the ankus, for both sultans made visits to Sufi hospices to seek spiritual counseling. A second possibility is that one of Amin ad-Din's murids was a master armorer who made the ankus as an offering to his revered pir. When the saint might have used the ankus is also difficult to determine. Shah Amin ad-Din A'la's name is inscribed on the basket hilt of a steel sword covered with calligraphic embellishment that is now in a private collection in Hyderabad, and the Gol Gumbaz Museum in Bijapur has a more or less similar ankus, also with Qur'anic inscriptions, in its collection. The sword and both elephant goads could have been carried in ceremonial processions, but it is not known whether this was Sufi practice.

J.M.

1. The information on Amin ad-Din A'la's life is based on Eaton, *Sufis of Bijapur.*

Published: Bilgrami, *Landmarks of the Deccan,* p. 62; *The Indian Heritage,* pp. 136–37, no. 448. (Because the last name in the inscription was misread as 'Ali instead of A'la, the ankus is incorrectly attributed to the early eighteenth century; the entry reads: "This probably refers to the *sufi shaikh* Sayid Shah Amin ud-Din 'Ali Husaini who died in 1150 AH/1737–8 AD.")

THIS ALARMING BUT handsomely sculptural forged steel weapon was designed to thrust fore and aft. As is clear from the carefully replicated shape of antelope horns, it was based upon primitive, probably tribal, prototypes, which initially were made from natural materials to which steel tips were added at a later stage of the evolution. Some examples were made with a shield over the grip to protect the hand.

Such weapons are associated with the Marathas—a hardy, warlike people descended in part from the Huns and Scythians—whose greatest leader was Shivaji (1627–1680), noted for his struggle against Aurangzeb. The Marathas gained renown as mercenaries in the employ of the Deccani sultans. From Malik Ambar, the Abyssinian chief minister of Ahmadnagar, they learned guerrilla warfare, which they mastered so proficiently that Maratha power soon spread through most of northern India. On the death of Shivaji,

204.
STEEL WEAPON IN THE FORM OF ANTELOPE HORNS
Maharashtra, 17th century
Length 33 in. (83.8 cm.)
Private collection

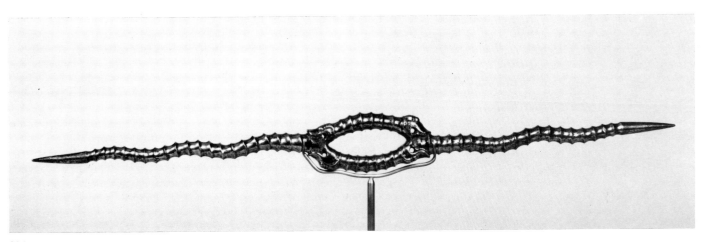

204

his son Sambhuji seized control. Detested by the Mughals for his cruelty, lechery, and addiction to wine, he was also feared by them. When eventually they captured and executed him, Aurangzeb arranged to educate his son, later known as Shivaji II, at court, an experience that so softened him that he became unfit to govern. Maratha rule then fell into the hands of the Peshwas (prime ministers), who soon assumed hereditary leadership. Within seven years of Aurangzeb's death in 1707, Maratha energy, ambition, and military skill enabled them to enter into an alliance with the Mughals, sharing with them the revenues of the northeastern provinces, in addition to controlling the territories already in their hands. In 1761, however, at the third Battle of Panipat, a huge army led by the Afghan ruler Ahmad Shah Durrani inflicted a major defeat upon the Marathas, from which they never fully recovered.

205

205.
'ALI 'ADIL-SHAH II SLAYS A TIGER
Deccan, Bijapur, ca. 1660
Opaque watercolor on paper
Folio: 11¾ × 15 in. (29.9 × 38.1 cm.)
Miniature: 8½ × 12¼ in. (21.6 × 31.1 cm.)
The Knellington Collection, Courtesy
Harvard University Art Museums,
Cambridge, Massachusetts

LIKE HIS FATHER and grandfather, 'Ali 'Adil-Shah II was concerned as much with art and literature as with statecraft and like them he aspired to create for himself the greatest of all Bijapuri tombs. But at his death, it was far less finished than his father's had been; and with its seemingly gothic arches open to the air, it now resembles a romantic ruin as painted by Caspar David Friedrich. Sultan 'Ali's reign was beset with tribulations. When he inherited the throne at the age of fifteen or eighteen in 1657, his succession was declared invalid by Emperor Aurangzeb, on the awkwardly personal grounds of illegitimacy. 'Ali's life was further soured by Shivaji and his Marathas, who formed an alliance against him with his erstwhile friend, the Mughal general Mirza Raja Jai Singh of Amber (see no. 233). Further struggles seemed futile. In 1666, Sultan 'Ali withdrew into the pleasurable insulation of his harem and the oblivion of wine. In 1672, he died of stress and calculated joy. He was succeeded by his son, Iskandar 'Adil-Shah, the last of the 'Adil-Shahi sultans of Bijapur.

As if in a glittering tableau vivant, Sultan 'Ali, resplendently dressed in gold, orange, and blue, smiles victoriously in his portrayal as a tiger hunter. The likeness is intensely Indian, bringing to mind gold coins of the Gupta dynasty in which deified heroes slay evil in the form of lions. His lips are stained red from chewing betel nut (pan), and his eyes are shaped like pipal leaves as he speeds a well-aimed royal shaft into the vitals of a beastly force of darkness—an inadequate surrogate for the encroaching enemy. The wicked tiger snarls from a rocky outcropping in which the artist has hidden amusingly dastardly grotesques. This heart of a miniature, the corners and lower section of which are missing, once included 'Ali's royal barge, of which only two finials remain. It was painted by the same hand as several wall paintings —large bouquets of flowers in splendid vases adorned with gold and lapis lazuli arabesques—in the Athar Mahal (Palace of Relics).[1] Despite the frustration of ruling a doomed state, Sultan 'Ali was an important and inventive patron.

1. For the wall paintings, see: Cousens, *Bijapur*, pl. LXXVII.

Published: Zebrowski, *Deccani Painting*, p. 140, fig. 110.

RESTRAINED, DIGNIFIED, MARVELOUSLY inscribed architectural reliefs abound in Bijapur. This relief from the Athar Mahal (Palace of Relics), with its bold Nasta'liq characters, demonstrates that artistic quality remained high virtually until the fall of the 'Adil-Shahi dynasty. Were it not dated, one would be tempted to assign this piece, on the basis of the style of the arabesques, to a considerably earlier date.[1]

1. For another panel from the same mosque, see: *In the Image of Man*, p. 97, no. 11.

Published: Frederic, *Indian Temples and Sculpture*, fig. 381.

206.
ARCHITECTURAL INSCRIPTION
From a fountain inscribed:
"Fountain from the Paradisical spring Kauthar," a chronogram for the date, 1082
Deccan, Bijapur, dated A.H 1082 (1671-72)
Basalt, $16\frac{3}{8} \times 24\frac{5}{8} \times 8\frac{5}{8}$ in. (41.5 × 62.5 × 22 cm.)
Archaeological Museum, Bijapur (2)

207

207.
PRINCELY DEER HUNTERS
Deccan, Bijapur, ca. 1680
Opaque watercolor on paper, 9½ × 18 in.
(24.1 × 45.7 cm.)
The Knellington Collection, Courtesy
Harvard University Art Museums,
Cambridge, Massachusetts

No MERE HUNTING scene, this picture—one of the last painted for the ʿAdil-Shahis—contrasts the static with the kinetic, tranquillity with violence, and invites allegorical interpretation. Against a hide-and-seek of clouds, reminiscent of the sky in Altdorfer's *Battle of Alexander* (Alte Pinakothek, Munich), a golden sunset caresses a softly feminine landscape—a stretch of hips, belly, and breasts, fringed by silhouetted trees. But the primary subject is two princes and a pack of hounds chasing deer. The older prince, immobile as an equestrian statue, rocks backward, amplifying the momentum of the active younger prince, who hurtles forward. We hear the golden bells of his horse's mane jingle, as to the right deer scramble to escape the crushing jaws of the

fierce hounds. From the left a squad of huntsmen approaches, to attend to the kill.

On the horizon at the left is a typical Bijapuri palace, and the landscape recalls the rolling hills of the ʿAdil-Shahis' hunting grounds. It is tempting to suppose that the younger prince is Sultan Iskandar himself, the last of the ʿAdil-Shahi line (see no. 208), enjoying a final outing before his kingdom fell to Mughal hands.

Published: Blochet, *Collection Jean Pozzi*, pl. L; Welch, *A Flower from Every Meadow*, pp. 130–31, no. 78; Zebrowski, *Deccani Painting*, pp. 144, 147, figs. 115, 116.

208.
THE HOUSE OF BIJAPUR
Inscribed: "work of Kamal Muhammad and
Chand Muhammad"
Deccan, Bijapur, ca. 1680
Opaque watercolor on paper, 16¼ × 12¼ in.
(41.3 × 31.1 cm.)
The Metropolitan Museum of Art, New York,
Purchase, Gifts in memory of Richard
Ettinghausen; Schimmel Foundation, Inc.,
Ehsan Yarshater, Karekin Beshir Ltd., Margaret
Mushekian, Mr. and Mrs. Edward Ablat and
Mr. and Mrs. Jerome A. Straka Gifts; The
Friends of the Islamic Department Fund, Louis
E. and Theresa S. Seley Purchase Fund for
Islamic Art, Rogers Fund, and gifts and funds
from various donors, by exchange (1982.213)

BIJAPURI PAINTING NEARED the end with a flourish in this miniature which both sums up the dynasty politically and harks back stylistically to the glory of Ibrahim ʿAdil-Shah II. Apparently a famous subject, of which several later versions are known, this large miniature was painted for the last Bijapur sultan, Iskandar ʿAdil-Shah, who came to the throne when he was four years old after his father's early death in 1672. He grew up under the control of a succession of squabbling regents, always threatened by the Mughals and the Marathas. Brave, determined, and precocious, he took over the reins of government while very young, and cleverly pitted his enemies one against the other. But on the death in 1680 of his fickle ally, the Maratha leader Shivaji, the cause of Bijapur became hopeless. In 1686 the eighteen-year-old sultan was captured by the Mughals, who annexed Bijapur. Iskandar's last fourteen years were spent imprisoned in Daulatabad Fort. After his death his corpse was returned to Bijapur, where he was remembered with tearful reverence. He was buried tombless in a garden—now a public park—beneath a simple cenotaph.

In this group portrait of the house of Bijapur, showing the dynasty from beginning to end, Iskandar is the dark-skinned twelve-year-old boy at the right, seated beside his father, Sultan ʿAli. In this painted curtain call, all of Iskandar's line are reassembled, nobly and characteristically attired and enthroned on a magnificent floral carpet. On the horizon, beyond the landscape painted in the style of 1590, the Arabian Sea reminds us that proud, dismembered Bijapur once included Goa.[1]

1. For later versions of this picture, see: Taylor, *Architecture at Beejapore*, frontispiece; Strzygowski, Kramrisch, and Wellesz, *Asiatische Miniaturmalerei*, p. 42, fig. 37, pl. 13; Manucci, *Storia do Mogor*, vol. 3, pl. XXXIV.

Published: Nouveau Drouot-Salle, Paris, June 24, 1982, lot 67; *Notable Acquisitions 1982–1983*, pp. 12, 14–15; Zebrowski, *Deccani Painting*, pp. 150–51, no. 118a, pl. XVII.

209.
CIRCULAR SALVER
Deccan, probably Golconda, ca. 1600
Copper, chased and engraved, with traces of
gilding, diameter 23⅞ in. (60.5 cm.)
Jagdish and Kamla Mittal Museum of Indian
Art, Hyderabad (76.1442)

THIS MAGNIFICENT COPPER salver is a rare survival of Indian Islamic metalware. In fact, it is the only Indian example of its kind. A Shiʿite inscription in elegant Naskhi script encircles the hamsa (sacred goose) set amid floral ornament in the central medallion. Superbly executed birds and beasts, both real and fanciful, hunt and fight in the broad outer band against an animated arabesque of floral motifs, and the cavetto and flattened rim are decorated with scrolling, intertwined stems. Most of the salver's original gilding has disappeared, perhaps from regular use. The quality and style of the design suggest that this masterpiece is a product of a Qutb-Shahi karkana (royal workshop) at Golconda, probably from about 1600.

The recent interest of scholars in the history, society, literature, and art of the Muslim kingdoms of the Deccan has led art historians to accept the existence of a distinct Deccani style in metalwork that, like Deccani painting, achieved its own unique character. For centuries before this salver was made, the Deccan had a tradition for metalwork. Deccani craftsmen produced objects not only for the innumerable temples in the region but for the courts of the Kakatiya, western Chalukya, and Hoysala kings. From the fourteenth to the seventeenth century, the Muslim states of the Deccan established economic and cultural ties with Iran, Arabia, and Turkey, but though Deccani art adopted certain of the artistic conventions of those countries, the artists and craftsmen of this plateau region of southern India had a different vision. Their creations are intimate and seem effortless. Although the resources of the Deccani sultans were humbler than those of the Mughals, some of these rulers were highly cultivated men who generously supported artistic endeavors.

Very little Mughal metalware of the sixteenth and seventeenth centuries has survived, and Deccani examples are even rarer. Most of the known examples are tinned copper objects produced for religious purposes, with finely proportioned bodies and meticulously engraved and chiseled—almost Safavid—floral arabesques and calligraphic inscriptions in Thuluth script. The only piece of Indian Islamic metalware comparable to our salver is a large Mughal wine bowl dating to the first quarter of the seventeenth century (no. 119). The decoration on the bowl, hunting scenes of horse and

209

elephant riders in a landscape filled with floral arabesques, was evidently designed by a Mughal painter. Scholars have now come to believe that the designs on several of the decorative art objects used by the Mughals were created by court painters rather than by the craftsmen who executed the pieces.[1] This exquisite salver must also have been designed by an artist of great ability for a discerning patron, who then had it executed by a master craftsman in his karkana. The design reminds us of the drawing of an "inhabited arabesque" (no. 210), which we have also attributed to about 1600.

The shape and general decorative scheme of the Mughal wine bowl to some extent follow Western Iranian tradition. Although certain details of the chased and engraved decoration on our salver are characteristic of Timurid and Safavid Iran, in its totality it is more Indian. The hamsa at the center is a common southern Indian, particularly Hindu, ornament, and the drawing is typically Deccani. Also Deccani in character is the inscription in the band surrounding the medallion, a Shiʿite version of the Kalima (the Muslim profession of faith) and the phrase "nasrun min Allah wa fathun qar[ib]" (Help from God and near victory; Sura 61:13). The inscription is written in cursive Naskhi script against scrolling floriates, and a narrow band of floral ornament with undulating stems surrounds it. Annemarie Schimmel has pointed out certain errors in the inscription that show it was executed by someone who did not know Arabic.[2] The mistakes in the inscription, the inclusion of a hamsa and yalis (mythical lions, also Hindu symbols), and the style of the drawing of some of the other animals lead us to suspect that the salver was executed by a local Hindu craftsman. But this is mere conjecture. The artisan could as easily have been a highly skilled but less than literate Muslim, and hamsas and yalis were part of the prevailing regional design tradition.

The richness and energy of the imaginatively conceived, action-filled decoration in the broad outer band confirm the salver's Deccani origin. Tigers, yalis, deer, a cow with a calf, bulls, horses, elephants, camels, dogs, cats, rabbits, peacocks, ducks, cranes, simurghs, griffins, and dragons engage in violent combat or run about playfully. The elephants, yalis, and bulls are drawn in a manner that is particularly Deccani.

The dramatic interplay of spirited animals, birds, and floral ornament, subtly deployed and harmoniously integrated, also gives the work an overall sense of order, clarity, and balance. The charm of the design is enhanced by the equally meticulous and sensitive execution. This salver is a key piece in the history of metalware in Islamic India and will remain so even when comparable examples are discovered.

J.M.

1. Mittal, forthcoming.
2. Personal communication, October 1982.

Published: *The Indian Heritage*, p. 145, no. 491; Mittal, "Indo-Islamic Metal and Glassware," p. 63, fig. 1 (det.).

210

210.
AN INHABITED ARABESQUE
Deccan, Golconda, ca. 1590
Reddish black line and touches of white on paper, 4⅝ × 2½ in. (11.6 × 6.5 cm.)
Jagdish and Kamla Mittal Museum of Indian Art, Hyderabad (76.588)

THE MUSLIM SULTANS who ruled in the Deccan during the sixteenth and seventeenth centuries, like the Bahmanid dynasty they succeeded, maintained close relations with Iran. The cultural, religious, and political ties between Iran and the Qutb-Shahi sultanate of Golconda were especially strong, not only because the founder of the dynasty had originally come from Iran but because the Golconda sultans, like the rulers of Iran, were Shiʿites. A number of Iranian theologians, soldiers, traders, and men proficient in the arts found patronage and a welcome abode at the Golconda court.

As does most Golconda art of the Qutb-Shahi period, this floral arabesque alive with mythical birds and beasts owes an undeniable debt to Persian traditions. Iranian designers also drew fantastic dragons, birds, and fish amid entwined tendrils and flowering stems, but this Deccani artist's extravagant creatures seem charged with special intensity. As usual, though the design may be borrowed, the interpretation is unmistakably Indian.

J.M.

Published: Welch, *Indian Drawings*, p. 67, no. 28.

211.
SONG FROM AN ILLUMINATED
DAKHNI MANUSCRIPT IN NASTAʿLIQ
SCRIPT

Deccan, Golconda or Bijapur, ca. 1625–35
Black ink, gold, and opaque watercolor on
paper, 5⅝ × 3½ in. (14.2 × 8.8 cm.)
Jagdish and Kamla Mittal Museum of Indian
Art, Hyderabad (76.1540)

THIS CALLIGRAPHY PANEL may be the opening page of a manuscript of poems composed by ʿAbdullah Qutb-Shah, ruler of the Deccani kingdom of Golconda from 1626 to 1672. Although in the political sphere ʿAbdullah's reign witnessed the waning of Qutb-Shahi power, in the field of literature it was a period of remarkable achievement, especially in the vernacular language, Dakhni. Several of the masterpieces of Dakhni literature, such as Wajhi's allegorical tale the *Sabras* (The Senses), Ghawwasi's *Saifuʾl-Muluk*, and Ibn Nishati's *Phulban* (The Gardener), were written under ʿAbdullah's patronage, and the sultan himself was an accomplished poet in Dakhni, combining his poetic skill with a knowledge of North Indian (Hindustani) classical music. Only a meager portion of his total literary output survives, in a unique but incomplete manuscript housed in the Salar Jang Museum in Hyderabad.[1]

The Dakhni song inscribed in Nastaʿliq script on this folio does not appear in the Salar Jang manuscript. The heading above the text, "dar maqam-i malhar" (in the Malar mode), indicates the song's musical mode, or raga (see also nos. 191, 269). In the subcontinent, raga Malar is traditionally associated with the rainy season and with rejoicing. The Hindustani idiom "malar gana," literally "to sing the raga Malar," is sometimes used simply to mean "to be merry."

In view of the obscurities of both script and language, we can propose only a rough translation of the poem:

> Come, friends, let us go and arouse . . .
> The rain clouds of the mountains.
> Let us adorn every tray with gems;
> Let us spread garlands of pearls around our necks;
> Let us make the devotee and dancer dance;
> Let us make them drink wine and let us give them
>   a taste of fun;
> Let us sing the song Malar;
> ʿAbdullah Shah, for the sake of the Prophet, brings
>   the rain.

The main charm of the page lies in the minute, lively decoration between and around the lines of calligraphy. The text of the poem, in two columns separated by a narrow gray band with a floral design, and the heading at the top of the page are written in elegant black Nastaʿliq script against unpainted rolling cloud forms contained by thin black lines. The second caption, in a rectangular frame with a green border, is written in red against a gold cartouche with arabesques on either side on a gray ground. The rest of the decoration is painted mainly in black ink and two shades of gold on a gold ground; there are buildings in the rocky landscape that surrounds the caption in the top panel, and in the landscape of the two vertical panels a lion and a tiger hunt deer and cows graze in undulating pastures.

This folio is almost identical in style and richness of embellishment to the *Kitab-i Nauras* (Book of Nine Sentiments), a well-known collection of Dakhni songs based on North Indian classical ragas composed by Ibrahim ʿAdil-Shah II of the neighboring state of Bijapur and transcribed in 1618 by the court calligrapher, Mir Khalilullah Butshikan. It is possible that ʿAbdullah Qutb-Shah followed his example and had his poetry equally lavishly illuminated. The name ʿAbdullah Shah in the last line of the poem could, however, also refer to Shah Shaikh ʿAbdullah ʿAidarus, the Sufi who miraculously cured Ibrahim in the 1620s and was hence greatly revered by the sultan and made his adviser. If that is so, the page may come from another manuscript by Ibrahim, perhaps also transcribed by Khalilullah, that is now lost. Whether it is from Golconda or Bijapur, this folio, like those from the *Kitab-i Nauras*, amply establishes the unique quality of the royal Deccani book pages.

J.M.

1. For the manuscript, see: Muhammad, *Divan-i ʿAbdullah Qutb-Shah.*

Ali Asani has made important contributions to this entry and translated the poem.

211

212

MUCH OF SEVENTEENTH-CENTURY India converges in this kalamkari (literally, worked with a pen), a delightful painted cotton strongly influenced by the art of Golconda, whose sway extended to the centers of textile manufacture on the Coromandel Coast. Contained in its theatrically flat façade is a visual fruitcake of motifs—Indian, Iranian, and European, Hindu, Muslim, and Christian—pleasing to every sort of taste, salable to anyone from a Golconda or Safavid nobleman to a rich Hindu merchant or European factor.

212.
KALAMKARI
Madras region, perhaps Pulicat, ca. 1640-50
Cotton, resist dyed, 8 ft. 3½ in. × 6 ft. 5 in.
(2.53 × 1.96 m.)
The Metropolitan Museum of Art, New York,
Gift of Mrs. Albert Blum (20.79)

During the seventeenth and eighteenth centuries, makers of traditional kalamkaris adjusted to European customers, who wanted bedspreads, bed curtains, and yard goods for their rapidly expanding markets. These extended as far as America, where many colonial houses boasted spritely patterns made by Indian artisans.

In the center, proud and happy parents admire their curly-haired babe, whose pose recalls that of the infant Krishna crawling as butter thief. The mother is richly jeweled, and her mustachioed husband seems to be a Muslim of high degree, even though his jama is tied in the Hindu way, under the left shoulder. Most of the other Indian gentlemen are Muslim, and several are dressed in Safavid style. Whether enthroned, hunting, riding in a bullock cart, on horseback, performing music, arguing, gossiping, drinking, or just milling about, they are almost as decorative as the ladies, who range from the mother to a yogini, from a musician to the refined and sumptuously dressed trio. Resembling the Three Graces out for a stroll, they seem destined to meet the gentleman of similar scale who waits at the right, his arm casually resting on his typically Deccani straight-bladed sword. Everyone in the picture is engulfed by flowers, blossoming in every nook and cranny and strung into the garlands that dangle from every cornice. Between the parents and the trio of ladies is a row of coffers, vases, bowls, cups, a crutch, and a walking stick, superbly adorned with dots, dashes, curlicues, and arabesques.

212, detail

The courtier at the right is balanced by two Europeans, probably traced from prints: a wide-eyed gallant on a rearing horse, and, below, a down-in-the-mouth traveler or merchant leaning against an Indian bolster. Except for him, every personage, bird, deer, horse, and bullock exudes cheerfulness. Down to the last squiggle of flower, crockery, or molding on the gimcrack façade, drawing and coloring flowed mellifluously at the hand of this anonymous but accomplished painter, who had sampled the world's artistic motifs and chosen some as his own.

This magnificent hanging—along with a companion piece in the Victoria and Albert Museum, London[1]—was not expected to outlast a few years of use; but its artist, and his family of fellow craftsmen, never stinted in following the many complicated ideas and procedures that went into its manufacture, an entire science of mordants and dyes, infinite numbers of washings, dryings in the air, masking out of areas not to be colored, and of course the exuberant act of drawing.

1. For the companion piece, which has identical floral borders, see: Gittinger, *Master Dyers*, pp. 112–13, no. 103.

Published: Morris, "An Indian Hanging," pp. 143, 149–52; Clousoz and Morris, *Painted and Printed Fabrics*, pl. III; Irwin, "Golconda Cotton Paintings," p. 38, fig. 5, pl. V; Irwin and Brett, *Origins of Chintz*, fig. 2.

THE SHAPE OF this armguard, called a dastana or bazuband, is typical of those used in the Deccan and southern India from the sixteenth to the eighteenth century. Both plates have a transverse elliptical rib at the wrist. The long plate, curved out at the top to accommodate the elbow, protected the outer forearm, and the shorter plate guarded the inside of the wrist. A gauntlet, probably mail, attached to the main plate would have covered the hand. Steel pins through the hinges, which are also steel and were originally silver plated, held the two plates together around the arm. An Indian soldier often wore only one vambrace, on his sword hand if he was on foot and carrying a shield, on his bridle hand if on horseback or, we presume, riding an elephant.

Most Indian armguards are made of steel. Some are plain; some are embellished with chased patterns or koftgari work (gold or silver inlay). Calligraphy is sometimes introduced into designs of floral motifs and arabesques, but this is the only armguard we know of where the entire surface has been covered with openwork calligraphy and engraved ornamentation. The calligraphy, exceptionally well-written Thuluth script, has been brilliantly executed in thick copper sheet. On the long plate, the ninety-nine names of the Prophet Muhammad and invocations to him are arranged in four rows on either side of the central rib, and the narrow band at the wrist contains another openwork inscription. An arched cartouche above the wrist, incorporating the transverse rib, encloses openwork and engraved floral decoration. The short plate has similar floral ornament in two panels separated by a plant motif and framed by a band of script in openwork, part of the Throne Verse (Sura 2:255) from the Qur'an. The edges of the plates are enriched and reinforced by narrow borders decorated with engraved trefoils. Few craftsmen would even attempt a project as exacting and time-consuming as this.

Such superb workmanship is rarely encountered on armor made for defense rather than purely for show, and we might at first think this vambrace was a ceremonial accessory for a king. But because the ornate copper overlay is supported from inside by a steel plate, we believe the armguard may indeed have been worn on the battlefield—by a king who was not actually fighting but directing his army from his seat atop an armored elephant. Armor inscribed with passages from the Qur'an provided the wearer with not only physical but talismanic protection and assured his victory.

J.M.

Published: *The Indian Heritage*, p. 137, no. 453.

213.
VAMBRACE
Deccan, Golconda, ca. 1650–60
Steel with gilded copper overlay,
length 13⅞ in. (35.2 cm.)
Jagdish and Kamla Mittal Museum of Indian
Art, Hyderabad (76.1526)

213

214.
ALBUM PAGE WITH VERSES IN
NASTAʿLIQ SCRIPT
Inscribed: "Faqir ʿArab"
Deccan, Golconda, ca. 1625–35
Opaque watercolor on paper, 6⅞ × 4 in.
(17.6 × 10 cm.)
Jagdish and Kamla Mittal Museum of Indian
Art, Hyderabad (76.1541)

TWO PERSIAN VERSES in praise of eyebrows are written diagonally across this album page on paper marbled in orange and green (see no. 198). Gold arabesques with touches of blue embellish the spaces between the lines of calligraphy, and floral arabesques are painted in colors on a lapis lazuli ground in the top right and bottom left corners. The graceful Nastaʿliq script, the matching curves of the sword-shaped arabesques, and the pattern of the marbled paper all convey the varying moods expressed by the changing shapes of eyebrows, echoing, in an abstract way, the words of the poem.

The cloud of marbling in the lower left corner contains the calligrapher's name, Faqir ʿArab. Mulla ʿArab Shirazi originally came from Shiraz, in Iran. It is said that he was not only well versed in ornamental writings and inscriptions but could write more than a thousand couplets a day. He was one of the expert calligraphers appointed by Sultan Muhammad Qutb-Shah of Golconda (r. 1612–26), who had a great passion for books and made many important additions to the royal library, to transcribe copies of rare manuscripts.

Mulla ʿArab's name also appears on a royal illuminated copy of the *Fawaʾid-i Qutb-Shahi* (The Benefits of Qutb-Shah), a collection of Persian prose and poetry compiled in 1630 by order of Muhammad's successor, ʿAbdullah Qutb-Shah (r. 1626–72). The manuscript, like this album page, is written in Nastaʿliq script, which had come into vogue at Golconda during the reign of Muhammad-Quli Qutb-Shah (1580–1612) and thereafter continued to be used for all secular manuscripts and inscriptions. Five calligraphers worked on the eighty-eight folios; ʿArab Katib (Arab the Scribe) and one other wrote the third part, dated A.H. 1040 (1631).

From the names of the five calligraphers who worked on the *Fawaʾid-i Qutb-Shahi* manuscript, as well as from other literary sources and the inscriptions on surviving Qutb-Shahi buildings, we can infer that most of the scribes at the Golconda court during this period were Persians from Shiraz, Isfahan, Tabriz, and Nishapur. Scholars, poets, painters, and calligraphers flocked to both the Mughal and the Deccani courts throughout the sixteenth and seventeenth centuries, for the Indian monarchs were famous for their lavish rewards for artistic talents. But Persians migrated in especially large numbers to Golconda, where the Qutb-Shahi dynasty was founded in about 1518. The steady influx was never greater than during Muhammad Qutb-Shah's reign, when the Peshwas Mir Muhammad Muʾmin and Shaikh Muhammad ibn Khatun as well as several key officials and merchants of Golconda were all Persians.

We are inclined to date this calligraphy to between 1625 and 1635. The opallike iridescence of the marbled paper, the perfectly spaced and elegantly written Nastaʿliq script, and the beautiful illumination in Shirazi style make the page worthy of an album for a book-loving sultan.

J.M.

215.
PEN BOX
Signed, on bottom: "Raqm-i banda
Rahim Deccani"
Deccan, style of Golconda, ca. 1680
Lacquer over papier-mâché, 1⅞ × 12 × 2¾ in.
(4.8 × 30.5 × 7 cm.)
Khalili Collection, London

SOME OBJECTS MOVE us with their intimacy. This small box conjures up appealing domestic scenes. In the Islamic world every educated person aspired to calligraphic excellence—for copying out Qurʾanic verses, for writing poetry, and for corresponding with friends and lovers. Boys and girls of good family learned not only to express themselves elegantly but to write letters as gratifying to the eye as to the mind. They became connoisseurs of writing materials. Lustrously black, mellifluously flowing inks, steel knives and scissors of surgical perfection to nib reed pens and to cut paper—all these enhanced the pleasure of penmanship.

Boxes for writing tools splendid as this one required months of artful toil by an entire workshop. Feather light and satin smooth but strong, almost impervious to water or ink stains, they were shaped and refined by a master of papier-mâché to satisfy a discerning clientele.

To the well-known artist Rahim Deccani, who signed this box, commissioned perhaps as a token of love, the challenge was as great as decorating a

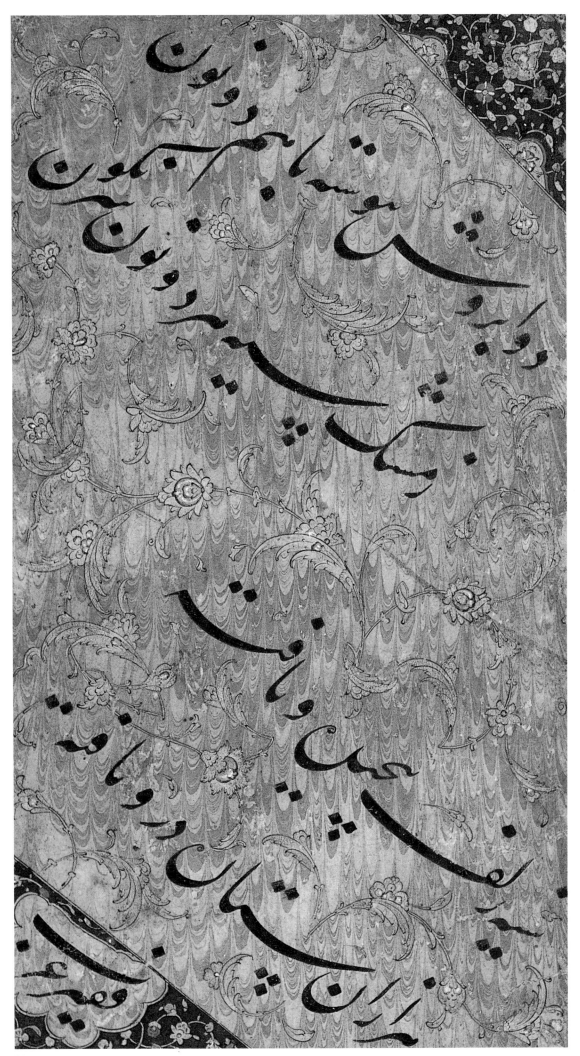

214

215, top

215

small room. On top, vignetted between lithely voluptuous sprays of leaves, are portraits of a lover, his beloved, and their attendants. Rows of sensitively ornamental flowers transform the sides into a garden, while the bottom, painted with grapevines in gold, promises a glass of wine once the letter has been composed.

Rahim's signing his name with the sobriquet "Deccani" suggests that he may no longer have been working in the Deccan, even though his markedly international mode, synthesizing Iranian, Deccani, and Mughal idioms, was formed there. His style is a gentle variant on that of an Iranian artist,

Shaikh ʿAbbasi, who headed a Golconda atelier with his two sons, Muhammad Taqi and ʿAli Naqi. Wherever this style was practiced—at Golconda, in Mughal India, or in Iran—the flavor was romantically exotic, and redolent of Golconda.

With its exquisite fineness of touch and unexpectedly forceful design, the Khalili pen box represents Rahim Deccani at the peak of his engagingly delicate style.[1]

1. On Rahim Deccani, see: Zebrowski, *Deccani Painting*, p. 201, pls. 169–76.

Published: Zebrowski, "Indian Lacquerwork," p. 337, pl. 3c (det.); Fehervari, "The Near East, the Middle East and India," pp. 159–60, p. 152, ill. (top and bottom only).

ONLY IN THE Deccan, and especially at Golconda, did painted horses resemble swans and scamper like dragons. Propelled from behind by a swirling tail, this graceful stallion prances through a network of twittering arabesques. Dagger points of his headgear notwithstanding, the determined but apprehensive young groom could not possibly control his snorting, airborne steed. Even the lion-skin saddle, its mask gazing pitifully heavenward, holds on for dear life.

Although this idiosyncratic, marvelously extreme picture defies attribution, its Iranian characteristics can be associated with Shaikh ʿAbbasi.

Published: Coomaraswamy, *Les Miniatures orientales*, p. 68, no. 109, pl. 67.

216.
HORSE AND GROOM
Deccan, probably Golconda, 3rd quarter of 17th century
Opaque watercolor on paper, 5½ × 8½ in. (14 × 21.5 cm.)
Museum of Fine Arts, Boston, Francis Bartlett Donation of 1912 and Picture Fund (14.699)

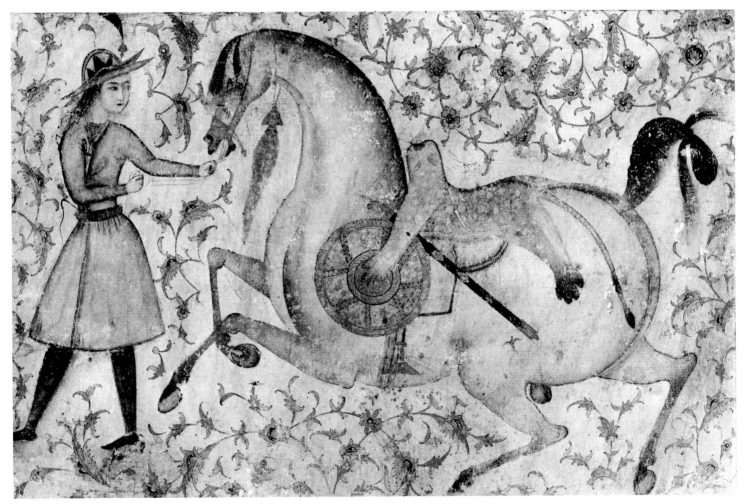

216

217

218

BIDRIWARE, SO CALLED because the technique is believed to have originated at the city of Bidar in the Deccan, is related to the brass and bronze wares inlaid with gold and silver long known in the Islamic world. Bidri objects are cast from an alloy chiefly of zinc with an admixture of copper and tin, often with a varying proportion of lead. They are then inlaid or overlaid with silver, brass, or sometimes gold. Finally, a mud paste containing sal ammoniac is applied, and when the coating is removed the alloy has been imparted a permanent rich matte black that provides a pleasing contrast to the encrusted design. The earliest known bidriware is a huqqa base inlaid with silver and brass, now in the Jagdish and Kamla Mittal Museum, that is inscribed: "On Rabi^c [10] 44 [1634] Najaf Quli, son of Nan, completed the work."

Bidar, capital of the Muslim Bahmanid kings in the fifteenth century and seat of the Barid-Shahi dynasty in the early sixteenth, remained the principal center of the industry, and bidri is still produced there and at Hyderabad. But during the eighteenth and nineteenth centuries, both Muslim and Hindu craftsmen made bidri objects at centers at Lucknow and Banaras in Uttar Pradesh, Purnea in Bihar, Murshidabad in West Bengal, and elsewhere. The simple, elegant shapes of seventeenth-century bidriware derive from Persian, Mughal, and Deccani prototypes, and the deeply inlaid decoration is based chiefly on Mughal and Deccani designs. Seminaturalistic floral motifs typical of all Mughal decorative arts at the time appear in bidri as well, yet the vibrant, uncrowded Deccani adaptations are charged with exceptional vitality; in the best examples the floral designs seem almost to burst with an explosive force.

This plate, one of the finest examples of early bidri, was made at Bidar sometime between 1650 and 1700. An accomplished craftsman sensitively and imaginatively rendered the originally Mughal design in teh-nishan work (the Persian translates literally as "sitting on the bottom"), a type of koftgari technique in which the alloy is deeply engraved and gold, silver, or brass hammered into the grooves and filed down until the finished inlay is flush with the surface. (In ordinary koftgari, very fine wire is hammered into shallower grooves.) The plate's interior is embellished with eight cartouches, each of which encloses a dianthuslike plant bearing six flowers against a background filled with tiny Chinese cloud motifs in the manner that became characteristic of Mughal and Deccani ornamentation in the sixteenth and seventeenth centuries. A chevron pattern decorates the flattened rim, and scrolling floral designs ornament the shallow cavetto, the spaces between the cartouches, and the band encircling the blank central medallion.

J.M.

Published: *The Indian Heritage*, p. 142, no. 481.

THE FORMS OF bidriware are infinitely varied and always useful: huqqa bases, containers for spices and for betel nut and the lime and spices to go with it, wine and sherbet bottles, salvers, dishes, cups, and many more. Always eager to attract new markets, the metalworkers of Bidar adjusted their styles over the centuries to satisfy all manner of clients. Deccani sultans and their courtiers, Mughals, Rajputs, and rich merchants, French, English, and other Europeans—all were offered irresistibly enticing objects, which were often kept as eye-pleasers in architectural niches.

Using tracings, designers of bidri objects borrowed motifs from textiles, architectural ornament, and many other sources, sensitively adapting them and changing the patterns according to their own good judgment and to their patrons' tastes. Although bidriware has survived in considerable quantities from the mid-seventeenth century onward, no two objects are quite alike. From decade to decade, the precise formula of its alloy of zinc, tin, and copper varied almost as much as its ornament. Presumably, the ateliers descended within families which maintained trade secrets, pattern books, and networks of customers through the years, offering goods of varying levels of quality and price based on metal content, workmanship, and design. In the late eighteenth century, craftsmen from Bidar may have moved to Lucknow and there developed styles pleasing to the local nawabs and their courts.

The Metropolitan Museum's huqqa base is distinguished for its bold yet delicate floral brass inlays, masterfully related to the globular form of the bowl.

218.
HUQQA BASE
Deccan, Bidar, last quarter of 17th century
Alloy inlaid with brass, height 6⅞ in.
(17.5 cm.), diameter 6½ in. (16.5 cm.)
The Metropolitan Museum of Art, New York, Purchase, Louis E. and Theresa S. Seley Purchase Fund for Islamic Art and Rogers Fund (1984.221)

A FISH (MAHI) was one of the nine royal ensigns (nine being the number of perfection) symbolizing the Mughal emperors' conquest of the world. In an imperial retinue, standard-bearers carrying replicas of the nine emblems rode before the emperor on elephants and camels. Mahi o maratib (literally, fish and ranks), denoted by the figure of a fish with two balls or other insignia, was one of the highest honors the emperor could bestow on a noble. W. Irvine, in his *Army of the Indian Moghuls*, describes a Mughal fish standard, meant to be placed horizontally on the point of a spear, as four feet long and made of gilded copper.[1] Though we have no documentary evidence, fish standards must also have played a ceremonial role at the courts of the Muslim sultans who ruled in the Deccan from the fourteenth to the nineteenth century. The Jagdish and Kamla Mittal Museum has two other Deccani fish standards, both brass and both of the eighteenth century, in its collection.

This iron standard was cast in two parts that are held together by rivets. There are two circular holes in one of the bottom fins and an elongated slit in the tail for attaching a clamp to secure the standard to a handle. Sculpted with a careful eye for naturalistic detail, the noble fish has finely modeled scales and six fins, two on its back, two on its belly, and one on each side.

219.
FISH STANDARD
Deccan, perhaps Golconda or Bijapur, 17th century
Iron with traces of silver overlay, length 23⅛ in. (58.7 cm.)
Jagdish and Kamla Mittal Museum of Indian Art, Hyderabad (84.1)

219

The eye sockets once held shining stones, and the entire body was covered with thin sheets of silver overlaid on crosshatching, a technique often used in the Deccan to enrich arms and armor. Quite apart from its actual use, this is a fascinating object and a stirring work of art.

J.M.

1. Irvine, *The Army of the Indian Moghuls*, p. 33.

220.
CALLIGRAPHIC HAWK STANDARD
Deccan, perhaps Hyderabad, late 17th century
Gilded copper, height 13¾ in. (34.9 cm.)
Victoria and Albert Museum, London
(I.M.163–1913)

ALTHOUGH MOST MUGHALS were Muslims of the Sunni sect, there were many Shi'ites in the Deccan, especially in Golconda and Hyderabad. Like the Mughals, they participated in processions to celebrate religious and state occasions as well as familial rites of passage. Holy men, rulers, courtiers, and multitudes of followers joined these parades, some riding elephants or horses, most on foot, and all dressed up for the occasion. Bobbing on poles above their heads, emblematic standards lent further meaning and majesty to the events, whether celebratory festivities or dirges in commemoration of the Shi'ite martyrs Husain and Hasan. This gilded copper hawk is strikingly designed in Tughra script with the religious formula known as Nadi 'Aliyyan:

> Call 'Ali, the locus of manifestations of miracles—
> You will find him a help in the vicissitudes of life.
> All grief and sorrow will pass
> Thanks to your rule [or saintliness], O 'Ali—O 'Ali—O 'Ali![1]

This apotropaic formula was apparently introduced by the Safavids of Iran, for there are no instances of its use prior to 1500. It became one of the most frequently used invocations from Turkey across to India and was reproduced on paper, metal, stone, and cloth to bring good luck and for protection. It is also engraved on small agate talismans worn by devotees.

1. Translation by Annemarie Schimmel.

Published: Wheeler and Jayakar, *Textiles and Ornamental Arts*, p. 63.

220

325

221

BEFORE AND AFTER the Mughal seizure of the Deccani sultanates in the late seventeenth century, Mughal governors, officers, and soldiers cultivated Deccani ways. The leisurely, almost excessively civilized attitudes of the Deccan were infectious, as can be seen in this portrait of a determinedly official Mughal in his magnificent garden, proudly presenting, or receiving, a small piece of paper. The gallant nobleman and his attendants and emissaries are as crisply silhouetted on the page as the formal garden is laid out, with immaculately ordered watercourses, manicured trees, and obediently symmetrical arrangements of birds and deer. If we can believe the artist, Allah-wirdi Khan's life had achieved crystalline harmoniousness. Only a small peacock in the foreground, turning away, defies the system.

The late seventeenth century was a time of artistic ferment. Mughal officers from the north spent many years in the Deccan, where they employed artists trained at the great Deccani courts, such as Bijapur and Hyderabad. Many of these painters, as well as craftsmen and musicians, migrated with their new patrons to northern India, where Deccani styles blended with Mughal and Rajput traditions (see especially nos. 241, 242, 248, 249, 260, 265, 267).

Published: Das, *Treasures of Indian Painting*, ser. 1, pl. II; Zebrowski, *Deccani Painting*, pp. 236–37, pl. XXII.

IN THE DECCANI outposts of the waning Mughal empire, even officers at comparatively minor courts lived with extravagant elegance. Atachin Beg Bahadur Qalmik, a Turkman by lineage, indulged his artistic whims when he was painted against a spreading landscape alive with birds beneath rain

222

clouds that augur well for the next harvest. Hiding within the pyrotechnically striped coat, flowered sash, and sumptuous turban, the man himself is blandly plain, far less impressive than his belled and ringleted page, running alongside, his saluting courtier, or his horse. Indeed, the high-stepping steed, with its corkscrewing yak tail and opulent saddlecloth and plumes, is unconscionably curried and coiffed. His dapples twinkle like stars through a waterfall of mane, which ends in fetlock-tickling curls.

Who was Atachin Beg who so poetically adored his stallion? We are unlikely ever to know. But this curiously stirring picture indicates that its patron deeply appreciated and helped shape a marvelously extreme phase of later Deccani art, one that was rocketed to yet more fanciful heights at the Rajasthani court of Kishangarh a few decades later (see nos. 248, 249, 250).

Although Burhanpur never ranked in importance with Delhi, Agra, or Lahore, it was a major center of learning and religious activity, with many madrasas. ʿAbd ar-Rahim, the Khankhanan, the most distinguished and discerning of all nonimperial Mughal patrons (see no. 161), lived there during the first quarter of the sixteenth century, and Prince Khurram (later Emperor Shah Jahan) chose Burhanpur as his headquarters prior to his rebellion against Emperor Jahangir. Many weavers from Sind and Tatta migrated to Burhanpur during the early seventeenth century, and their splendid printed cottons lent colorful dignity to Mughal and Rajput courts (see no. 179).

Published: Zebrowski, *Deccani Painting*, pp. 212–13, pl. 185.

223.
PECHHAVAI FOR A TEMPLE OR SHRINE
Deccan, perhaps Hyderabad, ca. late 18th century
Paint on cotton, 8 ft. × 8 ft. 6 in. (2.44 × 2.59 m.)
Museum of Fine Arts, Boston, Gift of John Goelet (67.837)

TEMPLES AND HOUSEHOLD shrines sacred to the Hindu god Lord Krishna usually had altars bearing images behind which hung pechhavais (that which hangs at the back). In themselves greatly appealing works of art, these painted textiles should be imagined in situ, not only as backdrops but with offerings of flowers, sweets, spices, and even models of bullock carts or boats arranged before them and being worshiped by priests and other devotees. This joyous pechhavai is partly based on temple hangings painted in Rajasthan at Nathadwara, site of the major Vaishnavite temple complex and of the image of Lord Krishna as Shri Nathji.

In the center of the composition, which is appropriate to Varsha, the season of rain, a kadamba tree, possibly symbolic of the god himself, is attended by six gopis, Krishna's devoted herdswomen. Mango trees heavy with fruit are at either side, and red and green parrots roost in the branches. Flowers, probably signifying nourishing rain, are showered from the skies by airborne deities, while in the lower register cows and gopalas—all associated with Vaishnavite worship—contribute to the divine mood.

Published: *The Rathbone Years*, p. 52, no. 36.

I am indebted to Kalyan Krishna for providing information employed in this entry.

223

Overleaf, 259, detail ▷

THE RAJPUT WORLD

No one knows precisely when and how the Rajputs first came to India. "History," as usual, blends myth with fact. Rajputs, whose name is Hindi for sons (putras) of kings (rajans), are legendary descendants of the sun and the moon. As Rajput lore recounts it, their primary ancestor, called forth by the gods to defend the Brahmin priesthood, rose from the flames of a sage's firepit atop Mount Abu in southwestern Rajasthan. According to scholars, Rajputs descend from the Iranian and Central Asian tribes—Parthians, Kushans, Shakas, Huns, and others—who invaded India between the fourth and the seventh century, moving down through the mountain passes in the northwest and across the Indus Valley into what came to be known as Rajputana, land of the Rajputs, and is today the state of Rajasthan. Like the Aryans who came by the same route during the second millennium B.C., the invaders were soon Indianized, adding yet another variation to the pattern as they were absorbed into the cultural, social, and religious mosaic that is India. They intermarried with the indigenous Indian tribes whose ancestry preceded even the Aryans' arrival, as well as with high-caste Hindu families who were partly of Aryan descent. They became Hindus and were incorporated into the second of the four classes of Hindu society, the Kshatriyas, warriors and rulers who are the protectors of the first class, the Brahmins.

Proud followers of an ancient code of honor, Rajputs rank loyalty to family and clan second only to their paramount duty to serve the gods and the Brahmin priests. The medieval Rajput world brings to mind Europe's age of chivalry. During the early Middle Ages, in the centuries following the demise of the Gupta empire and the empire of King Harsha (d. 647) of Kanauj that succeeded it, Rajputs ruled much of northwestern India. Maharajas, rajas, maharanas, ranas, raos, rais, and other titled heads of the thirty-six Rajput clans and their many cadet, or junior, houses established small kingdoms in Rajasthan and eventually controlled feudal territories to the north in the Punjab Hills and to the south and west in Central India. The wealthiest and most powerful of the patriarchs built massive fortified complexes to house and protect their many dependents and their armies, and their entire establishments sometimes spent part of the year at hunting lodges, pleasure pavilions, or military encampments. Their constant feuding, however, left the Rajputs ill equipped to face the armies of Islam that came in ever increasing waves after the tenth century.

There were occasions when Rajput states combined forces in unsuccessful attempts to defend themselves, but the alliances were temporary and never involved more than a few of the clans. Some of the princes allied themselves early on with the Muslims, and one by one the others either acquiesced or were forced to submit. The senior Rajput house, the firmly traditional Sisodyas who ruled over Mewar, in western Rajasthan far from the Muslim centers, stoutly opposed even Akbar's imperial ambitions. Their centuries-long struggle ended ten years after Akbar's death, when Mewar fell to Emperor Jahangir in 1615 and the maharaja of Mewar, like the other Rajput rulers, began paying homage to the Mughal court with revenues and soldiers for the imperial armies. As the Mughal empire crumbled in the eighteenth century, the princes once again took advantage of a political vacuum to expand their territories, only to retreat once more when the British replaced the Mughals as the major power in India. Although many of the rajas continued to maintain their states, the new Raj sent residents to oversee the courts and, like its predecessor, exacted tribute in the form of taxes and soldiers. When independence came in 1947, the Rajputs lost most of what was left of their power.

The pictures and objects assembled here reflect the Rajput world from the sixteenth to the nineteenth century, when it was becoming a more and more complicated blend of the indigenous and the foreign. The great Rajput fort and palace complexes that still stand, many of them now museums, are often confusing monuments to centuries of change and accommodation. The structures were originally massively built for defense, with provision against attack not only for the ruler and his household but also for the villagers and their animals. During the mid-seventeenth century, Jahangir's and Shah Jahan's magnificent palaces at Agra and Delhi influenced the forts of their feudatories, and living quarters increased in comfort and splendor. White marble replaced red sandstone, and flower patterned carvings, inlays, and textiles enriched courtyards and darbar halls. When Mughal power began to wane, rocked by the invasions of Nadir Shah and others during the eighteenth century, traditional Rajput ways were reasserted. Less threatened by the imperial armies, the maharajas no longer had to live in forbidding forts. City palaces like the one Jai Singh built at Jaipur came into vogue: still stoutly walled and defensible, but open to the sun and more spacious, with extensive courts and gardens.

After the early nineteenth century, when many of the chiefs of Rajputana signed treaties with the British, European styles became fashionable, radically changing the appearance of Rajput architecture, art, and life. The British resident assigned to each court brought with him family, staff, household furnishings, pictures, books, and bric-a-brac by the barrel. In due course, English architects such as Sir Swinton Jacob were designing grandly operatic "Indo-Saracenic" palaces for the adventuresome, rich Rajput princes. Always respectful of power and fascinated by England's culture, Rajputs admired and began to emulate the exotic English ways of life. They delighted in the spectacle, the "tamasha," of it all, and before long maharajas' costumes juxtaposed Mughal irises with Scottish plaids, and English tables, chairs, clocks, and mirrors began to crop up even in the zenana, where the women received them with a mixture of astonishment, delight, and horror.

The Rajput world was of course never composed exclusively of Rajputs. The Hindu caste system has been likened to a man: the Brahmins, priests and scholars, are his mouth; the ruling and military class of Kshatriyas are his arms; Vaishyas, farmers and merchants, form his thighs; and the fourth class, the Shudras, are the man's essential feet. Without the others, none of the classes or the thousands of castes and subcastes that they comprise could survive. At the Rajput courts, Brahmin priests presided over morning prayers and the continuous cycle of sacred rituals and festivals. Brahmins also served as teachers and, because all castes may accept food from their hands, as cooks. Vaishyas were hired to look after state funds and to provide many specialized crafts and services; one of their many subcastes sold sweets, others were musicians and artists. Shudras worked in the fields and the dairies and at carpentry, building, metalsmithing, and dozens of other occupations.

Tribal people outside the caste system also often played crucial roles. At Jaipur, tribesmen were the hereditary guards of the state treasure, and when a new ruler was installed the ceremony was not valid until the maharaja's forehead had been marked with the tikka by a member of the Mina tribe, who had once ruled the region. Other religious groups worked in professions that often paralleled those of Hindus. Jains were businessmen and administrators, as were Parsis. Muslim influence was scarcely felt in the Punjab Hills and remote areas of Rajputana before the eighteenth century, but at the Hindu courts of eastern Rajasthan and Central India Muslims tended to be omnipresent by the late 1400s, when the first of the pictures shown here was painted for a Muslim patron. Muslim nobility such as the nawabs of Tonk formed part of the feudal system of Rajasthan, and they were among the honored guests at Rajput marriages and gatherings.

The walls of the major Rajput palaces enclosed what amounted to large, self-sufficient towns. Even fairly modest Rajput homes invariably contained a shrine, a darbar hall for receiving guests, a mardana where the men of the household slept, and a zenana for the women and children (a custom borrowed from the Muslim home), as well as servants' quarters and rooms for cooking and dining. In a grand palace, the place of worship was often a large temple, the mardana and zenana each a sprawling complex of private apartments with its own servants and separate gardens and pavilions. As did the Mughal emperors (whose customs and architecture were based at least in part on Rajput prototypes), the head of the house ruled over what was often a large army and a vast number of workers, servants, and retainers. Stables and barns housed scores of elephants, camels, horses, and other animals. Beneath the palace, in a labyrinth of godowns, was storage space for foodstuffs, weaponry, clothing, carpets and furniture, tents and awnings, jewels and gold, and manuscripts and paintings. Each section had a staff, in some instances not just custodians but craftsmen and artists who could make almost anything the court required.

Like Mughal emperors and nobles, Rajput princes spent much time in tents, virtual cities of cloth and rope that included a portable palace complete with shrines, public and private audience halls, living quarters, a treasury, and an armory. When a Rajput prince of the standing of the maharaja of Jodhpur served in a major campaign, such as those of Shah Jahan or Aurangzeb in the Deccan, whole communities were away from home for years on end. When in the field, a prince was outfitted with two complete suites of tents, one of which he occupied while the other was being set up at the next stage of the march. (A Rajput or Mughal army moved at a rate that varied from a leisurely seven and a half miles per day to thirty-five on a forced march.) The raja traveled in stately progress, accompanied by an entourage of priests, wives, children, courtiers, musicians, dancing girls, artists, and domestic animals, in addition to the hunting and military establishments. A special commissary provided the princely household with water and food, some brought on camelback, the rest foraged and hunted for en route. The army looked after itself, buying food, clothing, weapons, and sweets and other luxuries from the merchants of an accompanying bazaar, which was also staffed with bankers and moneylenders. Food for the elephants and horses was provided either by a small army of grasscutters or by special merchants of the Banjara caste, who traveled very slowly (two miles a day) with as many as 50,000 bullocks laden with sacks of grain. By mutual consent, the Banjaras were never injured by the enemy.

Brilliant generals and mighty warriors though they may have been, the rajas of Rajasthan and the Punjab Hills were also often men of formidable intellect, architects, poets, and connoisseurs who surrounded themselves with highly skilled and talented scholars, artisans, and painters. We display here but a sampling of the output of the Rajasthani and Hill, or Pahari, ateliers during the more than four hundred years of Rajput patronage and artistry that nourished a great flowering of Indian painting.

The cultural traditions of the Rajput courts underwent a profound change after the establishment of Mughal rule in the sixteenth century. The series of Rajput alliances forged by Akbar soon after his accession to the throne in 1556 gave the courts of Amber (later Jaipur), Jodhpur, Bikaner, and Bundi a new prominence by their association with and exposure to the emperor's brilliant and cosmopolitan court.

Prior to the strongly secular influence of the Mughal court, Hindu painting was almost exclusively religious in nature. A resurgence of popular Hindu bhakti cults during the fifteenth century sparked renewed interest in the divinities of ancient India, notably in the two incarnations of Vishnu, the god Rama (hero of the *Ramayana*) and the youthful, dark-skinned cowherd god Krishna. Their exploits were celebrated in devotional texts and lyrics in both Sanskrit and the vernacular languages, and they also became popular themes for manuscript illustration. Books from the *Ramayana* and the *Mahabharata*, the love lyrics of the *Chaurapanchasika* of Bilhana, the tales of Krishna and Radha from the *Gita Govinda* of Jayadeva, the heroes and heroines of Keshavadasa's *Rasikapriya*—all these became the subjects of countless series of paintings distinguished by fluency of line and glowing color, whose figures and settings were suffused with symbolic meaning. Love, whether human or divine, remained the dominant theme of Hindu literature, as it had earlier been in Sanskrit texts.

Following the successive waves of Mughal influence in the sixteenth and seventeenth centuries, the local schools of Rajasthan and Central India assimilated elements of Mughal style in varying degrees. Malwa and Bundelkhand, for example, too remote to be much influenced by Mughal customs, remained closest to the bold drawings, simplified designs, and color schemes of the pre-Mughal style. The desert state of Marwar, by contrast, with its capital at Jodhpur, absorbed many elements of the Mughal style (notably evolving its own refined tradition of portraiture), but never completely lost its indigenous folk rhythms. The ranas of Mewar, who had so staunchly held out against the Mughal efforts to dominate Rajasthan, patronized a school of painting that produced an abundance of religious manuscripts in the early Rajasthani style; but after about 1700, Udaipur artists produced large and impressive paintings of the palace environs.

Portraits, darbar scenes, processions, and festivals were popular subjects, and they provide an excellent record of Rajput court life in the eighteenth century. The courts of Jaipur, Bikaner, Bundi, and Kishangarh, all of which were economically and politically linked with Mughal rule, were major centers of painting in the seventeenth and eighteenth centuries. They combined Rajasthani and Mughal features with ease and assurance, but they also developed their own conventions in the treatment of color and of landscape figures. Because of military contacts with the Deccan, the schools of Bikaner and Bundi received the added stimulus of Deccani style and color schemes. The Kishangarh school is best known for the stylized, attenuated portraits in a late Mughal style, often shown against an extensive landscape vista, that were created during the reign of the Vaishnavite devotee and poet Raja Sawant Singh (r. 1748–64). The Kotah school, occasionally indistinguishable from that of Bundi, the sister state from which Kotah was separated in the early seventeenth century, is best known for the large, dramatic, and minutely observed hunting scenes that it produced from about 1720 to 1870.

In the Pahari region of the Himalayan states, an area only some three hundred miles long by a hundred wide, indigenous traditions at the numerous minor Rajput kingdoms remained free of internationalizing Mughal influences far longer. Their rajas sent fewer officers and soldiers to serve in the imperial army, and the Mughal emperors rarely visited the more inaccessible courts in the Hills. Though their cultural background was similar to that of their southern counterparts in Rajasthan, the intervening expanse of the Punjab Plains kept them in relative isolation.

The origins of Pahari painting are still relatively obscure, but its earliest associations are with the court paintings of Basohli. These are remarkable for their taut line and vibrant and sophisticated color combinations, and paintings of Krishna and Devi are highly charged with an almost primitive intensity.

Although there is some evidence of Mughal influence even in the early phases of the Pahari tradition (in paintings from Bilaspur, for example), it was only in the second quarter of the eighteenth century that fundamental changes were introduced. This was the result of Nadir Shah's conquest of Delhi in 1739, after which artists trained in the Mughal style began emigrating to provincial centers in search of patronage. At such courts as Guler, Chamba, Jammu, Kangra, and Nurpur, these painters applied their refined technique to depicting Hindu poetical and devotional subjects. Thus the mature Pahari style was a combination of Mughal drawing techniques and Pahari lyricism: as in Rajasthan, the love of Krishna and Radha was a universal theme, and artists depicted it on all levels, from the spiritual to the erotic, often blending the two.

There was a short-lived renaissance of traditional styles when Mughal power weakened in the eighteenth century. However, the invasions of the Hill kingdoms by the Gurkhas, and their annexation by the Sikhs in the early nineteenth century, combined with the growing Rajput taste for European paintings and photographs, eventually deprived Pahari and Rajasthani artists alike of their much needed patronage, and in effect marked the end of India's great painting traditions.

224

MANY OF THE liveliest early pictures from the Rajput world illustrate romances, fable books, and Hindu epics, such as the *Laur Chanda*, the *Bhagavad Gita*, and the *Ramayana*, which combine moral and religious instruction and animated storytelling. Rajput courtiers, townspeople, and villagers learned about the gods and about life from these captivating tales, some of which they memorized as children and which became fundamental to their thought, much as Biblical tales in the Western traditions.

This miniature is from the *Laur Chanda*, a romance written by Mulla Da'ud for the chief minister of Firoz Shah Tughluq of Delhi in 1377 or 1378. It describes the frustrating love of the beautiful maiden Chanda for Laurik, each of whom suffered from being married to someone else. Eager to be together, the young couple plotted to elope. One night, as shown here, Laurik went to Chanda's house, where she was under guard in an upper room, and tossed up a rope ladder to her, and she climbed down to join him.

Working in a wiry, animated style related to Western Indian painting (see no. 31), the anonymous artist recounted the episode vividly, using only a few colors and swiftly sketched lines. Starry skies and a see-through house fix time and place; and the dramatis personae are projected as types rather than as individuals by formulaic, angular simplifications of feature and gesture. Nevertheless, Chanda's loving eagerness, her maid's apprehensive encouragement, the guard's obliging lassitude, and Laurik's muscular boldness are conveyed with directness and verve.

Published: *The Art of India and Pakistan*, p. 109, no. 398, pl. 82; Krishnadasa, "An Illustrated Avadhi of Laur-Chanda," p. 70, fig. 2; Khandalavala and Chandra, *New Documents of Indian Painting*, pp. 48, 133, no. 99, fig. 99; M. Chandra, *Studies in Early Indian Painting*, pp. 97–98, fig. 49; Khandalavala, "The Mrigavat of Bharat Kala Bhavan," p. 25, pl. 3; Krishna, "An Illustrated Manuscript of the Laur-Chanda," p. 276 and n. 5, p. 288, fig. 613.

224.
THE HEROINE ELOPES
From a manuscript of the *Laur Chanda*, or *Chandayana* (The Story of Chanda), of Mulla Da'ud
Uttar Pradesh, ca. 1450–75
Opaque watercolor on paper
Folio: 8¾ × 5¾ in. (22.2 × 14.5 cm.)
Miniature: 8⅜ × 4½ in. (21.2 × 11.4 cm.)
Bharat Kala Bhavan, Banaras Hindu University, Varanasi (5440)

A PARTICULARLY VITAL early group of miniatures from the Rajput world is represented by this battle scene, the four parts of which were recently recognized by Daniel J. Ehnbohm as forming a single composition.[1] For many years, probably for centuries, these fragments had been lost within a now dispersed, brilliant set of one hundred or more illustrations—in the same style, some by the same artist—to the *Bhagavata Purana*, the Hindu epic recounting the life of Lord Krishna.[2] Inasmuch as the Blue God does not appear in this dizzyingly charged scene, which bears no text on either the recto or the verso, the actual battle has not been identified. Ehnbohm has suggested, however, that it might be from a manuscript of the *Mahabharata* (The Book of Wars).

The *Bhagavata Purana* series has been dated by Jagdish Mittal to about 1541–42.[3] His argument is based on the presence of the numerallike marks in Devanagari style with which several of the horses shown are branded; the significance of these marks is evident in light of the following historical events. In 1537 Sher Khan, the Afghan leader of northern India, asserted his independence of the Mughals, overrunning Bengal. In 1539 he overwhelmed the army of Humayun and the following year annihilated the Mughal army at Kanauj. Humayun fled to Iran, and Sher Khan as Sher Shah Sur took control of the Mughal empire. He reigned until 1545.

The branding of Sher Shah Sur's cavalry horses was introduced between April 1541 and April 1542, when the army was in the area of Agra and Delhi.[4] The practice must have come to the attention of artists in that region. In all likelihood, the *Bhagavata Purana* series was being painted at that time and the artists incorporated the new feature in the battle scenes.[5]

As reassembled here, the picture is a noble and imposing example of a crucially important style among the infinity of syntheses that evolved in Indian painting. And within it, many earlier artistic strains can be identified —indigenous Indian styles, sultanate traditions, even vestiges from such ancient ancestors as the Sassanians, who contributed the pinwheel crown worn by the gray-bearded warrior in the fragment at the upper right.

225.
BATTLE SCENE
Four fragments constituting a folio from a dispersed manuscript of the *Bhagavata Purana*
Uttar Pradesh, Delhi or Agra area, or Mewar, 2nd quarter of 16th century
Opaque watercolor on paper
Folio: approx. 16½ × 20 in.
(41.9 × 50.8 cm.)
Each fragment: approx. 7 × 9⅜ in.
(17.8 × 23.9 cm.)

a. Jagdish and Kamla Mittal Museum of Indian Art, Hyderabad (76.119)
b. Collection Jagdish Goenka, Bombay
c. Collection Stuart Cary Welch
d. The Kronos Collections, New York

225a

225b

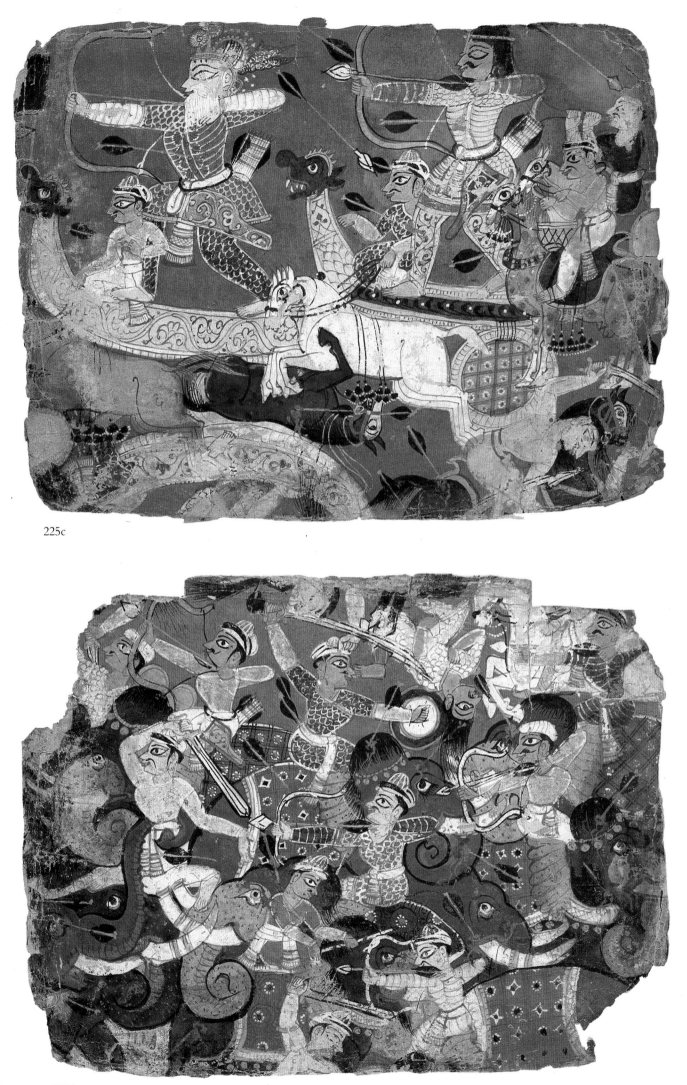

225c

225d

Marvelous to behold, this heroic melee is also highly instructive, enabling us through its scale to envision long lost murals from the area of Delhi and Agra prior to the absorption of the style into the all-encompassing new artistic synthesis under Akbar. With its crescendo of energy, animated gestures, and vivid thumbnail characterizations of men and animals, this style can be seen as a major element in the formation of yet another evolutionary stage during the early Mughal period. Indeed, it provided the dynamism to a defensible if very much simplified art-historical equation: the style of this battle scene combined with the imported Safavid idiom of Mir Sayyid ʿAli and ʿAbd as-Samad (see no. 84) to create Akbar's new synthesis, exemplified in the *Hamza-nama* (no. 91).

1. Daniel J. Ehnbohm made the important realization in the late 1970s that three of the fragments were from a single painting, a theory borne out when he saw the fourth, the Kronos miniature, in 1981.
2. Strikingly similar in style to the *Bhagavata Purana* series and to this battle scene are the illustrations to a manuscript dated 1516. See: Khandalavala and Chandra, *An Illustrated Aranyaka Parvan*. Also related is a battle scene, apparently the only surviving picture from another series. See: Welch, *A Flower from Every Meadow*, no. 5.
3. Personal communication, January 1985.
4. Irvine, *The Army of the Indian Moghuls*, p. 46.
5. Khandalavala and Mittal, "The Bhagavata," pp. 28–32, pls. IX, X, XIV, fig. 4a.

Published: Welch and Beach, *Gods, Thrones, and Peacocks*, pp. 24, 115–16, pl. 3a; Lerner, *The Flame and the Lotus*, pp. 146–47, no. 57.

226

THIS SHARP-EYED SCRIBE is as monumentally imposing as a yogi. Propped up like the tripod bearing his water flask, his knees held fast by a sash wound around them, he works smilingly. The portrayal perfectly exemplifies the indigenous tradition, experienced more by the mind's eye than by direct observation. The scribe's fingers bend unnaturally backward, totally contradicting our knowledge of reality, and—perhaps by inverting our expectation—impelling us all the more to feel the grip of his fingers and to hear the scratch of reed against paper. Our empathic response probably parallels that of Akbar, and it recalls Abu'l-Fazl's claim that Akbar's "[Hindu] artists surpass our conception of things."[1] *A Scribe* brings to mind Akbar's vivid little portraits of single figures, such as the one of Tansen (no. 106); similarly stark in its isolation against a flat ground, the figure is so extraordinarily moving because the artist painted from both his inner and his outer eye, each view enhancing the other.

The Bharat Kala Bhavan owns two hundred fifty folios of the *Mrigavata* series to which this miniature belongs. The text, written in the Kaithi script associated with eastern Uttar Pradesh, has been described by Karl Khandalavala as "a strange tale of love, fantasy, magic, and the supernatural."[2] It was composed by Shaikh Qutban in 1503, apparently for a ruler of the Sharqi dynasty of Jaunpur. Always lively, the pictures can be assigned to several artists of various levels of accomplishment, some like this one being masterfully incisive, others verging on the folkloristic. The scribe's simplified fish-shaped eye and zigzag profile are timeless formulas found even today in the carved and polychromed puppets of Rajasthan, and familiar here from the Bengali mortuary portrait (no. 46).

1. Abu'l-Fazl, *A'in*, vol. 1, p. 107.
2. Khandalavala, "The Mrigavat of Bharat Kala Bhavan," p. 27.

Published: Khandalavala, "The Mrigavat of Bharat Kala Bhavan," pp. 34–35, fig. 90, folio 32.

226.
A SCRIBE
From a manuscript of the *Mrigavata* of Qutban
Probably Uttar Pradesh, ca. 1525
Opaque watercolor on paper
Folio: 8 × 7⅛ in. (20.3 × 18.1 cm.)
Miniature: 5¼ × 5 in. (13.3 × 12.7 cm.)
Bharat Kala Bhavan, Banaras Hindu University, Varanasi (7957)

◁225d, detail

227

227.

227.
BILHANA MAKES LOVE WITH
CHAMPAVATI
From a manuscript of the *Chaurapanchasika*
(Fifty Verses of Chauras) of Bilhana
Mewar or Uttar Pradesh, mid-16th century
Opaque watercolor on paper, 6⅜ × 8½ in.
(16.3 × 21.7 cm.)
Bharat Kala Bhavan, Banaras Hindu University,
Varanasi (10515)

THE TEXT READS: "At this moment of my death, nay, even in my next birth,
I shall ever remember that swan in the cluster of lotuses of love, with her
eyes closed in the ecstasy of love, all her limbs relaxed, while her garments
and the tresses of her hair were strewn in disorder." According to legend,
the Sanskrit love poems of the *Chaurapanchasika* (Fifty Verses of Chauras)
were written in the eleventh century by Chauras, a young Brahmin who was
in love with the daughter of the ruler of Kanchinpur. The ruler was so
incensed by the young man's presumptuousness that he sentenced him to
death. While awaiting his fate, the poet put into verse his recollections of
happy days and nights of love. Another version of the story, followed in this
manuscript, states that the ill-fated young man was named Bilhana, the king
Virasimha, and the enamored daughter Champavati.[1]

In his miniature, the artist followed the spirit of the text as decorously
as the translator. Bilhana undresses Champavati with surgical scrupulousness
while Champavati averts her glance. The lotus petals on the edges of their
pavilion, however, glow with the flame of love.

The eighteen illustrations surviving from the series were acquired by
N. C. Mehta at Pratapgarh, near Mewar, and quite possibly they were painted
there. Since their discovery, they have been recognized as key documents of
Indian painting. The style, with its even, wiry outlines, coolly accomplished
brushwork, and crisp masterfulness, represents the Mewar idiom in full
ripeness, not at a more vigorous and experimental earlier stage such as we
find in the battle scene (no. 225).

1. For further comment on the series, see: *The Art of India and Pakistan*, p. 109, no.
396, pl. 81; M. Chandra, *Studies in Early Indian Painting*, fig. 69.

Published: Shiveshwarkar, *The Pictures of the Chaurapanchasika*, pl. v; Khandalavala,
"The Mrigavat of Bharat Kala Bhavan," pl. vi.

228.
BHAIRAVA RAGA
From a Ragamala (Garland of Melody) series
Chunar, Bundi school, dated 1591
Opaque watercolor on paper
Folio: 11½ × 7⅜ in. (29.1 × 18.6 cm.)
Miniature: 10 × 6⅛ in. (25.5 × 15.7 cm.)
Victoria and Albert Museum, London
(I.S. 40–1981)

THE GOD SHIVA, besmeared with ashes, takes his ease with two ladies in a
palace by night in this particularly intense and powerful version of one of
the musical modes, the Bhairava raga. The mood of the raga combines terror,
grandeur, seriousness, and awe-inspiring adoration. It should be performed
in autumn, before sunrise. While following the usual iconography, the artists
have underscored Shiva's severe asceticism and power and stressed his
meditative aspect. Seemingly illumined from within, the god sits on a cushion of lotus petals beneath the skin of the flayed elephant Nila (the Blue

One), whom he had slaughtered in his aspect as Bhairava (the Destroyer). His tiger pelt is tied by coiled snakes, and his knot of hair resembles his attribute, the lingam, from which emerges a small profile of a woman —visualized, perhaps, through his concentration. Shiva's expression is radiant, his third eye prominently crowned by the young moon. He wears a necklace of severed heads, and he plays the vina to an elegantly dressed lady, perhaps Parvati, who offers him pan (ground betel nut wrapped in a leaf). Both she and the chauri bearer are rapturously attentive.

The setting is royal and romantic. Facing a courtyard with a small pool and fountain with paddling ducks, Shiva and his devotees occupy a chamber rich with decorative carvings and tiles, golden vessels, gilded ornaments, and sumptuous textiles, including a carpet with floral arabesques. A peacock struts on the roof in front of a small pavilion, with chhatris at either side.

Although the mood of the picture is strongly devotional and Hindu, many of its elements are not. The duck pond, carpet, arabesque ornament, and tiles are standard furniture in Mughal and Safavid painting; and the palpable roundness of limbs, the heavily modeled, convincingly three-dimensional architecture, and the extreme fineness of handling all stem from Mughal prototypes. This is fully consistent with the history of the series to which this miniature, with its unusually rich borders, belongs. The last folio is inscribed in blue Nasta'liq script stating that it was completed at the time of midday prayer on February 25, 1591, at Chunar by "the pupils of Mir Sayyid 'Ali and 'Abd as-Samad, the slaves Shaikh Husain and Shaikh 'Ali and Shaikh Hatim, sons of Shaikh Phul Chishti."[1] When it was discovered that the raos of Bundi maintained a palace at Chunar, which adjoined Banaras, it became clear that the series must have been painted there for Rao Bhoj Singh of Bundi (see no. 245), one of Emperor Akbar's officers.[2] One could hardly cite a more dramatic instance of cultural and religious integration. This Bhairava raga, one of the most burningly devotional of Rajput paintings, whose iconography seems to have been established at Bundi, is not only the work of a Muslim artist, or artists, trained under formerly Safavid masters at Fatehpur-Sikri but is by the son, or sons, of a Muslim saint!

1. Skelton, "Shaykh Phul," has suggested that Shaikh Phul is the same saint of the Chishti order portrayed in *Shaikh Phul in His Hermitage* (no. 140).
2. For the 1591 Ragamala series, see: Beach, *Rajput Painting at Bundi and Kota*, p. 9; Welch, "Review of *Bundi Painting* by P. Chandra," p. 295n; Welch and Beach, *Gods, Thrones, and Peacocks*, pp. 33, 116, pl. 5; Welch, *A Flower from Every Meadow*, pp. 40–41, no. 17.

Published: *The Indian Heritage*, p. 57, no. 138; Topsfield, *An Introduction to Indian Court Painting*, pp. 33–34, pl. 21.

229.
ELEPHANTS AND WATER SPIRITS
From a manuscript of the *Gajendra Moksha* (The Deliverance of the Elephant King Gajendra)
Probably Ajmer, ca. 1640
Opaque watercolor on paper
Folio: 8⅜ × 12 in. (21.3 × 30.5 cm.)
Miniature: 7¾ × 11½ in. (19.7 × 29.2 cm.)
Collection Jagdish Goenka, Bombay (160)

BENEATH THE THREE summits of Mount Trikuta—one gold, another silver, the third iron—was a tranquil lake often visited by the elephant king and his herd. As described in the *Gajendra Moksha* (The Deliverance of the Elephant King Gajendra), an episode from the *Bhagavata Purana*, the valley was a resort of sportive siddhas (semidivine sky dwellers), gandhavras (heavenly musicians), kinnaras (horse-headed choristers of the firmament), apsaras (heavenly nymphs), and mighty sea serpents. Music played constantly, and celestial damsels made a playground of a nearby garden. Life was idyllic. But unknown to the carefree elephants, lurking in the water's depths was a crocodile demon who entangled the king in his tentacles and tried to drown him. For a millennium a battle raged between these well-matched forces of good and evil; it ended only when the god Vishnu, at last fearful of the outcome, interrupted his life of ease. He stepped from his throne, mounted Garuda (his half-bird, half-man vehicle), swooped down to the lake, and calmly spun a quoit, which—as the elephant king sank toward death—cut off the monster's head.

Few Rajput pictures are so liltingly paradisiacal. Within the deep blue strip of sky one senses the presence of the heavenly beings, while below we share the splashing and trumpeting of the king and of his wives and babes in the luminous lake. The master artist of this well-known series may have

229

come from Ahmadnagar in the Deccan (see no. 191). Attentively observant, and appreciative of the comical similarities between elephants' tails and trunks, he was above all an inventive colorist. The restrained palette—light blue water, deep blue sky, darkish gray elephants, and yellow-green shore and rocky islands, set within bright red borders—is touched off by the small electrifying charges of mint-fresh green lotus and parrots.[1]

1. For the painting from the same series showing Vishnu's destruction of the crocodile demon, see: Welch and Beach, *Gods, Thrones, and Peacocks*, pl. 13.

Published: Khandalavala, Chandra, and Chandra, *Miniature Painting*, pp. 57–58, no. 142a–d, fig. 99.

FOLLOWING THE CRISP formulas of painting from the so-called Malwa tradition of Central India, a stage has been set for carefully categorized lovers: black sky and slate blue landscape, white horizon line, dead white platform, trees growing like candy canes and feathers and inhabited by rowdy monkeys, and a peacock crying for its mate. Perhaps in emulation of artists of the Mughal court, Sukhadeva and several other artists employed by the Rajputs at this time foreswore their wonted anonymity and proudly inscribed their names on the backs of pictures. Sukhadeva deserved to be pleased by his series of illustrations to the *Rasabeli* of the early seventeenth-century poet Puhkara. In this one the stodgy monotonies of Malwa painting suddenly come to life. His brush danced dots, blobs, dashes, and long runs, in colors subtle as those of Japanese lacquer painters. Spiny accents of yellow and red

230.
THE BELOVED WHO PROPOSES LOVE
By Sukhadeva
From a manuscript of the *Rasabeli* of Puhkara
(folio 12)
Perhaps Bundelkhand, Malwa school, ca. 1660
Opaque watercolor on paper
Folio: 9⅞ × 7¼ in. (25.1 × 18.4 cm.)
Miniature: 9½ × 6¾ in. (24.1 × 17.2 cm.)
National Museum, New Delhi
(51.63/14)

enflame his dark green trees like a burning wind and transmit blue heat to the small figures. The hero, resembling a butterfly that has just alighted on a white rose, stands, sword in hand, blue as Krishna, and crowned with the god's peacock plumes. Either he awaits words from his nayika or he responds incredulously to those just spoken. For, unlike most heroines, she has taken the active role and proposed her love to him. Subtle Sukhadeva understood —and characterized her appropriately, with assertive gestures and a charming but knife-edged profile, and wearing a partly veiled bold-striped garment.

This picture represents seventeenth-century Central Indian painting at a slightly postclassical moment, when traces of far earlier, earthier gusto, reminiscent of the *Hamza-nama* (no. 91), are still evident in the patterned vitality of the trees. But the style here achieves a peak of synthesizing refinement, as seen in the fineness of the brushwork, the artfully controlled palette, and the individualized characterizations. Rooted in the indigenous Hindu tradition, the Central Indian schools responded strongly to sultanate painting traditions, which they soon absorbed; and in the present miniature, Sukhadeva reveals a further cautious acceptance of Mughal ways.

Published: Krishna, *Malwa Painting*, pl. 18.

"O MOTHER, MY whole being is in love with Biharilal [Lord Krishna]!" So wrote the blind poet Surdas (ca. 1483–1563), who lived in Agra and devoted his life to composing devotional songs in praise of the god Krishna. His words are inscribed on this blazing picture, in which Krishna plays the flute and leaps into the air with the gopis to the tune of trumpet, shahnai, cymbal, and drum. To express Surdas's plaintive ecstasy, the artist has frozen motion and sound, translating roars, thuds, clangs, and toots into silhouetted patterns of flagrant reds, oranges, yellows, blues, and greens. The artist very nearly splits our ears through our eyes.

Like Sukhadeva, who worked in the Malwa tradition (see no. 230), this painter transcended a style that normally falls flat. Mewar, too, had evolved its own variant of the early Indian tradition, and because of the firm resistance of Rana Pratap Singh (r. 1572–97) to Akbar's expansionism, its art remained free from Mughal influences well into the seventeenth century. Mewar's rulers, bearing the title of rana (rather than raja, rai, or rao) and tracing their ancestry to the sun, were the senior ranking Rajputs. For a quarter of a century, Rana Pratap Singh waged guerrilla warfare against Akbar. In 1576, the Mughals, combining forces with the rajas of Marwar and Amber, among others, and led by Akbar himself, drove Rana Pratap and his twenty-two thousand Rajputs to the rugged Aravalli Hills. Terrible slaughter ensued on the Plain of Haldighat. At last, with only eight thousand Rajputs still alive, the golden sun, symbol of Mewar, was seized from the rana and carried off. Ironically, the raja bearing the golden booty was killed, while Rana Pratap, on his great war-horse Chetak, made his legendary leap across a mountain stream to safety—and to prepare for the spring campaigns.

Although his followers were decimated and his capitals seized, the rana continued to resist the Mughals. His son, Rana Amar Singh I (r. 1597–1620), consolidated the state and maintained its independence against Emperor Jahangir, although his heir, Karan Singh (r. 1620–28), was later a welcome visitor to the Mughal court. Jahangir's friendly feelings toward him survived an episode that would otherwise have sparked imperial wrath. When Prince Khurram (later Shah Jahan) revolted against his father, the rana provided sanctuary. Indeed, on the death of Jahangir, it was in Udaipur, the capital of Mewar, that the prince was first hailed as emperor. Shah Jahan later restored parts of Mewar long held by the Mughals to Rana Jagat Singh (r. 1628–52). During his reign, the arts of peace flourished at Mewar. As in Shah Jahan's palaces, marble was lavished upon Jagnivas Palace on Lake Pichola, and ecstatic paintings such as this one were painted in reflection of newfound tranquillity.

Published: M. Chandra, *Mewar Painting*, pl. 3.

231.
THE DANCE OF KRISHNA
From a manuscript of the *Sur-Sagar* of Surdas
Rajasthan, Mewar, mid-17th century
Opaque watercolor on paper, 11 × 8⅝ in.
(27.9 × 22 cm.)
Collection Gopi Krishna Kanoria, Patna
(VK.117)

A "SECOND PARADISE," a poetical phrase for India, could refer to the bower of bliss around the lovers Rama and Sita. At last they are again together after the heroic adventures following Sita's abduction by the demonic tyrant Ravana (see no. 13). Rocks become pink clouds, and greenery and blossoms sprout from nowhere, giving form to the lovers' beatitude in this lyrical and unique picture by an unknown artist perhaps from Raghugarh (see no. 251). The thin line of white froth edging the lake, the cranes, the outlines of the trees, and the bursts of flowers tremble with expectation; Rama and Sita, whom the poetic master has joined in a central splotch of yellow, inhabit the picture's only zone of calm.

THAT ARMS AND armor should be viewed as sculpture is impressively demonstrated by this unusual helmet, artfully hammered into the form of an immaculately tied turban and ornamented with floral arabesques.[1] Unfortunately, there are no acquisition dates for it or for the accompanying shield, which is decorated with the same finely scaled, textilelike ornament in gold. On the basis of style, provenance, and sheer opulence, we can assume that they belonged to Raja Jai Singh of Amber (r. 1625–67). Known as the Mirza Raja, he served the Mughal emperor Aurangzeb, who elevated him to the

232.
RAMA AND SITA
Rajasthan, perhaps Raghugarh,
ca. 1740
Opaque watercolor on paper
Folio: 12¾ × 8⅞ in. (32.4 × 22.5 cm.)
Miniature: 11⅛ × 7½ in. (28.3 × 19.1 cm.)
National Museum, New Delhi
(51.34/50)

233.
HELMET AND SHIELD
Perhaps Agra, 2nd half of 17th century
Maharaja Sawai Man Singh II Museum,
Jaipur (2.3620)

233a

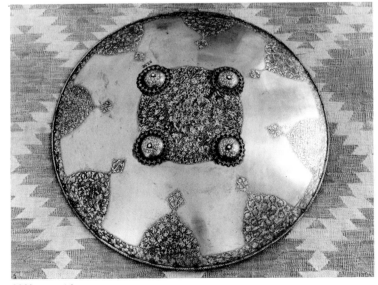

233b, outside

233b, inside

351

mansab of 6,000 horse and may have given him these superb objects. The emperor was well pleased with Raja Jai Singh on two counts: he betrayed the emperor's rival, Prince Dara-Shikoh, during the wars of succession, thereby easing Aurangzeb's way to the throne; and he also captured the Maratha leader, Shivaji, and brought him to the imperial court. Later, however, on learning that the emperor had broken a pledge to his prisoner, Jai Singh, in a characteristic display of Rajput chivalrousness and independence, enabled Shivaji to escape. Proud to the point of vainglory because of his presumed control over Mughals and Marathas alike, Jai Singh so angered the emperor that a plot was hatched against him. Aurangzeb promised the throne of Amber to Kirat Singh, the raja's younger son, if he would kill his father. He did so, at Burhanpur in the Deccan, by poisoning his father's opium; but the contemptuous emperor rewarded him not with Amber but with the small district of Kama.

The shield is lined with an unusual Italian ciselé velvet of about 1620 to 1650, handsomely decorated with flowers in a pattern that would have appealed to Mughal taste. Still attached is the embroidered seventeenth-century knuckle pad, which protected the hand of the bearer against the mighty blows sustained in battle.

1. There is an Indian helmet in turban form in the Musée de l'Armée, Paris, and another in the Archaeological Museum, Bijapur.

Published: Welch, *The Art of Mughal India*, pp. 123, 172, no. 69; *The Indian Heritage*, p. 138, no. 456.

234

234.
KNUCKLE PAD FROM A SHIELD
Amber, mid-17th century
Cotton, embroidered with silk and metallic thread, 5½ × 5½ in. (14 × 14 cm.)
Maharaja Sawai Man Singh II Museum, Jaipur (1352)

AT MUGHAL AND Rajput courts, small, seemingly trivial objects, rarely if ever viewed, were often as beautiful to see and touch as larger, more visible ones. This knuckle pad represents weeks, if not months, of painstaking and imaginative embroidering. It is tempting to believe that the maker was an amateur, some Rajput lady who lavished her devotion on stitching the colorful arabesques of this small object intended for her soldierly lover. More likely, it was made by a special craftsman who spent his life sewing, day in and day out, as had his father and his father's father.

This tender lotus bud of the battlefield springs open to reveal a threatening foliation of sharp spikes. Mughals and Rajputs, it seems, encouraged deadly flights of fancy from their armorers, who concealed daggers within swords, fashioned blades that spread apart inside the victim's gut, and fitted pistol barrels to the sides of dagger blades. Another cherished invention was the tiger claw, steel talons to be concealed in the palm of the hand and used to rip the flesh from an enemy's face.

ONE COULD NOT imagine a more powerfully Rajput dagger. Heavy, sharp, and well fitted to the hand, this imaginatively composed khanjar required most of the armorer's technical skills to create. The massive blade of watered steel, with an armor-piercing tip, is carved in low relief with what seems to be a collision between a horseman and an elephant on one face and a tiger hunt on the other. Tiger and elephant masks snarl and roar on the quillon and pommel of the hilt, the grip of which resembles entwining ropes, or cobras. Final touches of gold koftgari work enrich the finial and other parts of the hilt.

Although the form recalls the Akbar period dagger of about 1585 (no. 98), the carving of the blade suggests a later date, perhaps as late as 1670.

Published: *The Indian Heritage*, p. 131, no. 421.

235.
MACE IN THE FORM OF A LOTUS BUD
Rajasthan, perhaps Amber,
3rd quarter of 17th century
Steel, length 24 in. (61 cm.)
Maharaja Sawai Man Singh II Museum, Jaipur
(928)

236.
KHANJAR
Rajasthan, perhaps Kotah, 17th century
Watered steel, with koftgari work in gold, length
12⅜ in. (31.3 cm.)
Victoria and Albert Museum, London
(I.S. 86–1981)

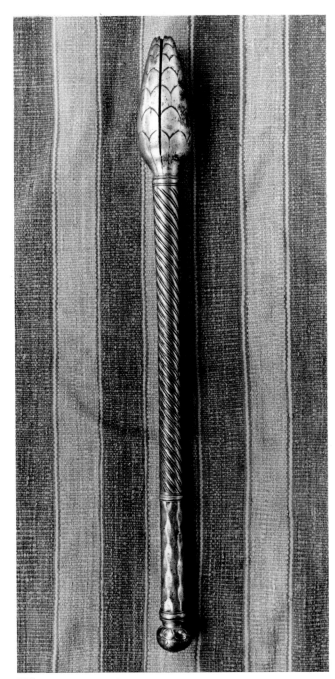

235

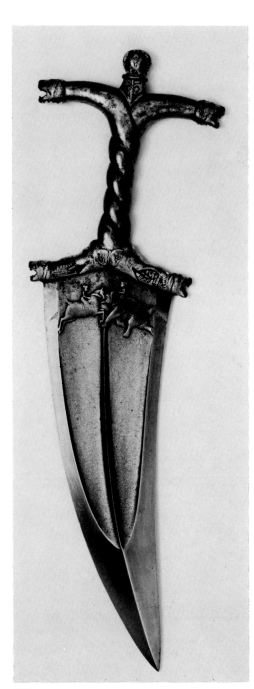

236

237.
TWO MATCHLOCKS

a. MATCHLOCK
Probably Rajasthan, late 17th century
Steel barrel with koftgari work; stalk of ebony
inlaid with mother-of-pearl and silver, length
39¾ in. (101 cm.)
Maharaja Sawai Man Singh II Museum, Jaipur
(1230)

THE FIRST GUNS were matchlocks, which appeared in Europe in the fifteenth century and thence spread to India, where they were first used in the sixteenth century. Their mechanism is simple: the guns are fired by pulling a trigger which in turn releases a movable arm (serpentine) carrying a lighted cloth fuse impregnated with wax (match) into a small pan of fine black gunpowder. The flame then enters the barrel through a drilled touchhole, setting off a reserve of coarser powder. Because they fire less promptly than

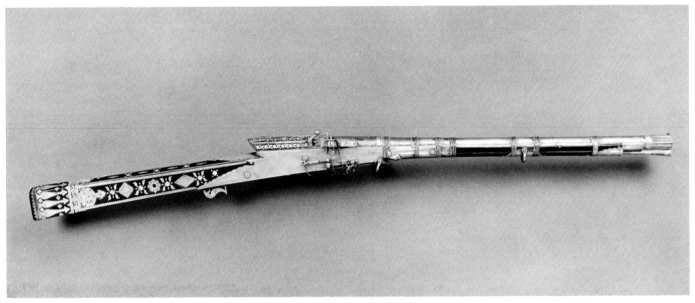

237a

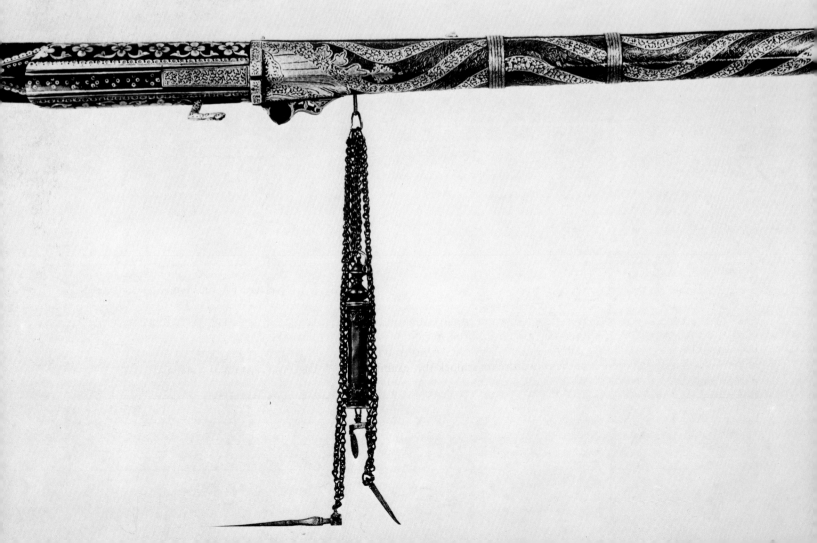

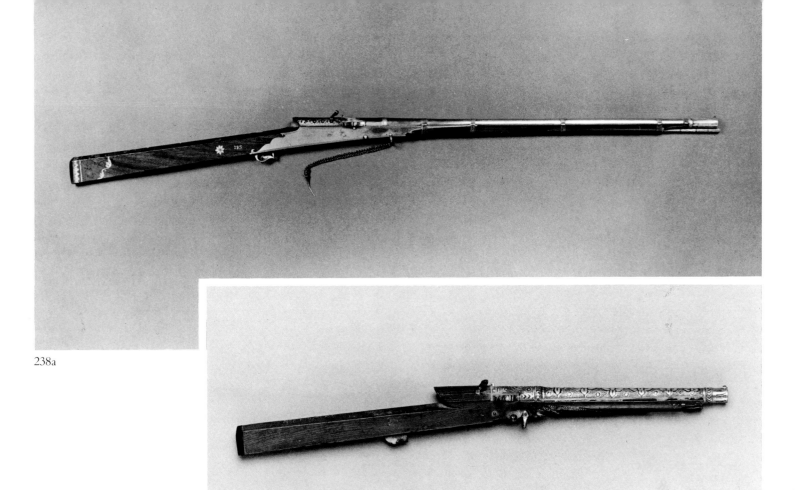

238a

238b

flintlocks, which evolved from the matchlock, their long barrels were usually rested on stands, or on the shoulders of obliging huntsmen. Slow acting and awkward, matchlocks were ill-suited to pitched battle, but they were fired at approaching enemies. They were particularly valued in the hunting field, and can be found in miniatures as early as about 1540. A portrait of Akbar in old age (no. 113) includes an imperial example, suitable for hunting, with a polychromed green stock; and Emperor Aurangzeb employs a matchlock to shoot nilgai in one of the most explicit Mughal hunting scenes (no. 176).

Like other Rajput arms, matchlocks were artistically pleasing objects, as attractive to the eye as to the hand. Barrels were made from watered steel, sometimes gilded or carved in relief with flowers or arabesques, and stocks were polychromed and inlaid with ivory birds, trees, and flowers. The comparatively spare and compact Jaipur gun appears to be the earlier of the two. The Figiel matchlock is the most sumptuous we have seen, and it retains the original kit of tools for loading, suspended from chains near the pan.

WEAPONS WERE enjoyable as well as serious matters in Rajput households. The scaled-down matchlock (a), ideal for shooting small game, must have delighted the heart of a Rajput boy or girl, for whom it would also have been an invitation to join in the adult activity of hunting. Already, however, he or she might have been given the miniature matchlock (b), examples of which can be seen in Rajput paintings among the toys of young members of the warrior caste.

Published: Welch, *The Art of Mughal India*, pp. 145, 173, no. 73.

b. MATCHLOCK
Probably Rajasthan, ca. 1700
Watered steel barrel; stock inlaid with ivory; gold ornament, length 66 in. (167.6 cm.)
Collection Leo S. Figiel, Atlantis, Florida

238.
TWO MATCHLOCKS

a. MATCHLOCK FOR A CHILD
Marwar or Amber, early 18th century
Steel with paint and gilt; rosewood, with paint and ivory inlay, length 35 in. (88.9 cm.)
Maharaja Sawai Man Singh II Museum, Jaipur (295)

b. MINIATURE MATCHLOCK
Amber or Jaipur, early 18th century
Rosewood, ebony, and steel damascened with gold, length 9⅞ in. (25 cm.)
Maharaja Sawai Man Singh II Museum, Jaipur (2302)

◁ 237b, detail

239.
FOUR ARROWS WITH IVORY POINTS
IN THE FORM OF DEER HEADS
Rajasthan, Kotah, mid-18th century
Average length 29 in. (73.7 cm.)
Rao Madho Singh Museum Trust, Kotah
(1419–1422)

THESE UNIQUE ARROWS, with blunt points carved with deer heads, were intended either to stun small game or as "hunting magic," to lure game into the field. They were probably made for one of the most ardent of Kotah hunters, Maharao Durjansal (r. 1723–56). According to Lieutenant Colonel James Tod, the usually informative author of *Annals and Antiquities of Rajasthan,* he was "a valiant prince, and possessed all the qualities of which the Rajput is enamoured: affability, generosity, and bravery. He was devoted to field sports, especially the royal one of tiger-hunting; and he had *ramnas,* or preserves, in every corner of his dominions (some of immense extent, with ditches and palisadoes, and sometimes circumvallations), in all of which he erected hunting-seats."[1]

Numerous paintings and drawings have survived from Rao Durjansal's reign, many of them depicting the hunt. Some attest to his innovative approaches to both art and the chase. A sketch, for instance, depicts him watching as a huntsman, hidden behind a musician playing the soothing melodies of a vina, stalks a deer.[2]

1. Tod, *Annals and Antiquities of Rajasthan,* vol. 3, p. 1530.
2. Private collection.

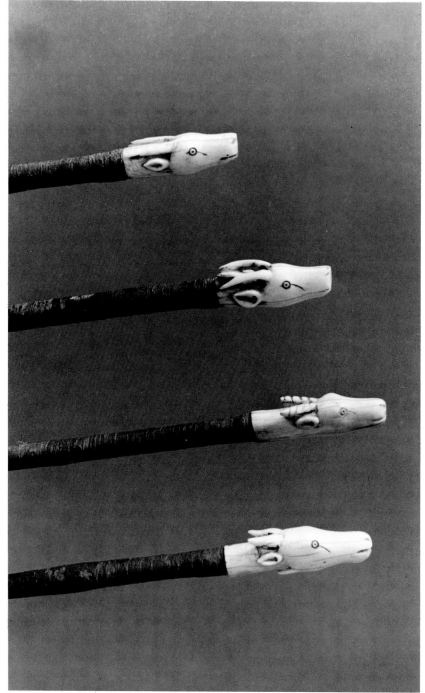

239

240

THIS LETHAL SCULPTURE, auspiciously shaped like a stylized makara, fired its charge from a fire-breathing muzzle. Now pacified by a cannonball wedged in its maw, it is usually assigned an honored, ceremonial post on the ramparts of the magnificent Jodhpur Fort.

The makara is one of India's most ancient symbolic images, harking back more than two thousand years to a time when the natural world was seen as both symbol and reality and fantastic creatures were invented to express the complexity of nature. Traditionally, festoons and strings of pearls poured forth from the gaping mouth of this crocodilian monster of the primeval waters, symbolizing the potent abundance of the sea. The motif has adorned the headdresses, earrings, armbands, and hip belts of countless Hindu gods and decorated the columns, brackets, lintels, and ceilings of the temples that house them. Its use for a cannon is at once strikingly original and a reminder of India's rich and ancient storehouse of memory.

IN 1657, WHILE serving Shah Jahan against Aurangzeb in the wars of succession, five Kotah brothers, wearing saffron-stained robes and bridegrooms' crowns dedicating them to victory or death, rode into battle. Only one survived. Following that proud but tragic day, Rao Jagat Singh (r. 1657–70) received the mansab of two thousand men from Aurangzeb, the very man responsible for the family tragedy. Like many Rajputs, Rao Jagat served in the Deccan, where he hired a brilliant artist, whom we have dubbed the Kotah Master, the painter of this animated portrait in which the prince's ardent spirits are symbolized by the preening, leonine sarus crane in the left foreground. In the center of the composition, Jagat, seated on a marble platform and surrounded by ladies and flowers, is the quintessence of a Rajput nobleman at leisure.

The artist so finely attuned to Rao Jagat was trained at Golconda in a draftsmanlike tradition that can be traced back to fifteenth-century Tabriz, ancestral home of the Qutb-Shahi dynasty of Golconda. From its beginnings, the Golconda school referred through drawings and tracings to earlier Iranian motifs and also maintained contact with the evolving newer modes, invaria-

240.
CANNON IN THE SHAPE OF A MAKARA
Rajasthan, Marwar, Jodhpur,
late 18th century
Bronze, length 49 in. (124.5 cm.), diameter
12 in. (30.5 cm.)
Mehrangarh Museum Trust, Fort, Jodhpur,
on loan from Maharaja Sri Gaj Singhji II of
Jodhpur (L17/1874)

241.
RAO JAGAT SINGH OF KOTAH IN A
GARDEN
Attributed to the Kotah Master
Rajasthan, Kotah, ca. 1670
Opaque watercolor on paper, 10⅝ × 7 in.
(27 × 17.8 cm.)
The Knellington Collection, Courtesy
Harvard University Art Museums,
Cambridge, Massachusetts

241

bly emphasizing excellence of drawing. When innovative Iranian artists such as Riza-yi ⁽Abbasi spun sinuous calligraphic lines and painted with spring-fresh colors at Isfahan for Shah ⁽Abbas I, Golconda artists usually followed suit. And when Rajputs with a penchant for art saw these Golconda variants on the Iranian mode, they invited the artists to join their ateliers. Thus, the heritage of Iran and of Golconda reached Kotah and enriched one of the memorable Rajput schools.

Although Rao Jagat spent most of his time in the Deccan, he kept in touch with his feudatory in Rajasthan, and probably visited it for extended periods. Accompanying him, his newfound artist became familiar with Rajput ways and places; and with Rao Jagat's encouragement, the Kotah Master painted the jungles, lions, tigers, and elephants of Rajasthan with the surging line once devoted to Iranian dragons, demons, and simurghs.

Published: Dickson and Welch, *The Houghton Shahnameh*, vol. 1, p. 233, fig. 282; Welch, "Return to Kotah," pp. 79–81, figs. 5, 6.

FRAYED FROM TOO frequent handling, the rhinoceros's mask lost, and the elephant's hind leg replaced, this picture nevertheless outpaces all other Rajput hunting pictures. Like the portrait of Rao Jagat (no. 241), it can be assigned to the Kotah Master, who continued to work for Kotah princes long after Jagat's death in 1670. During the reigns of Rao Kishor Singh (1670–86) and Rao Ram Singh (1686–1707), both of whom fought and died for the Mughal cause in the Deccan, the master expanded his repertoire to suit Rajput and, particularly, Kotah taste.

Paradoxically, hunting scenes, which had been a Kotah specialty since the state was founded under Rao Madho Singh (r. 1625–49), were invigorated by his Iranian finesse. Unlike his Turkman precursors who never saw the dragons they rendered so believably, he knew firsthand the pounding rush of elephants. More powerfully than Basawan's (see no. 88), his riptide line

242.
RAO RAM SINGH I OF KOTAH
HUNTING A RHINOCEROS
Attributed to the Kotah Master
Rajasthan, Kotah, ca. 1690
Opaque watercolor on paper, 12⅝ × 18¾ in.
(32.1 × 47.6 cm.)
Collection Stuart Cary Welch

242

charted hulking muscle and bone inside scratchy hide, enabling us to feel the thud of feet and the lashing of ropes, and to hear the clang of bells.

Published: Lee, *Rajput Painting*, cover, p. 45, pl. 36; Welch and Beach, *Gods, Thrones, and Peacocks*, pp. 43, 120, no. 27, pl. 27; Beach, *Rajput Painting at Bundi and Kota*, pp. 32–33, pls. LXVII, fig. 71, pl. LXVIII, fig. 72 (det.); Welch, "Return to Kotah," pp. 79–80, fig. 4.

243.
THE RANI'S SOUTH AMERICAN
MONKEY
Rajasthan, Mewar, ca. 1700
Opaque watercolor on paper, 17½ × 22 in.
(44.5 × 55.9 cm.)
Collection Stuart Cary Welch

THE PREHENSILE TAIL indicates that this monkey can be traced to South America. According to an inscription on the back of the painting, it was given by a Muslim nobleman to the rani (wife) of Rana Amar Singh II of Mewar (r. 1698–1710). As always, the history of politics and art mesh. Amar Singh II's father, Jai Singh, married a princess from the Rajput state of Bundi, who bore him Amar Singh. As so often happened in Rajput households, she was replaced in Jai Singh's affections by a second wife, who jealously conspired against the rightful heir. Strained relations between father and son worsened when young Amar Singh (playfully?) turned loose an enraged elephant in the streets of Udaipur. Unwilling to face his father's anger, the prince fled to Bundi, where he gathered a force of ten thousand men to attack his father. His army included many disillusioned noblemen of Mewar, who had suffered from Rana Jai Singh's indolence and imbecility. Inasmuch as three-quarters of the father's subjects joined the son's cause, Rana Jai saw that he

243

would be unable to crush the rebellion and proposed that Amar Singh maintain a separate court in exile until the end of his reign.

Cut off from his father, young Amar Singh became enmeshed in Mughal politics, sporadically supporting and undermining the cause of Prince Mu'azzam, one of Emperor Aurangzeb's sons, during the wars of succession. Despite the bitterness felt by many Rajputs toward Aurangzeb, Amar Singh signed a treaty with the Mughals once Prince Mu'azzam was established as Emperor Bahadur Shah I. And although harassed by the Rajputs, the emperor (whose mother was a Rajput princess) usually attempted to smooth relations with them. We suspect that one of his noblemen bestowed the exotic and handsome monkey upon Amar Singh's wife.

Zoos were among the pleasures of Mughal emperors, and the rani's monkey may have belonged to a simian dynasty maintained in the imperial gardens of Delhi. Certainly, the picture's artistic prototypes were the animal studies made by Mansur and others for Emperor Jahangir's albums (see nos. 141—44).

Published: Welch and Beach, *Gods, Thrones, and Peacocks*, pp. 47, 120, no. 26, pl. 26.

LARGE MINIATURES ARE rare in Indian art, and this panoramic battle scene —showing Bahadur Shah I (r. 1707–12) fighting against Maratha marauders in the aftermath of his defeat of his younger brother Kam Bakhsh—is unique. Swarming with men, horses, elephants, camels, bullocks, cannon, and rockets, the picture is divided by its three principal artists into three sections, in each of which only the major figures and their immediate entourages are recorded in the glory of full color. Everyone else is masterfully drawn in lean black line, occasionally highlighted with gold and modeled in grisaille washes. However fierce the subject, the pervading tone is orderly, the composition stitched together by the repeated diagonals of cannon, rockets, and spears, and effervescently dotted with round black shields. At the center of the Mughal armies, Bahadur Shah remains crisply aloof as he advances through the din.

Following the death of his ancient father, Aurangzeb, in 1707, the sixty-three-year-old Prince Mu'azzam crowned himself emperor as Bahadur Shah I, unaware that the empire was crumbling. Wars of succession followed, embroiling most of Mughal and Rajput India. After his long wait for power, Bahadur Shah optimistically led armies from Lahore to Delhi and Agra and across the Narmada River into the Deccan, invariably bettering his ambitious but less effective brothers. When Prince A'zam and his troops reached Agra Fort to seize the Mughal treasury, Bahadur Shah had already taken it. A soldier to the core, he is said to have spent only four nights in palaces (the rest of the time in tents) during the five years of his reign.

But Bahadur Shah's troubles were not over. While he was defeating Prince A'zam, Raja Ajit Singh of Marwar, eager to avenge Aurangzeb's vendetta against his family, attacked the imperial territories near Ajmer. Bahadur Shah again swooped into action, disciplining recalcitrant Rajputs with sword and diplomacy. After his armies had vanquished Ajit Singh at Merta, he forgave the rebel and elevated him to the rank of maharaja with a mansab of 3,500 horse.

Another Rajput rebellion sprouted just as the busy emperor was setting off for the Deccan to fight against his sinister brother Kam Bakhsh. The rebellion was led by Rana Amar Singh II of Mewar and by the patron of this giant battle scene, Sawai Jai Singh Kachhwaha. They brazenly killed the Mughal commandant of Mewar and seized Amber, which Bahadur Shah had recently—and annoyingly—bestowed upon Sawai Jai Singh's loyal younger brother.

Sensing that the Rajput troubles could wait, Bahadur Shah marched toward Hyderabad, where he offered peaceful terms to Kam Bakhsh, who rejected them even though most of his army had deserted. Deluded with notions of god-given invincibility, Kam Bakhsh led his sons and a small force against the imperial armies. The battle depicted in this panorama was

244.
EMPEROR BAHADUR SHAH I IN BATTLE
Inscribed: "a battle between Emperor Bahadur Shah against Purushottam Das Surhwaja and Sangaji Inglia of the Deccan," "painted by Gopal, Jivan, and Udai"
Rajasthan, Amber, early 18th century
Tinted drawing on paper, 8 ft. 11 in. × 32½ in. (2.72 m. × 8.6 cm.)
Maharaja Sawai Man Singh II Museum, Jaipur (AG–1401)

244, detail

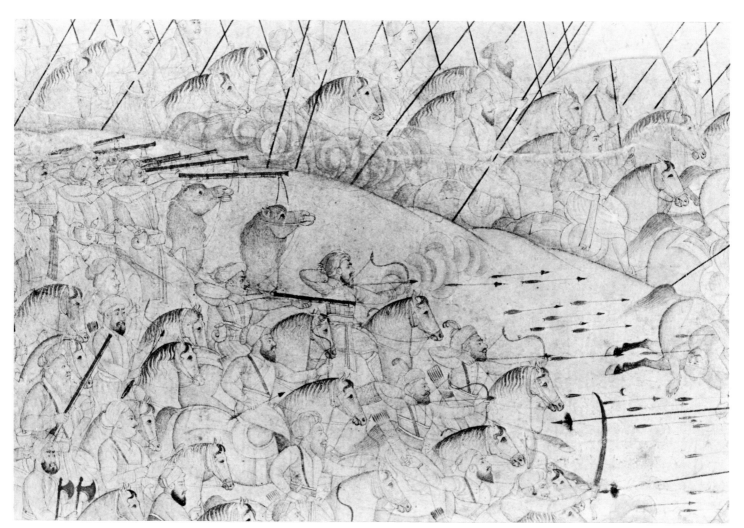

244, detail

244, detail

244, detail

fought on January 13, 1709. Rockets and arrows pierced the air. Kam Bakhsh was wounded at once. Streaming blood, he stormed on his elephant into the melee, firing arrows with demonic vigor until he was so weakened that he was surrounded and captured. Sixty-two bodies were found riddled by his arrows.

After Kam Bakhsh's downfall, Marathas entered the field, eager for loot; and they, too, were defeated by the imperial armies. Apparently, this stage of the battle is shown here. Later, Kam Bakhsh was brought in a palanquin to the emperor, who lamented the triumph over one so close. Surgeons were summoned, and Bahadur Shah himself washed dried blood from the wounds and put a cup of rosewater to his brother's lips. A few hours later, Kam Bakhsh died.

By May 1710, Bahadur Shah had returned to Rajasthan, determined to defeat the Rajput alliance; but before his armies had massed, word arrived of a more urgent problem—a Sikh uprising in the Punjab. Again the Rajput challenge went unresolved. Charity and forgiveness were substituted for war: the pleased but suspicious Rajputs were sent back to their states bearing gifts.

Bahadur Shah's afflictions were unending. Exhausted but still winning skirmishes against the Sikhs, he died at the age of sixty-nine in 1712. Perhaps, on learning the news, Sawai Jai Singh called for this panorama of battle, and pondered the portrait of his generous enemy, whose life was drained away by a succession of victories.

WITH THE AIRY grace of a ballet dancer, Rao Bhoj Singh of Bundi (r. 1585–1607) flicks a deadly arrow into the flank of a splendid lion, who snarls in death as he is followed by his sleek, saddened mate. The Kotah Master (see also nos. 241, 242) flourished in Rajasthan, where he accompanied the rulers on their daily rounds and in the hunting field, watched elephant combats, fished in the Chambal River, and established a brilliantly lively atelier that was to survive into the nineteenth century. Like his followers, he sketched everything that caught his eye; and in his finished pictures he combined portraits and animal studies from life with motifs inherited from a line of talented draftsmen that can be traced to Golconda and eventually to fifteenth-century Iran.

This historical subject—it shows an ancestor common to Bundi and Kotah who had served Akbar at the siege of Ahmadnagar—was commissioned toward the end of the master's career, when his expressive line had become more calligraphic, with pronounced thickenings and thinnings. In its dynamically lunging men and animals and its surging greenery, the artist synthesized his experience of lions, the jungle, and the Rajputs with his own ancient heritage, which included (unknown to him) lions that still snarl on Assyrian and Achaemenid stone reliefs.

Published: Welch and Beach, *Gods, Thrones, and Peacocks*, p. 48, no. 31; Beach, *Rajput Painting at Bundi and Kota*, pp. 35–37, pl. LXXXI, fig. 86, pl. LXXVIII, fig. 87 (det.); Dickson and Welch, *The Houghton Shahnameh*, vol. 1, p. 233, figs. 283, 284; Welch, "Return to Kotah," p. 85, figs. 9, 10.

245.
RAO BHOJ SINGH OF BUNDI SLAYS
A LION
Attributed to the Kotah Master
Rajasthan, Kotah, ca. 1720
Opaque watercolor on paper, 18¾ × 26 in.
(47.6 × 66 cm.)
Collection Stuart Cary Welch

Overleaf, 245, detail ▷

246.
RANA SANGRAM SINGH II OF MEWAR
Rajasthan, Mewar, Udaipur, ca. 1725–35
Opaque watercolor on paper, set with pearls
and precious stones, 16¾ × 11¾ in.
(42.6 × 29.9 cm.)
Collection Gopi Krishna Kanoria, Patna
(VK.117)

LUXURIOUSLY PRECIOUS with attached pearls and jewels—a Mughal practice (see no. 154)—this likeness of the Rajput patriarch Rana Sangram Singh II of Mewar (r. 1710–34) is also a searching characterization of an accomplished, successful ruler. His name means Lion of Battle, and he was admired as a powerful, just, and inflexible king who took advantage of the weakening Mughal empire to regain long lost territories.

Even when his political authority was fading, Emperor Muhammad Shah—Rangila, the Pleasure Loving (see no. 182)—was artistically influential. Had he not flung pearls with such princely abandon in Delhi, they would not have landed so pleasingly in Udaipur.

246

247

"THE DOMESTIC INCIDENTS of this, as of the preceding reigns, are without interest." So wrote Lieutenant Colonel James Tod on the subject of the maharaja painted here. Why? Because, we suspect, Zorawar Singh of Bikaner (r. 1736–45) spent most of his days at home. Geographically remote and insulated by the Thar Desert, Bikaner played little part in the imbroglios of Mughal power. Its merchants sent their camel caravans to distant trading centers, and the maharajas enjoyed their Rajput activities, celebrating festivals and marriages, looking after their zenanas, leading war parties against their neighbors, hunting, and cultivating the arts.

Maharaja Zorawar Singh's most notable artist was Ustad Murad, to whom we assign this hunting scene set beneath the artist's favorite citron sky. One of the outstanding Rajput artists, his style became increasingly personal over the years. Like the state of Bikaner itself, he turned from Mughal to Rajput ways, shedding imperial naturalism in favor of a highly

247.
MAHARAJA ZORAWAR SINGH
HAWKING
Attributed to Murad
Rajasthan, Bikaner, ca. 1740
Opaque watercolor on paper, 9¾ × 6⅞ in.
(24.8 × 17.5 cm.)
National Museum, New Delhi
(BKN.35)

mannered, nostalgic style appropriate to Bikaner's desert vastnesses. His vision came from within, and as he aged, figures, animals, and settings sweetened into slightly humorous poetic dreams. Serene figures are scaled according to whim, from the large and important maharaja to three-quarter-sized courtiers and minihuntsmen. Trees are twisted into fruitful candy canes, birds fly in arabesques, and horses grow rounder rumps, larger heads, and narrower girths and necks to facilitate our appreciation of their sensitive expressiveness.

Published: W. Archer, *Indian Miniatures*, pl. 45; Brijbhushan, *The World of Indian Miniatures*, pl. 25.

For other works by this appealing artist, see: Patnaik and Welch, *A Second Paradise*.

248.
A POPPY
Rajasthan, Kishangarh, ca. 1740
Opaque watercolor on paper, 7⅛ × 4⅛ in.
(18.1 × 10.5 cm.)
The Knellington Collection, Courtesy
Harvard University Art Museums,
Cambridge, Massachusetts

248

INDIA'S BURST OF flowers following the monsoon provided an ecstatic, scented fanfare to the coming harvests, and inspired dancers, painters, and lovers. Although we have rejoiced in Mughal blossoms, burgeoning on costumes and across tent walls, Jahangir's and Shah Jahan's floramania was in fact an imperializing of ancient forms transmitted to the Mughal court from the arts of Rajasthan and the Deccan. This glowing poppy, with chinks of sky visible between the petals, was painted at Kishangarh during the reign of Raj Singh (r. 1706–48), one of a line of rulers deeply concerned with painting.

Although one can only speculate upon pre-eighteenth-century Kishangarh painting, the style may always have been influenced by Mughal and Deccani art. Kishangarh separated from Marwar during the reign of Akbar, and seems to have maintained close relations with the imperial court throughout its history. Outstanding Kishangarh pictures, however, share few qualities with Mughal ones beyond exquisite fineness of finish and lively draftsmanship. If Mughal patrons and artists usually viewed the world with sunlit clarity, those of Kishangarh preferred a lunar vision, far more extreme and romantic than imperial art at its most poetic. This small painted flower, more mysterious and bewitching than most Mughal ones, exudes the peculiar darkling quality that lends fascination to some Kishangarh art and reminds us of the poppy's varied uses. Beautiful to the eye, it was also—in the form of opium—conducive to lackadaisical states of mind; and it provided the deadly element of pousta, the morning quaff forced by imperial order down the throats of unwanted Mughal princes locked in Gwalior Fort, easing them from rivalry to oblivion.

But what accounts for the art of Kishangarh's affinities with Mughal art? The explanation lies in Raja Rup Singh's (r. 1643–58) close association with Shah Jahan, who may have shared with him a taste for the romantic and poetic, and must have discussed with him such projects as the Taj Mahal and shown him paintings by Govardhan. These experiences, combined with the dynasty's long-standing intimacy with the Mughal court and an inbred penchant for intensely expressive literature and art, provided a basis for the Kishangarh pictorial style as we know it from the late seventeenth century onward.

Although little is known of Kishangarh history, its art reveals very strong connections with the Deccan, where Kishangarh princes must have held commands in the Mughal army. Indeed, the earliest Kishangarh pictures we have seen are by a late seventeenth-century artist trained in the Deccan, who soon adjusted his manner to Kishangarh's curious and unique variant of the Mughal mode. Perhaps he was trained at Burhanpur, one of the Mughal centers in the Deccan and the city where Shah Jahan's favorite wife, Mumtaz-Mahal, died in 1631.

Burhanpur was also famed for its textiles, especially painted cottons, such as the magnificent floor spread with decorative but sensitive red poppies against a white ground (no. 179). So similar are these poppies to the painted one that we believe the artist of the miniature was trained at Burhanpur, an idea borne out by the equestrian portrait of Atachin Beg Bahadur (no. 222), a painting from the Deccan, probably from Burhanpur, which could easily be mistaken for Kishangarh work.

249

AN INSCRIPTION ON the reverse side of the painting identifies the prince as Raj Singh, ruler of Kishangarh from 1706 to 1748. Himself an amateur painter, he was also a devout follower of the fifteenth-century Vaishnavite sage Vallabhacharya, who had propounded the doctrine of Pushtimarga (the Way of Grace), which promised salvation through personal devotion to Krishna. According to this cult, Krishna was to be clothed in rich garments and worshiped with ceremonial splendor; his devotees were to bring to him the same

249.
PRINCE RESTING AFTER A HUNT
Inscribed, on reverse: "picture of Maharaj Sri Raj Singhji"
Rajasthan, Kishangarh, ca. 1740
Opaque watercolor on paper, 8¼ × 12⅝ in. (21 × 32.1 cm.)
Collection Gopi Krishna Kanoria, Patna (GK.100)

249, detail

Krishna and Radha. Rajasthan, Kishangarh, mid-18th century. Opaque watercolor on cloth, 40¾ × 37 in. (103.5 × 94 cm.). Philadelphia Museum of Art

spirit of love and service (seva) that a wife brings to her husband and dedicate to him all their material belongings.

In his efforts to portray Raj Singh as the embodiment of all princely virtues, the Kishangarh artist clearly could think of no better way to honor his patron than to endow him with the attributes of his own favorite divinities. Like Rama, who is often shown holding the bow that he broke in order to win the hand of Sita, Raj Singh is portrayed seated and proudly erect, demonstrating his prowess with a bow and arrow. Grouped before him, in the shade of hauntingly congruent, perfectly balanced trees, is an entourage of admiring young women who recall, in their poses of reverence, the gopis who serve Lord Krishna. At some distance, two women bathe languorously in the lake, their dopattas trailing from the trees, unmistakably evoking the popular Vastraharana episode of the Krishna legend (see. no. 11). The delicate touch of the artist shifts from foliage, to blossom, to flowerlike hands, to a decoratively trussed black buck, to the horse, graceful as a swan, in this creation of a hunter's paradise.

Paintings from the reign of Raj Singh's eldest son, Sawant Singh (r. 1748–64), usually considered the major patron of the Kishangarh school, further document prevailing Rajput religiosity and illustrate the truism that we interpret our gods according to our personalities and needs. Sawant Singh's temperament joined worldliness with fervid religiosity, which inspired him to write devotional poetry dedicated to Lord Krishna and to abdicate seven years before his death. As a young man, he frequented the court of Emperor Muhammad Shah, in whose revels he must have participated. But ultimately, the riotous life of the Delhi court led to revulsion; and just as Muhammad Shah spent more and more time with Sufis and other devotees at Delhi, so did Sawant Singh devote himself to Vaishnavite practices at Kishangarh, participating in the sacred releases of the bhakti cult.

Among the best-known paintings from Sawant Singh's felicitous partnerships with his artists are the many extraordinary portrayals of Krishna and Radha. A particularly spectacular example is the large painting on cloth in the Philadelphia Museum of Art (left), which expresses Sawant Singh's exquisite worldliness and his spirituality in a highly scented amalgam of extreme courtliness and divine passion. In it, traditional Indian artistic ways emerge forcibly, as in the metaphorical interpretations of Krishna's leonine waist and shoulders and attenuated, sinuous eyes resembling leaves from a pipal tree.

250.
BY THE LIGHT OF THE MOON, AND FIREWORKS
Attributed to Nihal Chand
Inscribed, on reverse: "[a] gathering of the uninformed, wine-drinking, restless ones"; in Devanagri script, the same words, without reference to wine drinking
Rajasthan, Kishangarh, ca. 1740
Opaque watercolor on paper, 8½ × 6⅛ in. (21.8 × 15.6 cm.)
Private collection

SATIRE, BROAD HUMOR, and sexual explicitness enliven Rajput art far more frequently than Mughal. In this nocturnal gambol, they are blended with such masterful sleight of hand that viewers respond not to the painting's "depravity" but to its delicacy of handling. Only resolute study unlocks its tongue-in-cheek wickedness and follies: the fat old sot struggling to balance both cup and dancing girl—but preferring the former; a lightly attired bounding nymphet ringing her bells; perverse ladies enacting the friendly vices of the zenana; and a brazen couple of moderate ambiguity demonstrating their devotion with the devil-may-care freedom of turtledoves.

On the marble terrace, scattered with a tasteful still life of largely neglected sweetmeats, musical instruments, smashed bottles, and promisingly full ones, other guests add further spice to the human jumble. Three lady musicians, quibbling over a wrong note, screech, tear hair, and wallop one another in a vignette that needs only to be seen to be heard. Within the eye of the storm, huddled together for reasons left to the imagination, are a stonily profiled elderly lady (the genteel wife of the rotund host?), a black eunuch, and two disembodied faces so alarming that we avert our glance.

This miniature, with its biting, Goyesque grotesquerie and savage humor, must have been painted at a time when Sawant Singh had turned against the mundane and yet could be amused by the recollection of evil. His remarkably creative collaboration with his major artist, Nihal Chand, to whom we assign this picture on the basis of inscribed works, produced some of the most perfervidly dreamlike—at times nightmarish—pictures in all of Indian art.

250

251

251.
MAHARAJA DHIRAJ SINGH OF
RAGHUGARH SLAYS A BEAR
Raghugarh, early 18th century
Opaque watercolor on paper, 7⅛ × 10½ in.
(18.2 × 26.7 cm.)
Jagdish and Kamla Mittal Museum of Indian
Art, Hyderabad (76.363)

LIKE OTHER HINDU courts in the more remote areas of Central India, Rajasthan, and the Punjab Hills, Raghugarh was saved from many of the undermining influences of Mughal court culture by its geographical distance from Delhi. Relatively untouched by Mughal "refinement," Raghugarh painting remained closer to its folk roots, imbued with intense feeling and, at times, remarkable strength. Raghugarh was founded in the mid-seventeenth century by Lal Singh Kichi, a Chauhan Rajput, and flourished as an independent state until 1819, when it became a dependency of the neighboring state of Gwalior, ruled by the Sindhia family of the Marathas. Despite their meager resources, the Raghugarh rajas supported their local painters over a period of at least two hundred years. Their uninterrupted patronage is documented by paintings dating as early as 1660 and as late as the 1860s. Throughout this long history, Raghugarh painters, though they were influenced to some extent by their contemporaries at Kotah to the north and Malwa to the south, maintained their own distinctive idiom. No other Rajput school produced paintings of such uniform quality over so long a period.

In this painting, Raja Dhiraj Singh (r. ca. 1685–1725) hunts with his dog in the rocky terrain of his state. His strong, massive figure dominates the scene; even the ferocious bear seems more awed by the raja than concerned by either the dog biting him or the arrows piercing his upper body. The blue-gray of the landscape, exactly the color of the soil of Raghugarh, makes this an ideal setting for a solitary hunt. The bold brushwork and the peculiar way the bushes are painted, with thinned blue-black pigment that is more like watercolor than the gouache used in the rest of the painting, are found in other works done for Dhiraj Singh and his successors until about 1780.

J.M.

CRIMES OF PASSION were seldom depicted by Rajput artists, and never by early Mughal ones. This miniature describes a horrendous episode with the full detail of a police report. A husband, it appears, returned one night to find his wife and her lover in flagrante delicto. He drew his sword and killed the lover, and is shown here in the act of hacking at his terrified wife, who cowers on her charpoi, screams for help, and raises her arms to block the swift blade. As the sword descends, the artist stops the action, allowing us to explore the ill-starred house and courtyard, the principals of the drama, and the townscape.

He has documented a typical Rajasthani town, with whitewashed mud walls, organically arranged, pleasingly crooked streets, and immaculate small houses. In the courtyard, auspicious drawings (rangolis) painted in rice flour by the doomed wife on the threshold bring to mind more peaceful days. At the right, still wrapped in his blanket, is the family servant, sleeping through the noisy incident. Others have been awakened: a crone, perhaps the evil schemer who arranged the assignation, listens at the front gate; at the right, a disturbed neighbor staggers to his doorway, clutching a club; at the left, a couple look on with concern, the woman depicted as a sympathetic friend of the wife, the husband as a partisan of the outraged mate; and a woman peers down from yet another window.

Two comparably disturbing pictures are attributed to Gangaram, who may have worked at the court of Bikaner.[1]

1. For other works attributed to Gangaram, see: Khandalavala, Chandra, and Chandra, *Miniature Painting*, nos. 152, 153.

252.
MURDER IN TOWN
Perhaps by Gangaram
Rajasthan, Bikaner, ca. 1740
Opaque watercolor on paper, 7¾ × 11⅝ in.
(19.7 × 29.5 cm.)
The Knellington Collection, Courtesy
Harvard University Art Museums,
Cambridge, Massachusetts

252

253

253.
RANA JAGAT SINGH II OF MEWAR
HUNTING WATER BUFFALO
Inscribed, on reverse: "Nur ad-Din"
Rajasthan, Mewar, ca. 1745
Opaque watercolor on paper
Folio: 18¼ × 11½ in. (46.4 × 29.2 cm.)
Miniature: 17⅝ × 10⅜ in. (44.8 × 26.4 cm.)
National Museum , New Delhi (57.4)

DURING THE MID-EIGHTEENTH century, most maharajas, rajas, rais, nawabs, and thakurs, even the prestigious rana of Mewar—the titled world of Hindustan—followed the irresponsible example of Muhammad Shah and cultivated pleasure above statecraft. Confronted by the threatening Marathas, the Rajputs failed once again to unite. Rana Jagat Singh II, absorbed in merriment, preferred paying tribute to fighting. A fun-loving, inventive spendthrift, he sponsored festivals and elephant fights and encouraged idleness and dissipation. He was also a great builder, and visitors to Udaipur are still enthralled by his pavilions and palaces.

Much of his time was devoted to the celebration of festivals and seasonal hunts. Each occasion, such as the one represented here, in which the rana ritually slays water buffalo when the monsoon floods tributaries of Lake Pichola, was a production. For the more gala events, special costumes were designed in conformance with the seasons, times of day, and religious events; appropriate music was performed; and the royal kitchens concocted suitable delicacies for the assembled royalty, nobility, and guests. These extravaganzas went on for days, and were enjoyed by the entire community.

It is no wonder that Rana Jagat Singh, as producer, director, and leading performer in these frequent celebrations, commissioned his artists to paint them, and ordered them to record every detail. Invariably, these vividly colored, crowded, and theatrical compositions express the carefree joy of the rana, who often appears several times, carrying out his myriad responsibilities as master of ceremonies, sacrificer of animals, and host.

Published: Brijbhushan, *The World of Indian Miniatures*, pl. 23.

RANA JAGAT SINGH II's pleasures included building. Under his artistic direction, Lake Pichola and the palaces on its shores were transformed into a rococo stage for his fêtes, amours, hunts, and contemplation. Artists contributed to the projects, proposing and designing architectural details, executing murals, and later painting large views of the rana's marvels. This bird's-eye rendering of the lake pavilion (which has now been redesigned as a hotel), projects the delightful building, with its courtyards and gardens, through sweetly innocent eyes.

Published: *Painting in British India 1757–1857*, no. 27, fig. 6; Welch and Beach, *Gods, Thrones, and Peacocks*, pp. 48, 79, 121, no. 34, pl. 34.

254.
THE RANA'S LAKE PAVILION
Rajasthan, Mewar, Udaipur, mid-18th century
Opaque watercolor on paper, 15½ × 18 in.
(39.4 × 45.7 cm.)
Collection Stuart Cary Welch

254

255

256

255.
SILVER BOTTLE
Rajasthan, ca. 1700
Height 11½ in. (29.2 cm.)
Private collection

WEIGHTY, UNADORNED, simple in its lines, and subtly proportioned, this bottle could have held wine, water, or asha, a liqueur flavored with saffron and other spices. (Each court took pride in its own formula for this heady and relaxing drink.) Although the form derives from the long-necked zinc bottles of Rajasthan (intended for cooling by immersion in water mixed with saltpeter, which caused rapid evaporation), the shape of the zinc bottles may in turn have derived from less courtly bottles made from water buffalo hide. The bottle also reveals the influence of richly jeweled Mughal examples, and they, of course, closing the art-historical circle, were based upon Rajput prototypes. Bottles of this design, with their agreeable associations, were often placed in niches; and they are found, too, as *pietra dura* inlays in Mughal buildings.

256.
GILDED SILVER HUQQA BASE
Mewar, Udaipur, mid-18th century
Height 7¼ in. (18.5 cm.), diameter 6½ in.
(16.5 cm.)
Collection Colonel R. K. Tandan, Secunderabad
(RKT/S–169)

AROUND THIS SILVER huqqa base, eight cast and chased musicians and dancers, all women, perform, each framed within a graceful arched colonnade. Stylized flowers, acanthus leaves, and garlands further enrich this sumptuous object, which must have been made for a rana of Mewar, probably at his capital. According to their portraits, Rajput noblemen were rarely without a huqqa: while they ride, a servant usually trots along beside the horse, bearing the huqqa base, from which a tube extends to provide gratification; and even in the zenana, while the nobleman caresses a wife or infant, the huqqa gurgles away nearby.

Most of these attractive objects, often made of silver or gold, have gone into the melting pot, in keeping with the Indian penchant for recycling old artifacts into new. Paintings, however, reveal the astonishing variety of huqqa bases, mouthpieces, and "snakes" or tubes, which—like dagger handles and the appurtenances for betel nut chewing—were designed and worked with unflagging imagination. At Rajput courts, bases were cast and sculpted in the form of birds, elephants, dancing girls, and amorous couples; and zoo-morphic mouthpieces were lavished with the same degree of imagination and skill we associate with eighteenth-century French snuffboxes or Fabergé's Easter eggs. (See also nos. 123, 171, 218.)

ON A TORRID DAY before the monsoon, Maharaja Madho Singh (r. 1760–78) whiles away time playing chess in the mardana (men's quarters) of his palace. Clad only in paijama, he lolls on a royal charpoi while a servant shampoos (massages) his foot and a punkahwala freshens the air—and discourages insects—by tugging the cord of the punkah, a cloth-covered wood frame suspended above.

The artist composed this unusually intimate view of royalty at rest in the white-in-whites of marble, chuna (polished lime), and muslin, relieved by brightly colored, richly patterned stuffs, gold, and jewels. Seeing him thus at ease, one might not realize that Maharaja Madho Singh was an active, effective ruler, admired as a patron of science and learning. Had not dysentery cut short his reign after seventeen years, Madho Singh might have resolved the chief problem of the Jat rulers of Bharatpur and prevented the splitting-off from Jaipur of Alwar.

Published: *The Indian Heritage*, p. 60, no. 147.

257.
MADHO SINGH OF JAIPUR PLAYING CHESS
Rajasthan, Jaipur, 3rd quarter of 18th century
Opaque watercolor on paper, 13½ × 9½ in. (34.3 × 24.1 cm.)
The Knellington Collection, Courtesy Harvard University Art Museums, Cambridge, Massachusetts

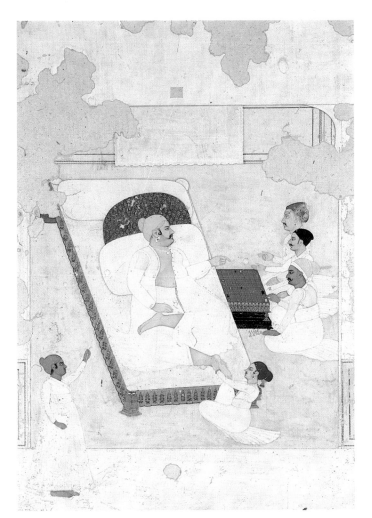

257

258.
MAHARAO UMED SINGH HUNTING
IN THE JUNGLE
By Shaikh Taju
Rajasthan, Kotah, dated 1781
Opaque watercolor on paper
Folio: 21½ × 32½ in. (54.6 × 82.6 cm.)
Miniature: 20¼ × 31½ in. (51.4 × 80 cm.)
Collection Wendy F. Findlay, New York

AT KOTAH, MAHARAO UMED SINGH (r. 1770–1819), a capable ruler who was also the best horseman and marksman in the country, was fortunate in being served by his uncle Rajrana Zalim Singh, one of Rajasthan's most dynamic statesmen. Zalim Singh so adroitly maneuvered matters, internal and external, that the state prospered in spite of the threatening Marathas. Affluent, protected, and spared the responsibilities of governing, the maharao was free to enjoy Rajput domesticity, to concentrate on religious rituals, and to perpetuate his family's enthusiastic pursuit of lions, tigers, and other game.

As before, the Kotah ateliers specialized in painting hunting scenes, which are among the liveliest and most compelling known. Under Umed Singh and the galvanic Zalim Singh, many of these shikar pictures were

258

painted in a highly appealing fresh idiom, apparently by an emerging wing of the ateliers staffed by masters such as Shaikh Taju, Hans Raj Joshi, and Bhimsen. Their ravishingly coloristic pictures were painted more broadly, in thicker, flatter pigments, and were far less draftsmanlike and more ornamental than those of the Kotah Master and his followers (see nos. 241, 242, 245). Shaikh Taju's manner brings to mind the rhythmic, consciously naïve jungle scenes by the Douanier Rousseau. Less addicted to drawing from life, the shaikh and his fellow artists painted plumper, sleeker deer and less ferocious lions, tigers, sloth bears, and wild boar, from their minds rather than from observation.

259

259.
BOUNDING HORSES
Attributed to Chokha
Rajasthan, Devgarh, ca. 1800
Opaque watercolor on paper
Folio: 10⅞ × 16 in. (27.5 × 40.7 cm.)
Miniature: 8½ × 14⅜ in. (21.7 × 36.5 cm.)
The Fine Arts Museums of San Francisco,
Achenbach Foundation for Graphic Arts,
Katherine Ball Collection (X71.42.426)

THESE NEIGHING, SNORTING, pounding horses, with lashing tails, high rumps, and unaccountably bedroom eyes, were painted at Devgarh, sixth among sixteen feudatories of Mewar. The land grant to this small state was bestowed in 1692, presumably along with the distinctive title of "rawat" conferred upon its chiefs. During the last quarter of the eighteenth century, if not before, Devgarh maintained small but busy ateliers in which a few artists painted strikingly original pictures. Perhaps because of the generous size of the patrons—one of whom was nearly seven feet tall and died at twenty-two after vainly struggling to reduce his bulk—Devgarh pictures are imposing, inhabited by buxom figures and animals.

Chokha, to whom *Bounding Horses* can be attributed, was the talented son of a gifted father, Bagta, who was also an artist. Brightly hued and crisp-edged, with sharply incisive characterizations verging on caricature, the older master's pictures were naturalistic and classical compared with his son's. For Chokha's style might be deemed the most peculiarly personal and empathic in all of Rajput art. To a critic from the imperial Mughal establishment, Chokha would have seemed a clumsy draftsman, a crudely awkward colorist, and a slovenly craftsman. To us, his flaws are essential to his engaging manner, which transcends academic shortcomings. *Bounding Horses*, one of his earlier pictures, painted under his father's disciplining influence, expresses Chokha's energy; and it also invites us into his imponderable, idiosyncratic world, where men behave like animals and humanized animals seem to be fully their equals, if not their betters.

260.
PECHHAVAI WITH GOPIS, COWS, AND
HEAVENLY BEINGS
Rajasthan, Jodhpur or possibly Bikaner,
late 18th century
Paint on cotton, 8 ft. × 8 ft. 4 in.
(2.44 × 2.54 m.)
Collection H. Peter Stern,
Mountainville, New York

PECHHAVAIS, HANGINGS PLACED behind sacred images, were important in Vaishnavite worship. This one, with its reverential gopis, the herdswomen with whom Lord Krishna disported in the groves of Vrindavan, would have been placed behind an image of the god in celebration of a particular time within his annual cycle. One of a set of hangings intended to be rotated according to the cycle of Lord Krishna's festivals and rituals, its fineness of design and execution suggests that it was painted for a shrine in a palace, or that it was a royal offering to another Vaishnavite place of worship.

In style it conforms to the mode of Jodhpur or possibly Bikaner, both of the Rathor clan. Although the art of Jodhpur is less well known than the traditions of its cadet branches at Bikaner and Kishangarh, it seems to be divisible into two modes: one secular and strongly influenced by Mughal and Deccani court painting, the other religious and of indigenous Rajput character. Despite its devotional subject, this pechhavai, perhaps the most exquisite we have seen, can be assigned to the secular branch of the Jodhpur or Bikaner ateliers.[1] The gopis resemble ladies from the royal establishment, and all their attributes, from jewels to fans, are of courtly splendor. Inasmuch as Jodhpur princes served as Mughal commanders in the Deccan, it is not surprising that the mango trees, with their ornamental and appetizing ripe fruit, recall those painted in Golconda and Hyderabad. In all likelihood, seventeenth-century Rathor princes, like those of Bundi, Kotah, and Amber, commissioned Deccani artists to paint pechhavais. On returning to Rajasthan, they brought not only the pictures with them but also, in many instances, the artists. And a century or so later, descendants of these artists turned for models to the pechhavais from the Deccan as well as to those from Nathadwara (see no. 223).[2]

1. Stella Kramrisch made the suggestion that this hanging might be from Bikaner.
2. For a comparable Deccani example, see: Skelton, *Rajasthani Temple Hangings,* no. 2.

261.
LORD KRISHNA'S COSMIC DANCE
(RASAMANDALA)
Jaipur, late 18th century
Opaque watercolor on paper, 26½ × 20 in.
(67.3 × 50.8 cm.)
Maharaja Sawai Man Singh II Museum, Jaipur
(AG-1382)

KRISHNA, THE DIVINE LOVER, was worshiped by most of the rulers of Jaipur, who dedicated their principal shrines to him. His cosmic moonlight dance at Vrindavan with his beloved Radha amid concentric circles of gopis—each of whom believed that he danced with her alone—is depicted in this large miniature of the Rasamandala, a Vaishnavite cosmogram. Targetlike, the composition flickers at the edges, gaining power, speed, and intensity of color toward the center, where a radiant Krishna and Radha, his favorite

261

261, detail ▷

among the gopis, dance with rhapsodic grace. From above, gandharvas in their flying chariots rain down flowers. The artist honored his patron, Maharaja Pratap Singh (r. 1779–1803), by painting the Blue God in his likeness.

Maharaja Pratap, who staged celebrations reenacting the divine dance in the courtyards of the City Palace, inherited the throne of Jaipur after his half brother's death in a riding accident. According to court rumor, the fall had been precipitated by a dose of poison administered on behalf of Maharaja Pratap's mother, who became regent. The maharaja was dominated by her until 1787, when he allied with the maharaja of Jodhpur and others against the Marathas, who were defeated at Tonga the same year. Within a few years, Maharaja Pratap, now considered gallant and capable, had spent more on victory celebrations than the cost of the war; and before long, the Marathas and others, lured by Jaipur's reputed riches, renewed their attacks.

Published: Mehta, *Studies in Indian Painting*, pp. 31–34, pl. 11; Das, *Treasures of Indian Painting*, ser. 3.

262.
TANPURA OF MAHARAJA PRATAP
SINGH OF JAIPUR
Rajasthan, Jaipur, late 18th century
Wood inlaid with ivory, length 37⅜ in.
(94.9 cm.)
Maharaja Sawai Man Singh II Museum, Jaipur
(T&C/Z)

HISTORIANS TOO OFTEN concentrate on battles, treaties, triumphs, and disasters, oblivious to the illuminating private moments of individuals, even of royal ones. This perfectly proportioned, meticulously inlaid tanpura—a rare survival of work by a great instrument maker—calls up the spirit of Maharaja Pratap Singh far more vividly than words about his victory at Tonga. Seeing it, we imagine the prince plucking its strings to supply the drone for singers or instrumentalists at recitals in Jaipur's City Palace.

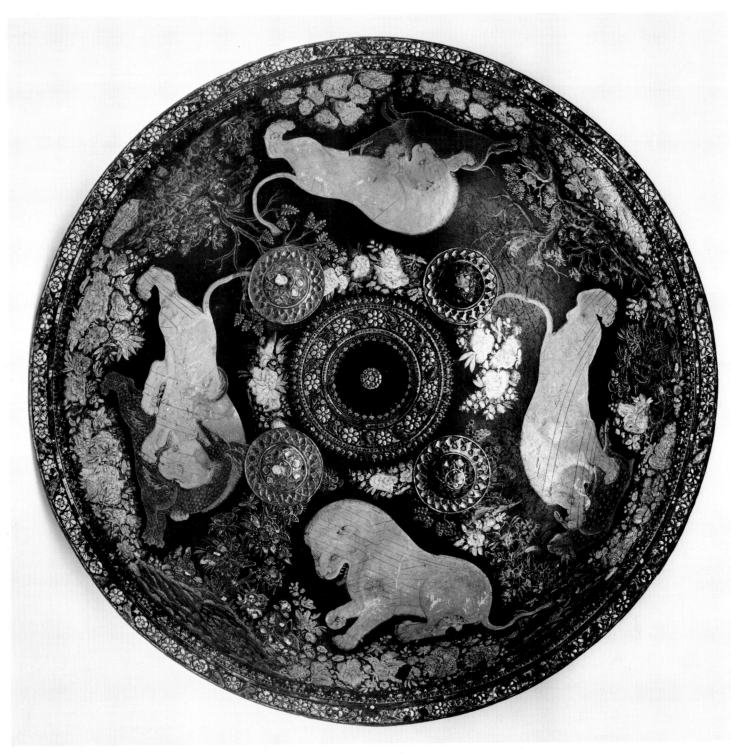

263

RAJPUT PAINTERS, LIKE those of European courts, were called upon to design or adorn princely accessories. Many craftsmen participated in the making of this shield. A leather worker removed the hair from the hide and tanned the skin for the man in the armory charged with preparing shields. The armorer cut it to shape, molded it over a wooden frame, stained and dried it, and with his helpers fitted it for straps before passing it on to the artist to ornament with flowers, appealingly curly lions—two of them in combat—and a border of spritely birds. In the meantime, the local jeweler, who probably plied his trade in the bazaar as well as in the fort ateliers, cast and finished the bosses, which were attached after the artist had completed his job. Such a fine shield must have been received with pride by its patron, who probably rewarded the craftsmen and often brought it out from the silahkana (armory), where it would have hung with countless others in tidy rows.

263.
SHIELD
Rajasthan, perhaps Kotah or Devgarh,
ca. 1800
Water buffalo hide, painted, with silver bosses,
diameter 23½ in. (59.7 cm.)
The Knellington Collection, Courtesy
Harvard University Art Museums,
Cambridge, Massachusetts

THE PUNJAB PLAINS AND HILLS

264.
MASK OF SHIVA
Punjab Hills, perhaps Kulu,
early 17th century
Bronze, 5⅞ in. (14.8 cm.)
Jagdish and Kamla Mittal Museum of Indian
Art, Hyderabad (76.972)

IN THE VILLAGES of the Himalayan areas of Kulu and Chamba such repoussée plaques, locally called mohras, are common. Most mohras represent Shiva, but masks of the goddess Devi and other deities were also made. The plaques are cast in bronze, brass, or sometimes silver. The head is sculpted in bold relief; the neck and shoulders are more summarily treated. Many scholars mistakenly believe these plaques were worn as masks like those used by dancers and actors. Stella Kramrisch beautifully describes their purpose: "Groups of such plaques or images, their metal faces gleaming, were—and still are—taken out of the temples on a palanquin in processions during religious festivals."[1] "Each mask is a thanks-offering. It is consecrated by a priest (*pujari*) and the shaman talks through the mask answering the questions which have been put to the deity. . . . Each village has its own masks. From their high position on the mountain on the chariot, they inspect the harvest. . . . These masks of deity, unlike those worn by men, are kept from year to year in the village as property of the deity. A tithe is collected for the preparation of new masks. The money is paid to the craftsmen through the clerk of the village."[2]

Mohras have been made for at least fourteen hundred years, in a bewildering array of sizes and styles. The known examples range from as small as two inches high to as large as a foot. In general, we can say that those made between the sixth and the fourteenth century are in the tradition of the classical bronzes of the region, and most of those dating from the fifteenth century onward are in folk style. On plaques of Shiva, whatever their style, the deity wears a lobed crown, beaded earrings, and two neck ornaments, one a beaded or cordlike necklace, the other a pair of wriggling serpents, symbols of Shiva and fertility. The flattened body below the face has two beadlike nipples, a mere suggestion of a chest. The hypnotizing stare of Shiva's three large, commanding eyes, wide open in a faraway gaze, and his divinely mysterious smile charge these plaques with special energy.

This extraordinary piece was manufactured by a technique often used for folk bronzes by craftsmen in Bastar, Bihar, Orissa, and Bengal but only rarely by the metal casters in the Hills. The envisioned metal image was first modeled in clay. When the clay was dry, the mold was wrapped with pieces of wax wire placed one against the other and pressed together until the form was completely sheathed. On this plaque the wax strips were purposely not smoothed, and the resulting ribbed effect has been used with great feeling to infuse the god's image with an added vitality. The beaklike nose and the large, downward-looking eyes are reminiscent of the earliest Pahari paintings from Basohli of carvings in wood and stone from the Himalayan states.

J.M.

1. Kramrisch, *Manifestations of Shiva,* p. 103, no. 83.
2. Kramrisch, *Unknown India,* p. 62.

265

265.
DEVI IS ADORED BY THE GODS
Punjab Hills, Basohli, ca. 1660–70
Opaque watercolor and beetle-wing cases
on paper
Folio: 8 × 12 in. (20.3 × 30.5 cm.)
Miniature: 7⅛ × 10⅞ in. (18.1 × 27.6 cm.)
Collection Kasturbhai Lalbhai, Ahmedabad

THIS IS ONE of the most captivating and profound of Indian pictures. Devi is shown here in the aspect of Chandi, "the Cruel One," created from the anger of the gods, who were then compelled to worship her. The setting, with its courtly pavilion and paradisiacal trees that seem to be ecstatic emanations from the musicians' fanfare, contributes to the religious mood. Seated on her throne, protected by tigers, four-armed Devi receives the homage of the assembled gods. Vishnu, also with four arms, stands to her left, while Shiva, with a third eye and boar's tusks, wearing a leopard skin, fans her with a chauri (yak-tail fly whisk). The four-armed and four-headed Brahma blows on a conch shell and plays a stringed instrument, and behind him Durga holds a sword and a pair of cymbals in her four arms. *Devi Is Adored* perfectly embodies the moment of classical ripeness in Hill painting's most traditional and compelling school. Basohli, a small state only twenty miles long and fifteen miles wide, gave birth to the earliest known Hill miniatures imbued with unmistakable and concentrated regional characteristics. A cadet branch of the house of Kulu, Basohli was founded in 1598 by Raja Bhupat Pal, who was said to be so strong that he could rub out the letters on a coin between his fingers. Bhupat Pal descended from the Rajput Balauria clan, a family associated with the holy city of Hardwar, near the source of the sacred river Ganges. A victim of intrigues, he was imprisoned by Jahangir in 1613. He was released in 1627 by order of Shah Jahan, who presented him with a robe of honor. After his murder in Delhi in 1635 at the age of sixty-two, Bhupat Pal was succeeded by his seven-year-old son, Sangram Pal. When he was twelve Raja Sangram Pal was summoned to Delhi, where he was praised for his good looks by the royal ladies. He remained in the Mughal capital for one year and then apparently returned to Basohli. He married a number of wives, seven of whom committed themselves to the flames in rites of sati following his death in 1673.

Iridescent with beetle-wing cases, exquisitely painted in colors rarely combined, boldly drawn, and charged with devotional power, this Devi was probably done for Raja Sangram Pal. Only the heightened courtliness and the extreme fineness of execution of Sangram Pal's pictures reflect his sojourn in Delhi. The goddess's robust features and intense gaze hark back to a more primal phase of Hill art, represented by the mask of Shiva (no. 264), and excite us with the prospect of discovering painted icons from the emergent phases of the Basohli style, when it may have been less refined but was surely more smolderingly passionate.

Published: *The Art of India and Pakistan*, p. 126, no. 511; W. Archer, *Indian Painting in the Punjab Hills: Essays*, pp. 6, 15, fig. 5; W. Archer, *Indian Paintings from the Punjab Hills: A Survey*, vol. 1, p. 35, no. 3, vol. 2, p. 17, no. 3.

COMPARABLE TO A superb folk melody artfully enriched with grace notes, the *Lady with Musicians and Pet Rabbits* evokes a refined court in the Hills, where aesthetic ferment was zealously encouraged at a very leisurely pace. This painting comes from a series depicting a poetic catalogue of nayakas and nayikas in various emotional states and amorous situations. Hours of massage, oiling, perfuming, combing, and costuming, all to entice her lover, preceded this heroine's lonely stroll through a garden as immaculately tended as she. Nevertheless, she appears slightly withdrawn and sad, and her attendant musicians are anxious. Forlorn she might be, but the connoisseur who commissioned this masterpiece encouraged his artist to draw forth, slowly and carefully, every nuance from each jewel, floral pattern, stripe, and sinuous line.

Inasmuch as Sangram Pal died without male issue, he was succeeded in 1673 by his half brother, Hindal Pal, who was ill-treated by his stepmother and forcibly detained in the palace until he came to the throne at the age of forty. Basohli painting as seen here probably stems from Hindal Pal's five-year reign, and may have provided a creative outlet for his housebound energies.

Published: W. Archer, *Indian Paintings from the Punjab Hills: A Survey*, vol. 1, p. 40, no. 5 (iii), vol. 2, p. 24, no. 5 (iii); Randhawa and Galbraith, *Indian Painting*, pl. 28.

266.
LADY WITH MUSICIANS AND PET RABBITS
From a Nayaka–Nayika (Lovers) series
Punjab Hills, Basohli, ca. 1670–75
Opaque watercolor on paper
Folio: 7⅞ × 12⅜ in. (20 × 31.5 cm.)
Miniature: 6⅛ × 10½ in. (15.6 × 26.7 cm.)
Collection Gopi Krishna Kanoria, Patna (GK.178)

266

266, detail

267.
TREES AND FLOWERS IN A LANDSCAPE
Punjab Hills, Kulu or Basohli, ca. 1680
Opaque watercolor on paper, 5¾ × 11⅞ in.
(14.6 × 30.3 cm.)
Collection Kasturbhai Lalbhai, Ahmedabad

PURE LANDSCAPE IS rare in Indian painting. Except for a few Jain examples, Indian pictures ordinarily contain a "subject," albeit no more than a single deity, figure, animal, or blossom. This flowerscape may have been the opening illustration of a literary series, meant to establish mood and setting. The idea for it may have struck a raja as he admired a Mughal textile, binding, floral border, or marble relief during a visit to Delhi or Agra. The wispy dragon clouds above the looming, rhythmically alive flowers and feathery trees recall the clouds, ultimately traceable to Chinese art, that occurred frequently as ornament in Mughal art after the early years of Shah Jahan's reign. Here, however, imperial motifs have been completely adjusted to the Hill style of the Balaurias as practiced at Kulu or Basohli.

267

IN LATER EPISODES of the *Ramayana*, Rama makes his way back to Ayodhya, after fourteen years in exile, to regain his kingdom. The long, drawn-out war in Lanka has ended at last; Sita has been rescued, the demon king Ravana who abducted her slain. The scene portrayed here is the auspicious moment of Rama's coronation within the seclusion of the palace walls. Surrounded by his followers and attendants, Rama sits enthroned in the palace at the left, while the women witness the ceremony from an adjoining building and the populace and the royal retainers, some with elephants and horses, wait patiently in the courtyard in the foreground. Rather than agitated gaiety and excitement, the mood is one of dignified calm as the people of Ayodhya give thanks in silent prayer for the happy end to the long ordeal and for the safe return of Rama, Sita, and Lakshmana. Like generations of Indian painters before and since, the sensitive artist has captured the emotions of the crowd not by gesture or facial expression but with color.

The same muted, refined palette appears in several other paintings, now in collections throughout the world, whose many compositional and stylistic affinities leave little doubt they were all painted by the same artist or group of artists, perhaps of the same family, who had either been trained in the Mughal style or descended from painters who had. In all of these paintings the figures, usually clustered in groups, are small in stature, with softly modeled faces. Men and women of rank wear Shah Jahani costumes, others raiments of local mode. The trees are often cypresses, sometimes tall with small, fine leaves, or, as here, large and full with feathery foliage in light to dark shades of green. Pairs of birds in flight break the monotony of the sky, a band the color of lapis lazuli that merges into a near-white stripe of clouds gently softening and fusing with a band of paler blue along the very high horizon.

In addition to four other folios from the *Ramayana* series, the group includes twelve folios from a *Bhagavata Purana*, a series of smaller pictures depicting gods and goddesses, ragamala paintings, a fragment showing two young girls, two pictures of horses, each with its groom, and several unpublished paintings in the Mittal Museum in Hyderabad. The folios from the *Ramayana* and the *Bhagavata Purana* seem to be by one artist. They are also earlier than the rest, probably dating from about 1670 to 1675. Both sets were drawn with a firm, sure hand, reflected in the confident outlines. The brushwork is similar, and vivid colors are often used in the same combinations. The paper is thin and smooth, the color surface rich and luxurious. Birds fly in the sky, the foliage is feathery light, and the figures have slightly enlarged heads, small eyes, and faces modeled with shading near the temples and along the hairline. The pictures also have certain recurring decorative and architectural details in common: the patterns on door hangings, the placement and striped designs of dhurries, the shapes and forms of cornices and turrets.

During the reign of Emperor Aurangzeb (1658–1707), when the court arts languished for want of patronage, Mughal-trained painters took service wherever there was comparative peace and a willing patron, and many found work illustrating Hindu subjects for Rajput rulers in Rajasthan and the Punjab. That it was also not uncommon for talented painters to migrate from one state in the Hills to another at the invitation of a raja often makes assigning exact provenances even more difficult.

Precisely where and when this group of pictures was painted has long been the subject of scholarly debate. So close are they in style to paintings done at Bikaner, in Rajasthan, that for many years it was assumed they were painted there. Recent studies, however, theorize that they were probably produced in the Hills at one of the Rajput courts that was strongly influenced by Mughal art and may have hired an artist or artists who had worked for a time for the Rathor princes of Bikaner.[1] Catherine Glynn assigns the paintings to the Hill school of Mandi and dates them between 1630 and 1645.[2] It is possible that some of them were indeed painted at Mandi. But there are more convincing reasons to suggest that most if not all of the miniatures in this group are early products, painted between about 1670 and 1700, of the workshop at Bilaspur (Kahlur), another of the important Pahari schools.

268.
THE CORONATION OF RAMA
From a manuscript of the *Ramayana*
Punjab Hills, Mandi or Bilaspur, ca. 1670–75
Opaque watercolor on paper
Miniature: 15 × 10¾ in. (38.1 × 30 cm.)
Jagdish and Kamla Mittal Museum of Indian Art, Hyderabad (76.232)

268, detail

Painting at Bilaspur seems to have begun during the reign of Raja Dip Chand, who came to the throne in 1650 and ruled until 1667. Dip Chand not only campaigned for Aurangzeb but almost certainly spent some time at the court in Delhi, an association that would very likely have created at Bilaspur a hospitable climate attractive to Mughal artists. And many features peculiar to this *Ramayana* series and the group of related paintings—the treatment of the sky, the drawing of the figures and their costumes, the tree types, ornaments, architectural details, and color schemes—are also found in paintings from Bilaspur.[3]

J.M.

1. See Khandalavala and Chandra, *Miniatures and Sculptures*, p. 24, fig. 73; Welch, *A Flower from Every Meadow*, p. 65, no. 33; Khandalavala, "Two Bikaner Paintings," pp. 301–4, pl. v, figs. 635–44; *The Indian Heritage*, p. 64, no. 160.
2. Glynn, "Early Painting in Mandi," including thirty-four figures.
3. Several of the Bilaspur paintings are published in W. Archer, *Indian Paintings from the Punjab Hills: A Survey*, vol. 2, pp. 170–77, nos. 5, 8, 9, 11, 13, 17–19; Lerner, *The Flame and the Lotus*, no. 62.

Published: Glynn, "Early Painting in Mandi," fig. 16.

269

269.
AHIRI RAGINI
From a Ragamala (Garland of Melody) series
Punjab Hills, Basohli, early 18th century
Opaque watercolor on paper
Folio: 8 × 7½ in. (20.3 × 19.1 cm.)
Miniature: 6⅞ × 6¼ in. (17.5 × 15.9 cm.)
Collection Gopi Krishna Kanoria, Patna
(BD.18)

ACCORDING TO MESAKARMA, a court priest of Rewa during the sixteenth century who composed verses on ragas (see no. 191), Ahiri ragini, the musical mode interpreted visually in this painting, sounds like a snake. Simply composed, with large, flat areas of hot color and a curtain flaring out to reveal a symbolically closed door, the picture is charged with mystery. Why does the sad, concerned young girl feed a snake? Does he represent Shiva? Is he a surrogate for her absent lover? Or both?

A RESPECTFUL HUSH surrounds Raja Sidh Sen (r. 1684–1727), the impressive, enormous raja of Mandi who is shown here with the commanders of his army. Fifty years old when he came to the throne in 1684, Sidh Sen lived to be one hundred. Credited with supernatural powers, he was said to possess a potent book of spells. He was also a great warrior and deeply religious. During his long reign, he founded two temples and welcomed the tenth Sikh guru, Govind Singh, when he visited Mandi in about 1697 (according to legend he arrived by air in an iron cage) to gain support against the Mughals. The guru granted Sidh Sen a boon: "When Mandi is plundered, heavenly balls will be fired," a prediction of invulnerability that held true until 1840, when Mandi was conquered by the Sikhs.

Mandi was founded in the tenth to eleventh century, an offshoot of Suket, which dates to the eighth century. The ruling family is descended from the Sena rajas of Bengal. Mandi painting is usually rugged and earthy, with darkly outlined silhouetted figures. The power, dignity, and rock-cut solidity of these pictures express a world in slow motion. The palette of dark greens, tans, indigo, and brownish reds well suits the Mandi artists' dignified portraits and their depictions of thick-limbed deities.

Published: W. Archer, *Indian Paintings from the Punjab Hills: A Survey*, vol. 1, p. 353, no. 6, vol. 2, p. 263, no. 6.

270.
RAJA SIDH SEN OF MANDI IN AUDIENCE
Punjab Hills, Mandi, ca. 1700–20
Opaque watercolor on paper
Folio: 17½ × 13⅞ in. (44.5 × 35.2 cm.)
Miniature: 13⅛ × 9⅛ in. (33.3 × 23.2 cm.)
National Museum, New Delhi
(62.1774)

270

271.
PATKA WITH DESIGN OF FLOWERING
TREES
Dacca, 18th century
Cotton, with metallic thread and beetle-wing
cases, 12 ft. ¾ in. × 23⅝ in. (3.62 m. × 60 cm.)
Museum of Fine Arts, Boston, Gift of
Denman W. Ross (24.433)

NATURE INTO ART: beetle-wing cases, here stitched on fine muslin woven with gold and silver metallic threads to create a paradoxically icy forest fire of iridescent ornament, were particularly admired in the Hills, where artists of the Basohli school applied them to favored pictures. Magically glittering, they are also brittle and fragile. Indeed, this patka is a tangible affront to practicality; its wearer must have had to be exceedingly careful lest his celestial radiance snag on a fingernail and flutter to earth.

Like so many precious goods that sparkled at Indian courts, this rare textile may not have been made where it was used. Inasmuch as Dacca, in eastern Bengal, was renowned for its cobweb fine cottons, this fabric may have been made there, but the finished piece would surely have been welcomed by any discerning court, whether in the Plains or the Hills.

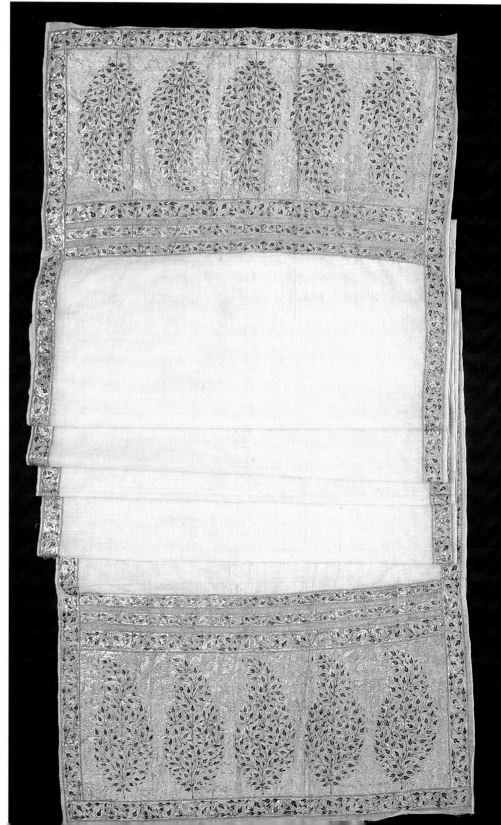

271

DEMONS, SWIMMING ELEPHANTS, sea monsters, bears, and several kinds of monkeys, assembled in a bright landscape planted with cypresses and plantains, make this large picture irresistible. But the painting is also a dramatic illustration to Part VI of the *Ramayana*, which recounts the adventures of Rama and his brother Lakshmana, who set out to rescue Rama's wife Sita after she was abducted by the demonic Ravana, tyrant of Lanka (Sri Lanka). Supported by an army of bears and monkeys, Rama and Lakshmana successfully laid siege to the golden fort of Lanka, slew the archvillain, and released Sita. Here Rama and Lakshmana, surrounded by their appealing army, discuss the proposed attack with Ravana's turncoat brother Vibhisana, whose knowledge of the golden fort interests them intensely. As they talk, two demons disguised as monkeys, spies intent on infiltrating the enemy's ranks, sidle over from the fort. The account of the episode from Valmiki's *Ramayana* is written on the back of the painting, which still bears marks left by the fingers of the storytellers who held it up to their courtly audiences.

This miniature was painted at Guler, where a fifteenth-century fortress dominates the view above the broad Ban Ganga River and large numbers of monkeys disport, making it an apt setting for the subject. Guler maintained a major school of Hill painting that can be documented from the late seventeenth through the nineteenth century. Guler artists were invariably accomplished and innovative draftsmen as well as colorists, and their pictures ranged from the stately to the humorous to the poignant and poetic.

Fifteen finished miniatures, a few barely touched with color, and fifty or more preparatory drawings for the exciting series from which this picture comes have survived.[1] All seem to be the work of a master artist with a genius for simple, bold composition and effectively dramatic presentation. Here, he laid out a lively and precise pattern accented by trees, arches, windows, and figures. With astonishing cleverness, he crowned the rightmost cypress tree with a delicate fillip, thereby joining the right and left halves of a design that would otherwise have broken in two. The artist's humorous psychological insight into the natures of men and animals is also in evidence here: each bear, monkey, and pair thereof should be inspected with care with an eye for zoomorphic waggery.

272.
TWO SPIES DISGUISED AS MONKEYS
APPROACH THE ARMY OF RAMA
From a manuscript of the *Ramayana*
Punjab Hills, Guler, ca. 1725
Opaque watercolor on paper, 23¾ × 32¾ in.
(60.3 × 83.2 cm.)
The Knellington Collection, Courtesy
Harvard University Art Museums,
Cambridge, Massachusetts

Overleaf, 272 ▷

272, detail

The series of illustrations to the *Siege of Lanka* was commissioned by Raja Dalip Singh (r. 1695–1741), chief of the Katoch family, which can be traced to the early fifteenth century, when it split off from Kangra. Dalip Singh came to the throne at the age of seven or eight. He was an effective, peaceful, and devout ruler, but he was apparently more interested in religion, the arts, and the quiet enjoyment of life than in governing. He turned over the administration of his state to his eldest son, Bishan Singh, in about 1725 and then to his second son, Govardhan Chand, when Bishan Singh died. Portraits of Dalip Singh show him at worship, playing polo, and—most often—conversing with his family and friends.

1. Ten other pictures from the series are in the collection of the Museum of Fine Arts, Boston; four are in The Metropolitan Museum of Art; and the Cleveland Art Museum and the British Museum each have one. An unfinished picture is in a private collection, and many of the drawings are in the Prince of Wales Museum of Western India, Bombay, and in the collection of B. K. Birla, Calcutta.

Published: Welch, *A Flower from Every Meadow*, pp. 74–75, no. 41; W. Archer and Czuma, *Indian Art*, no. 115.

273.
RAJA BALWANT SINGH OF JAMMU WRITING A LETTER IN HIS TENT
By Nainsukh
Punjab Hills, Jammu, ca. 1760
Opaque watercolor on paper
Folio: 8½ × 11¼ in. (21.5 × 28.5 cm.)
Miniature: 7¾ × 10⅞ in. (19.8 × 27.7 cm.)
Trustees of the Prince of Wales Museum of Western India, Bombay (33.108)

IN INDIA AS ELSEWHERE, works of art are enlivened and enriched by congenial, creative collaborations between artists and patrons. Without Jahangir, his "Wonders"—Abu' l-Hasan, Mansur, and Farrukh Beg—would have painted less insightfully, and in the Hills, Nainsukh's inspiration might have flagged without Balwant Singh of Jammu (1724–1763). Were it possible to overcome time and space to bring together these artists and patrons, exhilarating exchanges would be likely, for the Mughal emperor and the royal Jammu connoisseur surely had much in common, as did their artists. Jahangir and Balwant Singh appreciated life's trivia, and their congenial, ardent painters were of like minds. Jahangir would have applauded Nainsukh's intimate glimpse of Balwant Singh, shirtless, casually writing a letter while his bored servant lets droop the morchhal. And had Balwant Singh seen *Squirrels in a Plane Tree* (no. 141), his eyes would have flashed in recognition.

The Jammu house of Jamwal resisted the Mughal emperor Akbar but was forced to submit in 1588. Thereafter, it was compelled to send royal hostages to the imperial court until the early eighteenth century. During the late seventeenth century, however, Raja Kirpal Dev (r. ca. 1660–90), of the Bahu branch of the house, allied with Chamba, Basohli, and Guler to defeat the Mughal viceroy of the Punjab and drive him from the Hills. Painting at

Jammu is known from the late seventeenth century onward. Its greatest flowering occurred under Raja Balwant Singh.

The collaboration between Raja Balwant Singh and Nainsukh began in about 1744, when both were in their early twenties. Nainsukh was from Guler. He had been well trained as an exponent of both the Guler and imperial Mughal idioms, and he merged them harmoniously in his work, especially under the encouragement of the raja. The relationship between prince and painter is so well expressed by W. G. Archer that I cannot improve upon his words: "Nainsukh follows him round as if with a camera, snapping him as he finishes his toilet, is shaved by a barber, inspects horses, picnics in the country, releases his hawks, or camps beneath a shed. He shows him as nothing if not dignified but, at the same time, off-guard or in undress, the presiding genius, not of a feudal state, but of a rural household in which the humblest servant is allowed his little quirks."[1]

1. W. Archer, *Indian Paintings from the Punjab Hills: A Survey*, vol. 1, p. 195.

Published: W. Archer, *Indian Miniatures*, pl. 82; M. Chandra, *Indian Art*, pl. LIII; W. Archer, *Indian Paintings from the Punjab Hills: A Survey*, vol. 1, p. 206, no. 52, vol. 2, p. 151, no. 52.

AMONG INDIA'S MORE seductive depictions of romantic love are those painted in the Punjab Hills during the latter half of the eighteenth century, when Mughal naturalism combined with the tender lyricism of local traditions and Vaishnavite poetry. The synthesis could not be better exemplified than by *Krishna and Radha in a Pavilion*, a profoundly ecstatic vision of erotic passion and spiritual union. Symbolically illuminated by a lightning bolt, the godly couple embrace beneath an exuberant profusion of deliciously ripe mangoes and luminous flowers laced together by spiraling vines.

Raja Govardhan Chand of Guler (r. 1741–73) conducted what Ananda K. Coomaraswamy describes as "a delicate research into physical charm"[1] and encouraged his artists to apply the results of his discoveries in idealistically amorous pictures. A man of strong opinion, he went to war against the Mughal governor of the Jullundur Doab over an argument about a favorite horse, and won. The same disciplined, determined power that enabled Govardhan Chand triumphantly to enforce a whim may also have inspired his artist, who has painted Krishna and Radha not only with immense charm but with moving credibility.

1. W. Archer, *Indian Paintings from the Punjab Hills: A Survey*, vol. 1, p. 149.

Published: Brijbhushan, *The World of Indian Miniatures*, pl. 33.

To HONOR THE occasion of his marriage, which probably took place in 1781, Raja Sansar Chand of Kangra commissioned a series of illustrations to the *Gita Govinda* (The Song of the Cowherd), the twelfth-century Bengali court poet Jayadeva's story of the ecstatic union of Krishna and Radha, to whom the Kangra house were devoted. This page was the opening miniature. Nanda, the cowherd who was Krishna's adoptive father, has urged Radha to accompany Krishna home because he is afraid of the darkness. Graceful as dancers, the divine lovers stop to embrace on the bank of the Jamuna River, while around them, in a series of arboreal *pas de deux,* pairs of trees reenact the stages of their developing attraction for each other.

Seeing the Kangra Valley, lush, richly fertile, crossed by a gently flowing river in sight of the white-capped peaks of the Himalayas, deepens one's appreciation of Kangra painting. The supremely pictorial landscape, like many of the paintings from the Kangra court, is so prettily, excruciatingly beautiful that it very nearly palls. The ancient Kangra dynasty dates from as early as the sixth millennium B.C., centuries before the great classical Sanskrit epic the *Mahabharata* (The Book of Wars) was composed. But Kangra painting can be traced back no further than the reign of Sansar Chand, who came to the throne in 1775 at the age of ten. Sansar Chand was an ambitious

274.
KRISHNA AND RADHA IN A PAVILION
Punjab Hills, probably Guler, 3rd quarter of 18th century
Opaque watercolor on paper
Folio: 12¼ × 9 in. (31.1 × 22.9 cm.)
Miniature: 11⅛ × 7¾ in. (28.3 × 19.7 cm.)
National Museum, New Delhi
(51.207/23)

275.
KRISHNA AND RADHA: LOVE IN A DARK WOOD
From a manuscript of the *Gita Govinda* (The Song of the Cowherd) of Jayadeva
Punjab Hills, Kangra, ca. 1780
Opaque watercolor on paper
Folio: 7 × 11 in. (17.8 × 27.9 cm.)
Miniature: 6 × 9⅞ in. (15.2 × 25.1 cm.)
Private collection

275

ruler, but he also loved music, dancing, and, especially, art, both paintings
and brush drawings. The wealth and power of Kangra enabled him to indulge
his enthusiasm. He hired master painters from Guler, the waning cadet branch
of the Kangra dynasty, and encouraged them to work in a variant of the
Guler style, a blend of Hill and Mughal artistic ways (see nos. 272, 274).

The *Gita Govinda* series from which this page comes was painted soon
after Sansar Chand established his atelier. That he nurtured so remarkable a
set of paintings, one of Kangra's major creations, when he was only fifteen
or sixteen years old attests to his intense and precocious interest. Throughout
his political troubles, his delight in painting never waned. Under his patronage and direction, the work of the Kangra artists, particularly their idyllic
illustrations to Hindu literature, attained Botticellian grace and refinement.
(Court portraiture was usually treated less fastidiously.) In time, the reputation
of Kangra painting assumed almost legendary proportions, far beyond that
of any of the other Hill schools. In England, its naturalism, sweet poetry,
and fineness were especially appealing to critics who had been reared in the
comfortable shade of the Pre-Raphaelites.

Under his successors, the Kangra style persisted and spread, but without
Sansar Chand's disciplining attention it soon lost its purity. What had been
sweet soon became cloying, then coarse. Sansar Chand's wittily aristocratic elongated ladies in sinuous, subtly colored costumes gave way to a
generation of pleasing but wilted belles who would have suited Saint
Valentine's Day cards. Their granddaughters tended to be hardier women,
dumpy in comparison, with thicker hands, wearing brightly colored dresses
of little elegance. If their earthy appeal is sometimes warmly sensual and
they have gained in energy, one nevertheless regrets the passing of their
ethereal grandmothers.

276.
STUDIES OF A TIGER AT REST
Punjab Hills, late 18th century
Tinted drawing on paper, 7⅛ × 5½ in.
(18 × 14 cm.)
Government Museum and Art Gallery,
Chandigarh (L-8)

TIGER HUNTING WAS a favorite pastime of the Rajputs, Mughals, Sikhs, and most other Indian rulers—a time to test their mettle and enjoy the sport. Orphaned cubs were on occasion brought to palace compounds and reared as not quite tamable pets, fascinating to study but risky to handle. This amiable feline appears to have been domesticated. It seems to have obliged the artist by stretching out in its enclosure, both formally and with almost coy, topsy-turvy ease to reveal majestic stripes, a soft underbelly, and massive, disquieting paws.

276

Intent upon his sensitively accurate study of the marvelous animal, the artist has provided no trees, flowers, or figures that might have enabled us to place the painting at Kangra, Guler, Lahore, or some other atelier where late eighteenth-century Mughal technique and verisimilitude combined with the spirit of Hill art.

HANUMAN, THE HINDU monkey god, is shown here as one of Rama's forceful helpers at the siege of the demon Ravana's fort at Lanka, an episode from the *Ramayana* (see no. 272). Mountain vast, tall as a great tower, and agile as the winds, in one leap Hanuman could soar from Sri Lanka to the Himalayas to bring curative herbs for those wounded in battle. Despite his godly powers, he retained engagingly simian characteristics. His great tail, greased and ignited for use as a weapon in a hand-to-hand struggle against Ravana, brushed against Rama's encampment and set it aflame.

This image of the benevolent Hanuman, who roars like thunder and shakes the earth as he bounds to Rama's aid, was designed and embroidered in the Hills, probably at the court of Chamba, where the women in the zenana adorned many such coverings for gifts or offerings. Unusually large in size and boldly captivating in design, this piece underscores the close relationship between court and folk art. Whereas Chamba miniature paintings of comparable date were influenced by Kangra exquisiteness, this jubilant textile is zestful as a village festival.

Published: "Folk Textiles," pp. 279–80.

277.
LEAPING HANUMAN
Punjab Hills, Chamba, late 18th century
Cotton embroidered with silk and metallic thread, 29⅞ × 41⅜ in. (76 × 105 cm.)
Museum of Fine Arts, Boston, Helen and Alice Colburn Fund (1983.320)

277

278

278.
GENERAL JEAN-FRANÇOIS ALLARD
AND HIS FAMILY
Inscribed, at top: "painted at Lahore, 1838
A. D."; in Nasta'liq script: "General Allard
Sahib Bahadur, formerly a commander of
France, assigned to the army of H. E. Maha-
raja Ranjit Singh Bahadur Surgaba, may he
rest in heaven"; and at center: " to the most
generous Maharaja Ranjit Singh Bahadur in
the Province of Punjab"
Lahore, dated 1838
Opaque watercolor on paper, 8¼ × 10½ in.
(21 × 26.7 cm.)
The Knellington Collection, Courtesy
Harvard University Art Museums,
Cambridge, Massachusetts

THE SIKH BROTHERHOOD, a sect combining aspects of the Muslim faith (chiefly
worship of one god and a rejection of the caste system) with Hinduism, was
founded in northern India by the guru Nanak in the late fifteenth century. It
was not until the early eighteenth century, when Mughal power had begun
to wane, that what had been essentially a religious community changed
decisively to a political and military entity with territorial claims. By 1750,
large Sikh confederacies known as misls (bands of equals) held considerable
tracts of land. But the many misls were disunited, and although the Sikhs
took Lahore in 1767, it was only after the advent of their great leader Maharaja Ranjit Singh (r. 1780–1839) that they carved out their own state. Of
Akbar-like vitality and magnetism, Ranjit Singh, the Lion of the Punjab,
occupied Lahore in 1799, defeated the Bhangis, the most powerful misl, in
1801, and in 1802 captured Amritsar, site of the holiest Sikh shrine. Five
years later he added Ludhiana to his holdings, but in 1809 the British succeeded in confining him to lands east of the Sutlej River, thus preventing
him from aggrandizement beyond the Punjab.

A small, fiery, eagerly sensual man who was pockmarked and blind in
one eye from a childhood attack of smallpox, Ranjit Singh had a taste for
pretty girls and boys and a yen for a drink made from corn liquor, opium,
musk, and the juices of raw meat, described by the well-traveled English-
woman Emily Eden as "liquid fire . . . of which no European can touch a
drop."[1] Despite these enervating habits, he dominated the Punjab Plains and
Hills until his death in 1839.

Ranjit Singh's colorful establishment included a number of European soldiers of fortune, one of whom was General Jean-François Allard. Allard was born in Saint-Tropez (where his descendants still live) in 1785. He enlisted in a regiment of Napoleon's dragoons and at eighteen served in Italy for three years. In 1806, he was promoted to sergeant major in Joseph Bonaparte's bodyguard, and he later rose to quartermaster in a dragoon regiment serving in Spain. After suffering wounds, he was given a lieutenancy in the Imperial Dragoons of the Guard, and then became a captain in the 7th Hussars. He served under Napoleon during the One Hundred Days and was a captain of the Cuirassiers at Waterloo.

Following the downfall of his hero Napoleon, Allard, still addicted to the military life, voyaged east in search of a suitable career. Cairo, Tehran, and Kandahar proving unpromising, he went on to Lahore, where he arrived in March 1822. He persuaded Ranjit Singh to hire him at ten gold mohurs a day to train two regiments, one of dragoons, the other of lancers. After successful forays against the Afghans, he was put in charge of four regiments totaling 3,000 men and was soon assigned a further artillery force of 2,000. He married a beautiful woman from Kashmir, fathered several children, grew rich, and lived in luxury; at Anarkali, near Lahore, he built a splendid mansion (which later belonged to the maharajas of Kapurthala). But he never forgot La Belle France. His troops, the Francese Campo, flew Lafayette's flag, and on his chest the French Legion of Honor was pinned beside the Bright Star of the Punjab, a decoration he had designed for Ranjit Singh.

In 1833, distraught by the death of his daughter and the almost simultaneous loss of his savings when the Palmer's Bank in Calcutta collapsed, he asked permission to visit France. Ranjit Singh granted his request, but only reluctantly, insisting that Allard accept payment for the moneys owed him in shawls—30,000 rupees worth. So the general left for France accompanied by wife, children, and bales of textiles. Eighteen months later he returned alone to Lahore, and in January 1839 he died there of heart failure.

Inspired, alas, as much by loneliness as by pride, Allard had this Francophile conversation piece painted in Lahore and shortly before his death presented it to Ranjit Singh. The miniature was apparently based on a preliminary sketch for a family portrait Allard commissioned while he was in France between 1834 and 1836. The finished oil, by an artist of the Bouilly school, remained in Saint-Tropez (it was recently stolen from the Saint-Tropez museum, to which it had been lent by Allard's descendants), but Allard evidently carried the artist's sketch back to Lahore. In the Indian painter's version of the portrait, the romantic general, with his forked beard (one end of which he tucked behind his right ear the other behind his left when he ate) and wearing the decorations bestowed on him by Ranjit Singh and his idol Napoleon, sits surrounded by his family, including the beloved daughter he mourned and a son who resembles Bonaparte; the family is attended by servants, and the great mansion at Anarkali looms in the background—all a delightful commemoration of a curious international military life.

1. Eden, *Up the Country*, p. 197.

Published: W. Archer, *Paintings of the Sikhs*, pp. 82–84; Welch, *Room for Wonder*, pp. 124–25, no. 55; *The Indian Heritage*, p. 54, no. 108.

"SINGH" MEANS "LION," as is affirmed by this impressive likeness of the man who proved his capacity to succeed in the political jungle of the Punjab in the years following the death of Maharaja Ranjit Singh in 1839. In India, sitters past the first blush of youth were usually portrayed with emphasis on prestige and character. In one of the most biting characterizations in Indian portraiture, Gulab Singh's artist, who had been trained in the Kangra tradition, has stressed the maharaja's piercing stare, his turned-down mouth, and his jewels and sword, but the imposing attitude is foiled by the three tiny flowers he holds, almost mincingly, between thumb and forefinger.

279.
MAHARAJA GULAB SINGH OF JAMMU AND KASHMIR
Lahore, ca. 1846
Opaque watercolor on paper, 10⅝ × 8¼ in. (27 × 21 cm.)
Victoria and Albert Museum, London (I.S.194–1951)

279

Gulab Singh, a grand-nephew of Raja Balwant Singh of Jammu, the lively patron of painting (see no. 273), was born in 1792. He was a Rajput, not a Sikh, but he joined the army of Ranjit Singh, who admired his effectiveness as both soldier and statesman. In 1820, following his annexation of Kashtwar, Gulab Singh was designated raja and made governor of the Jammu Hills, to which Jasrota and Basohli were later added. Contemporary accounts of Gulab Singh's personality are somewhat contradictory, but fully in keeping with this portrait. Emily Eden found him "a horrid character,"[1] but the French scientist Victor de Jacquemont saw him as "a lion in war, but anything but a rose-water dandy . . . remarkably handsome and with the simplest, most gentle and elegant manners."[2] And G. T. Vigne, a British traveler who met him in 1835, described him as "only one of the better class of mounted sepahis (soldiers). . .[whose career] was stained by treachery and perfidy."[3]

In 1846, the year of this portrait, C. Hardinge, nephew of the British governor-general, penned a succinct sketch: "Gulab Singh is about 50 years in age and not only noted for his political acumen but for his physical activity and courage, which has never been disputed; his character also is free from those vices which have been attributed to his brothers, Rajahs Dhihan and Suchet Singh, and which pervade all orders of the Sikh nation, high and low. His features are regular, and the expression of his countenance more than usually mild, with an affectation of openness. Indeed, it has been remarked that a 'man might almost take him for his grandmother,' and the impression is certainly one which many who have conversed with him would form. He has remitted one fifth of the revenue paid by the Hill Chiefs in Kashmir, and by abolishing the rite of Sati in the Valley of Kashmir, as well as by making lenient settlements, has taken steps to conciliate the feelings of the Kashmirians, who have been more or less oppressed by the successive governors appointed by the Lahore Durbar."[4]

After Ranjit Singh's death, Gulab Singh gradually emerged as a new "Lion of the Punjab." For a few years he was admired by both the British and the Sikhs. He was recognized as maharaja of Jammu and Kashmir, and the Sikhs lauded him as the savior of the Sikh nation and protector of Ranjit Singh's heir, the boy maharaja Dalip Singh. But by 1849, when the Punjab was formally annexed to British India, Gulab Singh had already been forced from the Sikh political scene and had retired contentedly to his domain. A few years later, Dalip Singh, heir to the Sikh kingdom, was taken to England, where he bought a splendid estate, was befriended by Queen Victoria, and lived out his life in the style of an opulent English squire.

1. Eden, *Up the Country*, p. 135.
2. Jacquemont, *Letters from India*, p. 179.
3. Vigne, *A Personal Narrative*, pp. 250–52.
4. Hardinge, *Recollections of India*, pl. 14.

Published: Goetz, *Geschichte der indischen Miniaturmalerei*, pl. 16; W. Archer, *Paintings of the Sikhs*, pp. 52–56, 146–48, no. 25, fig. 50; Victoria and Albert Museum, *Indian Art*, pl. 49; Zebrowski, "Decorative Arts of the Mughal Period," pp. 175–76, no. 191; Topsfield, *An Introduction to Indian Court Painting*, pp. 45–46, pl. 39.

280.
OCCUPATIONS
By Kehar Singh
Kapurthala and Lahore,
3rd quarter of 19th century
Tinted drawings, 8⅝ × 7⅛ in. (22 × 18 cm.)
Government Museum and Art Gallery,
Chandigarh (1711, 1431, 1421)

a. ʿAJAB SINGH NIHANG, A SIKH HOLY MAN
Inscribed, at top: "ʿAjab Singh
Nihang caste Bahl Khatri born at
Nankana"; "painted by Kehar Singh
at Kapurthala"

b. A TURNER MAKING CHARPOI LEGS

c. A MAKER OF METALLIC THREAD OR TAPE

KEHAR SINGH, LIKE Ghulam ʿAli Khan of the Fraser Album (nos. 49, 50), whose work he may have known, was a humble artist whose talent and devotion to accurate observation enabled him to transcend the usual limitations of his period. Working in and near Lahore at a time when assorted European, Mughal, and Hill-school influences had reduced most art to pastiche, he served as a living camera, recording craftsmen, laborers, and other picturesque beings in sets that could have illustrated books on the tribes and castes of the Punjab, the sort of publication that was becoming popular among the English intelligentsia and their Indian circles. Possessed of an eye and feeling for human foibles, a darting, sure brush, and an anthropologist's dispassionate curiosity, he was a masterful draftsman.

Kehar Singh had a portrait photographer's gift for confronting subjects without causing them to freeze in self-consciousness. In the first of these

280a

280b

three tinted drawings, a Sikh holy man, such as one may still see in the Punjab, gazed comfortably at the artist as he worked. M. S. Randhawa described the obliging sitter's sect, the Nihangs, as "picturesque survivors of the 18th century. This sect was founded by Guru Gobind Singh. Maharaja Ranjit Singh, when he consolidated his power, made use of Nihangs as his suicide troops. They were a lawless lot who obeyed no authority. Their chief leader was Phoola Singh Akali who played a prominent role in the siege of Multan. The Nihangs wear conical blue turbans, on which they fasten a number of quoits. They wear cholas and usually carry swords, spears and shields on their persons. . . . Their headquarters are at Anandpur where they congregate at the Hola festival. They are fanatics and one of the sports which they enjoy during the Hola is desecration of the grave of Aurangzeb who they call 'Nauranga.' A raised mound is made to symbolize the grave of Aurangzeb and it is given shoe beating by parties of Nihangs.

280c

Apart from this pastime Nihangs enjoy drinking *bhang*, and they have given it the name of *sukha* or giver of pleasure."[1]

Kehar Singh's drawings of the shops of two artisans document their activities with encyclopedic thoroughness. Craftsmen, workshops, and tools are analyzed and delineated with an exactitude worthy of Diderot's illustrators, but it is also evident that the workmen interested Kehar Singh as individuals. One is reminded of Akbar's words on portraiture, for the Punjab artist also created pictures whereby "those that have passed away have received a new life, and those who are still alive have immortality" (see no. 106).

1. Randhawa, "Two Panjabi Artists," pp. 67–69, figs. 168–78.

Published:
a. Randhawa, "Two Panjabi Artists," pp. 67–69, fig. 168.

THE BRITISH PERIOD

Like the Mughals and other foreigners who came to India, the British were attracted by her legendary riches. Unlike the others, whom India absorbed, most of the British eventually returned home, unaware that they had been to some degree Indianized. But the depth of Britain's involvement with India, the jewel in its crown of empire, is apparent from the extraordinary nostalgia still expressed in the British Isles, nearly forty years after the departure of the last viceroy. Although the British in India are usually dismissed as greedy representatives of "the nation of shopkeepers," in fact many were cast in very different molds, from pirates to idealistic administrators, from scholars and artists to soldiers and seekers after the curious. Symbolically, the first Englishman in India was Ralph Fitch, an eccentric preromantic who came on foot in 1583 and explored India for several years.

In the decades following Fitch's extended walk, Englishmen came to India in a steady trickle. Most were merchants keen to emulate the successes of the Portuguese and Dutch in the spice trade. The East India Company was founded in London in 1599, and in 1600 Queen Elizabeth granted a charter to "the Governor and company of merchants of London trading into the East Indies." But the first voyage to Sumatra for spices, as well as silk, gems, camphor, and indigo, led to a glut in the pepper market. In 1611, discouraged by Dutch and Portuguese control of the East Indies trade, the Company opened a factory in India, at Machilipatnam, to deal in cotton and other fabrics. The following year Surat, near Bombay in western India, became the Company's Indian headquarters.

In 1615, King James I sent Sir Thomas Roe as ambassador to the court of the Mughal emperor Jahangir. When Sir Thomas showed the emperor English portrait miniatures, Jahangir enthusiastically ordered his artists to make copies and challenged the ambassador to detect them from the originals. According to the ambassador's own account, when he failed the test, due perhaps to poor light or an excess of diplomacy, Jahangir "creaked [boasted] like a northern man" at his artists' triumph. Sir Thomas's diplomatic skills also prevailed along other lines; he obtained trading privileges for the Company from the emperor in exchange for their providing the Mughals with a naval force to protect pilgrims on their way to Mecca. His rapport with Jahangir and other Indians was prophetic, for over the centuries where other aspiring merchants and colonialists —the Portuguese, Dutch, French, and Danes—eventually failed the British usually prospered.

British trade with India gradually increased. By 1641, Company factories had been set up at Madras, where the British built Fort St. George. Further expansion resulted from Emperor Shah Jahan's aversion to the Portuguese, who had failed to support him against his father, Jahangir. The Portuguese were forcibly driven from Hooghly, their major trading center in Bengal, and the Company opened a factory there in 1650. In 1661, Bombay also became Company territory, as part of the dowry King Charles II received when he married a Portuguese princess, Catherine of Braganza.

Company employees flourished. The career of Boston-born Elihu Yale exemplifies the successes that awaited bright and enterprising young Englishmen in India during the late seventeenth century. Yale joined the Company as a "writer" or clerk in 1671, and he persevered not only for them but for himself. By privately investing in Javanese pepper to sell in London he raised sufficient capital to acquire merchant ships, and in due course he not only married into the English aristocracy but was appointed governor of Madras. In 1714 and 1718, he made small donations of books and textiles to the Collegiate School in Saybrook, Connecticut, the school that was chartered as Yale University in 1745. Yale died in England in 1721 a very rich man and a model for the aspiring young.

Partly due to the erosion of Mughal power but also because of their ambition, energy, and toughness, British presence in India steadily grew. Irked when the Company threatened to take Chittagong in 1685, Emperor Aurangzeb (who succeeded Shah Jahan in 1658 and ruled for fifty years) seized Surat and ordered all Englishmen to quit his domain. But his words rang hollow. In the 1680s, the Mughals were hamstrung by the very extent of their territories and drained by their continuing campaigns in the Deccan. Far from leaving, the English deftly expanded their position, alternately standing firm against the Mughals and bribing them with such presents as clocks, good pieces of ambergrease, European fuses, and small field pieces. In 1691, at the little village of Kalikata near Hooghly, Job Charnock founded Calcutta, the city that was to become the major seat of British power in India. To protect the city with its lucrative access to the Bhagirathi and Ganges rivers, a convenient trade route up-country, Fort William was built in 1696, and by 1701 the English governor of Calcutta was powerful enough to ban all Mughal ships from the port. The Company was granted the privilege of collecting taxes and administering justice in Calcutta and three nearby villages.

Prior to 1700, most of the Englishmen who sought their fortunes in the India trade were hardy, rambunctious, and uninhibited, with just enough of the buccaneer in their characters to assure success. Job Charnock, who married an Indian woman and took pleasure in Indian food and Indian ways, typified his generation. Attuned to cooler climates and home-grown bacteria, many of these rugged pioneers succumbed to fluxes and tropical fevers. By the early eighteenth century, however, the lot of the British in India had so improved that positions with the East India Company were not only promising for the up-and-coming but desirable for gentlemen. In the words of an Englishman, Captain Alexander Hamilton, writing in about 1720: "Most gentlemen and ladies in Bengal live both splendidly and pleasantly, the forenoons being dedicated to business and after dinner to rest, and in the evenings to recreate themselves in chaises or palankeens in the fields, or to gardens, or by water in their budgeroes, which is a convenient boat that goes swiftly by force of oars."[1] It was possible to live extremely well in India and to retire to England rich as a nabob (from the Mughal title nawab, or governor). Stalwart young men of good family now joined the Company. Brave young women soon followed, but a high percentage of them did not survive more than a few monsoons, as is tragically apparent from the lichened inscriptions in Calcutta's graveyards.

British power in India was centered in Calcutta in the second half of the eighteenth century. In 1756 the nawab of Bengal, who like the governors of Oudh and the Deccan was virtually independent from imperial Delhi, was angered by the British because they had aided his enemies, the Marathas. He attacked Fort William, seized Calcutta, and captured 146 British citizens, whom he confined in the so-called Black Hole, a space measuring eighteen by fourteen feet. Many died. The Company protested to the nawab, and the Council in Madras, hot for vengeance, dispatched an army and a fleet led by the illustrious Robert Clive. Clive recaptured Calcutta in January 1757, and in June he cajoled Mir Jaʿfar, one of the nawab's generals, into treacherously advising the nawab to yield to the Company force at the Battle of Plassey. A few days later the nawab was murdered, and as his reward Mir Jaʿfar was enthroned by the British, now the major military power in India.

Power led to abuse. In 1762 Mir Qasim, son-in-law of and successor to Mir Jaʿfar, wrote a letter of protest: "And in this way your gentlemen behave; they make a disturbance all over my country, plunder the people, injure and disgrace my servants. . . . Setting up the colours and showing the passes of the Company, they use their utmost endeavours to oppress the peasants, merchants, and other people of the country. . . . They forcibly take away the goods and commodities of the peasants, merchants, etc. for a fourth part of their value, and by way of violence and oppression they oblige the peasants to give five rupees for what is worth but one rupee."[2] Robert Clive overcame such complaints in 1765 by compelling the weak Mughal emperor, Shah ʿAlam II (r. 1759–1806), to legalize the Company's position in Bengal. The Company was given the right to collect taxes, and authority was transferred from the Mughal governor to a deputy selected by the British, a puppet through whom they held total control.

Clive's crude methods were replaced by subtler, more up-to-date ones following the appointment of Warren Hastings as governor-general in 1772. Laws, taxation, and a rigorous judicial system now provided the stick with which the British controlled India, force being reserved for especially trying occasions. In 1773, Shujaʿ ad-Daula, the nawab wazir of Oudh, agreed to pay the Company two and one-half million rupees a year for maintaining a troop of Company soldiers in Oudh, which simultaneously buttressed British interests. The nawab wazir further agreed to receive at his court a permanent British resident, who was to ensure that Company policies were carried out. This pattern became standard in British India.

In his zeal for legality and honorableness, Hastings attempted to prohibit private trade among officers of the Company, a stand so unpopular that it contributed to his removal as governor-general in 1785. Hastings was impeached in 1787 on charges of being a moneymaker and oppressor. He was acquitted, but only after a rankling and financially draining eight-year trial. Lord Cornwallis, who became governor-general in 1786 and served until 1793, raised Company salaries during his first year in office and made private trading illegal.

Some of the British became truly devoted to India, Indians, and Indian culture. One such Englishman was Richard Johnson, who was employed by the Company from 1770 to 1790, serving at Lucknow from 1780 to 1782 and as resident at the court of the nizam of Hyderabad from 1784 to 1785. Like Warren Hastings and several other English connoisseurs, Johnson developed a taste for Indian art, especially Mughal and Rajput miniatures. Unlike most of the collections assembled by Englishmen in India, his remains intact. He sold the collection to the East India Company in 1807, shortly before his death, and it was maintained by the India Office Library in London until recently, when it was transferred to the British Library. Another Englishman sensitively and creatively appreciative of Indian culture was Sir William Jones, one of the founders, with Warren Hastings, of the Asiatic Society of Bengal in 1784. A judge by profession, Sir William was also an eminent scholar: he translated the Indian poet Kalidasa's drama *Sakuntala*, written in the fourth or fifth century in Sanskrit, into Latin and English.

For the elite, by the late eighteenth century Calcutta and Madras had become outposts of London. At receptions and balls, Company employees shone in costumes that would have been fashionably of the moment in London only six months earlier (the time required for shipment). Governor-general Lord Cornwallis, complaining that gentleman dancers were commonly too far gone in drink to venture upon any experiments demanding the preservation of the perpendicular, insisted upon improved comportment.[3] Distinguished couples such as Sir Elijah Impey, chief justice of Bengal, and his wife Mary, who hired Indian artists to paint family portraits and natural history studies (see no. 281), lived in great houses that were tropical transformations of grand Palladian designs.

In 1793 William Roxborough, who had been the Company's botanist in the Carnatic, was appointed first official superintendent of the Calcutta Botanic Gardens. In the name of science, specimens gathered from all over India were painstakingly and sensitively rendered in watercolor on imported English paper by Indian artists trained in the Mughal tradition.

Lured by the promise of ample patronage and the thrill of exotic places, English artists came to India. The landscapist William Hodges (1744–1797) traveled in India from 1780 to 1783. Thomas Daniell (1749–1840) and his nephew William (1769–1837) spent two years preparing their *Views of Calcutta*, large aquatints published in Calcutta between 1786 and 1789. The Daniells later visited South India and also went up-country to sketch monuments and landscapes in places as remote as Garhwal in the Punjab Hills. Tilly Kettle (1735–1786) and John Zoffany (1733–1810) also visited India, enjoying much success at the court of Oudh, where the nawab vied with British patrons for their services.

India had become so much a part of English life that it was included in the Grand Tour of George Annesley (Viscount Valencia), who visited Calcutta at the outset of the nineteenth century, when the huge Palladian Government House had just been completed. To the critics who said the building was overly grand, Annesley replied: "Remember that India is a country of splendour, or extravagance, and of outward appearances; that the Head of a Mighty Empire ought to conform himself on the prejudices of the country he rules over; and that the British, in particular, ought to emulate the splendid works of the Princes of the House of Timur, lest it be supposed that we merit the reproach which our great rivals the French have ever cast upon us, of being influenced by a sordid mercantile spirit. In short, I wish India to be ruled from a palace, not from a counting house; with the ideas of a prince, not those of a retail dealer in muslins and indigo."[4] By 1800 the Company officialdom of Calcutta, Madras, and Lucknow had become so worldly that serious interest in India of the sort evinced by Warren Hastings, Richard Johnson, and Sir William Jones was considered bad form, suited only to scholars and eccentrics. Nevertheless, British India prospered, even as its representatives became ever more remote from the people they increasingly dominated.

Richard Wellesley, governor-general from 1798 to 1805, signed a treaty in 1798 with the nizam of Hyderabad whereby the nizam agreed to expel all French officers, to accept a British resident, and to support six battalions of Company troops. In 1801 the British annexed the Carnatic and Oudh, and a few years later Arthur Wellesley (the future Duke of Wellington) won the Deccan, defeating a Maratha and French alliance of 290,000 troops with his army of 55,000. At about the same time Lord Lake took

Delhi and Agra, the Marathas sued for peace, and the Maratha leader Daulat Rao Sindhia accepted a resident at his court. In 1803 the British became the protectors of Shah 'Alam II, recognizing him as emperor but disregarding his wishes on all levels. The British resident at Delhi had in effect assumed what remained of imperial power.

The East India Company had become a powerful independent government with a bureaucracy larger than that of many nations. To prepare cadets for careers in India, the Company established Haileybury College in London. In 1813, on the urging of high-minded evangelicals who were eager to reform "the people of Hindostan, a race of men lamentably degenerate and base," the British Parliament passed the Charter Act, which declared its sovereignty over the Company's expanding dominions. Company representatives continued to administer the British-held areas of India, but they now did so in trust for the British government.

During the early nineteenth century the British made extensive progress into the interior of India, gaining paramountcy over Rajputana (Rajasthan) through what were called defensive alliances. From 1817 to 1823, the rulers of the states of Kotah, Mewar, Bundi, Kishangarh, Bikaner, Jaipur, and many others received British political agents and often paid tribute.

With increasing British control, many age-old Indian practices such as slavery and female infanticide were discouraged or outlawed. In 1829 sati, the self-immolation of widows on their husbands' funeral pyres, was declared illegal in Bengal. In the same year William Sleeman was assigned to investigate and eliminate thugs (from the Hindi word thag, meaning thief), "who sallying forth in a gang . . . and in the character of wayfarers . . . fall in with other travellers on the road and having gained their confidence, take a favourable opportunity of strangling them by throwing their handkerchiefs round their necks, and then plundering them and burying their bodies."[5] Three thousand thugs were convicted between 1831 and 1837, and by 1860 they had virtually disappeared. Despite such worthy paternalism, in 1833 Parliament took over the Company's possessions and established an Indian Law Commission with the aim of codifying a system of law and justice.

English was declared the official language of India by the British in 1835, and English was made the language of instruction in higher education, inasmuch as the purpose of education was seen as the dissemination of Western knowledge. Lord Macaulay, in his Education Minute, proposed the creation in India of an elite "Indian in blood and colour, but English in taste, morals, and intellect." In thirty years, he forecast, "there would not be a single idolator among the respectable classes of Bengal." By 1845, however, among the 17,360 Indian pupils being educated at government expense in all parts of India there were 13,699 Hindus, 1,636 Muslims, and 236 Christians.

The Mutiny of 1857, seen by many as a war of liberation, by some as a conservative reaction to the modernization forced on India by British rule, was the inevitable consequence of many years of accumulated offense, aggravated by the widening rift between the rulers and the ruled. Indian religious leaders, princes, landlords, and intellectuals alike challenged British authority. Smoldering resentment caught fire in January 1857, when the Brown Bess rifle was replaced by the Enfield in the Indian army. Rumor spread among the sepoys (Indian troops) that the cartridge for the Enfield, one end of which had to be bitten off, was lubricated with beef or hog fat, the former considered alarmingly contaminating by Hindus, the latter by Muslims. On February 26, in Bengal, soldiers refused to use the Enfield. Although no British troops were present the regiment was marched to Barrackpore, near Calcutta, and placed in irons. On March 29, the imprisoned soldiers were liberated and their officers were shot by comrades from other regiments. The mutineers then hurried to Delhi, where they persuaded the aged Emperor Bahadur Shah II to lead the growing rebellion. Although at this time only 40,000 of the 300,000 men in the Indian army were Europeans, the British eventually defeated the mutineers in a struggle notable for the atrocities carried out on both sides. In the aftermath, the British tried Bahadur Shah and condemned him to exile. The last Mughal emperor died a prisoner in Rangoon in 1862 (see no. 287).

In 1858, Queen Victoria issued a proclamation that was read throughout India: "For divers weighty reasons, we have resolved, by and with the advice of the Lords Spiritual and Temporal, and Commons, in Parliament assembled, to take upon ourselves the government of the territories of India, heretofore administered in trust for us by the Honourable East India Company." The title of governor-general became viceroy, and the Company's army was absorbed into the Royal Army.

After the Mutiny, British attitudes toward Indians hardened. John Lawrence, who served as viceroy from 1864 to 1869, aptly stated the post-Mutiny mood: "We have not been elected or placed in power by the people, but we are here through our moral superiority, by force of circumstances, by the will of providence. This alone constitutes our charter to govern India. In doing the best we can for the people, we are bound by our conscience, not by theirs."[6]

Queen Victoria was proclaimed empress of India in 1877. The Indian states and their princes and people were now vassals of the British sovereign. Lord Lytton (viceroy 1876–80) concluded that the government of India should seek support from at least one level of society and proposed that it be the aristocracy. The days of glamorously rich maharajas had come. They were soon joined by great Indian industrialists like Jamshed Tata, who opened the Empress Cotton Mill at Nagpur in 1887 and in 1907 founded the Tata Iron and Steel Company.

In 1901, the Raj seemed as permanent as Mount Everest, but the discouraging evaluation of a little-known Englishman, F. H. Skrine, proved to be a flash of foresight: "Here we stand on the face of the broad earth, a scanty, pale-faced band in the midst of three hundred millions of unfriendly vassals."[7] Forty-six years later, in March of 1947, Earl Mountbatten of Burma (great-grandson of Queen Victoria) became the last viceroy of India, and in August India and Pakistan became independent nations.

1. Hamilton, quoted in Woodruff, *The Men Who Ruled India*, p. 76.
2. Mir Qasim, quoted in ibid., p. 106.
3. Kincaid, *British Social Life in India*, p. 120.
4. Annesley, *Voyages and Travels*, p. 235.
5. Yule and Burnell, *Hobson-Jobson*, p. 916.
6. Lawrence, quoted in Edwardes, *Memorials of the Life and Letters*, vol. 2, p. 192.
7. Skrine, *Life of Sir W. W. Hunter*, p. 68.

281.
FOUR WATERCOLORS PAINTED FOR
MARY, LADY IMPEY
Probably by Shaikh Zain ad-Din of Patna
Calcutta, Company School, 1777–83
Opaque watercolor on paper

a. A FAIRY BLUEBIRD (*irena puella*)
   Inscribed: "pear tree, blue fairy, Zain ad-Din"
   21 × 28⅞ in. (53.3 × 73.4 cm.)
   Private collection

b. SAMBAR (*cervus unicolor*)
   16½ × 21¼ in. (42 × 54 cm.)
   Collection Sven Gahlin, Bath, England

c. MARY, LADY IMPEY, SUPERVISING HER
   HOUSEHOLD
   18 × 21 in. (45.7 × 53.3 cm.)
   Collection Lawrence Impey Esq.,
   Hampshire, England

d. THE IMPEY CHILDREN WITH THEIR
   ATTENDANTS
   14 × 20⅜ in. (35.6 × 51.8 cm.)
   Collection Lawrence Impey Esq.,
   Hampshire, England

MARY, LADY IMPEY, wife of Sir Elijah Impey, who was chief justice of Bengal from 1774 to 1782, lived in Calcutta between 1777 and 1783. During her brief stay, she employed three artists who signed themselves "of Patna" —Shaikh Zain ad-Din, a Muslim, and Bhawani Das and Ram Das, who were both Hindus—to paint a series of natural history studies. All three artists had been trained in the naturalistic Mughal tradition, which appealed directly to English taste, and they adapted comfortably to the technique of English watercolor on imported English Whatman paper, which came in larger sheets than could be readily found in India. Conceivably, these artists had already moved from Patna to Calcutta and were employed as natural history painters there prior to Lady Mary's arrival. If not, their earliest works for her, signed and dated to the year of her arrival, imply that they adjusted to the foreign Company manner with amazing speed—which would certainly have been possible, considering the disciplined tradition from which they had emerged.

Shaikh Zain ad-Din appears to have been senior among them. His pictures are the most inventive, touching, and painterly. His brushwork varied from hard-edged to soft, and he took pleasure in building up glowing passages of rounded, ample forms, often in palettes of startling originality. A bold yet gentle designer, he silhouetted his subjects amid ornamental profusion, simultaneously conveying their outer shapes with scientific accuracy and expressing their essences. He was also the most prolific of the

281a

three, but his work was uneven in quality; when he was bored by a picture, so are we.

Two hundred or more studies of flora and fauna, which are equaled for artistic discrimination only by those done for William Fraser (see. nos. 49, 50), commemorate Lady Impey's few years of patronage. Like the natural history studies painted in India for other private patrons and for the Company at their extensive gardens and menageries near Madras and Calcutta, the Impey series was probably commissioned more in the name of science than of art. Most of the pictures from the Impey collection are life-sized studies, but when the subject was too large, the precise measurements were penciled on the page.

The Impey pictures of birds, animals, and fish are the earliest dated examples of this genre painted for the British in India. They are also the liveliest, and they are outstanding for their sensitive and accurately observed depictions of flowers, foliage, and insects, which lend further credibility to the subjects. The Impey estate in Calcutta included a large garden, with ample space for a zoo and ornithological collections. (We have already seen a "jewel" of feathers, no. 184, plucked from a bird named in homage to the Impeys' contributions to ornithology.)[1] The convincing vivacity of their work argues that the artists painted from life, instead of struggling to reanimate bird and animal skins or stuffed specimens.

Both the studies reproduced here were originally signed by Zain ad-

281b

281c

Din. *A Fairy Bluebird*, painted at the outset of the Impey project, reveals traces of his Mughal training, perhaps at Lucknow, especially in the enamellike burnishing of pigments on the bird's eye and on the undersides of the guava leaves, with their rhythmically decorative veining. Following the procedure of his artistic ancestor, Mansur, the shaikh feathered this bright-eyed bird with minute brushstrokes. The engaging pose of the bird, camouflaged against a leaf; the delightful combination of blue, black, and green; and the subtle composition, the sinuously curving foliage balanced by large areas of open space, are all characteristic of the artist's original insight. The young female elk that posed for *Sambar* must have been a pet. The sambar is the largest Indian deer—a full-grown stag can weigh 700 pounds—but the Impey specimen, with her sensitive mask and sleek blue-gray coat, seems delicate as a gazelle.

Sir Elijah's years in Calcutta, which coincided with Warren Hastings's controversial term as governor-general, ended prematurely. (Four years after his return to England, he was humiliatingly impeached. But the charges were politically motivated and patently flimsy, and he spoke so eloquently, feelingly, and convincingly before the bar of the House of Commons that the case against him was shattered.) In anticipation of the Impeys' departure from Calcutta in 1783, these two paintings of their Indian domicile were commissioned. *Mary, Lady Impey, Supervising Her Household* and *The Impey Children with Their Attendants* are unequaled as nostalgic glimpses into late eighteenth-century Calcutta life among the upper classes. They can be attributed to Shaikh Zain ad-Din, who again reveals his Mughal training in the formally isolated figures and their proportions, as well as in the masterful

281d

arabesque patterns. Many enlivening touches—the peep into the Impey bedroom, with its four-poster bed and its dressing table laden with an arrangement of jars, brushes, and other appurtenances; the little Impeys scampering with their puppies or attended by devoted ayahs—must have been closely directed by Lady Impey, who deserves much of the credit for these entrancingly intimate Bengali conversation pieces.

1. I would like to thank Katharine Ray for making available to me the findings of her research on the Impeyan pheasant.

Published:
a. Hayter and Falk, *Birds in an Indian Garden*, no. 3.
b. *In the Image of Man*, p. 106, no. 45.
c. Archer, "British Patrons of Indian Artists," pp. 340–41, no. 3057; W. Archer, *Indian Miniatures*, pl. 100; Welch, *Room for Wonder*, pp. 23–24, fig. 3.
d. Archer, "British Patrons of Indian Artists," pp. 340–41; Edwards, *The British in India*, no. c4, pl. 3.

INTERNATIONAL CULTURAL EXCHANGES bore fruit in this portrait of a festooned and plumed odalisque attended by a mildly lascivious cockatoo. The three muses, an Ottomanesque tabouret, sphinxes, classical pediments, and a be-wigged lion licking what appears to be a vegetarian ice-cream cone further enrich the confection, which was painted for a connoisseur who may have taken it more seriously than we do.

Just as Akbar and Jahangir had urged their artists to borrow European exoticisms from engravings and other imported works of art, so did later

282.
ODALISQUE WITH A PARROT
Mughal, Lucknow or Delhi, early 19th century
Opaque watercolor on paper
Folio: 13⅜ × 17¾ in. (34 × 45 cm.)
Miniature: 10⅞ × 15 in. (27.5 × 38 cm.)
Chester Beatty Library, Dublin
(Ms. 69, no. 19)

282

patrons. In the early nineteenth century, highly skilled Indian painters plucked motifs from European prints with as much rapacity as conviction. Although one might suppose that pictures of this sort were commissioned for British households in India, they are more likely to have been painted for Indian aristocrats during the awkward years when Indians bravely adjusted to the foreign ways of the new Raj. Unused to European furniture, disinclined to sip tea or munch gateaux and crumpets, rajas and nawabs nevertheless generously redecorated erstwhile halls of public audience and, tolerating extreme discomfort, smilingly received distinguished British guests.

Published: *The Indian Heritage*, p. 52, no. 93.

283.
CAVALCADE OF THE KING OF OUDH
AND THE BRITISH RESIDENT
Mughal, Lucknow, ca. 1820
Bronze, 7½ × 15½ × 9½ in.
(19.1 × 39.4 × 24.1 cm.)
Ashmolean Museum, Oxford (1977.25)

THIS FESTIVE AND amusing procession in bronze illustrates the protocol-ridden, tragicomic complexities of Indian politics during the early nineteenth century. Lord Moira (governor-general 1812–23), urged by the Company's resident at Delhi to abolish the title of emperor and further weaken the sovereignty of Akbar Shah II (r. 1806–37), proposed instead that the Mughal ruler be demeaned by a subtle plot: the nawab wazir of Oudh, Ghazi ad-Din Haidar (r. 1814–27), was to be named king. In 1819, George III bestowed the august title on Ghazi ad-Din, who had earned it by lending the Company huge sums of money. But lest the former nawab wazir be overly honored, the governor-general insisted that the British resident at Lucknow be treated as his equal on all ceremonial and formal occasions.

Hats and elephants are crucial to the iconography here. Mounted on a state elephant, accompanied by his chief minister, Ghazi ad-Din proudly wears his new crown. On an equally large elephant rides the resident, wearing a chapeau bras, and next to him sits an adviser in a shovel hat. The king was described by Reginald Heber, lord bishop of Calcutta at the time, as a weak man who was dominated by a sinister, "dark, harsh, hawk-nosed" former butler named Agha Mir, who in addition to his princely salary was granted 23 million rupees a year as well as a bonus of 33 million.[1] If we are to believe history's allegations (which may come from biased sources), Agha Mir also plundered property and jewels galore.

Inasmuch as bronze figural sculpture had not been encouraged at Mughal courts, this piece, based on European example to satisfy a new market, would have been sculpted and cast by craftsmen whose previous repertoire had consisted of village icons and toys. Technically remarkable for casting and complexity, it invites comparison with early folk bronzes (see nos. 58–68).

1. Heber, *Narrative of a Journey*, vol. 2, p. 53.

Published: Digby and Harle, *Toy Soldiers*, pp. 9–10, pl. 8.

284

284.
EMPEROR BAHADUR SHAH II
ENTHRONED
Inscribed with the names and titles of
the four subjects
Mughal, Delhi, dated A.H. 1254 (1838)
Opaque watercolor on paper, 12⅛ × 14½ in.
(30.8 × 36.8 cm.)
The Knellington Collection, Courtesy
Harvard University Art Museums,
Cambridge, Massachusetts

TITLES GROW AS power declines, as is evident from a sampling of those inscribed on this portrait of the last Mughal emperor Bahadur Shah II (r. 1837–58): His Majesty the Shadow of God, Refuge of Islam, Propagator of the Muslim Religion, Increaser of the Splendor of the Community of the Paraclete, Progeny of the Gurganid (Mughal) Dynasty, Choicest of the Race of the Sahibqiran (Tamerlane), Exalted King of Kings, Emperor and Son of Emperor, Sultan and Son of Sultan, Possessed of Glories and Victories.

Toweringly crowned, weighted down with gold, pearls, emeralds, and epaulettes of gilded fur, and glorified by a radiant pale blue and gold halo, the emperor smokes a huqqa in the khas mahal, the private apartments in the Red Fort of Delhi. He is accompanied by two of his sons: Mirza Fakhr ad-Din, the heir apparent, and young Mirza Farkhanda. In the background, an attendant waves a morchhal.

Bahadur Shah II inherited the throne at the age of sixty-two, expecting that in his long-lived family (his father Akbar II died at eighty-two) he might reign for as long as twenty years. As a young man he had been a fine horseman with strength enough to draw the mightiest bows, which he aimed more accurately than anyone else in Delhi. All his life he hungered for mangoes. In his youth he could eat thirty at a sitting, but when he was older fifteen once made him ill for months. He was an able calligrapher and piously copied verses from the Qur'an; he delighted in planning gardens and buildings; and he was a connoisseur of women, literature, and music. His nom de plume as a poet was Zafar, and he signed his music Shauq Rang (Melody of Longing). At a time of imperial greatness Bahadur Shah might have been a Shah Jahan. It was his misfortune to be enthroned on a pastiche Peacock Throne in a dirt-streaked marble palace—always under the suspicious eye of a British agent—with no armies, no strong allies, and an empty treasury.

Until the Mutiny in 1857, Bahadur Shah's life was devoted to literature and to family matters. Inasmuch as he had many wives and children, and in 1848 as many as 2,104 descendants of the imperial family were living on his benevolence in the Fort in Delhi, he found it necessary to encourage formal gifts from visitors and to cadge money as best he could. But the financial management of his household in such straitened circumstances was not the worst of his domestic problems. His favorite wife, Zinat-Mahal Begum, who was seventeen and he sixty-two when they married, ferociously promoted the cause of their son, Mirza Jawan Bakht, as heir apparent over Bahadur Shah's eldest son, Mirza Fakhr ad-Din. Because he was admired and trusted by the citizens of Delhi and by Sir Thomas Metcalf, the Company agent, Fakhr ad-Din was confirmed as heir. But shortly thereafter, Sir Thomas and other Englishmen who had participated in the decision died mysteriously. Delhi rumor accused Zinat-Mahal of the crimes, and in 1856, when Mirza Fakhr ad-Din died suddenly under comparably odd circumstances, the begum was blamed with increased conviction.

When in 1857 the mutinous sepoys of Bengal marched to Delhi and begged Bahadur Shah to lead them, he agreed. Such a gamble appealed to the very old man, who, oppressed by Company rule, virtually powerless and moneyless, had long dreamed of restoring Mughal ascendancy (see no. 287).

Behind the emperor's halo and plumed crown (which was bought at auction by Queen Victoria for £500 after the Mutiny), we glimpse the pierced marble jali in the khas mahal and above it the marble relief showing the scales of justice balanced on a crescent moon. The miniature is flawlessly drawn and colored down to the last golden flourish, but it lacks the palpability that makes earlier Mughal painting so forcefully immediate. Was the artist hinting that the emperor's unfocusing eyes had been forced inward, that the emeralds of his crown were flawed and his "gold" lions starved, and that justice—of which he received so little—was no longer his to bestow?

Published: Welch, *Room for Wonder*, pp. 118–19, no. 52; Welch, *Imperial Mughal Painting*, pp. 118–19, pl. 40; *The Indian Heritage*, pp. 54–55, no. 109.

THIS SPECTACULARLY LARGE and detailed picture—the most informative and lively description of the Red Fort prior to its partial dismantling by the British after the Mutiny—was painted not for a Mughal but for a great Rajput patron, Maharao Ram Singh II of Kotah (r. 1828–66). Like the Delhi visits of other Rajput rulers, his was no mere courtly act. During the final glow of imperial sunset, the Mughal emperor was still revered as Hindustan's greatest ruler, privileged to bestow and confirm titles on maharajas and nawabs. He was also the living embodiment of a still creative and influential culture.

Bahadur Shah II's piety, literary and philosophical turn of mind, and advanced age had not sapped the court of mirth or love of life. Nor had they ended factional rivalries, scandal in the harem, or youthful high spirits. The emperor himself took pleasure in animal and bird combats, circus performances, pigeon breeding, dancers and musicians, and, of course, poetry. He also enjoyed the superb imperial cuisine—although his appetite faltered after someone attempted to murder him with a succulent kebab lethally spiked with the whisker of a tiger. If the maharao's visit was partly formal, he also went to Delhi for amusement, for an urban fling, and to enjoy the gossip.

A royal progress from Kotah to Delhi was a considerable undertaking in 1842. Priests, wives, dancing girls, musicians, artists, cooks, soldiers, courtiers, and a mob of servants were packed onto elephants, camels, and

285.
MAHARAO RAM SINGH II OF KOTAH VISITING EMPEROR BAHADUR SHAH II
Inscribed with names of individuals and places
Rajasthan, Kotah, ca. 1842–43
Opaque watercolor on cotton,
14 ft. 10 in. × 8 ft. 6 in. (4.45 × 2.59 m.)
Rao Madho Singh Museum Trust, Kotah (1003)

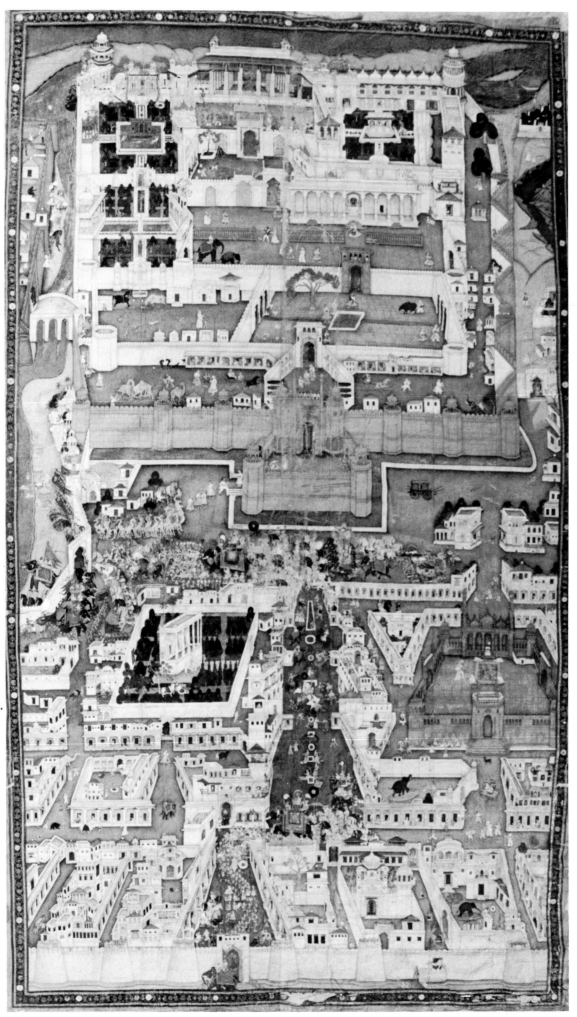

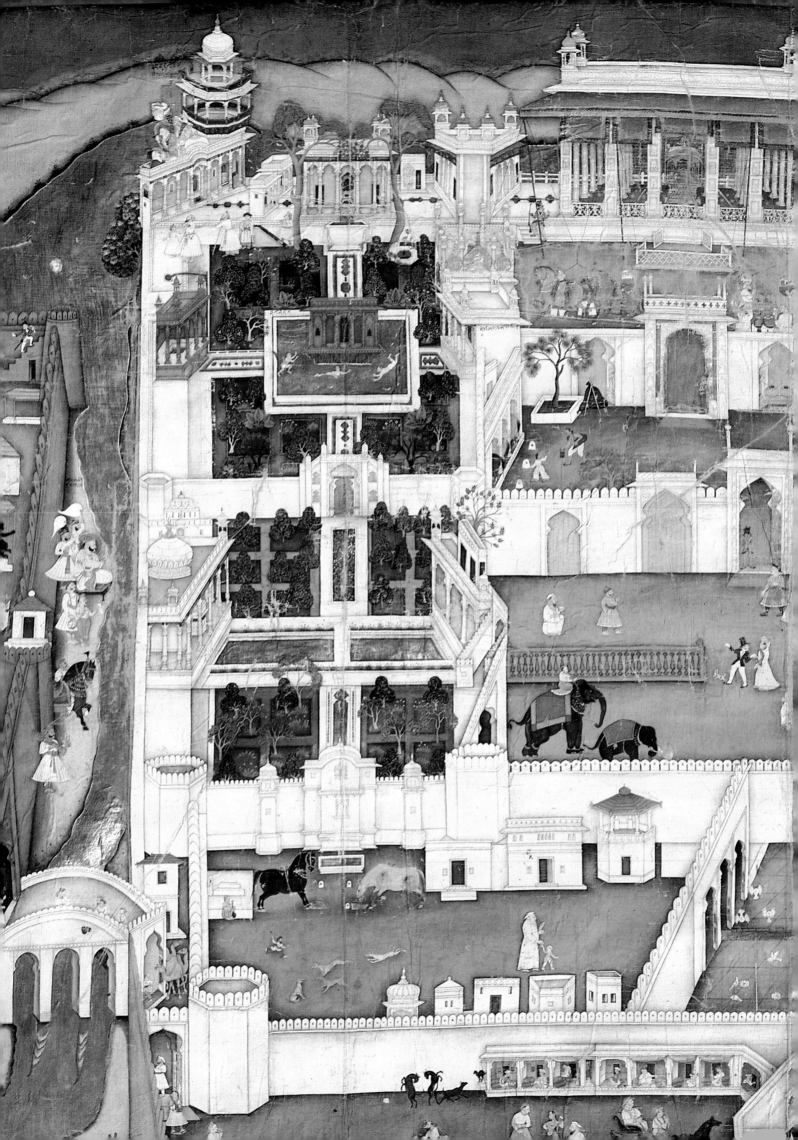

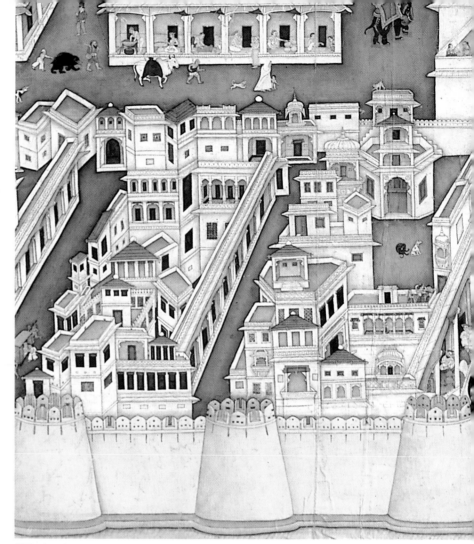

285, detail

horses in a great procession, which halted along the route, either visiting the forts and palaces of friends or staying in tents. Ram Singh was a blithesome ruler with a sense of humor (to jollify his court he once coaxed an elephant to mount the palace roof), and he urged his wittiest and most observant artist to record worthwhile moments during his imperial outing. This bird's-eye view of the Mughal capital, in which about twenty monuments are identified by the artist's inscriptions and which includes the neighboring markets, the Jamiᶜ Masjid, and views along the bank of the Jamuna, bubbles over with anecdotes and comical observations. Beaky nosed Bahadur Shah, in the upper left corner, accompanied by attendants and an Englishman (the Company agent?), has climbed to the highest level of the Fort's ramparts and seems to be attempting to sight his Kotah visitor through a brass spyglass. Meanwhile, Maharao Ram Singh, in the company of a priest, gazes at the Mughal bastions from the opposite side of a stream. Immediately behind them a monkey wearing a pointed cap and sitting imperiously beneath an awning also surveys the imperial prospect. Inside the palace, in the upper right corner, a cracker-jawed old begum protects the moral tone by keeping watch from a zenana window. Shopkeepers, craftsmen, pigeons, horses, scurrying dogs, elephants, leaping goats, and fighting camels crowd the byways. In the lower half of the painting and along its lower right edge, in the holy forecourt of the Jamiᶜ Masjid, a European couple appear locked in an embrace, and in a nearby enclosure an impatient elephant strains at its chains.

The artist's record of the Red Fort and environs is of great historical interest. Although he has compacted, bent, or twisted most of the buildings, courtyards, gardens, and streets to fit his upright rectangle, all were noted, usually in great detail. Besides the Jamiᶜ Masjid, three mosques are depicted: the Sonehri, Moti, and Fatehpuri masjids. The grand European style pillared

house and gardens of the notorious Christian Begum Samru are shown on the other side of the main thoroughfare. A former dancing girl who married a German, the begum became a great landowner at Sardhana, where she built a cathedral and maintained her own bishop. On the left side of the painting, below the bridge to Salimgarh, is the Nigambodh ghat with its temple complex with bathing platforms adjoining the fort walls. Within the fort, kitchens and stables are depicted at full tilt, and the pool around Bahadur Shah's garden pavilion at top left is asplash with swimmers. The pastiche replacement of the Peacock Throne occupies the diwan-i khas at top center. The gilded copper cupolas, which were later sold as scrap by the British, are plainly visible, as is much of the landscaping and the pavilions, most of which have been destroyed. Beneath the zenana at the right, the diwan-i am, which has since been cleaned down to the red sandstone, is shown radiant with its original chinar (polished white lime).

The unidentified master of this painting carried on the tradition of Kotah, where most of the artists were accomplished craftsmen who continuously sketched from life (see nos. 241, 242, 245). While in Delhi, he must have followed Ram Singh everywhere, taking notes at royal command of curious personages, animals, furniture, architectural details, and landscapes in his dashingly calligraphic style. On his return to Kotah the drawings and diagrams, some of which have survived, served as aides-mémoire for this giant tour de force, which must have been a major attraction when it hung at court. (The painting was later stored rolled up and brought out only for occasional delectation.) Although this pictorial travel diary developed from the minds of Ram Singh and his leading artist, one assumes that some of it was executed by other painters and apprentices in the Kotah atelier, which Ram Singh kept busy recording all—some might say too many—aspects of his sometimes ribald life.

286.
THE POET GHALIB
Inscribed: "picture of the noble
Ghalib of Delhi"
Mughal, Delhi, ca. 1855
Opaque watercolor on paper
Folio: 8⅜ × 7 in. (21.3 × 17.8 cm.)
Miniature: 6⅞ × 5 in. (17.5 × 12.7 cm.)
Red Fort Museum, Delhi (286)

MIRZA ASADULLAH KHAN GHALIB (1797–1869), perhaps the most admired of
all Mughal poets, wrote movingly in both Persian and Urdu. He began
writing Urdu verse at nine, but after he had compiled his first collected
works, when he was twenty-three, he preferred to compose in Persian. His
many letters provide vital and detailed accounts of nineteenth-century Mughal
life. At times visionary, at others serious or witty in his writing, he was also
a man of immense charm and on intimate terms with many of the aristocratic families of Delhi, Lucknow, and elsewhere. Occasionally unorthodox
in his behavior, he was fined on a charge of gambling in 1841, and in 1847 he
was imprisoned for maintaining a gaming house. But the stigma of a short
stint in prison was soon erased by invitations to the imperial court, where he
was commissioned by Bahadur Shah II to write a history of the Mughals in
Persian prose.

Until he was close to sixty years old, Ghalib was almost always short of
adequate funds to support himself, his wife, and her two orphaned nephews,
whom he adopted. But his situation improved in 1854 when he was appointed ustad to the heir apparent, Fakhr ad-Din (see no. 284), and at about
the same time he was awarded an annual stipend by the king of Oudh, Wajid
ʿAli Shah. He also wrote a letter requesting a grant from Queen Victoria.
When Fakhr ad-Din died (or was killed) two years later, Ghalib was appointed ustad to Bahadur Shah.

This sensitive but formal likeness was painted by one of the last imperial court artists when Ghalib was at the pinnacle of his success, a participant
in the all-night literary gatherings, called mushaiʿras, that were organized at
the Red Fort by the emperor and his heir apparent. For these artistically
serious and ceremonious occasions, special verses were composed on set
themes. Ghalib was noted for his dramatically effective readings. Had not
the Mutiny ended his career at court and dashed his hopes for patronage
from Queen Victoria, his later years might well have been more prosperous.

As it was, although the poet survived the horrors of the siege and its
aftermath, he was suspected of complicity for allegedly composing an inscription for the imperial coinage, several of his friends were executed, and
his brother's house was broken into by British soldiers. Troubled by ill health,

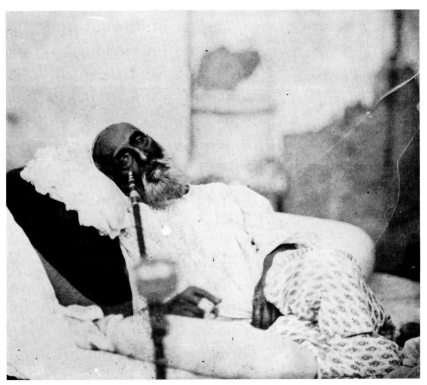

287

he nevertheless continued to work, serving as ustad to amateur poets and writing verse, criticism, and quantities of letters. Eventually he gained the favor of the British, and he received occasional stipends from his wealthiest disciple, the nawab of Rampur. When Ghalib died in 1869 at the age of seventy-three, most of the nobles and eminent men of Delhi attended his funeral.

FOLLOWING THE MUTINY, Bahadur Shah II was tried by the British and convicted of treason and rebellion. All royal property and revenues, as well as the monthly stipend of 10,000 rupees, were appropriated, and the former emperor and his household were exiled to Rangoon. The royal party of seventeen (six family members, three courtesans, and eight servants) lived in tents for their first few months in Rangoon. Later a teakwood house on stilts with four rooms, two bathrooms, and a small kitchen was constructed for them. Bahadur Shah occupied one of the sixteen-foot-square rooms; Zinat-Mahal Begum, Mirza Jawan Bakht and his family, and Mirza Shah ᶜAbbas and his mother, one of the concubines, lived in the other three rooms. The remaining prisoners were billeted in an old barracks beyond the ten-foot-high colonnade of the "palace." All were in the charge of Captain Davies, a kind and well-mannered British officer who spoke Urdu. He saw to it that they were adequately fed on the 430 rupees a month each person was allotted (eleven rupees a day plus an extra allowance on Sunday).

In exile, Bahadur Shah continued to compose poetry under his pen name, Zafar, during his remaining two and a half years. In 1862, at the age of eighty-seven, he was eased into death by a series of strokes over a period of eleven days. A few hours after he died he was buried without public ceremony, with neither tomb nor cenotaph, in a patch of earth surrounded by a simple bamboo fence that soon followed the last Mughal emperor into oblivion. His last direct descendant, who might have been the claimant to an empire, died recently in Calcutta.

This sensitive portrait was taken by an English military photographer, perhaps, as Howard Ricketts has suggested, a man called Captain Tytler.[1] The photograph is a moving record of the pathos of Bahadur Shah's last days, when he was afflicted with hiccups and his eyes were becoming glazed.

1. Personal communication, 1984.

Published: Worswick, *The Last Empire*, p. 76.

287.
BAHADUR SHAH II ON HIS DEATHBED
Perhaps by Captain Tytler
Rangoon, ca. 1862
Salt print, 4½ × 5½ in. (10.8 × 14 cm.)
Collection Howard and Jane Ricketts, London

288

288.
PALANQUIN
Rajasthan, probably Jaipur, ca. 1840
Gilded silver and gold, 11 ft. 9½ in. × 3 ft. 1 in.
(94 cm. × 3.84 m.)
Maharaja Sawai Man Singh II Museum,
Jaipur (AG)

MAHARAJA RAM SINGH II of Jaipur (r. 1834–80) came to the throne as an infant and reigned during the years when Rajput princes were adjusting to British ways. Without sacrificing traditional values, Ram Singh modernized his state by building and supporting colleges, hospitals, and charitable and learned societies. He was a devout Hindu, a worshiper of Shiva, but he was also the first great prince to master ballroom dancing and cut quite a figure as the vicereine's partner at Simla balls.

One of Ram Singh's many enthusiasms was photography. With the help of an Englishman named T. Murray, he set up studios and darkrooms in the palace and later established a photographic training school. Many of the photographs he took with Murray have survived, and they document the changes brought to Rajasthan by the British. In addition to many portraits and self-portraits and studies of sword hilts and ornamental glazed pottery made in Jaipur workshops, there are scenes of Britishers and Anglophile Rajputs riding to hounds, views of a bridge under construction and of the building of Rajasthan College, and photographs of Parsi actors in Shakespearean costume.

This splendid palanquin from Jaipur recalls the opulent magnificence of a great Rajput court in pre-Mutiny British India. Richly ornamented in a style uniting Hindu, Mughal, and early Victorian florescences, the palanquin is still brought out on religious occasions. But one likes to imagine Maharaja Ram Singh II being carried in it, at night, through City Palace corridors lighted only by torches. Inasmuch as Jaipur is noted for its jewelers, goldsmiths, and silversmiths, it seems likely that the palanquin was made there.

Sri Yadvendra Sahai of the Maharaja Sawai Man Singh II Museum graciously provided much of the information on Maharaja Ram Singh II and the court of Jaipur.

In the official catalogue of the lavish exhibition of Indian art held in the Kudsia Gardens of Delhi in 1903, Sir George Watt wrote, "Perhaps if any one article could be singled out as more freely discussed at the Exhibition than any other, it would be the Pearl carpet of Baroda." He explains that the exhibition contained two parts of what must have been a dazzling ensemble, the circular portion (not included here), which he described as a "veil or canopy," and "the rectangular carpet . . . one of the four such pieces that are said to have formed the carpet. . . . The entire series is believed to have cost Rs. 60,000,000. His Highness the Gaekwar is permitting these wonderful exhibits to be taken to Delhi. The field is seed pearls, the arabesque designs in blue and red being worked out in English glass beads with medallions and rosettes of diamonds, rubies, emeralds, freely dispersed." To his description, Watt added an account of 1879 written by Sir George Birdwood in his *Industrial Arts of India*: " 'The most wonderful piece of embroidery ever known was the *chaddar* or veil made by order of Kande Rao, the late Gaekwar of Baroda, for the tomb of Mahommed at Medina. It was composed entirely of inwrought pearls and precious stones, disposed in an arabesque pattern, and is said to have cost a crore (ten millions) of rupees. Although the richest stones were worked into it, the effect was almost harmonious. When spread out in the sun it seemed suffused with a general iridescent pearly bloom, as grateful to the eyes as were the exquisite forms of its arabesques.' . . . Needless to add," Watt continued, "this superb gift never went to Mecca."[1]

The patron of these astonishing objects, Khande Rao, the Gaekwar of Baroda (r. 1856–70), a transitional figure in post-Mutiny British India, more than anyone else set the pattern for extravagance associated ever since with maharajas. His enthusiasm for splendor brought British disapproval. "A spend-thrift, careless of his people, a lover of luxury and pomp," he was called by Colonel G. B. Malleson, writing in the days before the Raj encouraged princely lavishness.[2]

During the early eighteenth century, the Gaekwars were officers of the powerful Maratha Dhabari family, centered in Baroda. Their rise to power occurred in mid-century, when Damaji Gaekwar and his uncle Madhaji suc-

289.
THE BARODA CARPET
Gujarat, Baroda, ca. 1865
Pearls, rubies, emeralds, diamonds, and glass beads sewed on deerskin and silk,
5 ft. 7¾ in. × 8 ft. 7⅛ in. (1.72 × 2.62 m.)
Seethadevi Holding

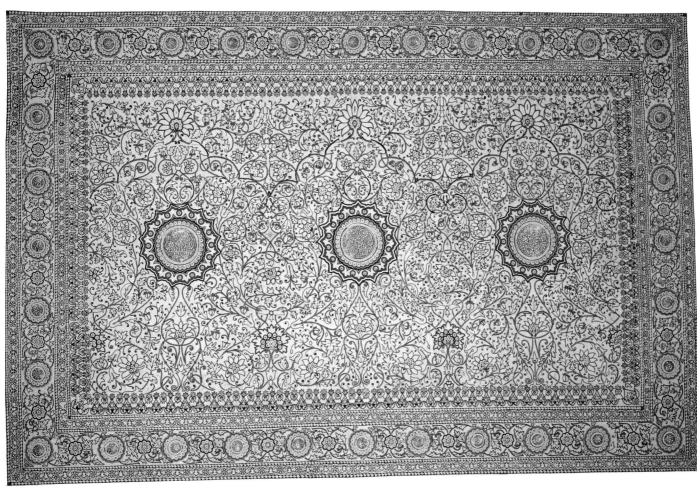

cessfully wrenched Baroda and the rest of the thriving state of Gujarat from the Mughals, who never regained it.

In 1862, the Gaekwar was officially addressed by the British as His Highness the Maharaja Gaekwar of Baroda. And by the time the carpet had been commissioned, he had identified his own cause with that of the British government. An attempt was made on his life by his younger brother, Mulhar Rao, who tried to poison him with a concoction of crushed diamonds. But Khande Rao survived; indeed, he flourished—somewhat to the dismay of his British overlords. In *The Rulers of Baroda*, F. A. H. Elliot wrote, "The economical spirit of the British period . . . would not admit of any extravagance. But [Khande Rao and Mulhar Rao] found themselves in a position to spend much money, and a great deal of it went towards enriching Brahmans, an easy method of acquiring a certain kind of fame. It is more difficult to explain, what undoubtedly occurred, how [Khande Rao] extended his charities to the Mussalmans, though we may not be far wrong in imagining that there was some domestic influence at work."[3] Despite Elliot's attempt to raise our eyebrows, it was entirely appropriate for the maharaja of Baroda, whose people included many Muslims, to include them on his list of charities. If the English critic's views were inspired, as we suspect, by the notorious lavishness of the present carpet, it is now time to reevaluate the Gaekwar's motives, and not only to respect his intentions but also to admire the masterful work of the jewelers of Gujarat who prepared this generous and respectful gift in honor of the Muslim community. However unbridled the opulence of its million pearls of excellent quality, of its fine diamonds, rubies, and emeralds beyond count, the design is suitably restrained and dignified, a classic arabesque descended from the Mughal tradition and probably inspired by the legendary jeweled covering ordered by Shah Jahan to adorn the cenotaph of Mumtaz-Mahal in the Taj Mahal. If one approaches with an eye only for worldly delight, or even amusement, one soon backs off, sensing a degree of underlying seriousness and religious devotion.

1. Watt, *Indian Art*, p. 444.
2. Malleson, *An Historical Sketch*, p. 251.
3. Elliot, *The Rulers of Baroda*, p. 329.

290.
MAHARAJA THAKHAT SINGH OF MARWAR RIDING WITH HIS COURTESANS
Rajasthan, Marwar, mid-19th century
Opaque watercolor on paper
Miniature: 23⅞ × 37 in. (60.6 × 94 cm.)
Mehrangarh Museum Trust, Jodhpur, on loan from Maharaja Sri Gaj Singhji II of Jodhpur

IN THE DECADES after Mughal power had weakened and before British influence was much felt in Rajasthan, painting at the courts regained intense Rajput character. This heroic portrayal of Maharaja Thakhat Singh of Marwar (r. 1843–73) galloping on camelback through the desert with an assortment of his women is a confident reassertion of traditional Rajput ways. As the inheritor of Maharaja Ram Singh's ateliers (see no. 288), Thakhat Singh encouraged his artists to yet bolder and more zestful pictorial experiments. Although one might miss the subtleties of characterization associated with earlier painting at Jodhpur, when artists and patrons looked to Mughal example, the swashing rhythms, audaciously balanced colors, and Rajput panache are delightful.

Thakhat Singh's long rule was problematic to the British. On the one hand, he had "done good service" during the Mutiny; on the other, he was considered avaricious, careless of affairs, and inaccessible. When Lord Mayo, viceroy from 1869 to 1872, held a darbar at Ajmer in 1871, and Thakhat Singh was told that the maharana of Udaipur would take precedence over him, he refused at the last moment to attend, even though the political agent and his own son explained that the question had long since been settled. After the darbar, the viceroy directed Thakhat Singh to leave the camp at Ajmer one hour before daybreak and diminished his salute by two guns.

Thakhat Singh was considered "incorrigible." His behavior was at odds with Victorian gentlemanliness and a way of life the British deemed essential to the pursuit of happiness in India. What might be called the Pax Britannica encouraged the Indian aristocracy to cultivate apparently secure existences, lived out in slow motion. Supported by their lands and revenues, India's major or minor nobilities enjoyed tranquillity, provided they con-

290

formed to the code of the Raj. Rebels, misfits, and those with troublesome (as opposed to harmlessly picturesque) eccentricities were delicately isolated, or crushed. What were the requirements? Willingness to follow a gentlemanly pattern, not to rock the ship of state, and to pay taxes. Charm, of course, was appreciated, and public spending even more so. Eyebrows were raised—and salutes, perhaps, lowered—if a prince did not encourage the economy by employing British architects, designers, and decorators to build palaces, guest houses, hospitals, schools, and parks and then outfit them with the best English goods. Indians of other classes, it was assumed, benefited from their largess.

For the diffusion of these views, public schools were founded in India to educate young Rajputs as almost-English gentlemen—and to discourage the princes from adhering too rigidly to traditional ways. Chiefs College Rajputana (also known as Mayo College) was a Rajput Eton staffed by English schoolmasters, whose grand students arrived with courtiers and attendants, as well as horses, polo ponies, and other royal essentials, and were housed in suitably palatial quarters. The princes studied British history and tales of colonial heroism, Shakespeare, Kalidasa, and the Lake Poets, and they were given some science, enough mathematics to tot up revenues, and lessons in deportment, cricket, and art. Youths taught to appreciate Landseer's tearful evocations of hunts in the highlands must soon have found pictures such as this one of Maharaja Thakhat Singh and his courtesans on the plains rather old-fashioned.

291

291.
FOUR REDDI RAJAS AT COURT
Probably by Garudadri Appaya
Deccan, Hyderabad, ca. 1875
Opaque watercolor on paper
Folio: 14¾ × 13¾ in. (37.6 × 34.9 cm.)
Miniature: 14⅛ × 12¾ in. (35.8 × 32.5 cm.)
Jagdish and Kamla Mittal Museum of Indian
Art, Hyderabad (76.419)

AT THE TIME this rather large group portrait was painted at Hyderabad, much Indian sculpture and painting was being done in the Company style, and the art schools established some decades earlier at Bombay, Calcutta, and Madras were fast spreading the influence of European painting. By the 1880s, European fashions had infiltrated court life even at Hyderabad, where the nizams of the Asaf Jahi dynasty who had ruled the state since 1724 had adhered staunchly to their old ways and customs. Painting at Hyderabad as yet showed no signs of the intrusive influence of the Company style, but photographers had already been welcomed at court. Mahbub 'Ali Khan, who during his reign at Hyderabad from 1866 to 1911 kept the most exotic and lavish court in India, appointed Lala Din Dayal court photographer in 1884 (see no. 296).

The Reddi rajas were Hindu agriculturists. Over the course of time a number of them had become landlords, and under the nizams some of them controlled sizable states and would have paid occasional visits to the capital. The raja who commissioned this portrayal of four Reddis at court, surrounded by their courtiers and attendants, was perhaps a traditionalist who preferred a scene imbued with the decorative charm only an Indian miniature painter's brush could give to a faithful but colorless photographic record. For despite the European sofa and chair and the glass lamps, and though its appeal is somewhat marred by the garish green and blue pigments and aniline dyes—European imports that were a common feature of post-1830 Indian paintings—this picture displays many of the refined, reserved, and gentle traits of earlier paintings from Hyderabad.

The miniature may be the work of Garudadri Appaya, who seems to have belonged to a family of painters from Shorapur, a state in the nizams' dominions that was ruled by Hindu rajas. The same fine brushwork and meticulous workmanship are found in other paintings by Shorapur artists.

J.M.

To UNDERSTAND AND appreciate the ample lady of this miniature, one need only look beyond the earmarks of time—the flowers, tassels, book, and chair—to recognize an Indian archetype: the forceful senior wife who protects traditional values as well as the family coffers. Stable and staunch, self-possessed, benevolent but firm, she is well known to everyone who has lived in India. We meet her here in Victorian guise, but she is better known from a famous sculpture of the first century B.C. that was found at Besnagar and is now in the Indian Museum of Calcutta.[1] The ancient likeness shows the same almost physical intelligence and has the same rounded forms, bespeaking fertility. She is draped in comparably contour hugging, rhythmically arranged clothing and wears remarkably similar jewelry, down to the last ankle bracelet and toe ring.

1. See: Codrington and Rothenstein, *Ancient India*, pl. IIa.

292.
A RATHOR PRINCESS
Inscribed: "auspicious one . . . Rathor . . .
Sri Rastan . . . princess"
Rajasthan, mid-19th century
Opaque watercolor on paper, 25¼ × 18½ in.
(64 × 47 cm.)
Private collection

292

293.
A PARSI GIRL
Bombay, ca. 1875
Ivory, height 5⅝ in. (14.4 cm.)
Trustees of the Prince of Wales Museum of
Western India, Bombay (31.92)

AMONG THE LEAST Indian of Indians, the Parsis, whose name derives from "farsi," or "Persian," are Zoroastrians who fled from Muslim persecution and emigrated to western India (first to Surat and later Bombay) at the time of the Arab invasions of Iran in the eighth century. Remaining to itself, the small community of Parsis in India (there are fewer than 100,000 in India today) has prospered ever since in mercantile and professional life. Their reliable efficiency and quickness appealed to the British, who sought their services, especially as ship chandlers, during the late eighteenth century, and also helped them gain positions as administrators and finance ministers at Rajput and nawabi courts.

Close contact with the British introduced the Parsis to international trade—and tastes. Chinoiserie as well as Européenerie enriched Parsi households, one of which contained this finely carved portrait of a daughter of the family wearing her paijama.

293, detail

294.
TANSI THAKUR BAG SINGH AND HIS COURT
Attributed to S. Ram Narayan
Rajasthan, dated 1880
Opaque watercolor on paper, 40 × 32½ in.
(101.6 × 82.6 cm.)
Collection Prince Sadruddin Aga Khan, Geneva

ONE SMILES WITH pleasure—and holds one's ears. Tansi Thakur Bag Singh, who ruled a small fiefdom somewhere between Jaipur and Udaipur, has overgenerously provided his guests with three musical entertainments. Two perform simultaneously: an English style drum-and-bugle corps in fancy dress at bottom right, and a troupe of home-grown musicians to whose tune the nautch girls spin on the red carpet. A woman seated beside her stringed instrument is shown at center right. In 1880, a thakur's life was not without amenities, and this picture brings together more than a three-ring circus of them. Accompanied by his son, Kunwar Gopal Singh, and his secretary, Khiali Ahmed, Tansi Thakur Bag Singh, comfortably dressed in kurta and

paijama and seated at ease on the throne, oversees his full darbar. The court is framed with a rhythmic arrangement of English gaslights, stallions and duck ponds, the thakur's pigeons and other birds, his artillery (firing salutes), a "Ferris wheel," a swing, a merry-go-round, and five gymnasts (in fact soldiers who have removed their shoes, solar topis, and outer garments). All this and more was composed and arranged with military precision against a stunning ground of striped dhurries by the talented and diligent Ram Narayan. Every significant figure here—from the thakur to his dancing girls, guards, and servants—has been portrayed in depth, apparently from photographic likenesses.

By 1880, painters were losing out to photographers at courts in India—if they had not already taken to the new art themselves in a scramble for patronage. To compete, painters had explored all avenues, from making painted copies of photographs, to painting over them, to, as here, adding portraits in photographic style to traditional compositions. Some artists became sign painters (their successors have participated in the recent artistic crescendo of film billboards); others, to make ends meet, designed colored lithographs of gods, goddesses, and worldly notables, or adorned the walls of rich merchants' mansions, or at wedding times enlivened buildings and courtyards with depictions of bridegrooms riding horses or elephants. Inasmuch as Ram Narayan achieved the best of both worlds, we assume that he prospered.

Published: *Octagon*, p. 19.

295

COMING UPON THIS lyrical coat, nostalgic as dried flowers in a book of verse, brings to mind some beguiling child taking the air with his ayah and bearer. Was he a princeling, the son of a rich merchant, or a toddling British administrator-to-be? By 1890 or 1900, Indian society had so changed that "royal" costumery was no longer limited to royalty. The spring-fresh cloth, a courtly flower garden that survived the defoliation of the Mughal empire, has leaves reminiscent of those in Jahangir's *Squirrels in a Plane Tree* (no. 141). Although the coat is tailored in late nineteenth-century style, the fabric was probably woven earlier, in the late eighteenth or early nineteenth century, by the same Kashmiri families who had spun, dyed, designed, and woven textiles for the emperors. Inscribed textiles of comparable design and technique were also made in Amritsar by Kashmiri craftsmen.

295.
CHILD'S COAT
Probably Amritsar, 19th century
Wool, length 28⅝ in. (72.7 cm.)
The Metropolitan Museum of Art, New York,
The Nasli Heeramaneck Collection, Gift of
Alice Heeramaneck (1983.494.10)

PHOTOGRAPHY WAS BROUGHT to India in the 1840s, and by 1890 it was a well-established professional and amateur activity, practiced by both foreigners and Indians. By 1849, F. Schranzhofer had opened India's first photographic studio; the Photographic Society of Bombay was founded in 1855; and the following year, the East India Company hired photographers instead of draftsmen. Soon ambitious lensmen were lugging awkward and heavy equipment to India's farthest reaches. Firms such as Bourne & Shepherd and Johnston & Hoffman offered superb prints of landscapes, archaeological monuments, animals, and people to an eager public.

Lala Din Dayal was the first major professional Indian photographer. Born at Sardhana in 1844, he studied at Thompson's Civil Engineering College in Roorkee, then was employed by the Public Works Department of Indore. In 1874, encouraged by Sir Henry Daly, who must have noted in him the rare combination of technician and artist, he began to study photography as an amateur. Maharaja Tukoji Rao II of Indore subsidized his early photographic work, which included portraits of the viceroy and of the Prince of Wales (later King Edward VII) when he visited India in 1875–76. The portraits were so admired that Din Dayal was asked to photograph the English darbars at Simla, the hill station to which the viceroy and his entourage moved during the hot months.

In 1884, Lala Din Dayal was appointed court photographer to H.H. Sir Mahbub ʿAli Khan, the sixth nizam of Hyderabad, who also gave him a fine house and a splendid title: Raja Musavvir Jung (Photographer Warrior). He was also the only photographer in India entitled to follow his name with "By Appointment, Photographer to Her Imperial Majesty, Queen Victoria." Talented as a businessman as well, he had ateliers at Indore and Hyderabad, and in 1896 he opened the largest photographic studios in Bombay. In Secunderabad, Raja Din Dayal and Sons enterprisingly established a special Zenana Studio for Female Photography, which was headed by Mrs. Kenny-Levick, wife of a London *Times* correspondent. Lala Din Dayal died in 1910, a year before his major patron, the nizam.

Lala Din Dayal's work is wide-ranging. His portraits far transcend the fashionable and documentary; his architectural and archaeological studies not only catch moods but are technically flawless, always sharply focused and undistorted by wall-toppling problems of parallax, and his panoramic compositions of elephants, tents, the nizam's armies, and cavalcades of distinguished visitors in carriages are of picturesque grandeur.

Photographic portraits, recorded point-blank by lenses, not filtered through painters' eyes and minds, can be magically closer to their subjects than paintings—provided the photographer is not only skillful but sensitive and concerned. Lala Din Dayal was one of the few photographers able to meet those conditions. In about 1890 he posed this alert, fawnlike princeling, talwar in hand, against a staged Tudoresque backdrop. This portrait of a pensive child, whose hauntingly mysterious intelligence outshines all the finery, stands apart from the era when maharajas were in fullest swing and most photographers concentrated not on the sitter's character but on the

296.
TWO PHOTOGRAPHS
By Lala Din Dayal
Deccan, Hyderabad, ca. 1890
Private collection

a. A YOUNG PRINCE
10⅜ × 7⅞ in. (26.4 × 20 cm.)

b. TWO PAIRS OF SWAGGED CURTAINS
11½ × 9⅛ in. (29.2 × 23.2 cm.)

296a

uninhibited royal flair for splendid jewels and raiment—costumes that would have stunned fin-de-siècle Paris or London. The prince's identity is unknown. At the studio of Din Dayal's successors, Mrs. Subas Chand very generously showed us the original ledgers. Though virtually all other photographs of the same numerical sequence are recorded, with their provenances and the names of the sitters, this one is unidentified, and the glass negative no longer exists.

296b

The pairs of swagged curtains, probably the least "important" of Din Dayal's images, are nevertheless artistically and nostalgically potent. Clogged, bunched, and surrealistically mounted, not around a door or windows but against an impenetrable wall, the hangings pique the imagination. Heavy tassels, fraying European stuffs, and staccato shadows writhe with the ache of East meeting West.

CHRONOLOGY

GLOSSARY

BIBLIOGRAPHY

INDEX

PHOTOGRAPH CREDITS

◁ 289, detail

CHRONOLOGY

compiled by Norbert Peabody and Woodman Taylor

The time frame for this exhibition begins in the thirteenth century, as the great dynasties of India's classical age are coming to an end: the Pandyas and Hoysalas of South India give way to the Vijayanagar kingdom; the Senas of Bengal are defeated by the Ghorids, as are the Chandellas in North Central India and the Chauhans in Rajasthan. The Great Tradition section of the exhibition derives its inspiration from this classical age, rooted in ancient Indian traditions. Similarly, the Tribe and Village section includes objects that are timeless, the reflection of customs which continue even today. The Muslim presence in India, beginning in the twelfth century, shapes Sultanate, Mughal, and Deccani art, but not without the influence of local traditions. The Rajputs of Rajasthan and the Punjab Hills, though adapting Mughal court culture, strongly retain their Hindu character. With the era of British rule, another foreign culture interacts with the fertile Indian environment.

973–1048   Al-Biruni, the great Muslim intellectual from the court of Mahmud of Ghazni, after thirteen years of travel in northern India describes Indian geography, philosophy, religion, and science in his detailed Arabic work *Kitab al-Hind*.

1106–67   Basavanna establishes the Virashaiva sect, later known as the Lingayats, which is devoted to the worship of the Hindu god Shiva through the dedication of one's body as his temple.

1193   Muhammad of Ghor takes control of Delhi. His former slave Qutb ad-Din Aibek establishes in 1206 the first Muslim sultanate in India. During this period, the expansive Quwwat al-Islam Mosque (fig. 2) and the monumental Qutb Minar are built.

1142–1235   Mu'in ad-Din Chishti brings the teachings of his Sufi tradition to India, founding a chain of succession that continues to this day. His tomb at Ajmer is a center of pilgrimage, especially on the anniversary of his death.

1253–1325   Amir Khusrau Dihlavi, court poet of seven kings in Delhi, is well known for his Persian lyrical poetry, his epical *Khamsa* (Quintet), and poetical descriptions of contemporary events. He is also reputed to have invented the musical instruments the sitar and the tabla, as well as the musical forms of qawwali and tarana.

1327   Muhammad Tughluq moves his capital from Delhi to Deogiri in the Deccan, renaming it Daulatabad, where he builds an impressive citadel (fig. 3).

1336   The kingdom of Vijayanagar, the successor of the great South Indian dynasties (fig. 1), is founded by two brothers, Harihara and Bukka. Their capital is renowned for its wealth and architectural grandeur.

1341   Muhammad ibn Badr Jajarmi composes the *Mu'nis al-Ahrar*, which is illustrated in the same year.

Fig. 1.   Vitthala Temple, Vijayanagar, begun in 1513. Photograph by E. D. Lyon, 1860s. Canadian Centre for Architecture, Montreal

1345   Hasan Gangu, the Tughluq governor of the Deccan, rebels to found the Bahmanid kingdom, with its capital at Gulbarga.

1345–58   Shams ad-Din Ilyas Shah proclaims an independent sultanate in Bengal with its capital at Gaur.

1347–58   Abu'l Muzaffar 'Ala ad-Din Bahman expands the Bahmanid state to include the provinces of Gulbarga, Daulatabad, Berar, and Bidar.

1352   Ibn Battuta, the North African geographer, describes his extensive Indian travels in his Arabic *Rihla*.

1377–78   Mulla Da'ud composes the *Chandayana*, the love story of Laur and Chanda, in Hindi. It is illustrated in the sixteenth century.

1398   Timur (Tamerlane) invades northwestern India.

Fig. 2. Quwwat-al Islam Mosque, Delhi, begun in 1192. Photograph by Samuel Bourne, 1860s. Fogg Art Museum, Harvard University, Cambridge, Massachusetts

Fig. 3. Fortress, Daulatabad, begun in 1327. Unidentified photographer, 19th century. Canadian Centre for Architecture, Montreal

1401 Dilavar Khan Ghori establishes the independent state of Malwa, with its capital at Mandu, in Central India.

1411–42 The reign in Gujarat of Ahmad Shah, who founds the city of Ahmedabad and builds many of its monuments.

1420–70 Zain al-ʿAbidin Badshah, an enlightened patron of scholarship, art, and architecture, rules Kashmir from Srinagar.

ca. 1440–1518 The mystic and poet Kabir opposes religious sectarianism and teaches the unity of Hindu and Muslim under one God.

1458–1511 Mahmud Begra, the famed Prince of Cambay, rules Gujarat, captures Champanir, and builds a large palace complex at Sarkhej.

1459 Rao Jodha, Rajput maharaja of Marwar, builds an impressive fortified capital at Jodhpur.

1469–1538 Guru Nanak, after a long religious quest through many religions, founds the Sikh religion.

1472 The great madrasa of the Iranian-born Mahmud Gawan is founded in Bidar, capital of the Bahmanids since 1422, to attract scholars from all parts of the Islamic world. The tiled façade and four-iwan construction are reminiscent of Persian architecture from the same period.

1484–1512 The Bahmanid kingdom fragments into five independent sultanates, all with related styles of painting and architecture: the ʿImad Shahi sultanate of Berar (1484–1574); the ʿAdil-Shahi sultanate of Bijapur (1489–1686); the Nizam-Shahi sultanate of Ahmadnagar (1490–1636); the Barid-Shahi sultanate of Bidar (1492–1609); and the Qutb-Shahi sultanate of Golconda (1512–1687).

1485 Birth in Bengal of Chaitanya, leader in the bhakti movement, who founds a sect devoted to the loving worship of Krishna.

1486–1516 Raja Man Singh builds his palace at Gwalior, combining Hindu and Muslim architectural elements.

1498 Portuguese explorer Vasco da Gama reaches Calicut by sea, thereby opening new trade routes for European merchants.

1500–1511 Nasir ad-Din Khalji, sultan of Mandu, continues his father's patronage of literature and painting, including the composition of the Niʿmat-nama and its illustration by Haji Mahmud.

1501 Bihari Lal, Hindi poet at the Jaipur court, composes his Sat Sai, later illustrated by many painters in the Punjab Hill courts.

1503 Sultan Sikandar Lodi transfers his capital from Delhi to Agra, a city that is to achieve architectural glory in the Mughal period.

1503–4 Hindi poet Shaikh Qutban composes the Mrigavata, soon illustrated.

1504 Babur, from the house of Timur, occupies Kabul, where his son and successor Humayun is born four years later.

1509–30 Krishnadeva Raya rules Vijayanagar, is patron of eight major Telegu poets, and builds the great Krishnaswami Temple at his capital.

1510 Affonso d'Albuquerque wrests the island of Goa from the sultan of Bijapur, making Portugal the first European colonizer of India.

1526 Babur defeats Ibrahim Lodi at Panipat and founds the great Mughal empire in India.

1530–56 Humayun, at the age of twenty-two, succeeds his father Babur as Mughal emperor and reigns for twenty-six years.

1532–1623 Tulsidas, a leading poet of the Hindu bhakti movement, composes a popular version of the epic Ramayana in Hindi, the Ramcharitmanas.

1540 Sher Shah Sur defeats Humayun at Kanauj and takes over the capital at Delhi. Humayun escapes to Sind, where his son Akbar is born in 1542.

1540–50 The Uzbek sultan ʿAbd al-ʿAziz of Bukhara commissions a manuscript of the poet Saʿdi's Bustan, copied by the calligrapher Mir-ʿAli al-Husaini with three paintings by Shaikh-Zada. This masterpiece is later bought by the Mughal emperor Jahangir, whose painter Bishndas repaints some of the miniatures.

1544 Humayun resides at the Safavid court of Shah Tahmasp, where he observes the leading Iranian artists at work.

1548–63 Surdas, a blind poet and a disciple of Vallabhachar-ya, composes the *Sur-Sagar* in praise of Krishna, a text that gains popularity and is often copied and illustrated.

1550 Humayun establishes his court at Kabul. One of the artists in his atelier is Dust-Muhammad.

1555 Humayun, defeating Sikandar Shah Suri at Sirhind, returns to India accompanied by the leading Safavid artists, Mir Sayyid 'Ali and 'Abd as-Samad.

Baz Bahadur declares his independence as sultan of Mandu. His love for Rupmati, a courtesan, is the subject of painting and poetry in both folk and court traditions.

1556 After falling from his library steps, Humayun dies. His son Akbar, at the age of fourteen, succeeds him.

1556–1605 During the reign of Akbar, the Mughal empire expands to include most of India. Akbar's conquests include Malwa (Central India) in 1552, Chittor (Rajasthan) in 1568, Ranthambor and Kalanjar (Rajasthan) in 1569, Gujarat in 1573, Bengal in 1576, Kashmir in 1586, Sind in 1591, Orissa in 1592, Baluchistan and Makran in 1594, Kandahar in 1595, and Berar, Khandesh, and part of Ahmadnagar from 1595 to 1601. Akbar's interest in other religions leads him to commission the translation and illustration of Hindu epics such as the *Ramayana* and the *Mahabharata*.

1557–1605 Akbar's artists undertake to illustrate the *Dastan-i Amir Hamza*, which comprises 1,400 large-format paintings in twelve unsewn volumes.

1565 A confederacy of Deccani sultans defeats Vijayanagar at the Battle of Talikota. Wadiyar Vira Chama Raja creates the state of Mysore from one of the areas not overrun.

1569 The monumental tomb of Humayun (fig. 4) is constructed in Delhi from red sandstone and marble.

1570–1600 Akbar's artist Basawan works on paintings for the *Tuti-nama*, the *Hamza-nama*, the *Darab-nama*, the *Anvar-i Suhaili*, and the *Divan-i Anvari*.

1571–85 Akbar builds an extensive capital at Fatehpur-Sikri (fig. 5), near Agra, centered on the tomb of the Sufi saint Salim Chishti.

1574 On a site given by Akbar, the Sikh Guru Ram Das builds the Hari Mandir in Amritsar.

1579 The Din-i Ilahi, an eclectic religious sect, is founded by Akbar, who professes universal toleration.

1579–1626 The reign of Ibrahim 'Adil-Shah II at Bijapur, during which art, music, and poetry flourish. The *Kitab-i Nauras*, a book of songs, is composed by Ibrahim himself (fig. 6).

1580 Akbar builds an ornate palace, later known as the Jahangiri Mahal, in the Red Fort at Agra.

Fig. 4. Tomb of Humayun, Delhi, begun in 1565. Unidentified photographer, 19th century. Collection Paul F. Walter, New York

1589 Akbar has Babur's autobiography, the *Babur-nama*, translated from Chaghatai Turkish into Persian and illustrated by his best court artists.

1590 Muhammad-Quli Qutb-Shah, a great builder and patron of poetry and the arts, founds Hyderabad and transfers his capital from Golconda.

1591 One of the earliest sets of Ragamala paintings, depicting musical modes, is executed at Chunar, possibly for a Rajasthani patron.

1596 The *Akbar-nama*, a chronicle of Akbar's reign, is composed by the court chronicler and poet Abu'l-Fazl and illustrated by the leading artists of the atelier. Abu'l-Fazl also writes the *A'in-i Akbari* and is an adviser and confidant of the emperor's.

1598 Basohli, the Punjab Hill state that later becomes known for its distinctive style of painting, is founded by Raja Bhupat Pal.

1600 Queen Elizabeth grants a charter to the East India Company authorizing it to conduct trade with India and the Far East.

1603 Shah 'Abbas of Iran sends an ambassador to Golconda. Cultural and political ties between the Deccan and Iran remain strong.

1604 Guru Arjun compiles the *Adi Granth*, the sacred book of the Sikhs.

1605 At Akbar's death, Jahangir assumes the throne. Artists in his workshop include Miskin, Basawan, Balchand, Daulat, Murad, Govardhan, Bichitr, Abu'l-Hasan, Mansur, Farrukh Beg, Aqa Riza, Muhammad 'Ali, and Manohar.

1612 Jahangir grants the British rights to set up factories at Surat, Ahmedabad, and Cambay.

1613–20 Jahangir sends an embassy, which includes his artist Bishndas, to the court of the Safavid ruler Shah 'Abbas at Isfahan.

1615 King James I sends Sir Thomas Roe to Jahangir's court as his ambassador.

1622–24 Nur-Jahan builds a tomb in Agra (fig. 7) for her father, Itimad ad-Daula, with exquisite jalis and *pietra dura* geometric designs inlaid in the finest marble.

1623 Tirumala Nayaka succeeds Virappa at Madurai, where he builds an impressive palace in a combination of architectural styles and also makes important additions to the great Minakshi Temple.

1625 Under the leadership of Raja Madhu Singh, Kotah becomes independent from the state of Bundi.

1626–72 'Abdullah Qutb-Shah, an accomplished poet who also maintains a large workshop of painters, rules Golconda.

1627–58 Shah Jahan succeeds Jahangir and reigns as Mughal emperor. Artists in royal workshops include Hashim, Chitarman, Govardhan, Bichitr, Payag, Balchand, Lalchand, and Murad.

1631 Mumtaz-Mahal, Shah Jahan's beloved queen, dies in Burhanpur while giving birth to her fourteenth child. Shah Jahan begins a tomb in tribute to her, the Taj Mahal (fig. 8).

1633 The Mughal army conquers the fortress at Daulatabad, thereby ending the 'Imad-Shahi dynasty.

1635 Shah Jahan inaugurates the Peacock Throne, which has taken seven years to construct.

Fig. 5.   Courtyard, Jami' Masjid, Fatehpur-Sikri, 1571–85. Photograph by Samuel Bourne, 1860s. Fogg Art Museum, Harvard University, Cambridge, Massachusetts

Fig. 6.   Ibrahim Rauza, the tomb of Ibrahim 'Adil-Shah II, Bijapur, ca. 1615. Unidentified photographer, 19th century. Private collection

Fig. 7.   Tomb of Itimad ad-Daula, Agra, 1622–24. Unidentified photographer, 19th century. Collection Paul F. Walter, New York

Fig. 8. Taj Mahal, Agra, begun in 1634. Paper negative by
J. Murray, 1850s. Collection Paul F. Walter, New York

1635–73 Raja Sangram Singh of Basohli, possibly influenced by a year spent in the Mughal capital of Delhi, is an enthusiastic patron of art in his Hill state.

1640s The *Padshah-nama*, a record of Jahangir's rule, is illustrated by Shah Jahan's leading artists.

1641 The East India Company sets up factories at Madras.

1648 Shah Jahan moves his capital from Agra to Delhi and establishes a new fort and city, called Shahjahanabad (fig. 9).

Shivaji revolts against Bijapur, takes over the North Konkan, and sets up his capital at Kalyan.

ca.1650 Prince Dara-Shikoh attempts to reconcile Hindu and Muslim beliefs in his *Majmaʿ al-Bahrain*.

1656 The Gol Gumbaz (fig. 10), mausoleum for Muhammad ʿAdil-Shah, is built in Bijapur with a dome almost as large as that of Saint Peter's in Rome.

1658–66 Shah Jahan is imprisoned in Agra Fort by Aurangzeb, his third son, who has usurped the throne. He dies there.

1671 The image of Sri Nathji is brought to Nathadwara from Mathura. The market for pilgrims' souvenirs and for pechhavais used in temple rituals leads to the development in Nathadwara of a center of painting.

1687 The French found a settlement at Pondicherry, south of Madras.

Aurangzeb conquers Golconda, thereby ending the rule of the last Deccani sultanate.

1689 Mughal armies lay siege to the Bijapur fort at Adoni, after which Maharaja Anup Singh of Bikaner, who served as a Mughal general in the campaign, is made governor of the fort.

1691 Calcutta (fig. 11) is founded by Job Charnock and soon becomes the main center of British mercantile activity in India.

1695–1763 During the reign of Raja Dalip Singh of Guler a series of large paintings illustrating the Hindu epic the *Ramayana* is commissioned.

1719–34 Maharaja Jai Singh II builds the Jantar Mantar observatory in his new capital at Jaipur (fig. 12).

1719–48 The reign of the ineffectual Muhammad Shah witnesses the collapse of the central authority of the Mughal empire.

1724 Asaf Jah Nizam al-Mulk, a Mughal governor of the Deccan, declares the independence of Hyderabad. The nizams of Hyderabad rule India's largest princely state until 1948.

1724–63 Raja Balwant Singh of Jammu takes pride in his court painter Nainsukh, who records his ruler's daily activities.

Fig. 9. Chandni Chowk, the main thoroughfare of Delhi (Shahjahanabad), built ca. 1648. Photograph by Samuel Bourne, 1860s. Fogg Art Museum, Harvard University, Cambridge, Massachusetts

Fig. 10. Gol Gumbaz, the tomb of Muhammad ʿAdil-Shah, Bijapur, built ca. 1656. Unidentified photographer, 19th century. Collection Howard and Jane Ricketts, London

1734	A darbar of all Rajputana rulers is held near Ajmer in the Jodhpur royal tent.
1739	The Iranian ruler Nadir Shah invades India and sacks Delhi, taking with him the Peacock Throne, the Koh-i Nur diamond, and 300 artisans.
1748–64	Poet and prince Sawant Singh of Kishangarh's eccentric activities are spiritedly captured by court artist Nihal Chand.
1757	At the Battle of Plassey, the East India Company defeats Nawab Siraj ad-Daula, thereby gaining control of Bengal.
1770–90	While serving in the East India Company, Richard Johnson forms a collection of Indian paintings that he later sells to the Company.

1775–1823	Through his interest in painting, Raja Sansar Chand makes Kangra a flourishing center of Punjab Hill painting. The Hindu texts of the *Gita Govinda*, the *Rasikapriya*, the *Sat Sai*, the *Ramayana*, the *Mahabharata*, and the *Bhagavata Purana* are lavishly illustrated by his court artists.
1777–83	Lady Impey, wife of Chief Justice Sir Elijah Impey, employs three painters from Patna, Shaikh Zain ad-Din, Bhawani Das, and Ram Das, to paint Indian flora and fauna and also to record the activities of her family (see no. 281).
1780–1839	Maharaja Ranjit Singh rules the Punjab with the help of European mercenaries such as Jean-François Allard (see no. 278).

Fig. 11. View across the esplanade, Calcutta. Photograph by Samuel Bourne, 1860s. Fogg Art Museum, Harvard University, Cambridge, Massachusetts

1784   Sir William Jones founds the Asiatic Society of Bengal to promote and publish research in the history, arts, sciences, and literature of India.

1795–1808   Thomas and William Daniell publish *Oriental Scenery*, with 144 aquatints of India made after paintings and drawings done during many tours there. This publication brings India into the parlors of many English homes.

1797–1869   Mirza Asadullah Khan Ghalib, the leading poet of northern India, writes poetry in Persian and Urdu for such patrons as the last Mughal emperor of Delhi, Bahadur Shah II, and the nawab of Rampur.

1799–1830   William Fraser arrives in India as agent of the governor-general. During his tours of duty in northwestern India, he employs at least two Indian artists, most notably Ghulam 'Ali Khan, to record the village life he encounters (see nos. 49, 50).

1800   Jaipur maharaja Sawai Pratap Singh convenes a conference of leading musicians, the proceedings of which are compiled as the *Sangit Sar*, an important Hindi treatise on music.

1801   The India Museum is established in London with the Sanskritist Charles Wilkins as curator. The museum, the precursor of the India Office Library, is to collect manufactures and natural products of India and to maintain a library.

1819   The Ajanta caves, with their outstanding murals representing Buddhist lore, are discovered, causing a reevaluation of early Indian painting.

1820–57   Maharaja Gulab Singh rules both Jammu and Kashmir.

1828   Raja Ram Mohan Roy, leader of the Bengal renaissance, founds the Brahmo Samaj, a form of Hinduism influenced by Christianity and Islam.

1833   The British Parliament takes over the Indian possessions of the East India Company.

1835–37   In the Goomsur Wars, the British try to stop the tribal Konds from continuing human sacrifice.

1837–58   The last Mughal emperor, Bahadur Shah II, is more concerned with composing poetry and practicing calligraphy than with events outside his domain of Delhi.

1841   The first permanent academic position for a professor of Sanskrit and Indology in the United States is created at Yale University. A year later, the American Oriental Society is founded in New Haven.

1842   Ram Singh II of Kotah (r. 1828–69) visits Bahadur Shah II in Delhi, an occasion that is the subject of a monumental painting on cloth by his leading court artist (no. 285).

1847   Wajid 'Ali Shah succeeds his father, Nasir ad-Daula, as king of Oudh, with its capital at Lucknow (fig. 13).

1850–75   Painter Kehar Singh records life in the Punjab (see no. 280).

1855   The Photographic Society of Bombay is formed, an indication of the extensive use of photography in India.

1857   The Indian Mutiny, also known as the first war of independence, begins with discontent among soldiers in Meerut and quickly spreads throughout northern India. In Delhi, Emperor Bahadur Shah II declares his independence and is then exiled by the British to Rangoon, where he dies in 1862 "without two meters of my own land for a grave."

1858   The British Crown assumes direct control of the East India Company.

Fig. 12. City Palace, Jaipur, with the Hawa Mahal at right, built in 18th century. Unidentified photographer, 19th century. Canadian Centre for Architecture, Montreal

Fig. 13. Kaiserbagh Palace, Lucknow, built in 1850s. Photograph by Samuel Bourne, 1860s. Fogg Art Museum, Harvard University, Cambridge, Massachusetts

Fig. 14. Rashtrapati Bhavan, New Delhi. Designed by Edwin Lutyens as the viceregal residence. Completed in 1931. Unidentified photographer, 20th century. From A. S. G. Butler, *The Architecture of Sir Edwin Lutyens*, London, 1950

1862   The Archaeological Survey of India is formed, with the object of identifying, documenting, restoring, and preserving the many monuments of India's past.

1875   Sir Sayyid Ahmad Khan founds the Muhammadan Anglo-Oriental College at Aligarh, where Muslims learn Western sciences and English. In the same year Swami Dayananda founds the Arya Samaj, a neo-Hindu organization, also dedicated to reconciling traditional ways with modern times.

The India Museum is established in Calcutta to house many newly discovered art treasures.

1877   Queen Victoria is crowned empress of India.

1884   Lala Din Dayal is appointed court photographer to the nizam of Hyderabad.

1885   The Indian National Congress is founded in Bombay.

1901   Rabindranath Tagore founds Shantiniketan, a school where traditional arts of India can be studied. Artist Nandalal Bose teaches students there to use indigenous techniques in a contemporary mode.

1905   The Prince of Wales Museum is founded in Bombay.

1911   At the Coronation Darbar in Delhi, King George V announces that the capital will be transferred from Calcutta to Delhi.

1913–31   Architects Edwin Lutyens and Herbert Baker design the capital buildings and develop a plan for New Delhi (fig. 14).

1917   Ananda Coomaraswamy, the renowned art historian, joins the Asiatic Department of the Museum of Fine Arts in Boston, due to the enthusiasm of Denman Ross, who funds the acquisition of the first major collection of Indian art in the United States.

1921   Victoria Memorial, a tribute to the grand British empress, is completed in Calcutta and includes a museum dedicated to the history of the British in India.

1924–33   The pre-Aryan sites of Mohenjo-Daro and Harappa are excavated.

1947   India gains independence. Earl Mountbatten, the last viceroy, is charged with the responsibility of transferring power. The subcontinent is divided politically into India and Pakistan; the eastern part of Pakistan becomes Bangladesh in 1971.

GLOSSARY

A: Arabic
H: Hindi
P: Persian
Port: Portuguese
S: Sanskrit
T: Turkish

ankus (S) elephant goad

apsara (S, lit. "essence of the waters") heavenly nymph, one of the seductive female dancers of the gods who take on any form at will

ashoka (S) flowering tree sacred to Shiva; in the *Ramayana*, Rama's wife Sita is held captive by the demon Ravana in an ashoka grove, and Hindu women have thus associated the tree with fidelity and purity

asura (S) demon in Hindu mythology

avatar (S, lit. "descent") incarnation of a deity, especially Vishnu, who appeared on earth in many forms, both animal and human

ayah (H/Port) nursemaid or lady's maid

begum (H/T) Muslim princess or lady of high rank

Bhairava (S) the Terrible One, the Hindu god Shiva in his destructive aspect; also one of the terrifying forms of the Vedic god Rudra, the Roarer

bhakti (S) loving devotion to a deity

bidri, bidriware (after the Deccani city of Bidar) metalware made from an alloy that is inlaid with gold or silver, then blackened

Bihari (after the province of Bihar) Indian style of Arabic calligraphy distinguished by its wedgelike forms

Brahma (S, masc. of brahman, lit. "all-pervasive power") first god of the Hindu trinity, the Creator

chakdar jama (P, lit. "split garment") four-pointed skirt introduced by the Mughals

chapati (H) flat, round unleavened bread

charba (P) copy or tracing; also the thin vellum used for tracing

charpoi (H/P, lit. "four-legged") simple bedstead or cot

chauri (H) yak-tail fly whisk

chhatri (H) kiosk with an umbrella-like dome

chhattar (H) umbrella

chitrakara (S) painter

chowki (H) platform

chuna (H) slaked lime; also plaster or stucco made of lime used for decoration on buildings

danda (S) staff or rod, a symbol of power, also carried to ward off evil spirits

darbar (P) court, or an official or royal public audience

darogha (P/T) superintendent

Dasara (H) Hindu autumn festival, a nine-day celebration of the triumph of good over evil

dastarkana (P) large cloth spread on the floor

deva (S, lit. "luminous") god

Devanagari (S, lit. "divine city writing") script used for Sanskrit and Sanskrit-based Indian languages, written from left to right

devi (S) goddess

Devi or **Mahadevi** (S) the Great Goddess, Shiva's consort, representing cosmic energy, or shakti. In her benign form the Devi is called Uma (Light), Parvati (Daughter of the Mountain), Bhavani (Giver of Existence); in her fierce aspect she is Durga (the Inaccessible One), Kali (the Black One), Chandi (the Cruel One), Bhairavi (the Terrible One)

dharma (S, from dhar, "to hold") in Hinduism and Buddhism, the unchanging moral law; man's ethical and religious duty

dhoti (H) long loincloth worn by Hindu men

dhrupad (H) classical style of Hindu vocal music

dhyana (S) meditation, contemplation

div (P) giant, gigantic demon

divan (P) collection of poetry (Arabic, Persian, Turkish, or Urdu) by a single author

diwan (P) gathering

diwan-i ʿam (A/P) hall for public audience

diwan-i khas (A/P) hall for private audience

dopatta (H) thin shawl of silk or muslin worn by women over the head and shoulders

farrashkana (P) workshop or chambers where carpets, rugs, and other items for a royal household were prepared and/or stored

Fatiha (A) first chapter of the Qur'an, a seven-line prayer recited very frequently; the popular Muslim rituals performed when the prayer is recited over food or sweets are also called Fatiha

gadi (H) cushion, especially the cushion on the ruler's throne

gandharva (S) musician of the gods, one of the guardians of the heavenly nectar

Ganesha (S) elephant-headed Hindu deity associated with wisdom and good fortune who as the Remover of Obstacles is invoked before any undertaking

Garuda (S) mythical figure—part bird, part man—identified with the sun, who is the emblem and vehicle of Vishnu; Garuda is believed to devour snakes and to be able to cure the effects of snakebite

ghanta (S) bell, one of the many objects used in Hindu ritual and one of Shiva's attributes, symbolizing creation; the tolling of a bell, said to contain within it the sounds of all instruments, protects against evil and harm

ghazal (A) short poem (in Arabic, Persian, Turkish, or Urdu), a monorhyme, written in one of the classical Arabo-Persian meters, whose main topic is love, divine or human

gopala (S) cowherd

Gopala or **Govinda** (S) the Cowherd, an epithet of the god Krishna, who grew up among the herdsmen and -women of Vrindavan

gopi (S) herdswoman; the gopis—symbols of human souls yearning for and enjoying union with God—fell in love with Krishna, and each of them believed she alone was his beloved

guru (S) teacher, especially of Vedic lore, and spiritual master to whom absolute obedience is due; also a title of the founders of Sikhism

Hadith (A) compendia of the sayings and traditions (hadiths) of the Prophet Muhammad, which were carefully sifted and collected in the late ninth century and are the basis for Muslim life

hakim (A) ruler, wise man, or philosopher, especially a physician who practices the system of Yunani, or "Greek," medicine

hammam (A) bathhouse

hamsa (S) goose (often translated as "swan"); in Hindu mythology the wild goose, a symbol of knowledge, said to feed on pearls, is the vehicle of Brahma: its graceful flight is akin to man's striving to achieve union with the divine

Hanuman (S, lit. "heavy jawed") resourceful monkey god, counselor to Sugriva the monkey king, who in the *Ramayana* helps Rama defeat the demon king of Lanka. Hanuman, son of the wind, possesses great knowledge and magical powers, and his image presides over nearly every village or town in northern India

harem (A) women's quarters, to which only the closest male relatives have access

haveli (H) large house, mansion

hijra (A, lit. "emigration") the Muslim calendar (a lunar calendar with years of 354 days), which begins with 622, the year of the emigration (hijra) of the Prophet Muhammad from his home town of Mecca to Yathrib, hence known as Medina (the City)

Holi (H) popular Hindu festival marking the coming of spring, during which the rejoicing participants throw red or yellow powder and liquids at each other

howdah (H) litter used on camels and elephants

huqqa (A, lit. "box") water pipe; also called a hubble-bubble

jali (A, lit. "open") stone or marble openwork used in screens

jama (P) garment or dress, specifically an overgarment

jamiᶜ masjid (A, from jamiᶜ, "gathering" and masjid, "place for prostration") congregational mosque where Muslims gather to pray, especially on Friday, when the sermon includes recitations of prayers for the ruler of the age

jauhar (H) rite of self-immolation, performed by Rajputs after a defeat

jharoka (H) window at which a ruler appears to be viewed by his subjects

jinn (A) spirit, which may be good, evil, or neutral, that is created from fire and has supernatural powers

Kaᶜba (A, lit. "cube") central sanctuary of Islam in Mecca, which all Muslims face during the ritual prayer; the black stone in its southeastern corner is circumambulated during the annual pilgrimage to Mecca in the last month of the lunar year

Kaithi (H) Indian style of script associated mainly with eastern Uttar Pradesh

kalamkari (P, lit. "penwork") fine arabesque and floral designs on textiles, created with hand-applied mordants

kard (P) Persian dagger with a straight blade and hilt

karkana (P) workshop

karma (S) in Hinduism, Buddhism, and Jainism, the law of cause and effect, according to which every action bears consequences either in this life or in future lives

katar (H) Indian thrusting dagger with a double-edged blade and a transverse grip between two parallel bars

kathakali (H) masked dance drama of South India, especially Kerala

khalifa (A) caliph, successor, either to a ruler or to a mystical leader

khanjar (A) curved dagger; the Indian type has a double-edged, sometimes double-curved blade and often a pistol-grip handle

khas mahal (P, lit. "special place") private apartments of a prince or ruler

kirttimukha (S, lit. "face of glory") lionlike mask that is a potent symbol of Shiva

koftgari (P, from kuftan, "to beat") metalwork technique in which gold and silver are hammered into an engraved steel surface

Krishna (S, lit. "dark") hero of ancient legend revered as the eighth avatar of Vishnu. Perhaps the most popular Hindu deity, Krishna is the object of a cult associated with the bhakti (devotional) movement in northern India; called the Blue God, he is worshiped in many forms, as an infant, as Gopala (the Cowherd), as the Divine Lover, as Bhagata (the Adorable One)

Kufic (A) angular style of Arabic writing used in early Qurʾans and in pre-1250 epigraphy

kurta (H) overshirt, tunic

Lakshmi (S, lit. "sign" or "token") goddess of fortune, the consort of Vishnu

lingam (S, lit. "mark" or "characteristic") phallic symbol of energy and fertility and of the god Shiva

lota (H) water vessel

madrasa (A, lit. "place of learning") Muslim theological college

Mahadeva (S) the Great God, epithet of Shiva, sometimes also applied to Vishnu

maharaja (H) great king or great prince, title of the most powerful Hindu rulers of the Indian princely states

mahout (H) elephant driver

makara (H) mythical aquatic animal, a kind of crocodile, which has magical and occult powers, usually related to the fertility of rivers, lakes, and the sea; the makara is the vehicle of Varuna, god of the waters of heaven and earth, and of Ganga, goddess of the Ganges, and it is the emblem of Kama, the god of love

mandala (S, lit. "circle") circular diagram of religious symbols used for meditative purposes by both Hindus and Buddhists; the Hindu temple seen from above represents a mandala

mansab (A) rank of an officer, usually in the Mughal army

mansabdar (A/P) someone who holds the rank of mansab

mantra (S) sacred word or formula carrying spiritual power

mardana (P) men's quarters

masjid (A, lit. "place for prostration") mosque

maya (S) illusion; in Hindu and Buddhist philosophy, the phenomenal world is but an illusory play

mihrab (A) prayer niche, placed so as to indicate the direction of Mecca; metaphorically, the place to which one turns in devotion

mirza (P) title of honor given to royal princes as well as to high officials, scholars, and noblemen

morchhal (H) peacock-feather fly whisk or fan

mudra (S) in Hinduism, Jainism, and Buddhism, hand gesture expressing a symbolic meaning

Muhaqqaq (A) decorative cursive Arabic script with very high verticals

muraqqaʿ (A, lit. "patchwork") album with pictures

muraqqaha-i latif maʿi taswirha (A/P) charming albums with pictures

mushaʿira (A) contest of poets reciting their own verse, usually in Persian or Urdu

naga (S) serpent, snake spirit

Nandi (S) the Happy One, the bull that is the vehicle of Shiva

Naskhi (A) simple cursive Arabic script

Nastaʿliq (P) "hanging" style of Arabic lettering used predominantly for writing Persian, characterized by strong movement from upper left to lower right

Nauratan (H, lit. "nine jewels") the nine specially selected members of Akbar's entourage

nawab (P/A, from naʾib, "viceroy") high-ranking official, often a governor or prince (origin of the English word nabob)

nayaka, nayika (H) male, female lover in classical Indian poetry

padma (S) lotus

paijama (P, lit. "foot dress") long, loose trousers, usually of thin material

pan (H) areca nut, lime, and other ingredients rolled in a betel leaf and chewed

pandan (H) box in which pan ingredients are kept

parda (P, lit. "curtain") veiling of women and, by extension, their confinement in their homes

pashmina (P) fine Kashmiri wool used for weaving shawls

patka (H) sash worn by the nobility

pechhavai (H) hanging for a shrine or temple of Vishnu, usually depicting scenes from the life of Krishna and symbols associated with his worship

peshwa (P/H) prime minister, especially among the Marathas

pousta (H) opium concoction, which is lethal in large doses

pranayama (S) breath control, practiced by yogis and also by Muslim mystics

puja (S) Hindu ritual of worship, homage

punkah (H) fan; formerly, a piece of cloth fastened at a door, sometimes sprinkled with water, which a servant pulled to and fro with a string to produce a soft, cooling breeze

qalam (A) reed pen used for writing Arabic characters

qalamdan (A/P) box for writing utensils

Qurʾan (A, lit. "recitation") the scripture of Islam; according to Muslim dogma the 114 chapters of the Qurʾan contain God's word as proclaimed through the Prophet Muhammad

Radha (S) the most beautiful of the gopis (herdswomen) of Vrindavan, mistress of Krishna

raga, ragini (S, from ranj, "to color" or "to tinge with emotion") fundamental musical modes on which classical Indian music is improvised, conceived as masculine and feminine and connected with special times and moods

ragamala (H, lit. "garland of melody") sequence of musical modes illustrated according to special iconographic traditions

rahl (A) Qurʾan stand

raja (H, from S, rajan) king, prince

rakshasa (S) demon who wanders in the night and can assume many animal and human forms

Rama (S) seventh incarnation of Vishnu and legendary hero of the great Hindu epic the *Ramayana*

Ramadan (A) ninth month of the Muslim lunar year, devoted to complete fasting (neither food, drink, injections, nor even the smelling of fragrance is permitted from dawn to sunset); the feast celebrating the end of the fast is a joyous occasion

rana (H) Hindu prince, ruler

rani (H) Hindu princess or lady of high rank

rao (H) king, prince, or chief; a Hindu title of honor

rasa (S) flavor, sentiment; also sap, juice, essence

Rihani (A) small, decorative Arabic script with short endings

rishi (S) seer, sage

rumal (P, lit. "kerchief to wipe the face") square cloth, often embroidered, used as a handkerchief, towel, or covering

sadhu (S) Hindu ascetic

safina (A, lit. "boat") small notebook, usually for Persian poetry, that is sewn at its narrower end

sarpech (P/H) turban ornament; the lower part is the arpati, the upper front the jigha

sati (S) self-immolation of a Hindu widow on her husband's funeral pyre

Shab-i Barat (P/A) night of the full moon of the eighth lunar month, Shaʿban, when it is said the fates of mankind are written in heaven for the coming year; Muslims celebrate Shab-i Barat with fireworks and the preparation of special sweets

shah tus (P, lit. "king's fleece") fleece left on bushes wild mountain goats have passed, the wool the finest Kashmiri shawls are made from

shaikh (A, lit. "old man") honorific name for the elder in a community, specifically a master of the mystical path

Shaivite worshiper of Shiva

shakti (S) divine power as embodied in the female, especially connected with Shiva's female counterpart

shamsa (A, lit. "little sun") rosette

Shiʿa or Shiʿite (A, from shiʿa, "sect") Muslim faction that holds that Muhammad's cousin and son-in-law ʿAli should have been the Prophet's first successor. The Shiʿa developed the concept of the infallible imam (leader), descendant of ʿAli and his wife Fatima, Muhammad's daughter

Shikasta (P) "broken" style of Persian calligraphy developed during the seventeenth century, often quite illegible

shish mahal (P, lit. "place of mirrors") hall covered with numerous tiny mirrors that reflect the light

Shiva (S, lit. "auspicious") third deity of the Hindu trinity, great ascetic who is both creative (symbolized by the lingam) and destructive (as Bhairava, the Terrible); Shiva is often represented as Nataraja, Lord of the Dance, whose powerful, ecstatic dance is symbolic of the continuous cycle of creation and destruction of the universe

simurgh (P) fabulous mythical bird whose colorful feather helps fulfill wishes; in mystical Islamic literature, the simurgh becomes the symbol of the divine

Sita (S, lit. "furrow") goddess of agriculture, Rama's wife and heroine of the *Ramayana*, in which she is abducted by Ravana, demon king of Lanka

Sufi (A, from suf, "wool") Muslim ascetic and mystic; Sufi fraternities, which developed in the twelfth century, were instrumental in carrying the teachings of the Prophet into the many borderlands of Islam, including India

Sugriva (S, lit. "he who has a beautiful neck") king of the monkeys, Rama's ally

Takht-i taʾus (P) the Peacock Throne, commissioned by Shah Jahan

talwar (P) sword with a long, curved blade

tanpura (P) stringed instrument used to provide a drone in Indian music

thakur (H) lord, master, or person of rank or authority

Thugs (H, from thag, "thief") religious fraternity of professional assassins who until they were suppressed in the nineteenth century prevailed in parts of Central and North India; they garroted their victims and offered them up to the goddess Bhavani (a form of the Devi)

Thuluth (A) monumental Arabic script often used in epigraphy

tikka or **tilaka** (H) mark of blessing or caste made on the forehead

tirthankara (S) one of the twenty-four saints whose teachings are the basis of the Jain religion

toran (S) gate or archway at a temple or stupa

tughra (T) especially in India, any artificially contrived form of Arabic writing, such as mirrored sentences, fenceworklike writing, or birds or beasts composed of meaningful words (a tughra was originally the handsign of a ruler at the beginning of a document, and later the word referred to a calligraphic emblem)

'urs (A, lit. "wedding") anniversary of the death of a Muslim saint, commemorating the union of his soul with God; the 'urs of a great Sufi attracts thousands of visitors, who enjoy communal prayer and music, as well as less spiritual entertainment

ustad (P) master of any craft

vahana (S) vehicle or mount of a deity

Vaishnavite worshiper of Vishnu

vina (S) ancient Indian musical instrument with one or more strings, a kind of lute

Vishnu (S, lit. "pervader") second deity of the Hindu trinity, the preserver of the universe who embodies mercy and goodness; to save mankind from suffering, Vishnu descended to earth in several incarnations; his first avatar was a fish (Matsya); the most well known of his avatars are the heroes Rama and Krishna

Yama (S) King of the Dead, in Hindu mythology the god who conducts the dead to the realm of the ancestors

yogi (S) Hindu ascetic; literally someone who practices yoga

yugas (S) the four ages or periods of the existence of the world, which total 4,320,000 years: krita- or satya-yuga (the "golden age"), treta-yuga, dvapara-yuga, and kali-yuga, the present "black age," the shortest of the four, after which the world will be destroyed, to be re-created in a new, similarly arranged system

zenana (P) women's quarters

BIBLIOGRAPHY

I. THE GREAT TRADITION

Allchin, Bridget, and Allchin, Raymond. *The Rise of Civilization in India*. Cambridge, 1982.

Archer, Mildred, "Company Painting in South India: The Early Collections of Niccolao Manucci." *Apollo* 92 (1970), pp. 104–13.

Archer, Mildred. *Indian Popular Painting in the India Office Library*. London, 1977.

Archer, W. *The Loves of Krishna in Indian Painting and Poetry*. London, 1957.

"Art of Asia Acquired by North American Museums, 1981." *Archives of Asian Art* 35 (1982), pp. 83–98.

The Art of India and Pakistan. Ex. cat., London, The Royal Academy of Arts, 1947.

Art of the Orient. Vol. II of *Handbook of the Collections in the William Rockhill Nelson Gallery of Art and Mary Atkins Museum of Fine Arts*. Kansas City, Mo., 1973.

Auboyer, Jeannine, and Goepper, Roger. *The Oriental World*. New York, 1967.

Banerjee, P. *The Life of Krishna in Indian Art*. New Delhi, 1978.

Barrett, Douglas, and Gray, Basil. *Painting of India*. Lausanne, 1963.

Brunel, Francis. *Jewelry of India: Five Thousand Years of Tradition*. New Delhi, 1972.

Chaitanya, Krishna. *A History of Indian Painting: Manuscript, Moghul and Deccani Traditions*. New Delhi, 1979.

Chandra, Pramod. "Notes on the Mandu Kalpasutra of A.D. 1439." *Marg* 12 (no. 3, 1959), pp. 51–54.

Chandra, Pramod. "A Unique Kalakacharya-kantha Ms. in the Style of the Mandu Kalpa-sutra of A.D. 1439." *Bulletin of the American Academy of Benares* 1 (1967), pp. 1–10.

Chandra, Pramod, and Ehnbom, Daniel. *The Cleveland Tuti-nama Manuscript and the Origins of Mughal Painting*. Ex. cat., Cleveland Museum of Art, 1976.

Chitra, V. R., and Srinivasan, T. N. *Cochin Murals*. Cochin, 1940.

Czuma, Stanislaw. *Indian Art from the George P. Bickford Collection*. Ex. cat., Cleveland Museum of Art, 1975.

Dahmen-Dallapiccola, A. L., and Goswamy, B. M. *Krishna the Divine Lover*. London, 1982.

Das, J. P. *Puri Paintings: The Chitrakara and His Work*. New Delhi, 1982.

"Decorative Arts." *Bulletin National Museum New Delhi* no. 1 (1966), pp. 10–23.

de Zoete, Beryl. *The Other Mind: A Study of Dance and Life in South India*. London, 1953.

Doshi, Saryu. "Illustrated Manuscripts." In *Heritage of Karnataka*, Banaras, 1985 (*Marg* 1985).

Fabri, Charles. *History of the Art of Orissa*. New Delhi, 1977.

Fickle, Dorothy H. "Karaikkalammaiyar, Saint and Poetess." *Bulletin: The Nelson-Atkins Museum of Art* 5 (no. 8, 1983), pp. 19–22.

Fischer, Eberhard; Mahapatra, Sitakant; and Pathy, Dinanath. *Orissa Kunst und Kultur in Nordost-Indien*. Zurich, 1980.

Ghosh, D. P. "Eastern School of Mediaeval Indian Painting (Thirteenth–Eighteenth Century, A.D.)." In *Chhavi: Golden Jubilee Volume*. Banaras, 1971, pp. 91–103.

Ghosh, D. P. *Mediaeval Indian Painting: Eastern School*. Delhi, 1982.

Ghosh, D. P. "Orissan Paintings." *Journal of the Indian Society of Oriental Art* 9 (1941), pp. 194–200.

Gittinger, Mattiebelle. *Master Dyers to the World: Technique and Trade in Early Indian Dyed Cotton Textiles*. Washington, D.C., 1982.

Goetz, Hermann. *The Art and Architecture of the Bikaner State*. Oxford, 1950.

Harle, J. *Temple Gateways in South India*. Oxford, 1963.

Heras, H. *South India Under the Vijayanagar Empire*. Reprinted, New Delhi, 1980.

Indian Painting: Mughal and Rajput and a Sultanate Manuscript. Ex. cat., London, P. & D. Colnaghi & Co., 1978.

Irwin, John, and Brett, Katharine B. *Origins of Chintz*. London, 1970.

Irwin, John, and Hall, Margaret. *Indian Painted and Printed Fabrics*. Ahmedabad, 1971.

Ishwaran, K. *Religion and Society Among the Lingayats of South India*. New Delhi, 1983.

Karanth, Shivram. *Karanataka Paintings*. Mysore, 1973.

Khandalavala, Karl, and Chandra, Moti. "A Consideration of an Illustrated Ms. from Mandapadurga (Mandu) Dated 1439 A.D." *Lalit Kala*, no. 6 (1959), pp. 8–29.

Khandalavala, Karl, and Chandra, Moti. "An Illustrated Kalpasutra Painted at Jaunpur in A.D. 1465." *Lalit Kala*, no. 12 (1962), pp. 9–15.

Khandalavala, Karl, and Chandra, Moti. *Miniatures and Sculptures from the Collection of the Late Sir Cowasji Jehangir*. Bombay, 1965.

Khandalavala, Karl, and Chandra, Moti. *New Documents of Indian Painting: A Reappraisal.* Bombay, 1969.

Kramrisch, Stella. *The Art of India: Traditions of Indian Sculpture, Painting and Architecture.* London, 1954.

Kramrisch, Stella. "Early Indian Ivory Carving." *Philadelphia Museum of Art Bulletin* 54 (1959), pp. 55–66.

Kramrisch, Stella. *Indian Sculpture in the Philadelphia Museum of Art.* Philadelphia, 1960.

Kramrisch, Stella. *Unknown India: Ritual Art in Tribe and Village.* Ex. cat., Philadelphia Museum of Art, 1968.

Kramrisch, S.; Cousins, J. H.; and Poduval, R. Vasudeva. *The Arts and Crafts of Kerala.* Cochin, 1970.

Lerner, Martin. *The Flame and the Lotus: Indian and Southeast Asian Art from the Kronos Collection.* Ex. cat., New York, The Metropolitan Museum of Art, 1984.

Lippe, Aschwin de. *The Freer Indian Sculptures.* Washington, D.C., 1970.

Losty, Jeremiah. *The Art of the Book in India.* Ex. cat., London, British Library, 1982.

Losty, Jeremiah. *Krishna, a Hindu Version of God: Scenes from the Life of Krishna Illustrated in Orissan and Other Eastern Indian Manuscripts in the British Library.* London, 1980.

Mittal, Jagdish. *Andhra Paintings of the Ramayana.* Hyderabad, 1969.

Mittal, Jagdish. "Portfolio." *Marg* 16 (no. 2, 1963), pp. 17–22.

Mohanty, B. C. *Patachitras of Orissa.* Ahmedabad, 1980.

Nagaswamy, R. *Masterpieces of Early South Indian Bronzes.* New Delhi, 1983.

Nagaswamy, R. "Tamil Paintings." In *Splendours of Tamil Nadu.* Bombay, 1980, pp. 103–24 (*Marg* 1980).

Nambiar, P. K., ed. *Census of India 1961. Volume IX, Madras, Part IX-A: Handlooms in the Madras State.* Madras, 1964.

Pal, Pratapaditya. *The Sensuous Immortals: A Selection of Sculptures from the Pan Asian Collection.* Ex. cat., Los Angeles County Museum of Art, 1979.

Panikkar, K. M. *A History of Kerala.* Annamalainagar, 1960.

Rajan, K. V. Soundara. *Art of South India: Tamil Nadu and Kerala.* Delhi, 1978.

Rarities of the Asian Art Museum: The Avery Brundage Collection. Ed. Karl P. Kramer and Robert J. Hills. San Francisco, 1978.

Rawson, Philip. *Indian Art.* London, 1972.

Rowland, Benjamin. "Indian Art." In *Praeger Encyclopaedia of Art.* London, 1971.

Sarkar, A. H. *An Architectural Survey of Temples of Kerala.* Delhi, 1978.

Sastri, K. A. Milakanta. *A History of South India from Prehistoric Times to the Fall of Vijayanagar.* Madras, 1958.

Sewell, Robert. *A Forgotten Empire: Vijayanagar: A Contribution to the History of India.* London, 1924.

Sharma, O. P. *Indian Miniature Painting.* Ex. cat., Brussels, 1979.

Sharma, O. P., and Vatsyayan, Kapila. *Krishna of the Bhagavata Purana, the Gita Govinda and Other Texts.* Ex. cat., New Delhi, National Museum, 1982.

Singh, Raghubir. *Kumbh Mela.* Hong Kong, 1980.

Sivaramamurti, Calambur. *The Art of India.* New York, 1974.

Sivaramamurti, Calambur. *South Indian Paintings.* New Delhi, 1968.

Spink, Walter M. *Krishnamandala.* Ann Arbor, 1971.

Srinivasan, P. R. "Bronzes of South India." *Bulletin of the Madras Government Museum* 8 (1963), pp. 1–396.

Talwar, Kay, and Krishna, Kalyan. *Indian Pigment Painting on Cloth.* Ahmedabad, 1978.

Van Lohuizen-De Leeuw, J. E. "Indian Ivories with Special Reference to a Mediaeval Throne Leg from Orissa." *Arts Asiatiques* 6 (1959), pp. 195–216.

Varadarajan, Lotika. "Figurative Kalamkari and Its Local." In *Chhavi 2: Rai Krishnadasa Felicitation Volume.* Banaras, 1981, pp. 67–70.

Watt, George. *Indian Art at Delhi 1903. Being the Official Catalogue of the Delhi Exhibition, 1902–1903.* Ex. cat., Delhi, Kudsia Gardens, 1903.

Welch, Stuart Cary. *Indian Drawings and Painted Sketches.* New York, 1976.

Zimmer, Heinrich. *The Art of Indian Asia.* New York, 1955.

Zimmer, Heinrich. *Artistic Form and Yoga in the Sacred Images of India.* Trans. Gerald Chapple and James B. Lawson, in collaboration with Michael McKnight. Princeton, 1984.

II. TRIBE AND VILLAGE

Allchin, Bridget, and Allchin, Raymond. *The Rise of Civilization in India.* Cambridge, 1982.

Archer, Mildred. *Indian Popular Painting in the India Office Library.* London, 1977.

Barbier, Jean-Paul. *The Art of Nagaland.* Ex. cat., Los Angeles County Museum of Art, 1984.

Birdwood, G. C. M. *The Industrial Arts of India,* 2 vols. London, 1880.

Boal, Barbara M. *The Konds: Human Sacrifice and Religious Change.* Warminster, 1982.

Brown, J. C. *The Coins of India.* Calcutta, 1922.

Chatterji, Suniti Kumar. *Kirata-Jana-Krti: The Indo-Mongoloids.* Calcutta, 1951.

Christie's, New York, December 1, 1982. Sale cat., *The Pan Asian Collection.*

Crooke, William. *The Tribes and Castes of the North Western Province and Oudh,* 4 vols. Calcutta, 1896.

de Zoete, Beryl. *The Other Mind: A Study of Dance and Life in South India.* London, 1953.

Elwin, Verrier. *The Art of the North-East Frontier of India.* Shillong, 1959.

Fürer-Haimendorf, Christoph von. *The Konyak Nagas.* New York, 1969.

Fürer-Haimendorf, Christoph von. *The Naked Nagas.* London, 1939.

Getty, Alice. *Ganesa: A Monograph of the Elephant God,* 2nd ed. New Delhi, 1971.

Gopinatha Rao, T. K. *Elements of Hindu Iconography,* 2 vols. Madras, 1914–16. Reprint and 2nd ed., New York, 1968.

Grigson, W. V. *The Maria Gonds of Bastar.* London, 1938.

Hutton, J. H. *The Angami Nagas.* London, 1921.

Irwin, John, and Hall, Margaret. *Indian Embroideries.* Ahmedabad, 1973.

Jayakar, Pupul. *The Earthen Drum: An Introduction to the Ritual Arts of Rural India.* New Delhi, 1981.

Journal of Indian Art and Industries 1 (no. 9, 1886), p. 69.

King, W. Ross. *The Aboriginal Tribes of the Nilgiri Hills.* London, 1870.

Kramrisch, Stella. "Kanthas of Bengal." *Marg* 3 (no. 3, 1949), pp. 18–29.

Kramrisch, Stella. *Manifestations of Shiva.* Ex. cat., Philadelphia Museum of Art, 1981.

Kramrisch, Stella. *Unknown India: Ritual Art in Tribe and Village.* Ex. cat., Philadelphia Museum of Art, 1968.

Mookerjee, Ajit. *Indian Primitive Art.* Calcutta, 1959.

The Ramayana of Valmiki, 3 vols. Trans. H. P. Shastri. London, 1976.

Ray, S. K. "The Artisan Castes of West Bengal and Their Crafts." In *West Bengal Census, 1951.* Ed. A. Mitra. Alipore, 1953.

Reeves, Ruth. *Cire Perdue Casting in India.* New Delhi, 1962.

Rivers, W. H. R. *The Todas.* London, 1906.

Schwerin, Kerrin Gräfin. "Heiligenverehrung im indischen Islam: Die Legende des Märtyrers Salar Mas'ud Gazi." *Zeitschrift der Deutschen Morgenländischen Gesellschaft* 126 (1976), pp. 319–35.

Singh, Raghubir. *Rajasthan.* London, 1981.

Skelton, Robert, and Francis, Mark, eds. *Arts of Bengal: The Heritage of Bangladesh and Eastern India*. Ex. cat., London, Whitechapel Art Gallery, 1979.

Sotheby's, London, July 7, 1980. Sale cat., *Catalogue of Fine Oriental Manuscripts, Miniatures and Qajar Lacquer*.

Sotheby's, New York, December 9, 1980. Sale cat., *Fine Oriental Miniatures, Manuscripts and Islamic Works of Art Including the Fraser Album*.

Spear, Percival. *The Twilight of the Mughals*. Cambridge, 1951.

Thurston, Edgar. *Castes and Tribes of Southern India*, 7 vols. Madras, 1909.

Untracht, Oppi. *Jewelry Concepts and Technology*. Garden City, 1982.

Venu, G. "Mudiyettu: Ritual Dance-Drama of Kerala." *Journal of the National Center for the Performing Arts* 13 (no. 4, 1984), pp. 5–13.

Wheeler, Monroe, ed. *Textiles and Ornaments of India: A Selection of Designs*. Ex. cat., New York, Museum of Modern Art, 1956.

III. THE MUSLIM COURTS

THE SULTANATE PERIOD

ʿAli, M. ʿAbid. *Memoirs of Gaur and Pandua*. Calcutta, 1931.

Arnold, Thomas. *The Library of A. Chester Beatty: A Catalogue of the Indian Miniatures*, 3 vols. Ed. J. V. S. Wilkinson. London, 1936.

"Art of Asia Acquired by North American Museums 1982." *Archives of Asian Art* 36 (1983), pp. 92–108.

Arts de l'Islam des origines à 1700 dans les collections publiques françaises. Ex. cat., Paris, Musée de l'Orangerie, 1971.

Atil, Esin. *Kalila wa Dimna: Fables from a Fourteenth-Century Arabic Manuscript*, Washington, D.C., 1981.

Barrett, Douglas. "A Group of Medieval Ivories." *Oriental Art* 1 (no. 2, 1955), pp. 47–51.

Barrett, Douglas, and Gray, Basil. *Painting of India*. Lausanne, 1963.

Boeheim, W., ed. "Urkunden und Regesten aus der K.K. Hofbibliothek." *Jahrbuch der kunsthistorischen Sammlungen des allerhochsten Kaiserhauses* 7 (1888), pt. 2, pp. XCI–CCCXIII.

Born, Wolfgang. "Some Eastern Objects from the Hapsburg Collections." *Burlington Magazine* 69 (1936), pp. 269–77.

Bussaberger, Robert F., and Robbins, Betty Dasher. *The Everyday Art of India*. New York, 1968.

Digby, Simon. "The Fate of Daniyal, Prince of Bengal, in the Light of an Unpublished Manuscript." *Bulletin of the School of Oriental and African Studies* 36 (1973), pp. 588–602.

Dimand, M. S. "An Exhibition of Islamic and Indian Painting." *Metropolitan Museum of Art Bulletin* 14 (December 1955), pp. 85–102.

Ettinghausen, Richard. "The Bustan Manuscript of Sultan Nasir-Shah Khalji." *Marg* 12 (no. 3, 1959), pp. 40–43.

Ettinghausen, Richard. *Treasures of Turkey*. Geneva, 1966.

Faris, Nabih A., and Miles, George. "An Inscription of Barbak Shah of Bengal." *Ars Islamica* 7 (no. 2, 1940), pp. 141–48.

Fraad, Irma L., and Ettinghausen, Richard. "Sultanate Painting in Persian Style, Primarily from the First Half of the Fifteenth Century: A Preliminary Study." In *Chhavi: Golden Jubilee Volume*. Banaras, 1971, pp. 48–66.

Grube, Ernst J. *Muslim Miniature Painting from the XIII to XIX Century. From Collections in the United States and Canada*. Ex. cat., Venice, Centro di Cultura e Civiltà, 1962.

The Indian Heritage: Court Life and Arts Under Mughal Rule. Ex. cat., London, Victoria and Albert Museum, 1982.

Indian Painting: Mughal and Rajput and a Sultanate Manuscript. Ex. cat., London, P. & D. Colnaghi & Co., 1978.

Ipsiroglu, M. S. *Saray-Alben: Diezsche Klebebände aus den Berliner Sammlungen*. Wiesbaden, 1964.

L'Islam dans les collections nationales. Ex. cat., Paris, Grand Palais, 1977.

Khandalavala, Karl, and Chandra, Moti. "A Ms. of the Laur Chanda in the Prince of Wales Museum." *Bulletin of the Prince of Wales Museum* no. 7 (1959–62), pp. 27–31.

Khandalavala, Karl, and Chandra, Moti. *New Documents of Indian Painting: A Reappraisal*. Bombay, 1969.

Kühnel, Ernst. *Die islamischen Elfenbeinskulpturen VIII–XIII Jahrhundert*. Berlin, 1971.

Lach, Donald F. *A Century of Wonder*. Vol. 2 of *Asia in the Making of Europe*. Chicago, 1970.

Lee, Sherman. *Rajput Painting*. Ex. cat., New York, Asia House Gallery, 1960.

Losty, Jeremiah. *The Art of the Book in India*. Ex. cat., London, British Library, 1982.

Manuscripts from Indian Collections. New Delhi, 1964.

Notable Acquisitions 1981–1982. New York, The Metropolitan Museum of Art, 1982.

Pal, M. K. *Crafts and Craftsmen in Traditional India*. New Delhi, 1978.

Pope, Arthur Upham, ed. *A Survey of Persian Art*, 6 vols. London, 1938–39.

Robinson, B. W. "Areas of Controversy in Islamic Painting: Two Recent Publications." *Apollo* 120 (1984), pp. 32–35.

Robinson, B. W. "Origin and Date of Three Famous Shah-Nameh Illustrations." *Ars Orientalis* 1 (1954), pp. 105–12.

Robinson, B. W. "A Survey of Persian Painting (1350–1896)." In *Art et Société dans le Monde Iranienne*. Ed. C. Adle. Paris, 1982.

Sakisian, Armenag Bey. *La Miniature persane*. Paris, 1929.

Schulz, P. W. *Die persisch-islamische Miniaturmalerei*, 2 vols. Leipzig, 1914.

Simpson, Mariana Shreve. *The Illustrations of an Epic: The Earliest Shah-Nameh Manuscripts*. New York, 1979.

Skelton, Robert. "The Niʿmat-nama: A Landmark of Malwa Painting." *Marg* 12 (no. 3, 1959), pp. 44–50.

Skelton, Robert, and Francis, Mark, eds. *Arts of Bengal: The Heritage of Bangladesh and Eastern India*. Ex. cat., London, Whitechapel Art Gallery, 1979.

Tardy. *Les Ivoires. Deuxième Partie: Antiquité, Islam, Inde, Chine, Japon, Afrique noire, Régions polaires, Amérique*. Paris, 1977.

Welch, Stuart Cary, and Beach, Milo Cleveland. *Gods, Thrones, and Peacocks: Northern Indian Painting from Two Traditions, Fifteenth to Nineteenth Centuries*. Ex. cat., New York, Asia House Gallery, 1965.

THE MUGHALS

Abu'l-Fazl. *Aʾin-i Akbari*. Vol. I, trans. H. Blochmann. Calcutta, 1873. Vols. II and III, trans. H. S. Jarrett. Calcutta, 1891.

Abu'l-Fazl. *Akbarnama*, 3 vols. Trans. H. Beveridge. Calcutta, 1897–1921.

Aga-Oglu, Mehmet. "A Fragment of a Rare Indian Carpet." *Bulletin of the Detroit Institute of Arts* 13 (October 1931), pp. 1–5.

Ansari, Mohd. Azher. "Palaces and Gardens of the Mughals." *Islamic Culture* 33 (1959), pp. 50–72.

Archer, Mildred. *Tippoo's Tiger*. London, 1959.

Arnold, Thomas. *The Library of A. Chester Beatty: A Catalogue of the Indian Miniatures*, 3 vols. Ed. J. V. S. Wilkinson. London, 1936.

Arnold, Thomas. *Painting in Islam: A Study of the Place of Pictorial Art in Muslim Culture*. Oxford, 1928.

Arnold, Thomas, and Grohmann, Adolf. *The Islamic Book*. London, 1929.

Art at Auction: The Year at Sotheby's Parke-Bernet, 1970–71. New York, 1971.

The Art of India and Pakistan. Ex. cat., London, The Royal Academy of Arts, 1947.

Arts de l'Islam des origines à 1700 dans les collections publiques françaises. Ex. cat., Paris, Musée de l'Orangerie, 1971.

The Arts of India and Nepal: The Nasli and Alice Heeramaneck Collection. Ex. cat., Boston, Museum of Fine Arts, 1966.

The Arts of Islam. Ex. cat., London, Hayward Gallery, 1976.

Babur. *The Babur-nama in English (Memoirs of Babur),* 2 vols. Trans. and ed. Annette S. Beveridge. London, 1922. Reprinted, New York, 1971.

Bancroft, Peter. "Great Gems and Crystal Mines." *Gems and Gemology* 17 (1981), p. 113.

Bariand, Pierre, and Poirot, Jean-Paul. *Larousse des pierres précieuses.* Paris, 1985.

Barrett, Douglas, and Gray, Basil. *Painting of India.* Lausanne, 1963.

Beach, Milo Cleveland. *The Grand Mogul.* Ex. cat., Williamstown, Sterling and Francine Clark Art Institute, 1978.

Beatson, Alexander. *A View of the Origin and Conduct of the War with Tipoo Sultaun: Comprising a Narrative of the Operations of the Army Under the Command of Lieutenant-General George Harris, and of the Siege of Seringapatam.* London, 1800.

Beattie, May H. *The Thyssen-Bornemisza Collection of Oriental Rugs.* Castagnola, 1972.

Bernheimer, Richard. *Romanische Tierplastik und die Ursprünge ihrer Motive.* Munich, 1931.

Bernier, F. *Travels in the Mogul Empire.* Ed. A. Constable. Westminster, 1891. Reprinted, New Delhi, 1968.

Bidpai. *The Anvar-i Suhaili; or the Lights of Canopus: Being the Persian Version of the Fables of Pilpay.* Trans. Edward Backhouse Eastwick. Hertford, 1854.

Binney, Edwin. *Indian Miniature Painting from the Collection of Edwin Binney, 3rd: Mughal and Deccani Schools.* Portland, Ore., 1973.

Binyon, Lawrence. *A Persian Painting of the 16th Century: Emperors and Princes of the House of Timur.* London, 1930.

Binyon, Lawrence, and Arnold, T. W. *Court Painters of the Grand Moguls.* Oxford, 1921.

Blochet, E. *Collection Jean Pozzi: Miniatures persanes et indo-persanes.* Paris, 1930.

Breck, Joseph. "An Early Mughal Painting." *Metropolitan Museum Studies* 2 (1929–30), pp. 133–34.

Brijbhushan, Jamila. *The World of Indian Miniatures.* New York, 1979.

Brown, Percy. *Indian Painting Under the Mughals, A.D. 1550 to A.D. 1750.* Oxford, 1924.

Bukhari, Y. K. "An Unpublished Illuminated Manuscript Entitled Fawaid-i Qutb Shahi." *Lalit Kala* 13 (1967), pp. 8–11.

Camps, Arnulf. *Jerome Xavier, S.J., and the Muslims of the Mogul Empire: Controversial Works and Missionary Activity.* Schöneck, 1956.

Caplan, A. "An Important Carved Emerald from the Mogul Period of India." *Lapidary Journal* 22 (1968), pp. 1336–37.

Chaitanya, Krishna. *A History of Indian Painting: Manuscript, Moghul and Deccani Traditions.* New Delhi, 1979.

Chandra, Moti. *Indian Art.* Bombay, 1964.

Chandra, Pramod. *The Tuti-Nama of the Cleveland Museum of Art.* Graz, 1976.

Chandra, Pramod. "Two Early Mughal Metal Cups." *Bulletin of the Prince of Wales Museum,* no. 5 (1955–57), pp. 57–60.

Chardin, Jean-Baptiste. *Travels in Persia.* London, 1720. Ed. N. M. Penzer. London, 1927.

Clarke, S. *Indian Drawings.* London, 1922.

Coomaraswamy, Ananda K. *Catalogue of the Indian Collections in the Museum of Fine Arts, Boston. Part VI: Mughal Painting.* Cambridge, Mass., 1930.

Coomaraswamy, Ananda K. "Notes on Mughal Painting, 2." *Artibus Asiae,* no. 3 (1927), pp. 202–12.

Correia-Afonso, John. *Letters from the Mughal Court: The First Jesuit Mission to Akbar.* Anand, 1980.

Das, Asok Kumar. "Bishndas." In *Chhavi: Golden Jubilee Volume.* Banaras, 1971, pp. 183–91.

Das, Asok Kumar. "Calligraphers and Painters in Early Mughal Painting." In *Chhavi 2: Rai Krishnadasa Felicitation Volume.* Banaras, 1981, pp. 92–97.

Das, Asok Kumar. *Mughal Painting During Jahangir's Time.* Calcutta, 1978.

Das, Asok Kumar. *Treasures of Indian Painting from the Maharaja Sawai Man Singh II Museum,* ser. 4. Jaipur, 1983.

Delhi Museum of Archaeology. *Loan Exhibition of Antiquities Coronation Durbar, 1911: An Illustrated Selection of the Principal Exhibits.* Calcutta, [1912].

Dickson, Martin Bernard, and Welch, Stuart Cary. *The Houghton Shahnameh,* 2 vols. Cambridge, Mass., 1981.

Dikshit, M. G. *History of Indian Glass.* Bombay, 1969.

Dimand, Maurice. "A Persian Velvet Carpet." *Bulletin of the Metropolitan Museum of Art* 22 (1927), pp. 247–51.

Edwardes, Michael. *The Orchid House: Splendours and Miseries of the Kingdom of Oudh, 1827–1857.* London, 1960.

Erdman, K. *700 Years of Oriental Carpets.* Trans. M. H. Beattie and H. Hertzog. London, 1970.

Ettinghausen, Richard. "Near Eastern Book Covers: A Report on the Exhibition History of Bookbinding at the Baltimore Museum of Art." *Ars Orientalis* 3 (1959), pp. 113–31.

Ettinghausen, Richard. *Paintings of the Sultans and Emperors of India in American Collections.* Delhi, 1961.

"Exhibition of Islamic Jades." *Oriental Art* n.s. 12 (1966), pp. 202–3.

Falk, Toby, and Archer, Mildred. *Indian Miniatures in the India Office Library.* London, 1981.

Ferishta, Mahomed Kasim. *History of the Rise of the Mahomedan Power in India till the Year A.D. 1612,* 4 vols. Trans. John Briggs. London, 1829. Reprinted, Calcutta, 1908–10.

Ferrão de Tavares e Tavora, Bernardo. *Imaginaria Luso-Oriental.* Lisbon, 1983.

Fontein, Jan, and Pal, Pratapaditya. *Museum of Fine Arts, Boston: Oriental Art.* Boston, 1969.

Foster, William, ed. *Early Travels in India 1583–1619.* London, 1921. Reprinted, New Delhi, 1968.

Gans-Ruedin, E. *Indian Carpets.* Trans. Valerie Howard. London, 1984.

Gascoigne, Bamber. *The Great Moghuls.* New York, 1971.

Goddard, Yedda A. "Un Album de portraits des princes timurides de l'Inde." *Athar-e Iran* 2 (1937), pp. 179–277.

Goetz, Hermann. *Bilderatlas zur Kulturgeschichte indiens in der Grossmoghul-Zeit.* Berlin, 1930.

Grube, Ernst. *The Classical Style in Islamic Painting: The Early School of Herat and Its Impact on Islamic Painting of the 15th, the 16th and 17th Centuries.* Geneva, 1968.

Grube, Ernst. *The World of Islam.* New York, 1966.

Habib, Irfan. *An Atlas of the Mughal Empire: Political and Economic Maps, with Detailed Notes, Bibliography and Index.* New Delhi, 1982.

Hambly, Gavin. *Cities of Mughal India.* New York, 1968.

Hassan, Zaki M. *Moslem Art in the Fouad I University Museum.* Cairo, 1950—.

Heeramaneck, Alice. *Masterpieces of Indian Painting in the Nasli M. Heeramaneck Collection.* New York, 1985.

Hendley, Thomas H. *Memorials of the Jeypore Exhibition 1883,* 4 vols. London, 1883.

Hendley, Thomas H. *Ulwar and Its Art Treasures.* London, 1888.

The History of Bookbinding 525–1950 A.D. Ex. cat., Baltimore, Walters Art Gallery, 1957.

Hofer, Philip. "A Collector." In *Approach to Drawings.* New York, 1963.

Hôtel Drouot, Paris, November 23, 1960. Sale cat., *Collection Sévadjian: Peintures et dessins de la perse et des indes.*

In the Image of Man: The Indian Perception of the Universe Through 2000 Years of Painting and Sculpture. Ex. cat., London, Hayward Gallery, 1982.

The Indian Heritage: Court Life and Arts Under Mughal Rule. Ex. cat., London, Victoria and Albert Museum, 1982.

Indian Painting: Mughal and Rajput and a Sultanate Manuscript. Ex. cat., London, P. & D. Colnaghi & Co., 1978.

Irwin, John. *Indian Embroidery.* London, 1951.

Irwin, John. *The Kashmir Shawls.* London, 1973.

Irwin, John, and Hall, Margaret. *Historic Textiles of India at the Calico Museum: Indian Painted and Printed Fabrics.* Ahmedabad, 1971.

L'Islam dans les collections nationales. Ex. cat., Paris, Grand Palais, 1977.

Islamic Art in the Kuwait National Museum: The al-Sabah Collection. Ed. Marilyn Jenkins. London, 1983.

"Islamic Jade." *Metropolitan Museum of Art Bulletin* 33 (1975), p. 48.

"Islamic Painting." *Metropolitan Museum of Art Bulletin* 36 (Fall 1978), p. 39.

Ives, Edward. *A Voyage from England to India in the Year 1754.* London, 1773.

Jahangir. *The Tuzuk-i-Jahangiri; or Memoirs of Jahangiri,* 2 vols. Trans. Alexander Rogers. Ed. Henry Beveridge. London, 1909–14.

James, D. *Islamic Masterpieces of the Chester Beatty Library.* London, 1981.

Jauhar. *The Tezkereh al Vakiat; or, Private Memoirs of the Emperor Humayun.* Trans. Charles Stewart. Santiago de Compostela, n.d.

Joyaux et saris de l'Inde du XVIIIe au XIXe siècle. Paris, 1983.

Katalog 1971: Ausgestellte Werke. Ex. cat., Berlin, Museum für Indische Kunst, 1971.

Kühnel, Ernst, and Goetz, Hermann. *Indian Book Painting from Jahangir's Album in the State Library in Berlin.* London, 1926.

Lall, John, and Dube, D. N. *Taj Mahal and the Glory of Mughal Agra.* New Delhi, 1982.

Lerner, Martin. *The Flame and the Lotus: Indian and Southeast Asian Art from the Kronos Collection.* Ex. cat., New York, The Metropolitan Museum of Art, 1984.

Leth, André. *Islamic Arms and Armour from Private Danish Collections.* Copenhagen, 1982.

Leyden, Rudolf von; Duda, Dorothea; and Roschanzamir, Mehdi. *Spielkarten-Bilder in persischen Lackmalereien.* Vienna, n.d.

Losty, Jeremiah. *The Art of the Book in India.* Ex. cat., London, British Library, 1982.

Lowry, Glenn, and Brand, Michael. *Akbar's India: Art from the Mughal City of Victory.* Ex. cat., New York, Asia Society, forthcoming.

Maclagen, E. D. *The Jesuits and the Great Mogul.* London, 1932.

Manuscripts from Indian Collections. New Delhi, 1964.

Martin, F. R. *The Miniature Painting and Painters of Persia, India and Turkey from the 8th to the 18th Century,* 2 vols. London, 1912.

Mehta, Nanalal Chamanal. *Studies in Indian Painting: A Survey of Some New Material Ranging from the Commencement of the VIIth Century to Circa 1870.* Bombay, 1926.

Metropolitan Museum of Art. *Art Treasures of the Metropolitan.* New York, 1952.

Metropolitan Museum of Art. *The Guennol Collection.* Ed. I. E. Rubin. Vol. 2, New York, 1982.

Migeon, Gaston. *Exposition des arts musulmans.* Ex. cat., Paris, Musée des Arts Décoratifs, 1903.

Mittal, Jagdish. "Indo-Islamic Metal and Glassware." In *An Age of Splendour: Islamic Art in India.* Bombay, 1983, pp. 60–71 (*Marg* 1983).

Moes, Robert. *Auspicious Spirits: Korean Folk Paintings and Related Objects.* Ex. cat., Washington, D.C., International Exhibitions Foundation, 1983.

Morley, Grace. "On Applied Arts of India in Bharat Kala Bavan." In *Chhavi: Golden Jubilee Volume.* Banaras, 1971, pp. 107–29.

Murphy, Veronica. "A Note on Some Recently Discovered Tipu Shawl Fragments in England and Comparative Material in the Bharat Kala Bhavan." In *Chhavi 2: Rai Krishnadasa Felicitation Volume.* Banaras, 1981, pp. 161–69.

Nath, Nardindar, and Khandalavala, Karl. "Illustrated Islamic Manuscripts." In *An Age of Splendour: Islamic Art in India.* Bombay, 1983, pp. 34–51 (*Marg* 1983).

Nigam, M. L. "The Mughal Jades of India." In *An Age of Splendour: Islamic Art in India.* Bombay, 1983, pp. 76–84 (*Marg* 1983).

Notable Acquisitions 1982–1983. New York, The Metropolitan Museum of Art, 1983.

Notable Acquisitions 1983–1984. New York, The Metropolitan Museum of Art, 1984.

Os Descobrimentos portugueses e à Europa do Renascimento: A mão que ao ocidente o véu rasgou. Ex. cat., Lisbon, Armaria, 1983 (Council of Europe, *XVII Exposicão Europeia de Arte, Ciencia e Cultura*).

Paintings from the Muslim Courts of India. Ex. cat., London, British Museum (Prints and Drawings Gallery), 1976.

Parke-Bernet, New York, December 15, 1962. Sale cat., *Classical and Near Eastern Art Collected by the Late Hagop Kevorkian.*

Perdigão, José de Azaredo. *Calouste Gulbenkian Collectionneur.* Trans. Hélène Bourgeois. Lisbon, 1969.

Persian and Mughal Art. Ex. cat., London, P. & D. Colnaghi & Co., 1976.

Pope, Arthur Upham, ed. *A Survey of Persian Art,* 6 vols. London, 1938–39.

Porter, Robert Ker. *The Storming of Seringapatam* London, 1803.

Raghaven, V. *Srngaramanjarai of Saint Akbar Shah.* Hyderabad, 1951.

Rarities of the Musée Guimet. Ex. cat., New York, Asia House Gallery, 1975.

"Recent Sales." *Oriental Art* n.s. 29 (1983), p. 308, no. 29.

Riegl, A. *Oriental Carpets.* Trans. C. Purdon Clark. Vienna, 1892.

Rogers, J. M. *Islamic Art and Design: 1500–1700.* Ex. cat., London, British Museum, 1983.

Russell, Ralph, and Islam, Khurshidul. *Three Mughal Poets: Mir, Sauda, Mir Hasan.* Cambridge, Mass., 1968.

Saksena, B. P. *History of Shahjahan of Dilhi.* Allahabad, 1958.

Sarre, F., and Trenkwald, H. *Old Oriental Carpets,* 2 vols. Trans. A. F. Kendrick. Vienna, 1926.

Schimmel, Annemarie. *Classical Urdu Literature from the Beginning to Iqbal.* In *A History of Indian Literature.* Ed. J. Gonda. Wiesbaden, 1975—.

Schimmel, Annemarie. *Islam in India and Pakistan.* Fasc. 9 of sec. 22 in *Iconography of Religions.* Ed. T. P. van Baaren. Leiden, 1982.

Schimmel, Annemarie. *Islam in the Indian Subcontinent.* Leiden, 1980.

Schimmel, Annemarie. *Mystical Dimensions of Islam.* Chapel Hill, 1975.

Schimmel, Annemarie, and Welch, Stuart Cary. *Anvari's Divan: A Pocket Book for Akbar.* New York, 1983.

Shah-nawaz Khan and 'Abd al Hakk. *The Maasiru-l-Umara.* Trans. H. Beveridge. Calcutta, 1911. Reprinted, New Delhi, 1979.

Shyam, Radhey. *The Kingdom of Ahmadnagar.* Delhi, 1966.

Shyam, Radhey. *Life and Times of Malik Ambar.* Delhi, 1968.

Sinkankas, John. *Emerald and Other Beryls.* Radnor, Pa., 1981.

Skelton, Robert. "The Mughal Artist Farrokh Beg." *Ars Orientalis* 2 (1957), pp. 393–411.

Skelton, Robert. "The Relations Between the Chinese and Indian Jade Carving Traditions." In *The Western Influence of the Chinese Arts from the 14th to the 18th Century.* Ed. W. Watson. London, 1972 (Colloquies on Art and Archaeology in Asia, no. 3).

Skelton, Robert. "The Shah Jahan Jade Cup." *Victoria and Albert Museum Bulletin* 2 (1966), pp. 109–10.

Skelton, Robert. *Shah Jahan's Jade Cup.* London, 1978 (Victoria and Albert Museum Masterpieces).

Skelton, Robert. "Shaykh Phul and the Origins of Bundi Painting." In *Chhavi 2: Rai Krishnadasa Felicitation Volume.* Banaras, 1981, pp. 123–29.

Smart, Ellen. "Six Folios from a Dispersed Manuscript of the *Babarnama.*" In *Indian Painting: Mughal and Rajput and a Sultanate Manuscript.* Ex. cat., London, P. & D. Colnaghi & Co., 1978, pp. 109–32.

Smith, Edmund. *The Moghul Architecture of Fathpur-Sikri,* 4 vols. Delhi, 1894–98. Reprinted, Varanasi, 1973.

Sotheby's, London, November 24, 1952. Sale cat.

Sotheby's, London, December 16, 1971. Sale cat.

Sotheby's, London, April 22, 1983. Sale cat., *Catalogue of Jewels for the Collector.*

Sotheby's, London, June 20, 1983. Sale cat., *Fine Oriental Miniatures and Manuscripts, Including Drawings from the Pan Asian Collection.*

Sotheby's, London, October 15, 1984. Sale cat., *Important Oriental Manuscripts and Miniatures.*

Soustiel, Paris, 1970. Sale cat., *Catalogue de la collection Jean Pozzi: Miniatures indiennes et orientales.*

Stchoukine, Ivan. *La Peinture indienne à l'époque des Grands Moghols.* Paris, 1929.

Stchoukine, Ivan. "Portraits moghols: La Collection du Baron Maurice de Rothschild." *Revue des arts asiatiques* 9 (1935), pp. 190–208.

Stronge, Susan. "Mughal Jewellery." *Newsletter of the Society of Jewellery Historians* 2 (July 1982), pp. 2–6.

Strzygowski, J. *Die indischen Miniaturen im Schlosse Schonbrunn.* Vienna, 1923.

Sweat of the Sun, Tears of the Moon: Gold and Emerald Treasures of Colombia. Ex. cat., Natural History Museum of the County of Los Angeles, 1981.

Tavernier, Jean-Baptiste. *Travels in India,* 2 vols. Trans. V. Ball. Ed. William Crooke. London, 1925. Reprinted, New Delhi, 1971.

Teng, Shu'ping. *Catalogue of a Special Exhibition of Hindustan Jade in the National Palace Museum.* Ex. cat., Taipei, National Palace Museum.

Titley, Norah M. *Miniatures from Persian Manuscripts: Catalogue and Subject Index of Paintings from Persia, India and Turkey in the British Library and the British Museum.* London, 1977.

Topsfield, A. *An Introduction to Indian Court Painting.* London, 1984.

Upton, Joseph M. "A Gift of Jade." *Metropolitan Museum of Art Bulletin* 25 (1930), p. 22.

Victoria and Albert Museum. *Indian Art.* London, 1969.

Walker, Daniel S. "Classical Indian Rugs." *Hali* 4 (1982), pp. 252–56.

Welch, Anthony. *Calligraphy in the Arts of the Islamic World.* New York, 1979.

Welch, Anthony, and Welch, Stuart Cary. *Arts of the Islamic Book: The Collection of Prince Sadruddin Aga Khan.* Ex. cat., New York, Asia Society, 1982.

Welch, Stuart Cary. *The Art of Mughal India: Painting and Precious Objects.* Ex. cat., New York, Asia Society, 1964.

Welch, Stuart Cary. *A Flower from Every Meadow.* New York, 1973.

Welch, Stuart Cary. *Imperial Mughal Painting.* New York, 1978.

Welch, Stuart Cary. *Indian Drawings and Painted Sketches.* New York, 1976.

Welch, Stuart Cary. *A King's Book of Kings: The Shahnameh of Shah Tahmasp.* New York, 1972.

Welch, Stuart Cary. "A Lion-King's Lion." In *Felicitation Volume in Honour of Smt. Pupul Jayakar.* Ed. Lokesh Chandra. New Delhi, forthcoming.

Welch, Stuart Cary. "Mughal and Deccani Miniature Paintings from a Private Collection." *Ars Orientalis* 5 (1963), pp. 221–34.

Welch, Stuart Cary. "The Paintings of Basawan." *Lalit Kala* 10 (1961), pp. 7–17.

Welch, Stuart Cary. *Room for Wonder: Indian Painting During the British Period 1760–1880.* Ex. cat., New York, American Federation of Arts, 1978.

Welch, Stuart Cary. "Two Shahs, Some Miniatures and the Boston Carpet." *Boston Museum Bulletin* 69 (1971), pp. 6–14.

Wilkinson, J. V. S. *Mughal Painting.* London, 1948.

Yule, H., and Burnell, A. C. *Hobson-Jobson: A Glossary of Colloquial Anglo-Indian Words and Phrases and of Kindred Terms, Etymological, Historical, Geographical and Discursive.* Ed. William Crooke. London, 1903.

Zebrowski, Mark. "Decorative Arts of the Mughal Period." In *The Arts of India.* Ed. Basil Gray. Ithaca, N.Y., 1981.

THE SULTANS OF THE DECCAN

Archer, W. G. *Indian Miniatures.* London, 1960.

Arnold, Thomas. *The Library of A. Chester Beatty: A Catalogue of the Indian Miniatures,* 3 vols. Ed. J. V. S. Wilkinson. London, 1936.

The Art of India and Pakistan. Ex. cat., London, The Royal Academy of Arts, 1947.

Barrett, Douglas. *Painting of the Deccan, XVI–XVII Century.* London, 1958.

Barrett, Douglas, and Gray, Basil. *Painting of India.* Lausanne, 1963.

Bilgrami, S. A. A. *Landmarks of the Deccan.* Hyderabad, 1927.

Binney, Edwin. *Indian Miniature Painting from the Collection of Edwin Binney, 3rd: Mughal and Deccani Schools.* Portland, Ore., 1973.

Blochet, E. *Collection Jean Pozzi: Miniatures persanes et indo-persanes.* Paris, 1930.

Blochet, E. *Les Enluminures des manuscrits orientaux—turcs, arabes, persans—de la Bibliothèque Nationale.* Paris, 1926.

Chaitanya, Krishna. *A History of Indian Painting: Manuscript, Moghul and Deccani Traditions.* New Delhi, 1979.

Chandra, M. "Portraits of Ibrahim Adil Shah." *Marg* 5 (no. 1, 1951), pp. 22–28.

Clouzot, Henry, and Morris, Frances. *Painted and Printed Fabrics.* New York, 1927.

Coomaraswamy, Ananda K. *Les Miniatures orientales de la collection Goloubew au Museum of Fine Arts.* Paris, 1929 (*Ars Asiatica* 13).

Cousens, Henry. *Bijapur and Its Architectural Remains.* Vol. 37 of *Archaeological Survey of India.* Bombay, 1916. Reprinted, New Delhi, 1976.

Dahmen-Dallapiccola, Anna Libera. *Ragamala-Miniaturen von 1475 bis 1700.* Wiesbaden, 1975.

Das, Asok Kumar. *Treasures of Indian Painting from the Maharaja Sawai Man Singh II Museum,* ser. 1. Jaipur, 1976.

Eaton, Richard Maxwell. *Sufis of Bijapur.* Princeton, 1978.

Ebeling, Klaus. *Ragamala Painting.* Basel, 1973.

Fehervari, Geza. "The Near East, the Middle East and India." In *Lacquer: An International History and Illustrated Survey.* London, 1984.

Frederic, Louis. *Indian Temples and Sculpture.* London, 1959.

Gittinger, Mattiebelle. *Master Dyers of the World: Technique and Trade in Early Indian Dyed Cotton Textiles.* Washington, D.C., 1982.

Goetz, Hermann. *Geschichte der indischen Miniaturmalerei.* Berlin, 1934.

Gowd, K. V. N. "Bidriware." In *Census of India 1961. Volume II, Andhra Pradesh, Part VII-A(3): Selected Crafts of Andhra Pradesh.* Delhi, 1967.

Gray, Basil. "Deccani Paintings: The School of Bijapur." *Burlington Magazine* 73 (1938), pp. 74–76.

Gray, Basil. "Portraits from Bijapur." *British Museums Quarterly* 11 (1936–37), pp. 183–85.

Haq, M. Mahfuzul. "The Khan Khanan and His Painters, Illuminators and Calligraphists." *Islamic Culture* 5 (1931), pp. 621–31.

In the Image of Man: The Indian Perception of the Universe Through 2000 Years of Painting and Sculpture. Ex. cat., London, Hayward Gallery, 1982.

The Indian Heritage: Court Life and Arts Under Mughal Rule. Ex. cat., London, Victoria and Albert Museum, 1982.

Irvine, William. *The Army of the Indian Moghuls: Its Organization and Administration.* London, 1903. Reprinted, New Delhi, 1962.

Irwin, John. "Golconda Cotton Paintings of the Early Seventeenth Century." *Lalit Kala* 5 (1959), pp. 11–48.

Irwin, John, and Brett, Katharine B. *Origins of Chintz.* London, 1970.

Kaufmann, Walter. *The Ragas of North India.* Bloomington, 1968.

Manucci, Niccolao. *Storia do Mogor*, 4 vols. Trans. William Irvine. London, 1907.

Mittal, Jagdish. "Indo-Islamic Metal and Glassware." In *An Age of Splendour: Islamic Art in India.* Bombay, 1983, pp. 60–71 (*Marg* 1983).

Morris, Frances. "An Indian Hanging." *Metropolitan Museum of Art Bulletin* 20 (1925), pp. 143, 149–52.

Muhammad, Sayyid. *Divan-i ʿAbdullah Qutb Shah.* Hyderabad, 1959.

Notable Acquisitions 1982–1983. New York, The Metropolitan Museum of Art, 1983.

Nouveau Drouot-Salle, Paris, June 24, 1982. *Miniatures orientales, miniatures mogholes et indiennes du XVIe au XIXe siècle.*

Paintings from the Muslim Courts of India. Ex. cat., London, British Museum (Prints and Drawings Gallery), 1976.

The Rathbone Years: Masterpieces Acquired for the Fine Arts Museum, Boston, 1955–1972, and for the St. Louis Art Museum, 1940–1955. Ex. cat., Boston, Museum of Fine Arts, 1972.

Schimmel, Annemarie, and Welch, Stuart Cary. *Anvari's Divan: A Pocket Book for Akbar.* New York, 1983.

Skelton, Robert. "Documents for the Study of Painting at Bijapur in the Late 16th and Early 17th Centuries." *Arts Asiatiques* 5 (1958), pp. 97–125.

Skelton, Robert. "The Mughal Artist Farrokh Beg." *Ars Orientalis* 2 (1957), pp. 393–411.

Skelton, Robert. *Rajasthani Temple Hangings of the Krishna Cult from the Collection of Karl Mann.* Ex. cat., New York, American Federation of Arts, 1973.

Soustiel, Jean, and David, Marie-Christine. *Miniatures orientales de l'Inde: Les écoles et leur styles.* Paris, 1974.

Stronge, Susan. "Decorative Arts." In *The Arts of Bengal.* Ed. Robert Skelton and Mark Francis. London, 1971.

Strzygowski, J.; Kramrisch, Stella; and Wellesz, Emmy. *Asiatische Miniaturmalerei.* Klagenfurt, 1933.

Talwar, Kay, and Krishna, Kalyan. *Indian Pigment Painting on Cloth.* Ahmedabad, 1978.

Taylor, Meadows. *Architecture at Beejapore.* London, 1866.

Topsfield, A. *An Introduction to Indian Court Painting.* London, 1984.

Varma, D. C. *History of Bijapur.* New Delhi, 1974.

Welch, Stuart Cary. *A Flower from Every Meadow.* New York, 1973.

Welch, Stuart Cary. *Indian Drawings and Painted Sketches.* New York, 1976.

Wheeler, Monroe, ed. *Textiles and Ornaments of India.* Ex. cat., New York, Museum of Modern Art, 1956.

Zebrowski, Mark. "Bidri: Metalware from the Islamic Courts of India." *Arts East* 1 (1982).

Zebrowski, Mark. *Deccani Painting.* London, 1983.

Zebrowski, Mark. "Indian Lacquerwork and the Antecedents of the Qajar Style." In *Lacquerwork in Asia and Beyond.* Ed. W. Watson. London, 1982 (Colloquies in Art and Archaeology in Asia, no. 11).

Zebrowski, Mark. "Transformations in Seventeenth Century Deccani Painting at Bijapur." In *Chhavi 2: Rai Krishnadasa Felicitation Volume.* Banaras, 1981, pp. 170–81.

IV. THE RAJPUT WORLD

Abu'l-Fazl. *Aʾin-i Akbari.* Vol. I, trans. H. Blochmann. Calcutta, 1873. Vols. II and III, trans. H. S. Jarrett. Calcutta, 1891.

Andhare, Shridhar, and Singh, Rawat Nahar. *Devgarh Painting.* New Delhi, 1983 (Lalit Kala Series Portfolio, no. 25).

Archer, Mildred. *Indian Painting in Bundi and Kotah.* London, 1951.

Archer, W. G. *Indian Miniatures.* London, 1960.

The Art of India and Pakistan. Ex. cat., London, The Royal Academy of Arts, 1947.

Askari, S. H. "Kutban's Mrigavat: A Unique Ms. in Persian Script." *Journal of the Bihar Research Society* 46 (1955), pp. 452–87.

Beach, Milo Cleveland. "Painting at Devgarh." *Archives of Asian Art* 24 (1970–71), pp. 23–35.

Beach, Milo Cleveland. *Rajput Painting at Bundi and Kota.* Ascona, 1974.

Brijbhushan, Jamila. *The World of Indian Miniatures.* New York, 1979.

Chandra, Moti. *Mewar Painting.* New Delhi, 1957.

Chandra, Moti. *Studies in Early Indian Paintings.* New York, 1970.

Crooke, William. *The Tribes and Castes of the North Western Province and Oudh*, 4 vols. Calcutta, 1896.

Das, Asok Kumar. *Treasures of Indian Painting from the Maharaja Sawai Man Singh II Museum*, ser. 3. Jaipur, 1979.

Dickinson, Eric, and Khandalavala, Karl. *Kishangarh Painting.* Delhi, 1959.

Dickson, Martin Bernard, and Welch, Stuart Cary. *The Houghton Shahnameh*, 2 vols. Cambridge, Mass., 1981.

In the Image of Man: The Indian Perception of the Universe Through 2000 Years of Painting and Sculpture. Ex. cat., London, Hayward Gallery, 1982.

The Indian Heritage: Court Life and Arts Under Mughal Rule. Ex. cat., London, Victoria and Albert Museum, 1982.

Irvine, William. *The Army of the Indian Moghuls: Its Organization and Administration.* London, 1903. Reprinted, New Delhi, 1962.

Kaufmann, Walter. *The Ragas of North India.* Bloomington, 1968.

Khandalavala, Karl. "The Mrigavat of Bharat Kala Bhavan: As a Social Document and Its Date and Provenance." In *Chhavi: Golden Jubilee Volume.* Banaras, 1971, pp. 19–36.

Khandalavala, Karl, and Chandra, Moti. *An Illustrated Aranyaka Parvan in the Asiatic Society of Bombay.* Bombay, 1974.

Khandalavala, Karl, and Chandra, Moti. *New Documents of Indian Painting: A Reappraisal.* Bombay, 1969.

Khandalavala, Karl; Chandra, Moti; and Chandra, Pramod. *Miniature Painting: A Catalogue of the Sri Motichand Khajanchi Collection.* Ex. cat., New Delhi, Lalit Kala Akademi, 1960.

Khandalavala, Karl, and Mittal, Jagdish. "The Bhagavata Mss from Palam and Isarda: A Consideration in Style." *Lalit Kala* 16 (1974), pp. 28–32.

Krishna, Anand. "An Illustrated Manuscript of the Laur-Chanda in the Staatsbibliothek, Berlin." In *Chhavi 2: Rai Krishnadasa Felicitation Volume.* Banaras, 1981, pp. 275–89.

Krishna, Anand. *Malwa Painting.* Banaras, 1963.

Krishnadasa, Rai. "An Illustrated Avadhi of Laur-Chanda in the Bharat Kala Bhavan, Banaras." *Lalit Kala* 1–2 (1955–56), pp. 66–71.

Lee, Sherman. *Rajput Painting.* Ex. cat., New York, Asia House Gallery, 1960.

Lerner, Martin. *The Flame and the Lotus: Indian and Southeast Asian Art from the Kronos Collection.* Ex. cat., New York, The Metropolitan Museum of Art, 1984.

Mehta, Nanalal Chamanal. *Studies in Indian Painting: A Survey of Some New Material Ranging from the Commencement of the VIIth Century to Circa 1870 A.D.* Bombay, 1926.

Painting in British India 1757–1857. Ex. cat., Brunswick, Maine, Bowdoin College, 1963.

Pal, P. *The Classical Tradition in Rajput Painting.* Ex. cat., New York, Pierpont Morgan Library, 1978.

Pant, G. M. *Studies in Indian Weapons and Warfare.* New Delhi, 1970.

Patnaik, N., and Welch, Stuart Cary. *A Second Paradise*. New York, 1985.

Randhawa, Mohinder Singh, and Randhawa, Doris Schreier. *Kishangarh Painting*. Bombay, 1980.

Shiveshwarkar, Leela. *The Pictures of the Chaurapanchasika: A Sanskrit Love Lyric*. New Delhi, 1967.

Skelton, Robert. *Rajasthani Temple Hangings of the Krishna Cult from the Collection of Karl Mann*. Ex. cat., New York, American Federation of Arts, 1973.

Skelton, Robert. "Shaykh Phul and the Origins of Bundi Painting." In *Chhavi/2: Rai Krishnadasa Felicitation Volume*. Banaras, 1981, pp. 123–29.

Solvyns, Balthazar. *A Collection of 250 Coloured Etchings: Descriptive of the Manners, Customs, Character, Dress and Religious Ceremonies of the Hindoos*. Calcutta, 1799.

Tod, James. *Annals and Antiquities of Rajasthan*, 3 vols. Ed. W. Crooke. London, 1920.

Topsfield, A. *An Introduction to Indian Court Painting*. London, 1984.

Welch, Stuart Cary. *The Art of Mughal India: Painting and Precious Objects*. Ex. cat., New York, Asia Society, 1964.

Welch, Stuart Cary. *A Flower from Every Meadow*. New York, 1973.

Welch, Stuart Cary. *Indian Drawings and Painted Sketches*. New York, 1976.

Welch, Stuart Cary. "Return to Kotah." In *Essays on Near Eastern Art and Archaeology in Honor of Charles Kyrle Wilkinson*. Ed. Prudence Harper and Holly Pittman. New York, 1983.

Welch, Stuart Cary. "Review of *Bundi Painting* by P. Chandra." *Ars Orientalis* 5 (1963), pp. 293–95.

Welch, Stuart Cary, and Beach, Milo Cleveland. *Gods, Thrones, and Peacocks: Northern Indian Painting from Two Traditions, Fifteenth to Nineteenth Centuries*. Ex. cat., New York, Asia House Gallery, 1965.

Yule, H., and Burnell, A. C. *Hobson-Jobson: A Glossary of Colloquial Anglo-Indian Words and Phrases and of Kindred Terms, Etymological, Historical, Geographical and Discursive*. Ed. William Crooke. London, 1903.

THE PUNJAB PLAINS AND HILLS

Aijazuddin, F. S. *Pahari Paintings and Sikh Portraits in the Lahore Museum*. London, 1977.

Archer, W. G. *Indian Miniatures*. London, 1960.

Archer, W. G. *Indian Painting in the Punjab Hills: Essays*. London, 1952.

Archer, W. G. *Indian Paintings from the Punjab Hills: A Survey and History of Pahari Miniature Painting*, 2 vols. London, 1973.

Archer, W. G. *Paintings of the Sikhs*. London, 1966.

Archer, W. G., and Czuma, Stanislaw. *Indian Art from the George P. Bickford Collection*. Ex. cat., Cleveland Museum of Art, 1975.

The Art of India and Pakistan. Ex. cat., London, The Royal Academy of Arts, 1947.

Barr, W. *Journal of a March from Delhi to Peshawur and from Thence to Cabul, Including Travels in the Punjab*. London, 1844.

Brijbhushan, Jamila. *The World of Indian Miniatures*. New York, 1979.

Chandra, Moti. *Indian Art*, 2nd ed., rev. & enl. Bombay, 1964.

Coomaraswamy, Ananda. *Rajput Paintings*, 2 vols. London, 1916.

Ebeling, Klaus. *Ragamala Painting*. Basel, 1973.

Eden, Emily. *Up the Country*. London, 1966.

"Folk Textiles from Chamba, Bengal and Western India: 18th–20th Century." *Hali* 4 (1982), pp. 279–80.

Glynn, Catherine. "Early Painting in Mandi." *Artibus Asiae* 44 (1983), pp. 21–64.

Goetz, Hermann. "An Early Basohli-Chamba Rumal." *Bulletin of the Baroda State Museum and Picture Gallery* 3 (no. 1, 1947), pp. 35–45.

Goetz, Hermann. *Geschichte der indischen Miniaturmalerei*. Berlin, 1934.

Goswamy, B. N. "Pahari Painting: The Family on the Basis of Style." *Marg* 21 (no. 4, 1968), pp. 17–62.

Goswamy, B. N. "The Problem of the Artist Nainsukh of Jasrota." *Artibus Asiae* 28 (1966), pp. 205–10.

Gupta, S. N. *Catalogue of the Paintings in the Central Museum, Lahore*. Calcutta, 1922.

Hardinge, C. *Recollections of India*. London, 1847.

In the Image of Man: The Indian Perception of the Universe Through 2000 Years of Painting and Sculpture. Ex. cat., London, Hayward Gallery, 1982.

The Indian Heritage: Court Life and Arts Under Mughal Rule. Ex. cat., London, Victoria and Albert Museum, 1982.

Irwin, John, and Hall, Margaret. *Indian Embroideries*. Ahmedabad, 1973.

Jacquement, Victor. *Letters from India: 1829–1832*. London, 1834.

Khandalavala, Karl. "Two Bikaner Paintings in the N. C. Mehta Collection and the Problem of Mandi School." In *Chhavi 2: Rai Krishnadasa Felicitation Volume*. Banaras, 1981, pp. 301–4.

Khandalavala, Karl, and Chandra, Moti. *Miniatures and Sculptures from the Collection of the Late Sir Cowasji Jehangir*. Bombay, 1965.

Kramrisch, Stella. *Manifestations of Shiva*. Ex. cat., Philadelphia Museum of Art, 1981.

Kramrisch, Stella. *Unknown India: Ritual Art in Tribe and Village*. Ex. cat., Philadelphia Museum of Art, 1968.

Lafont, Jean Marie. "Civil Service and Political Activities of French Officers of Maharaja Ranjit Singh." *Journal of Sikh Studies* 9 (no. 2, 1982), pp. 118–50.

Lerner, Martin. *The Flame and the Lotus: Indian and Southeast Asian Art from the Kronos Collection*. Ex. cat., New York, The Metropolitan Museum of Art, 1984.

Pal, Pratapaditya. *Bronzes of Kashmir*. Graz, 1975.

The Ramayana of Valmiki, 3 vols. Trans. H. P. Shastri. London, 1976.

Randhawa, M. S. *Kangra Paintings of the Gita Govinda*. New Delhi, 1963.

Randhawa, M. S. "Two Panjabi Artists of the Nineteenth Century: Kehar Singh and Kapur Singh." In *Chhavi: Golden Jubilee Volume*. Banaras, 1971, pp. 67–69.

Randhawa, M. S., and Galbraith, J. K. *Indian Painting: The Scene, Themes and Legends*. Boston, 1968.

Topsfield, A. *An Introduction to Indian Court Painting*. London, 1984.

Victoria and Albert Museum. *Indian Art*. London, 1969.

Vigne, G. T. *A Personal Narrative of a Visit to Ghazni, Kabul and Afghanistan*. London, 1840.

Vigne, G. T. *Travels in Kashmir, Ladak, Iskardo*. London, 1844.

Welch, Stuart Cary. *A Flower from Every Meadow*. New York, 1973.

Welch, Stuart Cary. *Room for Wonder: Indian Painting During the British Period 1760–1880*. Ex. cat., New York, American Federation of Arts, 1978.

Zebrowski, Mark. "Decorative Arts of the Mughal Period." In *The Arts of India*. Ed. Basil Gray. Ithaca, N.Y., 1981.

V. THE BRITISH PERIOD

Ali, Ahmed. *The Golden Tradition: An Anthology of Urdu Poetry*. New York, 1973.

Allen, Charles, and Dwivedi, Sharada. *Lives of the Indian Princes*. New York, 1984.

Annesley, George. *Voyages and Travels to India, Ceylon, the Red Sea, Abyssinia and Egypt in the Years 1802–1806*. London, 1809.

Archer, Mildred. "British Patrons of Indian Artists." *Country Life* 118 (1955), pp. 340–41.

Archer, Mildred. *Company Drawings in the India Office Library*. London, 1972.

Archer, Mildred. *Natural History Drawings in the India Office Library*. London, 1962.

Archer, W. G. *Indian Miniatures*. London, 1960.

Birdwood, G. C. M. *The Industrial Arts of India*, 2 vols. London, 1880.

Codrington, K. de B., and Rothenstein, William. *Ancient India*. London, 1926.

Devi, Gayatri, and Rama Rao, Santha. *A Princess Remembers: The Memoirs of the Maharani of Jaipur*. New York, 1985.

Digby, Simon, and Harle, J. C. *Toy Soldiers and Ceremonial in Post-Mughal India*. Oxford, 1982.

Edwardes, Emma. *Memorials of the Life and Letters of Major-General Sir Herbert B. Edwardes*, 2 vols. London, 1886.

Edwardes, Michael. *The British in India*. Ex. cat., Brighton, Museum and Art Gallery, 1973.

Edwardes, Michael. *The Orchid House: Splendours and Miseries of the Kingdom of Oudh, 1827–1857*. London, 1960.

Elliot, F. A. H. *The Rulers of Baroda*. Bombay, 1879.

Falk, Toby, and Archer, Mildred. *Indian Miniatures in the India Office Library*. London, 1981.

Fatesinhrao Gaekwad, Maharaja of Baroda. *The Palaces of India*. London, 1980.

Forster, E. M. *Abinger Harvest*. New York, 1936, pp. 318–24.

Hayter, Gael, and Falk, Toby. *Birds in an Indian Garden: Nineteen Illustrations from the Impey Collection*. London, 1984.

Heber, Reginald. *Narrative of a Journey Through the Upper Provinces of India, from Calcutta to Bombay, 1824–1825*, 2nd ed. London, 1828.

In the Image of Man: The Indian Perception of the Universe Through 2000 Years of Painting and Sculpture. Ex. cat., London, Hayward Gallery, 1982.

The Indian Heritage: Court Life and Arts Under Mughal Rule. Ex. cat., London, Victoria and Albert Museum, 1982.

Karaka, Dosabhai Framji. *History of the Parsis*, 2 vols. London, 1870.

Khosla, G. D. *The Last Mughal*. Delhi, n.d.

Kincaid, Dennis. *British Social Life in India 1608–1937*. London, 1938.

Knighton, William. *The Private Life of an Eastern King*. London, 1856.

Malleson, G. B. *An Historical Sketch of the Native States of India*. London, 1875.

Octagon: A Quarterly Journal for Discerning Collections 16 (no. 4, 1979), p. 19.

Qambar, Akhtar. *The Last Musha'irah of Delhi*. New Delhi, 1979.

Russell, Ralph, and Islam, Khurshidul. *Ghalib 1797–1869: Volume 1 Life and Letters*. Cambridge, Mass., 1969.

Sen, Surendra Nath. *Eighteen Fifty-Seven*. Calcutta, 1957.

Sharar, Abdul Halim. *Lucknow: The Last Phase of an Oriental Culture*. London, 1975.

Skrine, Francis Henry Bennett. *Life of Sir W. W. Hunter*. London, 1901.

Spear, Percival. *The Twilight of the Mughals*. Cambridge, 1951.

Watt, George. *Indian Art at Delhi 1903. Being the Official Catalogue of the Delhi Exhibition, 1902–1903*. Ex. cat., Delhi, Kudsia Gardens, 1903.

Welch, Stuart Cary. *Imperial Mughal Painting*. New York, 1978.

Welch, Stuart Cary. *Room for Wonder: Indian Painting During the British Period 1760–1880*. Ex. cat., New York, American Federation of Arts, 1978.

Woodruff, Philip. *The Men Who Ruled India: The Founders of Modern India*. New York, 1956.

Worswick, Clark. *The Last Empire*. New York, 1976.

Worswick, Clark. *Princely India: Photographs by Raja Deen Dayal (1884–1910)*. New York, 1980.

Yadav, K. C., ed. *Delhi in 1857*. Vol. 1: *The Trial of Bahadur Shah*. Guraron, 1980.

INDEX

Catalogue numbers are in roman;
page numbers are in *italic*.

476

PHOTOGRAPH CREDITS

Photographs of works in Indian public and private collections were specially taken for this publication in India by Sheldan Collins, The Photograph Studio, The Metropolitan Museum of Art. All other photographs were supplied by the lenders, with the exception of those noted below:

Crawley Wilkinson Associates Ltd., London   43, 87, 129, 141, 167, 183, 189, 200, 220

The Photograph Studio, The Metropolitan Museum of Art   18, 33, 34, 35, 36, 39, 41, 42, 51, 66, 69, 86, 98, 104, 116, 131, 135, 154, 158, 164, 170, 172, 173, 178, 184, 225d, 275, 296

Christian Poite, Geneva   289

Arthur Soll, Philadelphia   146

Stephen Tucker, New York   258

Harold and Erica Van Pelt, Los Angeles   180

Nicholas Vreeland, New York   32, 49, 70, 96, 97, 100, 117, 144, 150, 162b, 169, 194, 205, 207, 225c, 241, 242, 243, 245, 248, 250, 252, 254, 255, 257, 263, 272, 278, 284